RABBIT HOLE

THE VANISHING OF AMELIA EARHART AND FRED NOONAN

CHRIS WILLIAMSON

CONTENTS

For Evan

FOREWORD

In 2019, I was approached by Chris Williamson. He was creating a podcast about Amelia Earhart and wanted to interview me. Absolutely positive that he had confused me with someone else, I told him that I knew who she was but did not know anything about this story other than that she disappeared while flying her plane over the Pacific Ocean. It turns out he had not confused me with anyone else, and that he was looking for someone who was new to her story.

The show was called *Vanished: Amelia Earhart*, and it was meant to be a more succinct version of his already very popular interview show *Chasing Earhart*. This book has been adapted from the transcript of *Vanished*. Part of the goal of the podcast – and now, the book – is to showcase four theories of what happened to Earhart and her navigator, Fred Noonan, on July 2, 1937. On that day, Earhart's Lockheed Electra disappeared as it was approaching Howland Island, a very tiny chunk of land in the Pacific Ocean that would serve as a place for the pair to rest and refuel before finishing up their flight around the world. Anchored right off the coast of Howland Island was a ship – the US Coast Guard cutter *Itasca*. The *Itasca*'s job was to help Earhart and Noonan find Howland Island and make a safe landing. The crew of the *Itasca* were the last people to hear Earhart's voice.

She had been communicating with the ship right before her plane vanished. The radio logs from that conversation are available in the National Archives.

They are *haunting*.

At 8:43 a.m. local time, Amelia Earhart spoke her last known words. They were, "We are on the line at 157/337...will repeat message...we will repeat this on 6210 KCS...wait." What took place after 8:43 a.m. local time on July 2, 1937, has been the subject of heated debates by researchers for the last eighty-five years.

Over the years, those who have been researching Earhart and Noonan's disappearance have split into factions, each with their own theory of what happened. The four theories that *Vanished* highlighted and are presented in this book are (1) The Lockheed Electra crashed into the water near the coast of Howland Island, with Earhart and Noonan inside. The plane and its occupants are currently somewhere at the bottom of the Pacific Ocean.

(2) Earhart and Noonan made a slight navigation error that led them to nearby Gardner Island (now called Nikumaroro), where they safely landed and lived as castaways until they died. Earhart's and Noonan's remains are on Nikumaroro, and their plane is in the water off the coast of that island.

(3) Earhart and Noonan, facing a stronger than anticipated head-wind, realized halfway through their trip that they didn't have enough fuel. They turned around and attempted to fly back, but crash-landed on Buka Island in the Autonomous Region of Bougainville. The plane is currently nestled in the coral reefs off the coast of Buka, with the remains of Earhart and Noonan inside.

(4) Earhart and Noonan crash-landed in the Marshall Islands in the Pacific Ocean and were quickly taken captive by the Japanese. Earhart and Noonan died in Japanese captivity, and the plane was destroyed and buried in Japan.

When Chris approached me to be a part of the podcast, I was going through a significant life change. I had just left my two-year clerkship at a Texas Court of Appeals and had moved across the state to Austin, Texas, where I joined a criminal defense firm.

For the first time since obtaining my law license in 2016, I was a practicing attorney. The world that I had just jumped headfirst into was nothing like anything I was used to. I did well in law school and at my clerkship. I was – and still am – introverted and bookish. At my prior job, I was posted up at a desk in the attic of a hundred-year-old courthouse. My job was to do legal research and draft judicial opinions. I loved it and was very good at it. As anyone who has ever practiced criminal defense can attest to, my new job could not have been more different from my old one. Every day, I was in a new courtroom, in a new county, talking to dozens of new people – judges, prosecutors, clients, and court staff. I was cross-examining witnesses, talking to juries, and reassuring anxious clients. People were placing their lives and futures in my hands. For an introvert who thrives in a dimly lit room with a stack of books, it was a shock to my system. It all felt very chaotic and scary.

Why was a baby lawyer from Texas asked to give an interview on this subject? I believe this can be traced back to a comment often made when defending the "Japanese capture" theory. According to some of the researchers who support this theory, Amelia Earhart and Fred Noonan were seen by two hundred eyewitnesses while they were held captive in Japan. If someone was on trial for murder, the argument goes, and the State brings in two hundred eyewitnesses to the event, that's a slam-dunk case for the prosecution. Case closed. Is that *true?* Chris wanted to pursue this argument further and had a lot of questions. What kinds of evidence are offered at a jury trial? What about expert testimony and forensic evidence?

What happens if two experts have opposite opinions? What does *beyond a reasonable doubt* mean? How reliable is eyewitness testimony? I was sent a list of these questions, as well as a brief rundown of the four theories. The initial idea was for me to do a quick interview answering these questions and giving my thoughts on how the different types of evidence relied on by each theory's proponents might hold up in court. That interview became episode 8, "Trial by Jury." But like most people who delve into this mystery, it was difficult for me to step away. After recording my initial interview, Chris and I wondered what it would be like to take this argument even further. What if we took each of the four theories and presented them to a jury in a mock trial? That idea became the foundation for the rest of the podcast and for much of this book. (Actually, it would be more accurate to say season 1 of the podcast, as *Vanished* is now an ongoing show.)

Chris asked me to join *Vanished* as a co-host, and I graciously accepted. My primary job for *Vanished* is to "cross-examine" guests – to ask them the tough questions and see how well they can defend their research and their theories. But make no mistake – I have very much enjoyed working with all the show's guests and have tried as hard as I can to make the experience enjoyable as well as challenging. I have had the opportunity to interview and learn from experts in many different fields and have made many new friends. Some of my favorite moments of 2019 were spent in the Vanished Facebook group poring over maps and fuel calculations and old newspapers, sleuthing with a group of people I never met in real life. I worked on this case for almost a year (far less time than most of the people I spoke with). In that year, I developed my own opinions on what happened and what didn't happen. Some of those opinions will be found in this book, but most of them were shared off the record, in one of countless phone calls between Chris and me during the production of the show. There is one thing that I firmly believe: this case *is solvable*. I hope to live to see the solution. The work I did on this case *undoubtedly* made me a better lawyer.

I went into my very first real trial having already gained experience in working with and cross-examining experts, explaining complex legal issues to laypeople, and even writing opening statements and closing arguments. The fact that these experiences came from working on a podcast did not diminish their value. In addition, my work on this case gave me a very early interest in the flaws of various forensic science disciplines and eyewitness testimony. My research in these areas started here. To this day, the use of scientific (and pseudoscientific) evidence in courtrooms is a topic that I am particularly interested in and spend a considerable amount of time researching. But probably the more profound and long-lasting impact on my personal and professional life came not from researching Amelia Earhart's death, but from learning about her life.

Amelia Earhart was fearless. She repeatedly risked her life, broke records, defied convention, spoke her mind, and lived her life exactly the way she wanted to. There were a thousand reasons why it would have been easier for a young woman in the early twentieth century to back down from these things. Instead, Amelia chose to fly. She did so during a time when flying was incredibly dangerous and when society still widely believed that a woman's role was to marry, have children, take care of the home and be quiet. She broke through not only her own comfort zone, but everyone's. And America loved her for it.

If she could do that, then I could leave my attic and my books and my comfortable bubble to go live and fight in the chaotic world that is the American criminal justice system.

Amelia Earhart entered my life in a time when I needed someone to teach me to be fearless. I owe her a lot.

For me, the pages that follow are memories. Like a photo album, they are filled with all the nostalgia and emotion that comes with looking back on a wonderful and crazy year of my life. As you progress through this book, know that you are reading the product of decades of work on the part of many talented researchers and experts – some of whom you will meet and some you will not. But more importantly, you are about to read the product of many years of painstaking work coalescing all this research and collaborating with all the relevant players to bring everything together in one place. Chris's habit has always been to stay in the shadows, shining the spotlight on everyone but himself to amplify their work and their voices. I have no doubt that you will come away from this story, like I did, inspired by the life and death of Amelia Earhart and Fred Noonan and by the men and women who are working tirelessly to keep her memory alive. And for that, we all owe Chris a lot.

Jennifer Taylor
Winter 2021

PREFACE

Hey everyone. Fair warning:

What you're about to read was never *meant to be read.*

Everything that follows was originally part of season 1 of our podcast *Vanished*. Years ago, I had the idea for the show after nearing the end of the Chasing Earhart podcast. I was still hungry for more Earhart, but I had grown tired of the format in which we did that show. Of course, the decision to move on was made easier because at that time, I had interviewed nearly everyone involved in the Earhart case, both on the legacy and the disappearance side of things. For a long time, I'd had this idea of tackling this case in a way that hadn't been done previously.

Like everything in this story, it really began with several questions:

What if we put several of the major theories in this case on trial? What if we called all the relevant experts to testify and presented all the evidence for each major theory and allowed our audience to act as our jury? If *you* were on that jury, what evidence would convince *you*?

What comes next is the written transcript of that original idea. Everything contained within what is now season 1 of our show is before you. If you've heard the show though, things might feel a little different. By far, the most difficult part of this entire process has been the conversion of the following material from something you *hear* to something you *read*. Because of that, I have taken certain liberties. A lot of the structure from that original show remains intact. However, formatting has changed, and some statements have been slightly amended in order for it to go down a little easier. You'll also hear fresh retrospectives from some of the people who were involved in the original show and some who weren't. The result is an Earhart book that you'll consume differently than any that's come before.

That's my hope, anyway. As we dive in, you should know that while I've done everything in my power to make sure this book is smooth, it's not an easy read. There is a ton of information here. Dozens and dozens of men and women have come together to provide you with the most complete picture of Earhart's life and disappearance possible. I want to say *up front* that without their participation, what you're holding in your hands never happens.

I am forever in debt to everyone who has lent their remarkable talents to help make this happen. The following text is *absolutely* a group effort. Take your time as you go through this story. There are tons of little details that help close the gaps and tie things together.

While the Earhart case often leaves us with more questions than answers, it's important to know that everyone taking part in this book is doing so because they respect Amelia's legacy above all, and they want to contribute to upholding it.

It's my sincere hope that you enjoy this journey. Take it slow, consume it with great care, and follow the evidence, *wherever it leads.*

This text is a theoretical account of the events that occurred on the morning of July 2, 1937, and thereafter.

While she *was* declared dead in absentia on January 5, 1939, there are many who believe the disappearance of Amelia Earhart remains *unsolved*.

WHAT MAKES A LEGEND?

39.563751 |-95.114487

"To understand the legend, we must understand the woman. To understand the woman, we must understand the girl."

Chris Williamson

I'm standing on the banks of the Missouri River close to the corner of Santa Fe and Terrace Street in Atchison, Kansas. It's right before sundown in the middle of winter, and it's *cold*. Across from me is a home. In some ways, it's like most homes in Atchison: unassuming, two stories; quaint and indicative of the time. Its wood-frame Gothic Revival cottage style wouldn't normally be noticed if you weren't drawn to that style of the time.

However, this home? This home I'm standing across from *right now* is the birthplace of a legend.

If you've followed the *Chasing Earhart* podcast anytime during its run, then you're pretty versed in who Amelia Earhart was, what she stood for, and why so many people seem to care so much about her ultimate fate. A lot of attention has been paid to how Amelia's life ended and everything that's gone on since then, but not so many

1

people have looked at how it began. I've been guilty of that myself. So let's right that wrong now and talk about it. After all, I've always been a firm believer that you can't fully understand an ending until you fully understand the beginning. I said this at the beginning of the podcast, and I'll say it here again now. I am not an expert on Amelia Earhart. There aren't many subjects that you can study for the majority of your life and still be a newcomer. But when it comes to Amelia, I am very much a newcomer. The guests who made up the Chasing Earhart project and the guests you'll hear from in this book are the stars of the show.

Now with that being said, you may be asking yourself how *I'm* qualified to be doing this.

The short answer is I'm *not.*

We'll get back to that soon enough. For now, let's begin with the question that we asked in season 1, episode 1. Are legends *born* or *made?* It's a fundamental but appropriate question as we begin our journey together. To help answer that question, I decided to do what *anyone* in my position would do. I made a phone call…

"When he came home, he stumbled and lurched, and as they watched him go into the house, he was obviously and embarrassingly drunk. I don't think there's any question about it."

Susan Butler

From everything that I ever read about Amelia and all the telltale little sources and tales that I uncovered while I was researching the book, Amelia was always a very outgoing, very content, and very curious little girl from the time that she was a baby. I have a line in my book, where I think she told her mother, "If there was nobody around, I'd talk into my own ears."

Chris Williamson

In 2009, Susan Butler released *East to the Dawn*, which many people believe to be the definitive biography on Amelia Earhart. Years of painstaking research went into the creation of her work, tracing Amelia's story back to before she was ever born. I figured if you're starting at the beginning, it doesn't get any better. I wanted to begin with the people who surrounded Amelia during her upbringing. To understand the legend, you have to understand the people who provided her foundation, and that almost *always* begins with one's mother. In this case, *Amy Otis Earhart*.

Susan Butler

Amy was born in Atchison, Kansas. She was a very gutsy young girl; she loved horseback riding. She was a very bright girl. At her coming-out party in Atchison, Kansas, she fell in love and ended up marrying her husband, who was a man named *Edwin Earhart*. He was a lawyer who had also grown up in Kansas, although he had never been to Atchison before.

. . .

3

Chris Williamson

So we know a little about Amy Otis. She was quite a woman in her own right, as Susan describes. So what was it about Edwin that Amy found so appealing?

Susan Butler

He was good-looking; when he was younger, he was a very hard worker. He went to Field College on a scholarship and became a lawyer, but somehow the law did not work for him.

He was not a successful lawyer, although he was a charming man and a very good father.

He loved his daughters, Amelia and her younger sister, Muriel; he gave them everything they asked for. Amelia was a bit of a tomboy. He gifted her a BB gun, a .22 and a football. But he was not a successful lawyer, and that caused great problems. As he fell behind his peers, he started to drink, which of course caused much *greater* problems. When Amelia was young, she was insulated from all of that because she'd been sent to live with her grandmother; Amy's mother, who lived in Atchison.

Chris Williamson

We all have flaws.

For Edwin, it was alcohol. That flaw though, would haunt Amelia for the rest of her life and become something that many people believe would come full circle and tie into the world flight. But not with Edwin of course; with *someone else*. More on that later. But how did she *really* feel in her young age about her father's drinking?

Susan Butler

They used to play a game when they were in Des Moines, Iowa; cowboys and Indians. They waited for him to come home and when he came home, he stumbled and lurched. As they watched him go into the house, he was obviously and embarrassingly drunk. I don't think

4

there's any question about it. When she became an adult and was living with George Palmer Putnam, they were building a house in California. She would not let anybody in the house drink an alcoholic drink. She felt very strongly about it.

Chris Williamson

Although it's clear that he cared deeply for his daughters, Amelia's relationship with her father Edwin was a strained one. His alcohol abuse clearly had an effect on her for the rest of her days. However, Amy and Edwin weren't the *only* parental figures in Amelia's young life. And that brings us to her reason for calling Atchison, Kansas a crucial part of her foundation.

Susan Butler

Alfred Otis had been a dynamo, one of the early settlers in the town of Atchison. He was also an abolitionist, and he had been instrumental in starting everything that ever happened in Atchison, including the bank. At one point, he had a nervous breakdown and became very withdrawn, and that left his wife, Amelia's grandmother, whose name was *also* Amelia, adrift and alone. Amelia Earhart was such a charming little girl, the decision was made that she would go and spend her winter months going to school in Atchison.

She'd live with her grandmother and help cheer her up. Up until the age of twelve, she had a very different upbringing from Muriel, who lived in Kansas City with their mother Amy.

Chris Williamson

Muriel stays in Kansas, and Amelia heads off to Atchison to live with her grandparents. A lot of us can relate to Amelia's close relationship with her grandparents. After all, there are many of us who share that same kind of relationship with our own. I'm sure you've heard the phrase "It takes a village" before. I wondered if this was the case? What Susan said got me thinking, so I had to ask. Did Amelia really have two sets of parents so to speak, who contributed to the foundation of who she would eventually become?

Susan Butler

Yeah, absolutely. In fact, I think that's a very good description of her childhood. Her mother and her grandmother basically shared Amelia because she was a very self-reliant, interesting, and fun child.

Chris Williamson

She was different in a few *other* ways that would give us all a small glimpse of how Amelia would challenge the status quo all of her life.

Susan Butler

When she saw boys playing basketball at her school, a college preparatory school, she asked the top basketball player/teacher how to play basketball. Nothing stood in her way.

She was a very curious little girl, and she was very bright. I don't think she was knocking herself out to do a lot of studying, and she spent a lot of time with her cousins *"Katch" and Lucy.*

Chris Williamson

Katch and Lucy. More on them in a bit.

There have been a lot of books written on various theories regarding what happened to Amelia Earhart and Fred Noonan on the morning of July 2, 1937. But as I said earlier, this section of the story isn't about any of that. After talking to Susan about her extraordinary book, I wanted to drill down even further into Amelia's childhood and try to uncover some of the stories that aren't so famous. To understand the legend, we must understand the woman. To understand the woman, we must understand the girl. In order to do that, I need to talk with someone who has devoted their work to the years *before* Amelia became a legend in the skies.

"The story goes that she was at the top of the hill, and the kids were all watching. By the time she got to the bottom, there was a cart being pulled by horses that was coming through."

Chris Williamson

The above quote is from author J. A. Kiehl. She wrote *Amelia: The Town and the People That Loved Her*

She's written more stories that focus on the foundation of Amelia's character, like *Splat!* and *Meelie's Christmas*, which has a very special and personal meaning for me. I traveled out to meet with her in Lawrence, Kansas just about an hour away from Atchison.

Her books aren't about the disappearance, and they don't promote any theory. As Kiehl describes it, they're love stories, and they're personal.

J. A. Kiehl

She was surrounded by her grandmother and her grandfather, who were instrumental in her life. He would read to her at a very young age, and because of that, she began to teach *herself* to read. She could read before she entered elementary school, the *College Preparatory School of Atchison.*

Chris Williamson

I wanted to find out more. I was interested in some of the stories that aren't so widely circulated about Amelia when she was a little girl. And J. A. didn't disappoint.

7

J. A. Kiehl

Grandmother Otis's sister was basically a next-door neighbor. The Chalices had lived on the opposite corner of North Terrace in Atchison. I believe it was in 1899 that their house caught on fire during Christmastime. I think somebody forgot to extinguish a candle. So they decided to rebuild. It was a frame house, but it was a very large, impressive home.

They chose not to rebuild there, but instead, they decided to move up next door to the Otises, so you had two sisters living next door to each other. Today, though, there's separation.

There is a house now between where Amelia lived and where the Chalices lived. The Chalices had children, and Amelia was extremely close to her cousins, Katch and Lucy.

They played together all the time, and Grandmother Otis, having come from a wealthy family in Philadelphia, had always wanted Amelia to be kind of girly. She would arrange for tea parties, and I think in my mind, I can see Amelia rolling her eyes, thinking, "Why do I have to do this when I'd rather be exploring the caves on the bluff across from us?" That was something that she did so often, and actually, as a child, I did the very same thing.

Chris Williamson

Yeah. You just read that right. Amelia Earhart was a *spelunker*.

J. A. Kiehl

The caves are not very large. They're maybe twenty feet in depth at the maximum, but they're dotted all along that bluff. One of her favorite things to do was to go past the orchard fence, hop over and go down and explore the caves. Her grandmother was not too fond of her doing that, but Amelia was very daring, and that's what she wanted to do. She was also surrounded by other friends. She had a close friend named *Dolan*. That was not her first name, that was her last name. Her full name was *Catherine Dolan*, but the children simply called her Dolan. Another close childhood friend of hers was *Bailey P. Wagoner*. I can only imagine the things that they must have done together because they were both adventuresome children. She liked to do boyish-type things, and her grandmother was not too fond of that because she felt she should be more ladylike. Amy and Edwin, on the other hand, were very encouraging of her. It didn't make any difference to them if you were a girl and you wanted to play football, or you wanted to go sledding with the boys and have snowball fights and all of that. They thought it was wonderful.

Chris Williamson

Next, J. A. tells me a story that will be part of one of her upcoming books. A story that took place during one of the winters in Atchison.

J. A. Kiehl

It was a snowy day in Atchison. She and Bailey got up on top of the roof of a carriage house and decided to sled off it. And boy, did they fly! That was something very memorable for Amelia. They also did a lot of sleigh riding on their sleds down Second Street Hill, which was very steep. The story goes that she was at the top of the hill, and the kids were all watching. By the time she got to the bottom, there was a cart being pulled by horses that was coming through. I think all the children were horrified, but Amelia made it, and she slipped right between the wheels and past the cart, and she didn't get hit.

Chris Williamson

Amelia had the daredevil bug in her genes long before she ever got up into the sky. In fact, you might say her first flight came long before *Frank Hawks* took her up on December 28, 1920. Like a lot of Amelia's professional career, this one *too* was marred in controversy.

It's simply known as *the roller coaster incident*. Here's Susan Butler:

Susan Butler

She'd been at the world's fair. Amy had not let her go on the roller coaster there, so she got back to Atchison, and she decided to create her own roller coaster. She found some two-by-fours, and she propped them up on the edge of the shed. She had her uncle Carl, Amy's brother, helping her, and she made a box and had a wonderful time. The first time she went down on it, she somersaulted but then got herself back into shape, and it was evidently a great success. She took a ride on it, and then her friend Bailey Wagoner took a ride on it; it was a very creative thing for a young girl to do.

Chris Williamson

As Amelia grew, she faced new challenges. Moving around a lot made it difficult to find a source of stability. By the time she found herself in high school, Amelia was trying to make her way and decide on what she wanted to do with her professional life. Was she really known as "the girl in brown who walked alone"? A wonderful line that helps build the legend. But is it *true?*

Susan Butler

I found her yearbook, and that was *not* what was said.

The yearbook quote about her was "Meek loveliness is 'round thee spread."

By the time high school rolled around, her father had gotten a job in De Moines, Iowa, and it was there that he started to drink. By the time they got to St. Paul, they had rolled around a bit because he kept losing jobs and trying to find more jobs, so they had to keep moving. It wasn't until they got to *St. Paul Central high school* that she started to enjoy herself and play basketball. Edwin was such a disaster that he and Amy split. Amelia, Amy, and her sister Muriel, went to Chicago by themselves and took rooms in an apartment where some old ladies lived. It was there that Amelia went to *Hyde Park high school*, and that's where she graduated.

. . .

Chris Williamson

This is where it gets real interesting real fast. The next several years of Amelia's life were a whirlwind, with Amelia going through multiple incidents and experiences that would take her from a boarding school, to a stint as a nurse during World War I that would result in near death. From there, she takes on what *she thought* would be her lifelong career as a social worker.

But as we all are well aware, destiny was calling, and it had *other plans*.

Susan Butler

She went to *Ogontz*, which was a girls' boarding school. She was there for a year and a half, and she was there because her mother had come into some money. It was basically a girls' finishing school. Then she went up to Canada to visit Muriel, who was at school up in Toronto. This was in 1918. She was there when the Canadian soldiers were coming back from the war. She was there when the French flu pandemic hit, and she became a nurse's aide and went to work in Toronto hospitals, taking care of flu and pneumonia patients.

Chris Williamson

There's one thing about Amelia that a lot of people agree on.

She had a distaste for war.

Remember that.

It may come back into play in the future. At this point, another hotly contested aspect makes its introduction to Amelia's life: the chronic sinus issues that would plague her during her career as an aviator. It's also important to note here that her sinus condition and more importantly her treatment for it, *or lack thereof* depending on where you sway, will play a huge part in her disappearance.

Yes, you read that right.

Susan Butler

She had come from a very posh boarding school, and the moment she had a chance, she went to work taking care of sick soldiers without really any due regard to the danger.

She had a sinus condition that she carried with her all her life; she always had problems as a result of that. She was quite sick for a while but after she recovered, she decided to become a doctor, and at that time, it was quite hard to be a doctor. She ran out of money.

Of course, then she became a social worker.

That was more important. I really *do* think that if she hadn't been such a successful pilot and hadn't been grabbed by the moment when flying was the most important thing to everybody [sort of like space exploration is to us right now], I think she would have ended up as another *Jane Addams*, who ran *Hull House*. She was well on the way to being one of the top social workers in Boston.

Chris Williamson

Amelia Earhart, the social worker, the doctor, the *president*.

Was this woman simply a slam dunk for being the best at whatever road she decided to walk down? And perhaps more importantly, did Amelia Earhart conquer *fear?*

Susan Butler

She probably could have succeeded at *whatever* she did. She was well coordinated, she was smart, and she had a wonderful ability to stay relaxed.

She never seemed to get uptight about anything, which is why she was a record-setting pilot.

Whereas other pilots would get anxious and start to overplan, she *never overplanned*.

If she had extra time before a flight, she would curl up and take a nap. She was not a worrier. She was just a very successful person. I don't know how you explain why one person succeeds and another doesn't, except that she was always very aware of what she was doing. She always kept her mind on the task at hand.

Chris Williamson

Having said all of that, we can now approach the question that we asked at the beginning of this text. Are legends *born* or *made?* I had to ask Susan if it was a fair assessment for me to say that Amelia willed herself into becoming a legend?

Susan Butler

Yes, I think that is safe to say. I'm not sure whether she knew it or not, or whether she was just a natural leader. In my book, I have quotes from the other girls around her who said that they waited to see what she was going to do because whatever she planned was much more exciting than what they had planned. I think when she was older, she was aware that she was a really great influence. Her years at Purdue teaching women were, for her, great fun. She knew she was making a difference with the college girls who were following her around. They all adored her throughout her career.

Chris Williamson

The one thing that Amelia always encouraged people to do was dream and then do everything in their power to act on and accomplish those dreams. During my interview with J. A. Kiehl, I learned something that I hadn't previously known about Amelia, and picturing it gave me chills

J. A. Kiehl

I did not know this, actually, until I was sixty-six years of age. When I needed to think, I would go to the bluff across the street from where Amelia lived. I knew that was her childhood home. She had been my father's heroine, and he had some wonderful encounters with her.

I would go up and sit on the bluff and watch the river go by and dream my dreams. I would look back at her home, and I would think very seriously about her and what she had done.

I did that so many times as a child. At the age of sixty-six, I was asked to become a docent for the *Amelia Earhart Birthplace Museum*. One day, I was telling some children I was guiding through the museum about how I would sit on the bluff and dream my dreams.

Our manager at that time, the first manager of the museum, *Louise Foudaray*, came to me, and she said, "I did not realize you did that." And I said, "Oh yes. So many times. I would ride my bike over there." She said, "Do you know that Amelia did the very same thing?"

She said, "Show me where you used to sit." So we went out to the front porch, and I pointed to where I would sit. She pointed out and said, "Do you see that spot?" I said, "Yes." She said, "That is where Amelia sat, and she did the same thing that you did. She would dream her dreams there." She knew that because Amelia's sister Muriel, was still living, and she paid a number of visits to that home. She talked to Louise about it a couple of times, and it was *Muriel* who told Louise that story. So I sat about twenty yards from where Amelia had sat, and we dreamt our dreams *together*.

Chris Williamson

Louise Foudaray. Louise curated the Amelia Earhart Birthplace Museum in Atchison for thirty years. She was one of the most knowledgeable people in the world when it comes to Amelia. I had the pleasure of sitting down with Louise for the podcast and our documentary *Chasing Earhart*, and I cannot wait for everyone to hear from her.

You think you know stories?

You ain't heard *nothing yet*.

A little girl born into a loving family, but a family not without controversy. An adventurous spirit that would be nurtured instead of denied, and a name that the entire planet would remember *forever*.

Are legends *born* or *made*?

Can someone *will themselves* into greatness?

As William Shakespeare wrote in his play *Twelfth Night*, "Some are born great, some achieve greatness. And some have greatness thrust upon them."

J. A. Kiehl

Those people whom she knew, those people who loved her, whom she had so much of an impact on, *did* draw on her. Women are now on the map because of Amelia. She put women there for what she did and what she accomplished. I think that is absolutely wonderful. Many women, and *men as well*, look back and draw on that strength and ask themselves, "What was in Amelia that I want to exemplify?"

Susan Butler

When I was working on her years at Purdue as a teacher there, I put an ad into the yearbook, and I asked anybody who was a student at the time and remembered Amelia Earhart to write to me with their impressions about her. I got letters from these women who wrote me and said she changed their lives. One woman said she started out in home economics, but she wanted to be an engineer. The engineering staff at Purdue didn't want women to be in their classes, because they were all men, and they were all basically misogynists, according to these women. Amelia encouraged them all to go and do whatever they wanted, and that changed their lives forever.

Chris Williamson

Are legends born or made? I feel like I'm starting to believe that Amelia was a combination of both.

A THOUSAND WAYS TO DIE IN THE SKY

33.9454867 | -118.3998088

"All these people are running over, and Neta turns around, and Amelia is facing away; she's looking at the fuselage. Neta goes, 'What are you doing? These people are coming to see you!' And Amelia says, 'Give me a minute, I'm putting on lipstick.'"

Chris Williamson

I've been thinking about the early days of aviation, what a lot of people refer to as the *golden age*. Imagine the aeronautical environment and how new it was to be up in the sky. *The Wright brothers'* vision allowed people to experience a whole new perspective on life. The women who stood at the forefront of aviation during this time must have endured countless obstacles. Women like *Louise Thaden, Florence Klingensmith, Ruth Elder, Ruth Nichols, Bessie Coleman,* and *Ruth Law.*

A lot of Ruths in the early days of aviation.

Of course, Amelia Earhart was at the head of the pack. What these women faced in this new profession was unreal. The idea that they could be dismissed before trying to do what men had done causes the mind to reel. Looking back now, it's apparent that these women made

17

up the very foundation for what women are accomplishing today. Because a few brave women dared to dream and *act* on those dreams, we now have modern-day progress in aviation, aerospace, and STEM. Progress of course, didn't come without sacrifice, and it didn't come without *death*.

In that time, there were a thousand ways to die in the sky.

If we're talking about aviation history, we need to bring in someone who knows it *well*.

Someone who can relate to us the struggle, the sacrifice, and the glory that Amelia Earhart and the rest of these early pioneers of aviation experienced. Luckily, I know just the guy, and I happen to have his phone number.

"I talked to a young fellow whose grandfather stopped her for doing eighty on a back road, and he said once he realized it was Amelia Earhart, he let her off. I remember telling him, 'Oh darn, the ticket would prove that it really happened.'"

Doug Westfall

Aviation was exceedingly dangerous. The first fatal crash was a Wright flyer only five years after the Wright brothers had first flown. This is fairly soon to have that kind of fatality.

Chris Williamson

Since the inception of *Chasing Earhart*, Doug Westfall has become more than just a project guest. He's been a mentor and a close friend of mine. It's difficult to explain how we clicked after our first meeting, but we have similar personalities, and I have a hell of a lot of love and respect for him. Doug has written and/or published multiple books on the life of Amelia Earhart. Like J. A. Kiehl, his books are largely about the little things in Amelia's life, and they don't focus so much on the disappearance. Doug is a historian first, and because of that, this is the perfect introduction to a man who carries a vast amount of knowledge on the subject at hand.

Doug Westfall

In the 1920s alone, there were over 175 air crashes: unbelievable in that timeframe.

There *were* airship disasters of course, but those were few and far between. Some of the crashes would have up to a dozen people on board. Eventually, because of the death of Knute Rockne, the Department of Air Commerce Support, the forerunner for FAA basically, said no more strutted aircraft because too many were crashing. There were so many air crashes, planes were constantly being put back together. Amelia in her own right, had an *Avro Avian* from England that she'd brought over on a ship and *that* went down three times. These aircraft were not put together well; they were not made for the stress of air flight. They were made cheaply to keep the cost down, and even if you didn't have a crash, you were always trying to put something together to fix the aircraft. There was always a problem.

Chris Williamson

So now we've set the stage for what it was like in the sky during the birth of flight. Pretty scary, if you ask me. But the women? Not only did they face deck-stacking statistics during those days, but they also faced a whole additional set of obstacles. *Internal obstacles.*

Doug Westfall

The primary obstacle is cost. Aircraft could cost well over $1,000 then; multiply that by twenty just to be able to have an aircraft that you could fly, and of course, these are all biplane single-engines; typically three-cylinder engines; very, very dangerous and very low cost.

Amelia Earhart, Pancho Barnes, and *so many* of the early aviators had extreme struggles with men opposing them in this field, yet there were so few fliers that they all found a way of doing it one way or the other. Amelia Earhart included.

Chris Williamson

Let me make this clear. Women were *not wanted* in aviation. They were considered inferior to men. However, a few brave women would change everything once they were given their shot. They were out there waiting in the wings, and what they would end up accomplishing is nothing short of extraordinary.

Doug Westfall

I believe there were always women of this nature, there just wasn't a vehicle for them to perform. You also had women getting into motoring, using automobiles and racing. Once the mechanic age took off, it gave women an alternative way to show their stuff. It gave them an opportunity that they would never have in, say, the Victorian era. Obtaining access, a loan for an aircraft, getting training, and going flying occurred all over the country. *Neta Snook*, Amelia's first trainer, was a woman from Iowa, and she learned right there in Davenport.

Chris Williamson

People come into our lives for very specific reasons.

If you know anything about Amelia Earhart, the woman Doug just mentioned should be important to you. Neta Snook is a legend in her own right. She was the first female aviator out of Iowa, the first female student to be accepted to the Curtiss Flying School in Virginia, the first female aviator to run her own aviation business, and the first to run a commercial airfield. Her autobiography *I Taught Amelia to Fly* aptly captures the essence of her fame, and she was forever linked to what has become Earhart lore as Amelia's first flight instructor.

Doug Westfall

Amelia had seen her first plane in Iowa, but she rode in her first plane in 1922 at the Long Beach airshow, and one of the hangars is still there, amazingly. Her dad paid ten bucks for a ten-minute ride so she could go up. This is like, $120 today. She loved it, and it was only a short trip up north to the city of Belle, where she bought her first plane on time from *Kinner Air*. The woman running the shop there was Neta Snook from Iowa, and Amelia had been to Iowa; she had lived there as a youth. They struck up a conversation, and Neta agreed to teach her, and a few lessons later Amelia was flying a plane. Neta was also with her when she crashed her first plane out at *Mines Field*, which is now known as *LAX*. The two were taking off, and she was too close to the trees. They used eucalyptus trees as windbreaks to cut the wind at the airport because it's right off the ocean, but she was too close. She pulled on the stick to try to get the aircraft to go up higher, and unfortunately it stalled, and they kited

21

down gently into the grass and *did* damage the ship, but it didn't hurt either woman.

All these people are running over, and Neta turns around, and Amelia is facing away; she's looking at the fuselage, and Neta goes, "What are you doing? These people are coming to see you!" She says, "Give me a minute, I'm putting on lipstick."

Chris Williamson

Two of the most famous aviators of all time involved in a spectacular crash together, and Amelia Earhart is worried about her *appearance*. This is a look into the woman that Amelia would eventually become: self-aware and always promoting. Always showing that she had complete control over fear.

But what about the rest of the female aviators of the time?

Women like Florence Klingensmith, Ruth Elder, Ruth Nichols, and so many others? Were they self-aware, and did they know each other? Was there mutual respect between everyone for being in the same boat, so to speak? Did they ever come together as one?

Doug Westfall

Before the formation of the *Ninety-Nines*, which brought a lot of these women together in one group, there was camaraderie, but again, they're all from different cities all over America. They would come to these air shows and then split up; go back and never see each other again. The telephone was very expensive to use; you didn't stay in touch too often. Some of them wrote back and forth, but eventually, they'd meet at another air show in some other city like New Jersey, and they would strike up their friendship again.

They were very isolated in their efforts. Each one did their own thing, and then they would meet up at a certain point.

Chris Williamson

Like in comic books, the individual heroes would have their own adventures, slaying their own villains and obstacles, and when the time called for it, the heroes would come together.

Make no mistake about it, these women *were* heroes. That begs the question though, were there ever any rivalries?

Doug Westfall

I've never heard of a rivalry, not *one*. I know they would talk back and forth. Neta Snook won one of the derbies out here in LA, then turned around, got married, had a child, and never flew again. A lot of these women went through that pattern where they were independent and doing their thing up in the air, and then they found love, and that was it; they didn't fly again. One of the exceptions is Pancho Barnes; another one is, of course, Amelia Earhart. At the same time, most of these women slowly faded out of the limelight and had families and lives and just went on with it.

Chris Williamson

Pancho Barnes. Remember that name. She broke Amelia's speed record. Records *are*, after all, made to be broken. Her career was a fascinating one, and she often doesn't get the proper due that she deserves. Look her up; you won't be disappointed.

Doug Westfall

Both Amelia and Pancho were adventuresome; they were the ones out there. Look at their histories, their childhoods; they were the ones going down the hill on skates; they were the ones taking the risks; and they wanted the excitement. They wanted the adventure, and of course, aviation gave that to them in such great quantity. Winning awards and races also helped to boost their spirits, but it was their way of expression. Amelia only got married for business purposes; Pancho got married because her family told her, and she soon divorced. These women were really out there on their own. This is what they wanted, and it reflects in what we see in the histories of these women.

. . .

Chris Williamson

Earlier we talked about that quote in Amelia's yearbook that Susan helped us determine was *not* accurate. I kept going back to those words though, "The girl in brown who walks alone."

While the quote may not have been a true attribution written in Amelia's high school yearbook, the words do seem to fit her true nature.

Doug Westfall

This gave her an advent that allowed her to go farther and farther on her own; she didn't need anybody with her and she didn't have to take a train. She liked fast airplanes and she liked fast cars. There's a story about one of her Terraplanes, which would do eighty miles an hour, by the way. I talked to a young fellow whose grandfather stopped her for doing eighty on a back road, and he said once he realized it was Amelia Earhart, he let her off. I remember telling him, "Oh darn, the ticket would prove that it really happened."

Chris Williamson

How would you like to be *that* officer? Pulling someone over for speeding only to find out *that someone* was Amelia Earhart.

Unbelievable.

After talking with Doug, I got to thinking about what it must have been like to fly these incredible machines during those early days of aviation. How did the mechanics work?

What went through Amelia's mind during these flights? To gain some further understanding, I decided to consult a pilot. But not just any pilot...

*"It was inherently risky at the beginning because it was all new. In a lot of the
training that we do today, we look back and know that those lessons were
learned in blood."*

Chris Williamson

To say that aviation runs in the blood of *Boyd Kelly* would be an
understatement. He went to civil air patrol on scholarship and was
hooked on flying before ever learning to drive.

Like many of our Chasing Earhart project guests, he has ties to
Embry Riddle Aeronautical University, receiving his education there. He
went on to be a flight instructor and teach aviation classes all while
building his own flight time. He moved on to flying freight, which led
to his first commuter job, where he earned his first airline captain
stripes. Currently, Boyd works for a major US airline, flying interna-
tionally on the Boeing 777 with over ten thousand flight hours. In addition to flying, he runs the popular *Air Boyd* aviation YouTube channel
with an incredible 250 million views worldwide.

Boyd Kelly

The Wright brothers proved you could get something into the air.
You could do it, but you had to keep improving upon it as time went
on. The bigger challenges came with the things that we really take for
granted today; things like flying through weather, navigation, long
distances, the availability of airfields to land, fuel, things of that nature.

At the beginning, we really knew nothing about flying through
thunderstorms, for example, which is something we just don't do
anymore because it tears the aircraft apart.

This time period in the '20s and the '30s certainly predates any safety regulation for the most part. Even the *Airline Pilots Association, ALPA,* which represents a large part of the US aviation community for major airlines, got their start in the '30s specifically to address the issues that were coming about from flying mail and things back and forth across the country.

So it wasn't a fun time.

Open-cockpit biplanes, monoplanes – you're out there in the elements, and you can imagine on the east coast taking off in the fog *today* and trying to get your plane from New Jersey to Chicago and having to stop a couple of times. Your only real navigation is roads. At nighttime, they literally lit bonfires to navigate. You've got your leather jacket, but you're exposed to the elements. There's no GPS; there's no *Google Maps;* there's nothing. So the fact that we even got this far is pretty amazing to begin with. A single- or twin-seat biplane, much like the *Canary* she flew, is basically just cables and wires connected to a stick and an engine out front that was hand propped. There's no hydraulics, no flight computers, nothing. You're physically moving the airplane around. I'm reluctant to say that they were unsafe back then because these aircraft are still flying today.

In many cases, the engines themselves may not have lasted as long as they did today, but they certainly did their job. The aerodynamics that everybody looks at on a biplane still endure to this day. It wasn't an easy thing to fly, and in the case of a single-seat biplane, there's nowhere for a flight instructor to go. If you were lucky enough to find someplace that had a two-seat aircraft, you'd learn to fly in that, but then you're back in your single-seater flying around and learning by yourself again. You had to be a good pilot.

It was not going to work out for you if you didn't get the hang of it back then. I think it's probably a lot more forgiving today, but a lot of that is the technology and the ability to have a larger plane and to have someone go with you.

Obviously, having radios and things like autopilot are a big help today, but back then you learned, or you **died**.

Chris Williamson

I've heard a lot of crazy things since we started Chasing Earhart, but navigation by bonfire?

Now I've heard it all.

No GPS. Virtually no technology whatsoever. Just putting a pilot into an aircraft and then putting that aircraft into the sky.

Cross your fingers and hope you don't die.

Earlier we talked about obstacles that women faced, and I mentioned that they weren't wanted in aviation, but maybe I was wrong. Were women wanted? Were they looked down upon or even condescended to?

Boyd Kelly

Well, absolutely, and I think you'll find that a lot of it is indicative of the time period.

Women were supposed to be at home taking care of children and being housewives. You'll find that a lot of the books, particularly the children's books today you read about Amelia Earhart, focus on her attitude. She was told she couldn't do it or shouldn't be doing it, but she persevered, and that's what every single one of these women had to do, including Neta Snook, her first flight instructor.

A female flight instructor would have been *unheard of* in that time; they're still fairly rare today.

It's just the way that we've grown up historically. Math and science have typically gone to the male side and not so much the female side. At that time, women didn't go to work *period*, for the most part, let alone fly airplanes or teach people to fly around the world by themselves. It just wasn't done

Chris Williamson

If you know Amelia Earhart, then the Ninety-Nines should be very familiar to you. Amelia was crucial to the formation of the Ninety-Nines and was subsequently elected their first president. She was a hands-on president, participating in every meeting and writing letters to members herself. It wasn't just a publicity stunt for her; she took it very seriously. Thinking about the Ninety-Nines, I wondered out loud if Amelia and the founding members of the Ninety-Nines would be satisfied with the current state of women in aviation, a cause that they fought so hard for.

Boyd Kelly

I think they'd keep pushing.

I don't know that you'd necessarily say *satisfied* as a line in the sand. Someone like Amelia, who had a following, probably would have gone a lot further in her career. Perhaps even management of an airline, like many of the other pioneers did and certainly as some of our World War II aces did as time went on. I can't speak for women being a man, but there are certainly a lot more women at work who are getting interested in it. I do mentoring, and there are women all the time coming up to me, saying, "You know, I've always wanted to do this, but I got sidetracked with something else." There's always a lot of concerns I hear that simply aren't an issue nowadays. What if I want to have a family?

There are FAA rules regarding flying while pregnant. It certainly can be done, but I think someone like Amelia probably would have pushed further today and pushed those boundaries. We've had female astronauts. The number two head of NASA for a while was a woman. We've come a long way. Could we have come further?

Probably. It's hard to speculate too far. I think the women pioneers we had back in the day would have pushed even further in modern times. Their voices would have been amplified with the internet, social media, television and things of that nature. Those are tools that would have really pushed them along.

Chris Williamson

One of the many things that has always fascinated me about Amelia Earhart is her *legacy*.

This was a woman who continues to reach people through the

bridge of time, almost cheering women on from beyond. If you listen closely, you might hear echoes of her voice saying, "Hold on just a little longer." A little cheesy, I know.

We experienced tales of Earhart's reach every day during the Chasing Earhart project, and Boyd's personal experience isn't any different.

Boyd Kelly

It almost seems like it's been coming out more and more recently, and I just think it's the awareness of it. Certainly, things like this book are getting it out there. *Night at the Museum: Battle of the Smithsonian* had the Amelia Earhart character played by Amy Adams; it really starts to bring back a lot of it; it keeps her name circulating around. I live near Van Nuys, and there's an *Amelia Earhart Park* there. Just this week, I was at my son's school, reading *I Am Amelia Earhart* from Brad Meltzer's series. It was certainly one of the most popular books read in the classroom that day, and it just invokes that spirit. I think that everybody looks back at it and sees it as being a *can-do* attitude.

Not listening to *no* and persevering as all women aviators did back in that time was really an uplifting thing that resonates with everybody.

I *can* do it. And I *should* do it. I'm going to do it whether you're telling me to or not.

Chris Williamson

Imagine getting into an airplane, taking off and not knowing if you were going to land and survive.

Would *you* do it? Probably not.

Most people wouldn't take that risk. But Amelia Earhart knew something that most of us will never realize. The reward is worth the risk. The reward begets the glory. And the glory inspires.

Boyd Kelly

Imagine flying across the Atlantic by yourself, knowing that there's no place to stop, go to the bathroom, eat, refuel, or even take a nap. This was the same situation with Charles Lindbergh.

You're going to fly for seventeen solid hours by yourself across the Atlantic and hope you make it to the other side. You've certainly got to overcome an awful lot of things to do that by yourself. I've been sort of framing a lot of my discussions by talking about Amelia slightly differently. I'll tell people: "If I had told you that there was someone out there who designed their own clothing line and had become an editor for *Cosmopolitan* and was a best-selling author in addition to breaking all these records, you would probably think I was talking about any sort of social media or *YouTube* star today." But this was Amelia Earhart, and this was in the '20s and '30s, which is right after women had gotten the right to vote in the United States. To achieve that sort of fame in a time that didn't have social media or the internet is mind-boggling. Telephones were new. Newspapers and newsreels were *it*, and she was literally famous. She had to do all these other things to help get her flying career going and keep flying. That was all she ever wanted to do. Keep flying.

Chris Williamson

And keep flying she *did*. But we'll save that for later.

DESTINY

47.681271 | -53.254120

"She remembered when she received the call, and someone asked her if she wanted to cross the Atlantic or do some special flying. She thought it was a joke. She thought they were bootleggers who were looking for someone to pass off illegal alcohol."

Chris Williamson

So far on this journey, we've gotten to know Amelia Earhart as a little girl, spending her youth in Atchison before venturing out into the world with her family and then on her own. The times were tough then. A young Amelia Earhart had been bitten by the aviation bug and was wading into the unknown skies to begin a career that would send shock waves into the aviation world that are still felt to this very day.

Before we get to the shocking end that has been clouded in mystery for over eight decades, we're going to talk about Amelia's rise to a legendary status in American history.

See, Amelia didn't just tap the glass ceiling when she burst onto the scene.

She shattered it.

Records were set, goals were achieved, and a destiny was realized.

As we dive into Amelia's blossoming career, we examine how this woman looked aviation in the face and took it to new horizons. While it was relatively young, the aviation world wasn't ready for the boom that Amelia was about to lay on it. Her career didn't start with as much of a bang as she'd initially hoped though. In order to gain some insight as to why this was, I decided to reach out to *another* one of my remarkable friends.

"She was asked by a reporter why she was going from Hawaii to California and not from California to Hawaii. Her answer to that was, 'It's easier to hit a continent than it is to hit an island.'"

Michele Albion

For a while, there had been a number of pilots who had been interested in crossing the Atlantic, and there had been several attempts, all of them *unsuccessful.*

Chris Williamson

Michele Albion wrote one of my favorite Earhart books of all time. *The Quotable Amelia Earhart* gives the reader an inside look at the woman herself by using Amelia's own words to explain how she felt about a multitude of things, from aviation to motivation and everything in between. We get to hear Amelia's words describe her life as we read along and gain more insight than possibly any other book on the market today. As you listen to Michele talk, be on the lookout for quotes from the icon *herself.*

I can promise you that you'll hear something new.

Michele Albion

There was a promoter in New York named George Putnam, who was very interested in promoting a woman crossing the Atlantic. There was a pilot who lived in Great Britain named *Amy Guest,* who was very interested in being that first pilot, but her family was not supportive of this. Keep in mind that most pilots who made transatlantic journeys died, and they were not interested in having their relative pass away. So Palmer was looking for someone to fulfill the role, and they did a great deal of research before reaching out to Amelia Earhart, who at the time was working in a settlement house in Boston called *Denison House.* She remembered when she received the call, and someone asked her if she wanted to cross the Atlantic or do some special flying.

She thought it was a joke. She thought they were bootleggers who were looking for someone to pass off illegal alcohol.

Chris Williamson

Did you catch that name? Michele just dropped the name of someone whose fate was forever linked with that of Amelia Earhart. Let me add on to this for you. If you love aviation history like I do, there's a website you should be familiar with. *This Day in Aviation* chronicles aviation's biggest and most memorable moments and characters, from the Wright bros first flight to modern day record breaking flights. I highly recommend you look them up. In researching for the original podcast and now this text, I found and pulled the following beautifully written passage from their dedicated post to the 'Friendship' flight:

> *"The flight that would eventually be known as Friendship had been originally ordered by Richard Byrd for his Antarctic Expedition, but because the Ford Motor Company was a major sponsor, he made the decision to switch to a Ford tri-motor airplane. Byrd sold the new Fokker to Donald Woodward, heir to the Jell-O corporation, for $62,000."*

Yes, folks, we just connected Jell-O to Amelia Earhart.

> *"It was then registered to his mechanical science corporation of LeRoy, New York. Woodward then leased the airplane to Mrs. Frederick Edward Guest, also known as Amy Phipps or Amy Guest, for her to cross the Atlantic Ocean by air. It was Amy who chose the name Friendship for the airplane. Mrs. Guest was the daughter of Henry Phipps Jr., an American industrialist. She was married to Captain Frederick Edward Guest, a prominent British politician, former secretary of state, and a member of His Majesty's most honorable privy council. Amy Guest, however, was a multibillionaire in her own right"*

Yes folks, that's billion with a *B*. More from *This Day in Aviation:*

"Mrs. Guest was not a pilot, however, so pilots Wilmer Stoltz and Slim Gordon were hired to fly her airplane when her family ruled out her own transoceanic journey, and an "American girl of the right type" was selected to make the flight in her place. Enter Miss Amelia Mary Earhart, a social worker living in Boston."

Destiny, am I right?

"Although at this time Amelia was a pilot with approximately five hundred hours of flight experience under her belt, she did not serve as one of the pilots on this flight. She was, however, the aircraft commander. Instructions from Mrs. Guest's attorney David T. Layman to Stoltz and Gordon, dated May 18, 1928, were very specific on this matter:

'If any questions of policy, procedure, personnel, or any other arise, the deci- sion of Miss Amelia M. Earhart is to be final. That she is to have control of the plane and of the disposal of the services of all employees as fully as if she were the owner. And further on arrival of the plane in London, full control of the disposition of the plane and of the time and services of employees shall be hers to the same extent until and unless the owner directs otherwise.'"

Michele Albion

She had come to their notice because she had been interviewed by a Boston newspaper and she talked about how important flying was, especially for women. Out of the blue, she's invited to New York. She sits in Palmer's office for hours and waits, and she gets very angry. He said later that she was "as angry as a wet hen." Eventually, he proposes this transatlantic journey. Most people would say, "I don't think this is a great idea" or "let me think about it." She immediately said "yes."

She and a crew of two others would be flying from Newfoundland to cross the Atlantic and land in Europe; that was the goal. Of course, Charles Lindbergh had made the flight previously. She was not origi-nally slated to fly the plane; it was a possibility but not a probability. She was supposed to be, sort of in charge of the crew, and she had many duties. I recently saw an article where they were talking about how she didn't really do anything; she was just there, and that's *not true*.

She helped prepare the flight, she worked with the crew, and when they took off from Newfoundland on the Friendship, she was a valuable part of the crew. However, as they made the Atlantic flight, the weather was terrible; they had lots of equipment problems, and she did not actually fly. So she was the first woman to cross the ocean but not the first woman to *pilot a plane across the ocean*, and she fully acknowledged that. She said:

> "Stoltz did all the flying; he had to. I was just baggage like a sack of potatoes. Someday maybe I'll try alone."

She was criticized later by a woman's aviation magazine about not being the actual pilot, and that really got to her. It was that disappointment of not being able to fly on that flight that propelled her to make her first transatlantic flight in 1928.

After Amelia had gone across the ocean on the *Friendship*, she had been bothered a great deal because she received a great deal of praise. She received awards, but she didn't really feel like she earned the praise. She felt like she wanted to do something to earn it. She said it was:

> "A consummation of my desire to wipe out the idea that I was just a sack of potatoes on the *Friendship* trip."

Chris Williamson

As Michele just mentioned, Amelia Earhart became a superstar after the completion of the *Friendship* flight. While she saw it as an opportunity to use her newfound notoriety to educate the masses regarding women's ultimate place in aviation, she faced some pushback and criticism for her role in the flight. As if it was ever even a question, Amelia decided that she wanted to do the flight *again*, and this time she wanted to do it *on her own*.

. . .

Michele Albion

Most of the planning was done in secret.

They didn't want a lot of attention because so many of these flights failed. In May of 1932, she takes off from Newfoundland and travels across the Atlantic. It was a frightening journey, and she had limited tools for navigation. The original plan was to land in Paris, but then it was revised, and she hoped to land in Great Britain. She landed in Northern Ireland and very nearly came close to missing the entire continent. We think of this as, "How hard could it be?" Well, it was very difficult because they didn't have the kind of navigational tools that we have today; there was no GPS.

Chris Williamson

If Amelia was a superstar after the *Friendship* flight, crossing the Atlantic by herself catapulted her into the stratosphere.

Although she was taking on this task to prove that women belonged in aviation, she must have felt a sense of overwhelming vindication after completing such a terrifying flight.

Michele Albion

I think there was definitely a sense of vindication.

She received a Distinguished Flying Cross from congress, the cross of the knight of the Legion of Honor from the French government, a gold medal from the *National Geographic Society*, and it kept on going on and on. She got to meet *President Hoover*, of course. You would think that she would say, "Okay, I've accomplished everything I need to accomplish, and now I'm going to stop," but of course she didn't.

In August of 1932, she becomes the first woman to fly solo across the North Atlantic continent. Later, she's going to break the record for doing it *again* because she's going to do it a little faster this time. She won the *Harmon Trophy* three years in a row; then in 1935, she flew solo from Honolulu Hawaii to Oakland California. It was funny, she was asked by a reporter why she was going from Hawaii to California and not from California to Hawaii, and her answer to that was:

"It's easier to hit a continent than it is to hit an island."

Chris Williamson

Remember that quote. "It's easier to hit a continent than an island." She didn't know it then, but that sentence would be the foreshadowing to the end for Amelia Earhart.

Michele Albion

She had decided that she wanted to end her career with a world-wide trip, going all the way from one coast around the world to the other coast, and the Honolulu trip was sort of a dry run for that trip. She flew from Honolulu to California by herself, that was the first solo flight, and she did it without a hitch.

Chris Williamson

All these flights were leading Amelia to what would be her ultimate destiny: a trip around the world. As I was speaking with Michele about Amelia's career, she told me something that I'd never heard before, and it also serves as a foreshadow to an aspect of her world flight that would come into play on the morning of July 2, 1937.

Michele Albion

As she was flying back, they had a radio so they could communicate. She was communicating with the folks in Oakland, California, and they could hear her, but she cut out sometimes. At one point she said that she was "tired of looking at the water," and they heard "tired" and *only* "tired." They thought that she was too fatigued, and they were very worried about her landing. When she got to California, the tarmac was covered with emergency vehicles. She said:

"A special mental hazard was the sight of three fire engines and an ambulance in front of the hangar."

She, of course, landed without a hitch, but the crowd surged and just came out of nowhere and ran onto the runway before the propellers were stopped.

She was terrified that one of the propellers would hit someone.

Chris Williamson

What a story, right?

No matter how many experts I've talked with, I always wonder what their thoughts are on Amelia's ability to pilot an aircraft. After all, that's the very topic that will be called into question later when she's in Hawaii at *Luke Field*. Was Amelia Earhart *really* a good pilot, or was she simply *good enough* with an abnormal platform?

Michele Albion

For those who think that she wasn't a very good pilot, we need to put it in perspective.

Gore Vidal was in charge of American aviation, and Gore recalled as a young man sitting at the table and having all these pilots coming for dinner. He would always ask a few months or maybe a year later, "Whatever happened to so and so; how come we haven't seen this person?"

Well, they had *died flying*.

Amelia was a good pilot, she probably wasn't the *best* pilot, but most pilots couldn't get life insurance because their job was so dangerous. You might compare it to astronauts in the 1960s; everybody crashed and some survived, but most didn't. It's a very dangerous profession to be in. On top of that, she spent so much time having to promote herself that she sometimes didn't get the flying time that she needed. Male pilots usually had an advantage over female pilots because male pilots were mostly trained in the military.

Female pilots didn't have that opportunity, so in order to become a pilot, she had to do a thousand other jobs. She was a telephone operator, a photographer; you name it, she did it. When she became famous, she had to go all over the country constantly talking about aviation to promote herself.

So was she a *good* pilot?

Yes.

Was she probably the *best* pilot she could have been?

No.

She couldn't have done all these flights and broken all these records had she *not been* an accomplished pilot.

Chris Williamson

The interesting aspect to observe lies in the circumstances. Amelia Earhart was an exceptional pilot, but was she the best? Maybe I'm a little biased, but one thing is for certain.

The circumstances surrounding Amelia's career were *vastly different* than that of her peers'. As the face for women in aviation, Amelia spent more time in the promotion of not only *herself,* but the industry and cause that she cared so much about. Earlier, Doug Westfall told us that the women of the time all supported each other, and there was no resentment between the ranks. What about anyone else on team Amelia at that time? Was there tension?

Michele Albion

I think there was a great deal of resentment towards her, not because of *her* but because of Putnam, her husband. Her promoter was cutthroat, and he tried to put every other female aviator in the shade. However, when other pilots were asked about Amelia personally, they had a great relationship with her. She was a real team player, and she didn't believe that women's aviation could succeed unless women supported each other, which is why she founded the Ninety-Nines. She was individually loved, but not too many people appreciated her husband and his constant promotion of her while not promoting others.

. . .

Chris Williamson

Some people say that when you're at the top, the only direction that you can go is down.

Amelia didn't believe that.

Amelia believed that the sky was not only the limit, but it was also home. So it's not surprising that after crushing record after record, her quench to be better and push the envelope would get the better of her:

"The contemplated course covers about 27,000 miles. It will be the first flight (if successful) which approximates the equator."

Chris Williamson

Amelia Earhart wanted to fly around the world at the equator. She was always pushing herself. How did this idea come to her? Was it simply the next step in a career that had accomplished everything else? Or did Amelia Earhart want to do something *so* outrageous and *so* profound that she was willing to risk her *very life* to accomplish it?

Michele Albion

When asked why she was going to do the round-the-world flight, she said:

"To satisfy the ego that everyone exhibits sooner or later."

She wanted to go out on top; she wanted to do something that no woman had done before. She wanted to be in the record books, and she wanted to be an example for other women. She knew that it was dangerous:

"I'm more or less mortgaging the future to go on, but what are futures for?"

She was very aware of the fact that the flight would present a new level of danger. I'm sure she also knew that going around the world from west to east instead of east to west would make her journey much more difficult because that Pacific hop was very dangerous at the time. It's actually really shocking because the minute she crashed and they got away alive, she said:

"If we don't burn up, I want to try again."

Chris Williamson

The ground loop incident.

It's more than a crash. It's a turning point.

It's at this point that everything for the world flight changes. Some people say that it's at this point that Amelia Earhart sealed the fate of herself and of *Fred Noonan*.

Much, *much more* on the ground loop soon.

Michele Albion

She *did have* heart-to-heart conversations with her husband and with several women pilots before she took off. She knew it was danger-ous, and she knew that her chances of success were not good. The reason why her chances of success were not good wasn't just about the endurance that she would need for flying; there were also concerns about problems with navigation, which is why she had Noonan along. There were potential problems with getting fuel supplies in foreign countries where their standards were different; there were 1,001 things that could go wrong that had nothing to do with flying.

She knew her chances of success were questionable at best.

· · ·

Chris Williamson

And so, I ask you, would *you* do it?

Would *you* take the extreme risk of attempting a flight like this, at that time, with those kinds of odds stacked against you? Or did Amelia Earhart know something that we still don't know today?

Did she *know* that she wasn't going to return?

Michele Albion

I'm sure she was afraid, but fear wouldn't change anything. Just like anybody else who was a pioneer at that time and even today, it takes that respect for fear, that acknowledgment that you can't be motivated by it. It makes them do things that we all cower from.

Chris Williamson

Still with me?

We're just getting started on the world flight, I promise you, but there was a whole other aspect to Amelia Earhart's career that we haven't discussed yet. One of the most fascinating aspects of Amelia Earhart's career was the duality that it took on. With the great platform and promotional push that her business manager and eventual husband George Putnam would provide, Amelia Earhart became a household name. And I'm not talking about only within aviation.

I'm talking about straight-up iconography.

Amelia Earhart endorsed dozens of products, everything from luggage to vehicles to cigarettes and beyond. Very quickly she found herself in a career that had two sides, and those two sides were masterfully played by a woman who would become much more than a flyer. You can't discuss Amelia's aviation career without also discussing her endorsements, and for that, I knew exactly whom I wanted to bring in.

"In Philadelphia, they were introducing a new Packard automobile. She came out on the steps of the state building there, and there were tens of thousands of people. They probably didn't care much about the Packard; they wanted to see Amelia because at this point, she was an American icon."

Barbara Schultz

She didn't really go pound the sidewalk. Once she flew the Friendship despite only as a passenger, she was considered the number one person to endorse not just American aviation but all products in the United States. Lindbergh was there also, but he was not one to go out of his way to promote products.

Chris Williamson

An aviation historian first, *Barbara Schultz* is an accomplished pilot, author, and member of the Ninety-Nines, the group that Amelia Earhart helped found. Her book *Endorsed by Earhart: How Amelia Earhart Financed her Flying* is an intimate look at how Amelia parlayed her fame and notoriety into another fascinating aspect of her career that helped her achieve many of her aviation-related dreams. As Barbara tells it, Amelia quickly became America's sweetheart, and that translated into a burgeoning endorsement career.

Barbara Schultz

In order to have Earhart as a sponsor or endorse their products, brands would make a request. It was quite a coup, and I emphasize that phrase *quite a coup*, to *get* Earhart to endorse the new *Hudson Terraplane* automobile because when she was there, thousands of people literally came out to watch the christening.

Douglas's airplane the *Douglas Dolphin* was endorsed and christened twice by Earhart, once on *Clover Field*, which is now *Santa Monica*, and again at the grand opening of the *New Jersey airport terminal*.

She didn't really have to go out of her way to seek endorsements.

She endorsed a line of luggage with the *Orenstein Trunk and Luggage Company* just by chance because she met Orenstein at a social gathering. They had a discussion, and she said, "Well, that would work," so she endorsed a line of luggage and made a little bit of money off of that. She also participated in some of the designs and construction of the suitcases.

Chris Williamson

So come one, come all? Barbara's words got me curious. When it comes to endorsements, did Amelia ever draw the line or turn anything down?

Barbara Schultz

There were some things that she didn't think were appropriate. Putting her face on *Count Rapid,* for example. When George Putnam brought a project to her to create a children's felt hat with a headband that said "Amelia Earhart" on it, she also turned that down because she didn't want to misuse her image to influence children.

Chris Williamson

I would be remiss at this point if I didn't introduce you to a man who would change Amelia's life forever. Some would argue that without this man, Amelia Earhart would not have had her iconic success. George Palmer Putnam, *GP* as Amelia affectionately referred to him, saw a diamond in the rough when Amelia Earhart walked into his office in 1928.

That caused him to take her under his wing and make her the face for women in aviation.

This wasn't GP's first rodeo though. Just five years earlier, he helped catapult the career of someone you may have heard of by the name of Charles Lindbergh. It's safe to say that from this point on, Amelia Earhart was in the best of hands.

Barbara Schultz

He did serve as her manager, so all offers would go through him, and then occasionally, as with some of the ones I mentioned, he would come up with them on his own. She did turn those down. In Philadelphia, they were introducing a new Packard automobile. She came out on the steps of the state building, and there were tens of thousands of people there.

They probably didn't care much about the Packard; they wanted to see Amelia because at this time she was an American icon. Another reason was she was photogenic, just her image alone emanated sincerity and trust, so I think that had a lot to do with it. All of the potential endorsements were handled by Putnam. One of the major endorsements came along when *Pitcairn* autogyros were in production. You had people who wanted to purchase them who had to wait in line. *Beech Nut* were third in line, and they said, "We'll let you fly our autogyro as long as we can put 'Beech Nut' on the side, and then that way it's kind of a quid pro quo. You can fly the aircraft and at the same time endorse our products."

Chris Williamson

Since I have your attention, let me tell you a story. It may be my favorite Earhart story of all time. The following passage comes once again, from my friends at *This Day in Aviation*:

"An autogyro was a very expensive piece of equipment in 1930; approximately $15,000 back then. Only those people with financial backing or corporate sponsorship were able to afford one. From the public perspective, this new auto flying machine, which was able to take off from such a small piece of real estate, was truly a great human achievement. The gyroplane of 1930 was cutting-edge aviation technology. The autogyro was capable of flying at very controllable slow speeds without the risk of stalling the aircraft, yet was about as fast as any fixed-wing aircraft at the time. On December 19, 1930, Amelia Earhart went on a test flight in an autogyro that would become legendary. That day she became the first female autogyro pilot on the planet. On April 8, 1931, an autogyro sits on a field as Amelia looks the craft over. It

has four large fully articulating rotors of lightweight construction with support cables on the top to keep them from dropping too much when the aircraft wasn't being flown. Additionally, it featured a sleek rounded structure with short wings and upturned ends. As Amelia completes her checks, she surely has to think that this aircraft is made to set records. Earhart wore insulated coveralls that day and very joyfully and confidently enters the cockpit of the autogyro, placing her leather flier's cap on her head and adjusting herself on the parachute. She starts the engine and begins her attempt at the autogyro altitude record. Maybe it was for the press or maybe for the crowd. Maybe she wanted to ensure the ship had the power she would need, or it may have been that she wasn't fully focused on the task, but Amelia fell short on her first attempt at the altitude record."

Chris Williamson

However, this is *Amelia Earhart we're talking about,* and *failure is not an option.*

At this point, she took her own advice when she famously said:

"Women must try to do things as men have tried. When they fail, their failure must be but a challenge to others."

More from *This Day in Aviation:*

"Gathering her speed, Earhart pulled back on the stick and set the autogyro on its skyward search for the record books. As the altitude increased, the air became much thinner, which would bring the onset of hypoxia, a lack of oxygen to the brain. If she stayed too long at those higher altitudes, she could black out. The December air was cold, and at that altitude, it was even colder no one watched the altimeter continue to climb. The controls would continue to lose their effective- ness in the thin air, and her piloting skills would be challenged as she approached her mark. When no more could be pushed from the aircraft, Amelia pushed the stick forward after having attained the incredible altitude of 18,415 feet in a normally aspirated engine for a rotorcraft. Bringing the aircraft into a nice landing and rolling stop, Amelia entered the record books in one of the greatest aviation feats of all time."

Chris Williamson

What was it about this seemingly shy woman that changed the face of aviation forever? What did people see in Amelia Earhart that caused them to flock to her like moths to a flame?

Barbara Schultz

Well, I've often thought about that. Putting myself back in that time period in the 1920s, women were given much more freedom; the dressing was wild; their dancing was crazy; they were drinking. Here comes Amelia Earhart, this very quiet woman who as a passenger had the courage to get in an aircraft unproven, and fly across the Atlantic. I think she stood out as a representative of the modern woman and what all women aspired to be. Be courageous and do something to prove your self-worth. I don't think we're just looking at the '29 derby (the first national air race for women) that was considered by the general public as sort of a carnival act. If these women could fly, then anybody could transport or pilot an aircraft. So I think the emphasis was that this was a woman we could aspire to be. She's done more than we could ever dream in our lifetime. By seeing her, being around her and hearing her lectures, I think that gave people the ability to be part of that whole experience.

Most of the speeches that she gave were attended by women. I think it's akin to people who are sports advocates now; if they have a chance to meet one of their heroes, then they've shared a little bit in that hero's experiences.

Chris Williamson

Amelia Earhart was a worldwide icon. She didn't just belong to aviation; she *transcended* it.

A modern-day superhero, people would flock to wherever Amelia might be just to be able to say that they caught a glimpse of her and, if they were lucky enough, maybe even speak with her or get an auto-graph. We know this to be true because we continually heard stories during Chasing Earhart of people whose relatives had what we like to call an "Earhart experience" and still talk about how that experience affected them to this very day. As her career took off to new heights, Amelia Earhart had to quickly adapt and navigate a brand-new spotlight that she may not have expected to be a part of the equation when she started flying. Like everything else though, she took it in stride.

Barbara Schultz

Earhart doesn't shun being in the limelight because, for her, it was another way to promote aviation as a woman. To be as friendly as possible and connect with all the other ladies.

When she came back from the solo flight from Hawaii to Oakland, she got out of her airplane, and she had been in the air for, I don't know how long, but she was exhausted. She took time to simply answer the newspaper people's questions. I think that she probably would have appreciated being able to go sit down in the terminal on a couch and relax, but instead, I think it was all about promoting aviation. She would take the time to do that.

That's why she did two or three lectures a day sometimes, depending on how close they were in proximity.

She worked really hard to get out there and promote aviation. I think in 1935, she made something like $40,000, that's a lot of money, and that's just on her lectures.

Chris Williamson

Just in case you're wondering, $40,000 a year during that time is a little over 1.5 *million* dollars today.

But it wasn't *all* about the money. Amelia valued this part of her life perhaps more than anything else. It gave her the platform to directly influence women, and she was not going to let that opportunity pass her by. Like everything else in her life, she was presented with an opportunity, and she took that opportunity to a place that was surprising at the time.

Maybe not *that surprising* in hindsight.

She took it to college.

. . .

Barbara Schultz

It was a venue where she could share the knowledge that she had as an aviator, and she could share the process, perhaps applying some of her experiences that had not been successful. I think that would have been a practical career for her when she came back, and she would have embraced that. Giving lectures is about sharing your passion and sharing your experiences with other people. If you look at her record flights, those are great, but then the next week or the next month, somebody would break those records.

Her ability to connect one on one with individuals both during her lectures and also during her time at Purdue took her out of that perspective of being an aloof heroine. I don't think she was actually comfortable with that role, so by doing the lectures, she could show that she was just like anybody else who had gone out and done a little bit more.

Anybody could do what she could do, and that was the point.

Chris Williamson

Amelia's connection to Purdue was an important one. So important in fact, that we dedicated an entire episode of our *Chasing Earhart* documentary to it. *Vanished* also featured an entire episode dedicated to it as well. So will this text. Much, much more on Purdue coming up.

There is something I've been wondering about for a very long time, and it may be controversial to ask, but I think presenting this question allows us to look at the whole thing from another angle.

I wonder about Louise Thaden, Ruth Elder, Florence Klingensmith, Pancho Barnes, and all the others who were flying during that time. I wonder if *they were* in the same position as Amelia Earhart with the backing she had, would they have been as successful? Would they have had the same level of impact? If you take Amelia Earhart, *the woman,* out of the picture, and drop in anyone else from that era, do we have a difference?

Or was Amelia Earhart *truly* one of a kind?

. . .

Barbara Schultz

Well, I think there were a lot of aviatrixes who were as photogenic and as charming, but if you put Louise Thaden in there, and she accomplished everything that Earhart did, I think there would be some increment of less popularity. I think part of Earhart's popularity had to do with the fact that she resembled Lindbergh, and Lindbergh was the one who kicked off the big craze in aviation. So here we have a true *Lady Lindy*, and she'd fit that bill. She was the female counterpart for Charles Lindbergh, and you don't get any greater in aviation history than Charles Lindbergh. Now you have Amelia Earhart, who resembles Lindbergh, and I think that's part of why she was selected. We have *Lady Lindy* and *Lucky Lindy*. Maybe she (Louise) would have been more recognizable had she made some of the accomplishments, but not to the degree that Earhart did, just on the basis of what we're discussing. That resemblance to Lindbergh.

Chris Williamson

So it *was* Amelia. It was *always going to be* Amelia Earhart. Was it her destiny to go down in history as the greatest female pilot of all time, the best to ever do it? Perhaps it was.

Would the fame, glory and admiration come with a deadly price? Was part of Amelia's story forever linked with an ending that has become *so controversial* that it's debated to this very day? Is it really surprising that Amelia Earhart, America's sweetheart, would become a polarizing figure in her mysterious vanishing over the Pacific Ocean? Questions better served for a later discussion. One we will *most certainly have*. But before we get to *that* conversation, let's hear a few more words from Barbara.

3 Years Later: A Retrospective

Following her 1928 trans-Atlantic flight in the *Friendship*, Amelia Earhart became America's symbol of feminine triumph. It didn't matter that she sat in the back of the airplane, taking notes. Her achievement of crossing from one continent to another infused excitement into a movement toward women's independence, which began in the late 1920s. The press capitalized on reporting Amelia's achievements, placing her always photogenic image on the front page. Businesses, out of necessity, found unique ways to create additional fanfare for their products during the economic hardships of the 1930s. Publicity from the endorsements of a trailblazing pilot such as Amelia proved a guaranteed solution.

Amelia's newfound status enabled her to become a credible endorser of flight, more than any other woman pilot of her day. She took her role as a goodwill ambassador for aviation and women's rights very seriously. Through her lectures, radio broadcasts, and air tours as well as magazine and newspaper articles, Amelia heralded the benefits of the airplane and air travel. While Amelia proclaimed the benefits of aviation through various media, flying was her first priority. The sport required financing, however, and endorsements were the answer. She would make many during the next decade. Some were for goods traded in exchange for her name or image; others were monetary and supplemented her flights.

The first woman to fly solo across the Atlantic did not always welcome the opportunity to endorse a product. Amelia felt some were inappropriate, writing the following for the press in June 1928:

"Flying the Atlantic involves learning a lot more than I ever dreamed about when I accepted the invitation to take part in the flight of the *Friendship*. Ever since landing in England, I have been learning about what it means to be a public person, the center of some big event in the news that is interesting to people. Today, I have been receiving offers to go on the stage, appear in the movies, and to accept gifts ranging from an automobile to a husband. And I am caught in a situation when very little of me is free. I am being moved instead of moving. I am not going to commercialize my flight in the *Friendship*, and I will be happier when the pressure of life in the public eye diminishes."

George Putnam reflected on the subject of endorsements and public figures in his book *Soaring Wings*.

"I believe not one of the figures who have become popularly famous at one time ever imagined the sheer, thumping hard work of conscientious heroing…About getting financial help toward adventurous undertakings like AE's, there is nothing either illegitimate or unique. Indeed, it is the fact that it is possible for individuals to get a vicarious thrill out of having a financial hand in adventure which has largely kept modern expeditions going."

Specific to his wife, Putnam stated:

"If she could find people she believed in, representing something she believed in, which would benefit from the news she could create, she was willing and glad to make that news help underwrite her activities."

This was particularly true for Amelia's endorsement of *Lucky Strike cigarettes*, something for which she was highly criticized by the public. She explained her rationale for the company in her book *20 hrs. 40 min*:

"Cigarettes have nearly been my downfall. Not subjectively, understand, for my indulgence is decently limited; the count, I think shows that the restrained total of three for the current year. It's not what I did, but what I said, that caused trouble. I wickedly 'endorsed' a certain cigarette which was carried by the boys on the *Friendship*. This I did to benefit three gallant gentlemen – Commander Byrd to whose South Polar Expedition I turned over my own financial proceeds, and the companions on my flight who benefitted only if my name was used."

Over the next nine years, Amelia was able to fly thanks to her multitude of endorsements, setting records and promoting aviation.

The most appropriate backing came from aviation companies such as *Sperry*, *Veedol*, *Pratt & Whitney*, and *Mobil Oil*. Endorsements were given to emerging airlines – *Colonial*, *TAT*, *Maddux*, *Ludington*, and *Boston-Maine Airways*. Christenings were a large part of her testimonials – Standard Oil's *Essowing*, Parker Pen's *Fairchild*, Goodyear's *Defender*, and TAT's *City of New York*. In 1933, Amelia granted the *Orenstein Trunk and Luggage Company* permission to create a line of luggage in her name and with her input. The variety of luggage bore an assortment of labels bearing her name. Her red Vega was included on the early cases. Amelia endorsed a number of automobile companies – *Chrysler*, *Franklin*, *Hudson*, *Packard*, *Ford*, and *Cord* – often receiving one of their new models to drive.

Most profitable for Amelia were her lectures, which she did tirelessly. In 1935, she grossed $30,000. Audiences of all ages overflowed wherever Amelia spoke. Some, perhaps, were more interested in seeing her than absorbing the contents of her lecture. Venues included community and social clubs, schools, churches, awards banquets, and train stations. The theme of her speaking engagements was typically advertised as "Adventures in Flying," which informed the audience about her books or the state of modern aviation. Amelia's initial presentations seemed tentative at best, but in the later years, few if any women surpassed her in platform and dexterity and charm. Her abilities improved, and the crowds grew in size.

As a counselor in Careers for Women at Purdue University, Amelia may have made her greatest contribution to the advancement of women in aviation. In her own words:

> "The problems and opportunities of these girls were quite as much my concern as aviation matters. Perhaps I have something of a chip on my shoulder when it comes to modern feminine education. Often youngsters are sadly miscast. I have known girls who should be tinkering with mechanical things instead of making dresses, and boys who would do better at cooking than engineering. One of my favorite phobias is that girls, especially those whose tastes aren't routine, often don't get a fair break. The situation is not new. It has come down

through the generations, an inheritance of age-old customs which produced the corollary that women are bred to timidity."

Amelia would make a valiant effort to encourage her female students to *break the mold*.

Barbara Schultz
Summer 2021

THE RED SUN
40.6602418 | -73.7250994

"The Ninety-Nines were founded in 1929, I like to say, by Amelia Earhart and ninety-eight of her close friends. I would hope that all these years later, we're still fulfilling the original mission and vision of our charter members."

Chris Williamson

Thus far, we've waded into the career of Amelia Earhart, and we've discussed what separated her from the other aviators of the time. At this point, AE was soaring to heights the young world of aviation had never seen, setting record after record while also setting the example for women in aviation along the way. We've spent some time breaking down the various career paths some of the other key figures in Amelia's life took and how her career stood out and maybe pulled her away from everyone else in the field.

Now though, we're going to take a look at an aspect of Amelia's career that was a natural evolution of what she believed in and stood for.

We're going to talk about something that brought the pioneers of women in aviation together.

Well, *ninety-nine* of them at least.

Chris Williamson

To say that the Ninety-Nines are and always have been an integral part of aviation is an understatement.

Shortly before digging into this area of the story, I was gathering information on the early days of the group. I came across this passage from the official website for the Ninety-Nines.

Reading it will tell you all you need to know about their formation:

"On November 2nd, 1929, 26 women gathered at Curtiss Field in Valley Stream, Long Island, New York. The weather wasn't favorable and most drove in or came by train. The first order of business was the selection of Neva Paris as temporary chairman. Then the presentation of flowers to Viola Gentry who was recovering from a crash following an endurance record attempt.

"The women conducted their business in a hangar above the den of a Curtis Challenger with engines running as the work of the mechanics proceeded around them. Tea was served from a toolbox wagon on wheels, and eligibility and purpose were quickly decided upon.

"Membership would be open to any woman with a pilot's license and the purpose of the organization would be 'good fellowship jobs, and a central office containing complete files on women in aviation.' Choosing a name was a little harder though, some offerings were 'The Climbing Vines,' 'The Noisy Bird Women,' 'The Homing Pigeons,' and 'The Gadflies.'"

My personal favorite is *definitely* "The Homing Pigeons."

"Amelia Earhart and Jean Davis Hoyt put a stop to all that naming nonsense though and proposed that the name be taken from the sum total of charter members. Thus, the group was momentarily the 'Eighty-Sixes' then the 'Ninety-Sevens' and finally the 'Ninety-Nines.'"

The name and number stopped at *99*, but the membership there-after grew worldwide. Furthermore, if you search those charter members, you'll find a veritable hall of fame for women in aviation: Ruth Elder, Viola Gentry, Faye Gillis, Florence Klingensmith, Ruth Nichols, Louise Thaden, Mary Goodrich, Marjorie Stenson, and of course, Amelia Earhart.

Individually these women, *all of them*, had remarkable careers. But collectively, they changed the world. When we decided to include this as an episode during season 1 of *Vanished*, I had one choice, and one choice *only* as the guest to represent the organization that Amelia so loved. So much so, that I wrote a full interview for her before I ever asked her to join me.

Luckily for me and for everyone reading this, she said *yes*.

"Jackie Cochran was appointed by Congress as an ambassador to Japan to gather information on women's roles in the Japanese Air Force during the war. That was the guise for her going over there, but she never presented whatever report she should have to Congress after it was over with."

Lisa Cotham

The Ninety-Nines were founded in 1929, I like to say, by Amelia Earhart and ninety-eight of her close friends.

There was a recognition for the women pilots at that time that they needed an organization to support themselves and to promote women pilots from both a "Sports and breadwinning point of view." That was the language that was used to express the group to potential members. They also wanted to be able to tip each other off regarding what was going on in the industry. I would hope that all these years later, we're still fulfilling the original mission and vision of our charter members.

Chris Williamson

First and foremost, Lisa Cotham is my friend, and I'm lucky to know her.

She's a trustee for the Ninety-Nines and their public relations chairman. She's a pilot and all-around Earhart expert. Most importantly, she's keen on keeping the true history and legacy of both Amelia Earhart and the Ninety-Nines alive and well, and she does it with a tremendous sense of poise and a wonderful sense of humor. Lisa sat on our discussion panel during the 2018 Amelia Earhart festival in Atchison as the representative for the Ninety-Nines. On that panel, our moderator, Dr. Joshua Wolf, asked her about the history of the organization. She didn't disappoint *then,* and she didn't disappoint when she spoke with me for the podcast *either.*

Lisa Cotham

The first two years of the organization, it was under acting leadership while they were still struggling to find their way. In 1931, they elected their first president, and it was Amelia Earhart. We have documentation in our files in Oklahoma City of how extensive her involvement was. Of course, there was no internet or emails, so all their communication back then was by written letter or telegrams, and we have many of those correspondences in the files. I was amazed to see just how actively hands-on she was; she was constantly writing to the members to make them aware of events and circumstances and to invite them to travel with her to some events that she was participating in. She used her status as a quasi-celebrity, or maybe a *real celebrity*, to further the causes of the organization, but she didn't do anything for her own personal gain. She actually funded a lot of the early activities out of her own pocket, such as a uniform they were developing for all the members to wear.

She was in it to *make it succeed*.

Chris Williamson

How's *that* for putting your money where your mouth is?

We now know that Amelia wasn't only the official first president of the Ninety-Nines; she was also heavily involved in their early foundation. How did the other ninety-eight women feel about Amelia being the face of the organization?

Was Amelia Earhart a strategic business move for them?

Lisa Cotham

I'm sure from those charter members' perspectives, it was advantageous to have her.

There were other women in the organization who also had name recognition, like Louise Thaden, Pancho Barnes, and Faye Gillis Wells, but Amelia was definitely head and shoulders above them when it came to public awareness.

Chris Williamson

It's fascinating to hear about the early history of this incredibly influential group and some of the disagreements and egos that went into the early foundation. It goes to show you that while each one of the founding members cared deeply about the cause, it wasn't easy to make this formation successful right from the start. Some of the early meetings reflected some of this difficulty.

Lisa Cotham

In our archives at headquarters, we have the typed transcript of a meeting that was held in March of 1930, which was right after the formation, when they were still struggling with organizational structure, officers, and such. It was amazing, the arguments and the resolutions that were discussed at that time. It's about thirty-one pages long. It's a very interesting document showcasing the struggles and the thought processes that they went through as they were forming this organization to support women pilots. At one point, one of the members got put out about something, so she got up and left the room. I think one of the officers actually resigned at that time. There had been a problem, in that the ballot had been prepared for the initial elections, and one of the candidates on the ballot was tragically *killed*. Somebody just made some substitutions without getting back with the membership, so that caused a big tizzy over the process. I think that's what was more in view at that point. "Let's make this fair and do it the right way."

Chris Williamson

You'd think that there was a lot of thought that went into the formation of this hugely influential group, but history dictates that the Ninety-Nines may have been formed on spontaneity.

Furthermore, it was formed on a day that also ties *directly* into the history of aviation: August 18, 1929.

. . .

Lisa Cotham

Aviation had been around for twenty-six years at that point, and there had been cross-country races and closed-course air races that women were not allowed to participate in. So this race was created in 1929 for all women, and there were a lot of stumbling blocks; there were pre-race questionable events as well as some that took place during the race. There was one woman who may have suffered sabotage of her fuel line. Another one had contaminant placed directly into her fuel, and there was actually a fatality during the race as well. When those women finally arrived in Cleveland, Ohio, at the culmination of the race, they got together and said, "We need our own organization." That was the impetus for the foundation of the Ninety-Nines. They went from August/September of 1929 to the formation in November of 1929, so they did it rather quickly and all by snail mail.

Chris Williamson

August the eighteenth, 1929, is one of my very favorite days in aviation history.

The *women's air derby*. Look it up; that's homework for future discussion.

A dedicated section of this book on this very important date is coming at you just a little further ahead. When Amelia Earhart vanished seemingly into thin air on the morning of July 2, 1937, it must have had an impact on the organization that she helped found and cared so much about. After all, her fellow founders were close friends of hers. That got me curious as to how the disappearance affected them and what role she would have played had she returned home without incident.

Lisa Cotham

I don't know that it would have been a big part, but it would have definitely played a role.

I think Amelia was all about building up other women pilots and helping them achieve leadership roles, so I think she would have been

63

there as a mentor but not been out in front. Probably initially, after the completion of the world flight because of all the notoriety, but I think in the long haul, she would have been a backseat player, there to help support the women members in the organization itself.

Obviously, they were all friends with her and very upset by her disappearance, not just for *her* but because the attempt at the accomplishment failed. One of the results of the disappearance was that the organization chose to honor her by creating a scholarship fund in her name, and that first scholarship was issued in 1941 for $125 for an instrument rating.

As of today, we've issued about 750 scholarships totaling over $11 million to our members all in the name of Amelia Earhart. That's a massive impact that she had on our organization.

Chris Williamson

It's abundantly clear that Amelia Earhart's soul and spirit left a lasting impact on the Ninety-Nines.

Upon her disappearance and upon being declared dead in absentia, that impact, as Lisa mentioned, has been cause for the organization to create the Amelia Earhart Memorial Scholarship Award, which is still given out to this day. More on that in a moment. Another organization that I have a lot of respect for is the WASP. For those who don't know, Women Air Force Service Pilots have gone down in history as an important group that have fought for the right to be recognized by the United States government as intricate parts of the military. If you haven't heard of the WASP, I highly suggest that you look them up.

Impressive doesn't even begin to describe it.

The woman who started and championed that program was Jackie Cochran. Jackie Cochran was a very close friend and confidant of who? You guessed it. Amelia Earhart.

Read this next part very, *very* closely.

Lisa Cotham

A lot of the women who were in the Ninety-Nines were contacted or applied to be *WASP*.

Of course, the founder of the WASP, Jackie Cochran, was president of the Ninety-Nines from 1941 to 1943, so she knew the capabilities of the women and was right on target taking this concept to the military and making it happen. A lot of the women in the Ninety-Nines were WASP, and we still have a couple of living WASP who are *still* in the organization.

Right before Amelia left, she had some conversations with Jackie. After she disappeared, Jackie, who professed to have psychic ability, said she had received some messages from Amelia. They were not in competition, they both had their own goals, and they were close friends. She was appointed by Congress as an ambassador to Japan to gather information on women's roles in the Japanese Air Force during the war. That was the guise for her going over there, but she never presented whatever report she *should have* to Congress after it was over with.

Chris Williamson

It's often fun to speculate on what Amelia would have done with the Ninety-Nines and what she would think of their position in aviation during modern times. For that reason, I thought it would be a good idea to collect Lisa's thoughts on what Amelia might think of the status of her beloved organization *today* and the status of women in aviation, a cause that she championed so valiantly during her aviation career.

Lisa Cotham

I don't think the Ninety-Nines would have been as successful as it was in the early days without her. Obviously, there were other women who were achieving things, but because of the impact that she had on society, it brought attention to the organization and to the women who represented it. There's still a lot of hurdles out there that women have to jump through in order to achieve their career goals. Just about every woman involved in aviation gives credit to Amelia for paving the way. She really broke the boundaries, and she proved that women could do anything men could do. I think that she would be disappointed to know that women are still such a small percentage of the aviation industry. On the pilot side, we used to be able to look at statistics from the FAA, but they're not as easily obtained anymore. From my rough estimates, as of 2018, 6% or 7% of pilots were women, and that's a really low percentage over the course of ninety years.

I think she would be disappointed in that. I think she would also be amazed by the things that women *have done*. Everything from the space station and space shuttles to jet flights and all other types of flight. So yeah, I think she'd be really happy with what's going on.

Chris Williamson

Adding to those thoughts before we ended our chat, Lisa told me something that offers an interesting inside look at the early days in this remarkable organization. It was quite telling to hear of it because it reasserts the position of the organization and what they wanted to stand for. As we'll learn in just a moment, it's a position that hasn't changed much over the years.

Lisa Cotham

There was a letter sent to 117 women pilots in October of 1929, and it outlines their desire to form this organization. To quote from the letter it says:

"It need not be a tremendously official sort of an organization; just a way to get acquainted; to discuss the prospects for women pilots from both a sports and breadwinning point of view. And to tip each other off on what's going on in the industry. We're not particular whether you come by train, automobile, or on two legs, or just by mail, but we do hope you put in some kind of an appearance at the organization meeting of licensed women pilots."

That was signed by Faye Gillis Wells and several other women who were involved with the organization committee.

Apparently, there was some pushback on this because two months later, actually, on New Year's Eve, there was a letter from the acting president Opal Kunz to a potential member in New York, and this potential member seemed to have had a misinterpretation of what was going on. In some of the comments to this member from Kunz, she said:

"We are not fighting for anything. We're trying to bring about a different attitude towards the girl in aviation, where she is accepted as an equal rather than spoiled as something rare and very precious. In this organization of ours, it is hoped that we could encourage girls to enter flying schools with the determination not to accept any special consideration because of their sex."

Even back then, you can see how cognizant they were of the pushback and the possibility of special treatment because they were women. The letter even comments that because there were so many men doing these things, having a woman involved was a rarity, which is why it gained so much notoriety. They were not in it for any kind of special treatment. They just wanted to be treated as equals, which sounds a lot like what's still going on today.

Chris Williamson

After getting a good education of the foundation and the values of the Ninety-Nines from Lisa, I was naturally curious about how those values are being reflected in the current literation of the organization today. I wanted to find out if the Ninety-Nines still represented what Amelia wanted all these years later. There was only one person I could think of to call for that perspective.

I called the president. No, not *that one*. *This one*.

"Amelia provided hope for so many people; hope to strive, hope to learn by failure, and hope to succeed when everything is pushing back against you. 'What do dreams know of boundaries?' Nothing. Dreams know nothing of boundaries."

Jan McKenzie

We are an organization of over 5,700 licensed women pilots, and we're in forty-four countries.

Chris Williamson

Jan McKenzie learned to fly in a taildragger. Shortly thereafter, she became a 99. She's been an electrical engineer for over thirty-four years, something that Amelia Earhart would be *particularly* proud of. She's moved through the ranks of the organization, holding various chapter and international offices. She's also a former president of the Ninety-Nines. She's the perfect person to speak to on the topic of the Ninety-Nines in the modern age of aviation. Like Lisa before her, I'm grateful that she agreed to talk to me.

Jan McKenzie

We're astronauts and airline pilots; pilots who teach flight, and pilots who fly for pleasure.

We're pilots who are technicians, and we're pilots who are mechanics. First and foremost, though, we are women who love to fly. To honor that legacy, we've passed *on* our passion for applied women of all ages, particularly for young women. We do this through demo flights, scholarships, mentoring, and just generally helping women who want to start flying. We own and support the Museum of Women Pilots in Oklahoma City, and the Amelia Earhart Birthplace Museum in Atchison, Kansas. Those museums have helped educate and inform thousands of people about the magic of flight as well as the women pioneers who passed their love on to us, as we do now to others. We have second-, third- and even fourth-generation women pilots, professional military pilots, and racers and pilots who do it just "for the fun of it." We've made flying accessible to all races, classes, and income levels through the generous donations and bequests of our members.

Chris Williamson

It's really important to understand that the Ninety-Nines go out of their way to push **hard** when it comes to lighting the fire underneath women, young girls *especially*. It's a fundamental belief for the organization, the same way it was for its first president. The Ninety-Nines believe that women can do anything that men can do, *and they believe it to the very core*. As Jan explains, this is an organization that does not shy away from its history. These women are not afraid to get out front and put their money where their mouths are.

Jan McKenzie

As Lisa mentioned, since 1941, we've given out over a thousand awards totaling more than $11 million.

That's a thousand women whom we've helped with their aviation goals and dreams. In one year, we typically provide forty women an award to help them obtain their private pilot's license.

We also typically give over twenty scholarships every year for advanced ratings that are needed to help move up the ladder for commercial and ATP [airline transport pilots].

Right now, that fund, which is member endowed, is worth five and a half million dollars.

The Ninety-Nines have changed lives with these scholarships, and we continue to grow our abilities to support women worldwide, with whatever aviation goal they have.

· · ·

Chris Williamson

I originally met Jan at the annual induction of the International Forest of Friendship ceremony. I like to think of it as the Amelia Earhart Hall of Fame. According to its official website:

> *"The International Forest of Friendship is a living growing memorial to the world history of aviation and aerospace. It sits nestled on a gentle slope over-looking Lake Warnock on the outskirts of Atchison. It's made up of trees from all 50 states and 36 territories and countries around the world from which its honorees reside. Trees from George Washington's Mount Vernon estate, along with a tree from Amelia's grandfather's farm, and the moon tree, grown from a seed taken to the moon by command pilot Stewart Russa on Apollo 14 all reside there."*

> *"Winding through the forest are pathways honoring those who have or still are contributing to all facets of aviation and aerospace. The original path is called Memory Lane; it leads to a secluded circle of benches and a grove of trees. All of the forest walkways are five feet wide, and embedded in them are granite plaques with the names of over 1,400 honorees. Included in this illustrious list are markers memorializing such aviation notables as Charles Lindbergh, the Wright Brothers, Sally Ride, Chuck Yeager, Jimmy Doolittle, and Colonel Eileen M. Collins, the first woman to pilot a shuttle into space."*

> *"Memory Lane was designated as the first National Recreation trail in Kansas. In 1991, a beautiful gazebo was dedicated to Faye Wells in honor of her leadership of the forest as well as a waterfall in honor of Joe Kerrigan, for his many contributions as the founder and co-chairman."*

Nestled at the very back of the forest, as if to watch over her hall of fame and Atchison, Kansas, itself, is a statue of Amelia Earhart. The forest is open all year around from sunrise to sunset; I highly recommend that you seek it out if you're ever in Kansas.

Jan McKenzie

Faye Gillis Wells, who was a charter member of the Ninety-Nines and a noted journalist, along with Joe Kerrigan of Atchison, Kansas, co-chaired the forest from its very inception until their deaths.

Their sons and their families continue to stream world friendship through flight to this very day. The son of Amelia's husband, George Palmer Putnam, graciously provided a grant to help preserve the legacy of the forest and all that connects it to Amelia and *her legacy* with the Ninety-Nines today. It's a beautiful park and a peaceful place to contemplate how flying connects people all over, a message that Amelia was carrying on her last flight to all parts of the world.

Chris Williamson

When people ask me to describe Amelia Earhart in a single word, the word I use most often is *hope*. Amelia provided hope for so many people; hope to strive, hope to learn by failure, and hope to succeed when everything is pushing back against you. "What do dreams know of boundaries?" Nothing. Dreams know **nothing** of boundaries. My hope is that you're starting to see that.

Jan McKenzie

One of the most important parts of the Ninety-Nines' mission is to honor our unique history. One of our greatest treasures is the *Museum of Women Pilots*, which enables us to keep and share so many of these great women's legacies and share them with the community. We also cherish our Amelia Earhart Birthplace Museum to ensure that her legacy lives on. To expand our reach, we have displays on the Ninety-Nines at the Smithsonian Air and Space Museum. The staff at the Smithsonian have borrowed exhibit artifacts and have been loaned some of our most precious historical materials from time to time, and we will continue to have that relationship. The museum also maintains a large archive of historical documents available to researchers in the field. All of this keeps both the history and the legacies of our founders alive and well in the twenty-first century.

. . .

71

Chris Williamson

Where would our history be without museums?

The Museum of Women Pilots is located in Oklahoma City, and it was dedicated there in 1999. Located on the second floor of the international headquarters with over five thousand square feet of space, the museum contains displays and artifacts focusing on preserving the history of women in aviation: honoring their achievements of the past and recognizing current achievements. In addition, archives and other resources are maintained on-site as well, along with one of the largest collections of Amelia Earhart memorabilia in the world.

One of the goals of the museum is to inspire young women to enter the field of aeronautics.

AE would *definitely* approve.

You may have heard of the Amelia Earhart Birthplace Museum in Atchison. If you've been following our journey thus far, you know that I started all of this by standing on the bluffs across from Amelia's former home, now the museum, on a cold fall day. The construction of the home began in 1861 and has a long history. Annually, thousands of visitors tour the home to learn about the life of an icon. By the way, I say *life*, because the Birthplace, much like the Museum of Women Pilots in Oklahoma, prefers to talk about how Amelia Earhart *lived*.

Sound familiar?

Jan McKenzie

There's a saying, "To be something different, you have to see something different." We need to continue to share women's accomplishments in all fields of media today. We the Ninety-Nines provide examples where young women can see women in the cockpit when they walk onto an airliner, and they can read stories about women military pilots and see women going up into space as mission specialists and shuttle pilots. They see, and then they can believe, "I can do that."

As an electrical engineer, I didn't see women in science, math, and technology as I grew up. This is changing slowly; however, we need more encouragement by parents and teachers and counselors to ensure every young woman is aware of all the possibilities available in life, not just the traditional ones. Increased participation of the best and the brightest women has already occurred in medicine. It can only be good for the country and the world that the best people *for the job* are *in that job*, regardless of gender or race or nationality or whatever. The Ninety-Nines provide encouragement, mentoring, networking, and financial help to aid more and more women to make their dreams in aviation come true. Amelia as the first president, along with the other charter members of the Ninety-Nines, broke a mold to satisfy their dream of flight. Charter members started the Ninety-Nines to advance the state of women in aviation. As far as we've come, with only 7% of all pilots being women, we still have a long way to go, and Amelia would be cheering us on in this work.

She'd be astounded by the growth of the number of women pilots in the US. She would be proud of women's participation with male pilots in military and commercial fields. I think she would love that we are growing women pilot numbers worldwide. She would be proud of the organization that she and the other ninety-eight women pilots created in 1929, that it's alive and kicking and growing and inspiring and supporting women to do what she loved to do.

Amelia said, "Flying might not all be smooth sailing, but the fun of it is worth the price." I know she would see that we continue to represent what she believed in *then* and what we believe in *now*. If she could have been around to watch, I feel she would approve of how her successors have moved forward and faced the times to continue helping women's aviation grow from the ceiling of her time to where it is today.

She would expect us and our successors to keep growing and pushing to the fullest extent possible now and in the future. By continuing to do that, we will best represent what she believed and lived for.

Chris Williamson

You might be asking yourself *why* we've spent this time discussing an organization that played a very large role in Amelia's life? *Yes*, at the end of the day, this is an Amelia Earhart story. But to understand the story, we have to understand the aspects of her life that were most important to her. As we've learned here, in many ways the Ninety-Nines *are* her legacy. They are a living, breathing embodiment of all that she stood for. I now know that Amelia would have loved that her friends and fellow aviators kept the organization going and that today it's stronger than ever. While their first president vanished under what would become mysterious and well-debated circumstances, one thing *is not* a mystery.

The Ninety-Nines have been and always will be a part of Amelia Earhart.

Wherever she is.

AUGUST 18, 1929

41.4996562 | -81.6936813

"The women had to always look glamorous and be grateful and never show
any signs of being frustrated or tired. They always had to be appreciative of
the crowds, or else the newspapers would say, 'The women were out of sorts.'
They'd pick up on things like that."

Chris Williamson

We've covered a lot of ground in a short space up to this point. I
appreciate you hanging in there with me.

Everything we're covering, *all of it,* is going to be crucial to the
investigation into the vanishing of Amelia Earhart and Fred Noonan, I
promise you. So keep taking those mental notes. Keep looking out for
my bookmark recommendations as we go.

It's all relevant, and it all contributes something.

Just a couple of important areas left before we take a deep dive into
a case that's fascinated the entire planet for over eight decades. Before
we do that, a question to kick off the next segment:

What are some dates that you remember in *your* life?

Maybe a wedding anniversary or the birth of your child, or a date that something significant happened in your life, positive or negative. There are a few dates in the life of Amelia Earhart that would qualify as important.

How about January 3, 1921, the day that Amelia started flying with Neta Snook?

October 22, 1922, Amelia broke the altitude record that day, rising to fourteen thousand feet.

June 17 and 18, 1928, Amelia became the first woman to fly across the Atlantic as a passenger, the *Friendship* flight. We covered that.

How about July 2, 1937? The day she and Fred Noonan vanished forever?

We'll get to it.

There's another date that is synonymous with Amelia Earhart, and quite a few others, in fact. A date that not too many people know about. It's time we learned all about this date.

The woman's air derby, August 18, 1929.

Earlier, you learned all about the International Forest of Friendship in Atchison, Kansas.

A couple of years ago at the annual ceremony, I ran into someone else I had been wanting to talk to for a long time about our very next subject. Funny how the universe tends to bring people together when the time is right.

She's sort of a kindred spirit to me, in a sense. She's dedicated a lot of her life to studying the women's air derby. Her end goal was to create the definitive documentary on it, and she *did*.

Now she's here to take us *all* to school.

"The men, you know, have been somewhat worried about such a long flight for us. They seem to have visions of us smashing up all over the countryside. So the thing for us to do is to prove that their fears have been foolish."

Heather Taylor

Plenty of women, including Amelia, were in the first women's national air derby.

Chris Williamson

Heather Taylor has been researching the women's air derby for a long time. If there's a fact about the race, she knows it. If there's a rumor about the race, she's tracked it down and either confirmed it or debunked it. I don't think there's anyone on the face of the earth who knows this race better or more fluently than her. Trust me when I tell you we're all lucky to have her take part in this conversation.

Heather Taylor

It's multi-pronged, as so many things are. It was the golden age of aviation, so the national air races were a big component in the 1920s. General aviation, as far as airplanes being developed, really started around 1927. Before then, it was mostly the military that was into aviation. They were just starting to create airplanes for transportation and for commercialization around that time. In the early '20s, there were some national air races, but it was mostly showing off the military airplanes and how they progressed and how the soldiers flew them, that kind of thing.

By 1927, we were getting into more of the everyday man, and by then, the air races were becoming quite popular. *Elizabeth McQueen* was a philanthropist and a woman who was very interested in aviation. She decided to go to the national air races in 1928, when they were held in Los Angeles. There, she met some of the biggest stars of the day, including Charles Lindbergh. She also noticed that there were not many women. There were *no women* flying in that particular competition. Elizabeth McQueen is really the woman who came up with the idea of the national air race for women. She started contacting a bunch of women pilots whom she knew and asked about their interest in flying across the country for an air race, which would start initially in California and end in Cleveland, in 1929, where that year's air races were going to happen.

She started approaching air racing officials and women pilots to try to organize and gauge the interest. She contacted the national air racing committee to see about their willingness to do such a thing, and she gained the support of *Cliff Henderson*, who was the managing director for the air races. With the committee in tow, letters began to go out to women pilots.

There were about seventy women pilots in 1929, and she got at least forty to forty-five of them interested, initially. Over half of the women, maybe even three-quarters of the women, were interested in this race in the beginning. She started working on creating the rules and the race route and all kinds of things to set this all into motion.

Chris Williamson

I'm always a fan of promotion, so this woman, Elizabeth McQueen, sounds like my kind of girl. If I'm being honest, I'd never heard her name before. Naturally, I asked Heather to tell me a little more about this incredible woman.

Heather Taylor

Elizabeth McQueen was a very eccentric woman. She decided to create the *Women's Aeronautic Association of California*; it morphed into the *Women's International Association of Aeronautics* (WIAA). A lot of the leading people of the day, including *Mary Pickford, Mrs. Walter Beech* and other women, joined this organization that she started to make contacts with air-minded women who she said had "caught the spirit," meaning the aviation bug. She was very interested in airmindedness. That's sort of the buzzword of the '20s. Elizabeth was very patriotic, and she saw that women pilots could fly for patriotic reasons to help where they could with national security or flying ambulances or whatever the country needed.

When she initially thought about this air race, she started contacting people like Amelia to ask, "Would you be interested in this air race?"

Elizabeth McQueen was a high-society woman, and as I said, she was *very* eccentric.

She carried around a parrot on her shoulder that would ask people, "Do you fly, do you fly? I want to fly. Do you fly?" It was a female parrot named *Dick* that she carried on her shoulder. She always did the high-fashion luncheons, and if she had an idea, she stuck with it and saw it through. She got to know all these women because of the organization she created for women pilots, so she was a known name along with the other women in aviation. Often, she'd write these letters to Amelia or Ruth Elder or Ruth Nichols, women of their stature. The derby was just a matter of course. They couldn't email her, and even making phone calls wasn't as prolific as writing letters. That was more of the standard.

Chris Williamson

I want to meet this woman. And almost as important as that, I want to meet that parrot.

What a great character Elizabeth must have been. Think about this for a moment. You have Amelia Earhart and Ruth Elder who are...*superstars* at this point. If I'm Elizabeth, I'm going *right after them*. As a promoter, it's your job to hook the biggest fish possible to take part in your event. Hook the big draws, and everyone else will follow.

That's *exactly* what Elizabeth did.

Heather Taylor

Amelia and Ruth Elder were the most famous women at the time. Ruth Elder had almost crossed the Atlantic, and Amelia *had* crossed the Atlantic as a passenger. Amelia was interested because she wanted to prove her flying skills, not just that she could ride in an airplane across the Atlantic; she wanted to prove that she could fly as well.

Elizabeth *needed* these women.

Since Amelia and Ruth were both famous at the time, having them involved in the air race would bring a lot more attention to it, and of course, that's also what the air race promoters were thinking. First, having women pilots was going to be quite the draw. Having some of the most famous female names in aviation, like Amelia and Ruth, would be an even bigger draw. So they're looking at it from that perspective. Amelia and the other women who decided to fly in it are looking at it to prove that women can fly, that they are very capable, and that transportation and aviation are becoming a thing. The public needs to start being accustomed to that and getting comfortable with it because that's becoming the standard.

Elizabeth was not a pilot, but she was a great organizer and a great connector. She started asking the women like Amelia and Louise Thaden through correspondence *their thoughts* on what would make a good race.

Initially, Amelia, Pancho Barnes and some of the other women helped with creating the rules of the race, and Elizabeth sort of acted as the intermediary between the racing committee and the participants. Initially, Amelia suggested that they needed a woman on the committee, but they couldn't get that.

So the next best thing was to just give input on what they wanted. Amelia proposed only "a short triangular race at the airport itself," and guaranteed six entrants into the race.

Elizabeth had a *bigger idea.*

She wanted a cross-country race.

Initially, both the air racing committee and Amelia were thinking it would just be like a closed-circuit race at the national air races in Cleveland that year. Elizabeth basically said, "No, we need to do a cross-country race." There were a lot of men's cross-country races, but there hadn't been a women's cross-country race.

She wanted to go big. Eventually, Amelia agreed with her.

Chris Williamson

You have to give credit where credit is due. Elizabeth McQueen thought further outside the box than Earhart on this one. More importantly, she got AE on board, which I'm sure was no easy task.

Heather Taylor

Elizabeth suggested going from Santa Monica to Cleveland, and the racing committee wasn't too happy about that. They were afraid of the long flight. It's about 2,800 statute miles. Amelia's response to the situation was:

"The men, you know, have been somewhat worried about such a long flight for us. They seem to have visions of us smashing up all over the countryside. So the thing for us to do is to prove that their fears have been foolish."

Chris Williamson

If there was ever a quote that summed up Amelia Earhart's position in aviation, it's that one. What a powerful statement.

If Amelia Earhart and Ruth Elder were considered the big names in the air derby simply due to their aviation accomplishments at the time, they were just the tip of the iceberg.

The roster for the 1929 women's air derby reads like an aviation hall of fame. As Heather stated earlier, Elizabeth was able to bring together a remarkable group of women aviators to participate in this groundbreaking event.

Just listen to the names in that Heather's about to mention.

Heather Taylor

Over half of the licensed women pilots in 1929 signed up for the derby. There were seventy licensed pilots by then, and well over forty signed up initially. On race day at 2 p.m. on August 18, 1929, nineteen women took off with a waiver in place for one other woman to take off the next day. So there were twenty women who flew in the derby, and it started in Santa Monica, California, and went for nine days, ending at the national air races in Cleveland, Ohio. Bobbi Trout was one of the most famous women pilots in California. Louise Thaden had already broken several aviation records for the highest and longest flights.

You had two international pilots, *Thea Rasche* from Germany, and *Jessie "Chubbie" Miller* from Australia. Of course, you had Amelia; you had *Blanche Noyes* from Cleveland; *Mary Von Mach*, who was the first female pilot licensed in the state of Michigan; and *Edith Foltz* from Oregon. The one everybody loves is Pancho Barnes because she was full of personality and quite the showstopper, very flamboyant; she loved to shock people. She was sure to put on a show. There was *Phoebe Omlie*, who never gets enough credit; she was from Memphis, Tennessee, and was just a phenomenal pilot. She'd flown across the country for the Ford reliability tour the year before. She had been a wing walker and hung underneath airplanes just by chomping on a leather strap and holding on by that strap underneath the plane while it flew. She eventually became the first female to get a mechanic's license in 1927, and she's the first female on record to get the transport pilot's license.

Chris Williamson

What these women were known to do was nothing short of incredible.

This derby was no walk in the park, or maybe flight in the park would be more accurate.

This was a grueling, challenging race that was very dangerous to the participants. Everyone had something to prove.

Everyone.

For Amelia, as Heather stated earlier, she wanted to prove that she could fly. What I mean by this is she wanted to prove that she was more than the face of aviation. Maybe she wanted to prove that there was a *reason* she was the face of aviation. At any rate, this wasn't a nonstop flight from beginning to end, as you can probably imagine. But I'll leave the details to Heather.

Heather Taylor

The first day they started in *Santa Monica,* and they just went sixty miles to *San Bernardino,* and then they stayed the night. When they made these stops, they had to consider that they couldn't fly at night; they didn't have lights. Many of them were open cockpits, so you had the weather to contend with. They had limited gas; their gas tanks couldn't hold a whole lot more than four or five hours' worth of fuel at a time.

They only flew between five hundred to two thousand feet above ground most of the time, and they were flying over desert and mountains and all those kinds of things. They had to make frequent stops for the mechanics, but also because this was a publicity and promotional tour. They were on the front pages of every newspaper along the way. Wherever they landed, they had gigantic crowds meeting them and flocking for autographs and wanting to talk to them and touch them and see the planes because in 1929, not many people had even seen airplanes, let alone women flying airplanes.

Everywhere they stopped, they had the city honor them, and they had banquets to attend and crowds. Of course, the women wanted to spread aviation, but they also wanted to take care of their planes, and security could be an issue with the crowd.

So there was sort of a balance; the woman had to always look glamorous and be grateful and never show any signs of being frustrated or tired.

They always had to be appreciative of the crowds, or else the newspapers would say the "women were out of sorts"; they'd pick up on things like that. After leaving San Bernardino the next day, they flew over *Yuma* and stopped in *Phoenix* to stay the night. The next day, they went to *Douglas, Arizona,* and they stayed the night in Douglas. They went to *El Paso,* and it rained there. They had not planned on staying the night in El Paso, but thunderstorms grounded them, and they had no choice. The next day, they flew across Texas, and they had several stops along the way: El Paso to *Pecos* and a couple of other stops before landing in *Fort Worth.* From Fort Worth, they went to *Tulsa, Oklahoma,* and then to *Wichita, Kansas,* where they stayed the night. From Wichita the next day, on to *Kansas City* and then to *East St. Louis, Missouri.* They continued from St. Louis to *Columbus, Ohio,* and they spent their last night in Columbus, flying into *Cleveland* the next morning. It was the second day of the national air races, which was a huge, *huge* celebration with lots of other air derbies flying in, closed-circuit races happening, and exhibits happening with thousands of people coming in to see the latest planes and the who's who in aviation, from Charles Lindbergh to *Eddie Rickenbacker* to anybody you can name.

Chris Williamson

Incredible.

Naturally, after hearing Heather give us the blow-by-blow on the derby, I had to wonder about what this event meant to young people. I'm always thinking about that. For children of the day, the dreamers, seeing these larger-than-life women in person must have spread a message of hope *even then.* Heather weighed in on that.

Heather Taylor

It would have had to. I have met and showed my film to many WASP who flew in World War II. Many of them knew several of the women who flew in the derby. They carried that through, becoming pilots themselves. Phoebe Omlie, in fact, was a trainer to many of these women, who admired her and who ended up flying in World War II. They not only impacted young girls for the rest of their lives, but they also helped get some of the women into aviation. I also have articles of young boys who were so thrilled. One was like, "There's Ruth Elder. I can't believe I'm seeing her!" Boys and girls were just thrilled.

Chris Williamson

We don't have very many spoiler alerts in this book. In fact, this is our *first one.*

So if you'd rather find out for *yourself* who won this incredible race, stop now, and look it up.

• • •

Alright, if you're still with me, it's time to find out. As always, there's a little-known piece of information about the winner that not too many people know about. In this case, that piece of information is not about *who won*, but about *how many* winners there were.

Heather Taylor

There were two winners, because there were two classes of planes.

There was the small, light class plane, in which six of the women flew, and then there was a heavy class weight of plane, which had to do with the weight of the engine and the size of the plane. Thirteen of the women flew in those.

For the lightweight class of planes, Phoebe Omlie won, and she flew a *perfect race*. She didn't have any problems along the way.

For the heavy class division, Louise Thaden won the race.

Chris Williamson

Louise Thaden. I love this woman. What an incredible career.

If you're wondering about Amelia Earhart, well, she came in *third*.

I have a sneaking suspicion though, that winning this race wasn't all that important to AE.

As I said, she wanted to prove she could really fly. She was always about women in aviation *first*, and she loved her friends. Louise was her friend above all, and Amelia couldn't have been happier to lose the race to a woman she considered to be a dear friend.

Heather Taylor

Amelia and Louise were best friends; they were very close. She would have been thrilled for her. She and Ruth Nichols were also very close friends. On the final morning, before flying to the finish line, Ruth Nichols took her plane up for a test ride. At that point, she and Amelia were neck and neck; second and third place.

Ruth ended up crashing.

She came in for a landing, and there was a steamroller on the runway that she hadn't seen, and she ended up crashing into it. As a result of that, Amelia ended up in third place, where Ruth Nichols may have ended in third place; of course, we'll never know for sure. They had a friendly rivalry regarding who was going to win and who was going to come in second and third.

Amelia was all about promoting women in aviation. She said:

> "It was a privilege to be in the race because the girls were such good sports. Some had hard luck. It doesn't make much difference whether women fly, but we hope we have interested more women in flying and that more women will use the flying services and let their husbands and children fly."

Let me just say that right before the race, Amelia was the assistant traffic manager with Trans-Continental Air Transport (TAT). She said:

> "My job was to sell flying to women, both by talking about it and by watching details of handling passengers, which were calculated to appeal to feminine travelers. Justly or unjustly, air ticket sellers accused women of being the greatest sales resistance encountered; they wouldn't go up themselves and they wouldn't let their families do so."

One thing that the women in the derby were trying to do was prove that flying was *safe*. They were selling it to the public, and that's where that quote came from.

> "To me, the most important thing about the race is that it has brought the western and the eastern girls together where we realize the existence of each other. And it can appreciate that we all have the same view of things in general. It has been a great thing for aviation."

Chris Williamson
Enter the Ninety-Nines, right?
I hope you're starting to see how *all of this* comes together.

Heather Taylor

Before the derby, Amelia said:

"I am in this race in the hope that I might interest others in the industry. For that is what flying is, an industry, not only a sport, and certainly not a circus."

Chris Williamson

The more I continue to learn about this woman, the more impressed I am.

Amelia Earhart may not have won the race, but she saw the bigger picture. No one can ever question that.

One of my favorite aspects of the women's air derby pertaining to Amelia is *what she flew* during the race. The *Lockheed Vega* would forever be linked to AE. Really, the Lockheed brand would forever be linked to her. Heather told me something about this that I'd never realized, and it really puts into perspective how aviation was quickly evolving due to the popularity of its fliers, like AE and so many others.

Heather Taylor

In 1927, there were only two Lockheed Vegas that were built. By 1929, there were sixty.

You can see the growth in aviation just from the Lockheed Vega, which was one of the best planes of the day, and it helped emphasize the growth of aviation. As I previously mentioned, not many people had seen aviation other than in a military capacity. It was just becoming relevant for general transportation, and the women were the midwives to this. They were basically ushering the public from horses and buggies to cars and into the new age with aviation. One of the big things was "If women could fly, then you could fly," which was somewhat of a put-down, but it represented what the collective conscious was at the time. As far as the impact of the women, fourteen of twenty finished the race, which was the highest percentage of finishers for *any air race* up until that time. They proved they could fly, and that they were good pilots. More importantly, they could be taken seriously and make careers out of aviation. As we've already discussed, they could inspire future generations to come to a point where it wouldn't be seen as odd to see a woman pilot. From that point forward, there would just be *pilots.*

Chris Williamson

So are we there yet? What do *you* think? We started this segment by asking a question, and maybe it's a good bookend to end it with *another one.*

When you see a pilot who happens to be a woman, do you say to yourself, "There's a pilot?"

Or do you say to yourself, "There's a woman pilot?"

Do we still discriminate after all this time? What do you think Amelia would say all these years later about the current state of women in aviation? Do you think she'd be satisfied?

More questions than answers.

That may end up being a running theme for this story.

THE START OF SOMETHING NEW

40.4300927 | -86.926513

"When then Purdue president Edward C. Elliot brought AE into the fold, he was granting her a platform to do what she cared so much about doing, and that was to educate, influence, and inspire. She saw that opportunity as once in a lifetime. And we all know what Amelia Earhart does with once-in-a-lifetime opportunities, don't we?"

Chris Williamson

So far in this story, we've covered a lot of ground, and I've promised you that all of this information we've covered is going to tie in.

Next, it starts to do just that

In just a few short years, Amelia Earhart has become a household name. She's reached the zenith of her popularity, and at this point, she's nearly attained icon status. In 1935, just under two short years before she would vanish into thin air, she began an unlikely partnership with Purdue University. This new venture was an aspect of her life that she had been waiting for, for a long time. A chance to *"Get in on the ground floor"* and directly influence the women of the time. She relished her short time there, and as we'll learn, she looked forward to expanding that role when she returned from the world flight. Before we get to that, it's time to take you back to 1935 and West Lafayette, Indiana, to discuss the start of something *new* for Amelia Earhart.

Something she started but unfortunately never got to finish.

As we travel back to Purdue to discuss Amelia's short but powerful tenure there, I thought it'd be a great idea to start this wing of our story by speaking with someone who was *in the trenches*, so to speak, when it came to life on campus. As luck usually has it, I found the perfect guy, and he has *more than one connection* to Amelia Earhart.

*"The students feel empowered by having that connection to her, and it makes
Purdue that much more of a special place. If you talk to any Purdue alum,
they are obsessive. They really love Purdue and the Purdue experience, and
she solidifies that for so many."*

Andrew McGregor

My dad graduated from *Atchison high school,* my grandfather's
lived there since probably the late '50s or early 1960s, and he *still* lives
there. He founded the *Amelia Earhart Century Ride,* and he owns a bike
store now, but he taught auto mechanics and shop at Atchison high
school.

Chris Williamson

It's not often that I talk to a guest who ties to two different areas of
AE's life, but Andrew *is that guy.* Currently a visiting assistant
professor of history at *Texas A&M University,* Andrew earned his PhD
in American history at *Purdue University,* and he holds master's
degrees from the *University of Nevada* as well as *Baker University,* and
that ties him to the story. As you just read, though, he has ties to Atchison, Kansas, as well, *Earhart country.*

He's the perfect person to introduce us to campus culture at Purdue
pertaining to AE's influence there, and he had plenty of insight to get
us started.

Andrew McGregor

For most of my childhood, we'd pay visits to my grandfather in
Atchison. I remember driving by Amelia's house and learning about
her in the local museum there downtown.

She's always been one of those figures who has been very close to
childhood experiences with my grandfather, both with bike racing and
all the time I spent visiting him in Atchison.

• • •

Chris Williamson

What I really love about Andrew's connection to Amelia is the idea that after coming to Purdue, he decided to educate himself on her time there. As he teaches and molds, much like Amelia did when she was there, he *too* was learning more about the woman who carries such a massive influence over the university he was employed at.

Andrew McGregor

I didn't know much about her at all in terms of what she did at Purdue. I knew about her and her disappearance, I knew that she came from Atchison, but I didn't have much of an understanding of her life, or her journey, or what she did beyond being famous for disappearing and being an early female aviator. So when I arrived at Purdue, it was interesting to see that there's a dorm named after her. There's a statue outside that dorm; they have a great collection of documents there. It's sort of brought my life full circle.

I went to Purdue in the fall of 2011 after living in a variety of different places in Kansas; I've never *personally* lived in Atchison, although it was always this little bit of family connection. Coming to Purdue, for me, was a whole new learning experience about another side of Amelia that I didn't know, even though I thought I knew quite a bit about her from my childhood. I sort of learned alongside the students about what she had done. I tried to do what I could to read about her in the yearbooks, and in the archives as well. I wanted to get a sense of who this woman was, and how she represented an early moment in American history in terms of female education and movement into industry. She blazed exciting paths that we don't really think about women having opportunities to do early on.

Chris Williamson

That begs the question, though, what does the student body think of Amelia Earhart today? Surely not everyone automatically knows about her connection to the university in the years before her disappearance. Andrew filled me in on that.

. . .

Andrew McGregor

Some of them have no idea what she did there; a lot of them are just as ignorant as I was when they arrive at Purdue. They see her name, they see the dorm and the statue, and they're like, "Okay, that's the woman who disappeared, but what's her Purdue connection?" A lot of them have questions; they're sort of curious about her immediately.

Purdue has a very large STEM community. They have a lot of students who are interested in engineering. They have their own airport. Part of their direction is connecting them to that history by saying "Hey, you're not the first person to come here. This path is here; we've had major individuals come out of our university and work here." A lot of what I see at Purdue in terms of the faculty admin is that they're including her name as part of their recruitment and retention of female STEM students. I also see it on the other side, from the students; they feel empowered by having that connection with her, and it makes Purdue that much more of a special place. If you talk to any Purdue alum, they are *obsessive*. They really love Purdue and the Purdue experience, and she solidifies that for so many.

Chris Williamson

Go back and read that last part again. Did you catch it?

It's no secret that Purdue is a staple in the STEM community, but the fact that Amelia Earhart is being used in the recruitment of female students into their modern-day STEM programs makes me beam with pride.

I've been saying for a long time that Amelia Earhart was a pioneer in STEM. She was doing it before it was ever a thing. Purdue gave her the platform *then*, and they're spreading that word *now*. I couldn't agree more.

Since Andrew spent his time there on the ground floor teaching and discussing with students, the obvious question about impact and legacy there had to be asked. Just what *is* Amelia's legacy there?

. . .

Andrew McGregor

I think it's a tricky question to answer. A lot of this is my opinion, but I think Purdue has come late to understanding and celebrating its own history. Several years ago, they celebrated their quincentennial, which is their 150th anniversary. They're doing a lot to say, "Hey, look, this is where we've come from; this is who we are. This is our legacy." She's a huge part of that. I think her legacy has really helped Purdue rediscover itself over periods of time. Purdue is sixty-forty male; they've had a lot of problems recruiting, retaining, and focusing on women in higher education and in STEM. That's not just a Purdue issue, that's an *American issue.*

I think as Purdue has tried to be self-reflective and tried to understand itself and overcome some of those problems with gender, they really look to her and look to her legacy. I think she's helped Purdue in that sense.

I think her legacy at Purdue is, "Wait a minute, we can do this. We've done this before, we've always tried to do this, and it's part of who we are as a mission." I think discovering and rediscovering her legacy and celebrating her legacy has helped Purdue become reflective of those issues. I don't think most Americans know about the Purdue section of her career. If they're big Amelia Earhart fans, they might, but I don't think Purdue has necessarily done a great job of positioning itself as central to the narrative, and that might be somewhat *intentional.*

The Amelia Earhart story isn't a story about Purdue, it's about her, and they're facilitating that.

Their role in collecting and maintaining her collections, having all of her papers, and funding her airplane could be further explored and publicized. I think in terms of her legacy, I'm not sure they're recognized for having the rich collection and connection that they do in terms of her involvement there, and I'd like to see more of that. Her legacy looms larger than Purdue's in that regard. Purdue has her legacy there, but I think in terms of having faculty and student engagement, I would like to see Purdue put together some sort of publication. I think there's *so much* stuff there, we could put together a document that you can take into the classroom or take to the public and say,

"Here, read about this; this is women in STEM in the 1930s. This is Amelia Earhart in education." A lot of these issues we can address with a document that will make it easy for us to teach. Of course, I'm thinking about this from a teaching perspective but also from a public perspective.

This is a whole other side of her that nobody really knows about. There's a lot more they could do to get that story told. The work that you're doing with the podcasts and documentary are a really great part of that, but I would like to see something that maybe leans more towards the *written side*. That shows my own bias as an instructor. I love to bring pop culture figures into the classroom and discuss the unfamiliar side of their lives.

I always tell my boss that I use *familiar characters* to tell *unfamiliar stories*. I think you and Purdue are doing that really well. I would like to see even more.

Chris Williamson

Andrew gave us some interesting thoughts there. *Could* Purdue do more when it comes to honoring Amelia's legacy? Do they position themselves intentionally in a certain way when it comes to the disappearance? Maybe he's right. After all, this book *is* about asking questions and gaining clarification.

I think I need to call *another president*.

*"That plane and the entire project and mission was a Purdue mission. If it's ever recovered, it belongs to **us**."*

Mitch Daniels

I think Amelia Earhart's spectacular life and career would have kept her relevant with or without Purdue, but no institution has anything close to the relationship or the history that we do with her.

Chris Williamson

Mitch Daniels became only the twelfth president in Purdue University history. That was of course *after* the conclusion of his second term as Indiana's governor. According to Purdue's website profile:

"President Daniels launched a series of initiatives called Purdue Moves that provide bold answers to some of the greatest challenges facing higher education today."

The four pillars of Purdue Moves are affordability and accessibility, transformative education, world-changing research, and STEM leadership. Those last two are going to be particularly important to us, and they'll tie into the world flight.

Get that bow ready.

Mitch Daniels

As I'm talking to you, I'm looking at a photo that's been in my office of Amelia Earhart on our campus with then-president *Elliott* who brought her here in 1935. From then until the end of her life, this was her closest association. We are the library that has all her memorabilia and papers, and we've had several scholars work over the decades on sharing her story with others.

• • •

Chris Williamson

A little exposition if you haven't figured it out already. Of all the associations we've discussed thus far, perhaps no other looms larger over Amelia's life than her relationship with Purdue. As president Daniels will soon tell us, Amelia took her role *very* seriously.

This wasn't a publicity stunt for her.

This was the opportunity that she had been waiting for all her life.

When then Purdue president Edward C. Elliot brought AE into the fold, he was granting her a platform to do what she cared so much about doing, and that was to educate, influence, and inspire. She saw that opportunity as a once in a lifetime.

And we *all know* what Amelia Earhart does with once-in-a-lifetime opportunities, *don't we*?

Mitch Daniels

Purdue University has been at the forefront of a lot of important social transformations and phenomenon; another example is teaching international students; it goes back over a century here. It's not a recent phenomenon. Both educating young women and preparing them for careers in what today we call STEM disciplines has a very long track record here. President Elliot was certainly interested way back in the '30s in that. He'd heard her lecture on the subject of *Women after College* and was *so* impressed, he brought her here, hired her, and of course, we then supported her research and her personal aviation career for the rest of her life. Purdue University was the only university in the country, and it's still one of only a couple, that has its own full airport. Then and now, we have one of the finest aeronautics research and teaching colleges in the world, so it was a very natural fit.

Of course, the school was enthusiastic about her and raised outside money, in fact, to support her research, including the flight on which she was lost forever.

Chris Williamson

This was a mutually beneficial working relationship, and President

Elliott had the good foresight to recognize that. The prospect of advising at Purdue excited Amelia on a whole new scope. Neither party saw this as a publicity stunt but instead a way to inspire both men and women to follow the path that Amelia laid out or, perhaps even more importantly, to create their *own path*.

Mitch Daniels

I have to believe that it was an extraordinarily forward-looking action on his part. It had to be seen that way; she was such an outstanding person. If she were achieving equivalent feats today, I think she'd be a celebrity. So just imagine this in the 1930s when women who were attending schools like Purdue intended to return to the home afterward.

So of course, she was very extraordinary and would have been in any era, but certainly then she had a major impact.

Chris Williamson

The Amelia Earhart statue at Purdue refers to her as "an inspirer of dreams."

I couldn't say it better myself. I wondered if Amelia felt *then* what her statue there reflects *now*. So I asked President Daniels to educate me.

Mitch Daniels

I think she must have had some sense of it; it could not have escaped her attention that she was a unique and in-demand figure. Having read now so much about her, including the memoirs of people who knew her well, I think like so many pioneers, she would have wanted to see herself as an interesting and inspiring aviator *first*, and a woman behind that.

Chris Williamson

Often, we made the mistake at Chasing Earhart of assuming that Amelia's reach was more targeted to women than anyone else. While that may be true, we tend to underestimate her as simply being an icon for women. That would be amazing enough, but as President Daniels explains, Amelia was interested in reaching *students*, and it didn't particularly matter to her whether they were male or female.

She was going for the *biggest impact possible*.

Mitch Daniels

The building in which she lived while she was here is *still* here; I've been in it many, many times. It has a fairly small dining room, and she ate there apparently more often than not.

All our records show that students would angle for a chance to sit at her table, and my impression is that this wasn't just our young women but also our young men who were equally motivated by being around her. We *then*, as *now*, have a higher percentage of our engineering and aviation students who are women. There was an unusual number of young females around, and many of them had the same general career interests that she did.

Chris Williamson

It's important to note here that Purdue thought *so much* of their relationship with AE that they decided to get involved in her upcoming world flight by putting their money where their mouth was and financing her brand-new state-of-the-art Lockheed Electra 10-E.

It's all starting to come together now.

Mitch Daniels

We are now, and were at the time, a major research university. There was great interest here. Her principal interest wasn't flying as a stunt. It wasn't simply Lindbergh-type achievements, she really *was* interested in the physiological and psychological effects of long-distance flight; much in the same way we've studied the effects on humans during spaceflight. That was really what the money was raised for. That plane was described here as the *flying laboratory,* and she was taking it on long flights and carefully collecting data regarding what it meant to undergo the rigors of long-distance flight, sometimes with different pressurization and so forth. That's really what the around-the-world flight was going to be about.

It was about the pursuit of learning, which of course is central to the mission of Purdue.

Chris Williamson

Listen to what President Daniels just said.

Amelia was a... scientist, really.

This was a woman who not only wanted to fly for "the fun of it," but she wanted to use aviation as a tool to learn more about multiple aspects of science that continue to be taught and pursued today.

She was an innovator.

Add that to the list.

Don't worry, I'm keeping count.

One of my very favorite things to do when it comes to Amelia Earhart is to talk with my guests about the what-ifs. What would she have done if she had made it back safely from the world flight? How would her role with Purdue evolve? We never have a shortage of great answers to this question, so I had to ask President Daniels to weigh in.

Mitch Daniels

It's a fascinating question.

I believe it would have gone on for a while because she would have come back with a wealth of new information and scientific under-standings, which I'm quite certain she and other scholars here would have translated for the benefit of the aviation industry as it was at the time. I'd like to believe that it would have been a long-standing continuing relationship, but she was a very independent-minded person, as we know. It might well have at some point veered off into a different direction, but everything we know from her years here tells us that she really *did* enjoy the interaction with students and perhaps the motivation she provided them. We know for certain that she relished the companionship and the interactions with scholars, researchers, and scientists in the areas of aviation and aeronautics.

Chris Williamson

What I *wasn't* going to do was ask President Daniels what hypothesis he subscribed to regarding the disappearance.

There will be plenty of that coming at us all *real soon*.

But I *was curious* to learn about the fallout of the disappearance as it pertained to Purdue.

After all, Purdue was most certainly the closest working relationship that AE had at the time, and perhaps more importantly, it represented Amelia's potential future beyond long-distance flight.

Mitch Daniels

It hit much of America very hard; she was such a well-known figure at the time. It hit no place harder than here; so many people here knew her personally. More probably than any other place on the planet.

We had a very direct investment; that plane and the entire project and mission was a Purdue mission.

If it's ever recovered, it belongs to *us*.

I know that an event that struck home with millions of Americans and people outside the country probably had its epicenter right here at Purdue.

Chris Williamson

Purdue wants their plane back, and rightfully so.

If you're an Earhart historian, author, or just a fan, you've either visited the archives at Purdue or you *want to*. The archives at Purdue contain the most glorious collection of Amelia Earhart material that you could ever lay your eyes on, plain and simple.

Could that collection *someday include* a Lockheed Electra 10-E?

Well, you never know...

Mitch Daniels

Over many years, Purdue and Boilermaker alums have contributed money to missions that they thought might have a chance to find out what happened. To possibly retrieve the evidence, and maybe one day that'll happen.

We are the repository of her memorabilia and papers, even her poetry. Her family placed everything they had rights to *here*. With the passage of time and the overdue engagement of women in so many careers, *including aviation*, her remarkable achievements and character-istics probably *do* need to be nurtured from time to time.

We see ourselves as custodians or stewards, even, for that legacy.

Chris Williamson

We're almost there.

Before we dive into one of the greatest and compelling historical mysteries of all time, I want to remind you all of how everything we've covered up to this point *matters*.

As we go through this case, think about what Amelia meant to the collective conscience of the country, of aviation, and to dreamers every-where. Amelia Earhart has had a career up to this point that can only be described as magical.

And now she has a *plan*.

Fly around the world at the equator, a task that only someone like AE could dream up.

A challenge that many people think was a self-imposed death sentence.

As always though, Amelia didn't see that.

Amelia saw the struggle, the task, and the hope to continue to push herself to inspire, as she had been doing her entire career.

And now thanks to Purdue, she had her plane.

A plane that has gone down in history as the holy grail of aviation.

Get ready. This is where everything *changes*. But first, a message from a *very special* friend...

3 Years Later: A Retrospective

At a luncheon in New York on women's careers in 1934, Amelia Earhart spoke passionately about opportunities for women in aviation. The president of Purdue University, Edward C. Elliott, was in the audience. He was so impressed by Earhart's speech that he invited her to visit Purdue and give a lecture for the women students. A few weeks later, Earhart spoke at a banquet at Purdue on "Activities for Women After College." Her talk was a success, and after several discussions with President Elliott, a contract was finalized in 1935, to employ Amelia Earhart as a consultant in the Department for the Study of Careers for Women and a technical advisor in Aeronautics at Purdue University. From the autumn of 1935 until her disappearance in July 1937, Earhart served in this role.

As a land grant university, Purdue has always had a strong reputation in engineering, technology, and the sciences. Seemingly tucked away in northern Indiana, Purdue was the first university in the United States to own and operate its own fully equipped airport. This asset appealed to Amelia Earhart. She was passionate about two causes: aviation and equal rights for women. In her custom-created role at Purdue University, she had the freedom and means to advance both. As a career counselor, mentor, and role model for the growing number of women students enrolled at Purdue, she advocated for equal treatment of male and female students, increased enrollment of women in STEM courses, and encouraged women to consider pursuing careers after college. These ideas were radical for their time, when most women students were expected to marry and become homemakers after graduation.

As technical advisor to the Aeronautics department, Earhart interacted with classes of students, demonstrated new types of equipment, and shared her experiences as a pilot.

Most of her time was spent providing lectures, conducting conferences with Purdue faculty and students, and initiating studies on new career opportunities for women. Just as importantly, she served as an example of a successful modern woman for the female student population. She raised eyebrows by wearing pants on campus when women were not allowed to do so.

The co-eds, as the women students were called, were in awe of Earhart and competed over the right to sit near her when she took her meals in the dining hall. Always trying to gain weight, Earhart frequently drank buttermilk. After she began requesting it with her meals, the women students followed her lead, and buttermilk rapidly became an in-demand beverage on campus. When the women students observed that Earhart sat at the table with her elbows propped up, they asked why they couldn't do the same. The Dean of Women, Dorothy Stratton, responded by claiming that any student who had flown solo across the Atlantic Ocean would be allowed to eat with their elbows on the table.

Earhart enjoyed her interactions with students, but due to her demanding lecture schedule, she was only able to remain on campus for a few weeks at a time each semester.

While on campus, she stayed in South Hall, part of the women's residence halls on campus.

She frequently traveled from state to state, giving speeches and attending events. She had also begun thinking about what her next big flight would be. Earhart had already broken numerous flying records, and there were fewer *firsts* in aviation to be achieved. She spoke with President Elliott about her interest in conducting research at Purdue to better understand how fatigue and diet impacted pilots during long-distance flights. Although she initially kept her plans secret, she was already dreaming of breaking a new distance flying record. Earhart wanted to become the first pilot to fly around the world at its greatest distance, along the equator. To do this, she knew she would need a bigger, faster, and more modern airplane.

During a dinner party at President Elliott's home in 1935, Earhart spoke of her desire to conduct studies on how long-distance flying affected pilots. Before the evening was over, guest and university trustee David Ross offered to donate $50,000 as a gift toward the cost of providing an airplane suitable to serve as a *flying laboratory* for Earhart's research. Further donations totaling $30,000 in cash and equipment were received from J. K. Lilly, Vincent Bendix, and manufacturers Western Electric, Goodrich, and Goodyear. The $80,000 formed the basis of the Amelia Earhart Fund for Aeronautical Research at Purdue. These funds, provided to Earhart, enabled her to purchase a new, customized Lockheed Electra 10-E. The plane was modified to hold as much fuel as possible for long-distance flying, and was equipped with the latest aeronautical equipment, including a two-way radio and a Morse code key. It was in this airplane, this "flying laboratory," that Earhart and her navigator, Fred Noonan, disappeared during their second world flight attempt in 1937.

In 1940, Earhart's husband, George Palmer Putnam, donated Earhart's papers, photographs, medals, flight clothes, and other belongings to Purdue University. Purdue University Libraries' Archives and Special Collections owns the largest, most comprehensive collection of materials in the world created and owned by Amelia Earhart, ensuring her legacy remains alive at Purdue each time a researcher studies her papers. In further recognition of her impact on the university, one of the residence halls at Purdue was later named Earhart Hall, a student scholarship was established in her name, and more recently a statue of Earhart was erected on campus. The University Airport, where Earhart stored her plane while on campus and from which she made her first attempt at her world flight, remains; despite renovations over the past eighty-five years, the original hangar has been preserved, and the airport displays images celebrating its connection to the groundbreaking pilot. Perhaps most importantly, students today remain inspired by Earhart, and her relationship with the university is a point of pride for every Boilermaker.

Sammie Morris
Winter 2022

THE CHANGING

21.363888888889 | -157.96027777778

"Amelia Earhart has a plan and a plane. Now she needs a crew. This was going to be by far her most incredible flight ever, but even Amelia knew she couldn't do it alone. She needed to put a team together."

Chris Williamson

When we last left her, Amelia Earhart had an idea, and that idea was to fly around the world at the equator.

Because of her connection to Purdue University, she now had her vessel, a state-of-the-art Lockheed Electra 10-E that was dubbed the "flying laboratory." There are also a couple of characters who enter her life at this point, Characters who will forever be etched into history alongside her. One of them *especially.*

Next, we discuss the first leg of her world flight and where that leg took her: Hawaii.

All was well, spirits were up, and it seemed like Amelia Earhart was well on her way to adding *world flyer* to her already huge list of career accomplishments. Then, shortly after 5:40 a.m. on the morning of March 20, 1937, everything changed.

On takeoff at Luke Field, Amelia Earhart ground looped her aircraft. We'll talk a lot about that shortly. Pay close attention to the testimony throughout this section of our story. At the end, *you decide.*

Did Amelia Earhart make a potentially fatal error on takeoff? Or was something *else* at play?

As we start discussing the world flight, I need to bring in people who aren't just experts in aviation and Amelia Earhart, but Hawaii aviation *specifically.* After all, this part of the story takes place there, so why wouldn't I pull from all my sources and talk to people who know the story from the inside out? And boy, do I have the guest to get started. He's been waiting in the wings for a long time, and now he's finally arrived.

"Amelia Earhart needed someone who had the ability to navigate the skies. She needed someone who was considered one of the very best to ever do it. Enter Frederick J. Noonan."

Nick Augusta

Amelia Earhart decides to fly around the world, but she needs a crew, and she needs some expertise. This was no flight across the Atlantic, and it was certainly no flight across the Pacific from Honolulu to Oakland, as she did back in 1935.

Chris Williamson

Nicholas Augusta has a wide and varied background. He's sold coffee for the world's leading coffee company, ventured into the retail and wireless industry, flown airplanes, managed restaurants and has traded securities on wall street. He's a commercially rated pilot with a passion for aviation history in Hawaii and the Pacific. His first solo flight was from the very same runway on *Ford Island* where Amelia Earhart ground looped her Lockheed Electra. Currently he's building a website, hawaiiaviation.org, where the history of aviation in the Hawaiian Islands can be shared. He's also the voice of *Fred Noonan on Twitter and Facebook*, where he shares, often in real time, the events of 1937 and what it may have been like if Noonan himself were speaking.

Amelia Earhart has a plan and a plane, and now she needs a crew. This was going to be by far her most incredible flight ever, but even Amelia knew she couldn't do it alone. She needed to put a team together.

Nick Augusta

This was around the world at the equator, a huge undertaking. Enter *Harry Manning*.

Amelia first met Harry in 1928 when returning from England after her first flight across the Pacific aboard the Fokker F-7 named the

Friendship. Manning was the captain of the SS *President Roosevelt,* the ship that returned Amelia and her fellow crew members of the Friendship back to the US. While on board, Captain Manning struck up a friendship with Amelia, as they had mutual interests and had great conversations about flying and adventure. Manning was the youngest captain of the *United States Lines;* he was a well-respected ship captain, qualified nautical navigator, proficient with radio, and **was able to send and receive Morse code.** He was also a licensed pilot, having obtained his license in 1930. When the time came to get a crew together for the world flight, Manning was certainly at the top of the list.

Chris Williamson

Captain Harry Manning. According to Wikipedia*: "*

Harry Manning was an American master mariner, aviator, and an officer in the United States Navy Reserve. He's most noted for his heroic role in the rescue of thirty-two crew members from the Italian freighter Florida and for commanding the SS United States on her record-breaking maiden crossing of the Atlantic. He was among those honored in two ticker-tape parades: the first in 1929 as a crew member of the America and again in 1952 as master of the SS United States. He joined the United States Lines in 1922 and soon advanced up the officer ranks on the liners George Washington and Leviathan. He received his first command in 1927 as master of the President Roosevelt."

I have to tell you that this was a man whose reputation was no joke. He liked Amelia. He saw something in her. He *believed* in her.

Nick Augusta

Amelia asked him to join the project to fly the world. Manning's employer, the United States Lines, granted his request for a three-month leave of absence, and he was able to join the world flight. Manning's challenge, however, was that he was a nautical or maritime navigator, and he was not adept at the new science of aerial navigation. He needed to be confident in using the appropriate tools and procedures for aerial navigation and be prepared to calculate his positions much quicker, as an airplane moves much faster than an oceangoing ship. On February 13, 1937, Manning along with Amelia and her husband, George Putnam, flew the Lockheed Electra from New Jersey to Burbank, California, and en route, there was a problem. Manning made a mistake in celestial navigation that caused both Amelia and her husband to really question his aerial navigation proficiency. At one point, Manning had them over southern Kansas when in fact, they were over Northern Oklahoma. As Putnam stated, "He didn't even have us in the right state." They were really concerned, as was Earhart's technical adviser, *Paul Mantz*.

If he makes a mistake like that, how can he be expected to find Howland Island, a half-square-mile speck in the ocean 1,700 miles from Honolulu? As Amelia said before the flight, "It's much easier to hit a continent than it is an island."

This was the world flight's first problem.

Chris Williamson

We're seeing where Harry Manning was both beneficial to the crew of the world flight and maybe where he fell a bit short. Nautical navigation skills would be important to have on hand. However, this was a flight, after all, and Amelia Earhart needed someone who had the ability to navigate the skies. She needed someone who was considered one of the very best to ever do it.

Enter *Frederick J. Noonan*.

Nick Augusta

Fred Noonan came from a maritime background and had sailed across the oceans and really rose from the rank of an able-bodied seaman to that of captain of large oceangoing steamships. In 1930, he obtained a commercial pilot's license and then joined *Pan American Airways*, where he taught aerial navigation and, for a short time, served as Pan Am's airport manager in Port au Prince, Haiti. He would later return to Miami, where he instructed Pan Am's senior pilots in the fine art of aerial navigation for Pan Am's upcoming survey flights, as well as eventual commercial passenger and mail service across the Pacific in 1935.

Chris Williamson

According to Wikipedia:

Fred Noonan was born in Cook County, Illinois. His parents were Joseph T. Noonan, born in Lincolnville, Maine, in 1861, and Catherine Egan, born in London, England. The family was of Irish descent. Noonan's mother died when he was four, and three years later, a census report lists his father as living alone in a Chicago boardinghouse. Relatives or family friends were likely looking after Noonan. In his own words, Noonan "Left school in the summer of 1905 and went to Seattle, Washington," where he found work as a seaman.

At the age of seventeen, Noonan shipped out of Seattle as an ordinary seaman on a British sailing bark, the Crompton. Between 1910 in 1915, he worked on over a dozen ships, rising to the ratings of quartermaster and boson's mate. He continued working on merchant ships throughout World War I.

Serving as an officer on ammunition ships, his harrowing wartime service included being on three vessels that were sunk from under him by U-boats. After the war, Noonan continued in the Merchant Marines and achieved a measure of prominence as a ship's officer. Throughout the '20s, his maritime career was characterized by steadily increasing ratings of good, typically the highest work performance review.

Noonan married Josephine Sullivan in 1927, in Jackson, Mississippi. After a honeymoon in Cuba, they settled in New Orleans. Following a distinguished twenty-two-year career at sea, which included sailing around Cape Horn seven times, three times under sail, Noonan contemplated a new career direction. After learning to fly in the late 1920s, he received a limited commercial pilot's license in 1930, on which he listed his occupation as "aviator."

In the following year, he was awarded marine license number 121190, class master any ocean, qualifications required for a merchant ship captain. During the early 1930s, he worked for Pan American World Airways as a navigation instructor in Miami and an airport manager in Port au Prince, Haiti, eventually assuming the duties of inspector for all the company's airports. 1937 was a year of transition for Noonan, whose reputation as an expert navigator, along with his role in the development of commercial airline navigation, had already earned him a place in aviation history. The tall, very thin, dark, auburn-haired and blue-eyed forty-three-year-old navigator was living in Los Angeles. He resigned from Pan Am because he felt he had risen through the ranks as far as he could as a navigator, and he had an interest in starting a navigation school.

In March, he divorced his wife, Josie. Two weeks later, he married Mary Beatrice Martinelli of Oakland, California. Noonan was rumored to be a heavy drinker. That was a fairly common thing during this era. There was no contemporary evidence Noonan was ever an alcoholic. Although decades later, a few writers and others made some hearsay claims that he was.

Remember that last part, it's going to come back around later. Back to Nicholas.

Nick Augusta

With Noonan's work and helping pioneer Pan Am specific routes, as well as being the navigator for the famous *China Clipper* that flew across the Pacific from Alameda, California to Manila, it really helped seal his outstanding reputation as an aerial navigator. Without a doubt, Noonan was the most qualified person in aerial navigation in 1937. He was, as they say, the top of the pyramid.

Chris Williamson

Amelia now has Harry Manning, Fred Noonan, and her husband, George Putnam, as always, by her side for the first leg of the world flight. Let's keep in mind here that the first leg, like most of the world flight, went off without a hitch. It's a flight Amelia had made before. This time she's arriving in all her glory with her crew and her flying laboratory in tow.

· · ·

Nick Augusta

For the flight from Oakland out to Hawaii, Amelia and her crew departed at 4:17 p.m. on the afternoon of March 17, 1937. It was 2,800 miles to Honolulu and *Wheeler Field*. Paul Mantz was in the right seat and would handle the throttles and some of the flying duties while Manning worked the radios and navigated.

Noonan, having navigated across the Pacific twelve times before with Pan American, also assisted with the navigation. For Noonan, really, it was old hat. An hour out of Oakland, Amelia observed something that she had never seen before, *another aircraft in flight on a transoceanic flight*. This was the *Pan Am Clipper,* and it was also bound for Honolulu, having taken off from Alameda. This was really the first time the Pan Am pilots flying the Pacific had *also* seen another aircraft in flight.

It was at the time, apparently quite a significant sight.

You know, it's amazing when you think today that hundreds of flights cross the Pacific each and every day. In fact, there's a very cool photo of the Clipper in the Earhart Putnam collection at Purdue University taken from the Electra. You can see the Pan Am Sikorsky S-42 Clipper near a formation of cumulus clouds, and it's framed with the Electra's cockpit window.

Pretty cool.

The Electra continued on with the flight, and it was pretty uneventful with the exception of the right engine's propeller governor, which failed and kept the propeller in a fixed pitch for a time. This would clearly have to be addressed at Wheeler Field after they landed. At 5:45 in the morning on the eighteenth, they landed in the predawn light at Wheeler.

Fifteen hours and forty-seven minutes to Honolulu.

There are some wonderful photos showing a smiling and glowing Amelia and her crew on arrival at Wheeler. The first leg was completed, and a speed record was set on the route.

Not bad for the first leg.

Chris Williamson

Not bad *indeed*. Setting records along the way to potentially setting the biggest record of all.

Just another day in the cockpit for Amelia Earhart.

You might have noticed Nicholas mentioned *another character* who was part of the world flight crew, and he's one we haven't mentioned yet. He served as her technical advisor, and he would be an integral part of this leg of the world flight as well as her time in Hawaii over the next couple of days.

Nick Augusta

Fortunately, Earhart had Paul Mantz, a former Army Air Corps pilot, Hollywood stunt pilot and an outstanding aviator in his own right, serving as her technical adviser. Mantz advised Amelia's first solo flight from Honolulu to Oakland in January of 1935. Mantz was familiar with the techniques of Pan American airways and transoceanic flying.

They had several contacts among a very small and tight-knit community of navigators at the time, including Pan American's chief navigator, Fred Noonan. With the help of Putnam's contacts at the Bureau of Air Commerce, Earhart came into contact with Noonan.

Chris Williamson

According to Wikipedia:

Paul Mantz was born in Alameda, California, a son of a school principal, and was raised in nearby Redwood City, California. He developed his interest in flying at an early age as a young boy. His first flight on fabricated canvas wings was aborted when his mother stopped him as he tried to launch off the branch of a tree in his yard.

Sound *familiar?*

More research shows that at age twelve,*he attended the Panama Pacific Exposition in San Francisco and witnessed the world-famous Lincoln Beachey make his first ever flight in his new monoplane the Lincoln Beachey Special.*

Mantz took his first flying lesson at age sixteen, using money that he made from driving a hearse during the influenza epidemic of 1919. Although he had accumulated hours towards his private pilot's certificate, he quit flying altogether when he witnessed the death of his instructor. On September 24, 1924, he became a part of a famous aviation event when he lent his car battery to the Douglas World Cruiser that had dead sticked into a field on its way to San Francisco for a celebration of world flight.

He was invited to join the festivities at Crissy Field, where many noted military aviators tried to persuade him to pursue a career in military flying.

Now the first leg of their journey was behind them.

Amelia's time in Hawaii for the world flight was upon her, but this wasn't all play. There was work to be done. As Nicholas mentioned, the flight over wasn't completely without incident, and the Electra needed some attention.

In just a couple of short days, *everything would change.*

Nick Augusta

Having landed at the army's Wheeler Field, there's really much to do. Earhart, Mantz, Noonan, and Manning headed into Waikiki to rest and really prepare for the next leg to Howland. Mantz, however, later that afternoon would return to Wheeler Field. First off, the propeller governor on the right engine needed to be addressed, and after repairs were made, the right propeller still wasn't working correctly. The army facilities at Wheeler didn't have the equipment to address the problem, so both propellers were removed and trucked down to the navy's Luke Field on Ford Island in the center of Pearl Harbor.

The issue was eventually corrected overnight, and the propellers were brought back to Wheeler the following morning. The takeoff now for Howland would likely occur the following day on the afternoon of the nineteenth. Amelia promised that there would be no surprise takeoff like she did on her Honolulu-to-Oakland flight back in 1935. On that flight, she kept mum about it.

Well, this flight would *certainly* be different.

At noon on the nineteenth, Mantz took the Electra up on a short test flight and landed at Luke Field to have the final check run on the Electra's engines. The decision was made that the departure from Hawaii to Howland would now be from Luke Field; it was just a much better runaway environment there. An interesting side note too is when Mantz did the short thirty-minute test flight to Luke Field, he had with him his fiancée and the owner of the house in Waikiki where Amelia was staying. It certainly must have been a nice flight for those two passengers, for sure.

Chris Williamson

All systems go.

This was it.

They're getting ready for the most difficult leg of their journey from Hawaii to *Howland Island.*

That was the *original plan.*

But as we all know, things don't *always go according to plan.*

Nick Augusta

With the test flight, it really proved that there were no issues with the Electra, and it should be good for the takeoff to Howland pending weather conditions. Mantz ordered the Electra to be fueled and prepped for departure. However, the fuel being used from the Standard Oil truck was contaminated with sediment, and refueling was stopped at the request of Mantz. Fuel from the air corps was requested and ultimately used to fill the Electra's tanks. Earhart now pushed the departure to dawn on the twentieth, and she arrived in the morning at Luke Field at 4:30, along with Manning and Noonan. Mantz would not be continuing on the flight; he would be returning to Los Angeles with his fiancée to get married.

Noonan would handle the navigation to Howland and then get off

117

there, as he'd joined the world flight too late to acquire the necessary visas for the countries that were beyond Howland. Manning would continue on to Lae, and Darwin, Australia, where he would then deplane, and Amelia would continue around the world solo with the most difficult part of the flying behind her.

Chris Williamson

One by one like dominoes, Amelia's crew would leave the flight, leaving her alone to make history. The experts came together for various reasons to help Amelia Earhart accomplish something that had never been accomplished before. When their time was up, they would exit the flight and move into the history books.

But history would rewrite itself that morning like it has so many times before.

Nick Augusta

Mantz performed his final checks on the Electra, and at 5:30 a.m., Earhart, Manning and Noonan boarded, with Noonan taking the right seat and Manning taking the navigator's position in the rear of the Electra. Amelia started the engines up and immediately taxied to the north end of the runway for departure to the south.

Weather conditions were good, and some overnight rain showers had dissipated.

The winds were out of the south, less than two knots, and scattered clouds were at about three thousand feet; the weather looked good. When Amelia got to the end of the runway, she opened the throttles of both powerful 550-horsepower Pratt and Whitney wasp engines and proceeded down the runway. As the Electra gathered speed at the nine-hundred-foot mark, it swung to the right. Amelia immediately throttled the left engine back, whereupon the Electra was now veering to the left.

She was now entering what they call a *ground loop.*

The right wing was now low, with the weight of the Electra resting fully on the right landing gear. The right-hand gear suddenly collapsed, immediately followed by the left gear, and the Electra now skidded with a shower of sparks towards the left side of the runway and immediately turned into a 200-degree heading from its initial course down the runway.

Clearly it was a *very violent crash.*

Both landing gears sheared off, and the right wing and engine cells were severely damaged.

Both props were bent along with the tail rudder and stabilizer, and of course the oil and fuel tanks were ruptured and now leaking.

Fortunately for everyone involved, there was no fire. Earhart and Noonan both emerged from the overhead cockpit door, and Manning exited out the rear of the aircraft.

It was an absolute disaster, all in a matter of thirty seconds.

When we take a look at some of the photographs of the aftermath, we can see how violent the crash was. There's one photo of Amelia and Fred standing up through the cockpit door, and Amelia's face can only be described as having a look of dread.

Fortunately for the flyers, none of them were seriously hurt; they were very lucky. In one photo, we can see Manning on the left wing while Earhart gathers her things from the cockpit. We can only imagine what was going through his mind after being tossed about in the back of the plane. The photos are very telling, as we see the dawn sky starting to fade away, and we see *at this point, very little* of Earhart, Noonan and Manning. They sort of disappeared off the scene rather quickly. They left Ford Island and headed back to Honolulu.

We *do see* Mantz a lot, inspecting the crushed Lockheed Electra and directing its initial salvage. Within six hours, all of them would be on the SS *Malolo*, heading back to Los Angeles. Again, we can only imagine what's going through all of their minds while they're sailing towards Los Angeles and not in the air, six hours into a flight towards Howland.

Chris Williamson

Let's stop there. Before we recorded, Nick was kind enough to provide me with the official accident report at Luke Field. Strap yourself in, this is a long one. Keep in mind, this report is featured here without correction *intentionally*. The report reads as follows:

PROCEEDINGS OF A BOARD OF OFFICERS APPOINTED TO INVESTIGATE AND REPORT UPON THE CRASH OF MISS AMELIA EARHART'S AIRPLANE NR 16020 AT LUKE FIELD, OAHU, T. H., AT 5:50 A.M., MARCH 20, 1937, AND CIRCUMSTANCES RELATING TO HER ARRIVAL AND STAY AT WHEELER AND LUKE FIELDS, MARCH 18 TO 20, 1937.

PERSONNEL FOR THE BOARD

Major PHILLIPS MELVILLE, Air Corps, President (Luke Field)

1st Lieut. KENNETH A. ROGERS, Air Corps, Member (Wheeler Field)

1st Lieut. HARRY S. BISHOP, Air Corps, Member (Luke Field)

2nd Lieut. NORMAN L. CALLISH, Air-Reserve, Recorder (Luke Field)

This Board comprises the standing ACCIDENT CLASSIFICATION COMMITTEE, LUKE FIELD, T.H., (A.C. Circular 15-14, 3/1/34.) with the addition of one member from WHEELER FIELD appointed per oral order of the Commanding General, 18th Composite Wing.

Oral instructions to the Board were to investigate and render a detailed, confidential report on the circumstances of the crash of Miss Earhart's, Lockheed *"Electra"* airplane at Luke Field on the morning of March 20th, 1937, including, for record, an account of the preparation made for her arrival at Wheeler Field; her stay at that post; the transfer of her airplane to Luke Field; preparations for her take-off for Howland Island and a detailed report of all services rendered by the personnel of either post and the Hawaiian Air Depot, from the date of arrival until the airplane was shipped aboard the S. S. LURLINE, March 27th, 1937.

The Board was convened at Luke Field in accordance with the foregoing instructions at 8:30 AM, March 22nd, 1937.

Present: All members.

At this meeting, the instructions to the board were imparted to all members; arrangements made for the collection of signed statements from competent eyewitnesses; the Wheeler Field member was instructed to secure a statement covering the details of Miss Earhart's arrival and stay at that post; Headquarters at Luke Field, were called upon for a similar report. The Commanding Officer for Hawaiian Air Depot was called upon for a report of the facilities placed at Miss Earhart's disposal and services rendered by Depot personnel; disposition of the wrecked airplane; inventory of equipment, etc. Members of the Board who had not previously done so, then inspected the Luke Field landing mat, the wheel tracks of Miss Earhart's airplane, and the damaged airplane in the Final Assembly Hangar, at Hawaiian Air Depot.

The Board was adjourned, subject to call, at 11:30 AM, same date.

The Board was reconvened at the call of the President at 8:30 AM, March 24th, 1937, to review the evidence then available.

Present: All Members.

The Board was adjourned at 10:00 AM, same date, pending completion of these proceedings.

Due to the fact that Miss Earhart and her party left Honolulu aboard the S.S. MALOLO at Noon, March 20th, 1937, the Board was unable to obtain any statements from the personnel involved in the crash and has had recourse to Miss Earhart's statements to the Press as published in Honolulu newspapers.

After due consideration of the available evidence, the Board reconstructs the details and sequence of events from the time of Miss Earhart's arrival on the morning of March 18th, to her departure at Noon, March 20th, 1937, substantially as follows:

WHEELER FIELD:

Miss Amelia Earhart with Mr. Paul Mantz, technical advisor; Captain Harry Manning, navigator and Mr. Fred J. Noonan, co-pilot and assistant navigator, landed in her Lockheed *"Electra"* airplane, Department of Commerce No. NR 16020 at Wheeler Field, T.H., at 5:45 AM, March 18th, 1937, having flown from Oakland, California on the first leg of a projected *"Round-the-World"* Flight. Comprehensive preparations for her arrival previously made by the Commanding Officer, Wheeler Field were put into immediate effect. (See Exhibits B & C). The airplane was placed under cover in the hangar of the 75th Service Squadron and the personnel of the flight, after breakfasting at the quarters of the Commanding Officer, Wheeler Field, left for rest at the residence of Mr. Christian R. Holmes, Honolulu. No instructions were left by Miss Earhart or Mr. Mantz at this time relative to the care and maintenance of the airplane.

At the direction of 1st Lieut. Kenneth A. Rogers, Station Engineering Officer, Wheeler Field and under the supervision of Mr. Wilber Thomas, Honolulu representative of the Pratt & Whitney Aircraft Company and 1st Lieut. Donald D. Arnold, Engineering Officer, Hawaiian Air Depot, the personnel of the Station Engineering Department undertook a routine inspection and servicing of the airplane and engines. (See Exhibit B† for work performed).

Mr. Mantz had stated, on arrival, that for the last six hours of the flight, the right-hand Hamilton, constant-speed propeller had been frozen in a position of fixed pitch. Special attention was, therefore, paid to filling the propellers with fresh lubricant. At about 3:00 PM, Mr. Mantz returned to Wheeler Field and the airplane was placed on the flying line for test. The self-adjusting pitch mechanism of the right-hand propeller still failed to function. The engines were stopped, and the defective propeller removed for disassembly and inspection. The latter revealed a badly galled condition and that the blades were frozen in the hub due to improper or insufficient lubricant. As the necessary tools for dismounting the propeller and remedying this condition were not available at Wheeler Field, the left-hand propeller was also removed from the airplane and both propellers taken to the propeller section Hawaiian Air Depot, Luke Field, for reconditioning. The Depot personnel worked throughout the night on the propellers which were returned to Wheeler Field at 2:00 AM, March 19th, and re-installed on the airplane. (See Exhibits A & E). At this time, the hour of Miss Earhart's departure for Howland Island was still undetermined but it was generally understood that she would take-off late in the afternoon of March 19th, weather permitting. Mr. Mantz arrived from the city at 11:00 AM and was advised of the work that had been performed on the airplane and the propellers.

He requested that the airplane be partially serviced with gasoline and an adjustment made to the right-hand oleo leg. This was done. The airplane was then placed on the flying line for engine test. During this test, the propellers functioned perfectly. At about 11:15 AM, Mr. Mantz with Mr. Christian R. Holmes and Miss Terry Mines* as passengers took off for a test flight. Previous to the take-off he announced that he would land at Luke Field to have the airplane instruments checked at the Depot and if the landing mat at that station afforded better conditions for Miss Earhart's take-off, that he would remain there.

LUKE FIELD:

The Operations Officer at Luke Field was notified by telephone of Mr. Mantz's intention prior to his departure from Wheeler Field and steps were immediately taken to clear the airdrome. Mr. Mantz landed safely at about 12:00 noon. The landing was reported by telephone to the Operations Officer, 18th Composite wing, Fort Shafter. He was met by Brigadier General Barton K. Yount, Air Corps, Colonel Millard F. Harmon, Post Commander and Lieutenant Arnold, Depot Engineering Officer. Mr. Mantz stated at this time that the airplane engines and propellers were functioning excellently, and that Miss Earhart would definitely make her take-off from Luke Field at an hour to be determined after study of expected weather reports. After making arrangements for the refueling of the airplane by the Standard Oil Company, Honolulu, Mr. Mantz left for the city at 1:30 PM.

The Standard Oil gasoline arrived at Luke Field by truck at 3:30 PM and refueling through a chamois strainer was begun under the supervision of the Depot Inspector. Considerable sediment was observed in the chamois strainer and refueling was stopped at the order of Lieut. Arnold, who immediately notified Mr. Mantz by telephone of this difficulty. The latter requested that the airplane be refueled with Air Corps gasoline. Authority to do so was obtained by Lieut. Arnold from Lieut. Colonel Hume Peabody, Operations officer, 18th Composite Wing, who happened to be present. As there was a possibility of misunderstanding due to the gasoline situation, Lieut. Arnold requested that Mr. Mantz return to Luke Field and assume responsibility for the refueling in person. The latter did so, reaching Luke Field at 4:15 PM. After additional tests of the Standard Oil gasoline, Mr. Mantz again requested Air Corps gasoline and 515 gallons were serviced into the airplane from the segregator-equipped Air Corps refueling truck, of the 72nd Bombardment Squadron. (See Exhibit E, page 4). Servicing being completed, at Mr. Mantz's request, the airplane was placed in the Final Assembly

Hangar at 7:30 PM under guard. Somewhat earlier Lieut. Arnold had a telephone conversation with Miss Earhart and was informed she would take-off at 11:00 PM or at dawn, that the decision would be announced by 10:00 PM. Shortly after the return of Mr. Mantz to Honolulu, he telephoned that a dawn take-off had been decided upon and that Miss Earhart and her party would reach Luke Field about 3:30 AM.

During the night it showered heavily. The Depot personnel who had remained to work on Miss Earhart's airplane spent the night in the Final Assembly Hangar using cots and bedding furnished by the Commanding Officer, Luke Field.

The only visitors were one or two press representatives. At 3:45 AM, the airplane was placed on the apron, the area roped off and a heavy guard established. Traffic to the Fleet Air Base was halted, except for Navy personnel. Miss Earhart and party reached Luke Field via the Fleet Air Base at 4:30 AM. On arrival, Mr. Mantz requested 75 additional gallons of gasoline which were serviced, making a total of 590 gallons at Air Corps gasoline furnished and a total load of 900 gallons according to a statement made by Miss Earhart.

At 4:45 AM, a number of Press representatives arrived via the Navy. Due to the fact that the Luke Field ferry does not commence operations until 6:15 AM, there were no casual visitors or sightseers. At 5:00 AM, Mr. Mantz thoroughly inspected the airplane, including the tires, warmed up the engines and then shut them off. Miss Earhart then took her place in the pilot's cockpit and at her request, the Southwest floodlights were turned on for a short period to permit her to survey the runway. She decided to delay take-off until there was sufficient daylight to see clearly. At 5:30 AM, Captain Manning and Mr. Noonan boarded the airplane and Miss Earhart started the motors. At 5:40 AM, she taxied slowly to the Northeast end of the runway accompanied by the Luke Field fire truck (also termed the *"Crash Truck"*). Members of the work detail of the Hawaiian Air Depot stationed themselves at intervals along the west side of the runway. A special guard of enlisted men had previously been stationed at 200 feet intervals between the hangar line and the runway for the dual purpose of keeping the mat clear and to check the point at which the airplane left the ground. As Miss Earhart taxied down the mat, a Navy *"Grumman"* airplane taxied out from the Navy side and in spite of efforts by a Naval Officer to wave him down, followed her to the end of the runway and parked off the mat out of her way.

Flying conditions at this time were good; ceiling about 3,000 feet; wind southerly, not exceeding 2 MPH; visibility at the surface about 3,500 feet rapidly increasing with advancing daylight.

THE CRASH:

On reaching the end, Miss Earhart turned and after a brief delay opened both throttles. As the airplane gathered speed, it swung slightly to the right. Miss Earhart corrected this tendency by throttling the left-hand motor. The airplane then began to swing to the left with increasing speed, characteristic of a ground-loop. It tilted outward, right wing low and for 50 or 60 feet was supported on the right wheel only. The right-hand landing-gear suddenly collapsed under this excessive load followed by the left. The airplane spun sharply to the left sliding on its belly and amid a shower of sparks from the mat and came to rest headed about 200 degrees from its initial course. The fire truck had followed along the side of the mat during the take-off and reached the scene within a few seconds as did the observers nearest the crash. There was no fire. Miss Earhart and her crew emerged unhurt. The visible damage to the airplane was as follows:

Right wing and engine nacelle severely damaged, left engine nacelle damaged on under side, right hand rudder and end of stabilizer bent. Minor damage to the underside of the fuselage. Both propellers bent. The engines were undamaged. The oil tanks ruptured. The damaged airplane was roped off under guard as promptly as possible by the Officer-of-the-Day. All unauthorized persons were cleared from the mat and the work of salvage initiated by the Depot Engineering Officer without delay. The greater part of the gasoline was first pumped from the tanks into a refueling truck. Depot personnel then commenced to disassemble the airplane, preparatory to removing it from the mat. All loose property of technical or personal nature was collected under the supervision of an officer and placed for safe keeping in a stock room at the Depot. The work of removing the damaged airplane was continued in spite of steady rains and was completed by 6:00 PM at which time the airplane was housed in the

Final Assembly Hangar pending disposition. At 9:00 AM, Mr. Emil Williams, Department of Commerce Inspector arrived at Luke Field for the purpose of investigating the crash. By order of the Wing Commander, he was accorded every assistance and permitted to interview and take statements from witnesses. On March 25th, the Commanding Officer Hawaiian Air Depot, issued orders that the work of disassembly be continued, and the airplane prepared for shipment to California. This work was completed March 26th and the airplane delivered to the representative of the Young Brothers Company for transfer by barge to Honolulu. It was shipped, addressed to Miss Amelia Earhart, Burbank, California, aboard the S.S. Lurline, which sailed for San Francisco at Noon, March 27th, 1937.

FINDINGS:

The Board finds that Miss Amelia Earhart with Mr. Paul Mantz, technical advisor, Captain Harry Manning and Mr. Fred Noonan landed in Lockheed *"Electra"* airplane NR-16020 at Wheeler Field, Oahu, T.H., at 5:45 AM, March 18th, 1937; that adequate preparations had been made for her arrival by the Commanding Officer, Wheeler Field; that the personnel of the Station Engineering Department under competent supervision carried out a thorough check of the airplane and engines; that a dangerous condition of the propellers was discovered and remedied at the Hawaiian Air Depot; that subsequently the propellers functioned perfectly; that the airplane was flown to Luke Field at Noon, March 19th, 1937; that at this time it was announced by Mr. Mantz, technical advisor for Miss Earhart, that she would take-off from Luke Field as the mat afforded better conditions than Wheeler Field; that during the afternoon 515 gallons of Air Corps gasoline were serviced into the airplane at the request of Mr. Mantz and on authority of Lieut. Colonel Hume Peabody, Operations Officer, 18th Composite Wing; that this was later increased to 590 gallons making a total gasoline load of 900 gallons according to a statement by Miss Earhart; that at about 9:00 PM, March 19th, Luke Field was notified that the take-off would be made at dawn; that Miss Earhart and party reached Luke Field at 4:30 AM, March 20th, 1937, and that the airplane, including the tires, was inspected by Mr. Mantz shortly thereafter; that Miss Earhart with Captain Manning and Mr. Noonan as crew taxied out for take-off at 5:30 AM; that take-off was made from Northeast to Southwest; that after a run of approximately 1,200 feet, the airplane crashed on the landing mat due to the collapse of the landing gear as the result of an uncontrolled ground loop; that lack of factual evidence makes it impossible to establish the reason for the ground loop; that as a result of the crash the airplane was damaged to an extent requiring major overhaul; that no injuries were suffered by Miss Earhart or her crew; that approximately 50 square feet of the Luke Field landing mat was damaged necessitating replacement; that no other damage was sustained by government or private property.

The Board finds further that every reasonable facility and service requested by Miss Earhart or her representative, Mr. Paul Mantz, was accorded by the Station Engineering Department, Wheeler Field and by the Hawaiian Air Depot; that no requests were refused; that Miss Earhart's technical advisor, Mr. Paul Mantz, landed the airplane on the mat at Luke Field about Noon, March 19th, 1937, at which time he inspected it and pronounced it suitable for her take-off for Howland Island; that her decision to use it was based on his recommendation; that the nature and condition of the Luke Field landing mat had no bearing on the causes resulting in the crash; that in a signed statement to the Press (See Exhibit O) Miss Earhart stated: *"The runway is excellent and every facility for safe flying available"*; that, subsequent to the crash, prompt and efficient action was taken by the Engineering Officer, Hawaiian Air Depot, to remove the damaged airplane from the runway and to safeguard it and the technical and personal property it contained; that it was subsequently shipped to Miss Amelia Earhart, Burbank, California, on board the S.S. Lurline sailing from Honolulu, March 27th, 1937, in compliance with orders of competent authority based on the written request and authorization of Miss Earhart.

CONCLUSIONS:

It is the conclusion of the board that every reasonable assistance and facility was accorded Miss Earhart by the 18th Composite Wing to facilitate her flight and that no claim of negligence or responsibility in connection with her crash can be sustained against the personnel, equipment or facilities made available to Miss Earhart by the Commanding General, Hawaiian Department.

<u>RECOMMENDATIONS:</u>

None. Signed, Philips Melville Major Air Corps President Department Air Office.

Chris Williamson

There have been many ideas, suggestions and theories as to *what exactly happened* that morning.

In reading the official report and talking to Nicholas, one can conclude that maybe Amelia Earhart simply made a mistake; it happens.

But was it a fatal one?

This incident forced the postponement of the rest of the world flight until the Electra could be properly put back together again. More importantly though, this incident forced a change in direction for the flight, bringing the aviators *west to east* instead of *east to west*.

Did that ground loop essentially seal the fate of Amelia Earhart and Fred Noonan?

As I spoke with Nicholas, he informed me of *another incident*, this time attributed to navigator Fred Noonan, that I hadn't previously known about, and it may be a potentially telling piece of information when it comes to the aviators eventually flying to and locating Howland Island.

Nick Augusta

On a flight aboard one of Pan Am's Clippers in 1936, while flying from Midway Island to Wake Island, the Pan Am team on Wake Island radioed the approaching Clipper that based on their direction-finding equipment, the inbound Clipper was two hundred miles *south* off course, passing Wake Island. Captain Musick, who was Pan Am's chief pilot and had flown many times with Noonan, asked him if this was correct, and Noonan told him it wasn't and to just continue on for another twenty minutes and they should sight Wake Island. Musick responded by saying that they were "not flying another twenty minutes but in fact were turning north then."

Indeed, after turning north, Wake Island appeared.

Upon landing at Wake, Captain Musick told Noonan that he had better bone up on his navigation. I think this is important, as it really reminds us that aerial navigation *can fail* due to many factors, including human error. It reminds us that these fliers and navigators in the 1930s were doing something dangerous and very unforgiving. We call it the "human factor," which often plays a significant role in aircraft accidents, and we see that to this day.

Chris Williamson

I often wonder about this question. If you're reading this and you've heard our podcasts, you've probably heard me ask it quite a few times. If Amelia Earhart had successfully taken off from Luke Field that morning, are we *even* discussing this world flight in the same context decades later?

Was that *one* mistake *really* the key, or would the results have been the same, only much sooner in the flight?

Nick Augusta

Did the ground loop have a direct impact?

I would say yeah, it certainly did because it changed the dynamic of the flight.

Obviously, the crew members were going to change at Howland and at Darwin when Manning was to get off, and then Amelia was going to go solo the rest of the way. It's interesting that Noonan and Earhart flew around the world together with, really, no problems all the way up to approaching Howland. It definitely changed the outcome of the flight, It's kind of a sad thing, and you just wonder what would have happened if they had reached Howland and then continued on.

Would Amelia have done it?

I think she would have.

I think historically, we would have seen Amelia complete the around-the-world flight. On the voyage back to the west coast aboard the *Malolo*, I'm sure there was some soul-searching by *all of them*.

Manning's leave was coming up, and the repairs to the Electra would likely take too long. He'd have to return to the United States Lines before long. I know *Time* magazine ran an article about Manning that showcased his *own admission* of being a stubborn bullheaded introvert and an unsmiling perfectionist with a passion to run a perfect ship. One can possibly guess that, by looking at the newsreels or the photos of Manning arriving in Los Angeles. Maybe he didn't want to have anything to do with this around-the-world flight. If you take a look at the photos and the news reels themselves, his demeanor is one that's like, "I can't believe I'm involved with this mess."

He almost looks uninterested.

Chris Williamson

After learning about the ground loop from Nicholas and reading the accident report, I felt a little bitter, and I didn't want all of you to feel the same way. I didn't want you to feel that Amelia's legacy in Hawaii was just the ground loop. Sure, it was a big deal, but Amelia's Hawaiian history went far beyond that one trip. In preparing for this part of the series, I reached out to various contacts that I've made during Chasing Earhart, and everyone recommended *the same guy*.

When Nicholas recommended him, I knew I was on the right track.

"What I find interesting is that Amelia kept a secret about a flight she was making. So she was capable of doing that. Am I reading too much into it? Maybe."

Burl Burlingame

Hawaii is one of the most remote inhabited places on earth.

Mark Twain called it a "Necklace of Islands." Aviation basically helped unify the islands with the rest of the world, so aviation was really important to Hawaii. The first planes came out here on New Year's Eve 1911 and have been here ever since.

Chris Williamson

Burl Burlingame is the *very definition* of a historian.

An author, newspaperman and former curator, he has more knowledge on Hawaiian aviation than anyone I've ever had the pleasure of speaking with. He's the kind of expert whom experts recommend you talk to when *they* don't have the answers you're looking for.

And he's a master storyteller. I hope you'll see that.

Burl Burlingame

In early 1935, she pulled a sort of trick on Hawaii. She came out here with her husband and her mentor Paul Mantz and brought what she called her "red bus." Lockheed said she was here to do tours and she wanted to fly over and around the islands in her red bus. She did a lot of real high visibility tourist stuff, flying to the neighboring islands, visiting hula troops, planting a tree on Hilo which is still standing by the way, with her name in front of it. While all this was going on, Paul Mantz was preparing the airplane. One evening, she took off and didn't report in until she was more than halfway to California beyond the no-return point. They did not tell anyone that she was making the first solo flight between Hawaii and the mainland, not for the first *woman* but the first *person*. She aimed at the mainland from Hawaii because the target is bigger, but she flew from here to the Bay Area and was only a couple of miles off course and landed at Oakland field.

Chris Williamson

What a great story.

What I find interesting about *that* story is that Amelia kept a secret about a flight she was making. So *she was* capable of doing that. Am I reading too much into it?

Maybe.

Moving on.

Burl Burlingame

She had been involved in a few crashes in the past, and I think they were afraid of her having to turn back because of some mechanical failure when she was short of the no-return mark.

So they kept it under wraps.

Of course, it was a stunt in some ways. A lot of male pilots derided her abilities, but none of them could match her instinct for publicity. By the time she landed in Oakland, there were thousands of people very excited to see her land, it caused a tremendous wave of excitement, and people flooded the airfield in Oakland.

Chris Williamson

Interestingly enough, Amelia wasn't the only one on the world flight crew who had a history with Hawaii. Paul Mantz and Harry Manning had been to the islands on numerous occasions. Pan Am, Fred Noonan's organization, spent time perfecting aerial navigation there. As Burl explains it, Hawaii has deep roots in multiple facets of Amelia Earhart's life and inner professional circle.

Burl Burlingame

Manning had been in and out as a ship navigator and as an aviation professional. Mantz certainly had been in and out; he passed through there several times. Pan Am, of course, did the pioneering flights. The thing is, is that aerial navigation, particularly on great circle routes, was something that was really a new science. These were the guys who were pioneering it, and it was all being invented as they went along. The guys who knew how to do it were in a very small circle, and they all knew each other.

Chris Williamson

How would you like to be *in that* inner circle?

Earlier we got Nicholas's take on how Hawaii ties into the world flight and the ground loop incident in particular, but I wanted to ask Burl for his take on that day. After all, every expert you talk to perhaps can give you a different piece of the puzzle or a different perspective, and that's what this investigation is all about.

Burl Burlingame

The original idea was to fly around the world as close to the equator as possible, which was an around-the-world flight that had not been done yet.

She was determined to break that record.

At that time of year, which was March 1937, weather conditions dictated that they go around the world in a clockwise direction. So they took off from Oakland and flew to Hawaii, and actually, they took off from Oakland in rainy conditions, fully loaded with four people on the airplane: two navigators, Mantz and Earhart. They took off from a rainy field in Oakland, they flew successfully, landed at Wheeler, and started servicing the airplane.

They had problems with the propeller icing up at altitude, and Mantz asked the army to service the propellers.

One of the interesting things about the flight is how much help they got from the military without going through Washington.

. . .

Chris Williamson

Lightbulb!

Did you read that? Let me repeat it. "What's interesting is how much help they got from the military without going through Washington."

I sat *right up* when I heard him say that.

You should have too.

Burl Burlingame

The military is always happy to help, and they took the propellers off, they took them down to the propeller shops out on Ford Island, and the army technicians got them in shape and put them back on the airplane. Mantz test flew it, said it was fine, and they moved the airplane down to Ford Island and Luke Field and prepared it for takeoff there. All of this was done pretty quickly. Basically, they were here for only about thirty-six hours, but local commanders had a lot more autonomy at the time simply because it took longer to get okays from Washington, and it's always better to beg for forgiveness than to be turned down. There's a famous picture of the Electra being fueled at Oakland field, and Mantz is standing on the wing, and the sailors are fueling the airplane. It's obviously raining, but they are filtering the fuel as it's loaded into the plane. Mantz was a real stickler for fuel quality, and when the plane was moved down to Luke Field, they checked the filters and started loading it up with fuel from a civilian fuel truck. Those filters were showing particles of metal, so Mantz refused the fuel and asked for a new load. The civilian fuel truck was switched with another truck, and it *also had* metal particles, so Mantz then asked for all military fuel. The Army Air Corps said, "No problem," and completely fueled the plane with army fuel.

Chris Williamson

I'm *liking* Paul Mantz more and more by the second. If I'm flying around the world, I want *him* to be my technical adviser. Oh, and *another* lightbulb.

Military fuel.

I hope you're taking notes.

Back to March 20.

Burl Burlingame

The conditions were very similar between there and Oakland; it was a rainy morning, and it was dark. The runway on Luke Field was made up of crushed coral soaked with oil to make it dense.

Oakland field was cement, which made it harder. There were no lights on the field. The navy and the army shared Luke Field. Actually, the army version was Luke Field, and the navy version was Naval Air Station Pearl Harbor. For example, they were preparing for the flight, and a navy airplane started up and waddled right into the path of Earhart's airplane, and they had to wave it off because no one had told the navy this was happening.

A lot of onlookers showed up, and they realized they couldn't see the edges of the runway, so they handed everyone flashlights and asked them to line up on the edges of the runway about one hundred feet apart. This didn't illuminate the runway, but she could at least tell where the edges of the runway *were*. Remember, this was a *predawn takeoff.* Mantz started the plane up about 5 a.m., got it running, and she took over and started takeoff at about 5:45 a.m., went down the runway, and apparently the one wing lifted higher than the other, and she over controlled somehow, according to the official report, and the wings slammed down, which made the tire burst. The landing gear dug into the ground, the plane spun around, breaking the other landing gear, and that was it.

Chris Williamson

What I was really curious about here was the toll this accident had on Amelia and the crew.

Nicholas alluded to it before, but for Amelia, this was a failure on another level, on a world stage.

I wondered how that affected her mentally.

. . .

Burl Burlingame

She'd been in accidents before. Luckily it happened in civilization, as it were. They were able to get on an ocean liner within an hour or so and get back to the United States and start planning.

They also asked the army to disassemble the airplane, clean it up, and ship it back. And the army went, "Okay, no problem," which is interesting *also*.

This airplane was in the middle of an operating field with fuel soaking in. Every picture you see of guys working on the airplane, there are guys standing around with fire extinguishers. The plane was damaged but not *severely*. The damage was primarily in the landing gear and the engine cells with some twisting of the wings. One of the things that I understand but am not absolutely sure on is that the technical specifications for that airplane are based on the *pre-crash* specs.

After the airplane was repaired and put back into service, it was not retested for speed and distance. So the specs *may have* been off.

Chris Williamson

What Burl just said should be alarming to you. If you're not following, let me fill you in.

The original build for the Electra as Amelia received it from Purdue was tested thoroughly for speed and distance. Those factors were crucial to the success of the world flight.

However, the version of the Electra that was received *after it was rebuilt **was not** tested*.

That was the version Amelia and Fred would take around the world. It wasn't tested; therefore, there wasn't 100% assurance that *this version of the plane* could endure what the *original version could*.

Really think about that.

In the end, Amelia's impact in Hawaii is like it is everywhere. It looms over the island, and the monuments to her legacy are found all around.

Burl Burlingame

There's the monument to her that was created by the local chapter of the Ninety-Nines, over near Diamond Head, and it was the last place people were able to see her airplane as it flew away on its way to the mainland for the 1935 flight. It's a nice monument, and it's interesting; it shows the airplane high above the waves. The plaque is bronze, and it's fairly corroded, but the metal around the airplane is bright from people touching it. There is a time capsule buried in the monument, but the city has not decided to open it yet.

I was a newspaperman for a long time, and I had a coworker at the newspaper who was an older woman, and she was probably the best writer I'd ever met. When she was a little girl, she met Amelia Earhart at an airshow on the mainland, and Amelia bent down, looked her in the face, and told her she could be anything she wanted to be.

This woman said she just never *ever* forgot that for the rest of her life.

There are people who make other people feel like they can do more, just by the power of who they are.

Earhart was like that. She may not have been the world's greatest pilot, but she was one of those people who made aviation what it is today.

Chris Williamson

And with that, my time with Burl was over. Little did I know that I'd be publishing the last work before his untimely passing. It goes to show you how fragile all of this really is.

But Burl would want us to continue, so *that's* what we're going to do. Our time in Hawaii is over, and now armed with all the knowledge and the history, we're ready to take on the biggest historical mystery of all time.

And we're going to do it in a way that you've never experienced before.

Next up, jury selection for the trial of the disappearance of Amelia Earhart and Fred Noonan begins.

This is the trial of the century, and *all of you* are involved now.

TRIAL BY JURY

*"Follow the evidence. **Wherever** it leads."*

Chris Williamson

When I decided to do *Vanished* as a podcast series and, subsequently, as the book you're reading, the first question that I asked was, "How do we approach a case like this in a way that hasn't already been done? How do we make it interesting and fun even?" The idea for what you're about to read came to me several years back, and it took us almost a year to produce a single part of the original podcast series. As we stand right now, we've journeyed through Amelia Earhart's childhood and adolescent years, her time in Canada after the war, her introduction to aviation and her *extraordinary* career. We've looked at causes and events that meant a lot to AE, such as the Ninety-Nines, the air Derby of 1929, and her extraordinary ties to Purdue University.

When we last left her, Amelia experienced failure, not for the *first* time in her life, but on a stage and a level that was unlike anything she'd ever faced to that point. I've pored over this case for a little over twenty-two years now, and I've spoken to some of the top minds in the world regarding what happens next.

Some of those minds disagree with each other, aggressively at times. There are aspects of this case that begin on the day that she and Noonan disappeared, July 2, 1937, and have had constant developments occurring to this day. One thing's for certain; what's been done up to this point hasn't yielded any major results. As we wrapped up our time at Purdue, I told you that you were all about to take part in the trial of the century.

Now that trial *begins.* We can't look at this thing with a business-as-usual approach. It's time to shake things up. It's time to get under some people's skin. It's time to take this entire case, all eighty-five years of it, and burn it *all* down.

Before we get to the courtroom, something was almost embarrassingly obvious to me. I *don't know* how a jury trial works. Sure, I've seen movies and read books, but I don't know the first thing about trying a case like this one. Up to this point, I've been going this entire thing alone. But if we're going to do this *in this way*, I now need a partner. I've been waiting to say this for a long time.

I need to lawyer up. As fate would have it, I found the perfect person.

Now it's time for the world to meet her.

"We want the judge to apply the rules of evidence to determine whether an expert should be allowed to testify before that jury hears what the expert has to say. Because once they hear it, they cannot unhear it."

Jen Taylor

I think that you have so many different competing theories that it would probably be more appropriate to look at it as *four different trials.* What I mean by that is you take, say, theory number one, whatever that theory is, and you put that theory on trial. You establish what the evidence is, you test that evidence, and you determine whether you can prove that theory to whatever burden of proof you've decided to use.

For example, if you're using an analogy of a criminal trial, you would ask, "Did this theory get proven beyond a reasonable doubt?" Then you would move on to the next one, and you would kind of look at it as you would look at criminal trials; it would be the "State versus theory one" or the "State versus theory two." I think it would be a really good way of looking at it, and I *do think* that it's absolutely possible. The analogy is not going to be perfect, because when you have a criminal trial, a lot of it is going to focus on constitutional rights and things like that. Obviously, that's not going to be an issue here, but I think in terms of testing the evidence, testing witness credibility, and testing scientific theories, I think that looking at it in the context of a criminal trial is a really good analogy.

Chris Williamson

Jennifer Taylor is a passionate and dedicated attorney who believes that preparation, attention to detail and a strong work ethic are the keys to winning a case. That makes her my perfect partner to tackle this one. Jennifer completed her undergraduate degree in political science at Lamar University in Beaumont, Texas, graduating magna cum laude.

She attended law school at South Texas College of Law, where she met friends and future partners Jared Smith and Brad Vinson. While a law student, Jennifer focused on gaining as much real-world experience as she could. Experiences such as her internship with the army judge advocate general's core and her participation in two of South Texas's legal clinics allowed Jennifer to work closely with clients and help them navigate an often confusing and complicated legal system in order to obtain the results they wanted.

Academically, Jennifer focused on honing her legal research and writing skills, serving as editor in chief of *Currents: Journal of International Economic Law.* Jennifer graduated South Texas summa cum laude. Her academic success led to her appointment after law school as a judicial law clerk for the 11th Court of Appeals in Eastland, Texas. As a clerk, Jennifer worked closely with appellate judges on a wide range of criminal law issues such as post-conviction DNA testing, the Fourth, Fifth and Sixth Amendments, and admissibility of evidence, including expert testimony in complicated sexual assault and murder cases.

Her work at the court instilled in her a set of values that she carries with her throughout her career, including work ethic, honesty, compassion, and a desire to fight for truth and justice. You're going to be hearing a lot from Jen as we journey throughout this case. In fact, she'll be in the courtroom observing the events that transpire. Maybe I can even persuade her to cross-examine a few witnesses. After each day in court, I'll meet with her to get her observations and her ideas on the witnesses of the day and her thoughts on the case as we progress through it together. But for now, Jennifer has to take me and *all of you* to school on some basic principles of a jury trial case.

Jen Taylor

There are five different burdens of proof; they are *reasonable suspicion, probable cause, preponderance of the evidence, clear and convincing evidence,* and *beyond a reasonable doubt* is the highest.

Obviously, the most important ones in criminal cases are going to be probable cause and beyond a reasonable doubt, because probable cause triggers an arrest, and beyond a reasonable doubt is needed for a criminal conviction. To briefly go over what all of these things mean and maybe to help give it context, *reasonable suspicion* is at the very bottom.

That just means something above a hunch; you have something that allows you to articulate a reason for why you think something is happening. It's more than just a gut feeling. It's a very low standard. This is the standard that's used when you do a "stop and frisk," or you pull somebody over while they're driving. *Probable cause* are facts and circumstances from a reasonable trustworthy source that would warrant a belief by someone of reasonable caution that a crime has occurred *or* is about to occur. That's the definition in Texas that we use.

Like I said, you need probable cause to move forward with an arrest. So when we explain to a venire panel (anyone who's going to potentially be on our jury), we use this analogy of houses when we talk about probable cause. We show a picture of a house that is barely standing, but it *is* there. It's run-down; it's got holes; it's super old; no one really lives in it.

But if you were in an emergency and you needed shelter, the house *would* work. This is our visual of what probable cause looks like. It's okay, but it's not really going to get you what you need. It's just *okay* for now.

Above probable cause is what's called "preponderance of the evidence." This just means more likely than not. Fifty-one percent of civil trials operate under a preponderance of the evidence, burden of proof. So if somebody's money is on the line, then your burden at trials is to prove that more likely than not this thing happened.

Above that is "clear and convincing." That means that enough evidence to provide a firm belief or conviction as to the truth of the allegations ought to be established. So it's not quite "beyond a reasonable doubt," but enough to give you a firm belief or conviction. The example that we give most often to prospective jurors are CPS cases. To terminate someone's parental rights, you have to prove by clear and convincing evidence that someone is an unfit parent. We also use this standard in Texas for actual innocence. Once you've been convicted of a crime, you must then show in post-conviction that you're *innocent* by clear and convincing evidence. It lowers the burden just a little bit for you and makes you prove by clear and convincing evidence that you're *actually innocent*.

Then of course, the very last one is "beyond a reasonable doubt." You need that to obtain a criminal conviction. Again, we don't have a definition for it, so we use analogies. The analogy that we use goes back to that run-down house. The next slide is going to have a picture of a mansion. That is what the state needs to build you in order to obtain a conviction in this case. They had the house; that's why my client was arrested, that's why he's sitting here today, but that's not the end of the story. Now the state has to build you this mansion. That's where we end that section of our explanation, and we move into "What does everyone think?" and "What is reasonable doubt to you?" Because to everybody, it means something a little bit different.

Chris Williamson

How often is a trial decided on something that's beyond a preponderance of evidence? How often is it that it's just circumstantial evidence that's built up enough to make a conviction?

Jen Taylor

Quite often. I don't have statistics for you, but in my experience, the majority of the time we will have nothing *but* circumstantial evidence. I think in order to answer that question, you really have to understand what the difference is between *direct* and *circumstantial* evidence. A lot of people think that they know what that means. As an example, say you're inside and you don't have any windows in your office, so you can't see outside. You're inside for eight hours, you walk outside, and it's overcast, and there's water all over the ground, and people are putting away umbrellas, but you don't see rain. You *know* that it rained, yet you have no direct evidence that it rained because you actually didn't *see* any rain; you only see the results of the rain. The water on the ground, people putting away their umbrellas and the overcast sky, all of that is circumstantial evidence. You would be crazy to say, "Oh, but I can't prove it rained." No reasonable person would say that it didn't rain. Just because you have nothing but circumstantial evidence, that doesn't mean that you cannot prove your case beyond a reasonable doubt; you *can*. What matters is what *is* that evidence, how strong is that evidence, and how credible are your witnesses?

Just because you don't have direct evidence, eyewitness testimony of what happened or DNA evidence, that doesn't mean you can't prove it. It happens all the time in court. *All the time.*

Chris Williamson

If you're prosecuting or defending a case and you have 200 eyewitnesses who put somebody there, all 200 of them can't be wrong, right? How does that work? When you have one eyewitness who can put someone in jail for murder for the rest of their life, and then you have something like this that's got potentially over 200 from various backgrounds, is that a slam dunk, or am I mistaken here?

Jen Taylor

That's an overwhelming number, don't get me wrong. I don't think you would ever have 200 witnesses to anything in a criminal case. First, a judge wouldn't allow that. What *I* would want to know before I really answer your question is, what are these witnesses actually saying they saw? Did they say, "I saw Amelia Earhart?" Or did they say, "I saw a white woman over there?" Did they say, "I saw a Lockheed Electra?" Or did they say, "I saw a plane?" So I think that you're right in terms of having that many people saying exactly the same thing; that carries a lot of weight, it *really does*. With a jury, eyewitness testimony in my experience probably carries almost as much weight as DNA. People tend to believe someone who says, "I saw something, and I have no reason to lie." Why *not* believe them? Unless there's a reason why. Maybe you're forgetting, or you're mistaken.

Corroboration by 199 *other* people is really hard to beat. I wouldn't say it's a slam dunk because I would need to know what exactly it was they saw. How do we know that they saw what they think they saw? How do you know that they're remembering it correctly?

If your question is just that we have 200 people saying the exact same thing, I think that carries a lot of weight.

Chris Williamson

Let's break this down; how does a jury trial case actually work?

Jen Taylor

The very first thing that's going to happen that's going to trigger the criminal justice system being involved is a crime is committed, and then at some point, maybe immediately, maybe a few weeks later, or maybe a few months later, an investigation into that something happening could take place. Depending on what it is, that investigation can take days, it can take weeks, or it can take years. That's going to involve people, typically law enforcement, talking to witnesses, gathering evidence, testing that evidence, writing reports, and taking pictures. They'll do all of those things until they're satisfied that they think they know what happened. Then they're going to conclude their investigation, put all their evidence together, and they're going to send it to the county or district attorney's office.

That's phase one.

At some point during this investigation, an arrest is likely going to be made. They can't make that arrest until they've established probable cause, as we discussed earlier with our burdens of proof. Once they feel like they've made it to that point, they can obtain a warrant. There are various exceptions to having to obtain a warrant, but in any event, you have to have probable cause. They will make an arrest, charges will be filed, and then the county or district attorney's office is going to determine, "Okay, do we want to charge this case? What do we want to charge it as?"

Usually there's an intake attorney who does this. They will look at the file, they will look at everything that law enforcement gave them, and they will compare that to the penal code. In Texas, we have the Texas penal code, and they're the ones who make the decision, not the police officers. They will pick something out in the code; they might pick *several things* out in the code, depending on how bad the crime was. They will take that information for, say, a felony to a grand jury. From there, the grand jury will either indict or not. The burden of proof there is *also* probable cause.

That's all they need to move forward.

The defense does not have a right to participate in these proceedings, they don't even have the right to know what's going on in those proceedings; they're all behind closed doors.

The grand jury hears it, and if there's probable cause to move forward, you will get an indictment.

Once you get the indictment, *then* they have to share the evidence with you. When I say "you," I mean "your attorney." You'll get all of it, and now for the first time, there's *two* sides. There are adversaries; there's "the state," and there's "the defense." They all have the evidence, and they're looking at it. The defense might do *their own* investigation. Then you're going to have pre-trial motions, you're going to have to settle constitutional issues, and you're going to have to negotiate with the prosecutor to see if you can agree on a resolution to this case. If you're talking about going to trial, then that means you've reached an impasse. You don't agree on the best resolution for this case, or one person is saying they're completely innocent. Maybe we don't think that the offer is fair, and maybe we think we can get a better resolution in front of a judge or jury. Whatever the reason, negotiations have completely broken down, and now we're going to trial.

Chris Williamson

What happens on the day of the trial? Can you explain how opening statements work? I know it's a summary of the evidence, but walk us through that if you can.

Jen Taylor

Right, so on the day of the trial, the first thing that you're going to do is pick your jury. You go through that process, and then once the jury is in panel, you will give your opening statement. Actually, to back up a little bit, once the jury is in panel, the very first thing that happens is the state reads the charging instrument into the record. That's really important because that places *on the record* what you're being charged with. What you're being charged with is what they have to prove beyond a reasonable doubt. Every single element of that offense has to have proof beyond a reasonable doubt.

Chris Williamson

How is the jury selected, and what does that entail? Can we walk through that?

Jen Taylor

In Texas, for a felony, you want twelve jurors, and for a misdemeanor, you want six. If you're on a felony, you're going to have a bigger panel than you are on a misdemeanor.

Regardless, you're going to have a bunch of people come into this room, they're all going to sit in the gallery, and the attorneys are going to be in front. In federal courts and in some jurisdictions, the judge will ask the panel questions, but in my jurisdiction and in some others, the attorneys get to ask instead. Either way, what you're going to do is try to have a conversation with those jurors. It is the *only time* you actually get to talk to them, so it's really important because you want people on your jury whom you at least somewhat know. You don't want strangers there; you want the people whom you can get to discuss how they feel and what they think.

We call it jury selection, but it's really more like jury *deselection.* What happens is everyone's sitting down; they're numbered 1 through 100 or however many. If nobody gets struck, then the first 12 get impaneled onto the final jury. What you're doing is, you're saying, "I really don't like juror number two"; if no one strikes juror number two, then that juror is going to be on my jury, so I need to strike number two. If I don't like juror number 98, I will probably only strike them if I feel like we're creeping back there, if that makes sense.

The way I always do it is I start explaining general concepts, but I don't spend too much time on that. I might make sure everyone understands that the state has the burden of proof and not us. I make sure everyone understands "innocent until proven guilty." These are really big concepts that you really need to understand if you're going to be on a jury. I take a little bit of time just to make sure we all know what that means. Then I will ask open-ended questions. I might say, "This is a case where state is alleging that a plane went down in the middle of the ocean, and right then and there, Amelia Earhart and Fred Noonan died at sea." Whenever we talk about something like that, we're trying to show that there's reasonable doubt. What does reasonable doubt look like to you? We'll get open-ended questions, and people will start talking about things, and they'll say, "Well, I would want somebody who would have witnessed it," or, "I would want physical evidence." They open up about the things they expect, and that's good for the state as well as the defense. It lets you know 95 out of 100 of these jurors don't think that they can find this kind of case beyond a reasonable doubt unless you have physical evidence.

If that's the case, that's going to let you know when you go in that if you don't have physical evidence, you're going to have to find some other way to prove your case beyond a reasonable doubt. Maybe you want to bust the panel because all of these people hold it against you that you don't have physical evidence. You get them talking; you get them thinking about it early on. You're not allowed to give specific facts; that's called "asking a commitment question," and that means that you're trying to get a juror to commit to a set of facts *before* they're actually impaneled. That's not allowed, but what you *can* do is you can give general concepts, and you can say, "This is going to be a case where you have a plane that goes down and two people are never seen again. What kind of things would you expect to see in a trial like that?" It gets them talking, and it's really just a way for you to know who your jury is. It helps them when they're going into trial. It helps them understand the basic underlying concepts before they start hearing evidence.

Chris Williamson

From a legal standpoint, if any of these theories are going to present their list of expert witnesses, what goes into selecting that expert witness? What qualifies them to be an expert?

Jen Taylor

Let me give you an example. I'm a defense attorney, and I just received a new client into an indictment.

I've done a bunch of investigation, and we'll just say this is a simple DWI case. The state has taken a blood sample of my client. They have run that through a blood test, and that test comes back, and it alleges that my client's blood-alcohol content was a .22, way above the legal limit. I've talked to my client, and my client says, "That's crazy. I had one drink."

There's no way that number's right. Now I have to find myself an expert because clearly that blood number is wrong. So the first thing I'm going to do is I'm going to talk to people.

I'm going to say, "You've done a lot of good work with blood; you know a lot about gas chromatography. Can you take a look at this and tell me what you think?" At that point, that person is a "consulting *expert*" because all I want is their opinion. I'm not asking them to say anything, and they're not in front of a jury doing anything. Once they're a consulting expert, they are a part of our defense team. They share in all of the confidentiality responsibilities, and they're just going to give me an opinion on the stuff that I give them. *Then* I'll decide from there what to do with that.

I might look at this expert's report, and it might say "I reviewed everything, and none of the standard operating procedures were followed; this evidence was handled very badly; it wasn't refrigerated like it was supposed to be." I might see all of these problems, and from there, I can do one of two things: if it's something that is simple enough that I think the jury will understand just by cross-examining the state's expert, then I might choose to do that. Why might I choose to do that? Well, the expert might be unavailable, or it might be hard to get them down if the client can't afford to pay their testimony fee; any one of those things. If it's a situation where I think the subject matter is a little bit more technical than people can understand, then I might ask this expert, "Hey, what you found is very helpful for us, will you come testify?"

In the legal world, most of the time, there are experts we know already; they have a reputation in the community. Most of the time, that's how we're going to find people, but that's not *always* the case. Sometimes, something novel comes up, and you need something new. So you just do research; you call around and try to figure out who might be available to help you out. A lot of times, it's going to be based on who's available and who's willing to work with us, of course. You're going to look at their history of testifying and ask qualifying questions. Have they ever testified before? What does their education look like? How long have they been in their field? Have they ever been published? Things like that. Of course, if they're incredibly well known, that's going to be helpful, but they're all going to be incredibly expensive. So cost is something that we would look at too.

Chris Williamson

Can an expert be disqualified?

Jen Taylor

Yes. Expert witnesses and science generally in the legal world have a long and contentious history. This is probably one of the things that gets people the most upset because scientific testimony is very powerful testimony. If you get somebody up there who says, "I have a bunch of credentials, I'm a scientist, and on this subject, I know more than any person in this room, and this is my opinion," that carries a lot of weight.

Of course, there's a long history of conflict between the defense bar and the state or the government trying to litigate what is allowed in court and what isn't. One of the early cases on expert witnesses is a case called *Fry v. United States*, and that was out of the DC circuit. That case was decided all the way back in 1923. It was a murder case, the defendant was convicted of murder in the second degree, and one of the things used to convict this person was a really crude and early form of lie detector test where, essentially, they would measure your blood pressure while you were being interviewed.

The idea here is, if you are nervous, then your blood pressure goes up; but if you are talking freely and not hiding anything, then you have a normal blood pressure. Complete junk, but they used this crude lie detector test to convict Mr. Fry of murder. That was appealed, obviously, and the DC circuit at that time in a very short opinion said, "Unless something is accepted in the scientific community, then you cannot bring it to court." *The general acceptance test* is what it became known as. Is this test *generally accepted* in the scientific community? This caused a lot of problems because for any kind of novel science that was not accepted yet in the scientific community, you couldn't use it, no matter how good that science was. On the other hand, things that have been used forever while accepted in the scientific community might not be good science.

About fifty years later in 1973, the federal rules of evidence were adopted, and those are still used today.

There have been changes, obviously, but the federal rules of evidence are going to be the rules that are going to govern what evidence is admissible and what evidence is inadmissible. Up until that time, we didn't have anything like that; we just had common law. Everything was set down in the 1970s, and it included a provision on the use of expert testimony. Rule 702 of the federal rules of evidence as it read when it was adopted states:

"If scientific, technical or other specialized knowledge will assist the trier of fact (meaning the jury) to understand the evidence or to determine a fact in issue, an expert may testify there to." Rule 702.

It didn't say anything about general acceptance in the community; it's not mentioned.

That causes a problem because we have fifty years of everybody relying on Fry, but then you have the rules of evidence that just came in. Those give what appear to be a completely *different* rule. We fought about this for a really long time; it actually took twenty years of people fighting over this before the supreme court addressed this question.

Fry I think is important to understand because a little less than half the states *still* use the first standard. The federal courts do not use the first standard; my jurisdiction does not use the Fry standard. The standard that is used now in a little over half of the states and in the federal courts is the standard that was articulated in *Daubert v. Merrell Dow Pharmaceuticals* in 1993, roughly twenty years after the federal rules of evidence were first adopted. In that case, mothers were suing the pharmaceutical company because they had been taking anti-nausea medicine during pregnancy, and they were alleging that it caused birth defects in their children. There were competing scientific theories on whether that was the case. On one hand, you had scientists who said, "This has been studied; here are roughly thirty papers on all the studies that have been done. All of those studies say this drug does not cause this birth defect; case closed." The other side says, "Hey, wait a minute, we have about eight experts here, and they have done some newer additional testing, and their findings contradict those old papers of yours." Well, under Fry, if we're looking at what's generally accepted in the scientific community, then you'd have to favor the thirty or so papers. Whereas under the rules of evidence, that was not clear.

The US Supreme Court finally took this up, and they adopted this entirely new test. I think it's better, and the majority of states, including the federal courts, have now adopted it. This is called the "Daubert test." The Daubert test asks whether it is relevant and reliable.

Those are the two things: it has to be *relevant*, and it has to be *reliable.*

To determine whether it is relevant and reliable, it gives you five factors that you should look at. The first one is whether or not the scientific technique can be tested or has been tested. This factor asks whether there have been independent empirical studies; is there empirical data out there? The second factor is whether the theory or technique has been subjected to peer review and publication. Has it been published? Have other scientists had an opportunity to comment on it, and what have they said? The third factor is the known or potential rate of error; how likely is it that you're going to get the wrong answer when you apply the scientific technique and question to the facts? That's important to know.

Chris Williamson

Boy, that's the key there for sure.

Jen Taylor

That specific factor becomes incredibly contentious. The fourth factor is the existence and maintenance of standards controlling the technique's operation. Simply put, *standard operating procedures.* Does your lab, does your study, whatever organization you are, do you have standard operating procedures in place? That's actually very important in any trial. If you're going to call an expert witness, especially from a crime lab, I want to see your standard operating procedures so that whenever I compare those to what you did, I can make sure you've followed them.

The fifth and final factor is general acceptance. To what extent has this scientific theory been accepted in the relevant scientific community? We didn't get rid of the general acceptance test; it's just not the end-all, be-all anymore. It is one of several factors that we use to determine whether or not scientific evidence is relevant and reliable: that's the key.

Something else that the Daubert court said, which has probably been grabbed on a little too hard by certain courts, is, "The inquiry envisioned by rule 702 is, we emphasize, a flexible one." That sentence has also stirred up quite a lot of controversy because what the Daubert court envisioned is this idea of the judge as gatekeeper. We want the judge to apply the rules of evidence to determine whether an expert should be allowed to testify *before* that jury hears what the expert has to say.

Because once they *hear it*, they cannot *unhear it.*

Chris Williamson

You hear that all the time: "I'm going to ask the jury to disregard what that witness just said."

Jen Taylor

Not happening.

Chris Williamson

Yeah, so that never really happens, right?

Jen Taylor

Right. And you can ask the judge to give what's called a "limiting instruction." I almost laugh at those words because what the judge is going to do is to say, "You've just heard X, Y and Z, but I want you to consider that for the limited purpose of…" meaning, don't consider it for guilt or innocence.

Fat chance of that happening.

Or he's going to ask you to disregard it entirely. People are going to try, but people are people, and they heard what they heard. They *also* heard you get mad about it, so, okay.

Chris Williamson

I guess one of the ways you could tie that to the Earhart investigation is the Freedom of Information Act requests that Les Kinney has filed, over two hundred of them, with the United States government, requesting release and access to the Earhart files that are allegedly being contained. When you have someone who has the credibility of Les Kinney testifying to the fact that these documents are there and they could in fact change history, can this testimony *be enough* to cause a subpoena of that information, or would the judge hear something like that and ask the court to have it stricken from the record?

. . .

Jen Taylor

The first thing that comes to *my* mind when I think of somebody saying, "I don't want to give you this information" is the Fifth Amendment.

This only applies to the person on trial. If they don't want to testify, *they don't have to,* and you are not allowed to hold that against them. The reason why we remind the jury of that a thousand times during trial is because it's very, very hard not to. I *do* think it's safe to put those aside in a case like this, because nobody is on trial. Nobody's going to be losing their life. As hard as it is for me to put those considerations aside, I think when you have somebody who holds a key piece of evidence and they're unwilling to share it with you, the natural inclination is to hold it against them.

For example, in a criminal trial, the state has a constitutional obligation to share with you what's called "Brady evidence." If they have evidence that is damaging to their case and it is material, they must give it to you. Constitutionally they must give it to you.

Additionally in Texas, we have what's called the "Michael Morton Act." Their discovery obligations are expanded somewhat. The point being, if they have an obligation to give you something and they don't, that's a problem. Typically, what you're going to get is a continuance, you're going to get more time, and then they must give it to you. There *are* cases where, say, it gets destroyed, it gets lost, or they claim that it gets lost; they're not going to give it to you; you're not going to get it. You have the ability to make what's called a "spoliation argument." You can say, "They damaged or lost this evidence; it's absence should be held against them. You should assume that the reason why they didn't give me this evidence is because it's damning to their case." In civil law, I think that happens a lot more than it does in criminal law.

Chris Williamson

Theoretically then, if Kinney takes the stand and he states that the US government *has* these documents – it's not theory, it's a fact – can the court then force the government to release those documents?

• • •

Jen Taylor

No one can *force you* to do anything.

The judge can hold you in contempt, dismiss your case, or threaten to do whatever they're threatening to do. At the end of the day, what matters is what's more important to that advocate. Is it more important that I prove my case in trial? Is it more important that I win? Or am I willing to take a loss because I want to hold on to this evidence?

Chris Williamson

I want to ask you about the term "smoking gun." That's been something that's been thrown all around this case by multiple people involved in different camps. Ric Gillespie on our very own show referred to something that he dubbed as the "any idiot artifact."

Something that can be presented that, "any idiot" can look at and be convinced of its validity. Legally speaking in a case like this, what would be considered a smoking gun?

Jen Taylor

Phrases like "reasonable doubt" or "presumption of innocence" and even words like "circumstantial indirect evidence" all have meaning legally. We can provide you with a definition of them. "Smoking gun" is not a legal concept, so I can't really give you an accepted legal definition for it. That's referring to a piece of evidence that has only one reasonable explanation.

Why did I phrase it that way? Well, because what are we looking for?

Reasonable doubt.

If you can only explain it in one way and there is no reasonable alternative explanation, then that means that this piece of evidence is what proves the case beyond a reasonable doubt. If I'm looking at a criminal trial, that's how I would be looking at it.

Chris Williamson

I guess the most obvious question I have after that is, is the smoking gun *only* achieved when we have remains or the plane itself? Can you look at something like two hundred eyewitness accounts that range from firsthand accounts of people interacting with Earhart and/or Noonan or the plane, and military personnel who apparently have no reason to lie and say *that's* your smoking gun right there?

Jen Taylor

It certainly depends on what exactly they're saying, but I think it *could*. In these cases, when you're looking for something and you're trying to find the one thing to hang your hat on, I think that becomes a little difficult because often there's not going to be *one thing*. Like I mentioned earlier with the rain example, I see water on the ground, I see somebody putting away an umbrella, and there's overcast skies. But what is the smoking gun here? There isn't one. Does that mean that *it didn't* rain? No. I think that it's somewhat misleading to say, "You need a smoking gun; I've given you a smoking gun." A lot of the time, you're not going to have one. I think to fixate on that is a little bit misguided. Yeah, if two hundred people witness a murder, then of course that's a smoking gun, but that's never going to happen. It all goes back to the question of what they witnessed.

If two hundred people say they saw a person in a certain place, that's evidence that person might have been there.

It's *not evidence* of anything else *other* than that. I think a smoking gun, of course, helps you if you can be that person who finds it. *Then* you have a huge advantage over everyone else. To hold it against somebody because they *haven't* found it, I think is misguided.

Chris Williamson

Call me crazy, but talking with Jennifer *actually* gives me confidence that we can do this.

When word got out about what we were doing here, it stirred up a lot of curiosity within the aviation and podcast communities. This is such a robust case that people *actually* started reaching out to ask me how we were going to present this thing. As usual, there were no shortage of people who wanted to give me their own thoughts on what we were about to try before we ever tried it.

I thought it might be a good idea to reach out to a couple of guys who might be very familiar to you.

Guys I'm proud to call my friends.

Think of it as a pep talk before opening statements and first witnesses are called.

If you're reading this book, you're likely familiar with them. They don't know this, but *without them*, what you're reading wouldn't have been possible.

"You have to consider all of the evidence and everybody's theory so you can try to find a common thread running through. Often, you can find one. This is a flight that was charted up until a specific point that we know of. From that point, it's a leap of belief and faith."

Chris Williamson

I just wanted to talk with you guys before we embark on this thing because we're trying to do something that's never really been done. This case has become so watered down now; you guys know that better than anybody. It's one of those situations where you have to ask yourself what you can bring to the table that hasn't already been there. So we're trying to do this as a jury trial. You guys have been doing this for a long time, a lot longer than me. What do you think of what we're attempting to do? Is it even logical?

Scott Philbrook

Yeah, I think it's a really good approach because it's going to take an analytical angle on it that really hasn't been done before. There's a reason that the jury trial system is our system in the United States; it's because it's so effective. It's a really fair way to take a look at anything that might have happened, especially something like this. It gives you a template to explore all the angles and rule out what might not be possible or cast a reasonable doubt on some of these theories.

Forrest Burgess

You have five or six major theories with a bunch of sub theories that range from the most simplistic outcomes to the most crazy or conspiratorial. With a court case, you must find one angle that you're going to pursue from all the evidence. It will be really interesting to see what that main through line *is* here with the story of her disappearance. You have to consider all of the evidence and everybody's theory so you can try to find a common thread running through it. Often, you *can* find one. This is a flight that was charted up until a specific point that we know of.

From that point, it's a leap of *belief* and *faith.*

Chris Williamson

I can't begin to put into words how surreal it feels to call Scott Philbrook and Forrest Burgess *friends.*

Back when I was doing pre-research for what would become *Chasing Earhart,* I decided to model our podcast after their wildly successful show.

I can tell you *without hesitation* that we never got close.

That's a nod to just how great they are. *Astonishing Legends* is one of the most popular podcasts on the planet, even though Scott and Forrest are very humble about their success. They've now become more involved in the Amelia Earhart/Fred Noonan investigation than they probably ever wanted to, but I can always call them and talk about the latest developments. They've helped me to look at things in a logical way on more than one occasion. I can think of no better men to weigh in on this. Back to the pep talk:

Chris Williamson

As we're preparing to attempt this, I'm looking at all the evidence that we've amassed over the last several years for the project, and it's odd, because if you look at all these different theories, every theory has a different representation of data and a different type of evidence to support it. You have eyewitness testimony in some cases, you have tangible physical evidence that people are presenting, you have forensic evidence, you have circumstantial evidence, and you have the "official story" when it comes to that day.

This is one of those cases that seems to have it all.

I wonder what's going to make *the most* sense to people who are going to read through this. What do you guys think makes the most sense evidence wise to you?

. . .

Scott Philbrook

For me personally, I'm in an unusual spot, and I can't speak for other people; everyone has to come to their own conclusions. When we first talked about this, it was one of our early series when we started our show. We mentioned the idea of "confirmation bias," which certainly doesn't *belong* to the Amelia Earhart mystery, it belongs to anything that you're investigating. For the Amelia Earhart disappearance, confirmation bias should be next to it in the dictionary. Everyone who has their theory is bending the information that they're taking in; whether it's Leo Bellarts's testimony or other evidence, they're trying to figure out how that fits with what they personally believe. That's what everyone does, and that's something to keep in mind when you think about real court cases.

We've all seen enough *Datelines* and *2020s* to know that everything looks a certain way when you're looking at it through that filter of confirmation bias.

When we started out and first came to this, I had a predilection for the Japanese capture theory, and part of the reason I did was because it had a lot of eyewitness testimony. Now, anyone will tell you that eyewitness testimony is highly fallible, but it was a high number of people. One of the things that Forrest and I do might not work in a court case. We actually try to look at the human side of what we're investigating, not just the empirical evidence. When you're studying folklore and legend like we do, most times you *don't have any* empirical evidence. When you get some, that's a gift. We have to deduce things based on what people have said and what eyewitnesses have said. That was the theory that I was leaning towards, and I still have a propensity to believe in it. However, with Bill Snavely's discovery of the aircraft in Buka and everything going on there, I have a strong belief in the possibility that Buka might be the end game for Amelia's aircraft. I think Forrest will tell you there might be a combination.

Forrest Burgess

It might be the end game for *a* Electra.

Or maybe *the* Electra.

Going back to the question of what would appease a modern-day jury or audience here, in the modern sense, it's DNA. That exonerates people now on death row; cold cases have been reexamined and settled because of a piece of DNA that could be *years* old. We're seeing this currently in the news right now with a few people who were not known for murder and have been found out: really old cases. There are three elements that I see it boiling down to:

There are *two people* and *one airplane*. In the case of the *two people*, what would solve that? The DNA of Amelia Earhart, the DNA of Fred Noonan, and her *exact* plane. The plane that they know she took off in and that serial number.

Now, what is down at Buka?

Well, it looks pretty good right now that it's something very *similar* to an Electra, possibly very *likely* an Electra. Is it her plane? What happens when you find a combination of those? "We found a serial number, it's an Electra 10-E, it's got a man and a woman in there, but it's not them." Maybe you find another plane and it's a man and a woman, but they were passengers in the plane. What happens if you find that it's an Electra and it's *one* of them, but it's not *exactly her plane*? All of these scenarios *except* for both of them being confirmed with DNA and the serial number on her plane solves that riddle. It answers that mystery once and for all.

Any other combination and you've got a whole new mystery on your hands.

Chris Williamson

If Snavely's team pulls DNA from this wreckage, is that case closed?

Scott Philbrook

Well, I don't know that it is.

That's a hard thing to find, and who knows if they found anything like that? If they did, there's a whole other series of circumstances associated with it. If there's any human remains, they obviously have been underwater for eighty-five years. It's my understanding, based on papers that I've read and researched for this particular case, that DNA and bones in saltwater are usually unusable after as little as twenty-four to thirty-six hours. There's a 10,000% reduction rate or something like that in the amount of available DNA. On the other hand, what Forrest is saying works literally and figuratively. It's not only human DNA, but the plane has DNA, like he said. The serial number is the plane's DNA; there's factors about an Electra 10-E that are exclusive to an Electra 10-E. So that's a kind of DNA that you can get on the plane, and that would answer a lot of questions too, regardless of whether or not you are able to identify any human remains in it.

It *does* get complicated.

Forrest and I both have a propensity to believe in the Jaluit Atoll picture. Regardless of the circumstances and the controversy surrounding that photo, to us, it seems like a believable photo. That picture doesn't necessarily make sense in connection with Buka, but as far as we're concerned, what's happening in Buka *and* that photo are on even ground right now. Other people who are investigating the story, especially from other angles, will tell you, "Oh well, no, you can't have both of those." What Forrest is suggesting is that maybe you *can have both of them*. Maybe they *were* taken hostage, and maybe this is also a 10-E. Like he said, we've got a whole new mystery or, as the US government might call it, *a mess*.

Forrest Burgess

It doesn't solve anything.

The only scenario that works is if everything she took on board is intact as far as the manifest she would have had. If the serial numbers match up to her plane, that's the airtight DNA evidence. If it's crystal clear that it's *both of them*, then I think you put that to rest.

If there's any wiggle room there, then all these other theories people thought were crazy have to be looked at as well. What is going on? How did this get here? If it's another Electra 10-E that maybe has a spy camera on it, what's going on then?

Scott Philbrook

Well, then, yeah, you're looking at the possibility of two 10-Es. Getting into that whole spy idea and the idea that FDR wanted to get a map of the theater because he saw the war coming. It sounds like a Le Carré book, but you start to get into the idea of a double. In *that* case, what if you find remains associated with someone who was technically a look-alike and you can't get DNA from them? How are you going to identify that positively? It could be that person could have actual garments of her clothing, but *not be* her. I know that seems far out, but it's a hard thing to rule out too.

Crazier things have happened in the course of American history.

Forrest Burgess

There's a combination of things that sometimes happen. I believe with certain mysteries that we've looked at, there could be two or three simple things happening at once to convolute a scenario that makes it even more mysterious. When that happens, it baffles people because you don't know where to separate those. Where does one start and the other one begin? We've looked at the JFK assassination, another one of the greatest mysteries of the twentieth century. My view has changed, and I think Scott's has as well. There could have been two things that happened during that incident that overlap and make it even more confusing. They may be totally separate but happening simultaneously. You try to fit those pieces together, and they don't fit because how is that possible as a result of a single motivation? From a single actor, how are these things possible, the magic bullet theory and all that? My point about Amelia is that there could be several things going on that in and of themselves are not all that complicated or conspiratorial, but overlapping them *creates* a very complicated mystery.

Scott Philbrook

Traditionally when you do an investigation, you investigate a particular line of thinking, and you work backwards. You say, "Well this is what I think happened, and I'm going to investigate it from this angle."

The point is, that if more than one thing is going on, or something more complicated is going on, and you're closing your mind off to other possibilities, then you're going to throw away evidence that may be significant just because it doesn't align with the concept that you're trying to put together.

Chris Williamson

So what we're saying is that, really, at this point in the case, everything is on the table, and everything needs to be looked at.

Scott Philbrook

Absolutely, yeah. Because you know what, it *could just be* crash and sink. There's no reason it can't be that. We don't have an actual proven plane yet, so we can't take anything off.

Nothing has been ruled out.

All of the theories are viable until some kind of DNA, either literal or figurative, aircraft or people, comes back. Or you have some kind of hard-and-fast proof that whatever you're recovering from wherever you're looking specifically belonged to her.

If she was killed in Saipan, buried and the bones were removed, then maybe you would have to find a fragment on Saipan and identify from there. There's a set of skeletal remains where it might be possible to recover DNA from if you can find that hole that was supposedly dug that she was placed in.

Forrest Burgess

Even if you can't retrieve DNA from bone material, you can determine the sex of the skeleton. You can determine the height and get weight in a close range, so that's very helpful in itself.

. . .

Scott Philbrook

That's true.

Forrest Burgess

So you don't *need* DNA. In this case, we *want* DNA. We want conclusive proof in that form, but you will get even closer if you could find skeletal remains that were matched pretty closely to what we know about them. It doesn't totally close the case unless, again, you have their plane. *Then* maybe you can rest.

But what is the main mission here out of all these theories that have all these people doing research? The main goal should be to find her. To find her and Fred and find out what happened to them. *Not* to prove your *own* theory is right.

Scott Philbrook

That's right.

Forrest Burgess

If your theory is wrong, you should be able to abandon that and look at something else, and that's one thing that we like regarding Bill's attitude toward Buka. He's open to other possible scenarios. He's found one that he thinks is likely, but he's not so married to it that he's not going to look at anything else. That's the approach that we have when we go to look at any mystery we're studying.

Consider everything, and *then* make your choice.

Don't just brush aside something because it seems ridiculous to you at the outset, because more often than not, you're going to look like a fool later on.

Scott Philbrook

For me personally, it's far more intriguing to live in a world where I have a strong belief in both Japanese capture *and* Buka. On a scale, both of those cups would have the same amount of weight for me. I like being in that spot as opposed to saying, "Oh, no, I refuse Buka." The other thing about that is, if you're a strong proponent of crash and sink or the castaway theory, it doesn't make sense to say that you're not going to investigate something else.

Forrest Burgess

Well, that's ego.

Scott Philbrook

We need to be looking *everywhere* for her.

We don't know where she went, and we need to find out. She deserves the discovery and for her ending to be known.

Forrest Burgess

I believe it's totally okay to have your concern and your funding go to what you believe is the most likely scenario using some clues that you found. It's also important though, that while you're doing that, others can advance *their theory* and go research that. Be supportive, because it doesn't do anybody any good to cut other people down based on their theories.

You see that a lot because that's human nature. That's the way humans operate; we're very competitive.

We should be open to following the evidence wherever it takes us. Getting back to your scenario, that's what a prosecutor *should do*. Follow the evidence. Sometimes we see in court cases that they've got a particular agenda, and some things brought up by the defense are shoved aside, ignored or not brought into evidence.

Scott Philbrook

Next thing you know, the wrong person has been put on death row or is in jail for decades, and then later, they get exonerated, and they get out, but they only get exonerated if they agree not to sue. All those years of their life are gone because whoever was the prosecutor was so fixated on an idea, they couldn't accept the possibility that it *wasn't right.*

Forrest Burgess

You see that with juries as well. People making the decision who are supposed to be the objective persons coming in and hearing the evidence; a lot of that is also emotionally based. Hopefully you can put aside your personal biases and look at all the evidence.

We say this on the show. Wherever the story takes us, that's where we're going. Along the way, don't be afraid to form an opinion.

Harkening back to what Scott said about the Japanese capture theory, when we first started looking at it, it began to make sense to me. Again, it's anecdotal evidence, but a lot of it is circumstantial evidence from people who claim to have seen her.

Well, how many people does it take to start taking it seriously? Let's investigate that. Let's not just dismiss these people; there seems to be quite a few of them, over two hundred. So what's going on there?

Let's at least tie off that knot so we can look at other stuff. We're of the mind of looking at everything and forming your opinion based on your own personal logic. Try *not* to let your emotions get the best of you and see what happens.

It's a fascinating journey, and by no means is it coming to an end.

If she *does* turn out to be at Buka, if that *is* their plane, then there's still a story there.

You'll have to piece the puzzle together. How did she get there? Is it exactly as Bill thought, or was there some other reason? What's the story there?

It doesn't end if we find the plane. It's just a whole new chapter.

Chris Williamson

So follow the evidence *wherever* it leads.

· · ·

Scott Philbrook

That's right.

Chris Williamson

"Follow the evidence wherever it leads." I always feel better when I talk with those two.

Thanks, guys.

It's getting later in the evening on what I've affectionately dubbed "trial eve," and I have one more phone call to make.

When you grow up wanting to be an investigator, you search for people to look up to.

People who are a representation of what you consider to be the example in your field. A while back, I took a chance and reached out to someone I've admired for a very long time. You might say he's a bit of a hero of mine when it comes to studying cases like this.

I really was overwhelmed when he agreed to talk to me.

Being able to talk about a case, *this case,* what I've adopted as *my case,* with one of the people I've admired from afar, right before I take it all the way, is something that I can't *really* articulate at the moment.

But I have his phone number, so I called him. And as he was about to ramp up press on his newest book release, he was kind enough to give me a personal perspective that I never imagined I'd have.

"I actually have hope that it will be solved. There have been finds. Some of these modern-day, deep-sea dive companies that are well funded have enough people who are interested in the outcome and want to know; they're not going to stop. You're a good example of that."

Chris Williamson

I guess my first question for you is sort of an obvious one. When you look at a case like this, with so many different camps working so many different theories, is the investigation process for you different than any other case? Or is this really business as usual for you?

Buddy Levy

I think you have to always get as much information as possible that's out there, read *widely*, be *open* to all sorts of possibilities, and then take it from there. I'm a big believer in following your gut and your hunches, but also to not have a preconceived notion of where you're trying to head if you can possibly avoid that. Because going that way, you shut yourself down from being open to alternate possibilities.

Chris Williamson

According to his website:

"Buddy Levy is the author of seven books. His work has been featured or reviewed in the *New York Times*, the *Wall Street Journal*, *USA Today*, the *Washington Post*, the *Washington Times*, *Kirkus Book Reviews*, *Publishers Weekly Book List* and the *Library Journal*. He's also appeared frequently on national radio, including *The Dennis Prager Show*, *NPR*, and *Rudy Max's World*. He was the costar for twenty-five episodes from 2010 to 2012 on the History Channel's hit docuseries *Brad Meltzer's Decoded*, which aired to an average of 1.7 million weekly viewers and is still airing reruns today."

Truthfully his résumé could go on all day. If by some chance you *haven't* heard of his work, you should look him up. To me, the work Buddy and the rest of the team did with *Brad Meltzer* should be viewed as the gold standard for the investigation of historical mystery.

I can't *believe* I'm talking to him.

Chris Williamson

I've talked to Brad a couple of times about this case, he really loves it. In fact, he mentioned to me in passing that he really wanted to do a *Decoded* episode on it. Was there ever any talk amongst the team about taking this investigation on back when you guys were doing the show?

Buddy Levy

There was. Especially because of our work on the *DB Cooper case*, which remains to this day the only unsolved skyjacking in American aviation history. They're not really similar other than there's airplanes involved, but I think when there's something that is unsolved, it gets Brad's attention for sure. There were so many different avenues that we wanted to go down with *Decoded*, and there were always discussions when McKinley, Scott and I would be driving around during downtime about other things that intrigued all of us. So it definitely was in the wheelhouse for sure.

Chris Williamson

I want to ask you about investigative techniques because I know you guys kind of deployed a lot of different techniques during the show, and I'm sure in your own personal work as well. I know you touched on having a hunch and following that, but are there any other specifics that you can give me regarding specific investigative practices that you use?

Buddy Levy

I come from an academic background, in the sense that I'm a book writer and researcher.

I always start kind of old school in a way. I start at the library, which I know seems sort of quaint now. Because of the databases that are available now and the broadening ability for us to find information through the internet and using all sorts of interlibrary loans, you can access almost anything from a computer. I *do* like to go to the origins and go back.

As a person who writes books about history, on the book jacket, I'm often called a historian.

I call myself a *narrative history writer*.

I think that it's really important to use everything you can and to learn all the history that you can about a particular subject and start at square one. Not necessarily starting at what the most *current* knowledge is on something, but going all the way back to the beginning. I really like using the old-school models and talking to research librarians who are incredibly knowledgeable, especially those who have areas of expertise and specialization. Just read vast amounts. It's not really sexy sounding, but I like rolling up my sleeves and putting on the white gloves and going into the archives. I wrote my first New York book on the frontiersman Davy Crockett, and there's theories there about whether he perished at the Alamo or got away and actually went and lived in Mexico under an assumed name. It was really fun to be at the Tennessee State archives in Nashville or *be* at the Alamo or at the University of Texas in Austin and looking at original documents.

I'm a bit old school in that way.

Chris Williamson

This case really has become so robust; it's the eighty-fifth anniversary now.

Buddy Levy

Unbelievable.

Chris Williamson

Yeah, it is. Our team has been using the inductive reasoning method when looking at this case because we feel that every piece of the puzzle matters, since nobody's found that smoking gun, so to speak, and I don't know that they ever will.

Buddy Levy

Mm-hmm.

Chris Williamson

I was wondering, what are your thoughts on using that approach to investigate a cold case like this? As an investigator, do you *want to* see every piece of the puzzle, regardless of what people might think of it, so you can make determinations for yourself?

Buddy Levy

Absolutely. Even things that at the gut level may seem to be a little bit outside of the purview or far-fetched. The work that we did on *Decoded* involved a great number of conspiracy theorists, and it was always really important for us to give every expert that we were talking to the same amount of deference and interest and to listen really carefully. I'm always scribbling furiously in my notebook. You have to look at every single piece of evidence that exists because you might overlook something, for one, and also, I think there's a point at which things might start to add up. I'm a big proponent of inductive reasoning, even if it's a conspiracy theory. I know that there are some pretty interesting ones involving the Amelia Earhart case. It would be a mistake, in my opinion, to dismiss out of hand any theory as an investigator.

Chris Williamson

How do you determine what makes sense to you and what should be thrown out?

Buddy Levy

That can be really difficult because sometimes things start to *feel* right, but there might not be enough corroboration for them to develop any kind of impetus or momentum.

Another example from *Decoded* are the theories that there's gold in Fort Knox. What's happened to it? It's really tough because, like you say, barring a smoking gun, you're often talking about speculation. You need multiple sources that point you in the same direction.

Now, it's *also possible* there could be an outlier, where the one source that's pointing in the direction is actually right, but I often fall back on Occam's razor. The simplest explanation is the right one, or the best one. Then again, that's not 100% foolproof, is it?

Chris Williamson

Definitely. And I'm so glad that you mentioned that because my final question is going to be about Occam's razor. I know every investigator looks at this a little bit differently, but in your personal professional opinion, what holds the most water in a case like this?

Buddy Levy

Well, *you've got* her last dispatch, right?

Chris Williamson

Right.

Buddy Levy

With that, there's some information that gives us rough coordinates and direction. A last known correspondence, I think, has to weigh a lot. Then of course, you circle back to everything that led up to that moment. In the case of Amelia Earhart, that last known dispatch is really crucial, because at that point, you can start to use science and math to project out and speculate on how much fuel she might have had at that point. Clearly, we knew a direction. It sort of narrows down the field of inquiry, as far as a potential location.

Chris Williamson

We were talking about corroboration earlier. I want to ask you about eyewitness testimony. There's a lot of talk about this supporting evidence being less than credible, so to speak. When it comes to something like the Japanese capture hypothesis, you have over two hundred eyewitnesses putting Earhart and Noonan somewhere in the Marshall Islands. That's sort of a tricky situation, because on the one hand, I know eyewitness memory can be skewed, and the truth can get watered down as it's passed down from generation to generation. On the other hand, you have *two hundred people*.

Can you give me your thoughts on something like that?

Buddy Levy

When you get into a number like two hundred eyewitnesses corroborating evidence, I think that becomes *very difficult* to ignore.

I have had firsthand experience where eyewitness testimony proved to be erroneous, a personal experience where my wife was accused by a person, and it was a case of mistaken identity. She had to pass a lie detector test and go to court over a false identification. When we're talking about two hundred, even through the lens of decades and generations, that's *really significant* to me. I would have to look very carefully at that theory if there was that much corroboration.

Chris Williamson

The official explanation of the disappearance of Amelia and Fred is that they ran out of fuel somewhere in the vicinity of Howland Island, and that the plane rests approximately eighteen thousand feet beneath the surface and remains there to this day. It would appear that logic is on the side of that theory and that it dictates its accuracy. Then you have these other theories that have different types of supporting evidence, and they believe that they're, in fact, the *true fate* of Amelia and Fred. My question is, from the outside looking in, does Occam's razor have the upper hand here? Or can logic only take you so far when there's no bodies and no plane?

Buddy Levy

Yeah, that's a tough one.

I think Occam's Razor probably *does have* the upper hand, but we have technology that wasn't available through many years of search and inquiry, including the ability to do all sorts of scanning of the sea floor using small unmanned submarines to go to great depths.

I'm personally not going to be satisfied until we have an answer, because I just think history deserves the answer to what happened to these great Americans. I think that science and technology should be brought to bear in this case, more so than ever, because it's just getting more and more powerful. I know they're costly, but I think in this particular case, it's worth it.

Chris Williamson

It seems like an insurmountable job. Is it your opinion that this case will be solved?

Buddy Levy

I have hope that it will be.

There *have been* finds. Some of these modern-day, deep-sea dive companies that are well funded have enough people who are interested in the outcome and want to know; they're not going to stop.

You're a good example of that.

Chris Williamson

Ha, yeah. Right.

Buddy Levy

They're not going to stop looking.

Chris Williamson

Oscar Wilde once said, "The truth is rarely pure and **never** simple."

We've come a long way together. Now it's time to take this case apart and challenge the evidence in a way that's never been attempted.

I think I'm finally ready. I hope you are too.

"When we get to the end, all the evidence presented and all the experts who have testified before you will help you arrive at a verdict on the biggest historical mystery of all time."

Bailiff

ALL RISE!

All those having business with this court stand forward, and you shall be heard.

Judge

Is the project prepared to make an opening statement?

Chris Williamson

Thank you, yes, Your Honor.

The facts of the case are these. On the morning of July 2, 1937, world-famous aviatrix Amelia Mary Earhart and her navigator, Captain Frederick Joseph Noonan, leave Lae, New Guinea, at roughly the three-quarter mark of their equatorial world flight. At this point in the trip, they're 22,000 miles in, with just 7,000 miles to California; 2,556 miles from Lae lies Howland Island. This was to be their final refueling point before returning to Hawaii.

It was to be a roughly eighteen-hour flight. Harry Balfour, a radio operator from Guinea Airways, set up a schedule for him and Earhart to make radio contact on the hour.

Soon after the plane left Lae, Harry noted that headwinds were stronger than anybody had thought. He sent transmissions to Earhart with this information three times in two hours, but Amelia didn't seem to receive them. These would have been crucial because headwind speeds could have affected flight speed, fuel consumption and the length of flight. Around 2:18 p.m., Amelia's transmission, which had been blocked earlier, was finally received by Balfour in Lae. She gives her speed at 140 knots and an altitude of 7,000 feet: "Everything okay."

A little over an hour later, her next transmission states that she climbs to 10,000 feet. This may be uneconomical in terms of fuel usage, and it's unclear why she made this climb. This transmission also seemed to be delayed. They seem to still be on course though, and many experts believe that at this point, Amelia would have made the necessary adjustments to combat the headwinds.

As they near Howland, it's believed that the Electra was down to her last ninety-seven gallons of fuel.

The Coast Guard cutter *Itasca* lay in wait off the coast of Howland to help guide Earhart and Noonan in once they came into sight. It's believed that all was well because the signal strength readings from the Electra kept getting stronger and stronger as she apparently got closer and closer. You'll hear testimony from Leo Bellarts, the chief radioman on the *Itasca*, who will testify to the fact that he thought she was *so close* that he stepped outside the radio booth to look for her plane. One of Earhart's last transmissions was "We must be on you but cannot see you." She followed that with "Gas is running low."

Her last transmission came in at 8:43 a.m. "We are on the line 157/337. We will repeat message. We will repeat this on 6210 kilo cycles. Wait." There have been some conflicting reports, but this final transmission may have also included "We are running north and south." Leo Bellarts reported that Amelia's voice sounded frantic. On July 7, five days later, the USS *Colorado* began to search the waters to the southeast of Howland. The *Lexington* arrived on the scene soon after, from its base in San Diego, to join the fray. They all kept searching until July 18.

To this day, neither Amelia Earhart, Fred Noonan nor their plane have ever been found.

These are the facts of the case.

And they are *undisputed*.

That's right. The story I've just told you is the exact same story that you're going to hear from Leo Bellarts, and it's the exact same story that you're going to hear from the United States government.

Now…the representation of *other theories* are going to try to pull off a little magic act here. There may be a little misdirection, stories of rituals, memories and other theories that they wholeheartedly believe to be the truth.

They might even try to cut into a few people for you.

Each expert will testify to their own truth about what happened that day eighty-five years ago and thereafter, and it will be up to you, our jury, to determine what evidence has convinced you when all that is said and done. So that we can present an even balanced case, the project is also going to bring into the fold our own witnesses, who will testify in general areas of expertise. Witnesses who have no iron in this fire.

One thing's for sure, it's going to be entertaining.

When we get to the end, all the evidence presented and all the experts who have testified before you will help you arrive at a verdict on the biggest historical mystery of all time.

These are the facts of the case. And they're about to be challenged.

"I think you certainly have enough for reasonable doubt, and that's really all you need in order to get one theory off. You need enough reasonable doubt to be able to have a defense attorney say, 'I know everybody thinks they're crossing the ocean, but what about all this other stuff?' "

Chris Williamson

The project would like to begin by calling *Tad DiBiase* to the stand.

Mr. DiBiase, for over twelve years, you were an assistant United States attorney in the District of Columbia, and you prosecuted homicide cases for most of those years. In January of 2006, you prosecuted the second *no-body* murder case tried in DC and have specialized in no-body cases ever since. You track no-body murder cases, trials, and investigations, and your online table of no-body murder trials lists over five hundred no-body murder trials in the United States alone. You've also consulted with law enforcement agencies throughout the United States and Canada, and you're the author of the book *No-Body Homicide Cases: A Practical Guide to Investigating, Prosecuting and Winning Cases When the Victim is Missing.*

Mr. DiBiase, my first question for you today is simple.

Are these types of cases like the Amelia Earhart and Fred Noonan case *solvable*, even when there is yet to be remains found?

Tad DiBiase

They *are* solvable, Chris, but they're much, much tougher than an ordinary murder case.

The reason for that, of course, is when you don't have the body, you don't have the main piece of evidence in a murder case. I often liken it to being in a hundred-meter race, and the perpetrator gets to start at the sixty-meter mark. He's going to beat you even if you're Usain Bolt, because he has a huge head start for someone who's committed a murder and successfully gotten rid of the body. A body can tell you *where* the murder happened. Did it happen in a home? Did it happen outdoors? Did it happen at a place of employment?

The body can also tell you *when* the murder happened. Did it happen yesterday? Did it happen an hour ago? Did it happen two years ago? Most importantly, the body tells you *how* the murder happened. Was this person stabbed? Shot? Did they die in a plane crash?

Did they die because they were poisoned? Strangled? When you don't have the body, you don't have any of that information. That's what makes a no-body case so uniquely challenging. You don't have the most important piece of evidence.

Chris Williamson

Are these cases more common than one might think? Do we know any numbers or statistics pertaining to no-body cases?

Tad DiBiase

Well, I *can* give you some numbers, because that's one thing I *do* track. They are incredibly rare. I've been studying these cases now for probably close to thirteen years. In that time, I've found 526 cases that have gone to trial in the United States, and that doesn't count pleas.

It only counts the cases that actually went to trial. That goes back to the early 1830s. The United States has a much higher murder rate than virtually any developed country and probably most undeveloped countries. So, when you're talking about that, it's an incredibly small percentage. I discovered at one point in the last twenty years, there's been about 120,000 murder trials. To have only 526 in the life of the United States for the most part, that tells us that these cases are still incredibly rare.

What's also interesting too is half of those 526 cases have occurred since the year 2000.

Chris Williamson

Mr. DiBiase, will you please explain the term *victimology* to the court?

. . .

Tad DiBiase

Victimology is the idea that in order to understand your murderer, you have to look at who your victim is.

What are the things about the victim that may have led to him or her being murdered, and that can mean different things. For example, if you have a murder victim who is married, has children, has a regular job that she went to five days a week, and was very regular in everything that she did, she's going to have a very different victimology than maybe someone who's a sex worker, a drug abuser or an alcoholic. That doesn't mean that one case is more important than the other; it just means that the people those two women encountered in their daily lives are likely *very* different. You have to look at those two people and ask, "This person was a working woman, mother and wife. Who is she going to encounter who might want to murder her?" Someone who's a sex worker is going to be encountering very different people. In order to understand who your pool of suspects might be, you've got to look at that particular victim's victimology. Who would they come in contact with on a regular basis that might lead to them being killed?

Chris Williamson

How does victimology play a role in a case where someone has vanished?

Tad DiBiase

In this particular case, the most obvious likelihood is a plane crash because this is someone who's flying a plane. I have not studied the Amelia Earhart case to a great degree, but when you start to look at her in particular, you *do learn* that she was pretty independent; she was ahead of her time as a woman. She was someone who would be considered a feminist.

You start to think about what other categories she'd fall into that might lead to someone wanting to murder her? She was a US citizen in a time where there was great global conflict, those types of things. Those are the things you look at if you're looking at theories and asking yourself, "How would this person have likely met their demise?" Of course, number one still is that she was flying an airplane at a time when that was dangerous to do because the equipment wasn't as good. You could also look at it and ask, "Well, if she did land successfully, why might she disappear?" Ordinarily you would think people would be excited about having found this person. "Oh, we rescued Amelia Earhart, a well-known United States citizen!" Then you start to ask, "Well, who might want not want to rescue her? Who might not want people to know that they had found her?" Those are the types of things with victimology that you look at when you're trying to solve a case for a person who's vanished.

Chris Williamson

Can you inform us all of some of the ways prosecutors might tell us that somebody had died when there's no body in play?

Tad DiBiase

In this day and age, it's much easier than it was in the past, and there's one particular reason why:

It is just much easier today to determine whether someone disappeared because we all leave behind these electronic trails that people didn't leave twenty years ago, let alone eighty-five years ago. We use credit cards, we use cell phones that ping on cell towers, we send text messages, we use Facebook, Instagram, Snapchat – all of these things that leave behind a very distinct electronic trail. When those things stop, it's much easier to say, "I don't think this person is missing. I think they're actually dead."

People don't stop leaving those electronic trails. When you go back in time, obviously in the 1930s, it was a lot harder to prove that someone was dead and not just missing. You could say in the case of Amelia Earhart or someone else that they went to Mexico or Europe, and it would be very hard for someone in the United States to disprove that theory because how are they going to contact people over in Europe? What's interesting in this case though, unlike an ordinary person, Amelia Earhart in 1937 was *very well* known.

Her *face* was well known.

That's a little bit different than Joe or Jill, an ordinary person who might not be very well known. It'd be much harder for people to swap this person. Here, you'd have a greater chance because she was well known in terms of what she looked like.

Chris Williamson

Mr. DiBiase, how difficult would it be to show a time, cause, and a place of death when you have no body to work from?

Tad DiBiase

Well, the difficulty there is if you have no body, you don't have a scene, and that makes it awfully difficult. When you have a scene, there may be blood left behind, there may be DNA left behind; you have a better chance of saying, "Okay, I see." If you have, for example, an indoor scene where a woman is missing, maybe you go into the house and find blood.

Maybe it's spattered on the wall, and you have a high velocity spatter, so you think a gun was used. Or maybe it's not quite as high a velocity, so it might be a knife or blunt force.

When you have some possibility of knowing where the scene is, you just have a better chance of understanding how the murder may have occurred. You can also have people who can give you information about that: "Well, I know he had choked her before." Then you can ask if that is a possibility. Maybe she was choked to death. When you have no body and no scene, you just have no information at all to determine shooting, stabbing, or even strangulation, any of these things.

It makes these cases so uniquely difficult when you just have no idea at all.

. . .

Chris Williamson

Pertaining to this case, we have a situation where no bodies or remains have ever been recovered. If the plane exists, we don't know where its resting place lies. There's no evidence of the vanishing whatsoever. Based on the rules you've laid out to the court today, would the disappearance of Amelia Earhart and Fred Noonan qualify as uniquely difficult to prosecute?

Tad DiBiase

If I were a prosecutor, I think I'd like this case based on the theory of her crashing the plane for a couple of reasons: one, it would strike most people as the most logical. You always want to have a motive in any case as a prosecutor. That's why when you have a dead wife, the husband's always a great suspect because *of course he has motive.* I know you're married; I'm married; we all get frustrated with our spouses; it doesn't mean you murder them. But everyone who's married understands that as a possible motive.

Here you have a great motive in your suspect of the ocean and the crash, because she's flying a plane, and there was some sense that there was difficulty in terms of landing and making radio communications with the people who are sending out the radio signals. They knew there was some difficulty, and people can just rationally believe in 1937 that the navigation was not as sophisticated, and the equipment wasn't as good. That fits in terms of what you think *might make* the most sense.

The problem with the other suspects is it's hard to imagine her being alive and not have other information about it out there unless someone wanted to keep it quiet. It's hard to think of reasons why you'd want to keep it quiet because she was very famous. People might want to benefit from having rescued the famous aviatrix. In that sense, I think those theories become harder to figure out regarding what the motive for those suspects might have been.

. . .

Chris Williamson

If Occam's razor is the chief backing for the official explanation of the disappearance, how far does that take you when you have other theories that have supporting evidence such as circumstantial, eyewitness testimony, forensic science and maybe even a plane?

Tad DiBiase

You start off with asking, "Where's the last place this person was seen?"

It's no different in a regular no-body murder case. "Oh, they were with their husband, and the husband has admitted they had an argument." Well, here you have something very similar.

Where was the last place she was seen?

In Lae at takeoff.

Where was the last place she was heard?

In her airplane over the ocean.

That we can confirm, putting aside the eyewitnesses for the moment. She was in an airplane, possibly running out of fuel because it was kind of tight on how much fuel she was going to have to make it to Howland Island. Also, you have some circumstantial evidence that seems to fit.

As we've learned, back in 1937 eyewitness testimony was like gospel, right? You didn't get any better than that. You didn't have forensics, you had fingerprints. We really accepted eyewitness testimony to a very high degree back then, and it's now come to light that maybe eyewitness testimony *isn't as accurate* as we thought. When you look at wrongful convictions that are proven to be wrongful through the subsequent use of DNA, the most common area for wrongful conviction is eyewitness testimony. Back in 1937, it may have been considered very strong. As a prosecutor looking back now, the argument could be made that even with two hundred people, who knows if it was suggested to them that that's who it was? Were they *really* independent observations of one another? I would rather have forensic evidence.

That's why most no-body murder cases are not made by eyewitness testimony because most of the time, the murders are not witnessed by other people because they tend to be of a domestic nature. Those things happen in the quiet of our homes. Most no-body murder cases are made through one of two ways: they're made through forensic evidence such as DNA, fingerprints, hair fiber, those types of things. The second way they're made is via a confession to friends and family. Although eyewitness testimony *does happen,* in no-body murder cases, they're way down the list of a quantum of evidence that you might get.

Chris Williamson

If you are unable to produce the details of a no-body vanishing or death, how difficult is it to obtain a conviction?

Tad DiBiase

That's what's interesting, Chris, because one of the things I was fascinated by when I started studying these cases is I thought the conviction rate was going to be really low.

What I discovered is the exact *opposite.*

The no-body murder conviction rate is actually running right now at about 86%; 86% of the cases that go to trial get a conviction of some charge. Typically, it's a murder charge, or sometimes you have kidnapping; 86% of the time you're getting a conviction of one of the top counts. Generally, not first-degree murder or capital murder, but usually second-degree manslaughter, things like that. That to me seems completely counterintuitive.

Particularly when the conviction rate on murder cases nationwide is about 70%. You're talking 16% or 17% higher in a no-body murder case. The reason for that is only the very strong cases go to trial. Because of the inherent weaknesses in these cases while the person is still missing, those cases usually don't go. A prosecutor is only going to take a strong case to trial, and I'll use my case as an example. The case I tried when it went to trial was the twentieth murder trial I'd done as a prosecutor, but it was by far the strongest case I had. I had a lot of forensic evidence, I had a confession to friends and family, *and* I had a confession to the police. So I had all three of what I call the "legs of a no-body murder stool" that a prosecutor and police officer would want to get. That's why the conviction rate in these cases is actually quite high.

Chris Williamson

Mr. DiBiase, one of the most difficult aspects of this case is the passage of time. As you and the court are well aware, it's now been eighty-five years since the disappearance of Amelia Earhart and Fred Noonan. How does the passage of time affect the likelihood of new witnesses coming forward and new physical evidence being presented?

Tad DiBiase

It's very interesting because as time goes on in no-body murder cases, what you discover is that it's a balancing act. On the one hand, your chance of finding a body significantly decreases, particularly depending on where you live. If you live in Florida and you've been missing for three years, you are probably never going to find that body because of the temperature in Florida. Bodies decompose more quickly in hot, humid climates than in, say, Alaska, where you have a greater chance of finding a body.

The flip side is, of course, the longer it goes, the greater chance you have of proving the person is *not missing* but is instead *actually* dead. If you haven't heard from someone in seventeen years, you can be pretty certain they're not living in Europe or they're not hidden somewhere; they're probably dead. What happens too is the longer the case goes on and the colder it gets, you find that more people are willing to come forward and confess things.

Maybe because they're no longer in a relationship with the person who's the suspect, or maybe because the suspect is now incarcerated for something else and they feel more comfortable talking. Maybe it's been so long and maybe your suspect died, or the person just doesn't fear them anymore, so they're more comfortable talking about it, and that is actually a very common feature of those cases.

What's interesting here is you don't have to necessarily find Amelia Earhart's body, which presumably no one will ever find unless it's buried somewhere. You could certainly find the plane, which would be a huge piece of evidence in this case because she's so clearly associated with the plane at the time she disappeared. I think you have the benefit of time passing so that if she did not crash into the ocean, if she somehow landed safely and was captured, for example, you might have the Japanese government more willing to talk about it *now* than they certainly would have been back in 1937 when they were on the brink of war with Europe and the United States.

Obviously now our relationship with Japan is much different. You'd expect that if *they did* discover something, they'd be more willing to share it with us. Time can sometimes actually strengthen a case, which seems a little counterintuitive.

Chris Williamson

Are you saying that finding the Lockheed Electra 10-E would be equivalent to finding the remains of Earhart and Noonan?

Tad DiBiase

I think so because if you find the plane on the bottom of the ocean, that tells you something pretty strongly regarding what happened. If you find wreckage of the plane on an island in the middle of the Pacific, that also tells you something. That, to me, is the equivalent of finding a body. If you were to find out that we all thought they crashed in the ocean, and they *didn't*, that I think completely changes the complexion of the investigation. It's not exclusive to say they had to have died if they crashed into the ocean.

To say that they successfully landed the plane somewhere, that really changes everything.

· · ·

Chris Williamson

Is voir dire more difficult when we have no body?

Tad DiBiase

It *is* more difficult.

If you take away one thing from my discussion with you about how to investigate and how to prosecute these cases, it has to be that you have to eliminate anyone from your jury who can't answer the following question: "If the government proves to you beyond a reasonable doubt that the defendant murdered the victim, but there is no body, could you still vote guilty?"

If they've answered *yes,* they can sit on your jury.

If their answer is *no,* they can't sit on your jury.

If you've already front-loaded it by saying the government has proven beyond a reasonable doubt that the defendant murdered the victim, but there's no body, you have to get rid of anyone who says no. Even if there's no body, I'm not going to find someone guilty. That's what's called a "for cause challenge." The court must eliminate that person because you have to be able to find someone guilty even if there's no body. That makes these a little bit difficult because you have to get the court to *allow you* to eliminate that person without having to use what we call a "peremptory challenge," which are the optional challenges a prosecutor and defense attorney get to use. You cannot have someone on your jury who says, "Well, even if they prove it beyond a reasonable doubt, if they don't have a body, I'm not voting to convict."

You can't have that.

Chris Williamson

Earlier, you spoke about a potential murderer confessing to a friend or family member and then that person coming forward to testify. We know this as "hearsay." In this case, the equivalent of hearsay is original people who were alive at the time who interacted with Earhart, Noonan or the Electra and have now passed that information down to their children or others. How does hearsay affect or not affect a case like the one we're presenting here?

Tad DiBiase

The hearsay rules don't change based on the charge. Even in a no-body case, the hearsay rules are still present. What *is* different though is that there's a very big exception to the hearsay rule that has a number of different names; it's been called "admission against interest" or "declaration against penal interest." What it basically means is if a defendant says something that is against his interests, such as, "I killed Amelia Earhart," that's going to be permitted in the court of law because even though hearsay is ordinarily *not* permitted, the court says people don't typically make statements like that unless they're true. It's so inculcating towards themselves, and that's true even for non-defendants when they make statements that are against their interest. It may be "I assisted someone in capturing Amelia Earhart, and we ended up holding her for three months, and then she died." Those types of statements would still come in. So the hearsay rule doesn't change in a no-body case; those same rules still apply.

Chris Williamson

Mr. DiBiase, the court is familiar with *Rich Martini*, a researcher on the Japanese capture hypothesis, and his video recordings of Mr. Robert Wallack and other military personnel who shared their experiences with potentially a big piece of supporting evidence in this case: the briefcase found on Saipan. Unfortunately, these brave men are no longer alive to tell their story to this court. My question for you, sir, is, can their video testimony evidence as it was told to Rich Martini be included in support of the Japanese capture case?

Tad DiBiase

That's a closer call. The difficulty would lie in those witnesses being available for cross-examination.

If those witnesses could come to court and be cross-examined about that discovery, that typically would be permitted. If the witnesses *aren't* coming in, then it's a little bit harder to put on their testimony. If you had a video of her passport, that probably would be allowed because they'd be able to have other experts look at it and ask, "Is this a legitimate passport or not?" You have to kind of break up a little bit and ask, "What are we playing the video for?" Is it because we want the testimony of these people who said they found it, or is it just to ask, "This is what was found. Does it appear to be a passport?" You have to slice through it to determine what's going to be allowed and what's not going to be allowed.

To me the main suspect, as I said, is always going to be the ocean.

But if you were to go to trial on that, I think you certainly have enough for reasonable doubt, and that's really all you need in order to get one theory off. You need enough reasonable doubt to be able to have a defense attorney say, "I know everybody thinks you're crossing the ocean, but what about all this other stuff?"

Here, I think you certainly have enough reasonable doubt.

Now the difficulty for *you* is to have one theory predominate that you can prove beyond a reasonable doubt. That's the *real* challenge.

Chris Williamson

Thank you, Mr. DiBiase, no more questions.

Your Honor, at this time, I'd like to ask the court for a recess and request that we reconvene shortly to continue calling witnesses.

Bailiff

ALL RISE!

LAST FLIGHT
-6.7015456 | 146.9429657

This section of our story contains a transcript of historical archival audio footage. I'd like to thank both Elgen Long and Dave Bellarts for allowing us to feature this testimony here in this text.

"We must be on you but cannot see you."

Chris Williamson

On June 29, 1937, a tired Amelia Earhart and Fred Noonan touch down in Lae, New Guinea, having reached the three-quarter mark of their record attempt at circumnavigating the globe. Long days of flight had brought Earhart and Noonan to the likes of Brazil, Dakar, Bangkok and Darwin, Australia, just to name a few. Though she was anxious to complete her long journey and fly into the record books, the next day, June 30, 1937, AE sent a telegram to her husband, George Palmer Putnam, that read, "Radio misunderstanding and personnel unfitness.

Probably will hold one day." What these personnel problems meant has been debated for many years.

Were they related to Fred Noonan?

Whatever the issues might have been, AE didn't let them derail her plans. She and Noonan took off from Lae on the morning of July 2, 1937, at 10 a.m. local time.

It was the last time anyone would ever see them.

While Earhart's plane was in the air, the Coast Guard cutter *Itasca* was waiting to guide her into Howland Island. However, due to her friend Gene Vidal no longer being at the Bureau of Air Commerce to direct subordinates to smooth her way, some of the ship's communications were on a bandwidth that she didn't have the ability to receive. There were other difficulties: a radio direction finder on Howland that would work with Earhart's higher-bandwidth equipment required batteries that were drained by the time she would be in the area. Fourteen hours and fifteen minutes into her flight, the *Itasca* received a first, somewhat garbled transmission from Earhart. "Cloudy weather." Though the messages themselves would grow clearer, the content remained worrying, as when Earhart radioed, "We must be on you but cannot see you."

She apparently only received one message from the ship, though the *Itasca* had been transmitting for hours. While continuing to broadcast, the radio strength for communications indicated she was close. However, Earhart remained unable to see Howland Island. The weather around Howland was clear, but there *are* reports of clouds about thirty miles northwest, and if Earhart had flown into clouds and bad weather along the way, it could have prevented Noonan from taking the sightings he needed to navigate precisely.

There's also *some* evidence to indicate that the charts that Noonan and Earhart were using were not entirely accurate. Earhart's last transmission, made twenty hours and fourteen minutes into her flight, indicated that they were going to continue "running north and south."

The Electra never made it to Howland.

Now we dive into the events that occurred while AE and Noonan were at Lae, some controversial and some head scratching. We'll also climb aboard the Electra and try to unravel the beginnings of one of the greatest mysteries of all time.

What *actually* happened to Amelia Earhart and Fred Noonan that day?

Our trial continues as we bring someone to the stand *you'll never see coming.*

Now that opening day of the trial is behind us, I had to collect my thoughts and try to digest everything that's unfolded as we've begun this descent. More importantly, before I begin day two of this trial, I wanted to catch up with my *now partner* Jennifer, to get *her* thoughts on Tad's testimony and on what we're about to cover on the second day of this incredible experiment.

What we're going to try to pull off next is quite groundbreaking, and I wanted to ask her how *to do it.*

Pre-Trial Discussion

Chris Williamson

What did you think of the first day of the trial? How did you think it went?

Jen Taylor

I thought Tad did a phenomenal job on the stand.

It's undeniable that he is *the* expert on prosecuting and investigating a no-body murder case. I've read his book; it's amazing. He really knows his stuff. I thought the most interesting part of that conversation was when he was talking about victimology. Having a thorough understanding of your victim, and so, in this case, *Fred and Amelia*, who they were, and how they spent their time, the fact that she was famous. Is he as famous as she is? I know that he talked about her fame and said, "I don't know how famous she was, but I'm thinking Lindbergh. I'm thinking Babe Ruth kind of fame." What does it mean to be famous in 1937 versus being famous in 2022, where we have Instagram and Twitter and twenty-four-hour news cycles? It just got me thinking about a lot of things, so I thought that in particular was really interesting.

Chris Williamson

When we talk about this case in media, I always try to push for Noonan as much as I can, because there was a second person in that plane. We really try to shine the spotlight on him, but unfortunately, there is not a whole lot of information on Fred Noonan. He was newly remarried at the time that he disappeared with Amelia Earhart, and his wife, *Bea Noonan*, sort of went into hiding after the disappearance.

When she went into hiding, that was basically the last that most people ever heard of her, and he never had children. So there's not really much lineage there, and it's really kind of sad. We want to make sure Fred Noonan gets the spotlight he deserves, and we're actually working now on trying to track down genealogy for Noonan, for some interesting potential evidence for the Buka hypothesis to try to see if we can get to any kind of extended family in any way, shape, or form. I think a lot of people, when you ask them, would say he was key to the vanishing.

Jen Taylor

Yeah. Based on some of his testimony there, as we move forward, I think those are definitely questions that we should keep in the back of our mind.

How famous was she? Did that fame extend to her image? Of course, people knew her name, but did they also know her face? I know, most of us weren't around in 1937, but especially with young people today, if someone's famous, you are going to recognize that person if you see them on the street. We have social media. When you're famous, people know what you look like. I think maybe that's something we take for granted today. Maybe it was the same in 1937.

When he spoke about victimology, I thought back to everything leading up to this. We've been doing exactly what he said, learning about who she was, learning why she was doing what she was doing, and maybe trying to get a better understanding of her as a person. In that way, maybe we could understand what happened to her. I thought that those were all great points. Another thing that really struck me about him and his testimony was that he obviously does not have a pet theory yet. A lot of these people you've talked to, and a lot of these people who are going to weigh in from this point forward, already have an idea in their head about what happened to her. Some of them, probably *a lot of them*, are not going to be shy about telling you what they think when they come to testify.

They're going to defend their theory. That's what they're coming to do.

He's not really in that position, and I think he's a really inspired choice for that. He *did say* that he leaned toward a certain theory, but he also indicated that there may be reasonable doubt for the crash and sink theory. You can definitely see that he is open, and he hasn't made up his mind yet. Anytime you have an expert on the stand that up front, who is willing to say, "Hey, I'm not here on behalf of anybody. This is what I think, and this is why I think that," that's something that's really rare. On the flip side of that, it also kind of changes your tactic when you're cross-examining them, right? You don't have to be as aggressive with them. If you have an expert on the stand, and you know for a fact that they're not going to change their opinion, it will do you no good to start asking them questions in an effort to get them to change their opinion in front of a jury because it's not going to happen.

You would be wasting your time.

Chris Williamson

Yeah, you make a good point. I like that he told me on the record that our job would be to really sway the jury by saying, "Hey, look at this over here. Yes, we know the official explanation for the disappearance of Amelia Earhart and Fred Noonan is that they crashed just shy of Howland Island somewhere, but look at what all these other theories have to offer." That was really interesting.

Jen Taylor

And in the real world, that *does* happen.

If you were prosecuting a murder case, for example, there's limits on how you would do that, but you *can* do it. For example, if he was a prosecutor, and he was trying to prosecute my client for a murder, and we didn't have a body, I as the defense attorney could say, "Here are some alternative theories about what could have happened to her. Here are some leads that the police didn't follow." Maybe I represent the husband. I know he mentioned most no-body victims are females, and most of the time, it's going to be a boyfriend or husband. Let's say I represent the husband, and I think it was an intruder, I think that somebody came into her house and burglarized and killed her that way. It's really hard to actually put somebody else on trial who's *not present* to defend themselves.

So a judge will often say, "Look, you can't go into that. We're not going to have a trial on two people at once." What you *can do* is you can say, "There's evidence out there that maybe points to something else having happened. Maybe the police didn't do a thorough investigation and follow all the leads." You can still get that stuff in, but you have to frame it a little bit differently. What we're doing here is we're putting *four theories* on trial. We are in a unique situation where we can say, "Actually, we have a whole other line of evidence, and we can follow it, and we have the time to do that." It's really cool, what we're doing.

Chris Williamson

Yeah, I think it was interesting, especially starting off by calling general expertise. You're a defense attorney; he's a prosecutor. Obviously, you're going to come at something like this from a different point of view. Is there anything that he said on the stand that you *didn't agree with* professionally speaking? Or is there anything that you would have come at differently? Was there anything that you had a hard time with?

Jen Taylor

There's nothing that I would say I disagreed with professionally. I *did* notice that when he was talking, he said, "My first instinct would be to maybe prosecute the ocean; maybe she crashed and sank." I just kind of laughed at myself a little bit when I heard that, because when you first approached me, and I started looking at everything, my first instinct was almost the *opposite*. I want to hear more about a conspiracy theory involving her being a spy. That's where my mind went. I think it just goes to show you that when you have a certain job, it *does* affect how you think about things. If he's a prosecutor, and he's worked for the government, it would totally make sense for his starting point to be, "This is what happened, this is easy to understand."

This is what the government said happened. Why not start there?

Whereas *my first instinct* when I hear something that the government has told me is to say, "No, don't trust any of it; *question everything*." And of course, that doesn't mean that I don't think he's biased at all. I don't think he's married to crash and sink; he even said himself that he wasn't. Maybe somebody else would disagree, but if there's evidence of crash and sink, I'm totally happy to hear it. I don't think it's necessarily going to affect our ability to look at everything, but my point is that it doesn't matter who you are; it doesn't matter how long you've been studying this case. Every single person comes at a problem with their own personal experience. We all have these little biases, and recognizing them is important.

Anytime somebody says anything, you always have to ask yourself if they have these internal biases that might be influencing them to say certain things over others.

Chris Williamson

Now that we've talked a little bit about what happened on the first day of the trial, I want to get into what we're about to tackle because what we're about to do with one of the witnesses we're going to call is really sort of groundbreaking. One of the main points of contention for what happened to Earhart and Noonan between Lae and Howland and maybe crashing and sinking in the ocean is fuel. You've been tackling this pretty aggressively in the last couple of weeks in our Facebook group, doing personal research and prepping for our next section. Tell me some of the stuff that you've uncovered. Let's get into the fuel a little bit because that's one of the areas that we're going to talk about a lot when we question specific witnesses a little later.

Jen Taylor

I started with Bill Snavely and the Buka theory because he's the one more than anyone else who has said she started with 950 gallons of fuel. That's always been one of his main points. He's arguing she could only carry that much due to weight capacity. I think there's even a statement about this in Mary Lovell's book *The Sound of Wings*. I actually found that statement as well. To walk you through how I researched this, I had heard from you that Bill Snavely got that number from that book. I went and grabbed that Kindle book, and she *does* discuss fuel at length in appendix B. She had a number of footnotes in her book that explained where she got these numbers from. She says Fred Noonan told a local reporter the night before that they had put 950 gallons of fuel into the plane. There's a little footnote there, and it says that she got *that* from a newspaper article dated July 7, 1937, and she names the newspaper. After quite a lot of time on the internet, I was able to find an image of that *exact* newspaper article.

Chris Williamson

Right, you showed it to me, we talked about it via text, and then I stuck it in the Vanished Facebook group, and we started discussion there.

Jen Taylor

Right. Okay, so a couple of things:

If you read the article, the wording is not really clear on that information coming from Fred Noonan. Fred Noonan said something to the effect of "We are two tons overweight," something like that. Then the article goes on to talk about how much fuel the plane had; how much food and what rations they had; things like that. The way that it's worded, that information could have come from Fred Noonan, but it's not clear that's what happened.

Okay, so we don't know for a fact that number came from Fred Noonan. Where did that number come from? That's the first thing.

She *also* mentions in her book that Lae used *imperial gallons* instead of *US gallons*, and she mentioned that maybe some of this confusion could have been because we're talking about apples and oranges. I looked into that a little bit further, and I think she's right about that.

I think she might be wrong in her conclusion that it had 950 gallons.

She isn't clear, and the article doesn't say 950 US gallons. It also doesn't say 950 imperial gallons. It just says 950 gallons; it leaves it unspecified. You can go to Google and pull up a converter, and you can convert 950 imperial gallons to US gallons. If you do that, it brings up 1,140.9 US liquid gallons. Also, there's a letter written by James Collopy written on August 27, which is actually almost two months after the original news article came out, and it appears to contradict the article. In it, he says that, "according to Captain Noonan, the total fuel capacity of the aircraft was 1,150 US gallons, and 64 US gallons of oil." They left Lae with a total of 1,100 US gallons. He even gets very specific and states that, "one tank contained only 50 gallons of its total capacity of 100." So he's very specific, but he also says 1,100 US gallons. It's possible that they're actually saying the same thing; that 1,100 US gallons is the same as 950 imperial gallons, and that the reporter and the letter are both right. Because we're not being specific enough about our unit of measurement, and that's where the confusion comes in.

I don't know how many fuel tanks it initially had, but I know that there were some added because they were going to be doing long-distance flights, and they knew that they needed more fuel. My thinking is if adding an additional fuel tank is going to add weight to the plane, why do it unless you're *actually* going to use that fuel tank? If you're only flying around with 900 or 950 US gallons of fuel, then you have an extra fuel tank that you don't need. If the total capacity for one tank is 100 gallons, then to me, it still seems like you're adding too many tanks, and you're adding weight that's completely unnecessary. I would think that they're going to use as much of it as they can.

I don't *know*, but again, I don't know anything about planes. That might be something that you'd want to go into with some of the people who are coming later. People who are smarter than I am and know more about it than I do. What do you think?

Chris Williamson

I agree with you; you make some good points. On that note, I talked to Robert Wheeler for quite a long time about this, and he basically came to the same conclusion that you just did regarding imperial gallons versus US gallons. He said he spoke with Gary Lapook, and actually, Gary put some information out there in our Facebook group that sort of proves that.

That's going to put a damper on Bill Snavely's Buka theory, **but** it should be noted that Robert Wheeler *does* believe that Bill Snavely is very much onto something, and that very well *could be the plane* at Buka.

It's one of those things where we don't know what we don't know.

There's so much vagueness to it. Every once in a while, you get something that's very, very specific, but for the most part, there's a lot of vagueness, or there's a lot of conflicting reports coming from all over the place. You're left trying to discern what the actual report is. What is the definitive opinion on this? It's really not unlike multiple experts on a stand challenging each other; one for the defense, and one for the prosecution disagreeing on the same report, disagreeing on the same test, or getting different results in the same type of test. It's the same concept here.

Jen Taylor

Yeah, I think this is why it's always important to start with the data and then move to a theory instead of starting with a theory and trying to work backwards and find data that *fits* that theory.

Chris Williamson

Well, that's called confirmation bias.

Jen Taylor

Right, of course, absolutely. A lot of times when you have competing experts with competing opinions, you'll find when you dig down that maybe they're using different science. *Or* maybe they're *both* using good science and good methods, but the information that they're getting might be different. That's always something that you need to explore as well. This is a big one because it doesn't *seem like* 950 versus 1,100 versus 1,150 gallons makes a big difference, but it turns out that it makes a *very big* difference on some of these theories.

· · ·

Chris Williamson

When you factor headwinds and the type of weather they might have faced into the idea, all that stuff adds to the fray.

I think it's possible that maybe they just had a very bad day.

There's all kinds of stuff that they didn't anticipate. During my conversations with Robert Wheeler, he's mentioned that the headwinds actually *were* anticipated, and they did count those headwinds into it. It's one of those situations where you have to go with what you know and what the history tells you. History tells you that she was en route to Howland Island with Fred Noonan and that they incorporated a multitude of potential issues into their flight plan. They never established a two-way radio connection; that was one of the most interesting aspects of it. Howland is a floating needle in a haystack; it's almost invisible from the sky *especially* if it's cloudy. There's the question of why Amelia Earhart dropped down to 1,000 feet below cloud cover. Really at 1,000 feet, you cannot see Howland; I can almost certainly tell you it's an impossibility. We have this thing that we do with kids when we do history day talks, and we try to explain and relate to them what they were up against and how difficult it was to spot this island. I stole this idea from Doug Westfall, who's a good friend of mine, so all credit to Doug on the following:

> You take the kids outside, and you take a pen or a pencil with you. You lay the pen/pencil on the cement, and you have them back up maybe twenty-five or thirty feet down. Then you have them lay their head on the ground and ask them if they can see the pen. Most of the time, they can't see the pen because it's thirty feet away and it's not visible. Well, then you tell them to walk a hundred feet down and ask them if they can see the pen. That's basically what they were up against. It was almost impossible to see Howland on that particular day, and I think it scared her. All things considered, it could have been a multitude of little things that just added up.

Jen Taylor

That seems to happen in life. There's not ever just *one thing* that goes wrong. It's going to be a thousand things going on at the same time, so I can definitely see that.

Chris Williamson

What's very interesting is she basically foreshadowed this exact problem. She said before they left Hawaii for the flight that if anything is going to go wrong, it's going to be in this leg. When I heard that the first time, it really sent chills up my spine. It's almost like she foreshadowed her own death if that's actually what happened.

During my conversations with Bob, I asked him the same question that we're going to be talking about shortly as well as during our crash and sink segment, and that question has to do with signal strength and radio communication. As far as Earhart and Noonan are concerned, how far out can that Electra be from the *Itasca* while pulling an S-5 signal? An S-5 is the strongest signal strength that they can pull at the time. If you're pulling a signal strength 1 or 2, you're a thousand miles out or maybe even thousands of miles out; you're barely detectable. If you're pulling an S-5, according to Wheeler, you're around the two-hundred-mile mark. That's where you'll start to pull S-5s. Earhart indicated they were two hundred miles out, one hundred miles out. "We must be on you but cannot see you." At this point, you start to see some of the data and some of the math line up with what the crash and sink hypothesis is basically stating. She simply ran out of gas, and that plane lies 18,000 feet below the surface of the water as we speak right now.

Jen Taylor

There are so many other questions, then, if that's the case.

One of the collateral consequences of me looking through dozens and dozens of newspaper articles from 1937 was her husband, George Putnam, had apparently told reporters around that time that the plane should float indefinitely, and that was repeated in newspapers quite a bit. The media hung onto that statement because everyone was really hopeful that they would find her. That's what he was telling the media; that *that plane* on *no fuel should have* been floating. So they should have been able to find her if they knew she was within one to two hundred miles of the island.

Something else that I never knew until reading these newspaper articles from around this time was that there was a US Navy ship that encountered really bad weather when they were looking for her there. When I say really bad weather, we're talking hail and snow.

We're on the *equator.*

When I read that, I thought that was so weird because it's July, but they were encountering ice and things like that. They couldn't look for her because the conditions were too bad, so they had to call off their search. I didn't really get a whole lot of information about how long they were out there, when they had to pull back, and when they were able to go back after that. Maybe she *was there*, and if there wasn't bad weather, maybe people would have been able to find her. Maybe the bad weather moved the plane and caused it to sink at a faster rate than it should have.

Once you start trying to answer one question, you get five more questions. Then you have to find the answers to those. It's been a little frustrating.

Chris Williamson

That's the *very definition* of a rabbit hole.

I've talked to multiple people who agree with you who say, yes, the plane would have been like "a ping pong ball with wings," and it could have floated indefinitely. However, Elgen Long, who was an aviation pioneer and was really the pioneer of the crash and sink hypothesis, says the plane would have sunk almost immediately. So does Tom Dettweiler, who readers will hear from shortly; he agrees with that. It really depends on how she was able to put the plane down on the water. If she was able to *pancake land* the plane and put the plane down in a soft enough manner that they could have floated, it's *possible.* If she put the plane down in a nosedive, which is unlikely, or if she put the plane down and one of the tanks got pierced or something like that, then that tank starts to fill with water immediately. It doesn't take long for the plane to go down.

The other argument if I'm playing the devil's advocate here, is that if she *was in fact* able to put the plane down on the water and let's say they were able to float for a while, then all of the post-loss radio communications that we'll get to during the castaway episode would directly dispute that. The radio on the Electra would not have been able to send those post-loss radio signals if the radio was submerged in water, which tells us that the Electra *had to have been* on land. If we're going to follow the thread that she ended up continuing on and actually running into Nikumaroro, then that's how she was able to actually send out the post-loss radio signals, which, by the way, all happen to triangulate to what area?

Nikumaroro.

Jen Taylor

That's another question I will definitely have when we get to that theory. These islands that she was supposedly at, have they been searched? How thoroughly were they searched?

Chris Williamson

There are so many experts who are involved in this case, and there are multiple camps.

It's not just prosecution versus defense here. It's a four-way trial; that's really what this is.

There are so many people who vehemently disagree with each other and present their own set of data with their own facts. How do we now as a team determine which experts to put on the stand? How do we determine which experts to cherry-pick from the bunch, to best represent all these different hypotheses?

Jen Taylor

We put all of them on the stand. *All of them.*

Of course, there are all of these things that we talked about in our previous segment regarding making sure that rule 702 and the rules of evidence have been satisfied. We don't want to give somebody a platform when they're obviously repeating junk science or if they obviously don't know what they're doing. That's what that is for. When you are looking at rule 702 and Daubert, this is supposed to be a flexible analysis. That's just step one; that's the judge's gatekeeper role. Is it something that is reliable and something that is relevant?

If it is, then let the jury hear it.

If every side has their experts and they can sufficiently show that this is somebody whom we can rely upon, then let us hear it because at the end of the day, the more information that a jury has, the better.

They can make a more informed decision, which is what we want. What we *don't want* is to give them things that *sound* great because it's coming from somebody who's claiming to be knowledgeable. Turns out that it's just complete junk, and that's what rule 702 does. It keeps out the things that are going to skew in favor of injustice. If every person has their own opinion, and they have something that can back that up, let's get it all out there, and then we can break it down for the readers. "Okay, this is what they were saying, this is why they said it, and here are the reasons why other people have a different opinion."

Chris Williamson

Yeah, well, speaking of putting everybody on the stand, right off the bat, we're about to throw a curveball at our readers that I don't think they're ever going to see coming.

Jen Taylor

I can't wait.

Chris Williamson

The last thing that I wanted to ask you about before we continue to trial is the video of the takeoff at Lae. I know that you've studied these types of videos for modern-day DUI cases and things like that. A lot of people agree that while Noonan may not have been obviously drunk the morning they took off, he very well could have been hungover. You've seen the clip. Give us your thoughts on the clip from a criminal standpoint.

Jen Taylor

I don't see any signs of intoxication on that video. No signs of impairment on that video at all. I know it's only a few seconds that we get, and the video itself is less than a minute long. Even less of that is Fred Noonan, so there *is* that caveat. To be completely honest, I don't see anything that would convince me that he's intoxicated, like none at all. I know that this is maybe a little bit different, but when you're doing a DWI investigation today, we typically have a lot more information available to us. We'll have a dashcam video, maybe somebody will take a sample of their breath or blood, or they'll be doing a field sobriety test and you can pay close attention to whether or not they're losing their balance or whether they can divide their attention. That's one of the things that you're really going to look for when you're trying to determine whether somebody's too drunk to drive. Can they divide their attention between two different things?

For example, when you're doing a field sobriety test, you'll tell them, "I want you to stand in this position with your feet here and your arms here, and I want you to listen to the instructions I'm about to give you."

Then you tell them how to perform the test, and one of the things you're looking for before the test even starts is can they stand there in that position like you've asked them to and also listen to your instructions?

That requires doing two things at once, which is what driving requires. You have to be able to listen to somebody and also drive, pay attention to the road signs, and pay attention to other people in traffic. When they pull you over and say, "I need your license and your registration," they've asked for two things on purpose so that you can look for two things at once. While you're doing that, they might ask you other questions. While you're looking through your wallet, you'll likely hear, "Where are you coming from? Where are you headed?" They're doing that on purpose when they pull you over because they're determining whether you can do two things at once. Can you listen to them *and* respond appropriately to their questions *and* also look for your insurance card like you've been asked? If you can't do that, you fumble with those things, and that's going to be their first clue that *maybe* you're intoxicated.

They're going to ask you to step out of your vehicle, or they're going to ask you if you've been drinking, things like that. When I see *this though*, he's excited and he's happy. He's there getting ready for takeoff. He's jumping onto the plane. He's pulling her up. I don't see any kind of imbalance. I don't think that there's anything there. If all the evidence you had of intoxication is just that video and nothing else, I would say that you've done a terrible job. You have no evidence *whatsoever* that he was intoxicated that day.

Chris Williamson

I agree 100%. Now, we're heading into day two of the trial, and we're going to be putting a couple of experts on the stand today. How do you think it's going so far?

Jen Taylor

I think we're doing great so far. Tad ended his testimony by stating he thinks it makes sense that she crashed into the ocean and sank. I know that's also the official explanation given by the US government. I think that's probably a really good place to start. Let's figure out what happened when she took off, and let's figure out whether or not the official explanation is something that actually holds water, *no pun intended.*

.   .   .

Chris Williamson

Yeah, let's not make this easy. Time to throw readers that curveball.

There is *so much information* jammed into the series of events that comes next.

If you think about it, the entirety of the podcast (and this book) has led to this *very moment* in time.

This is our crime scene.

These are the events that led to the vanishing of Amelia Earhart and Fred Noonan.

It's important to call the right people to the stand to give the appropriate perspective on the morning of July 2, 1937. Of all the people we could call as an expert witness, I think we found the perfect person.

After the events of day two of the trial, all of you will have a solid foundation for everything that's going to come after. Now, there's nothing left but to get *back into* the courtroom and lay this thing out.

Time to swear in.

"I can't say definitively what happened; I can just tell you what I think based on all my reading. She's already been established as one of the most famous Americans of all time. As long as it's a mystery, it will continue to be a topic."

Chris Williamson

The project calls *Aaron Habel* to the stand.

Mr. Habel, you're the co-creator of the *Generation Why* podcast, and you've been studying true crime cases for a very long time. You covered the Earhart case in great detail early in your run, and you've been involved in the Chasing Earhart project as a guest. You have a unique general perspective in this case and can speak as an expert regarding why this case in particular has captured the imagination and the attention of the entire world for over eight decades. My first questions for you today are why are you so intrigued by this investigation, and why did *Generation Why* want to cover it?

Aaron Habel

Well, I wanted to cover it because one of the first shows that I ever latched onto and became a huge fan of was *In Search Of* with Leonard Nimoy. If you know about that show, you know they covered this case. The brilliant thing about *In Search Of* was it not only introduced you to the mystery of what they were talking about, but it gave you some of the history. Even though it's mystery, they made you *even more* intrigued than you already were going into it. If you watch that episode with Amelia Earhart, it just sucks you in, and it gets you thinking

You have this famous woman who just disappeared.

What happened to her? You go through the possibilities; "Oh, maybe she was seen later."

It just gets your mind working. You get excited because everybody knew who she was.

· · ·

CHRIS WILLIAMSON

Chris Williamson

Does the Amelia Earhart case cause you to change your approach in the way that you study the investigation and everything contained within? Are there special circumstances here?

Aaron Habel

I pretty much look at it the same way. I just tried to factor in who the person was, and what they were doing. Is it something they were *actually good at*? If there's a flight that's missing, if there are people who were scuba diving, what is their expertise level, and where were they headed? So you kind of try to follow where they were going. With her, you look at the radio contact. There are just so many factors here, but you take it where you feel the evidence is leading you.

Chris Williamson

Mr. Habel, you just mentioned looking at someone's character and using it as a factor to determine what might have happened. I'd like you to elaborate on that for the court, please.

Aaron Habel

The simplest way that I can put it is many of these theories that say that she crash-landed somewhere and was brought back secretly or ended up in Japan and was held hostage – all these different theories don't really fit her personality to me. She was such a strong personality; she didn't bow down before *anyone*, let alone the government. A lot of those theories to me just don't hold water, and I think that if she *had survived*, she would have made her way back, and she would not have been quiet about it.

Chris Williamson

In your professional opinion, what happened to Amelia Earhart and Fred Noonan on the morning of July the second?

. . .

Aaron Habel

I think they ended up in the water. I think it's that simple.

I have a lot of respect for Amelia Earhart, and I think that if she had somehow survived and made it to land, I don't think you could stop her from getting back to America and doing this all over again. A lot of people will say all these things like "Oh, she must have been taken hostage, or maybe she survived on this island," but I just think that Amelia Earhart was the kind of person who was always ready to get back up into the air.

The fact that she never came back, to me, says that she was in the water.

Chris Williamson

If, indeed, the Electra crashed into the ocean somewhere near Howland Island, why do you think this case continues to thrive in the general public? Why is the official explanation for the events that took place that morning *not enough* to put this case to bed?

Aaron Habel

It's a **real mystery**. I have my opinion, so does everyone else, but it's still a mystery. I can't say definitively what happened; I can just tell you what *I think* based on all my reading.

She's already been established as one of the most famous Americans of all time. As long as it's a mystery, it will continue to be a topic

Chris Williamson

From a general historical perspective, is it *really* surprising to you that pertaining to her disappearance, Amelia Earhart would become such a polarizing figure?

. . .

Aaron Habel

No, not really because she was unique at the time. She was the one who was out there trying to empower women to become pilots, saying, "Let's do this, get out there and start flying!" As we know, back then, women weren't really welcome in a lot of different industries. Even when it came to passion for flight. It wasn't like they couldn't do it; it's that no one was ushering people into that who *weren't* men. She was actually saying, "Hey, let's do this!" She was inspiring women to fly.

Chris Williamson

Now, Mr. Habel, we all have our opinions on the events of that day and thereafter, but in the eyes of the general public, is the disappearance of Amelia Earhart and Fred Noonan in fact *solved*?

Aaron Habel

No, it's unsolved. Like I said, I have my opinion, and if anyone asks, that's what I say. But there isn't enough evidence to say "case closed."

Chris Williamson

Do you think that'll ever change? Will we *ever have* a definitive answer here?

Aaron Habel

I don't think so.

Chris Williamson

Mr. Habel, one of the most fascinating pieces of information that I've come across are the letters that the Amelia Earhart Birthplace Museum in Atchison Kansas continues to receive from children all over the world who continue to write letters to Amelia, hoping that *maybe* she'll write back. Do you think these types of facets add to the tragedy of a loss like this?

Aaron Habel

No, because the way I would look at it is her dream didn't die *with* her.

Chris Williamson

The government has given us an explanation for the disappearance, yet, for the most part, the general public isn't buying it. Can you explain that?

Aaron Habel

The government said it. It's that simple. A lot of people just *don't* trust the government.

Chris Williamson

We know that pertaining to this case, over two hundred Freedom of Information Act requests have been filed and denied by the US government. We *also know* that an Earhart file *does in fact exist* and that very few people have seen it. My question is, is it possible that the United States government *may know* more than they let on about the events of that day?

Aaron Habel

Well, you'd be surprised, but I hear this all the time, even on things you would consider mundane. People like to hold on to the data. I'm not sure that they have *more*, but it also might be one of those things where they get lots of requests for Amelia Earhart or DB Cooper, and they just don't care anymore. Maybe it's just as simple as "let's just move on, you guys keep messing with this, but we have modern things to worry about."

Chris Williamson

Is there a reason that the general public continues to latch on to this woman in particular?

If this were anyone else, would it matter as much as it has?

Aaron Habel

Well, she stands out in history. She pushed the envelope, and she was setting records.

More importantly, she had the loudest voice in the room, and she *was* talking. She was telling people what she wanted them to know. She had a message, and that message got out, and somehow even though it's 2022 now, that message continues to get out, which is pretty phenomenal. Her passion for flying was *so* intense that when she set about doing that, nothing was going to get in her way. That singular focus is what makes people so good. This goes for *anybody doing anything*. If you have the kind of focus she had, then you could accomplish amazing things too.

Chris Williamson

Later when some of the hypotheses are presented, we're going to be talking pretty heavily about eyewitness testimony. Before we get to that though, can you please tell the court your thoughts on the merits of eyewitness testimony being used to support a given theory?

Aaron Habel

It *can be* good but only in certain circumstances. If you just have someone who saw someone for the first time especially, they can get it *way* wrong, and it can be really bad.

We've seen cases where people have been incarcerated, and then later, it turns out they do DNA testing, and it was someone who looks *somewhat* like them, but it wasn't that person who got incarcerated.

Chris Williamson

In your opinion, does the *amount* of eyewitness testimony change anything? Do the merits of the person testifying about seeing Amelia, Fred Noonan *or* the Electra make any impact on whether that particular evidence holds water?

Aaron Habel

Well, they saw *something*, but we have nothing left to present anyone as evidence. We just have these stories. It wouldn't surprise me that people make up stories so they can be part of something. I have a real problem with knowing how she spoke and how she conducted herself, what her personality was like, that she would just be quiet and just go away. I just don't see that.

Let me just say this; I don't think they should ever stop looking. I think as long as we have people who are curious and have the means, I think they should keep the search up to try to find the answer.

Chris Williamson

A lot of people would say that the Lockheed Electra 10-E that Earhart and Noonan vanished in would be the holy grail of aviation if ever found. Would it be fair for me to refer to *this particular plane* in that way?

Aaron Habel

I think that's entirely possible because of who it was who was piloting the plane and the story that goes along with it. This was supposed to be her last flight. That was something that she had set as the goal. Once she does this, where does she go from there? How does she top it?

. . .

Chris Williamson

Earlier, you said that you believe Amelia and Fred simply crashed into the ocean.

However, by your own admission, there is no proof of that fact. Just now, you stated that we should keep looking. Why, in your opinion, is it so important for this case to have an ending?

Aaron Habel

I think this could end any number of ways and still be satisfying.

To me, it's satisfying that it's a mystery because it gets your mind working, and you think about the possibilities, and you go down all those rabbit holes. I might not put a lot of stock into many of those, but it's *still* interesting, and I've read through them.

It might also be cool to find the plane even if we don't find remains with it. Maybe we *do find* remains; you just never know. That could be an ending; *now* we have the answer. I think though for some people, if you answer it, it diminishes it a little bit. She's this legend that we never got back. It's almost like she *did* keep flying into the sunset. Well, now we have the answer, and she just ditched the plane. She didn't have anything else to do. I think we should keep looking because that's part of honoring the mystery, trying to figure out which aspects work and which ones don't.

If they never find her, I think having her life end with a mystery is still fascinating.

In fact, it *might be* the *most fascinating* ending that you can have in this case.

Chris Williamson

Thank you, Mr. Habel, no further questions.

*"We could hear her voice just as easily as I'm hearing yours, and I'm deaf in one ear now. I tell you, you could hear it all over the shack and even outside the shack. Really loud and clear. **I mean it.**"*

Chris Williamson

Your Honor, the project calls as its next witness chief radio operator of the USS Coast Guard cutter *Itasca, Mr. Leo Bellarts.*

Mr. Bellarts, this is an honor, sir. Thank you for your service and for being here today.

Mr. Bellarts, I want to start my questioning by asking you about your communication with Lae, New Guinea, and Harry Balfour. Can you tell us if you had *any* communication with them, and did they assist at all?

Leo Bellarts

We had no contact between the ship and Lae, New Guinea. We couldn't work that distance.

Of course, their frequencies were different than ours, the lower frequencies, you know?

We couldn't work that distance anyhow.

Chris Williamson

You're saying the skip and communication weren't right for you?

Leo Bellarts

No, we didn't even pay no attention. We figured we'd get briefed through the regular channels. Washington, Honolulu or San Francisco. The briefing, well, that's another story.

Chris Williamson

Can you please tell the court about your personal communications with *Harry Balfour* and Lae, New Guinea?

Leo Bellarts

I wrote him a letter. In fact, I got back several letters. He said:

"Many thanks for the information you sent me in your letter, as I did not know that you had sent out any homing signals for Amelia Earhart."

He was absolutely not aware of it; he couldn't even hear the plane frequency even when we started at night. He didn't care at all whether he kept track of us or not during the night.

"Furthermore, I can guarantee that her radio equipment **was in good order when she left.**" And this guy here was an operator when I got this.

Chris Williamson

Mr. Bellarts, can you read the words from Mr. Balfour in his letter to you regarding what Amelia Earhart left behind with him when she left Lae, New Guinea, that morning?

Leo Bellarts

"One important factor that you have to know is that she handed me her radio facility book the morning she left. Plus a lot of papers as well as her pistol and ammunition. I did not see the takeoff, as I was QRL VJC Rabaul."

In other words, he was busy working traffic with Rabaul but made a QSO contact about ten minutes later after she took off.

"I also sent a 500 KC signal for her to check her DF if she wanted to make sure it was okay."

But 500 KC was no use to her because she didn't have that; she couldn't work on that frequency; that was the sad part of it.

"Inside her facility book was all her radio brands concerning her communication arrangements with the Itasca, suggested frequencies to be used, and she could not have remembered all the information that these papers contained. Perhaps she left the facility book by mistake. So that would account for her not keeping her schedules with you" [that is with the *Itasca*] "I know these papers contained all the arrangements she had made because I had station copies, some as far back as her arrangement with Batavia radio, which was prior to Lae."

We corresponded quite a bit.

Chris Williamson
Did Mr. Balfour ever give you copies of anything or any indications of any kind of message that he might have received from her?

Leo Bellarts
He received nothing. Nothing after she took off.

Chris Williamson
You're saying that Mr. Balfour never worked her at all after she took off from Lae?

Leo Bellarts
No, no.

. . .

Chris Williamson

He never gave her any position reports that you're aware of?

Leo Bellarts

Well, the only position report was what you've got. You've got that.

Chris Williamson

Mr. Bellarts, in order to make it clear for the court, I'm going to ask you to repeat the words that she radioed to you as you wrote them down in the *Itasca* call logs. There's been a lot of speculation as to exactly *what* Amelia Earhart said and how her tone was when she spoke to you. So that the court and the jury is *clear*, can you please read from the *Itasca* call logs now?

Leo Bellarts

Okay:

"KHAQQ TO *ITASCA*. WE ARE ON THE LINE 157/337. WE WILL REPEAT NORTH AND SOUTH THIS ON 6210. WAIT."

And that was *it*, brother.

Chris Williamson

Mr. Bellarts, can you tell the court about the radio direction finder that was aboard the *Itasca*? Was that of any use to you at all in the search?

Leo Bellarts

This was a new piece of equipment as far as we were concerned. It was a portable high-frequency direction finder, and it came from the navy. I don't remember who brought it down, actually, but I believe the district radio electrician from the Honolulu Coast Guard district HM *Anthony* arranged that we get that direction finder. It was a breadboard type with a loop on the top. Strictly portable. And they brought that aboard, and we had never seen it. Nobody had seen it. (Frank) Cipriani was the same way. I figured Cipriani would be the logical man because my men knew the ship, and he didn't know the ship.

Chris Williamson

So since he didn't know the ship, he needed something to do. You assign him to the radio direction finder, correct?

Leo Bellarts

That's right, so he went onto the beach.

Chris Williamson

Cipriani had just joined your crew; he was new, correct?

Leo Bellarts

Temporary. He was a temporary man. He went over on the beach, and it was just as good.

As far as that goes, Cipriani was on the island for quite a long time. We didn't even pick him up; we didn't want him. He stayed with his equipment, and we took off. Anyway, we had fairly good contact. That direction finder was as good as nothing.

Chris Williamson

Mr. Bellarts, is it accurate for me to say that on the island with the finder, Cipriani was only able to hear Amelia Earhart on one single instance?

. . .

Leo Bellarts

He didn't know if he heard her or not, actually. I don't think he actually, *positively* identified it.

Chris Williamson

Well, he could hear *you*, correct?

Leo Bellarts

Oh yeah, well, gee whiz, you could hear me without an antenna! That direction finder was inoperative. I didn't know it until *after* we came back and picked Cipriani up. But a lot of speculation on the direction finder kinda gripes me because one person described the thing up to four or five hundred pounds! Honest to criminy sakes, the man didn't have good sense to say something like that! I can carry it under one arm; it wasn't heavy. It didn't weigh as much as a TV set, not by far, because one man could handle it.

Chris Williamson

Mr. Bellarts, can you tell the court a little about the direction finder itself? How was it built?

Leo Bellarts

If you have any idea what a direction finder is, you know there's a breadboard, the unit itself, the receiver part, and then there was a loop on the top. Oh, if I recall rightly and possibly it was maybe a foot in diameter. Whoever designed that, well, he should've designed one more and then quit. He didn't even have slip rings in there. The wires came down, and there wasn't a stop on it either, so you could turn it 180 or 360 and stop.

There wasn't any stop on it, and when it came back aboard ship, I was very interested in it, and I looked it over.

Hey, this thing's *dead!*

I started checking it out, and I looked at it, and here were all the wires twisted up like a bunch of rat's tails!

Chris Williamson

Now that you've enlightened us about that, let me ask you something about the direction finder, then. Howland Island reported a signal to you on a bearing of 3105, and this was when they possibly felt that they had sighted her to the north. Howland had taken a bearing that they believed to be northwest, correct?

Leo Bellarts

It's possible. As I say, I don't know when the thing went haywire.

Chris Williamson

In this log, there seems to be one point that's fallen into great contention since the log has been released, and that's fuel. At one point Amelia mentions that she's "running low on fuel." There seems to be contention as to whether there were thirty minutes of fuel left or whether something else was at play. Is there any way that you can clear that up for the court?

Leo Bellarts

Well, the only solution is what's in the log:

"KHAQQ" (in other words, Amelia Earhart) "CALLING *ITASCA.* "WE MUST BE ON YOU BUT CANNOT SEE YOU BUT GAS IS RUNNING LOW."

Now *that* is what's said, and this is the rest of it:

"GAS IS RUNNING LOW. BEEN UNABLE TO REACH YOU BY RADIO. WE ARE FLYING AT 1,000 FEET."

And bingo, she turns the thing off. Not saying a call or a "go ahead" or this or that or the other thing. That's what made us as operators disgusted with her. She would say something like that and then hang it up and apparently wouldn't even turn the receiver on. We didn't know if she had the receiver off or on or what.

We received *nothing*.

Until she got *stuck*.

She saw that her number was coming up, and then she started scratching, pretty much.

She should've done it that way the *first time* she heard or called us. She should've listened to us. She apparently didn't listen for us at all. That's what really disturbed us to no little bit. She'd come on and just tell you, "The weather is overcast," this, that and the other thing and hang it up. She never tried to establish contact until the last quart of gas she had, let's put it that way.

"BEEN UNABLE TO REACH YOU BY RADIO. WE ARE FLYING AT 1,000 FEET."

We thought *that* was terrible too.

Chris Williamson

Let me stop you right there, Mr. Bellarts, and argue this point. What if Amelia Earhart dropped the plane to 1,000 feet in order to get below the clouds, which has been another point of contention in this case?

Leo Bellarts

Those clouds were not that thick.

232

Chris Williamson

Was there any indication of any kind of a line of storms to the north at that time?

Leo Bellarts

Not that we could see. There were puffy clouds, and there was plenty of blue in between them.

Chris Williamson

So as she gets closer and closer, two hundred miles out, one hundred miles out, she speaks the words that have gone down in history:

"WE MUST BE ON YOU BUT CANNOT SEE YOU."

You must have wanted to leave the radio shack and go outside to…

Leo Bellarts

I actually *did* go outside and stand right outside the radio shack and started listening like that. Any second! Actually, we had people out on deck. We thought she was going to be flying right down the way. Oh man, she came in like a ton of bricks. I mean that.

Chris Williamson

Our records say that she only carried a 50-watt transmitter. There's a lot of confusion about her radio. Mr. Joe Gurr, who installed all of her radios down in Burbank, California, at Paul Mantz's hangar, stated that she only carried a 50-watt transmitter. This would make her daytime 3105 signals able to put her pretty close to you.

Leo Bellarts

In the early morning, the signals carry pretty good.

Chris Williamson

Mr. Bellarts, to the best of your knowledge, could the USS *Ontario* or the USS *Swan* hear her at all, or did they even have the ability to monitor for her?

Leo Bellarts

Neither one of them, as far as I know, were monitoring.

Chris Williamson

And you knew that the Electra couldn't send code at all?

Leo Bellarts

Well, that's why when we use code or what we call *ICW*, when we use that, boy, we would go about two words a minute or slower.

Chris Williamson

Am I correct in saying that she could have had ships take a bearing on her by simply holding down a single key?

Leo Bellarts

Oh man, yes. Actually, that direction finder, that was my pride and joy because I've had an awful lot of experience on a direction finder, and of course now they're practically obsolete. As far as ships are concerned, *they are* practically obsolete.

Chris Williamson

Could the *Itasca* send out voice on the 7500 kilocycles frequency?

Leo Bellarts

Sure. Certainly. We could ship back and forth. Very easy.

Chris Williamson

Was there a transmitter set up for *all* the frequencies that morning?

Leo Bellarts

We could check any one of those. That's all we had to do is turn around, and there you are.

Chris Williamson

Were the men on Howland, Baker and Jarvis, listening in during this whole thing?

Leo Bellarts

Yes, if their batteries were up. In them days, there's nothing but a dry battery option check. And they had to charge the array batteries, so to speak. So it was a little problem.

Now as far as Baker is concerned, and Jarvis, neither one of them were in on the deal at all.

Chris Williamson

Now, you were working Baker at that time; however, we can't find anything in any log that would indicate that anyone asked them if they had heard Amelia Earhart. Is that right?

· · ·

Leo Bellarts

They *were* asked at one time, and they came back negative.

Chris Williamson

Mr. Bellarts, if we can please go back to the fuel aspect of the last flight, can you educate the court and our jury on where the thirty-*minute number* or *about a half hour* figure originated from?

Leo Bellarts

I'll tell you how that happened, I believe. After the flight, I think it actually took place. I don't recall if it was going into Honolulu on our way north, or if it was from Honolulu going back home to Frisco, I don't recall.

But I remember the old man was down there. Thompson, Baker, and myself. I don't know if Sutter was there. But anyway, the old man, Baker and myself and I think it was the navigator if I'm not mistaken because he had to put some of the stuff in as far as the ship's log is concerned. They were concocting up a long letter, sort of a search report. And that, I think, was put in that report.

They shouldn't ever have put that in; they misquoted.

But what I read you, *that* is what came over the air.

Chris Williamson

It appears that she heard you a single time on the 7500 frequency, is that correct?

Leo Bellarts

I don't think she even tried to hear us half the time.

The static was maximum on three megs, so she made a big mistake changing to three megs. You see, what he [Balfour] originally described was that when she was coming in, he was working on 62, and she shifted right after she took off, apparently, and dropped down to three megs. That's all we ever heard.

Chris Williamson

Now, according to written statements from Harry Balfour, he was in contact with her for a time.

Leo Bellarts

Coming in. Coming in, yes.

Chris Williamson

Mr. Bellarts, when Amelia and Fred are inbound and she's communicating with you, "I'm two hundred miles out. I'm one hundred miles out. We must be on you but cannot see you." When reading the logs, it doesn't come across as if they felt they were lost. So what I want to ask you now is was there any change in her demeanor or the tone of her voice she was using, anything?

Leo Bellarts

Actually, her voice…

We could hear her voice just as easily as I'm hearing yours, and I'm deaf in one ear now. I tell you, you could hear it all over the shack and even *outside* the shack. Really loud and clear. I mean it. She was a woman. We heard her, quite a few times, you know. But that last one I'm telling you if she would have broken out in a scream, it would have sounded normal.

She was just about ready to break into tears and go into hysterics. That's exactly the way I describe her voice now, and I'll never forget it.

She was just on the verge of just saying, "oomph" and letting it go. She was on the verge of going into hysterics.

I *mean that.*

· · ·

237

Chris Williamson

Thank you, Mr. Bellarts, for your testimony today. No further questions.

Your Honor, at this time, I'd like to call a recess and reconvene with the *crash and sink hypothesis.*

Bailiff

ALL RISE!

85 YEARS
LATER

18,000 FEET
0.8075145 | -176.61687

"Until we have that plane, in my mind, there are other possibilities. Even if the people on the stand today say, 'Highly improbable,' well, that may be, but until we find her plane, and until we find her resting place, I think there's always other possibilities."

Chris Williamson

July 2, 1937, is a day clouded in judgment.

Many people believe that it was the last day in the remarkable lives of Amelia Earhart and Fred Noonan. For those people and everyone investigating this case, their investigations begin on that day. Earlier in this text, we talked about specific dates and the importance of those dates in our lives.

What if you knew when the last day of your life would be?

Would you want to know how your life would end? Or would you want to go fearless into the horizon like Amelia and Fred did?

In the following pages, we're going to lay the foundation for the greatest mystery of all time.

Every crime has a crime scene, and every crime has evidence. Now we're going to lay the evidence for this story out, and at the end of day three of the trial, you'll know exactly what that evidence *is*, and just how heavily that evidence is leaned on by the experts who are called to testify before you. Next, for the very first time, we're going to put the first of four remarkable theories in front of you, our jury.

It's time to unravel July 2, 1937, with witnesses, evidence and testimony for *crash and sink.*

Pre-Trial Discussion

Chris Williamson

Lots to unpack here. We had Aaron Habel's excellent testimony, and we were able to bring Leo Bellarts back, in a really special curveball for our readers. What did you think of *that* testimony?

Jen Taylor

I think Bellarts's testimony was just amazing. It's really unique to be able to hear from somebody who was *actually there*. He actually heard her, so he can testify to what she sounded like, and that is something we're not going to get from anybody else.

Chris Williamson

I agree. For a case like this, you have to figure out how you can bring that kind of testimony into play. I know that's not normally done, and we're kind of bending the rules there, but when you're looking for eyewitnesses or something as close to an eyewitness as you can possibly get, how could we not? How can you not have him there to say his piece? When we get back into court, we'll start talking to certain witnesses who will reference him. A lot of the people who represent crash and sink or support that theory will talk about relying on his testimony because he was there. So to not have that would just not be as powerful as actually having him take the stand. I think that was really cool.

Jen Taylor

Yeah, there's so much you miss from just reading a transcript. We have the radio logs; we know what she said. We have the little notation there that says it was coming in at S-5, but that's not the same as hearing somebody say, "I heard her, and she was so loud that I stepped outside and thought that I'd be able to see her." Just towards the end there when he was describing the panic in her voice, that's not something you can get from reading the transcript, and I thought it was really powerful to be able to hear that.

Chris Williamson

Indeed, *very* powerful. The first time I heard that, it sent chills up my spine because you hear a lot of stuff in documentaries that cover this story; they say things like, "She was whistling into the microphone; she was trying to whistle to get a bearing and a steady sound so the *Itasca* could pull a bearing and try to get an idea of where she was at." When you hear Bellarts talk about it, he states very specifically she was not whistling. It was more like a high-pitched scream into the microphone. It almost seemed like she was begging for someone to save her life. We talk so much about her being fearless, and indeed I stand behind that 1,000%, but that was just very heartbreaking to hear an icon of that stature in those final moments. If she did just simply run out of fuel and crash into the ocean, I can't imagine being in that cockpit and going through that.

Jen Taylor

If you look at it in the context of that maybe being her final moments on this earth, it gets very eerie, and it was just really powerful to hear what he had to say about it. It gives it that human element. We can sit here and debate what happened all day long, and we can look at the logs, and we can listen to people talk about the science and the math and the technical aspects of it, but it was really good to have that here. To show why we're doing this, to have the human element brought back into it. I really like that.

Chris Williamson

Shout out to Scott Philbrook, whose words earlier gave me the idea to attempt that. On the flip side of that, Aaron Habel. We're both big fans of the *Generation Why* podcast, and they're no strangers to the Earhart case *themselves*. What did you think about him giving his opinion on it? He's a pretty straight shooter; he always has been on everything *Gen Why* covers, especially the Earhart stuff.

Jen Taylor

Oh yeah, I thought that he made some good points especially when he said, "Maybe the answer is the mystery." He doesn't subscribe to anything other than crash and sink, but he loves reading about it, and he loves going down these rabbit holes. I can relate to that because since I've started working on this with you, I have gone down so many rabbit holes myself; Lord knows I've spent more hours than I should reading about stuff and following little trails. That's the fun part. At the end of the day, hopefully we can figure out what happened, or maybe we won't, but the journey is the fun part. So I really liked that aspect of his testimony.

Chris Williamson

Yeah, part of the journey is the end.

Moving on to our next day in court, we're going to put our first theory on trial. You know, I've been doing this for a long time. I've been talking to a lot of these folks who will testify next. It's not going to be the first time I've spoken with them; we have history. They've appeared on our *Chasing Earhart* podcast; some of them sat on our panel in Atchison in 2018. We've had experience with them. There's a boxing metaphor that I like to use in relating historical context and theory on a given piece of history, and it goes like this: If you're a champion of some kind and you're defending your title, all you have to do is *not lose*; that's it. It's up to the challenger to take that title *from you*. I feel like the science regarding the S-5 and everything that we're probably going to hear about next when it comes to crash and sink is *really* solid. If somebody were to topple that science or present something that could rival it or even trump it, for lack of a better term, it's going to have to be *earth shatteringly good* for that to actually take a precedence.

. . .

Jen Taylor

I think Tad sort of hit on this earlier; I think we talked about the reasonable doubt being in the other four theories. The other four hypotheses are where your reasonable doubt lives.

Crash and sink has the radio logs, and they have the data to back up this theory. What keeps people coming back and what keeps this from being a "mystery solved" scenario is that they haven't actually found the plane. So there's the possibility that it can be somewhere else. It's these other people coming forward and saying, "Actually, we have evidence that she may have been in Saipan" or "Actually, we have evidence that she may have been on Nikumaroro." I think that it's great that we're starting with crash and sink because we can lay the foundation for that hypothesis and why so many people believe that is what happened. There's a reason why that's the official story, so we start there, and then we can ask, "Do you have anything that refutes that? Do you have anything that can steer us somewhere else?"

It's got to be something that rises to the level of beyond a reasonable doubt because that's what we're trying to do here.

Chris Williamson

Well, that's *your job*. I'm the one who has to put up all these reasons why people should believe that this particular theory is it. You're the one who actually has to disprove all of that, so I apologize in advance, but it is what it is. You're going to have your work cut out for you.

Jen Taylor

I should *never* have answered the phone a couple of months ago when you called me.

Chris Williamson

Into the storm you go.

I can almost promise you this. They're going to double down. Signal strengths don't lie; this is according to the experts you're about to hear. Fred Noonan's navigation was spot on, and there's no reason to question that. I think a lot of people are going to refer back to the belief in Amelia Earhart and what she was saying. That's going to be key. They're going back to, "We must be on you but cannot see you." They're going to lean heavily on the idea that she was clearly stating she was somewhere near Howland Island, somewhere near the *Itasca*, and there's no reason to question that. They're going to really push hard on the evidence and the *Itasca* logs like you said. That's the only solid evidence that exists, and until something comes along that overrides those, or adds to those maybe, the logs are gospel. They're going to double down on their trust for Noonan's skills and rightfully so. I don't think it's going to be a surprise that those are going to be the key factors that almost all of these experts are going to lean on.

Jen Taylor

You also have to keep in mind that we still haven't found the plane. We don't know 100% that's where she's at. If this is what really happened to her, then how do you explain two hundred people seeing her in Saipan? How do you explain signals that sounded very much like they were coming from Amelia and Fred *five days later*? That leaves a lot left unexplained.

I'm not quite so sure yet. *We'll see.*

Chris Williamson

I want to find out if there's anything else they're going to lean on besides those key factors.

We talk a lot about the simplest explanation being the most likely one, Occam's razor. I'll probably question them about that and get their opinions on it. My question for you is, do you think you can get any one of them, if not *all of them*, to admit that it's possible that something *else* could have been the result of what happened that morning?

Jen Taylor

I don't know, we'll have to see.

. . .

Chris Williamson

Yes, we will. I just want to make it clear, my position here is to put everything out in an unbiased format, as much as we can, anyway. I'm going to present every one of these theories, not only crash and sink, but as we move to *castaway* and then to *Japanese capture*, I'm going to give everything I've got as far as all the data that supports a particular theory because I think all of them are worth looking at. We have no plane; we have no wreckage; we have no oil slicks on the ocean; we have nothing to go by. We just have these two people in a plane who vanish into thin air eighty-five years ago, and that's all we've got. We're going to present a lot of data in this case, but until we get to one theory in particular, the one thing we *don't have* is a plane.

Jen Taylor

Until we have that plane, in my mind, there are other possibilities. Even if the people on the stand today say, "*Highly improbable,*" well, that *may be*, but until we find her plane, and until we find her resting place, I think there's always other possibilities.

"Many of us who have been doing this for a long time have heard the stories. Some of the people who make money off these alternate histories know damn well that's not what happened, and they couldn't care less because it's how they make their living."

Chris Williamson

The project calls *Brian Dunning* to the stand.

Mr. Dunning, for those who don't know, explain to me what it is you specialize in.

Brian Dunning

I'm a science writer. My specialty is the science behind urban legends, mainly separating real history from pseudo history, facts from fiction, that kind of thing. Anything in the pop culture where there's public misinformation and there's actual lessons to be learned from the real science or real history behind something.

Chris Williamson

You've been doing this a long time, so let me ask you this: With cases like this one, is it really surprising that so many theories would spring from a vanishing of this magnitude in order to give the world a reason for the events of that day?

Brian Dunning

No. All you have to do is turn on the History Channel to see how much misinformation there is about historical events. *Ancient Aliens,* alright? You can just take it from there.

That's why we see so many of these nonsense crackpot theories being promoted on TV networks and everywhere else you turn. The real history is seemingly less interesting, but all the proof and data in that history is all right there for anyone who wants to actually go find it.

It may not be as *sensational*, but it's *there*.

Chris Williamson

Why do you think people seem to gravitate towards situations that have more controversy and more question marks than the actual story?

Brian Dunning

I think you just used all the words right there. Sensationalism sells. People love that there's some mystery. People like to think that there's some secret mysterious explanation for things they've heard in the past. That's why you'll see all these alternate theories being promoted on TV; it's to get that *eyeball share*.

Chris Williamson

I want to give you two *whys*, and you can give me your thoughts on each one. The first *why* is, why do you think that it's so important for this story to have an ending?

Brian Dunning

It's not so much that it needs an ending because it's not likely to have one.

I think what's important about this particular story is that Amelia Earhart was an early pioneer of women in science. Her legacy should be remembered as an inspiration to young girls. Instead, what we're seeing is all these crackpot theories cloaking that legacy with all of this nonsense pseudo history.

That's the tragedy.

I think that's why it's important that we keep our eye on the *true* history of who she actually was, what she actually did, and ultimately what finally became her resting place, which is the least interesting of her accomplishments.

Chris Williamson

The second *why* is, if the official explanation backed by the United States government states that Earhart and Noonan crash-landed in the vicinity of Howland Island, why is it that a very large portion of the public just can't seem to accept that as the end?

Brian Dunning

They've never been told that. What they've been told is what you see when you turn on the History Channel, and you find all of these silly ideas like they flew instead to this island four hundred miles away, or they were captured by the Japanese. One thing or another. That's really the only airplay that the Amelia Earhart story has been given. I think there was a *Nova* episode about what happened to the airplane, but absent of that, it's been one miniseries after another on the History Channel or Nat-Geo that you have promoting these false histories.

Chris Williamson

Mr. Dunning, can you explain Occam's razor for me?

Brian Dunning

The explanations actually get pretty complicated, but to oversimplify it, it means that the explanation that requires the fewest new assumptions to be made is the preferred explanation. The one that's more likely to be true. If you see a light in the sky, a simple explanation might be, "Oh, it's an alien spaceship," but really that's introducing new assumptions about the world, like that aliens are out there and are visiting Earth. So instead, we look for the one that *doesn't* require us to make changes to the world as we know it in order for that explanation to be likely true.

Chris Williamson

In *your* coverage of this case, we've come across a term called *manufactroversy*. I wonder if you can explain that term to me.

Brian Dunning

That's when you have a story that's not especially interesting and you want to *make it* interesting, so you make up stuff about it. Any time you turn on any sort of news today, you're hearing a lot of manufactroversy. That shouldn't come as a great surprise to anyone. Everything from "this particular food is poisonous and is going to kill you and you should avoid it" to whether there's a bigfoot running around in the woods. There are all kind of these manufactroversies, and certainly the Earhart story is full of them.

Chris Williamson

Can you tell us what *verifiable evidence* is?

Brian Dunning

Well, it's the opposite of anecdotal evidence. Anecdotal evidence has a place; an anecdote is something that *can't* be tested or verified. Someone tells a verbal story, "Hey, I saw Elvis last week." That's anecdotal evidence. Maybe it suggests a direction for research. Maybe I can go to where that guy says he saw Elvis, but that by itself certainly doesn't constitute proof that Elvis is still alive. By the same token, when we look at the anecdotal evidence that Amelia Earhart had all these alternate fates, that clearly contradicts where we know her plane went. The reason all that evidence is anecdotal is because nobody has actually picked up something and brought it to us that we can look at, study, test and verify.

"Ah, yes, Amelia Earhart is the only possible explanation for this piece of garbage," whatever it is.

Chris Williamson

Can you explain what confirmation bias is?

Brian Dunning

Confirmation bias is the native tendency that we all have; we all do this. We tend to prefer information that confirms our previously existing beliefs or notions. So in this case, someone who's promoting any given false history of Amelia Earhart, they're going to look at everything that could possibly be conceived as being consistent with the version of the story *they* prefer, and that's what they're going to promote. They're simply going to ignore everything that contradicts their version of the story. That's where confirmation bias comes into play, kind of continually echo chambering these particular versions of the story with bad information and ignoring all the good information that they don't like.

Chris Williamson

Mr. Dunning, take me through the events of that day. What happened on the morning of July 2, 1937?

Brian Dunning

What happened was they were on the last leg of their flight from Papua New Guinea to Howland Island to refuel. They were given a radio direction finding beacon to follow, and they had, of course, voice radio once they got a close enough distance for communication.

They had a reasonably good enough plan to make it to Howland. Aviation was not new in this part of the world; US Navy aircraft carriers had been flying planes all over the place for decades. The Pan Am Clipper flying boats were just about to start *their* service. So aviation was not new in the Pacific Ocean; we did know how to navigate a plane from Papua New Guinea to Howland. The Coast Guard cutter that was on station at Howland, the *Itasca*, was set to help them refuel there. It refueled every plane that came in; Amelia Earhart was just one in a long line. This wasn't anything super extraordinary that we were trying to do, and we understood what the challenges were. When they came overhead and finally got into radio contact, that meant they were very close. They weren't at any of these other islands; that was simply not possible with the voice communication happening.

From the information that she was able to provide, she couldn't see the island, but they thought they knew where they were. We're pretty sure what happened is they missed the island because it was right in the setting sun in their eyes. When the sun came up, they went over the island, and they began their search pattern. Between forty and two hundred miles to the northeast was where the radio operators determined the signal was coming from.

They continued their search pattern in that area until they ran out of fuel sometime just after 8:43 a.m.

Chris Williamson

In your opinion, sir, what went wrong that morning?

Brian Dunning

Well, I have no reason to believe that the foremost experts who were actually present got anything wrong. Everything that we know seems to jive with that account pretty well. It seems that it was just unfortunate that there was probably a bit of a tailwind they didn't properly correct for. It probably pushed them a little bit further past the islands, so they were a little bit further than they thought they were when they got there.

I think it's probably as simple as that.

It's absolutely *not* an uncommon story in plane navigation problems.

. . .

Chris Williamson

Do you think we can attribute what ultimately happened that morning with several small things going wrong?

Brian Dunning

Depending on what those things are, possibly.

Chris Williamson

Mr. Dunning, if Amelia Earhart and Fred Noonan had Harry Manning on board with them and would have had the ability to send Morse code out to the *Itasca*, are we having a different discussion right now?

Brian Dunning

Yeah, I think everyone's been universally in agreement on that. The fact that they didn't *know* Morse code was crucial. Morse code transmits much farther than voice, certainly back in the 1930s.

Voice communication is useful only for very close range. What's so frustrating about it is they were very close to Howland. They're talking back and forth until they ran out of fuel.

It's a sad story. With Morse code, they would have been able to say, "Hey, we're not on the direction-finding beam." They could have said whatever they needed in order to help themselves.

Chris Williamson

Considering the headwind factor, do you think that if they had successfully been able to take off from Hawaii the first time and make Howland Island their first stop as opposed to being one of their last, we'd have a different historical result?

Brian Dunning

I don't think I'd be able to speculate on that with sufficient authority.

Chris Williamson

As it stands right now, is Amelia Earhart's Lockheed Electra 10-E the holy grail of aviation in your opinion?

Brian Dunning

I think it's certainly one of the most famous missing planes. If you want to call it that, sure.

I think that's a reasonable description.

Chris Williamson

If there's one aspect of this case that's apparent, it's that everyone, no matter what hypothesis they're working, is pretty sure they have it right. Whether it's the evidence they're using to prop their theory up or whether it's something else entirely, everyone feels that they have the answer. What is it about this theory that makes you so certain that Amelia and Fred simply crashed into the ocean?

Brian Dunning

Well, first, I don't agree with your premise that everyone believes that they have it right.

Many of us who have been doing this for a long time have heard the stories. Some of the people who make money off these alternate histories know damn well that's not what happened, and they couldn't care less because it's how they make their living.

Whether that's writing a book or taking money to conduct expeditions and making a TV miniseries. So I don't agree with your premise that everyone believes that they have it right.

My version of the story is absolutely open to being changed if new information comes forward. That hasn't happened since 1937.

I've had no reason to change the version of events as they were recorded at the time they happened. I don't think you could say the same for some of the other people promoting alternate histories, I don't think they're open to admitting they were wrong and changing their theory.

Chris Williamson

What kind of evidence would it take to sway you?

Brian Dunning

Find the plane.

Chris Williamson

I only have one final question before I pass the witness. Do you think the vanishing of Amelia Earhart and Fred Noonan does anything to damage their respective legacies?

Brian Dunning

Yes, I absolutely think it does, because now people are going to remember Amelia Earhart *as* "The woman who was taken captive by the Japanese and tortured," or they're going to remember some nonsense version of the story that didn't happen when instead, they should be remembering her as a pioneer, particularly for young girls. An inspiration and a pioneer of women in STEM. She was definitely a woman in the sciences, and I think everyone who is familiar with her story would agree with that.

That's where her legacy best lies.

Chris Williamson

Thank you. Pass the witness, Your Honor.

Cross-Examination of Brian Dunning

Jen Taylor

Okay, Mr. Dunning, it's fair to say that your job title is *professional skeptic*, is that correct?

Brian Dunning

I call myself a science writer. I basically do research to see what the true science and true history behind urban legends and myths in popular culture are.

Jen Taylor

When you were talking to Mr. Williamson, you used the terms *pseudoscience* and *misinformation*, is that correct?

Brian Dunning

I use those terms a lot, yes.

Jen Taylor

So it's fair to say that when you're going to start writing about something, you've already made a decision in your mind that this is a topic concerning pseudoscience and misinformation?

Brian Dunning

No, not at all. If you look at the body of my work, it doesn't bear that out at all. That's part of the excitement of what I do; we never know what the outcome is going to be until we actually get in and talk to the real experts and find out what the state of knowledge is on a situation.

. . .

Jen Taylor

What's the name of your podcast?

Brian Dunning

It's called *Skeptoid.*

Jen Taylor

But you don't think you're a skeptic writer?

Brian Dunning

Well, you know, it's a problematic term because different people think it means different things. I wish I'd chosen a different title for the show, but yeah.

Jen Taylor

And you do acknowledge that you are a writer and not a researcher? You're not actually out there doing the science.

Brian Dunning

No, I'm not a research scientist, I'm a science writer. My job is to talk to the research scientists and report it to the general public. What's going on in the world of science or history, whatever it is we're talking about.

Jen Taylor

Okay. And of course, you know where I'm going with these questions, because you also talked about confirmation bias.

Brian Dunning

Yes, that's something that comes up a lot in my work.

Jen Taylor

Of course. And you would agree that this is something that probably *all of us* carry with us.

Brian Dunning

Oh, definitely.

Jen Taylor

I know we're going to disagree on this term, but as a *professional skeptic*, you write about things where you believe people have come up with these crazy conspiracy theories and they have no basis in fact or science.

This is your experience; this is where you come from.

So whenever you look at a problem, do you think it's fair to say that you might have a little confirmation bias as well?

Brian Dunning

That's a point that I make all the time. The first step is understanding and recognizing that we *all* have confirmation bias and all kinds of perceptual errors and problems in our thought processes. Understanding that I bring that to the table every time I sit down to research a topic that's a key important first step.

Jen Taylor

Okay, so let's also talk a little bit about Occam's razor because that was brought up earlier. Can you give me, just one more time, your definition of Occam's razor?

. . .

Brian Dunning

The explanation that requires the fewest new assumptions is the one to be preferred.

Jen Taylor

We as humans almost have a psychological tendency to prefer the simple over the complex in most cases. You would agree with that?

Brian Dunning

Well, yes, but don't conflate simple with the fewest new assumptions because they're not the same thing at all.

Jen Taylor

I guess to kind of step back a little bit, not talking about *this specific issue* and really not even talking about anything specific to conspiracy theories or anything, but *generally*, in the world that we live in, people these days tend to prefer the simple over the complex. You have to think about the way headlines are written, and the way advertisement is developed. It's designed to grab people's attention because they can't really pay attention for longer than how long it takes to give a sound bite. I know it's a generalization, but you would agree with that?

Brian Dunning

Certainly. I'd use the word anecdotal instead of simple because with simple, it's not clear what we're talking about. We can say that you see a light in the sky "Oh, it's an alien spaceship." That's a very simple explanation, but it's not the one that requires the fewest new assumptions. We have to be careful about terminology so we don't get the wrong idea.

• • •

Jen Taylor

Occam's razor is often used in science.

Brian Dunning

Occam's razor is often used in debate. I'd say it's not really part of the formal scientific method.

Jen Taylor

No, no, and that's partly where I'm going. It's often used as a tool in science, sometimes even in theology or in philosophy. It's used as a tool to compare two different theories or two different ways of looking at things. It's just a tool that is used to discern which one we like better; you would agree with that?

Brian Dunning

It would certainly be a tool that would aid you in deciding what direction to go for more formalized research, yeah.

Jen Taylor

But it's not always 100% applicable. I don't know if that's the right word, but we do have, in science especially, things like quantum mechanics and the standard model of quantum physics. We have string theory, we have, in theory, all of these things. If you were to apply Occam's razor, then you would probably be discounting a lot of good theories that do actually explain how the world works. Under Occam's razor though, it wouldn't necessarily mean that you would get to the right answer.

Brian Dunning

And that's why I say that Occam's razor isn't really a tool that's used in the formal science process. It's more of a philosophical device.

. . .

Jen Taylor

Okay, I think we're mostly on the same page, then. Occam's razor is a tool, but when you were on direct, Chris said some people use this as the *end-all, be-all* of what they call the crash and sink theory.

My point is that's not necessarily appropriate because what you should be doing is you should be gathering data, correct?

Brian Dunning

Yeah, I mean Occam's razor doesn't tell us "Oh, here's where the plane is" or anything like that. If you were to apply Occam's razor in this case, certainly everyone who was there who recorded and experienced that day would kind of be our default standard model of what happened, and it doesn't require any new assumptions as we see with all of the other kind of fringe theories that have emerged in the ensuing decades. People who have essentially had to make up things that can't be coordinated with the facts of the case, would meet new assumptions, i.e., they suddenly flew hundreds of miles, they suddenly got captured by a friendly nation; you know, all kinds of things that can't be matched up. These would be new assumptions that we've introduced. If we want to apply Occam's razor, then we eliminate all of the new assumptions about the world and new assumptions about history. New things that don't fit with what we actually know.

Jen Taylor

Anytime you're doing an investigation, whether it be an accident or a criminal investigation, you are going to start with certain assumptions. The key is to make sure that at the end of the day, you're following the evidence. I know that we had somebody on the stand earlier, Tad DiBiase, who came in and said, "Oftentimes we have a missing person, for example, most times, in these no-body murder cases [he called them], they're going to be a woman, and most of the time it's going to be the husband or the boyfriend." That is an assumption. It's also an assumption that law enforcement officers typically start with, and so long as they continue to follow the evidence and not get too locked into this assumption, then everything is fine. Once they get so locked into the mindset of, "No I'm not going to deviate from this idea I already have in my head," then we start to get problems, and we start to see injustice.

I think we're on the same page.

Brian Dunning

Generally, yeah. Heuristics like that are certainly a valuable part of a job like law enforcement.

Jen Taylor

Oftentimes, evidence might exist to contradict an assumption that somebody starts with, and it might be ignored, or it might be explained away. A lot of times, the reason behind this is this principle of Occam's razor that people use in investigations. They say, "Well, this is the explanation that makes sense, she had a contentious relationship with her husband or boyfriend, and she's disappeared." I know there's other conflicting evidence that shows up. I'm not saying that *you* are doing this, I'm not saying this is happening here today, but I am saying that it *does happen*. People use this Occam's razor idea almost as a benefit to their *own* confirmation bias. It can be harmful as well as helpful in some cases if we're relying too much on it.

Brian Dunning

Is that a question? Certainly, all sorts of people are susceptible to all kinds of reasoning errors, certainly.

Jen Taylor

I believe you talked about conspiracy ideation, and you talked about the tendency for certain groups of people to gravitate towards conspiracy theories, and you gave some examples. I think you talked about the 911 truther movement and things like that. What I want to do is, I want to try to lock down the difference between a conspiracy theory and a distrust of the government. Is this like a spectrum? When in your mind do you say, "That's a conspiracy theory"?

Brian Dunning

I think the term conspiracy theory is overused. People apply it a little bit too broadly because, oftentimes, people will refer to any strange belief as a conspiracy theory, and that's not necessarily what a conspiracy is. When we use the term conspiracy theory, what we're *really* referring to is false conspiracy theories. Claims that there was some secret cabal in the government or in finance or whatever it is colluding to perform some illegal, immoral act, usually against *the people*. Most of these are false conspiracy theories.

Jen Taylor

So a conspiracy, as the name would suggest, would require people acting in cahoots with one another?

Brian Dunning

Yes.

Jen Taylor

Typically, the government is involved and is in cahoots with some-body who *does not* have our best interests at heart. That's typically what we're looking at?

Brian Dunning

In many cases, but the thing about conspiracy theories is that they *do* cut equally across all demographics, and it's not all groups of people who see the government as the bad guy.

Although that's the case with many conspiracy theories, it's not with *all of them*.

Jen Taylor

I think what I'm getting at here is there are several different hypotheses about what happened to her *other than* what we're calling the crash and sink theory. Some of them might go into conspiracy theory territory, but not all of them do.

What I want to do is go over each of them and get your opinion on whether you think that it counts as a conspiracy theory. The one we're going to be talking about next is what some people call the *castaway theory*, that she overshot a little bit, and there were navigational errors that led them to end up on Nikumaroro Island, where they were castaways there for a little while. Regardless of whether the evidence supports it, would that classify as a conspiracy theory?

Brian Dunning

No, I classify that as just alternate adventure fiction, basically.

Jen Taylor

Okay. Another one is the *Buka theory*. She knew she was going to run out of gas; she turned around and started going back the way she came and landed in Buka. That also seems similar to castaway, and that's not really a conspiracy theory. Would you agree with that?

Brian Dunning

Yeah, I mean, if you want to call these conspiracy theories, then that's okay. Who are the rest of the conspirators and what are they up to here? You don't have those elements in those stories.

· · ·

Jen Taylor

Right. Then we get to the more controversial ones; the first one being that she landed in the Marshall Islands and was captured by the Japanese. Would you qualify *that* as a conspiracy theory?

Brian Dunning

Yeah, that particular story is one of the Japanese military/governments deciding to cover something up for some reason. So that one, *yes*.

Jen Taylor

Based on your understanding of the theory, who were the conspirators? Was it our government? Or was it just the Japanese government? Were they in cahoots together?

This is a really weird way to ask the question because there's so many different versions of this story, but who would be the conspirators in that theory, generally?

Brian Dunning

I would refer you to the guy's book who made that one up.

He's gonna understand his version far better than I would. Basically, anyone who is *in* on the secret. That's the definition of a conspirator in that sense.

Jen Taylor

So the US government and the Japanese government. Possibly Amelia Earhart herself. I think this theory has a lot of people working together.

Brian Dunning

To whatever degree those parties are implicated, yeah.

. . .

Jen Taylor

Of the three alternate theories of what happened to her, one of them you classify as a conspiracy theory, two of them you would not.

Brian Dunning

I would say so, yeah, but that's hardly the distinctive characteristic of these things.

They're simply goofy inventions that don't line up with what we know happened on that day.

Jen Taylor

If we just want to focus on the two that we have agreed probably *aren't* government conspiracies, they're just alternate theories. For example, the Nikumaroro Island theory, what about that makes it *goofy* as opposed to just a different calculation of where she may have landed and died?

Brian Dunning

These are all Elvis sightings, basically.

Elvis Presley died. He was at the hospital, they did a postmortem on him, and we have his body. We know for a fact that he died. We don't really bother to look into Elvis sightings from that point. We already know that's not what happened, and we have the same case here. We have people who were there that day who were present during the entire event until she went into the water. We know what happened on that day, so we don't really bother to give any credence to these later versions of history that pop up that people essentially invent. That's why I'm using the phrase *fictional adventure stories*. There's no part of them that could fit into what *we know* happens, so we don't really bother to look into them too deeply.

. . .

Jen Taylor

But there *is* a difference between the Elvis sightings and what we have here. With Elvis, people saw him die, right? That's how you know. I understand why people think that's a little bit different than somebody who has literally disappeared; she was declared dead in absentia because she was never found. So do you not think *that* factor gives a little bit more credence to people trying to find her? They're trying to find her resting place. If we haven't found her, can you *really* say that the crash and sink theory has been ***definitively proven?***

Brian Dunning

Well, yeah, there's certainly physical boundaries of what happened. We know that because of the radio signal strength.

We know that there's a very small box in which she existed in.

We know that with the amount of fuel on board, she could not have gone anywhere outside that box, simply by the laws of nature.

We have a pretty good idea of where that plane is.

It's in 18,000 feet of water.

That's the difference between this and the Elvis case. The body is a little bit deeper than we're able to retrieve, but it's really the same thing. You keep using the term "crash and sink theory" or "crash and sink hypothesis." That's like saying, "the Apollo moon landing hypothesis." A lot of people were involved, and people were there when that happened. We have all the history on what happened that day. We don't *need* to bother looking into stories of the moon landing being a hoax. We don't need to investigate stories of Amelia Earhart being somewhere *other* than inside that little box where the *Itasca* crew was talking with her. The whole thing is kind of silly at face value.

Jen Taylor

You mentioned fuel. Have you ever seen contradictory statements about how much fuel she took off with? Are you aware of that at all?

· · ·

270

Brian Dunning

Oh, certainly. Virtually everyone who has tried to promote an alternate version of this has come up with alternate scenarios for how much fuel they're trying to claim she had on board. That simply doesn't match with what's *actually* known.

Anyone can make stuff up.

Jen Taylor

Do you know what the two competing numbers are as far as how much fuel she had off the top of your head?

Brian Dunning

No. I don't have it in front of me, no.

Jen Taylor

So the official, *and I say "official"* report that said she had 1,100 or 1,150 gallons of fuel versus the alternate claim that she had 950 gallons of fuel, you're aware of that?

Brian Dunning

She didn't tell us how much fuel was left on board when she said she was low on fuel. So we don't know the exact number that was left on board. We know it was certainly not enough to reach any other land from there. Although, like I say, it's possible for anyone to make up anything they want that supports whatever alternate history they're pushing.

The one thing wrong with that idea is that suddenly, magically, she had a lot more fuel than she did. You can *claim* that, but if they were lost in the immediate vicinity of Howland as they reported, and as the *Itasca* crew was able to verify, why then wouldn't they say, "Okay, we're lost?"

Instead of continuing to search for this island that's in their imme-

271

diate vicinity, they're now going to fly to an island four hundred miles away that they can't navigate to because they're lost *right now*. They don't even know what direction to head, and they're *not* going to tell anyone. They're not going to tell the guys on the *Itasca*. It's physically impossible because of the fuel numbers, and it's strange credibility from every logical perspective.

Jen Taylor

Well, two things: My first question is not really a question, it's just a clarification. The official number that's in the report was that she had 1,100 or 1,150 gallons. This other number is actually a lower number, 950. That's where Buka comes in, because *that* theory says she had way *less* fuel, not *more fuel*.

Brian Dunning

You're talking about the turn around and go back theory?

Jen Taylor

Yes, the turn around and go back theory.

Brian Dunning

Okay, I thought you were talking about Nikumaroro.

Jen Taylor

Well, kind of, but yeah. That theory specifically really relies on that lesser fuel number.

Brian Dunning

Well, again, there's no reason to even investigate that, because we know that she *did make* it all the way. She was right there in radio communication with the *Itasca*, so why are we even bothering to have this conversation? It's absurd at face value.

Jen Taylor

Okay. Going back to the fuel number just briefly. That was in news articles around the time that she disappeared. I'm not clear on why you're classifying that as a number that's been made up? It might be a number that's inaccurate. I guess I need further clarification on where you're getting the idea that this is a number that somebody simply made up in order to support a certain theory. This is a number that was in news media articles at the time.

Brian Dunning

What I'm saying is that people make up facts to support their version of the story. I'm not making any specific claims about any specific numbers right now. As I said, I don't have them in front of me. If you want to talk about the numbers, then I would refer you to Coast Guard historians. They would be happy to testify here and discuss the specifics with you.

Jen Taylor

The best evidence that we have that Amelia Earhart crashed and sank near Howland Island is going to be the radio logs, which show that the *Itasca* was receiving transmissions from Amelia at a signal strength of S-5. Would you agree with that statement?

Brian Dunning

Not just the signal strength, but the entire radio conversation that was had.

Jen Taylor

The things that she was saying.

Brian Dunning

Yeah. This panned out exactly as planned and exactly as everyone expected it to. They went where they said they were going; we confirm that they got there. There are really no significant holes in what happened that day. That's why we don't really say, "Okay, maybe none of what happened that day was real. Maybe we were all imagining, and maybe one of these alternate histories happened." We just don't bother with stuff like that.

Jen Taylor

Is it possible that she was wrong and was giving the *Itasca* incorrect information?

Brian Dunning

Well, certainly within the bounds of the signal strength stream, we know that she was in the ballpark of where they *thought* they were. If you say that she was wrong, pick out a *specific* statement she made.

Sure, there's room for error, but the margin of uncertainty is relatively narrow, because they couldn't have been far away based on the signal strength and the clarity. The fact that they were able to have that voice communication.

Jen Taylor

One of the things that Buka relies on is this idea that there was a storm over Buka, and she was indicating that there was bad weather. The people who were on the *Itasca* and at Howland Island were reporting that there was *not* bad weather. There were some clouds, but there weren't any storms or anything like that.

You just said that we need to trust what she said. If she's saying,

"I'm flying through a storm," how do you reconcile that?

Brian Dunning

I don't say that we need to trust what she said as if we're relying strictly on trust because that's not the case. We're relying on physical evidence, i.e., the signal strength and the simple physical testable nature of radio communication in 1937.

Jen Taylor

Why would she say that she was flying through a storm if she didn't see bad weather?

Brian Dunning

I'm not able to speculate on that. I can't speculate as to what was in her mind. What I *can report* is the physical characteristics of what happened on that day.

Jen Taylor

If she's saying two things – "bad weather" and "I'm at a specific location" – one of those things is relying on her direct observation, and one of them is relying on the assistance of Fred Noonan and the calculations he's made.

Which do you think is *more* reliable, her observations about what she sees outside, or her observations about where she is based on Fred Noonan?

Brian Dunning

We know they at least arrived at the approximate area of where they were trying to go based on their navigation. There's no arguing that point; they were physically there at Howland, in the vicinity.

• • •

Jen Taylor

But no one *saw* them. They looked outside and didn't see them.

Brian Dunning

No, certainly you rarely see a plane unless it's very close. Because of the radio communication, there's no alternate explanation possible for *how* they could have been anywhere else.

Jen Taylor

Are you aware of claims that Amelia Earhart was flying through storms or bad weather that day?

Brian Dunning

I have heard those elements added to some of the alternate histories, yes.

Jen Taylor

If she was claiming that she saw bad weather, do you think that it's possible she was incorrect about that? Where is this claim coming from? Do you think it's inaccurate?

Brian Dunning

Well, certainly nothing like that came out of Amelia Earhart's mouth. What she *did report* earlier in the flight was that they had clouds and it was overcast, but there was no mention of storms, and we know that the weather was clear at Howland Island itself. Once they came into the daylight, they were past the overcast weather.

Jen Taylor

So it's just your belief that she didn't see storms, *not* that she did.

She absolutely didn't, and she never said that. That's your belief based on what you've read?

Brian Dunning

We know that the transcripts don't record her mentioning *anything* about storms, and we don't have any record from the navy or the Coast Guard regarding storms. Trying to stretch *clouds and overcast* into a storm is a bit of an exaggeration, I think.

Jen Taylor

When we're talking about things that come from Amelia, your point is she said she was close; the signal strength was very high, corroborating that. She never said anything about bad weather, which would be expected because Howland Island did not have bad weather.

That's your contention that this is what happened, and this is how we know?

Brian Dunning

It's not my contention, it's what the record shows.

Jen Taylor

Let's switch over to Nikumaroro Island. I know we talked about the post-loss signals a little bit off the record. Is it your belief that those didn't exist or didn't come from her?

Brian Dunning

It's the position of the Coast Guard and the navy that those signals had nothing to do with Amelia Earhart.

Signals like that are picked up all over the world all day every day, just random radio bits and snips, and people choose to interpret them however they wish. Obviously, the Nikumaroro Island people are selecting anything they think *might be* consistent with their version of what happened. They're trying to characterize the *post-loss signals*, as they're calling them, as being associated with Amelia Earhart, and there's no reason why anyone should think that.

Jen Taylor

Was there a female voice in the post-loss signals or not?

Brian Dunning

Again, when we're talking about Elvis sightings, we don't bother to spend a heck of a lot of time on them.

You can turn on *any* radio in the world and find a female voice, and you can ask anyone who believes *your version* of the story if they've heard of such reports, and they'll say *yes*.

These are anecdotal reports of unidentifiable radio transmissions that are *consistent* with random noise that we hear all day every day. They're *absolutely not* empirical evidence of anything.

Jen Taylor

Let's say a female pilot is missing and there's a signal coming in from a female voice indicating that she's injured or that she's been in a plane crash. You can understand why you should follow that evidence and verify whether it's true or not rather than just dismiss it offhand.

Brian Dunning

You're speaking about things that specifically, explicitly *are not* in the record. These transmissions were not recorded at the time. These are stories that were added *decades later* by people who were passionately seeking to promote and support an alternate history of events. These things are not part of the actual record of what took place on that day.

· · ·

Jen Taylor

So you're not aware, then, of Australia and New Guinea newspaper articles from 1937, during the search, containing reports of signals believed to be her? Whether they were or not, you're not aware of the fact that people were reporting this as early as July 1937?

Brian Dunning

People report things all the time. You have to remember Miss Earhart was literally the most famous person in the world, probably certainly the most famous *woman* in the world.

It's not unlike what happened with Tupac Shakur. Immediately, you're going to have all kinds of people throwing out, "Oh, this happened, that happened." None of these were recorded by the people who were actually doing the search and whose job it was to follow up on every piece of evidence no matter how small. That tells us that these were not part of the legitimate historical record of what took place.

Jen Taylor

I understand that people heard things but didn't see things. Do you think they *should have* followed up on these, as you call them, *anecdotal sightings*?

Brian Dunning

I'm not aware of anything that should have been followed up on that wasn't. The fact that they didn't record these tells us that there were no reliable reports made. Again, I go back to these being Elvis sightings. You're saying someone saw Elvis wearing a yellow shirt three days later. Shouldn't they have followed up on that? *No.*

Jen Taylor

When you say *reliable,* you mean reliable in the opinion of the Coast Guard and the people searching?

. . .

Brian Dunning

In the opinion of the entire body of the US Navy, the US Coast Guard, the Japanese Navy, pretty much everyone who was involved in the search.

Jen Taylor

Sometimes, having a healthy *distrust* of the government is okay. It's not always a *bad* thing to want the government to prove the claims that they are making. Would you agree with that statement?

Brian Dunning

The whole definition of skepticism is applying a higher standard of evidence, and that should be applied everywhere.

Jen Taylor

Even to the government, correct?

Brian Dunning

Certainly, to the government, to whoever it is.

Jen Taylor

I have no further questions, Your Honor.

"Everything just went against her, and that's what we usually find in these disasters. It's not one thing that causes the disaster, it's the sum of a lot of little things."

Chris Williamson

The project calls Tom Dettweiler to the stand.

Mr. Dettweiler, can you please tell the court what it is you specialize in?

Tom Dettweiler

Basically, I'm an operations expert. I have forty-five years of finding things that have been lost in the ocean and recovering them. I've done a lot of really tough projects, projects that other people have looked for and failed to find. So that's my expertise, *finding things*.

Chris Williamson

And so the court and the jury are aware, can you list some of the cases you've personally been involved in?

Tom Dettweiler

Probably the most well-known for the public is the *Titanic*. I was Dr. Ballard's operations director when we went and found *Titanic*, and I've led a couple of expeditions back to *Titanic*.

My personal favorite and most rewarding was finding the *Dakar*, which was the last Israeli submarine. The *I-52* as well, which was a lost Japanese submarine. There's been quite a number of other shipwrecks as well as other things people have lost on the bottom of the ocean.

Chris Williamson

How long have you been studying the Amelia Earhart case in particular?

Tom Dettweiler

We started really looking for Earhart in 2001. We were introduced to Elgen Long, and we listened to his case, and then we started doing our *own* research, putting together an area where we thought she might be. We decided in 2002 to conduct our first expedition to search part of that area.

Chris Williamson

When you were first introduced to this case on a professional level, had you had any previous thoughts or ideas on what might have happened on the morning of July 2, 1937, or did you come into this with an open train of thought?

Tom Dettweiler

I'd say probably a pretty open train of thought. I'd never studied Earhart in detail, but I'd heard all the theories, that she was still alive and that she'd been captured by the Japanese and everything else, but I really didn't put any stock into those. I thought it was quite likely that she was lost in the ocean someplace, but really hadn't put much investigation into where that might be.

Chris Williamson

You mentioned Elgen Long just now. When you spoke with him, what evidence did he present to you, and what evidence have you personally reviewed regarding the events of that morning?

Tom Dettweiler

Well, virtually all of it. I think the key is some of the other theories tend to cherry-pick their data, and what we've always done at Nauticos is put all the data together and then consider it as a whole, and let's see what falls out. We put together every hard piece of evidence that we could find; we had a group of radio guys who did extensive work with the radio signals, the strengths reported and those sorts of things. We did fuel analysis, just about everything we could think of, considering such a long passage of time had occurred, and much of the data hadn't been recorded in any great detail. We put that all together into one package and then started considering what that package meant. What results fell out of it naturally?

Chris Williamson

And the evidence that's contained within that package you just mentioned has obviously helped you form an opinion, correct?

Tom Dettweiler

Right. In my mind, she very clearly ran out of fuel, just as she told us, and she was short of the island for various reasons and was unable to find it.

Chris Williamson

Can you tell the court what you believe happened on the morning in question?

Tom Dettweiler

Well, first of all, she had a very tough route to fly. She was flying to a very small island out in the Pacific. It was the only island that was set up to receive her so she could continue on. So it's very important that she find that island. Weather reporting in between wasn't really good. She had weather from where she took off in New Guinea and question-

283

able weather in between. There were not a whole lot of landmarks that she could work with, so it was a tough and very long flight path. It was approaching the maximum range of the airplane, so she had to do it pretty much perfectly. When she took off from Lae, she was very heavy. She had a very defined flight plan that had been done for her by experts, and she unfortunately had to violate that flight plan very early on because of clouds and storms over Bougainville.

She had a headwind that was stronger than had been reported, and that was going against her the entire way. When she got out to the islands, there were some low-lying clouds that she had to fly below, which limited her visibility as she was approaching the island.

Navigation in those days was relatively limited; we didn't have the satellites and everything to aid in navigation in those days. She just simply got to the point where she thought the island was, she was starting to run low on fuel, and she couldn't understand why they weren't able to see the island. She started flying patterns that she thought would help her find it.

She took a potential sunline and then used that sunline to start flying a relatively north and south course back and forth, hoping that from her side of the airplane, she could see the island. She felt she should have been over it at that time. The Coast Guard ship *Itasca* was also making smoke, trying to help her see the island, but at the time, because of weather conditions, there's photographic evidence that shows that the smoke was just kind of not rising very high but instead just dropping back to the surface. So she may not have been able to see that.

Everything just went against her, and that's what we usually find in these disasters. It's not *one thing* that causes the disaster, it's the sum of a lot of little things.

Chris Williamson

One of the aspects of that morning and that situation that most everyone seems to agree on is how difficult Howland Island would have been for Earhart and Noonan to see. Can you explain what they were up against when it came to spotting Howland?

Tom Dettweiler

Yeah, well, one thing is she was flying *into* the sun. It was rising in her face, so that would have made it much more difficult to see the island. Just the fact that there's no elevation in the island whatsoever; it's very, very flat. There are no landmarks on the island, there's no buildings, there's nothing like that, and the ship was sitting just beyond the islands. So there was very little in the way that would have caused contrast with the sky under those conditions.

Chris Williamson

Another area of contention is the fact that Amelia dropped the Electra to an altitude of one thousand feet, which would have put her *below* the reported cloud cover that morning. Can you talk about why she might have done that?

Tom Dettweiler

She really had no choice; there was a cloud layer. She wouldn't be able to see through the clouds unless she just happened to fly over a hole at the time that was right over the island.

So she felt her best option was to be *below* that cloud layer, cross over the island, and at some point, be beneath that cloud layer.

Chris Williamson

Mr. Dettweiler, can you tell the court what a *pancake landing* is, please?

Tom Dettweiler

A pancake landing is really a controlled crash. A plane is not meant to really pancake; it's meant to land on wheels and roll. When you pancake, you simply try to flare the airplane so that you're putting the maximum flat surface down on the water as gently as you can, and hope that it skids for a while on its belly to lose speed, as opposed to rolling on the wheels. The plane is not made to do that. It takes a lot of skill from the pilot to be able to do it. In the case of the Lockheed Electra, it's a very nose-heavy airplane. That would tend to limit its ability to be able to successfully pancake.

Chris Williamson

Now once the plane hits the water, does it sink right away? Does it float for any period of time?

Tom Dettweiler

It would probably float for a little bit of time. It would probably start collecting water in the nose and eventually go down that way. It's not going to float for a very long time, we don't think. It didn't float very far *horizontally* before it started its downward spiral.

Chris Williamson

Mr. Dettweiler, in your expert professional opinion, is this a recoverable aircraft?

Tom Dettweiler

It probably is.

You've got to remember; airplanes are built *very* strong. They're lightweight, but they're very strong. It was built out of materials that were purposely picked to try to limit corrosion. In the deep ocean, a lot of the corrosion factors are not in heavy concentration, so you don't have a lot of oxygen. You have *cold* temperatures, and that tends to slow corrosion. It probably *is* in pretty good shape and probably recoverable. You would have to be prepared to deal with the fact that corrosion would occur at a very accelerated rate once you picked it up and exposed it to oxygen again, so you'd have to have a way of either submerging it again or keeping it wet to allow for restoration as quickly as possible.

Initially picking it up, I think, would be probable.

Chris Williamson

You've been studying this a long time now, and your credentials are impeccable. Your opinion carries a lot of weight in the scientific communities. What is it about this theory in particular that makes you *so* confident that it is the most *probable* cause for the vanishing of Amelia Earhart and Fred Noonan?

Tom Dettweiler

I think we have to *believe Amelia.*

She wouldn't have been making up those last conversations for any reason. She was *telling us* what was happening; she was over the island. According to her navigation, she couldn't understand why she *wasn't* seeing it, and she was running low on fuel. The question lies in that she didn't give us a whole lot of detail about what she did at that point. We have to make some guesses as to what maneuvers she was flying and those sorts of things. She gave us a little bit of detail, but not quite enough. We have to believe what she said, and that's exactly what she told us. The other thing is the hard evidence. It corresponds with the fuel analysis, and it was happening exactly when we thought it should happen. The radio analysis, you know, you can't argue with that unless the Coast Guard guys were making up their data. They were recording a scenario of increasing signal strength, which can only conclude she was approaching the island. They thought she was very close.

All the hard evidence, and everything that's known for certain, all add up to this one scenario.

Chris Williamson

Thank you, Mr. Dettweiler. Pass the witness.

Cross-Examination of Tom Dettweiler

Jen Taylor

Mr. Dettweiler, earlier you gave the court an opinion about what happened to Amelia Earhart. You believe that she crashed near the vicinity of Howland Island, is that correct?

Tom Dettweiler

Right. We've literally recreated the entire flight from the time that she left Lae, New Guinea, up until the time she was making the radio broadcasts to *Itasca*, as she was approaching Howland Island. We've tried to recreate the winds and what effects they had.

We did a fuel study on how long that plane could fly on the fuel load that it had. What was available for her should she have an emergency? The most compelling was the radio signal strengths recorded by the *Itasca*, which fit the scenario of her approaching the island and running out of fuel *exactly* when she said she was running out of fuel and not being able to find the island because she was obviously in the wrong position.

Jen Taylor

Say I'm at the *Itasca* and I'm receiving a signal from Amelia Earhart. How am I able to figure out what that signal strength is? I know that there's various classifications. I don't think we went over this in direct, so can you just explain to the jury what the different classifications of signal strengths are?

Tom Dettweiler

Yes, on a modern radio you have a meter that gives you a signal strength of 1 through 5.

In those days on the *Itasca*, they did not have a meter like that, so it was based on the operator's subjective evaluation. We actually have run tests with a large number of operators to see if they were in agreement, and as experienced operators, they do agree with each other on what a representative signal strength is. It's based on how understandable and how intelligible the broadcast is, how loud the broadcast is, how easily it's separated from the background noise, that sort of thing. So, there's a lot of factors that go into it, but it's all based on the experience of the operator themselves. *They* [the *Itasca* radio room] wrote that down in their logbook, so it *is* a bit subjective, but they recorded on numerous levels as she was coming in, and it fits the scenario of her flying toward the island.

Jen Taylor

Are there any other environmental factors that could affect signal strength? Like say, if the weather was bad that day, or if she was flying through a thunderstorm or anything else? What kind of environmental factors might affect the signal strength?

Tom Dettweiler

Unfortunately, a number of environmental factors could influence the signal strength. The cloud level as an example, the low cloud layer can bounce signals that can travel farther and seem louder potentially than they really are. We've tried to recreate all those kinds of scenarios with different weather conditions, different vehicles, different ground planes, which is a technical term for the radios, to come up with parameter limits. What's the least range that the weather could have an impact? What's the farthest range it could have an impact? That sort of thing.

Jen Taylor

And based on all of that, even if it's only slightly possible, do you think that it *is* possible for an S-5 signal strength to be received by the *Itasca* if she wasn't within the distance that she was saying she was? In other words, is it possible for her to have been *somewhere else* yet somehow still receive an S-5 signal strength?

. . .

Tom Dettweiler

With the frequencies that she was using, there's only a limited range or window that signal can fall in and *still be* recorded as an S-5. At the time she made that broadcast, she was within that window of range, so she was close. Now what we're *missing* is, she didn't give us a whole lot of information about what her last moments were. We only know that she was running low on fuel, we know that she was making some maneuvers to try to improve her chances of seeing the island, but we don't know what happened beyond that.

So *it is* possible that she turned and flew away from the island. We don't know.

Jen Taylor

Okay. The two alternate theories for what happened to her involve turning around and going somewhere else because she was running low on fuel. That would be the Buka theory, which says that she turned around, went back to Buka and landed there. The other one would be the castaway theory, where she ended up on Nikumaroro Island and was a castaway there for a while. Do you think either of those are a possible final resting place for her plane based on the evidence that you've seen?

Tom Dettweiler

I will never say *anything is impossible.*

I've been surprised numerous times in the ocean. I *won't say* that, but it's very unlikely.

Buka is a very long way away. She definitely would not have had enough fuel to get back there had she been in the vicinity of Howland Island when she made that decision.

Nikumaroro Island is unlikely because the only island out there that was set up to receive her was Howland Island. She had to get there if she was to survive. Anywhere else, there was a very good chance that she would not survive the landing or the long stay before anybody found her. So it's unlikely that she would have made that decision to go somewhere else with the low amount of fuel that she had.

She would have instead, we believe, done everything within her power to improve her chances of finding Howland Island.

Jen Taylor

I know there have been a number of what we call post-loss signals. Are you aware of those? Do you know what I'm talking about?

Tom Dettweiler

Yes.

Jen Taylor

Part of the hypothesis that she ended up on Nikumaroro Island relies on these signals. Do you have an opinion as to whether those signals came from Amelia Earhart?

Tom Dettweiler

I firmly believe that they did not. None of those have ever been verified. The chances are that if she put the airplane down *any place*, it would not have been possible to send those signals because the airplane had to be running in order to do so. So it's very unlikely that she would have been able to do that. In *numerous* modern events and disasters, we have had repeats of false radio messages being sent. It's very, very common. Most people don't know that. It's a strange quirk of human nature that there are some people who get their kicks literally by sending a false radio broadcast out, pretending that they're somebody they aren't. It's unfortunate, because it sends searchers in the wrong direction.

Jen Taylor

I understand that your opinion is that these *did not* come from Amelia Earhart. For the sake of a hypothetical, if we put that aside, and she had somehow managed to keep her plane intact enough to send out those signals, what tools are available to try to figure out where those signals are coming from? How would that work?

Tom Dettweiler

There really aren't any tools anymore, because not enough information was recorded about the radio signals to utilize it for recreation of where they might have come from.

We're really only dependent on the information that people recorded and said they heard.

Jen Taylor

So we don't have any information about say, for example, the signal strength of those signals, because they were being picked up by ham radio operators?

Tom Dettweiler

Yeah, in most cases, they would have been radio signals that had already gone through several skips and that sort of thing to make that distance.

Jen Taylor

And for people who don't understand the term *skip*, that just refers to the environmental factors that we talked about earlier that might affect signal strength?

Tom Dettweiler

Skip is essentially a radio signal not following a direct path, but actually bouncing several times. With each of those bounces, the accuracy of being able to pinpoint where that signal came from decreases.

Jen Taylor

Okay, I want to swing back to Buka for a minute. Doing a little bit of research, I came across an article in 2012, when at the time, there was a lot of buzz regarding Secretary of State Hillary Clinton and searching for the plane in a location *other* than Howland Island. Do you think this means Dr. Ballard subscribes to the theory that the plane might be on Nikumaroro Island?

Tom Dettweiler

I think Ric Gillespie literally cornered them and presented his case, and you know, he can make a *very compelling case*. I think based on that being the only evidence they had, they said, "Yeah, it sounds plausible."

Jen Taylor

There is a lot of evidence out there for him to go look at regarding the official explanation.

That's what our government has told us. "This is what happened; she crashed near Howland Island." Do you think he just maybe isn't *aware* of all that other stuff? I guess I'm trying to understand why he's appeared to have jumped on that bandwagon?

Tom Dettweiler

I think at that point in 2012, he just hadn't done complete research of what evidence was available. He was basing that on what he had heard from Ric Gillespie, I'm sure.

Jen Taylor

Do you know if he still subscribes to this theory now?

Tom Dettweiler

No, I don't know.

Jen Taylor

You haven't spoken with him about it?

Tom Dettweiler

No.

Jen Taylor

Is there anything that we *haven't* talked about that you think is important? Anything we should address in front of the jury in terms of evidence for this or any other theory that you want people to know?

Tom Dettweiler

My company Nauticos that I worked for, their specialty was doing what we call "re-navigation." Re-navigation is based on taking all of the evidence, weighing each little piece of evidence based on how reliable it is, putting it all together, and seeing what comes out of that whole pile of evidence. I think most of the other theories pick and choose which evidence they want to use, and you really can't do that. You have to consider everything and then see where that points you, and sometimes it's quite different from where you might think it is based on just your gut or a few pieces of evidence that your brain may be considering. That is what we've done; we've tried to continually improve that data set.

Even to this day, we are still doing research and adding to that data set, and we still keep coming up with basically the same conclusion.

· · ·

Jen Taylor

Earlier we talked about Buka and Nikumaroro. I know you're aware that there's *another theory* that she ended up in the Marshall Islands and was kidnapped by the Japanese. A lot of people saw her on Saipan. When you say, "We're looking at all of the evidence and all of the data," does that *include* these eyewitness statements and these videos that supposedly are out there showing items that belonged to her? Are these things that you took a serious look at when you were trying to determine where she might be?

Tom Dettweiler

It does. We have run the re-navigation algorithm on all the other different theories to see if they were *even plausible,* and all of them have maybe a very *slight* probability. They're not impossible, but the primary result always ends up pointing towards Howland Island and crashing in the ocean. It's very unlikely that she would have done any of those other things. You have to consider that she *did* have enough fuel to get to any of these places. In most cases she didn't. If you go back and you *really read* the eyewitness accounts, they don't say they *saw Amelia Earhart.* They say they saw a *Caucasian woman,* or they saw a *tall Caucasian man.* I'm sure there were lots of incidences of that during wartime.

Jen Taylor

That's going to be one of the major issues in this case once we get to that theory. In 1937 Japan, how common is it for a white woman traveling with a white man to be there? This was Saipan, so we weren't in wartime yet. We were on the brink of war. Do you have an opinion on how *likely* it would have been that they would have seen somebody who was Caucasian who was *not them?*

· · ·

295

Tom Dettweiler

You have to remember that at this time period, there was lots of missionary work out in the islands, and that would have run against what the Japanese effort *was* there. It is quite possible that they would have taken those people as prisoners just to eliminate that missionary effort.

Jen Taylor

I understand your opinion is that Howland Island is most likely where the plane is. But between Buka, Nikumaroro and the Marshall Islands, do you think that any of those three would be more likely than the other two? Or do you think they're all equally unlikely? In the unlikely event that you're wrong about Howland Island, where would you look next?

Tom Dettweiler

Again, the probabilities are so slight. I've talked to Bill Snavely about Buka. I want to think that he will be able to prove that the airplane at Buka is Amelia's. I've told him that then we have a bigger problem, and that's trying to explain how it *got there.* The evidence doesn't support it being able to get there. That might even be another scenario where she was captured, and the Japanese took the airplane there to dispose of it. That's very, very unlikely, but I'm not ruling it out. Nothing is impossible, but the probabilities on comparing all of the evidence just keep pointing back to the fact that she fell short of Howland Island.

There is no reason *not to* believe what Amelia was telling us, and that is that she was where she thought the island was. They're not seeing the island, and they're running low on fuel.

There's no reason to believe that she did anything different. She would not have falsely broadcast that bit of information.

Jen Taylor

Is it possible that she was *incorrect* about where she was? I understand that navigational errors are possible. How likely is it that a navigational error, if any, would have been *so* great that she was way off regarding where she was? Do you think that's possible?

Tom Dettweiler

It's very, very unlikely because Noonan was a good navigator. He was the person who was recruited from marine duty because he was *such* a good navigator, they wanted him to teach the Pan Am pilots how to navigate across the oceans. He certainly knew how to navigate, and there's no evidence in any of the other legs on the flight, despite having run into even more severe conditions, that he was not able to navigate. It's very, very *unlikely* that they would have been *so far off* that they would have ended up on some other island.

Jen Taylor

What about Snavely's observation that the things she was saying were simply misinterpreted and that in fact she had already turned around? His theory is that she said she was turning around, but that part maybe wasn't heard. Everything *else* that she said later has to be listened to through the lens of her thinking that everybody understands she's going towards Buka. When she says "I must be on you but cannot see you. I'm two hundred miles away. I'm one hundred miles away," she's *actually really* talking about Buka. Do you think that that holds water at all?

Tom Dettweiler

We do what's called a *nodal analysis* where each time she gets to a decision node, and she has to make a decision, we try to list all of the different decisions she might make and then evaluate how likely those different decisions are. That would take into account that something was misinterpreted.

We've tried to go back over the records extensively to make *sure* that we have exactly the right wording. We tried to get verification of that from other operators who were present.

Elgen Long interviewed literally everybody who was involved in this *firsthand* prior to those people passing away, and we have all those tapes to listen to. We think that we've come up with the *best* interpretation, and again, it comes down to the fact that if *she did* get all the way to Howland Island, she did not have enough fuel to turn around and fly back to Buka.

Jen Taylor

Thank you, no further questions, Your Honor.

"When we first got the team together, we looked at the data, and I think it was Rod who first said, 'This can't be done.' Well, what do you mean it can't be done? 'The data is too qualitative.' Engineers like quantitative data. So I said, 'Okay, that's it? You want me to go back to Nauticos and say it's impossible?'"

Chris Williamson

Your Honor, the project calls Mr. Tom Vinson to the stand.

Mr. Vinson, can you please tell the court a little about your professional background and your specialty?

Tom Vinson

I worked for Rockwell Collins. I started in 1974 in engineering and operations and then moved into program management. We were working in high-frequency communications, putting airborne communications into military aircraft, mostly for the US Air Force. Most of my career was in government systems, where we were installing all sorts of situational-awareness datalinks, satcom and high-frequency communications, which the Earhart problem is all about. High-frequency communications. I spent thirty-five years at Rockwell Collins and retired. I still teach some of their program management.

Chris Williamson

I'd like for you to tell the court how you were pulled into the Earhart/Noonan investigation in a professional manner and tell us a little about the team you put together to look into the data and investigate this case.

Tom Vinson

I really didn't get into it until I got a phone call in October of 1998. We were Rockwell International at that time. I got that phone call, and it was actually from my vice president general manager, Bob Chiusano. He calls and asks, "Would you mind looking at the Amelia Earhart flight scenario and their HF communications?" "Oh yeah, sure, we could take a look at that; who's doing this?" And he said, "Well, there's a company called Nauticos that reached out to Collins." Collins had been well known in airborne communications and avionics system solutions since 1933. They're world renowned in avionics communication navigation solutions for modern aircraft.

My first question was, "I wonder if we ought to pull a team together." I was president of the Collins amateur radio club at the time, so we got together a team of radio amateurs from the club, but they were by no means amateur. We're all radio amateur hobbyists. These guys whom we worked with over there are just experts in their fields. They're world-class engineers. A couple of the team that we called out on this are Rockwell engineers of the year recipients.

The first person I called on my list was Rod Blocksome. Rod is a senior system engineer in high-frequency communications. We brought in our chief corporate pilot Larry Brown; Dan Resler, he's an HF propagation expert. That's what he did for his living. We got into military projects where that was very important. Charlie Snodgrass was a navigator on C-130 using bubble octants. We had Don Grim, another engineer of the year recipient; he was currently in software development and autopilots' safety NTSB, those kinds of projects. Overall, just a brilliant engineer who's still on the project.

Brian McCoy, who is kind of MacGyver. When we got into having to do things like run antenna setups and receive sites and things like that, he would pull these things together and rig things up for us. Tom Hefner, a mathematician statistician whom we needed to bring in for some heavy mathematics on the problem. Roger Hatcher performed antenna and computer modeling for what we call *NEC pro*; he worked on the antenna modeling for her aircraft antenna, trying to figure out what that thing looks like. So that was our initial team, and we called in other engineers and scientists as we needed who were also hams.

Everywhere we went, we had to draw upon people who were really willing to help. We were given this task to look at her high-frequency radio communications, and that three hours turned into over *three thousand hours* of engineering work. Never in my wildest dreams would I have ever thought that eighteen years later, I'd still be working on the project and helping to see if we can find the lady.

Chris Williamson

Mr. Vinson, I'm a logical thinker. This is eighty-five-year-old wreckage sitting at approximately eighteen thousand feet below the surface of the water in the middle of the biggest ocean on the planet.

Was this something you believed to be *possible* at the time you were asked to look into it?

Why did it intrigue you so much?

Tom Vinson

When we first got together, Nauticos provided the data to us. We had this stack of research that we had to work through, and that would be the task. The ship logs, radio logs, the type of equipment that was on the *Itasca*, and the configuration. That *does* take a little while to figure out.

How is that thing configured, *really*?

For the *Itasca*, what kind of receiving antennas or transmitting antennas did they have; did they add the slopers? What kind of power were they running? There's all kinds of data.

When we got into it, we looked at the ship logs, and what's kind of funny is that these were radio operators on the *Itasca*, for the Coast Guard. They're sitting there typing on what they call *mills*. They're a typewriter, but they're all capitals, and they're typing out what she's saying, the date and time, that kind of thing. They're typing in radio operators' shorthand. What was kind of funny is that it was just second nature for us to read that.

People who are *not* radio amateurs would read it and go, "What's all that?" For example, it would say QSA3, QSA4 or 5. Well, in the Q signals of radio amateur speak, those are signal strengths. As she got closer and closer to the island it went 2, 3, 4, 5. When we first got the team together, we looked at the data, and I think it was Rod who first said, "This can't be done." What do you mean *it can't* be done? Well, the data is too *qualitative*. Engineers like *quantitative* data. So I said, "Okay, that's it? You want me to go back to Nauticos and say it's impossible?" And they just froze; everybody just sat there.

Finally, they said, "Wait a minute; let's take another look at it." Then the attitude changed because it isn't like we *don't know* anything about the radio. We *do know* it's a 50-watt AM radio. We *do know* what the manufacturer is, and we can get that schematic. We know what the antenna is. We know what power levels are running. If it's impossible, what more resources and data would we need to *make it* possible? What are the things that have holes in them, and how could we quantify whether those holes are in the optical modeling or the software modeling? Do we need an actual field test run in real time by flying an airplane at one thousand feet, running the power, measuring the signal strength over salt water, all those things?

Well, we did that down in Melbourne, Florida. Understanding all of that, what you find is that with a group of engineers who are aviation, electronics, and communication experts, it's like waving raw meat in front of sharks. I think you just get hooked. It's a mystery, and you don't think about it. When we started getting into it, you kind of get to know who this woman was and what she stood for. What the surroundings of the culture were at that time. She goes across the ocean, and they have ticker-tape parades down in New York, and she's doing her own fashion line, luggage promotions and all these things. She's teaching as an adjunct professor at Purdue. All these things are going on, and you start to realize that *yes*, there's a mystery there.

It's the last great mystery of the twentieth century.

She is a *part of our Americana.*

She *is* our history and part of the fabric and being of what it's like in America as a culture of Americans, pushing those boundaries.

Chris Williamson

A lot of the work that your team has done has been based on a foundation of replication of the original scenario and the events of July

2, 1937. How important is it for the investigation and the results of that investigation to replicate as much of the original events as possible?

Tom Vinson

We think it's extremely important to get as close to the original as we can. Of course, that's very difficult to do. Even now, Chris, asking "Golly, can we get an L-10 or Beech 18 and get as close to the original configuration as we can?" Can we get the data regarding Noonan and how he navigated and what she was saying when she was flying? What did the signal strength tell us about how far away she was? All that data led us to say, "Oh yeah, she was around Howland Island." She was looking for the island. She wasn't hundreds and hundreds of miles away in the Marshalls or three more hours away down at Niku. That's why we're crash and sink. If it would have led to her being three hundred miles away with a signal strength at 8:43 in the morning, then we'd think differently. There was no decreasing out with those last three transmissions.

They were *all* S-5.

Leo Bellarts stated earlier that she was so loud he stepped outside and looked up, expecting her to fly through the rigging. With the errors they had in their instruments in 1937, and the accuracy of Fred Noonan's navigation, you could be at the end of his navigation solution, where he should be at the island because he could never get the bearing. They were always asking for the bearing to the ship or trying to take a bearing.

That was also another problem. She says, "We must be on you but cannot see you; gas is running low." Well, "we must be on you" is the end of his navigation solution, right? "We must be on you but cannot see you" is outside visual range. You have to do certain *other* actions. You're done, because you've done everything, and all you have is that sun shot for the line of position. That's what's tragic is that when Leo Bellarts was saying, "She was so loud, she's flying through the rigging," he was expecting to see the plane.

Chris Williamson

One of the most crucial pieces of data that Rockwell Collins has used are the Pan Am manuals, which are largely influenced by Fred Noonan. Can you tell the court how those manuals have assisted you in your investigation, and can you talk a little about Fred Noonan's navigation that morning?

Tom Vinson

Fred Noonan was basically *the guy* for Pan Am to open up the Pan Am Clipper navigation routes across the Pacific. His development of island fall navigation and his techniques are in essence what are in these manuals, as he was the training guy. He was the one who was setting the standard.

People will say, "Oh, he wasn't that good."

I just don't understand that.

I know there's rumors that maybe he had a drinking problem, but you know, you look at Lae, New Guinea, that morning on that video, and you see Fred Noonan jump up on that wing to help Amelia. He wasn't hungover. He was sharp *then*. Now, how sharp was he after twenty hours of flying in that eggbeater? With pilot fatigue and decision-making, that is very difficult navigation when you're crossing the equator, and you're crossing the dateline.

You have sign changes going on in the mathematics there. He could miss one sign and be off.

The radio signal strength will convince you that he was smack there, man. He was *there*.

He was taking the sunlight because Amelia said she was on the line of position 157/337.

Of course that's what he would do, he would take a sun shot, and we think that's probably what happened. She transmitted and said, "Two hundred miles out." Thirty minutes later, she says, "About one hundred miles out." Well, they're not traveling at two hundred miles an hour, so what happened?

Well, the sun was in between there, and Fred Noonan is able to get a good sun shot, which determines your east/west position, plus or minus. He thinks he could do it plus or minus five miles. He knows what he's doing, and he probably had it plotted. He would have been able to shoot the sun and understand plus or minus to that.

Chris Williamson

Mr. Vinson, it's been eighty-five years. Is the optimism still there for you? Is the question not *if* but *when* we'll find this wreckage?

Tom Vinson

That's a great question. Of course, we're still optimistic. It's a *big* ocean. Even if you have an area of several thousand square miles, that's a lot to do. When you have to do a towed array, you're only moving at two knots. So, you know, you can *walk that fast*. The signal strength, the data and the research lead us towards the idea that the airplane was close.

They were around Howland Island, so they say, "Well, now, since you've said that, you've come up with this area that wasn't in that area. Now what do you do?" Well, we were actually *one of four* independent analyses, and we didn't know this at the time, by the way. There were *three other groups* that were analyzing the problem different ways, using different methods. When we got together, finally, to say here's our output from our project, they came up with their plots, and we came up with our plots. You can basically draw a line around the perimeter of all those four. So it's not like the data led you off elsewhere. This is a big area, so then you have to go down a decision tree.

We've created a decision tree matrix. When we add our pilots and navigators together and ask, "Okay, here's the first decision point, what would you do?" What would *they* most likely do? It may not be the same. So you kind of work through those, and we had these wonderful conversations about what they would do. As you go down through that decision tree, you've come up with, "This is my probability. These decisions put us over here." Well, now, if that area is discounted, that's good information. *That's* good data. So what we're saying now is we go back to the decision tree, make refinements, take out the area that's been searched where we're 99.5% sure it's *not*, and say, "Okay, they must have made a different decision here." Then we go off on *that route* and see where that leads.

You get to a point at the end game where, if she's chasing cloud shadows, how do you know what they did then, right? You have to kind of stick with Fred Noonan and how he navigated. They're navigating smartly and still thinking rationally. When you get down to it, do we think we'll find it? Yeah, you know, I think it'll be found. That airplane is out there, and it's a big ocean.

Chris Williamson

Thank you, Mr. Vinson. Pass the witness.

Cross-Examination of Tom Vinson

Jen Taylor

Mr. Vinson, earlier I heard you saying that over at Nauticos, you guys conducted a little experiment. From what I understand, this was an attempt to verify the signal strength of what are believed to be Amelia's last transmissions to the *Itasca*. Did I understand that correctly?

Tom Vinson

Well, it started out to be a little experiment, but it ended up being over three thousand hours of actual engineering work, modeling simulations, and field trials.

Jen Taylor

Okay. And can you just summarize in a few sentences what you guys found out at the conclusion of that work?

Tom Vinson

Okay, well, there were two aspects of it:

One is to come up with basically a back calculation on the signal strengths S-2, 3, 4, and 5.

The signal strength is getting stronger and stronger as the aircraft moves towards Howland Island and the *Itasca*. With the modeling, simulation, and field experiments that we did, we're quantifying, not range rings, but range donuts with a distribution along that for S-2, 3, 4, and 5. The conclusion from that data just on the signal strengths will lead us to surmise that during her last transmission at 8:43 a.m., she was close. She got close to Howland Island and, of course, never showed up. While I'm not at liberty, of course, to say what the actual results were, the data all points to her being within one hundred nautical miles of Howland Island, certainly.

The second aspect of it was trying to get into Fred Noonan's training manuals for navigators and how he navigated. Researching the Pan American archives for his navigation methodology, if you will, and the training manuals that Pan American airways had for their navigators that Fred Noonan authored and created for the students. With that, we try to come up with a bearing. So you have *range* and *bearing*. At the end of that, we came up with a *most likely* or *highest probability* area. The whole reason for that is that Nauticos wanted to try to narrow down search areas, because it's very expensive to go out there. You want to be the most efficient with the dollars that you have on any expedition. So that's kind of the conclusion. Coming up with an area. We were just concentrating mainly on the signal strength communications and our HF communications and then the navigation part of it. Comms and navs.

Jen Taylor

When you're doing this, I'm assuming you're starting with the data from the *Itasca* logs that say, "This is what she was saying, and this is the signal strength that she was coming in at." Is that what you're starting with?

Tom Vinson

That's some of the foreground data, sure. There's background *and* foreground data that was given to us. The *Itasca* logs, the historical data, the type of equipment that was on the aircraft, the types of HF communications equipment that was on the *Itasca* – all of that was basic data that we had to start with.

Our original conclusion from that data was that we needed *additional* data if we were going to come up with a range for each one of those signal strengths. We need to make it more quantitative to come against that. You actually have real data, meaning quantifiable data. That set us off on a whole other track of design of experiments. Working with the type of transmitter she had, the kind of power output, the type of antenna that she was using, and what kind of radiated power she'd have from it. What would the decrease in signal strength be over salt water at one thousand feet versus distance? All of those things go into making design of experiments that would gather data, and then *from that* data, see where it takes us; basically, see where it leads to.

Jen Taylor

Okay, and the end result you're looking for is a location or an area of possible locations that she could be. That's the end goal of doing something like this.

Tom Vinson

Right, a high, higher, highest probability area. Try to narrow that down to a couple of thousand square miles.

Jen Taylor

Does a study like this assume that the data is correct? In other words, if say the signal strengths, for example, were incorrect, would that change the end result significantly?

Would you have to assume that the signal strengths were recorded correctly at the time in order to be able to rely on the end result?

Tom Vinson

Sure. Well, that's a good question.

The validity of your initial data would always affect outcomes Having said that, you have chief radio operator there, Leo Bellarts, and these trained radiomen who are on the *Itasca*.

They do that every day; they're communicating *every* day. There are definitions for each signal strength S-1, 2, 3, 4, and 5. So they're trained when they have these signals to be able to ascertain pretty closely what those signals are. That's where they put QSA2 or S-3 or 4 or 5 as she got closer. We have to assume that based on the definitions of each one of those, that's how they were trained in the Coast Guard.

That is, they were trained radio operators, and they were probably pretty correct.

Jen Taylor

Okay. So I think for the most part, most of us by now understand that it was on a scale of 1 through 5 with S-5 being the best signal strength and S-1 being the lowest signal strength. But can you break it down for us a little bit more? What's the difference between, say, an S-4 and an S-5 or an S-3 in an S-4? When Bellarts says it was an S-5, what does that *actually* mean?

Tom Vinson

Well, that's another good question.

There are definitions for each one of those. The main thing you really notice is there's this whole thing called "signal to noise." As a signal gets stronger and stronger, you can hear the presence of the signal *actually* getting stronger. If I'm talking louder, you'll see that it's getting stronger.

When you're at an S-1 or S-2, you're coming up out of the noise from a distance, and the noise drops off. So these operators know. You used to hear them say on TV shows, "You're loud and clear."

Well, once she gets to S-5, there's no background noise; it's all good audio. You might hear the prop noise, but not the atmospheric or basic radio noise. It's all very clear audio. That was the point where Leo Bellarts in an interview in 1974 said that she was *so* loud that he looked out the hatch, expecting her to fly through the rigging. So he was expecting to see her. That's pretty impressive knowing what I know *now* about the radio and the antenna and the power levels.

Jen Taylor

Is there anything, either environmental factors or anything else, that could have made a signal *sound* like an S-5 when in fact it shouldn't have been? Is there any reason why Bellarts would have been getting an S-5 even though she wasn't as close as she should have been?

Tom Vinson

They're hearing what they're hearing. That's an actual signal. It's an actual high-frequency radio signal. If it's *that* loud, it's not a thousand miles away or even four or five hundred miles away.

When it's an S-5, it's in the vicinity.

Jen Taylor

Okay. So you started out with these transmissions, all of them recorded as S-5 signals.

You started with that, and you guys conducted this study with this, among other data. I know I'm probably very much oversimplifying it, but you arrive at what you believe is a good location. I understand that this was done by Nauticos. I understand that probably a lot of it is confidential. Does that mean that the *actual study* itself and the actual math and engineering involved has not been looked at by anybody *other* than Nauticos?

Tom Vinson

Yes, good question.

You know, we're a group of engineers and scientists from Rockwell Collins. So even in our design methodology, we would have non-advocate reviews, intermittent design reviews and what have you. That's the same kind of process we had as we went along. As we generated the analysis and design of experiments and reports, we had other eyes looking at each one of those reports and challenging them. One of them was a professor of electrical engineering from Delaware as well as other people. We know a lot of electrical engineering people from Iowa State since we're *in* Iowa. Some of the other universities there looked it over. So far, there's been over twenty reports written about various aspects of the problem. It's a huge and complex problem. The non-advocacy was a very key point. To have other people looking at it and surmising, including pilots, navigators, engineers, and other technical people was important.

Jen Taylor

Were each one of these groups looking at everything that you did? Or did one look at *one aspect* and someone else look at *another aspect*, if that makes sense?

Tom Vinson

Yeah, I guess it'd be like if someone went to ask you to review a book they were offering, and you had certain expertise in your abilities, but you read the *whole* book, and then made comments against it.

That's kind of the way the process worked. They would go through it, and if something didn't *sound* right, or if a methodology might have been improperly set up, they'd ask us, "Well, did you think about this, or did you think about that aspect of it?" People would often noodle on it and change the design of the experiment or retest based on those comments.

Jen Taylor

All of these people who were helping out and giving feedback, did they *know* that you were working on Amelia Earhart? How much information did they have?

Tom Vinson

Well, they knew what the project was; it's pretty hard *not* to.

. . .

Jen Taylor

On the subject of Amelia Earhart's transmissions, there were, as I'm sure you're aware, claims made that there were possibly post-loss signals. Some people believe they were hearing Amelia and Fred Noonan after they had disappeared. Have you heard of those claims?

Tom Vinson

Yeah, I mean, the post-loss thing…after she went missing, there's nothing else recorded from the *Itasca*, but there *were* a lot of comms going on. The navy was out there with many ships, and there's a lot of communication happening. So, you know, people were listening.

Of course, people have shortwave receivers. When up-close things were going on during the search, one of the hams said he'd hoaxed it. We hear that on the air, even today, when you have a group out on a rare island that people want to work, they'll get on and actually *pretend* like they're that station. You're not *really* talking to that station or hearing the real station.

We call those *pirates.*

Amateurs, by the way, *were involved* in this whole project when she was flying west from California initially. They set up communication with radio amateurs who would be on a link and on nets to be able to follow her around as part of her safety margin. When she decided all of a sudden to go *east*, many of those people were disgruntled about all that was going on. If you look at some of the things that she was saying, there's no content to them. If you put yourself in someone's position after that, they would be saying, "Yeah, you know, we flew south, or we did this," or what have you. There's just nothing there content wise, position wise, or anything like that. So we don't give much credence at all to the post-loss. Same with Betty's notebook.

I, along with thousands and thousands of radio amateurs, operate on what's called the "80 meter band." That's three and a half megahertz, and *she was on* 3.1, 3105 kilohertz. That's 33.1 megahertz. With her running a 50-watt AM transmitter into an eleven-foot piece of wire on top of her aircraft, two and a half hours *after* sunrise, there is just no possible way that Betty was hearing her transmitting on 3105 at 08:43 in the morning *Itasca* time.

It's eight hours later over in Florida. It's in the afternoon in Florida. Once that sun comes up, there's a D-layer of your ionosphere that is ionized and makes your signals go shorter and shorter and shorter in distance. At nighttime that goes away. For those who listen to AM radio, that's why you can hear clear channel stations at night. It's because the delay or the ionosphere has gone away, and the geometry of the signal propagating over the ether is further and further. There's no way Betty heard that on 3105 kilohertz. So they have to come up with another reason why she wrote those things down, and it *could be* that it was a *March of Time* radio show or something like that. I've read what the other group has put up for Betty's notebook and Howland Port is mentioned. Well, Howland Port was an early name for the Staten Island dockyards. That was called Howland Port. So personally I think she was hearing radio stations fade in and out that are New York based and what have you, where they used to act out the news. That's my personal opinion.

But it's like a nose, everybody has one. So...

Jen Taylor

Are you aware of whether or not we have any information today about the signal strength of those signals, regardless of who they came from?

Tom Vinson

Not like we had from the *Itasca* by bona fide radiomen. There's the receiving station up in Hawaii, for instance, that had direction finding capability from Pan Am, things like that.

If you look at Makapuu Point, that receiving station was for the Pan Am flights going north and west, and that direction finding is going through a mountain. The direction finders there just don't work very well anyway for something *that* south.

• • •

Jen Taylor

I don't know if you've seen this, but I believe there have been claims that you can take the post-loss signals and triangulate the location of where they're coming from. Is that something you are aware of?

Tom Vinson

Sure, sure, and that's to the point. One of the DF stations they use as an example there was at Makapuu Point. The mountain's blocking that direction to the south, so it's not a very good triangulation.

Jen Taylor

Do you have an estimate of how much fuel she had left when she says, "We're on the line 157/337"? Is it possible to estimate that at all?

Tom Vinson

Yeah, that's been done. We had a professor from Cal-Poly who did a fuel analysis on that and came in basically around that time plus or minus. There's always a statistical variation amongst that when you do those. We had one of our Rockwell Collins engineers do a fuel analysis and break the flight into nine segments. We took all the basic Lockheed aircraft data and generated an Excel chart that you can plug into for each of those nine segments. That data came up with a fuel analysis. At 07:42 she was saying, "We must be on you but cannot see you," at the end of their navigation. "But gas is running low. Been unable to reach you by radio."

Well, *how low* is that?

One hour later is our last transmission, and we know from the radio data that she was within one hundred miles at 07:42. It takes three hours to fly down to Nikumaroro. She had just heard the *Itasca* transmit for the first time. She heard them at 08:00 hours, when she's circling and trying to get a bearing from them. Once she's heard them like that for the first time, and that's the only place where help is, to me it seems highly unlikely that once you have a voice *and* a signal, you would fly and see if that signal from the *Itasca* is getting stronger or weaker. If it gets *weaker*, you don't want to fly *away* from it, you want to fly *towards it*. Otherwise, we now think based on *our* data that she was close, and at 08:43, when she says, "Wait," that's where we believe that the engines coughed, and she had to throw down that mic and trim out the aircraft for a dead-stick landing. From one thousand feet, she'd have less than a minute before she'd be on the water. So it's a sad deal, but that's just what the data looks to. When we started this, none of us really knew anything much about it. We heard that maybe she had been on an island, but as we got in and then analyzed the radio from a radio standpoint and did all these experiments, we said, "Oh yeah, she tells us she was close."

The answer lies in the ocean. The airplane does anyway.

Whether she got out or not, that's still a mystery.

Jen Taylor

My last question, then, is do you think it is *at all possible* that after the *Itasca* could no longer hear her, she kept flying for an additional three hours? Do you think that's *at all* possible?

Tom Vinson

No, we don't think that's plausible at all, and of course, another group does. That's *their* hypothesis, and that's okay. To us, the data just doesn't show it's there. Again, we're doing the HF comms and the nav. The data doesn't lead us in that direction. Did you ever take debate?

Jen Taylor

Yes.

Tom Vinson

Okay. Well, one of the rules of debate is *thou shall not argue your point based on a premise, assuming your premise is true.* Have you heard that?

Jen Taylor

Yes, I have.

Tom Vinson

Okay. You heard recently about Buka; they found some aircraft near New Guinea.

Jen Taylor

Right.

Tom Vinson

Okay. So these people are saying, "Oh, she turned around, and this could be the L10-E. This could be Amelia." And you hear it in the news.

Jen Taylor

Yes.

Tom Vinson

Well, that would assume that she turned around *before* her PNR, or point of no return.

That's what the assumption is, of which there are no facts that substantiate that whatsoever. However, in fact, there *are* facts that state she got closer and closer based on those *Itasca* logs. She was actually pretty close. So they base that then on a false-premise argument. They base their argument, assuming that it's true, on the fact that she turned around, and then they want money to go look for that aircraft.

The problem with flying down to Nikumaroro is there are a lot of other higher probability scenarios for why things may or may not be there. Like the *Norwich City* grounding in World War II. There was a British colony. There's a lot of other things there, in fact, that would say she couldn't get there in the first place because she said she was low on fuel.

They have three or four more hours of fuel left from then on? If you had three hours of fuel left, I'm not sure you'd say you're "low on fuel."

Jen Taylor

Do you think that it's possible that Amelia survived?

Tom Vinson

You know, that's a hard question. Of course, no one knows.

I guess it's *possible*.

If she got out, she could maybe float out there towards the Marshall Islands.

However, if you look at that aircraft crashing on the ocean, no one practices that. A light aircraft with those engines out in front like that would go nose down very quickly. The very end of the nose would probably be eight to ten feet underwater at least, and that hatch is not a sealed hatch. It's not a pressurized compartment like aircraft are today, and water would come through very quickly. So if they survived the initial impact, almost immediately she would be in a very desperate situation with water rushing in and not being able to go out that hatch because of water pressure. She would have to go through to the bulkhead and back up the plywood that's sitting on top of the fuel tanks to get out.

So it's a precarious thing. Once the aircraft is found underwater, it'll be interesting to see if those hatches are closed and if the seatbelt is still buckled, or her shoes and leather jacket and things are still in the aircraft.

They're there.

Those are all things that are part of the mystery that finding the aircraft would reveal.

Jen Taylor

Thank you, no further questions.

*"She didn't have any problems or distress in the previous messages, and we know the signals are getting stronger with each one. 06:45 is stronger than 06:14. 07:42 is stronger than 06:45, and at 07:58, she's circling. They should have at least seen the island or been on it at 07:42. Almost fifteen minutes later, something's **very wrong** here."*

Chris Williamson

Your Honor, the project calls *Dana Timmer* to the stand.

Mr. Timmer, I.want to establish right off the bat how far you go back with this case. Can you briefly tell the court *when* you first got involved in a professional manner?

Dana Timmer

On March 19, 1993, I built an airplane, and I flew up to San Jose and met Elgen and Marie Long. That's when I *really* got started down this path of trying to find this airplane.

Chris Williamson

Mr. Timmer, the court has heard from Mr. Dettweiler and now Mr. Vinson regarding their involvement, and the names Elgen Long and Nauticos seem to intertwine pretty tightly with all of this. But you were there *first*. Can you give the court a summary of the deep-ocean searches in the years since 1999?

Dana Timmer

There are a variety of people who have been out in the deep water.

In 1994, Elgen and I discussed this project with Art, Mike and his team. So I was working with Elgen from '94 on through '98. We were having a tough time raising all the funds and actually getting out into the water.

In 1998, Elgen decided to try his luck with Nauticos, and he went off and pursued *that* avenue, and I continued my efforts with our friend Mike and a fellow named Guy Zions, who's part of our team. We actually were *the first* out there in 1999. That was the first ever deep-water search for the plane. Then subsequently, there's been four more or so since then. That's the early history, anyway.

Chris Williamson

Mr. Timmer, at this point, I think the project has established pretty soundly that the USS Coast Guard cutter *Itasca* was consistently pulling signal strength 5s as AE and Noonan were inbound to Howland Island. When Leo Bellarts was on the stand, he said something that struck me as quite interesting, and it's been heavily talked about here in court today.

He said that "he stepped outside but neither saw nor heard the Electra anywhere on the horizon." Additionally, as a material witness, he testifies to "no cloud cover whatsoever," yet we have no plane.

Can you explain that?

Dana Timmer

Well, you can easily get an S-5 radio signal in the radio room and step outside and *not* be able to hear or see an airplane ten, fifteen or even eighteen miles away. You just wouldn't. And remember, the wind is going from east to west, so the sound would be getting carried away from the *Itasca*. There's nothing unusual about getting a really loud signal strength in the radio room and not being able to go outside and actually see or hear the airplane.

The weather, as you know, is a very dynamic thing. There weren't any clouds at the *Itasca* at Howland. As Amelia was approaching a couple of hundred miles out, she *could have* had some, but remember she's coming out of the darkness. She's going from dark to low light to the sun coming up, and she would have gone up in altitude, eight thousand or ten thousand feet, however high she was at that point. In the early light, the occlusion would have looked a lot more severe than it probably was. In hindsight, she probably did not need to drop down to one thousand feet. As the day got brighter, she would have seen that those clouds were not as dense as she would have thought under a low-light situation.

Chris Williamson

So what's the story here? Did Amelia Earhart and Fred Noonan just have a *really bad* day? Is the simplest explanation *really it* after all this time? Walk us through some of the standout transmissions that AE sent out that morning.

Dana Timmer

Regardless of what theory you're operating under, whether it's Saipan or any of them, the only hard evidence we have are the *Itasca* logs of what Amelia was saying, and the relative signal strength of those signals. The operators in the *Itasca* were very skilled at determining an S-1 from an S-5.

That's what we need to focus on.

Those radio signal strengths and what Amelia was saying. Just to go through it very briefly, 06:14, early morning, Amelia says she's two hundred miles out. That position would have been from Fred Noonan, and the star sight that he had gotten roughly about an hour before the last star sight he took. You can take that to the bank; they were about two hundred miles out. They already started asking for a bearing at that time. At 06:45, they were about one hundred miles out, and there's a lot of controversy about that, because they *couldn't* have gone one hundred miles in half an hour. Amelia was not trying to give a definitive position; she was trying to establish radio contact. That *was not* Fred's position; that was something Amelia probably figured, "Well, half an hour ago, we were at two hundred." Instead of saying

"118 point whatever" like you would do today with a GPS, she just said, "About one hundred miles out," and she's also asking for a bearing. Then at 07:42, "We must be on you but cannot see you. Gas is running low." This is the first sign of distress.

She didn't have any problems or distress in the previous messages, and we know the signals are getting stronger with each one. 06:45 is stronger than 06:14. 07:42 is stronger than 06:45, and at 07:58, she's circling. They should have at least seen the island or been on it at 07:42.

Almost fifteen minutes later, something's *very wrong* here.

She's circling when, in fact, if they had kept on it for another ten to fifteen minutes, they would have seen the island, but they lost it at 07:42, and now they're not focusing on where the island is, straight ahead. She's to the left, to the right, and just a couple of minutes later, she's going off the schedule. She started the search. Most celestial navigators who have studied the case have her deliberately offsetting one side or the other of Howland. You have to advance your position far enough and then fly down. That's where the 157/337 line comes in.

But they didn't do that.

I know this is not going to go over well with some of the other celestial navigators out there, but they never did that offset approach. They flew straight into the island. They were short at 07:42 and thought they should be there at 8:00. They must have missed it. The last transmission at 08:43 is, "We're flying north and south on the line 157/337."

South is *very* critical. I know some people want to say *north*, some people want to say *south*, but she said, and this was in the *Itasca* log, *"Flying north and south"*.

So she was in a search pattern after missing the island. This is something called the "Chichester line of approach." That deliberate offset to one side or the other of the island.

That will help you with any north/south error, but it *doesn't* do anything for your east/west error.

Chris Williamson

Mr. Timmer, I want to drive this point home to the court because I think it goes to show how *little* history would have to be altered to tell a *different* story. If the Electra had Captain Harry Manning on board to send out Morse code transmissions, are we having a different conversation historically speaking today?

Dana Timmer

Oh, I think there's a good chance that is correct. Morse code would have been a very good skill to have for either Amelia or Fred. The *Itasca* is sending out A's so they would have something to home in on. One thing that's important is if Amelia was coming in from the north on that 157 line, she would have said something at either 07:42 or right around there. I don't know if your readers know how an RDF works. There aren't very many of them around anymore, but you need to know roughly where the signal is coming from.

The RDF antenna is that little loop on top of the cockpit of the Electra. You don't just turn these things around and around 360 degrees. You're looking in a quadrant.

The *Itasca* would have been expecting Amelia from the *west*, not from the north. I'm sure this line-of-approach procedure was not communicated to the *Itasca*. The lack of her saying "inbound from the north" or something to that effect tells me that they did not do that.

That's one of the reasons why I don't think they came in on that line-of-approach procedure, but rather flew straight in and then got there too late to ever go off one side or the other and perform that approach.

Chris Williamson

When Mr. Dettweiler was on the stand, he spoke briefly about the kind of condition we could expect the Electra to be found in *should it be* found. I wonder if you could expand on that for the jury a little more and talk about what kind of condition we could expect the Electra to be in, and what kind of condition some of the artifacts contained within her would be in.

. . .

Dana Timmer

Things retrieved out of the deep ocean, the *Titanic* for example, are in *remarkably* good condition.

The fact that they brought up a violin from the *Titanic* and newspapers that were *still* readable is incredible. Recently, a camera was found in a World War II trench, that belonged to a Soviet soldier. *Remarkably*, from that camera, they were able to develop one of the photos. This camera had been in a ditch in mud and water for the last seventy-seven years, and they were able to develop one of the shots that was on that roll of film. The deep ocean is a great place to preserve something.

I think we'll find that airplane pretty well intact.

I think they probably did a reasonable job of ditching it, and it would have sunk relatively soon after being on the water. It's down there in the vicinity of Howland, and I think it'll be an amazing time capsule for what happened.

Chris Williamson

Can you discuss just how plausible or even probable some of the other options might be when it comes to some of the other destinations that are currently being investigated?

Dana Timmer

In this case, I've never seen anything that has convinced me of any of the other theories.

If Amelia miraculously found a known from an unknown, obviously they wouldn't know where they were. Say, for example, they had flown three hundred miles to the south and landed on an atoll, there would be a very nice hard-packed sand runway at low tide on the island.

That is where you would have put the plane down, *not* on a reef. It would have ripped the landing gear off. Certainly, if you were able to put the plane down on the reef *without* ripping the landing gear off and make a successful landing, then you would have been able to slowly taxi the plane up to the high watermark and wait for help.

Theoretically, she should have been able to take off again and complete the flight. So I've never seen anything in any of the variety of theories that has convinced me that anything *other* than ditching and sinking near Howland Island was the fate of that flight. That's my take on it.

Chris Williamson

Talk to me about navigation. Let's try to get ahead of what the defense may argue regarding the possibility that Fred Noonan could have been suffering from exhaustion and therefore wasn't at his best ability to perform the duties of which he was there to do that morning.

Dana Timmer

There's always an inherent error in celestial navigation. It could be very small, but it's not GPS.

I don't think Fred made very much of an error at all.

You know, there was obviously *some.* They were behind where they thought they were, and we know that from "we must be on you" at 07:42. They continue to fly straight ahead towards the island. We *know that* because the signal strength got stronger, so it was just *very* unlucky that they couldn't even see the island from eight miles out, which is not a great error at all. After a 2,556-mile flight, they got very unlucky, but probably the downfall and the reason they missed the island was because of poor preflight planning.

The radio and the time, the schedule. Amelia is on Greenwich mean time, and the ship is on local time, which was, oddly, eleven and a half hours from Greenwich. So being out of sync on the radio work and being off on the schedule because of poor preflight planning between the *Itasca* and Amelia *really added up* to their downfall. They needed that RDF bearing to gain direct communication in spite of Fred doing a very good job of getting them *very close* to the island.

Chris, there's one more thing: As you know, there's some confusion around the *Itasca* putting out smoke. In the log, it says it was ten miles. Well, if you're the emitter, how do you measure ten miles? We know that these soot particles are very heavy; they tend to be pulled down by gravity rather quickly. A ship at station is *not* going to put out a ten-mile smoke trail possibly, when it was steaming up to the northwest after her last transmissions with the right atmospheric condition.

There's a picture of the *Itasca* putting out smoke that morning, and it's not going anywhere.

There wasn't this big smoke trail to follow. In hindsight, Amelia and Fred probably *should have* left two hours earlier, 08:00 instead of 10:00 in the morning. They would have been closer to their last star sight, which is a lot more accurate than certainly a sunrise shot would have been, because you get three stars, and you get a fix as opposed to just *one* line.

Chris Williamson
Thank you, Mr. Timmer. Pass the witness.

Cross-Examination of Dana Timmer

Jen Taylor

Mr. Timmer, earlier we heard a phrase that I don't think we have heard yet, so I'm going to ask you to clarify it for us. A little bit earlier you used the phrase "ditch and sink." So far today, we've been using the phrase "crash and sink." I just wanted you go over what that term means and what the *difference* is between *ditch and sink* and *crash and sink.*

Dana Timmer

For me, the difference between *crash and sink* and *ditch and sink* is that *ditching* is a more controlled situation. Amelia reported she was at one thousand feet. She would have been gliding in once the fuel was exhausted as opposed to an uncontrolled approach into the ocean, or a hard smash like Air France had over the Atlantic. *That* was a crash and sink situation.

The plane hit the water at a very high rate of speed and broke apart into many little pieces.

Ditch and sink is controlled, as I said, where Amelia was gliding the plane in and *hopefully* doing a good job of putting the plane onto the ocean surface with minimal damage and maximum safety for the occupants of the plane. That's the distinction that I make between crash versus ditch.

Jen Taylor

Okay. You mentioned that this has to do with how well she was able to control that landing.

Do you have an opinion on whether the plane would have floated for a time or whether it would have immediately gone down?

Dana Timmer

Well, I guess it depends on what *immediate* means. Not within minutes, we're not talking about that. But with the center of gravity and the tanks being empty, it would have been quite forward, so once on the water, the nose would have gone vertical basically and straight down. The plane would have been floating with the tail up in the air, and then water would ingress into the fuselage and slowly start to sink.

How long?

That's *very hard* to say pertaining to the plane staying on the surface.

An hour would be a long time, in my opinion. Probably more like a half an hour, something like that.

Jen Taylor

So certainly *not* long enough for anyone searching for her to have been able to find her *above* water.

Dana Timmer

That's correct, yes. The *Itasca* left Howland Island after her 08:45 transmission. They could not have been thirty-five miles northwest, the area they went to search, for a good couple of hours. The plane would have sunk before they got up there. They were the only ship in the area to perform a search.

Jen Taylor

I know that we already went over this a little bit on direct examination, but if the jury was going to go deliberate right now on which theory was the correct one, and you had to give them a handful of pieces of evidence that you think are the *most* important things for them to pay attention to, what would those things be?

Dana Timmer

The best evidence available in this case would be Leo Bellarts's testimony. He was in the radio room. He was an expert radioman. He knew how strong Amelia's signal was coming in and what she was saying, which are in the logbooks, of course. I would listen to Leo Bellarts and what he had to say, which is she was coming in "loud and clear."

Her voice got more and more anxious as the transmissions went on. In her last transmission, she was *very* stressed. That's not somebody who is flying off to another island to go try to find an atoll or try to land somewhere. She *knew* she was very low on fuel at 07:42.

Leo Bellarts and the *Itasca* logs are the best direct evidence we have. Anything other than that is getting into more and more conjecture.

I would recommend the jury listen to that.

Jen Taylor

Mr. Timmer, let's say, hypothetically, that tomorrow or next week, you find a plane in the vicinity of Howland Island that you believe could possibly be Amelia's plane, what are some of the things that you might be looking for?

Dana Timmer

Well, first of all, a Lockheed Electra 10-E. Hopefully Amelia put it down mostly intact, and I believe we'll find an airplane that is *fairly* intact. In the deep ocean, things are very well preserved, as I said earlier. I think we'll still see her registration number on the wing. The leading-edge paint may still be there, the orange paint. If we find an Electra, then I think we will be quite certain that it's Amelia's airplane, but we *will* be able to find other characteristics. The numbers may be faint, but if you look at pictures of objects in the deep ocean, the *Indianapolis* for example, recently found by Paul Allen's group, there's still paint on the ship. There are identifying marking numbers. Of course, our goal is to recover the airplane, so we will be able to certainly get *inside* the airplane. I think Fred's charts will still be in there.

There'll be a lot of forensic evidence that will identify that airplane as Amelia's.

. . .

Jen Taylor

I have heard the theory tossed around that possibly there were *multiple* planes and that there could have been decoys out there. Given what you know about the Lockheed Electra and about what was going on at the time, do you think it's *possible* that there could be *more than one* plane that might fit the description of Amelia's?

Dana Timmer

That's not my interpretation at all. The logistics and possibility of pulling something like that off is astronomical.

I guess anything's possible, but I would *really* have to see two airplanes in order to convince myself that something like that happened. It's just nonsensical domain. I don't have any real specifics on that; we *do know* that Amelia was in the vicinity of Howland Island at 08:45 on the morning of July 2, 1937. We know that because she was coming in loud and strong. She said, "We must be on you." We'd have to discount *everything* Amelia said and the evidence we have from the *Itasca*.

Now, was there *another* plane somewhere *else*? Another Lockheed Electra flying over some Japanese mandated islands, taking pictures? I guess anything's possible.

But the probability of something like that seems too astronomical to me.

Jen Taylor

I know that there have been a number of different people out there with a number of different claims being made that the plane has been found in various locations. Either a complete plane or, in some cases, pieces of a plane. When someone makes a claim like that, what are you looking for to determine *in your mind* whether or not that plane could have been found in another location?

Dana Timmer

Well, an identifiable piece. A scrap of aluminum or a shoe or a pocketknife or something like that doesn't *have* a registration number on it that could be linked to the airplane.

Jen Taylor

We know that the plane was modified, that there were fuel tanks added in order to accommodate long trips. Let's say somebody was to find a plane, and the serial or registration number was no longer legible and we couldn't get to it. Do you think that it's *enough* for somebody to say, "We see a Lockheed Electra that has been modified in the way that we knew Amelia modified it," would *that be* enough if you were unable to get a registration number from a plane?

Dana Timmer

That's a tricky question.

I suppose multiple planes could have been modified the same way, theoretically. *In theory,* you could have two identical Lockheeds that were just like Amelia's with the extra fuel tanks. I'm assuming, then, that there's going to be more to identify. If it's in the deep ocean, we should find plenty of evidence to support the airplane being hers. I think you probably know that with the *Titanic*, they brought up newspapers, seven letters and all sorts of identifiable objects. I expect we're going to find things like that as well with Amelia's airplane. Now, if it's just some scrap of something, it'll certainly be a lot harder.

It *could come* from the airplane, but it could *also come* from a lot of other things as well.

There *could be* an identical Lockheed out in the Pacific. If *in fact there was* a spy mission, which I think you're alluding to, and they flew over Japan, then you could theoretically have a duplicate.

But that second plane is not going to be near Howland Island.

It'll *only be* Amelia's.

. . .

Jen Taylor

I have no further questions for this witness, Your Honor.

Chris Williamson

Your Honor, at this time, both parties reserve the right to recall witnesses for future testimony. However, the project would like to reconvene next to present the *castaway hypothesis.*

Bailiff

ALL RISE!

LEFT FOR DEAD
-4.67327 | -174.52486

*"Everybody's entitled to their own opinion.
They're not entitled to their own facts."*

Chris Williamson

As we opened crash and sink, we began by saying that the ocean where Amelia Earhart and Fred Noonan lost communication with the *Itasca* was the foundational crime scene for this case.

But what I didn't tell you then is that this investigation has *multiple crime scenes*.

Next up, we explore theory two in this eighty-five-year-old case, and it takes us roughly 405 miles away from Howland Island to the shores of *Nikumaroro*. It's time to put arguably the most controversial and well-debated hypothesis in this case on trial with experts, exhibits and testimony for *castaway*.

Pre-Trial Discussion

Chris Williamson

On our first full day in court, so to speak, we presented what's known as the "crash and sink hypothesis," and we had Brian Dunning, Tom Vinson, Tom Dettweiler, and Dana Timmer, a *stacked* guest list, take part in that. I think it pretty much went like I thought it would. They talked about the same stuff, they referenced the same things, and they leaned on the same pieces of evidence. You got a chance to cross-examine *all four of them*; what's your takeaway from that?

Jen Taylor

I think it's pretty strong. It's got the benefit of Amelia Earhart saying what she said, and it's easy to listen to that and think, "Dang, she was describing exactly what was happening."

It also has the benefit of being simple. I think what they're saying props up what Leo Bellarts said in the segment *before*, which was pretty compelling. There are things that are *still questionable*, like what happened after that last *universally accepted transmission*?

Did she die right then, or did she have additional flight time? Could she have made it anywhere *else* after that? That's, of course, going to be a *huge question* going forward.

Chris Williamson

Yeah, you make a good point. I made an analogy/prediction at the beginning of crash and sink that they *really are* the ones to beat in this case. They have the science, they have the *Itasca* logs, they have Leo Bellarts, and they have the official government explanation behind them to back this particular theory. Two things: you've had a chance to cross-examine that team, but *we don't know* yet what we're going to walk into regarding castaway or any of the other theories we're presenting. Knowing all of that, do you think everyone else has the burden of proof here?

Jen Taylor

Yes, I *actually do*.

Going forward, you have to ask yourself two questions: The first question is going to be, "Did the proponents of this hypothesis prove their case beyond a reasonable doubt?" The *other question* that you should ask yourself is, "If they didn't, is the evidence that I just heard enough to create reasonable doubt that she crashed and sank off the coast of Howland Island?" That's a totally *different* question. So maybe you read through an entire segment, and you think, "Number one might be out, but number two? Now I have enough of a question that I have reasonable doubt that crash and sink happened." Does that make sense?

Chris Williamson

It *does* make sense, and I think you're spot on with that. Because *now you know*. You have the foundation, right? What you just read in the last part is what the US government backs, and it's the historically reported and accepted foundational story. If they went down in the ocean, and the plane lies at roughly eighteen thousand feet below the surface of the water, then *that's* your crime scene.

But now we move roughly 405 miles away from Howland to an island that has been a centerpiece for this investigation. For at least the last thirty-five years or so, you cannot talk about the search for Amelia Earhart and *not* hear about TIGHAR, the International Group for Historic Aircraft Recovery. Names like Ric Gillespie, Dr. Tom King, and Dr. Richard Jantz have come into the fold and dominated the airwaves and media in this case, there's no question about it. The idea here is that Noonan might have sustained a fatal injury as a result of the landing, and she may have ended up on an island all alone, left for dead.

This is the first one out of the gate after crash and sink. What are *you* looking for in this particular theory?

Jen Taylor

I think you kind of answered your own question. You hear this all the time, "She could have gone this way. They might have landed over here. It's plausible that she could."

A lot of *could haves* and *maybes*. But the evidence *has to show* that what you're saying *did happen, not just that it could have happened*, right?

Chris Williamson

Right.

Jen Taylor

If there are other things out there that explain the evidence that you have, then *it's not* evidence beyond a reasonable doubt that Amelia Earhart and Fred Newton *landed there*, it just means that she *could have* landed there.

Chris Williamson

What questions do you have here? What are you looking forward to hearing about *the most* regarding this particular theory?

Jen Taylor

Well, I guess to answer that question, I'll give you a list of questions that I had going into it before I talked to anybody. One of the biggest feathers in TIGHAR's cap is the post-loss signals. Radio transmissions that supposedly came from Amelia Earhart and Fred Noonan.

Chris Williamson

Yep. That's a big one.

Jen Taylor

So my first question is, did they *actually come from her*, and how do they know that? My second question is, can we use those signals to determine her location? In addition to the signals, you have, of course, the bones that were found, and I understand that we're going to get into those *extensively* coming up. But that, of course, is a huge question. Whose are they, and how confident are we? With the remainder of the artifacts, I'm going to be asking how confident these experts are that these artifacts came from either her plane or from her? Another huge question that I have is, *is it even possible* that she got to Nikumaroro?

In the last segment, everyone was so sure that she would not have had any fuel left after she made that final transmission. The big question that should really be looming over this whole thing as we get into it is, can we know if that's wrong? Was it even possible? I understand there are things that we can't know, but given what we *do know*, is it even possible that she could have made it from where she was all the way to Nikumaroro Island and be able to land there? Those are my questions going in.

Chris Williamson

As I mentioned, this is really the *first* of the alternate theories regarding what may or may not have happened that day. For the readers who maybe never heard our original show, *my job* is to do what I've always done and try to prove this hypothesis beyond a reasonable doubt using the data that's contained within it. I need to use the expert witnesses contained within this theory to prove to the jury that this is something that should absolutely be considered probable. In my opinion, all of what you're about to read is plausible. In order to be successful, I need to elevate that to probable.

We have to figure out what stands out. Like I said, all these theories have different types of evidence. Some of these theories have what I like to refer to as a "holy trinity of evidence." If castaway has a trinity, it's going to be the archaeological collection of evidence on Niku-maroro, including the bones. It's going to be all of the other items that have been found in the expeditions to this island, items like the freckle cream, the shoe, TIGHAR artifact 2-2-V-1, which is the patch panel off of what they're saying is the plane.

And of course, the post-loss radio signals, which you just mentioned. My job is to highlight that trinity of evidence through a variety of different witnesses and section this off into different areas that, when added together, build a cohesive case. I have three options in this case *as a whole*. *Telling, showing* and *proving*. It always begins with a story, that's the tell. The show is me laying out a different ending based on the evidence we have. And with that, if we *can't prove it unequivocally*, the hope is that we can cast *enough doubt* to have people look over from crash and sink and give some attention to some of these other theories.

Jen Taylor

And in order for you to get there, there's a lot of different sciences involved. We've got some archaeology, some anthropology, and a handful of *other* different fields. Those are all going to be critical for us when it comes to moving that line from *plausible to probable*.

Chris Williamson

Yeah, there's a handful of fields coming together for this *one* partic-ular theory; it's going to be interesting.

Vanished has become known for the deep dives we take, and for everyone reading this, you're about to *experience* one.

Opening Statements

Chris Williamson

If there's *one name* that's *synonymous* with the Amelia Earhart investigation, it's the International Group for Historic Aircraft Recovery. Today, the project is going to pull *multiple experts* from *multiple fields* who are *all going to tell you the same thing*. The likelihood of Amelia Earhart and Fred Noonan landing their plane on the tiny island of Nikumaroro is not only *plausible*, but *probable*. The project is going to pull witnesses to discuss a multitude of evidence, including fifty-seven post-loss radio signals *deemed credible* and picked up by major outlets in the days *after* Amelia and Fred vanished. This will prove that they did not in fact land in the ocean, but instead they had to be on land in order to send out those radio signals. We're also going to discuss a multitude of artifacts found on Nikumaroro over the course of the last thirty plus years, including the widely talked about *Nikumaroro bones* that made worldwide headlines just a few years ago.

And that's just the beginning. After today, you'll have no doubt that Amelia and Fred *did not* meet a watery grave. In fact, after the evidence is presented here, you'll be *more confident than ever* that Amelia Earhart's end, while equally as tragic as crashing and sinking, includes a valiant fight for her own life on an island all alone.

Jen Taylor

Today, all of you continue to sit on our jury. *You* are the ones who get to decide what the belief is in this case. So right now, I get to talk *directly to you*. When we last left, Amelia Earhart and Fred Noonan were attempting to send radio transmissions to the *Itasca* in order to establish communication with them. In order to establish where they were so that they could land *as planned* on Howland Island at approximately 8:45 in the morning, *Itasca* time.

The *Itasca* received a radio transmission from Amelia, and *she told them* she was "on the line 157/337," that she was going to "repeat north and south." And then she said, "Wait," and the transmission ended. There have been a number of transmissions that were heard by either the *Itasca* or various others *since that time,* and we're all going to disagree on whether or not those came from her. But that transmission you just read right there? *That* is the last transmission that *everyone universally agrees* came from Amelia Earhart. You heard Leo Bellarts testify that the above transmission came in at an S-5 signal strength, and that he heard it loud and clear. She was in fact *so loud* that he had to run outside and look because he thought that she was coming in right above his head.

Unfortunately, she wasn't. She never made it to Howland. Leo Bellarts never heard from her again after that. That's why we're here today. We are here today because the project will have you believe that Amelia and Fred *survived.*

During our crash and sink segment, you heard evidence that *that testimony* was her *last.*

She ran out of fuel right then and there, and she crashed into the ocean. The project has told you what *it expects* the evidence in this case is going to be, and as they present this evidence to you, I want you to pay very close attention to what is *missing.* You will hear people testify that Amelia Earhart and Fred Noonan might have flown south by southeast along the 157/337 sunline. That they *probably* had enough fuel to make it all the way to Nikumaroro. That the signals picked up in the following days *could have* been coming from Amelia and Fred and that those signals could have been coming from Nikumaroro Island.

You'll hear about subsequent expeditions that have been made that have uncovered possible artifacts from their stay on the island. You'll hear about pictures that have been taken, and you'll hear about human remains that have been found.

Today you're going to hear a few words and phrases *a lot*:

Might have.
   Probably.
   Could have been.

You are going to consume what at times might feel like an over-whelming amount of material evidence. *I call it* "evidence" because it's going to be admitted into evidence for your consideration. As you read through all of it, pay attention to what's *missing*. Pay attention to what they *don't give you*. I would also like you to pay special attention to the science in this case. You're going to hear today from a number of experts in a variety of different fields. Archaeologists, anthropologists, photo identification experts, and RDF radio experts have been brought together to astound you in a very cool magic trick that the project is attempting to pull off.

As they all testify, keep in mind what we talked about during jury selection. Are the methods being used *reliable*? Have they been subject to peer review? For each of these experts, it's not enough that they came here with their opinion. How they reached that opinion is important as well, if not *more important*.

Remember *who* has the burden of proof in this case.

What Amelia Earhart and Fred Noonan *might have done*, what they *probably could have done*, what this evidence *possibly shows* isn't good enough today.

They **cannot tell you** they've *solved the mystery*.

Today, they need to *prove it to you*.

*"I disregard the crash and sink theory primarily because she transmitted signal on July 3. It was agreed that she would transmit at a specific time on a specific frequency, and they heard the carriers at that time on those frequencies. So it **had** to be her."*

Chris Williamson

Your Honor, the project calls *Mr. Richard Olson* to the stand.

Mr. Olson, can you tell the court what your background is and inform us of your professional area of expertise?

Richard Olson

Well, the reason I am interested to a certain extent is because I'm a ham radio operator.

I've been one for over sixty years now, and *because of that* I became very interested in engineering. I have an undergraduate degree in electronic engineering from Cal Poly in San Luis Obispo. I then went on to study nuclear engineering, and I have a PhD *for that* from Stanford. So I've always had a keen interest in engineering and electronics.

Chris Williamson

Before you got into this case and took a harder look at the evidence being presented, did you have any preconceived notions or ideas regarding the fate of Amelia Earhart and Fred Noonan? Did you more or less accept the conclusion that they went down in the ocean somewhere near Howland?

Richard Olson

I think I more or less believed that. We knew that she was lost, so to speak. The way I got involved was I got a call from *Discovery*, and they wanted to know more information about my background as a ham radio operator for a special on Amelia Earhart they were doing.

After that call, I started looking more into it, and that was what caught my interest.

Chris Williamson

Before we get into the post-loss radio signals that occurred in the days after July 2, 1937, I'd like you to tell the court how radio signals would have worked back in the time of the world flight.

Richard Olson

A couple of things worth mentioning, they had moved to a higher frequency at that time.

Previously, aircraft were operating around 1600 kilohertz, but for Amelia Earhart, Pan Am moved to a little higher frequency. They were operating around 3 megahertz. Because of that, you can generally cover greater distances because you have what's called the "ground wave" and the "sky wave." It was clear that they heard her. We can get into "radio cracking" and stuff like that later. Apparently, they were going to try to put out a homing signal. I'm not too sure how well her aircraft was equipped to receive that signal. One of the things that was done during her airplane rebuild and modification was they removed her rotatable RDF antenna. So, she no longer had that.

Chris Williamson

Do we know what kind of an effect that antenna would have had on the Electra being able to communicate with the *Itasca* that morning?

Richard Olson

There were a couple of things; the *Itasca* was presumably putting out a homing signal of some type. Because she didn't have a rotatable antenna, she couldn't tell what direction that signal was coming from. Previously, her aircraft also had an antenna that they could just roll out the tail of the aircraft. That particular antenna was an extremely efficient antenna because you could adjust its length and get it working at maximum efficiency.

That type of antenna gives you much better coverage. If you want a good antenna, it's got to be up high and clear of everything else. During the rebuild and modification, that was also removed and replaced with a fixed antenna that installed toward the front of the aircraft and ran between the front and tail sections. It kind of looked like a triangular-shaped antenna. That was clearly not as efficient an antenna as her original one. There seems to be a running theme of replacing her onboard equipment with equipment that wasn't as reliable. There's mistake *number one.*

Chris Williamson

Mr. Olson, are you saying that it's possible that a lack of proper equipment could be the culprit for the events of that morning?

Richard Olson

The *sole culprit?* Well, that's a whole *different* question.

They basically started off with state-of-the-art equipment. They presumably had the best equipment that was available at the time. I think the fact that they changed their antenna arrangement was unwise. It wasn't as good as it could have been, especially when there are stretches like Lae to Howland in play. They had no one on board who was fluent in Morse code. Mistake *number two.*

Chris Williamson

Previously, experts representing the crash and sink hypothesis testified that because the *Itasca* was constantly pulling S-5 signals, Amelia and Fred *had to be* in the vicinity of Howland Island, meaning around or under the two-hundred-mile mark. However, she ends up on Nikumaroro; she's well *out* of that two-hundred-mile max range. Can you talk about how it would have been possible for the *Itasca* to be pulling signal strength 5s while the Electra was on Nikumaroro over four hundred miles away?

Richard Olson

Well, it's *possible*. These are all estimates in terms of how far signals will carry. We've not yet reached the range where we start talking about "skip distances." When Pan Am had their RDF stations, those were much further away.

I disregard the crash and sink theory primarily because she transmitted signal on July 3. It was agreed that she would transmit at a specific time and on a specific frequency, and they heard the carriers at that time on those frequencies.

So it *had to be her.*

I don't think there was *anyone else* masquerading as her. The other aspect is that the way her equipment ran, in order to transmit, she had to run the engines. At that time, the transmitter used something called the "dynamotor," which is a generator that generates high voltage for the transmitter. In order to operate that item, they had to operate the engines. Well, if she sank, then that's not happening, is it? There's no way they could have been transmitting at that time.

I'm pretty convinced that that plane landed somewhere, maybe on an island or on an atoll.

It did not go into the water, because she was certainly transmitting.

That plane *had to be* above water.

Chris Williamson

Mr Olson, there are a handful of islands between Howland and Nikumaroro. Can you tell the court how triangulation of post-loss radio signals seems to point to the Electra being on Nikumaroro?

Richard Olson

If you look at the data and triangulate the three signals that were received on July 3, those particular signals *do seem to indicate* Nikumaroro. There's a lot of uncertainty in any measurement. In any measurement, you need to try to reproduce the result. With any measurement you have systematic errors. So there's always an uncertainty, and in fact, I think later, they *did run* some tests with the *Itasca*, and they determined the readings could be off by 20 or 30 degrees. It's pretty clear that we don't know exactly where she was, but in my view, it has to be somewhere in the South Pacific.

Chris Williamson

Mr. Olson, in your expert professional opinion, the likelihood that the Electra was *in fact not submerged* and was on land is pretty high?

Richard Olson

Oh, absolutely.

Chris Williamson

There are fifty-seven *credible* post-loss radio signals that were picked up by multiple sources from various points in the days after Earhart's final agreed-upon transmission. Does that lend even more credence to the credibility of these signals, knowing that major significant sources *also* picked them up?

Richard Olson

I think what's perhaps *most credible* is the fact that the three Pan Am listening stations all heard them at the same time. They were able to use their radio direction capability to determine where those signals were coming from. Is it possible that they were heard on the East Coast? Yeah. I'll put my stock in them.

Chris Williamson

Knowing the science like you know, and knowing radio signals like you know, is it obvious to you that these post-loss radio signals were *in fact coming* from Amelia Earhart?

Richard Olson

Oh, I think so, yeah. I'm convinced that this was Amelia Earhart.

Chris Williamson

TIGHAR's report states that the quality of these received signals would have been *quite poor*. Is that something that you would agree with?

Richard Olson

Yeah, that's right. I think they were poor. If you look at some of the reports, they said they could only hear a carrier. What that means is she was using an AM radio, and when you turn that on, it puts out a continuous wave. Now, it was unfortunate that she didn't have a radio operator, because a good radio operator would actually hear it, and he would be able to send Morse code. Even a *weak* Morse code signal is very readable. In order to hear a *voice signal*, it takes a stronger signal because you're modulating it, and the amount of information that you're transmitting is more difficult. Had they sent a Morse code signal, an operator could have easily copied that message.

Chris Williamson

Before crash and sink was presented, we heard from Chief Leo Bellarts who testified that he felt they were *so close* to the *Itasca* that he stepped outside the radio room, expecting to see or hear her on the horizon, yet he *saw nothing,* and he *heard nothing* Could that be because at that time they were nowhere near Howland Island but, *instead,* were *much closer* to Nikumaroro?

. . .

Richard Olson

Well, that's *possible*. A lot of times, signal varies with time of day. They could have had a strong signal at one time, and then later, it could be something else entirely.

Chris Williamson

Mr. Olson, is there any doubt in your mind that the Lockheed Electra flown by Amelia Earhart and Fred Noonan during the world flight ended up on Nikumaroro Island?

Richard Olson

Well, I can't say it's Nikumaroro with 100% certainty. I think she clearly landed somewhere in the South Pacific.

Chris Williamson

Thank you, no further questions, Your Honor.

"It's mistake after mistake after mistake. It's not a mystery, it's a mix-up, and you can see the errors."

Chris Williamson

Your Honor, the project calls *Ric Gillespie* to the stand.

Mr. Gillespie, I'd like you to start today by telling the court about the post-loss radio signals that were picked up in the days *following* July 2, 1937, that TIGHAR has studied and compiled over the course of your working hypothesis.

Ric Gillespie

Something that had been bothering me for a long time is the body of evidence represented by what *we call* the post-loss radio signals, the radio distress calls that were heard for five days following Earhart's disappearance.

The *one call* that gets everybody's attention is the call heard by a fifteen-year-old girl in St. Petersburg, Florida, Betty Klenck, who kept a notebook. The phrases that she transcribed are just so emotional and poignant. There are things that Betty couldn't possibly know that are true. Betty's gotten a lot of attention. Her notebook has been featured in documentaries and articles, on and on. But there's so much more than just Betty's notebook. How can I draw attention to the *rest* of the evidence?

I started to go through and ask myself how I could present this stuff. We could have titled graphs that show how the credible post-loss signals match the tide conditions on the reef at that time.

Maybe I should go through it, reception by reception, because what a lot of people don't realize is that 88% of those transmissions were heard by professional radio operators and government radio operators, *not* housewives listening to their shortwave sets. There were a few of those, but most of the signals were heard by the *Itasca* or by the operators on Baker Island. They were heard by operators in Hawaii, the US Navy, and we need to show that.

So I got back into it, and I started to put it together.

As it often happens, when you get back into a body of original documentation, you see things you hadn't seen before. One of the things I quickly realized is that the credible signals only occurred, with very few exceptions, *at night* when the tide is low. It's not like they go on continually or randomly through those periods, when she's able to run an engine to recharge the battery that the radio depends upon. The signals come in little batches. There's an active period somewhere in the ballpark of about an hour. Then she's silent for an hour and a half, maybe two hours, and then she's back on for another hour or so. It goes on like this until the tide comes back in *or* daylight comes, and she has to stop.

There's *got to be* a reason for a pattern like that. I don't know the reason, but we have a hypothesis that we're going to test. We know that to recharge that battery, she has to run the engine at a speed of at least 900 RPM. Paul Mantz, Amelia's technical adviser, *said that* back on July 3, 1937, when he was asked about these radio calls and her ability to transmit. He said, "She's got to keep that battery charged, and she can do it by running the engine at 900 RPM. Doing that will burn about six gallons an hour."

In 2009, we went to Covington Aircraft Engines in Okmulgee, Oklahoma, and they put an R-1340 Pratt & Whitney Wasp engine on a test stand for us with the same kind of eclipse generator that Earhart used, and we *verified* what Mantz said. Yes, you can put a charge on that battery at 900 RPM, and you're going to burn about six gallons an hour.

Fine.

Well, I got to thinking about that. When I noticed this pattern, I thought, "I wonder if 900 RPM is enough to keep that engine cool under those circumstances." Even at night there's a fairly high ambient temperature. So I called the guys at Covington back up and asked what they thought about that. They said, "Oh, no, 900 RPM isn't going to keep that engine cool." I then asked them, "Well, how long is it going to take for it to get too hot?" Their response to that was, "After a couple of hours, you're going to see cylinder head temperatures and oil temperatures getting into the red, so you're going to want to shut down."

"How long is it going to take to cool off enough to try again?" "Oh, an hour and a half, two hours." Okay, well, that sounds exactly like what we're seeing. We can test this experimentally, and we *will*. All I need is somebody with the same engine, and we'll park it on a ramp, run the engine at 900 RPM, and we'll see how long it takes to cool down. We can test this stuff; that's how science works. We saw other patterns and relationships, and we knew that we had *more here* than just a rehash of old stuff we'd been trying to talk about for years. This is really worth a major study.

We put it together as a complete study, we gave everybody everything they need to verify what we're talking about, and we put it out there on Earhart's birthday. Because we have credibility with the media, they picked it up. That's how that happened.

Chris Williamson

Earlier you mentioned the name Betty Klenck. I'd like you to expand on the significance of her experience and the journal that's been a major pillar in your case for the court, please.

Ric Gillespie

Betty Klenck was fifteen years old in July of 1937. Her father worked for the electric company, and he had rigged up a rather fancy antenna for their commercial home radio.

He wasn't a ham; he wasn't a licensed amateur; neither was Betty, of course. She's just a kid who likes to listen to the radio, and she would spend a lot of time with it, cruising around on a shortwave dial, listening for foreign stations, foreign music, whoever she could get. She kept a notebook by her radio so that she could jot down the lyrics of her favorite songs, make notes about when different movies were playing, make sketches, things like that. This particular afternoon, she was listening to the radio and cruising the dial as she often did and was astonished to stumble upon what *sounded like* Amelia Earhart calling for help, and these were *anguished calls* for help. Amelia was arguing with and trying to deal with a man who was with her who was acting irrationally. Betty grabbed her notebook and just started copying down the phrases she could make out. The signals came in and out, and they weren't always clearly intelligible, but she wrote down what she could. This went on for, like, an hour and three-quarters, during which time her father came home from work and heard this.

He was excited about it, and he ran next door to his neighbor, who *also had a radio*, but didn't have the antenna setup the Klencks had. The neighbor couldn't get anything on his radio. When the signal and transmission stopped, Betty's father said, "We've got to get word to the Coast Guard." He took Betty's notebook, and he went down to the Coast Guard station in St. Pete and said, "Look, my daughter has been hearing these radio distress calls from Amelia Earhart. I heard them too. You've got to get the word out." And the response he got was, "Yeah, yeah, yeah, people are hearing this; we're on top of it. Don't worry about it; we got it." He couldn't get them to really pay any attention. He went back, and he was *very frustrated*. For years, he tried to get somebody to pay attention, and everybody just blew it off. Betty even wrote to Fred Goerner in the 1960s and said, "Look, I heard this stuff. I copied it down." Goerner said, "Yeah, well, that's all very interesting, but there's really nothing we can do with that." So Betty gave up. She kept the notebook, but she didn't try to get anybody to listen, she just gave up.

In 2000, we got some press, as we periodically do, and we got a call from Betty's neighbor, a guy named John Hathaway. He said, "Look, I've got a neighbor, she's an older lady who has this story about how she heard Amelia Earhart calling for help, and she wrote down what she heard in a notebook. She still has her notebook, but I'm not sure she'll even talk to you. She's so frustrated, but what she heard sounds like it matches what you're saying might have happened." I wanted to talk to her and see if she'd share her information with us. I talked to Betty on the phone, and she agreed to let me and my wife come out. They were in Illinois at the time, and her name was Betty Klenck-Brown at that time. Her husband was dealing with Alzheimer's and not in very good shape. We went out to Illinois and spent several hours with Betty, going through her notebook with her, and we videotaped that interview. We came away thinking that this really *sounds legitimate.*

Betty actually gave us the physical notebook to evaluate, and we checked the notebook.

It's a genuine notebook dating to 1937. All of the other notations she made in the notebook about songs she'd heard and all of that fit.

The notebook is *real.*

We started looking at it and sharing it, and the more we did, the more people recognized the same thing that we recognized. This is an incredible, almost *too intimate picture* of two people who are desperately trying to save their lives in a terrible situation.

Chris Williamson

On Amelia Earhart's birthday a few years ago, TIGHAR put out a report detailing post-loss radio signals. As we get into that report, I'd like you to tell the court who was listening to these signals and what exactly was being heard.

Ric Gillespie

Well, it was an all ships, all stations bulletin that the navy put up, and they put that out on the guard frequency that all ships at all stations always monitored. Anybody out there in the Central Pacific would receive this message: ships at sea, land stations, *anybody.* So there is no *list* of who received it, it was an all ships, all stations bulletin. It would be up to them whether they wanted to tune up those frequencies and listen for them or not. Pan American *did listen,* but they were limited because their direction-finding stations in Oahu, Midway and Wake were *also servicing* the Clipper flights that were going across.

When they had a Clipper flight inbound, they had to be on that frequency. They had to take care of their own business. When they weren't taking care of company business, they were listening, and they heard signals, and they were able to take bearings on several levels.

That's who was listening on the primary frequencies.

Chris Williamson

Accidental witnesses are also mentioned in this report. Now a lot of folks might ask how it would be possible for there to be accidental witnesses to something like this *in the first place.*

Can you explain that?

Ric Gillespie

Sure. It's not controversial at all.

She's putting out wavelengths of her primary frequencies, 3105 and 6210. At the same time those signals are going out, the radio is *also sending* multiples of those signals. Not intentionally, it's just the way the radio was made. They're called "harmonics"; they're higher frequencies than the primaries. Today, radios are shielded from doing that, because you can't have all this stuff on those frequencies going out over the airwaves, but *in 1937,* radios weren't shielded like that.

There was less concern about it because there was less radio traffic around to interfere.

Today, Earhart's radio would be called *very dirty,* because it's sending out all these spurious signals on harmonics. Well, the thing about harmonics is, they travel much further than the lower frequencies, they travel in a direct line of sight, but they also bounce off the ionosphere and can come down *anywhere.* It's not predictable, and it's not reliable as a means of communication, but if you happen on that frequency in a location where those signals are hitting, you'll pick it up.

So what you have are these people cruising their dial very much the way people surf the internet these days. People would just cruise their shortwave dials, looking for foreign stations, other news, or whatever, and they would be twisting the dial and suddenly hear somebody talking.

They tune in on it, and boom, there's Amelia Earhart calling for help. And they're just astonished by this. They're hearing her far better than the people who are listening on the primary frequencies out in the Pacific because those primary frequencies are fairly short range. Her airplane radio was not intended for worldwide communication. It was just meant to communicate a few hundred miles to local airports and stations. What the people out in the Pacific are hearing on the primary frequencies is sometimes just a carrier, somebody is transmitting on this frequency, and nobody *should be*. By law, it's a frequency that can only be used by US registered aircraft trying to call a ground station. That's why the *Itasca* had to get special permission.

Sometimes they're hearing an unintelligible voice. Somebody's talking; they can't understand what they're saying. That's not at all unusual with HF radio. If you've ever listened to HF radio, even when you've got a good connection, if atmospherics or something interferes with it, the signal can go from clearly understandable to not. She had gone past Naru on her way, trying to find Howland Island the *night before*. The operator at Naru had heard her the following night, when she had to be down. He hears the signals, and he can recognize the voice without the hum of the plane in the background. People out in the Pacific are hearing a lot of calls that they *think* are her, but they can't get a lot of information from them. The people who are getting a lot of information are the people who stumble upon the frequency, and there's not very many of them.

There were nine *credible receptions* around *North America*. Interestingly enough, even though the people who picked those nine up didn't know each other, they tell a consistent and deteriorating story of the situation. She's on a reef, the navigator's hurt, and then *after the third day*, she started to become worried about rising water.

Chris Williamson

When you're working a case like this and people who aren't associated with this flight or this search start coming out of the woodwork to give reports on something that they can't explain, and those all start to match up, how does that affect your hypothesis? Where does that fit into the rest of the case you're attempting to make for Nikumaroro?

• • •

Ric Gillespie

It's been critical.

The hypothesis is that Earhart was trying to find Howland Island but didn't. In trying to find Howland Island, she did exactly what she said she was going to do. She was running on the 157/337 line, which didn't bring her to Howland but *did* bring her to another island.

She's low on fuel, and she lands on the only place there is to land. The dry reef that's smooth like a runway.

She makes a *safe landing*. That's one thing we have a hard time with. Everybody wants her to crash.

She *didn't crash*; she made a safe landing.

She had to have, because she sent these radio calls. This goes on until rising tides and surf washed the airplane over the edge of the reef, leaving her and Noonan, who may have never made it out of the plane. She's literally marooned on a desert island, where she survives for a time, but eventually dies as a castaway at a campsite on the far end of the island, which happens to be the *best place* on the island for a castaway to hang out because of its particular characteristics.

Her bones are found in 1943 years later and misidentified by the British. The artifacts found with her, like parts of her shoe, are apparently thrown out because they're judged by the British to be of no importance. We hope we can find them, but three expeditions to Fiji have not turned them up.

I'm afraid they're *gone*.

We *do have* the British report, their full investigation that *does include* the doctors' measurements of the bones, which Jantz used to determine, as you know, to be a better than 99% chance that the castaway was Amelia Earhart. It's a very consistent story told by totally independent lines of evidence that are quantitative. These are documented signals. A radio signal, even though it's invisible, is a *thing* just like an artifact. If it's recorded at the time, as these were, it's a piece of evidence. We put people in jail because of cell phone signals. We kill people with drones because of electromagnetic signal records.

This is *hard evidence*. The bones are written documented evidence from the time. This is quantitative stuff.

The only mystery to me is *why* there's still a public perception among many that there *is* an Earhart mystery.

There's still more we can learn, and we're trying. We're going to continue to develop the data, we have a huge amount of data that we've assembled in thirty years of investigation, but *we know what happened.* The only explanation I have for the resistance among the public to accept this is the general problem we have in society these days of rampant science denial. Climate change, vaccinations, evolution, you can go right down the list.

That's the problem. All we can do is put up the hard evidence, and fortunately, it's increasingly being accepted.

Chris Williamson

But, Mr. Gillespie, the commanding officer of the USS *Itasca*, *dismissed all these signals.* If they're such a crucial piece of evidence in this investigation, wouldn't he have treated them as such?

Ric Gillespie

Oh, well, you're asking me to ascribe motivation, and I never met Warner Thompson. I've read a lot of what he wrote, and I know that his report is largely what is *often* known as "cover your butt." America's sweetheart aviator had disappeared on his watch, and he was very concerned about that. The whole episode had been terribly embarrassing for him. There had been no search plan formulated before Earhart disappeared, so when she *did disappear*, he's totally unprepared.

He's making it up as he goes along, and then there was this horrible incident on July 5, where the navy radio operator in Wailupe, Hawaii, gets this fragmentary code message that they interpret. It's very poorly sent code, and it's just phrases. We don't know how to break down the phrases because they didn't break them up. But it said, *"281 north Howland call KHAQQ beyond north. Don't hold with us much longer. Above water shut off."*

Thompson interpreted that "281 north" to mean they're floating around in the water, calling for help 281 miles *north* of Howland. That's what that means. So off he goes with the *Itasca* chugging along there, and he reports back to the Coast Guard headquarters in Hawaii that they interpret her to mean that she's in the water 280 miles north, and they're headed that way. Press representatives are hanging over the shoulders of radio operators in Hawaii, and they hear this.

"Oh, okay! They're on their way to rescue her!"

Well now, it's getting dark; it's coming up on nighttime. The *Itasca* is getting close to this place 281 miles north of Howland, and they're looking on the horizon, and somebody sees what *they think is a flare*.

Wow.

They send a radio message that's heard in Hawaii:

"We see your flares; we're on our way!"

Well, the press picks that up, and everybody goes crazy. The *Itasca* is getting inundated with these calls and offers for exclusive photographs of the rescue, the whole thing. They get to this place, and of course, there's nothing there. They get a message from the guys back at Howland Island, saying:

"Yeah, we see those things too; they're meteors."

The whole thing was *just such an embarrassment.* When it's all over and everybody's headed home, they've got to explain all this. The radio messages that everybody thought were quite genuine at the time hang over this thing like a ghost. They've got to *get rid of them.* So they make all these allegations; "Yeah, these were investigated and found to be hoaxes." Well, yeah, there were *some hoaxes*, but they were passive hoaxes. We've seen no evidence that anybody was out there transmitting signals pretending to be Earhart.

The hoaxes were people saying that they heard something they couldn't possibly have heard. So they had to get rid of the messages.

Thompson's report misstates all kinds of stuff; I go through it in *our* report.

It's full of demonstrably false statements. George Putnam and Paul

Mantz didn't buy it for a *second*. They were absolutely convinced that she was up there on an island someplace and she'd been left to die. They tried for years to raise the money to do their *own* search but were never able to do it.

Really, what we've done is pick up where somebody *should have* picked up back then.

Chris Williamson

Mr. Gillespie, one of the aspects of the search that criticizers of the castaway hypothesis use to contradict this theory is that there *was indeed* a flyover of the island during the search for Earhart and Noonan. So I'll ask you now, was there *in fact* a flyover of the island, and were ground crews ever deployed there during the search?

Ric Gillespie

No people were put on the ground at any of the islands.

The only islands that were searched were the islands in the Phoenix group. Well, no, that's actually not quite true; the *Itasca also* went over into the Gilbert Islands and made inquiries.

They didn't search, they asked people. The Gilbert Islands were densely populated, and they were British colonies, so that was easy. The Phoenix islands are uninhabited except for *one* of them.

They *did* put three airplanes from the battleship *Colorado* over the islands, searching for an airplane because they knew that in order for these signals to be genuine, there had to be an airplane on the ground, on its wheels, so they ought to be able to see it. By the time they get to the Phoenix Islands, the airplane's gone. They look down, and they don't see an airplane. They *do see* what the senior aviator described as "clear signs of recent habitation," but they were under the impression that all these islands had native work parties harvesting coconuts, with white supervisors. They weren't terribly surprised by the signs that somebody was there. They couldn't get anybody to come out and wave to them, so they eventually decide that no one's home.

They left, and the island was crossed off as searched, and that was the end of that. Now, *the next island* they searched that afternoon was Hull Island. There was a coconut operation there, so when they fly over Hull, they see huts, and they see natives standing on the roof, waving shirts or something. The senior aviator decides he's going to land in the lagoon there. John Lambert lands his plane in the lagoon; he can't taxi up to the shoreline because on all these islands, the lagoons are calm enough to land on if you can avoid hitting the coral heads. You can't get close to the shoreline because it gets too shallow. So he's sitting out there in his U-3 Corsair, and the white supervisor comes out in a canoe and talks with him. He says:

"Where on earth did you guys come from?!"
Lambert says, "We're looking for Amelia Earhart."
He responds with, "You're *what?!*"

He had no idea that Amelia Earhart had disappeared *anywhere*. He had a radio, but it could only be used to send code and communicate with his superiors. Back in June, there had been a solar eclipse up there. And he *knew* there was going to be a solar eclipse; it was well known. He'd been having trouble with his workers; they didn't want to work on Sunday.

He told his workers, "If you don't work this coming Sunday, I'm going to block out the sun to punish you." They said, "Yeah, right," and they didn't work on Sunday. On Monday, sure enough, a dragon eats the sun, and they figure the only way he could have arranged this was with that radio he uses, so they stormed into his radio shack and beat the living daylights out of his radio. His radio was out of commission until it was replaced in *August*.

So the Hull Island radio cannot be a source of post-loss radio signals suspected to be Earhart. That's why he didn't *know anything* about Earhart. Lambert takes off, and they search the other Phoenix Islands, but they don't land on any of those. They just assume that those signals have to come from an airplane *on land*, and we've looked on land; there's no airplane. Therefore *somehow* those signals must have been bogus. Once the *Lexington* shows up, the rest of the navy search takes place in open ocean, looking for floating wreckage or life rafts, and finds nothing. At the end of it, they say, "Well, she apparently just ran out of gas, looking for a tiny island in a big ocean, and she sank without a trace."

Chris Williamson

Do you think if the search teams were to have taken that same approach with Nikumaroro Island, that we'd be having a different conversation historically speaking? Would they have found them alive?

Ric Gillespie

We can only speak for Earhart, whose remains were found at this castaway campsite, along with food remains: burned fish, bird bones, and turtle bones. That indicates she had been alive for *certainly weeks, maybe months*. The navy overflight happened just a week after she disappeared, so yeah, Earhart was still alive. We can't speak for Noonan; we don't know what happened to him.

But Earhart was there someplace. If they had landed at Nikumaroro, he'd have the same problem he had at Hull; he can't go ashore and poke around. All he can do is sit out there on the lagoon.

Now, if she was someplace where she could get to the shore and wave to him, that'd be great, but we have no idea. We don't know where she was. If she was back in the shade, as any sensible person *would be* during the day, it can take ten minutes to get out to the beach through that dense vegetation.

I *know*. I've *been there*.

I also know that if you're on that island and an airplane or helicopter flies over, you don't know until they're right overhead because there's so much ambient noise from the surf and the trade winds. You don't hear them coming.

Imagine being on that island hoping for rescue, and seeing an airplane show up but fail to see you and leave.

You're screwed.

It would be *horrible*.

. . .

Chris Williamson

So, Mr. Gillespie, we have D. W. Hoodless examining the bones on Nikumaroro Island and determining them to be *male*.

Then we have the commanding officer of the *Itasca* dismissing these post-loss radio signals, attributing them to something *other* than what you've determined they *in fact are*.

Is this whole thing just certain people in certain positions making the wrong decisions regarding the data that's being presented to them?

Ric Gillespie

Sure. It's mistake after mistake after mistake. It's not a mystery, it's a mix-up, and you can *see* the errors. It's more difficult to ascribe motivation to the people who made the errors.

We know that the captain of the *Itasca* had kind of a bad attitude toward the whole thing.

It was never his idea to support the Earhart flight. *Now,* this is something he's assigned to do. They've got this Earhart flight, and they're supposed to send her the weather and signals that she can home in on. That's what they're supposed to do. They deliver the people who have fuel for her and are going to greet her and help service her airplane; that's their job. For the British, this whole story is just an amazing case. An administrative, almost unintentional head in the sand. You've got the high commissioner in Fiji, who is suddenly presented with this situation where a junior officer in one of the most remote parts of his domain in the Central Pacific has found what *could be* the remains of America's famous lost aviator, and this is September of 1940. The Battle of Britain is on, and England stands alone against Nazi Germany. Churchill was desperately trying to get Roosevelt to get Congress to provide more support; the American public is still very isolationist. It's a very delicate time diplomatically for Sir Harry Luke in Fiji.

To contact the Americans about this means he's going to have American press all over him, and he's going to have to deal with the

American government. So he says, "No, we're going to keep this investigation right here within Fiji. We're not going to send the bones down to the anatomy department at the University of Sydney," which was what was recommended. Hoodless was the principal of the Central Medical School, which was *not* a medical school in the way we think of a medical school. They didn't train doctors, they trained native medical practitioners, first responders. Hoodless didn't have any specific training in this, but he looked at the bones and applied the formulas available to him. But he misapplied them and came up with the conclusion that they were from a short, stocky man. Well, that's good news because now we don't need to worry about contacting the Americans, we can just forget about all of this, and that's exactly what they did. The whole incident disappeared. It wasn't intentionally hidden or anything, it just ended up in the file along with all the other records of the Western Pacific High Commission that disappeared like the Ark of the Covenant in the last scene of *Raiders of Lost Ark*. Until *we found* the file. It took ten years for us to track down this file in an obscure archive in England. Then we had the whole thing. It really *did* happen. We had Hoodless's report and all of his measurements. At that point, it became very apparent.

Chris Williamson

The very first time I spoke to you, you told me something interesting. You said that originally, you wanted nothing to do with this case. Now over thirty years later, do you ever think about the direction that TIGHAR *might have gone* had you chosen *not* to get involved in the search for Amelia Earhart and Fred Noonan?

Ric Gillespie

Well, honestly, no. We got involved in it reluctantly. If our initial investigation had not revealed that there might be something to it, we'd have walked away from that. We'd have probably concentrated *more* on the mystery of the *White Bird*, which I'm very impatient to get back to.

I think there's a lot more to be done there, and I think there's a chance that we can wrap that up as well. What we've proven to be good at is original source historical research. It's open source. It's through our members. It's *not me*, it's the people we've attracted to the organization. The historians, the scientists, the forensic experts, and the everyday people who have a great capacity to slog through the detective work and look for the original source material. It's just a powerhouse of research capability. It's my job to take the *results* of that research and help direct it toward what we hope are productive avenues, and present that information to the public for them to react to *any way they want*. It's not up to me to tell people *what happened* to Amelia Earhart.

I have to *show them*.

I have to show them what *we have found* that happened to Amelia Earhart, and they can accept that or not; it doesn't change the facts.

Everybody is entitled to their own opinions; they're not entitled to their own facts.

They can interpret facts any way they want to and form their own opinions.

All we can do is present the facts.

It's up to everybody else to decide for *themselves*.

Chris Williamson
Thank you, Mr. Gillespie. No further questions, Your Honor.

"Things just started adding up, and once you have that body of evidence, you have to start applying things like Occam's razor. Is there a simpler explanation for this? There isn't."

Chris Williamson

Your Honor, the project calls *Mr. Jeff Glickman* to the stand.

Mr. Glickman, can you tell the court a little about your education and your professional background?

Jeff Glickman

Sure, my background is in computer science. I was trained at the University of Illinois at Urbana Champaign, and I have a strong background there academically in image processing and pattern recognition. I got into the forensic side of things, as many people do, as a related activity to their primary area of academia. Forensics, as you probably know, means simply to argue. There are about three hundred different fields under the umbrella of forensics.

Chris Williamson

Can you give the court an overview of the science of forensic analyzation and processing, please?

Jeff Glickman

It varies pretty widely depending upon what the particular case or subject material is. The essentials of it have to do with creating some kind of imagery, whether it's from a regular camera, a film camera, a digital camera, or a surveillance camera, some of which might be in the form of moving images. I'm always careful to say that because moving images are really just sequences of still images. How they are taken, stored and managed can vary significantly, depending upon whether they're analog or whether they are of a digital origin. The kind of processing really depends upon the case. It's very hard to say. You have to be very specific about what kind of case, and from there, you can dive into what kind of processing might be amenable to that specific problem.

Chris Williamson

Mr. Glickman, the item known as "the Bevington Object" and said photo attached to that object have become a pillar of the castaway hypothesis. Regarding the age of this photo, is anything special being done when it comes to its investigation, or is this simply the same process as it always is?

Jeff Glickman

Both, actually. The nature of older film is you have to deal with something called *film grain*.

This is the molecular composition of the photo emulsion. The older the film, usually the grainer it is.

It has a larger grain size, and even the shape of the grain changes. How you choose to do the processing may vary because of that. In particular, some of the processing you may choose to use may interact in a positive way *or* a negative way. With source media, notably in digital photography, the pixels are square, but subsequent processing and storage of that digital imagery may also affect the way that you process them, and I'll give you a couple of examples.

In film grain, the grain is laid out in irregular patterns on the photo motion layer. If you drew a vertical column or horizontal line, you wouldn't really know whether or not you're going to intersect the grain and what percentage of the grain you might intersect, assuming you are looking at a sufficiently resolute image. If you compare that to digital photography, everything's *rectilinear*, so you're going to find that all of these pixels will align.

In the case of digital imagery, and particularly if it's images that have been stored in a compressed form, like a JPEG image, you're going to run into blocks of pixels, sometimes eight by eight, sometimes other sizes, thirty-two by thirty-two, that are going to behave differently than adjacent blocks. This is because of the way that JPEG images are stored. So the choice of processing is highly sensitive to the original source media. It's very important that you're able to trace backwards and find that origin of materials so you're able to process it with as little artifact as possible. That means when you're processing, there's the potential to introduce false information. You want to hold that to a minimum and certainly understand the way in which you're affecting the subsequent imagery.

Chris Williamson

I know that some cases might take longer than others, but in a *general sense*, how long might it take to come up with a conclusion on an image and deliver those results to a client?

Jeff Glickman

There's no typical answer to that. I've had cases where we've been able to give very quick and accurate work within twenty-four to forty-eight hours, which is about as fast as you can go. Of course, in forensics, the report is actually more important than the processing. Frankly, I've had other cases where a decade has gone by.

In order to be able to get processing accomplished, sometimes the technology just isn't there at the time that we start the case.

Chris Williamson

Mr. Glickman, can you tell the court how your work on this hypothesis and this image in particular began?

Jeff Glickman

Yeah, happy to do that. I think the year was 1995. I think I saw Ric on a television show or newscast or something, and he was describing some issues that they were having with the project, including interpretation of imagery. I thought this was something I could probably lend some expertise to, so I picked up the phone, and I called him. I said, "Look, this is a field I'm an expert in; perhaps I can help you." He took me up on the offer, and I've worked with him now for close to twenty-five years.

Chris Williamson

Was the idea here strictly that you could help *prove* this hypothesis, or were there other reasons that you might have wanted to get involved?

Jeff Glickman

Well, probably both. It's just a good thing to give something back. If there's opportunities to do work on a pro bono basis, I try to do that from time to time.

Chris Williamson

At this time, I'd like to offer project's exhibit 4, which is TIGHAR's 2017 report on the Bevington object.

Jen Taylor

I'm going to object under *federal rule of evidence 705 and under Daubert.*

Judge

Overruled. The report is admitted.

Jen Taylor

Thanks a lot.

Chris Williamson

Mr. Glickman, tell us how you got introduced to the Bevington image and tell the court what your initial thoughts were on it.

Jeff Glickman

Yeah, it's a funny story. I met Ric, and initially, he had sent me a bunch of negatives for images.

I don't know what year it was but probably somewhere around 1998 or 2000. We were looking for a water-collection device, which had been reported anecdotally, and which I *did eventually end up finding* in the imagery. So I have this collection of negatives, which just basically went to cold storage. About a decade later, Ric said, "Hey, we're going back to the island. Do you mind just taking a look at some of the historical imagery?"

This particular image was interesting in that you could see a large horizon of the island, in addition to the SS *Norwich City*, which is an old ship. Just by happenstance, Ric had focused in and essentially cropped a digital copy of the image, which he kept back at TIGHAR headquarters in order to focus in on the SS *Norwich City*, which really was the only thing of interest in the image. Now *I had* the original uncropped negative *here*. When I started researching for the 2010 trip, I just reviewed all the imagery, and I ran across an anomaly in this particular image that just didn't make visual sense. Something cognitive told me that this is not a normal sort of image defect; it's very, very small on the negative. There are so many defects that you can have due to processing, due to film staining, any number of sources.

It's *easy* to overlook something like this.

Starting in 2010, I spent the better part of a year looking at this image, and after a year's worth of analysis and processing, I came to the conclusion that this was actually something *on the reef*. My interpretation of it at the end of that period was that it was part of a landing gear assembly with part of a tire attached to that landing gear assembly.

I reported that to Ric, and then Ric, of course, took that to some other folks for review. We always do things with confirmation.

Chris Williamson

And how did you arrive at the determination that this was a landing gear in this image that you were studying?

Jeff Glickman

You first try to rule out possibilities.

What kind of defect could this possibly be? Defects on film tend to have certain specific patterns to them. One thing they *don't* tend to do is they don't tend to create an appearance of shadows, because if there's an appearance of a shadow, then that's suggestive of something originating from the imagery instead of coming from the film surface. So you look for contradictions in information, and they're often adjacent on the image. From there, you can keep working up the abstract concept hierarchy. When you eliminate the possibility of it being something related to the film or the film processing, then you move to it being something that the camera actually took an image *of*. What are all the potential possibilities? What can be included or excluded?

Eventually, that took me to the examination of engineering drawings for the Lockheed airframe.

We went down the path of looking at the landing gear assembly, the circular portion being related of course, to the tire, as we now know. In doing so, Ric remembered that there was some historical imagery of one of Earhart's crash landings.

We compared the failure of the landing gear assembly in *that crash* to the object that was on the reef, and there were some remarkable similarities between the two.

Probably because of the kind of stress that was put onto the landing gear assembly. We *do* know from the engineering work that was done on the airplane that the lateral stress load that can be placed on the landing gear was quite small. When there's lateral stress, it could cause the landing gear to snap off. Things just started adding up, and once you have that body of evidence, you have to start applying things like Occam's razor.

Is there a simpler explanation for this?

There *isn't*.

Chris Williamson

Is it difficult to remain objective while you're working on something that appears to be more and more *like* what you're thinking it might be?

Jeff Glickman

For objective analysis, excitement is a hazard. It's not something you really want to do.

You want to separate the emotions from the analysis and make sure you stay on the straight and narrow.

Chris Williamson

What were the conclusions of the others Ric took the data to? Did they agree with your findings?

Jeff Glickman

I had no involvement with that portion of it, which is all for the better. Again, you want to keep these silos of information separate to make sure that the analysts don't contaminate each other's opinions.

Chris Williamson

Thank you, Mr. Glickman. No more questions.

"The trouble is, it's very hard to disprove a negative. If you're trying to prove that Earhart did not land on Nikumaroro, the only way you're going to prove that is by finding her someplace else."

Chris Williamson

The project calls *Dr. Tom King* to the stand.

Dr. King, can you please tell the court where your professional specialty lies?

Dr. Tom King

My training is in anthropology and archaeology, and I've been working in that field for fifty plus years. Mostly, I work in and around historic preservation law, though I'm not a lawyer. I work with local communities and Indian tribes and folks like that to help them use the historic preservation laws to protect places that are culturally and historically important to them. I kind of fell into the Earhart thing by accident.

Chris Williamson

Can you elaborate a little more on how you got involved in the Earhart Noonan case and tell us how long you've been studying this now?

Dr. Tom King

I've been dealing with the Earhart case since 1988. I was working then for an agency called the Advisory Council on Historic Preservation in Washington, DC. Ric Gillespie of TIGHAR called us up, looking for advice regarding standards for preserving historic aircraft. Ric and I talked over the months that followed, and one day he called to ask a question about the archaeological ethics of managing artifacts that might be found if they found Amelia Earhart. He told me that they were going to undertake this project to look for Earhart on this unin-habited island in the South Pacific. About that time, I was fleeing government. I survived the Reagan administration, but not the first Bush administration.

He was talking about the first day covers, and I remember telling him that he wouldn't find paper products from a crashed airplane on a tropical island that had been there at that point for fifty plus years. I went on to tell him that I'd done archaeology in the South Pacific, and if he needed an archaeologist on this thing, to let me know. I joined the first expedition and got hooked.

Chris Williamson

When you came aboard the project, was there something in partic-ular that piqued your curiosity regarding this potential outcome?

Dr. Tom King

Ric Gillespie had been approached by these two guys, Tom Willie and Tom Gannon, who were retired aerial navigators. They had come to him with this hypothesis; they said, "Look, Noonan would have been using the same methodology that we were trained to use."

That would have involved using his celestial navigation to plot a line of position running perpendicular to their route and advancing it by dead reckoning until he calculated that they should be on Howland Island. If they couldn't then see Howland, they would fly along that line of position until they found it or ran out of fuel and went into the drink. The line of position would have been 157/337 degrees.

Well, Earhart in one of her last universally accepted transmissions says, "I'm flying on the line 157/ 337." Okay, you take the 157/337 line, and you plot it *through* Howland Island.

To the south, it hits Nikumaroro after an hour or so of flying. Ric said, "Look, she obviously went toward this island." Tom Willie and Tom Gannon said, "Yeah, isn't that interesting? Too bad they didn't search there." Ric was surprised, and he said, "What?! They didn't search there?!" Well, no, they *didn't*. Ric concluded that it ought to be searched, and that made sense to me. That was what attracted me to the idea in the first place. That and the fact that I *love* the South Pacific. I had done archaeological work there, and I just thought it would be a kick to go to another island that was completely uninhabited and see what it was like.

Chris Williamson

Before you got involved in this hypothesis, had you had any previous thoughts on what might have happened to Amelia Earhart and Fred Noonan?

My father was on Saipan at the end of World War II in military government. He had heard a lot of Earhart stories, and his attitude, which he brought back and conveyed to me, was basically that she ran out of fuel and went into the drink, and that was pretty much what I assumed.

In the late 1970s, I was assigned to help set up historic preservation programs in the new governments of Micronesia, and I was based *on* Saipan, so I heard the Earhart stories, and I didn't pay much attention to them.

It wasn't my business to go *look* for Earhart.

It was my business to set up historic preservation programs, but I kept hearing these stories, and I thought, "Well, these are interesting rumors, but that's about all." I had no particular preconceived notion except a sort of general bias toward what we *now call* the crash and sink hypothesis.

Chris Williamson

The stories that you mentioned your father told you and that you yourself had heard regarding Saipan, are those the *same stories* of Earhart and Noonan potentially being under Japanese capture there?

Dr. Tom King

They were usually second or thirdhand stories of people seeing

Earhart or people seeing a person *they interpreted to be* Earhart in Japanese captivity, yes.

Chris Williamson

Dr. King, as someone who has studied this case and this theory in particular, can you give the court your professional opinion on what happened on the morning of July 2, 1937?

Dr. Tom King

Well, I don't know that I have an opinion as such. My guess? They got to what Noonan calculated to be the vicinity of Howland Island, they couldn't see Howland well, and they couldn't make radio communication with the *Itasca*. They looked around for a while and said, "Well, hell, we can't find it, we had better fly along the line of position until we do find it." Flying north was not a very good option because if they were north of Howland, they would have been flying into nothingness. In theory, they would eventually see Howland.

My guess is that perhaps after flying north for a time or flying around in circles for a time, they flew south southeast along the line of position and eventually came in sight of Nikumaroro.

Chris Williamson

Dr. King, can you please give the definition of a *hypothesis* to the court?

Dr. Tom King

A hypothesis is an educated guess that can be tested.

Chris Williamson

Is there a general difference between a *hypothesis* and a *theory?*

Dr. Tom King

Yes. A theory is a much more developed body of thinking, with analysis, and so on. The theory of evolution, for example, is a very developed, robust body of thinking about how species evolve. It's *not* known fact, but it's pretty well nailed down. We have a very strong idea of how evolution works. We have a whole set of mechanisms that are built into theories. A hypothesis is a much more flexible term, and it's very loosey-goosey. It's basically something that you come up with.

I've lost my car keys. My hypothesis about where my car keys are is that I left them on the kitchen table. I test that hypothesis by going and looking on the kitchen table. Whoops, they're not there. Well, then, we'll have to reformulate the hypothesis and say, "Maybe I dropped them in the toilet." We then test that hypothesis, and we go forward like that.

Chris Williamson

Having said that, would it then be safe for me to say that a hypothesis would be foundational and would graduate into a theory if there was *enough information* to support that evolution?

Dr. Tom King

Oh, I suppose. You're getting into something that's really a matter for general semanticists and people who are into the philosophy of science to respond to that. Theory is just something that you apply to something rather general to which you can apply a lot of principles. We talk about the theory of relativity and so on. A hypothesis is simply a much more flexible term.

Chris Williamson

Okay. Let's move on to the archaeological aspect of what's been collected and studied on Nikumaroro. Aside from the much discussed and debated Nikumaroro bones, can you tell the court a little about some of the standout pieces that have been collected during the course of the last thirty plus years on that island?

Dr. Tom King

There are *two locations* on the island where we've done significant archaeological research and come up with considerable data: One is the colonial village that was occupied from 1939 to 1963, and it's very apparent that people there were harvesting or quarrying airplane parts, bringing them into the village to use mostly in handicrafts. To inlay boxes with them, to make hair foams, maybe fish lures, a variety of things like that. We found such things in the colonial village.

Aircraft aluminum was usually cut into pieces and sometimes made into specific things like hair combs. Sometimes it is demonstrably from a liberator bomber. There was a liberator bomber that went down on Canton Island about 150 miles away, and we know that people were back and forth between Nikumaroro and Canton. *Some* of the aluminum, perhaps *all* of the aluminum undoubtedly came from Canton Island, but a lot of the aluminum does not appear to be military.

The thing about military aluminum is that it's usually painted with zinc chromate paint, and it often has serial numbers on it and things like that. We have a lot of aluminum that does not have zinc chromate and does not have serial numbers and is the kind of aluminum, thickness and weight wise, that was found in Earhart's plane. We have a little bit of Plexiglas, too, that's the same thickness and curvature of the windows in Earhart's plane. We have this big piece, TIGHAR artifact 2-2-V-1, that has been the subject of considerable analysis at TIGHAR. TIGHAR also has photo imagery of the airplane at Lae shortly before takeoff. That gives TIGHAR and its experts a much better basis for comparison with this large chunk of aluminum found in the colonial village in 1991.

There are other artifacts from the village, and the nice thing about the village is that it collects stuff. People were collecting stuff and bringing it in. The difficulty with the village is the same thing: people were collecting stuff and bringing it in. They collected it from all over, and of course they lived there for a long time. There's all kinds of confusion in the village. We found a flashlight from the 1930s, and it's the kind of flashlight that Earhart *probably had* on her airplane. It's also the kind of flashlight that lots of *other people* probably had. So colonial village is one place.

The other place is the seven site at the southeast end of the island. It's called *the seven site* because there was a natural seven-shaped clearing in the vegetation at that point. It's pretty much gone now; we've destroyed it. We have historical evidence that human bones were found there in 1940. Thirteen human bones, including a cranium, a mandible, long bones and so on that were sent to Fiji for analysis and lost in Fiji during World War II.

The analysis by a medical doctor at the time reported they probably had an adult European or mixed-race male. Reanalysis of his notes by a modern forensic anthropologist suggests that it was maybe a female about Earhart's height and character. So yeah, we don't know. We think that that discovery took place at the seven site. In 2017, we had forensic dogs confirm that a human body had decomposed at seven site.

At this site, we found a number of what amounts to campfire features. Somebody was camping, and they were cooking fish, birds and turtles. The way they were procuring particularly the fish and the turtles was *not the way* that local people procured them. For example, there was basically a random selection of fish from the reef, whereas local people knew what kind of fish to procure; they're selective about it. Whoever was camping at the site was not being selective. We found similar kinds of things with shellfish and so on, that gets into a lot of detailed analysis.

There were also some very interesting artifacts, including a number of fragments of what appears to be a woman's compact, a little rectangular compact with a mirror, and rouge. It appears to be the size and shape of a compact that we have photographs of Earhart holding during the world flight, so that's pretty interesting. We also have a little jar that apparently contained freckle cream. Earhart had freckles and apparently was not very happy about them. She was very careful about how she was perceived by the press, so it's not *implausible* that she would be carrying a bit of this freckle cream, which was a terrible mercury-based substance to dab on her freckles and make them fade away. We can't say that was the case, but it's a possibility. There are artifacts like that plus a number of *others* from the 1930s that came from the United States that we found around the fire features at seven site. That's everything in a nutshell.

Chris Williamson

What does all of this data and information that's been discovered *do* for the theory? If we were to remove Amelia Earhart from this equation, would we be able to say that an amount of data this large helps bring this theory from the realm of possibility to that of a probability?

Dr. Tom King

Again, it's a hypothesis. It's not a theory.

I think it is a *plausible hypothesis*, and the evidence supports it. We don't have evidence refuting it. Of course, the trouble is, it's very hard to disprove a negative. If you're trying to prove that Earhart did not land on Nikumaroro, the only way you're going to prove that is by finding her someplace else, and we, frankly, haven't looked *someplace else*. We don't have the money or time to go out and look elsewhere. Nikumaroro is where we've looked, and we found evidence that appears to support the hypothesis. Now, some of what we've found turns out *not to support* the hypothesis. We had evidence of this sextant box that was found in 1940 on the site, and it turned out to be a US Navy surplus sextant box. We thought, "Wow, that obviously belonged to Noonan."

Well, John Kada recently and rather definitively showed that it didn't belong to Noonan, it came from the USS *Bushnell*, which visited the island in 1939. We don't know how it got from the *Bushnell* to the seven site, but it does not appear to have come from Noonan.

We were wrong about that, and that happens *all* the time.

We're right about some things and wrong about others. One of the problems with the seven site is that a lot of people have done stuff there. The colonists did stuff there, the Coast Guardsman who had a station just a quarter mile away did stuff there, and everything archaeologically on the site is in the top ten centimeters of the deposit. So it's all mixed together, and it's difficult to sort stuff out. It's a problematical site. Right now, the evidence we have all points toward Earhart having camped there for a time and died there.

Chris Williamson

One of the aspects of what TIGHAR has done that's very admirable is the fact that most of, if not all of, their data is published and available for review. In some cases, it *has actually been* peer reviewed by outside sources. Scientifically speaking, what is the benefit of peer review for a case like this? Does it lead more credence to what you're trying to prove?

Dr. Tom King

Well, peer review, I think, is a rather badly misused term. People make it more official and formal than it really is. This is a public activity, and we have expert colleagues and people with a lot of different kinds of knowledge who looked at our data and can reflect on it. It's very important to have those reflections and observations, and John Kada is a good example of that. He came out of nowhere, as far as I'm concerned, but he had the initiative to go out and do the research to show that we were *wrong* about the sextant box. That is a very important kind of peer review. Whether it shows us that we're right or wrong on a given piece of evidence, it's very, very important. I'm working with and being open to our peers. I don't know what a peer *is* anyway, *everybody's* my peer who happens to be alive today, and I'm happy to hear from anybody and comment on what they say. It all helps inform the pursuit of the hypothesis.

Chris Williamson

Dr. King, how has your personal opinion of this case, this hypothesis, and the work that's been done over the course of the last thirty years evolved for you?

Dr. Tom King

I think it's fair to say that when I got involved in 1989, it was pretty much a lark. "Oh, hey, let's go to this uninhabited island to look around, and maybe we'll find this airplane." Well, that was idiotic, there was no way we were going to find an airplane sitting on Nikumaroro, but we didn't know that at the time. We bashed about in the bushes, looking for an airplane, and obviously didn't find it. Then more data came in, and we came to look at the project and the situation from different angles. I've learned a lot about how you do research from this project, and in terms of how my opinion has changed, I have become, if anything, *more convinced*. *Yes*, this is basically a correct hypothesis, and we've got the right idea.

I am more than willing to entertain *other* hypotheses.

I've been trying to get somebody to go out and check Tom Maxwell's Orona hypothesis, because I think it's very interesting, and it would blow our hypothesis *completely* out of the water. It's an interesting idea, and I think it needs to be objectively pursued. That being said, the Nikumaroro hypothesis looks to me like the most likely one to be right, and we've got a good deal of evidence to support it. I really would like to see that evidence worked up in a standard scholarly format and made available to the world. I don't know how that's going to happen; I'm no longer associated with TIGHAR. I don't know that anybody in TIGHAR is oriented toward organizing all the data and getting it into a form that the world can use, but I think that's an important thing that needs to be done.

Chris Williamson

Thank you, Your Honor. Pass the witness.

Cross-Examination of Dr. Tom King

Jen Taylor

Dr. King, you just mentioned that you're no longer associated with TIGHAR, is that correct?

Dr. Tom King

Yes, I was the volunteer, senior archaeologist for TIGHAR and was on their board of directors.

Jen Taylor

Okay. Are you comfortable going into *why* you're no longer associated with TIGHAR?

Dr. Tom King

Oh, sure. How can I say this...I disagreed with some of the approaches that were taken by the organization's leader, Ric Gillespie. Ric has, over the years, become increasingly impatient with people who disagree with him, and he particularly disliked the fact that I published a novel interpreting what happened to Earhart. He felt that was deeply irresponsible and contrary to his interpretation of scientific methodology, and I took strong issue with that. I took strong issue with his insistence that we sort of back away from work on land on the island and focus on trying to find the airplane *underwater*, which I think is a fool's errand. He disliked that, so we had a lot of disagreements and could not reach a meeting of the mind. Eventually, he decided I should leave, and I eventually *did*.

Jen Taylor

Okay. You mentioned searching on land versus searching in water. You call it a "fool's errand" to search for the plane in the water; can you elaborate on that? Do you think that the plane is impossible to find at this point?

Dr. Tom King

Assuming that what happened is what *we think happened*, it's most likely that the plane is broken up into tiny little pieces and has pretty much been absorbed into the reef, which makes it extremely difficult to locate. The notion that somebody is going to find a great big chunk of it offshore is foolish. You can sink a lot of money into looking for airplane parts on a reef, and I have objected to devoting our time and money to that as opposed to focusing on work *on land*, where we know we have found evidence and there is productive work to be done.

Jen Taylor

Can you elaborate on why you believe the plane is broken up into little pieces as opposed to one larger piece? The people working crash and sink feel that the plane would be intact, and the people working Buka will likely tell us that the plane is intact but enveloped by coral. What is it about this hypothesis that *you have seen* that tells you the plane would be broken up?

Dr. Tom King

Well, there are places where planes can be intact in the water. Obviously, planes can be intact in the water just like lots of stuff can be. But there's water and then there's *water*.

The situation on Nikumaroro is that you've got a reef flat where we think that Earhart and Noonan put the Electra down. The reef flat ends at a reef edge. That is an extremely high-energy environment where surf comes up and breaks on the reef edge. Anything that is caught on that reef edge is going to be torn to pieces. Now, if the airplane manages to float off that edge more or less intact at a distance and then sink, okay, it's going to be down there more or less intact at great depths. The reef goes down very, very quickly. It's a sheer drop to a great depth, something like seven thousand meters. Maybe some big piece of the plane is somewhere way down at the base of the reef, which makes it very hard to find in its own right. *Or* I think it's more likely that the plane was hung up on the reef edge and battered to little bitty pieces by the surf. It's a different situation for crash and sink because they're thinking that she went into the drink in the open ocean. There's nothing to do there but sink in a more or less *intact condition*. The Buka folks, as I understand it, think that she came down in a relatively protected environment and simply went in and sank. So the environments are different, and the potential for preservation is different.

Jen Taylor

You also talked about searching on land; you're an archaeologist?

Dr. Tom King

That's correct.

Jen Taylor

So your specialty is looking on the island and actually digging on the island, trying to find historic artifacts that might support the hypothesis that Fred Noonan and Amelia Earhart lived on Nikumaroro for some time, that's correct?

Dr. Tom King

We're not just looking for artifacts. We're looking for data that relates to the hypothesis that Earhart and Noonan wound up there. Maybe it supports it, maybe it refutes it, but we're looking for information that relates to the hypothesis.

Jen Taylor

You mentioned several today. I know you're particularly interested in the compact found there. Do you think that's the strongest piece of evidence that it was Amelia Earhart and Fred Noonan there at that site?

Dr. Tom King

I don't believe in smoking guns, *okay?*

I don't believe in getting into making statements regarding a strong or weak piece of evidence. It's the accumulated body of evidence that matters. I like the compact because I think it's fairly definitive, and it's an interesting little piece of evidence that when put together with the freckle cream jar and the other skin lotions and the pocketknife makes for a very attractive picture.

The problem is, of course, that there were other people there who could have brought them.

Sorting everything out is extremely difficult because the artifacts and fire features are all at the seven site in this very difficult place to work because it is a coral-rubble ridge at the southeast end of the island where everything is in the top ten centimeters. So you can't say "Oh, well, this is earlier than that because it's deeper in the stratigraphy." There is no real stratigraphy, everything is layered together, so that makes it complicated. It's very easy to misinterpret the data, but the data is still there to be interpreted.

Jen Taylor

In the legal world, we use this phrase called "the totality of the circumstances." What you're telling me is that *you're confident* that based on the totality of the circumstances, and the totality of the evidence you've seen, somebody who *was not a local* was camping at what you're calling seven site. Am I understanding that correctly?

Dr. Tom King

Yes, you're understanding that correctly.

Jen Taylor

I know you've already acknowledged that it could be a number of other castaways, and we don't know for sure yet that it was Amelia and Fred. Am I understanding *that correctly as well?*

Dr. Tom King

Yes, you are.

Jen Taylor

You've made it clear that you don't believe in smoking guns. If that's the case, then at what point in *your mind* would you say, "We've done it. We have been able to show with certainty that Amelia Earhart and Fred Noonan were there?" Is there ever going to be a point where you reach that level? What is it that you're looking for that will allow you to say "mystery solved"?

Dr. Tom King

I don't know that I'd *ever* say that, and that doesn't particularly trouble me.

Certainty is not something that I'm very familiar with in life.

We may reach a level of certainty at some point, or we may never reach it. If we ever get back to the island, the big thing we're looking for is human remains that contain testable DNA. Whether we can find such remains, remains to be seen, as it were.

Jen Taylor

The reason why I ask a question like that is because there are people associated with this hypothesis who strongly believe this is the answer. As you heard earlier from Mr. Dunning during our crash and sink segment, people who have alternate hypotheses are not only wrong, but *so wrong* that we shouldn't even give them a platform to speak. When it comes to this hypothesis, I'm trying to understand why there's such certainty if we *don't have* a smoking gun, and it seems unlikely that we ever will. What is it about this hypothesis that convinces people to think, *no*, this is the *only right answer?*

Dr. Tom King

Well, what is it about *any hypothesis* that makes people think that?

Jen Taylor

Let me *rephrase*, then. What *evidence* is out there that makes people think this is the only right answer?

Dr. Tom King

I think you look at the body of evidence, starting with the line of position and the fact that the island is on the course that Earhart said she was flying in her last universally accepted radio message. Then you have all the post-loss radio messages, some of which were received by stations with radio direction finding equipment. When you plot there, the bearings on those radio messages cross in the vicinity of Nikumaroro. You take that and add things like the Bevington object and the photograph from 1937 that appears to show the landing gear of a Lockheed Electra sticking up off the reef at the location where we think she landed. You take that information, in addition to the pieces of airplane that we found in the colonial village, and the material from the seven site, and put *all* of it together.

I think it presents a pretty convincing case. Now, I say "a pretty convincing case." Others say, "Proof! We've got it! Case closed!"

Well, I don't believe in closed cases pretty much *ever*, but that's just a difference in approach.

Jen Taylor

During crash and sink, we had guests say, "We have to trust what Amelia said." So let's go through some of those things now. "KHAQQ calling *Itasca*. We must be on you but cannot see you. But gas is running low. Been unable to reach you by radio. We are flying at one thousand feet." You're familiar with that?

Dr. Tom King

Yes.

Jen Taylor

She said she was running low on fuel. I know there's been a lot of debate about what that *means*.

What does that mean *to you?*

Dr. Tom King

Well, she thinks she's running low on fuel. What's *important* is what's that mean to *Earhart*? I don't think anyone can really say.

Jen Taylor

Do you have any thoughts on what she said in that same transmission regarding flying at one thousand feet at that time?

Dr. Tom King

No, I'm not a pilot. I'm not an aerial navigator. Why she would have chosen to fly at one thousand feet is not something that I can comment on with any authority at all. Many other people have, and they've come up with different sorts of interpretations, which I think are very interesting, but that's not something that I can comment on.

Jen Taylor

I want to ask you about the transmission that you were speaking of earlier, "KHAQQ to *Itasca*. We are on the line 157/337. Will repeat message. We will repeat north and south. We will repeat this on 6210." My understanding based on reading this is that *she believes* she was low on fuel at 7:43. At 8:43, about an hour later, she's sending this transmission saying they're going to start going north and south on the sunline at 157/337. By the way, there's a little notation here that says the signal strength is coming in at an S-5 at this point. So an hour later, would you agree that based on this, she's still close, and she's still trying to find the island?

Dr. Tom King

She's doing exactly what the aerial navigators who initially proposed the Nikumaroro hypothesis to TIGHAR told us she would be doing. They had laid out their line of position, they advanced it by dead reckoning until they calculated that it should run through Howland, they didn't see Howland, so they flew north and south on 157/337 along the line of position, hoping to see it. They were doing that presumably at different altitudes trying to see it. A perfectly rational strategy.

Jen Taylor

She was also trying to establish communication with the *Itasca*, and she was at certain points trying to get them to get a bearing on her.

Dr. Tom King

Yes.

Jen Taylor

It looks like she was calling in every half an hour or so, trying to reach them. Would you agree that's the pattern we're seeing?

Dr. Tom King

I really turn to Ric Gillespie's interpretation for that because he's looked at this in really considerable detail, and I think that he and others' analysis makes a lot of sense. She did a bad job of working out with *Itasca* exactly *when* they were going to communicate with each other.

She apparently lost her belly antenna on takeoff from Lae, which seriously compromised her ability to communicate. The result being she couldn't communicate with the *Itasca*, and they couldn't get a bearing on her.

So they were out of luck.

Jen Taylor

The point of my question is that she was attempting every so often to get in touch. Here at 8:42, she's calling in again, "We are on line 157/337," and the signal strength is coming in really strong. At this point, she's still close, but that's her last transmission.

How do you explain the fact that she abruptly *stops* sending signals?

Dr. Tom King

Well, there are all kinds of things we don't know.

We don't know what the condition of her radios were. There are all kinds of reasons that she might have been unable to commit to continuing communication. How do you account for a negative? We really can't. She may have been communicating like crazy, and for one reason or another, something didn't work, and her calls didn't come through.

Beats me.

It's not a simple matter of them being close because the signal is strong. It's a lot more complex than that. There are a lot of variables that come into the picture at that point, *none of which* I understand, that may affect her signals. I just don't think we can say definitively *why* she wasn't heard after a particular point. There were all the post-loss signals that were heard. It's not my area of expertise, and I will happily rely on the experts for their opinion. It's not a simple matter of, "We stopped hearing her, so she must have gone into the drink."

Jen Taylor

Sure, and I understand that the signals are not your area of expertise, but even on TIGHAR's website it's acknowledged that *some of those signals* that were coming in were proven to be hoaxes. How do we know which one is real and reliable that we can use to try to locate them as opposed to somebody just sending something out?

Dr. Tom King

Oh, I think it's largely guesswork. There are things with the post-loss signals that Ric has looked at, and I think it certainly makes sense. You look for the esoteric things a hoaxer couldn't come up with. If she's down on an island, are there specific things she's referring to that make sense in terms of the island that a hoaxer wouldn't know about? Some of those kind of work out, but it's really very much a guessing game.

Jen Taylor

I have no further questions for this witness, Your Honor.

"I think you approach every artifact with the same degree of objectivity and try to see whose story this artifact is telling, realizing that at the end of that process, you'll have an interesting story no matter who it might be."

Chris Williamson

The project calls *Mr. Joe Cerniglia* to the stand.

Mr. Cerniglia, can you tell the court where your professional background lies?

Joe Cerniglia

It's quite far away from Earhart, but maybe *not* if you think about it. I am a senior consultant for Aetna Incorporated, and I work in the field of data analysis for health insurance.

Chris Williamson

Most people generally accept that Amelia Earhart and Fred Noonan crashed in the ocean near Howland Island. Can you tell the court what process you went through to go through the evidence in this case and ultimately make a determination that she and Noonan likely ended up on Nikumaroro?

Joe Cerniglia

I was interested in her disappearance, but I didn't *start* with the disappearance, because I thought that was something that was too far out there to fully understand. I wanted to consider her *life first* and then, maybe in time, try to look at that. I had always thought that the crash and sink hypothesis was the *correct one* simply because it was the most logical from the standpoint of the Pacific being very large. I eventually reached the level of maturity in which one begins to understand that one has to think for oneself and realize that everything that you read or hear is to *some degree* mediated.

There's no perfect objectivity.

Everyone is trying to persuade and tell their story. Once you begin to understand that, you begin to think for yourself. When I came to that point, that is when I read Elgen Long's book on the disappearance.

I found it very well written, and I thought it to be very logical. After that, I turned to the Nikumaroro hypothesis and started reading about that on the TIGHAR website and in the books that had been written by Dr. Tom King and Ric Gillespie respectively, *Amelia Earhart's Shoes* and *Finding Amelia*. As I was going through those, I felt like it was pretty esoteric. I had seen a lot of different lines of evidence, but nothing that really resonated with me. So I began to think that if any of this is holding water, there should be something in it that resonates. I began looking at some of the artifacts, and I asked myself, "What if there was something about one of these artifacts that was unknown or undiscovered that I could figure out?" Maybe I could find a way to relate that to Amelia. If I could do that, that might be a sign or an indication that there was something to the Nikumaroro hypothesis. This is a way for me to arrive at something on my own. I started with an artifact that I was able to identify as having a high probability of being a bottle of St. Joseph Lindemann, which to me resonated with the 1930s, but I wasn't positively sure of that. At the time, I became very excited about that because it seemed to me at the time that the island surely didn't have a very big history of inhabitation. With anything you found there, all you'd have to do is relate it to the timeframe in which it came and see if you could pin it onto the Electra and you're done. The island is not necessarily the far side of the moon, but it *has had* its share of occupation.

It's not Central Park either, by any means, it's very remote, but it *has seen* diverse people from different backgrounds. It's very difficult to take an artifact and show that it's from Amelia Earhart or that it solves the Amelia Earhart mystery. The preponderance of evidence is key. I think you approach every artifact with the same degree of objectivity and try to see whose story this artifact is telling, realizing that at the end of that process, you'll have an interesting story *no matter who that might be.*

Chris Williamson

Mr. Olson testified earlier regarding radio bearings. Let's talk a little bit more about the radio direction bearings. This is another element that hasn't received as much attention as some of the other aspects of evidence for this hypothesis. Can you elaborate for the court on those, please?

Joe Cerniglia

We have several radio direction bearings from three points in the Pacific: Wake Island, Midway Island, and Oahu. Those three radio direction finding stations were top-of-the-line equipment for the time.

This was large, sensitive equipment, and it took a few minutes to get a bearing, but once you did, it was much more accurate than what you could do from an airplane. Four out of five of those bearings cross in the area of McKean Island and Nikumaroro Island. Oahu took two sightings: 215 degrees and 213 degrees for Oahu, Midway took a sighting that was 115 degrees from Midway, and Wake took a sighting that was 144 degrees from Wake. The fifth sighting from Midway was one that didn't cross near McKean or Nikumaroro, but the first four also coincide with the 157/337 sunline that Noonan took and that Earhart described in one of her radio messages. That line is crossing the direction bearing lines.

While I realize that signal strength is said to be a very powerful indicator of how close she was to Howland at any given point, one of the main points of argument for Nikumaroro is what happens *after* the loss of the flight.

Receptions were picked up. As weak and wobbly as they were, most of them converged on the Phoenix Island area, which is McKean and Nikumaroro to a very, *very* close degree.

Chris Williamson

At this time, I'd like to offer project's exhibit 10, which is a copy of the *Chater Report*.

Jen Taylor

No objection.

Judge

Project's exhibit 10 is admitted.

Chris Williamson

Mr. Cerniglia, can you walk the court through the *Chater Report* and discuss its contents and its significance?

Joe Cerniglia

What's most interesting is the fuel load that the Electra carried on takeoff. There's a lot of debate about how much fuel they had when they took off heavy from Lae. Eric Chater was the general manager of Guinea Airways on Lae. He wrote a report on Earhart's activities at the airport, including her departure from it. The report itself was lost for many years in a filing cabinet of all places. It came to light after TIGHAR began its work, and it was really invaluable in establishing some of the facts as to Earhart's fuel load and the maintenance issues when she left Lae. The report states that they had 1,100 US gallons when they left for Howland Island, and according to Fred Hooven, that should have been enough to take them to Howland with roughly three and three-quarter hours of flying time *left*, which was more than enough to reach Nikumaroro if need be. They could have reached that point pretty much wherever they were on that line of position, north or south of Howland.

Chris Williamson

At this time, I'd like to offer project's exhibit 11, which is a copy of Fred Hooven's 1982 report.

Jen Taylor

No objection.

Judge

Project's exhibit 11 is admitted.

Chris Williamson

Mr. Cerniglia, much of this court may not be aware that the originator of the Nikumaroro hypothesis is a gentleman by the name of Fred Hooven. For those who are not aware, can you educate the court on who Mr. Hooven was and what his belief was regarding the world flight?

Joe Cerniglia

Fred Hooven is really the true founder of the Nikumaroro hypothesis. I think it really all starts with *him*.

He was a professor of engineering at Dartmouth College's Thayer School of Engineering.

He was born in 1905, in Dayton, Ohio, right near the home of the Wright brothers, and he got to know the Wright brothers as he was growing up. He was the inventor of the radio direction finding compass that Amelia Earhart used on her aircraft, but later *rejected* because she thought it was too heavy and would consume too much fuel. He had an advanced version of the radio direction finder loop that was attached over the navigation station of Fred Noonan on the top of the plane. Amelia wanted to use the more primitive RDF bearing finder. The difference was that the one she wanted could only give you a bidirectional reading.

That means that the signal you were trying to home in on was either to the left or the right of you depending on how the loop coupler is oriented to the plane, but you didn't know which. Because of that, you don't know which way to turn. Fred Hooven's RDF basically allows you to have a readout on the console of the airplane that would tell you *which way* to turn, but Earhart had that replaced with the more primitive version. Hooven thought this was a very bad mistake. He thought that if she had what he suggested, it would have been as influential in saving the flight as knowing Morse code would have been. So when we talk about not knowing Morse code, we have to also think about that Hooven direction finder. In 1982, Hooven decided to do a study of his own and try to look into what really happened to Earhart.

He began to focus on these radio direction finder bearings. This is Fred Hooven speaking in 1982, before anyone else had been talking about Nikumaroro:

> *"Statistical analysis of the direction finder bearings, even allowing a very modest estimate of their probable accuracy, indicate that the probability that three Pan American bearings out of four and one bearing taken from Howland should all coincide. These three Pan American bearings should also jointly coincide with the 157/337 position line. The fact that all these lines intersect in one of the only areas where there is any land is a further reinforcement of the assumption of the presence of the Earhart plane in the Phoenix area.*
>
> *"Without the other rather convincing indications of the identity of the signals heard, this evidence is sufficient to eliminate the official reconstruction of events from further consideration."*

What he's saying here is that the government's reconstruction of events that demonstrate crash and sink should be *eliminated* because of these direction finder bearings. He goes on to say:

> *"Most undeniable, however, is the evidence of the radio direction finders. Five bearings were taken on the weak wavering signal reported on the frequency used by the Earhart plane. Four of them plus the 157/337 position line in the last message all intersected in the general area of the Phoenix group. This constitutes positive evidence of the presence of a transmitter in that area, which could only have been that of the downed plane. No hypothesis purporting to explain the events of the last flight can be credited that does not offer a plausible explanation of these signals and why they originated along the*

plane's announced position line at the only location except for Baker and Howland, where there was land."

That's where it all starts, in some ways. You could almost say everything else is icing on the cake. It's not necessarily dispositive, but I don't think it's been very well disproven, or even attacked so successfully, that these radio direction bearings should be ignored.

Chris Williamson

Switching gears to the archaeological side of things, you mentioned earlier that you took it upon yourself to study at length some pieces that were found on the island. Can you educate the court regarding how a body of archaeological evidence like we have in support of the castaway hypothesis helps to support the idea that Amelia and Fred may have in fact landed at Nikumaroro?

Joe Cerniglia

Well, I think it certainly helps it.

One of the questions I always end up asking myself and one that probably needs further research to some degree is *how likely is it* that all of these things we're seeing could be found on other islands in the Gilberts? Would we find them in the Solomons? Would we find them in Fiji?

This is exactly the kind of thing we would expect to see if Amelia Earhart was a castaway and had perished on this island. We're seeing too much aluminum for comfort. We're seeing a lot of signs of sedimentation and overwash in the village that demonstrates definite sea activity from typhoons bringing stuff in from the sea onto the shoreline and driving it into the jungle areas.

There's been fifty-five years of non-inhabitation of Nikumaroro Island since its abandonment in 1963 due to a lack of water. Fifty-five years compared to twenty-four years of settlements by colonists, so more than double that time has amassed in which things can be swirled around and coughed up from the sea. We see evidence of things having cropped up in certain flotsam pieces, like flip-flops and things like that. We also see things like pressure-treated wood.

Pressure-treated wood *should not* be something you find on this island. Nikumaroro should be an *exporter* of wood, not an *importer*. I could list a dozen more examples, but these things could be explained in a number of ways. You could explain them as being from the Coast Guard, or you could certainly explain them as part of a former colony.

We have to make so many excuses for things that are piling up that it begins to become tiresome after a while. There will *always be* doubters, and I have doubts myself. I have doubts that we have found a definitive answer that will actually put all doubt to rest. I think we're just not there yet, but I *also* think that these artifacts, some of which I've *personally discovered* on the island, are very, *very* intriguing.

Chris Williamson

Mr. Cerniglia, after all the evidence that has been looked over, and after considering the evidence in support of this particular hypothesis, is it your professional opinion that Amelia Earhart and Fred Noonan ended up on Nikumaroro Island and ultimately perished there?

Joe Cerniglia

Yes, I would say it definitely rises over the 50% certainty mark. I might even be prepared to say in terms of probability that it lies somewhere in the region of, say, 80–85%, if you look at all the evidence. I realize, however, that for people who may not be devoting as much attention to it as I have over the last ten years, that number could well be lower, and they would much rather appreciate something that would just summarize it for them and give them a definitive answer. I wonder, however, if that definitive answer can easily be found.

It could cost $100 million to find it.

I think it's there somewhere.

But we're talking about an island that is surrounded by very deep water, and it's been eighty-five years. Things are in bad condition. The traces are very hard to read. I wonder sometimes whether it *will* be done. I think it *could* be done, but whether it will be done with the technology we have today is a different question.

It may not be, and I have to reconcile myself to that.

I should add that the crash and sink people probably have to reconcile themselves to that as well.

Chris Williamson

Thank you, sir. Pass the witness, Your Honor.

Cross-Examination of Joe Cerniglia

Jen Taylor

To get started, I'm going to ask you a really easy question. What does *beyond a reasonable doubt* mean to *you?*

Joe Cerniglia

Well, I think that's a standard of *law.* You probably have a better definition than that, as a lawyer, but to me, reasonable doubt means *near certainty.* When someone says *beyond a reasonable doubt,* I think of it as nearly certain; certain *enough* for some sort of legal decision.

Jen Taylor

Okay. What I want to *first* start with are the radio logs from the *Itasca,* and I'm going to go through the ones that I think are important. The first one being at 6:15 a.m. when Amelia Earhart calls in and requests a bearing and says that she's about two hundred miles out. *[Just a sidenote, but Judge, most of this I'm just going to be reading into the record. If you have any reason to disagree with my accuracy, just let me know.]* So at 6:15 she wants a bearing. She's saying that she's about two hundred miles out. So far, we're on the same page, correct?

Joe Cerniglia

I believe I've heard that one. If anything in terms of the detail was incorrect about the time or something like that, I wouldn't be in a position to say right now because I don't have those logs in front of me. That is definitely something I have heard that she said.

Jen Taylor

Well, *here,* let me show you.

. . .

Joe Cerniglia

I'm not doubting it.

Jen Taylor

This is the one I'm going to read verbatim. At 6:15 like we said, Earhart calls in and requests the bearing. She said she's about two hundred miles out. At 7:42, she says, "We must be on you but cannot see you." She *also states* that she's running low on fuel at this point.

Would you agree that's when this happened?

Joe Cerniglia

It sounds familiar, that's all I can say. It sounds very familiar to me.

Jen Taylor

Okay.

Joe Cerniglia

You have it right in front of you. It sounds like you're reading directly from the log.

Jen Taylor

I am.

Joe Cerniglia

Okay.

Jen Taylor

At this point, we have no idea what she means by *low on fuel*. We just know that she says that.

. . .

Joe Cerniglia

I could expand on that, but *yes*, we don't know exactly what that means.

Jen Taylor

Then at 7:58, she says, "We're circling but cannot hear you." Two minutes later at 8 a.m., she says, "We record your signals but cannot get a minimum." Do you know what that means, *cannot get a minimum*?

Joe Cerniglia

Yes, but could I go back to the circling part?

Jen Taylor

Yeah, let's go back to the circling part at 7:58. "We're circling but cannot hear you."

Joe Cerniglia

Do you notice on circling where it's crossed out? It almost looks like an overtype.

Jen Taylor

I see that, yes.

Joe Cerniglia

In other words, there's some uncertainty there about what that word may have been.

These might not be perfect.

. . .

Jen Taylor

Can you see where it says "KHAQQ S-5"? *This signal* was coming in at an S-5.

Joe Cerniglia

That's interesting because I hadn't been able to read that before. It's been crossed out and re-typed over for some reason; there's something below it. It's not very readable, but it sounds as though that might have been something that even at an in S-5, they weren't hearing very well. The thought has been that perhaps what they *really said* is "We are listening but cannot hear you." That makes more sense in the context of the sentence, and of course, *circling* doesn't make a lot of sense from a flying standpoint if you're on the line of position.

Jen Taylor

Well, she's *not* on the line *yet*. She doesn't say that she's on the line of position until about forty- five minutes later. We don't actually know if she was on the line of position the entire time, or if she had been circling. I can give you your point though; it does look like the wording may have changed.

Joe Cerniglia

Yeah, I just wanted to mention that and not as any part of the broader approach or argumentation, I just wanted to mention that the circling part has been disputed.

Jen Taylor

What I did want to go ahead and point out is that from 6:15, when she first requests the bearing, to 8 a.m., about an hour and forty- five minutes elapses. In that time, she's saying she "cannot get a minimum." So for an hour and forty- five minutes, she believes that she's near Howland Island, yet cannot get a bearing.

So this is an attempt that takes almost *two hours.*

At 7:58, she says, "Cannot hear you." Two minutes later, she says, "We record your signals but cannot get a minimum." My understanding is that at 6:15, she begins to get close, she's about two hundred miles away, and she starts to get closer, and the logs confirm that because we start to see increasing signal strengths. At this point, she still can't hear the *Itasca;* she's either not responding at all or not responding appropriately to what she's been asked.

Finally, at 8 a.m., "We record your signals, but cannot get a minimum." She's finally able to hear them after an hour and forty- five minutes of trying to reach them. Does that sound like a fair interpretation of the radio signals so far?

Joe Cerniglia

Sounds good to me.

Jen Taylor

Okay. Forty- five minutes after the 8 a.m. signal at 8:44, that's when we get, "KHAQQ calling *Itasca.* We are on the line 157/337. Will repeat." Then there's the notation about going north and south. "We will repeat this on 6210." Then she says, "Wait," and the message cuts off. She's saying she's on the line, she's going to repeat the transmission on 6210, and this particular signal is coming in at an S-5 signal strength. She says, "Wait," and doesn't complete that thought. That's the last time the *Itasca* hears from Amelia. Would you agree with everything that I've said so far?

Joe Cerniglia

Not exactly. That is the last *universally accepted transmission* the *Itasca* received from Earhart.

There were additional transmissions that *Itasca* recorded as having possibly been from Earhart. There was not universal agreement afterward.

Jen Taylor

Okay. Do you know how long it took for the *Itasca* to receive this next signal?

Joe Cerniglia

It would have been July 2, 1937, at 6:00 p.m. *Itasca* time.

Jen Taylor

Six p.m., okay. So, either way, at 8:44 a.m., that's her last transmission for *at least* ten hours.

Would you agree with that?

Joe Cerniglia

This is graded as an *uncertain signal* in my catalogue. You'd have to put a qualifier on that because if they *did* actually receive this from Amelia, it was in a weak and unreadable voice on 3105.

Jen Taylor

Right, and I am not yet ready to concede that this *was* a signal from her.

Joe Cerniglia
Okay.

Jen Taylor

I'm just saying that at the very least, they stopped receiving signals from her for at least ten hours.

Joe Cerniglia

Possibly.

Jen Taylor

Would you agree with that?

Joe Cerniglia

I would personally have difficulty accepting that, but I could see why some people might make that argument.

Jen Taylor

Earlier in trial, you heard Leo Bellarts talking about what he was hearing when he was hearing these last signals at 7:58 and 8:44?

Joe Cerniglia

Yes.

Jen Taylor

So you're aware that he describes them as not only *loud and clear*, but he describes panic in her voice at 8:44?

Joe Cerniglia

Yes, yes, I recall that.

Jen Taylor

So at 7:42, she says that she's "low on fuel," and then an hour later at 8:44, she's now panicking. My question is based on these two points: Why is it *reasonable to assume* or *believe* that she had hours of flight time left?

Joe Cerniglia

I don't know the answer to that, but I could certainly provide scenarios where that's possible.

Jen Taylor

Okay.

Joe Cerniglia

If what happened is what we're *thinking*, she's already gone into her fuel reserve, which is about 15 to 20%. So fuel is running low; she's losing the opportunity to complete the mission that she set out for herself, which was to land on Howland and then continue the flight. That's looking like an increasingly remote possibility. It's also looking like the possibility for losing their lives is increasing. So things are getting very tense, and it's a *big* ocean. She and Fred Noonan are going to have to come up with something.

Jen Taylor

Hypothetically, if you're lost somewhere, and you're calling out for a familiar voice to answer you for almost two hours, and all of a sudden, you hear that voice, would it be reasonable to then turn around and go in the opposite direction and leave the area *entirely* after you've just spent such precious time searching for a response to your signals?

· · ·

Joe Cerniglia

It's perfectly reasonable given the navigational logic. Perhaps I would say this: it might seem like a gutsy move to turn around and start flying south southeast, but this is what the line of position is for. Remember, they weren't flying directly to Howland anyway, they were flying to intentionally miss it, that's the *landfall approach* that navigators use all the time. They had to turn left or right in order to find Howland on that navigational line, which, *by the way*, I should mention was actually set at sunrise some hours *before* they reached Howland, and it was an advanced line of position, done by time and dead reckoning. They realized that they'd reached the line as they advanced it on the map. You have to take it at sunrise because that's when the angle is where it's supposed to be.

When you've reached the line, you're supposed to turn for the island. If you're confident that your line is correct, whichever direction you're supposed to turn, you should eventually see Howland, and you probably have a good general idea of *when* you should see it if you're not. It's very hard to see even in fairly *good* weather. You could look for a while, but at some point, you're going to realize you're cutting into your fuel reserve and there are other islands that you have as options. That being the case, one of them is only forty miles away, *Baker Island*. It might make sense to start turning south. She *did say*, "We're heading north and south." That doesn't necessarily mean a rapid north and south movement. It could very well mean that they're going to head north for a little while and then south for a little while until we see one of these other options. You have Baker, McKean and Nikumaroro. It makes perfect sense that any one of these islands could potentially save your life, although they're not equally trustworthy in terms of a landing. They all present some possibility for life. There's really no possibility for life by ditching in the water. That's *certain* death.

Jen Taylor

Earlier during direct, I heard you say that the decision to fly south southeast if they couldn't find Howland would have been intentional, and you just mentioned it again just now. That was Fred Noonan's backup plan, that's what he was going to do if they couldn't find Howland.

I'm still not really clear on this; if they had heard the *Itasca, why go into backup plan mode?*

Joe Cerniglia

I think the act of hearing them and taking a bearing are not necessarily the same thing.

You would be hearing them on 3105 or 6210. To take a bearing, you'd have to go down to something like 500 kilocycles. I think they might have been a little unclear about how they were supposed to be taking bearings and what signals they were supposed to be on, all while flying the plane as well. There's no radio operator on board, you've got to know where to be taking the bearing, and your equipment has to be working properly. We're not sure exactly if it was. It would seem from what we were able to observe that her trailing antenna, which was a receiving antenna, was not working properly or might have even been torn off during the takeoff at Lae.

Jen Taylor

Okay. So it's your belief that in that period between 8:00 and 8:44 while all of this is going on, that's when they decide to give up on Howland?

Joe Cerniglia

Well, maybe not *give up*, but I understand why you might think that.

We don't know exactly where they were when they made the turn. If they were left, they would turn south, if they were right, they would turn north. We just don't know *where she was* on the line. It's not possible to say with certainty what giving up really means. Noonan could have played that a number of ways.

If you're a navigator and you realize the geography of the line of position and what it stands for in that circumstance, you likely also realize that you've got opportunities for survival, maybe a safe landing on some of these reefs. A backup plan, *yes*, but they weren't anticipating that so many things would go wrong. I don't think that Noonan or Earhart were in any mood to give up trying to find land of some sort.

Maybe their thinking was that if they landed on *any* island, they could maybe take off again. If you're keeping an optimistic viewpoint, you might realize that if you can just reach land, everything might be okay.

Jen Taylor

Up until that point, she had been transmitting to the *Itasca* every thirty minutes to an hour.

Why all of a sudden would they stop trying to communicate, and not say anything until at least ten hours later?

Joe Cerniglia

I'm glad you asked that. If you're going to land somewhere, wouldn't you be transmitting that? Wouldn't you be announcing where it is you think you're at?

Jen Taylor

I think that's reasonable.

Joe Cerniglia

Number one, we don't know if every transmission she made was heard. If things were working as they should, they should have been heard.

The second possibility is, maybe because you're not hearing anything and you've been so concerned with saving yourself and your navigator, that you've stopped thinking about the *Itasca*. The *Itasca* is no longer of any use to you, and you're on your own to find an island; therefore you might not be transmitting.

There's a third scenario though, which is that *something* was heard, and it just didn't get recorded. Perhaps they *did* transmit, and the documentation of it is very shadowy. There are whispers about a later transmission putatively *pre-loss*, but it's not in a lot of the records.

Jen Taylor

Okay. How many hours of flight time does it take to get from Howland Island to Nikumaroro Island?

Joe Cerniglia

It's about four hundred miles away.

Jen Taylor

Three hundred fifty nautical miles.

Joe Cerniglia

Yeah, four hundred statute miles. So that's three or four hours of flight time.

Jen Taylor

Do you have any reason to *not believe* that at the 8:44 mark she was pretty close to Howland Island? Like under a hundred miles?

Joe Cerniglia

We don't know exactly *where they were*. The signal strength at an S-5 doesn't necessarily give us an idea of the distance. We don't know how far south or how far north they might have been. A lot of people, including Fred Hooven, have proposed the idea that they were up to ninety miles south of Howland when the last transition was made, but I don't think he knew either.

I can mention one radio phenomenon, and it's called the "3105 doughnut." A peculiarity in the antenna's transmission pattern meant that if the plane was closer than about eighty nautical miles, there's less than a 10% chance that the *Itasca* would hear Earhart *at all* on 3105 kilocycles at maximum strength, as recorded in the cutter's radio log. What this basically means is, if you think of a doughnut, and the hole of the doughnut goes around Howland, *in that hole* is basically a dead zone. Where you'll pick up the strongest signal is *just beyond* that hole where the doughnut begins again. There's another thing called "the skip zone," and some have proposed that it's just as simple as saying that the plane was too far away for good reception of ground wave. I only add that one because it's not necessarily where the aircraft *is* that tells you how good the reception is. You could get a very good skywave from a certain distance out, but skywave would only be received when you were a certain distance away. A little less strong of an argument there, but it's also possible that it plays a factor. The third thing is the "solar cycle," but that has to do more with the propagation of harmonics, which are received by people far away.

I think that there has been some agreement in the past that distance is not absolutely known *simply* by signal strength. There are ways to account for the Electra perhaps being farther and farther out than was claimed by Earhart's transmission.

Jen Taylor

Based on the signal strength that the *Itasca* was receiving, we can estimate that even if we were to give her a head start of up to 100 miles south by southeast, that would give her another 250 nautical miles to go. Is that fair?

Joe Cerniglia

Perfectly fair.

Jen Taylor

Earlier, you said it takes about three and a half hours to fly to Niku-maroro from Howland.

Joe Cerniglia

Yep.

Jen Taylor

I actually have in front of me, and this is *again* based on TIGHAR's website, that the cruise speed of the Electra was 130 knots. Knots, of course, translates to *nautical miles per hour*.

Ric Gillespie believed it would take her about two hours and forty-one minutes to get there. There's a report from TIGHAR's website called *Beyond Betty*; it's a twenty-eight-page report. Do you know the one I'm talking about?

Joe Cerniglia

Mmmhmm.

Jen Taylor

On page 10 of that report, TIGHAR claims that her likely landing time was 11:30 a.m. Nikumaroro time.

As the court is *now aware*, Nikumaroro is an hour *ahead* of Howland, so that would put her landing time at 10:30 *Itasca* time. Do you agree with that so far?

Joe Cerniglia

Mmmhmm.

Jen Taylor

Her last signal to the *Itasca*, again, an S-5 signal, was at *8:45 a.m.* How much time does that give her between sending that last signal with "we are on the line" to then being able to land at Nikumaroro? How much time does that give her?

Joe Cerniglia

I'd have to search the specs of the flying time and the flight speed of the Electra, but I think it's around 150 miles an hour. If you can cover 450 miles in three hours, while it's probably a little bit less than three hours, it would be three hours if you're rounding to the nearest hour.

Jen Taylor

Correct. But *Ric Gillespie says* it takes two hours and forty minutes to fly from Howland Island to Nikumaroro.

How do you reconcile that?

Joe Cerniglia

Well, what we have here is something that's not quite adding up, and maybe that means that someone's a little bit off in their calculation. I don't know where, but it's a little bit off.

Jen Taylor

Let me back up a little bit and try to explain where some of these numbers come from.

What *I'm looking at* are charts that TIGHAR compiled based on post-loss radio signals.

They took all of the ones that they thought were credible, and they put them on a chart.

They also overlaid on that chart, high and low tide on Nikumaroro Island. They determined that she would *not have* been able to land if it was high tide. They took that piece of information and the first post-loss signals that *they believe* came from Nikumaroro Island, and they used *that* to narrow down a window in which she *had to land*.

Based on that, they determined that 11:30 a.m. Nikumaroro Island time was more than likely when she landed.

Joe Cerniglia

I see where this *may* be going.

If we have little discrepancies of a few minutes or even half an hour to forty-five minutes or something, then *we could be off* in our tidal calculations. We could have her ditching into high tide, and that could perhaps detract from the hypothesis that she was landing at a safe time.

Jen Taylor

11:30 a.m. Again, this is 10:30 a.m. *Itasca* time, which only gives her an hour and forty-five minutes to make it there. Otherwise, she's there *too late* to hit that landing time, and some of the post-loss signals that TIGHAR believes are Earhart, and Ric Gillespie just testified to, **could not possibly have been** Earhart.

She wasn't there yet.

Joe Cerniglia

Well, I've *been* to Niku, and I can tell you a little bit about what it's like. The tide comes in, but it doesn't go right up to the tree line. If the tide is higher, then that means to some extent you'd have a lower quality landing because you're going to have to bring the plane up into areas that are a little bit more jagged, and that could possibly damage the aircraft on landing. When I spoke to Betty a few years before she died, she told me that one of the things she'd heard but was not mentioned in her diary was "one wheel is up" or "one wing is up" something like that. That seemed to indicate some sort of damage to the plane beyond what she had said.

As far as the tide is concerned, you have to remember that we're trying to determine what a tide was eighty-five years ago. Perhaps they're not perfect, and we might not be spot on in this analysis of where the tide was at a given point in time. If we're a little bit off, then that could change the analysis. Overall, I think it seems to indicate when transmissions became impossible because a few days later, the water was rising to the point where you couldn't turn the propeller anymore and you're beginning to lose the aircraft. That makes sense because that's when the transmissions stop.

Jen Taylor

I get all that, but *again*, I'm reading from the report. Whoever wrote this report for TIGHAR says the earliest the aircraft could reasonably arrive is roughly 9:45 a.m. At that time, the reef is dry, but the tide is coming in. Based on the aircraft's landing speed and tire size, the water level on the reef must be no more than six inches for a safe landing, and that closes the arrival window at 11:30 a.m. So what this report is saying is that she could not have possibly landed *after* 11:30 a.m. because the tide would have been too high.

Joe Cerniglia

Well, it's a very interesting point you've raised.

I am always fascinated by people who are able to find a critical weak link that, if true, could be a game changer. I'm not sure that it corresponds to as precise a reality as I think they end up convincing themselves that it is. If mistakes in calculations were made, it certainly doesn't invalidate the *whole thing*. I'm just saying that the tolerances of accuracy, the significant error here that's allowable, maybe the window, shall we say, could be a little bit looser than what they're claiming it is.

Jen Taylor

This seems like a *pretty critical error.*

If they know for a fact, based on the data in this report, that she *could not have* sent a signal, then they would deem it *uncredible*; but if that data is *wrong*, it screws up the whole report, and we *can't trust any of it.*

Joe Cerniglia

Well, I think that's what I've been arguing against. *Maybe* it screws up *some* signals. Let's take an extreme example and say that this is *all* incorrect. The signals were still heard by somebody, or even several individuals heard them. Perhaps there's a real fatal flaw in the casting itself, but that wouldn't necessarily cast a dim light on the 183 radio messages that *were* received.

Jen Taylor

That's the second time you said 183, the number *I got* was 120 that were reported. You have found 63 more of them that I have not heard about.

Where are you getting that number?

Joe Cerniglia

I'm going off a spreadsheet, and some of those might actually be transmissions from the *Itasca*, so they wouldn't necessarily be post-loss signals. I could redo it, but then I'd have to count up my spreadsheet again. *Your number* could be accurate if there are 60 signals. There were 183 that were either transmissions or receipts, I'd have to go through it again. We could pause, and I could do the count; it wouldn't take that long.

Jen Taylor

I think that explanation is fine if you're including what we'll call the *pre-loss* signals. That accounts for the discrepancy, I think. Fair enough.

The next thing that I want to do is see if we can agree on how much fuel it would have cost based on this report. We've now discovered that maybe some of the tidal data is wrong, so we're not sure how much we can trust it. Let's go ahead anyway and continue to use the report that TIGHAR has put out and see if we can agree on how much fuel at a minimum she would have needed to land and send all of the signals that TIGHAR has deemed credible.

I did the math, and I came up with a number. I'll walk you through how I did it, and just like the radio signals, if at any point you disagree with my methods or how I got there, then feel free to say so.

The way that I approached this was I looked at all of these charts starting on page 10.

There are a number of charts and graphs where TIGHAR has mapped out all of the credible signals, and they came up with seventeen of what *they call* "active periods." During those periods, that's when they believe she was sending out signals, and during those active periods in order to send out those signals, her engine had to have been running. Are we on the same page so far?

Joe Cerniglia
Correct.

Jen Taylor
Of those seventeen active periods, five of them had only a single signal that they believed to be credible. Because I couldn't really tell how many minutes she needed, I completely took those out of the equation. A negligible amount of time; let's just *throw out* five of them. So I ended up with twelve active periods. I won't go through all of them, but for example, period one was from 6:17 p.m. to 7:10 p.m.: *fifty-three minutes.* They do this for each active period. I went and added them all up, and I got twelve hours and forty-two minutes of *active time* for her where we know that her Electra had been running. That's step one. Are we good so far?

. . .

Joe Cerniglia

There's a lot of variables in fuel consumption when you're flying an airplane that we haven't taken into account yet. I should mention that Kelly Johnson, who was the chief engineer for Lockheed, said that an Electra 10-E fully loaded with gasoline should have a range of 4,500 miles.

Jen Taylor

We'll get to Kelly Johnson in just a bit because I have questions about his flight plan as well.

Joe Cerniglia

That was probably unreasonably optimistic; he *did* calculate that with no wind. You'd have to do everything right, which almost never happens. All I'm saying is that there are a number of variables that could in theory affect the amount of fuel that is used and the amount of fuel that you have left. From all that we know, Earhart was actually quite good at managing her fuel. She had taken the trouble to learn that. She had her Cambridge analyzer, which enabled her to lean out the carburetor, and she could lean out the carburetor when she was parked as well, which would make for a less rich fuel mixture and could also decrease the fuel consumption. So there are ways to conserve gasoline while you're parked on the reef that would probably expand the amount of fuel you had in order to transmit. There are also factors in the air such as wind speed, tailwinds, and headwinds. How many turns are you making? What's your altitude? Your altitude has a great effect on fuel economy. There are probably a lot more that I can mention. So we don't know. It's not a simple mathematic equation.

Jen Taylor

I understand all of that. What I'm trying to do is just take the time that TIGHAR has determined she was active and multiply that by how much fuel they believe she would have burned. In this very same report, they indicate that Paul Mantz had communicated that 900 RPM would be the lowest engine speed needed to charge the battery; however, the propellers at that speed would not be strong enough to keep the engine cool. That's where TIGHAR comes up with these active periods followed by inactive periods. It was a kind of cycle going back and forth. She needed time to let the engine cool off so that she could turn it back on. We have no way of knowing whether or not she *actually did this* and kept it *exactly* at the 900 RPM mark, but because we know that's the minimum needed to charge the battery, we can assume that you can use the 900 RPM number. Additionally, TIGHAR has performed some experiments with their own engines in order to determine how much fuel is burned per hour if you're just sitting there running your engine at 900 RPM. The number that they came up with was *6.4 gallons per hour.* All I did was, I took twelve hours and forty-two minutes, which is the minimum time she was active and running her plane at 900 RPM, and I multiplied that number by 6.4 gallons. The result I got was *81.28 gallons* of fuel at a *minimum* that she would have needed if all the post-loss signals that TIGHAR believes to be credible *actually are* credible. That's all I did. I understand that's a reality we can never know, because we weren't there, and there's a lot of unknowns.

I'm really trying to get the lowest number possible, because I really want to give the benefit of the doubt to the hypothesis.

Joe Cerniglia

Sure, sure.

Jen Taylor

You also have to take into consideration that five of those signals, I completely discounted.

I'm also assuming that the beginning of the first signal is in an *active period* and the end of the last signal is in an *active period,* and that is exactly when she cuts the engine on and off.

That's probably not reasonable either. You might disagree, but I think that this is a pretty solid minimum number.

It could be higher.

I don't think it could be lower.

Joe Cerniglia

You have definitely given the benefit of the doubt, no question.

Jen Taylor

And that brings us *now* to Kelly Johnson, so let's talk about Johnson's report; it's called *Report Number 487*. This report laid out a flight plan for her. You're, of course, familiar with what I'm referring to?

Joe Cerniglia

Yes, and I've read it over again just today. He did make the effort to try to communicate to Earhart how to manage her fuel effectively under certain conditions. It appears from what we can see that she was concerned about it and was doing it.

Jen Taylor

There is an original report and a revised report, but according to that report, the general idea is that at ten thousand feet if she had followed this plan, she should have been consuming 38 gallons per hour.

Joe Cerniglia

Yes, correct. I've no reason in the world to dispute what you're saying except to reiterate what was said earlier, and that is that consumption of fuel is subject to all the variables that I mentioned and perhaps a few more.

. . .

Jen Taylor

I know that the report goes into more detail about how much she should be consuming at takeoff, and it takes into account her increasing in altitude. That was all accounted for in his plan.

Joe Cerniglia

I should add as a parenthetical that I was shocked at how poor the fuel mileage is. We're talking, like, 2.8 miles per gallon on these early planes; it was just astounding to me. I had never thought about that before.

The actual miles per gallon on a Lockheed Electra is shockingly low, which is why they had to carry 1,100 gallons of fuel or something near that to get to where they were going.

Jen Taylor

I'm not a mathematician; I went to law school.

I was able to do the simple addition and multiplication earlier, but for *this*, I decided to defer to Ric Gillespie's calculations. In 2015, he posted in the TIGHAR forum, and that post was then copied over onto their wiki. He determined that if she followed the rules, and if she followed the flight plan to the letter, when she hit the line of position, she would have had 190 gallons of fuel left. Have you seen that quote?

Joe Cerniglia

I'm sure I've seen it. I'm willing to accept that's what he said.

Jen Taylor

I know that you mentioned the Hooven report before, and I know that there are *other* interpretations out there. Do you have anything that would dispute what Ric Gillespie came up with?

If so, *now* would be the time.

· · ·

Joe Cerniglia

If I took some time, I might be able to find a different opinion, but I don't have another opinion about what he said. I don't have anything to dispute him with there.

Jen Taylor

Okay. For the record, what Mr. Gillespie did was he took the amount of fuel that they started with; 1,100 gallons, and he made all of the calculations in the report and just said, "Well, if she followed it to the letter, she would have had 190 gallons left. And 190 gallons left at 38 gallons per hour gives you five hours of flight time." That's what Gillespie said.

Joe Cerniglia

Let me stop for a second and say that I *do recall* that Hooven's math was different. Hooven stated that he believed the Electra was ninety miles south of Howland at the time of the last message and would've had about ninety minutes of flying time to McKean Island, which is close to Niku. He has their fuel supply lasting them for about three hours and forty-five minutes of flight time.

Jen Taylor

He disagrees with Ric. Ric actually gives her *more*.

Joe Cerniglia

Yes.

Jen Taylor

He gives her 190 gallons with five hours of flight time left. To give your hypothesis the benefit of the doubt, I'm going to start with Ric Gillespie's numbers because they give her more time.

. . .

Joe Cerniglia

Okay.

Jen Taylor

We don't know where on the line of position she is, but as we discussed earlier, based on the signal strength that the *Itasca* is receiving, we know that she's probably within one hundred miles of the *Itasca* with 190 gallons of fuel, if she had followed the flight plan to the letter.

Would you agree with that?

Joe Cerniglia

According to the Lockheed specs prepared by W. C. Nelson in May of 1936, if you have 1,100 gallons of fuel, then you're getting 2.8 miles per gallon. As you're consuming fuel, the plane is getting lighter, and you can actually fly further. If you multiply that 2.8 miles per gallon by 1,100 gallons, that's 3,080 miles, which gives you a roughly 500-mile window of safety for reaching Howland.

Jen Taylor

Do those specifications indicate what altitude you're getting that fuel economy?

Joe Cerniglia

I just did that very quickly, back of the envelope. That goes against my *own reasoning* that you've got to take into consideration more than that. These were just basic specs about what her miles per gallon were.

Jen Taylor

So then, let's go back to Ric Gillespie's number because I'm sure he spent a lot of time getting there.

Earlier, we discussed the minimum amount of gas that she would have used while on Nikumaroro to send those signals, and we arrived at 81.28 gallons. I actually went ahead and subtracted that number from 190, and I rounded down. In order for her to get to Nikumaroro Island *and* send the post-loss signals, she needed to use no more than 109 gallons of fuel. Do you have any issue with that?

Joe Cerniglia

I'm just having trouble visualizing the math. You're starting with 1,100 gallons, and she has a certain number of gallons that she needs to transmit.

Jen Taylor

Start with 1,100. Gillespie uses Kelly Johnson's report to conclude that on the line of position, she had 190 gallons *left*. The reason why I'm subtracting 81 is because she needs to land on Nikumaroro with *at least* that many gallons.

Joe Cerniglia

Well, if I were to comment on that, I would say that someone has probably made an error.

I can tell you that this is probably *one area* that has maybe not received the greatest amount of attention. Other than Ric, I know of no *real fuel expert within the team*. We're a little bit short in that regard. It's always possible that a mistake was made in a calculation or something, but the basic point that I'm making is that if she was following her fuel program the way she should have and not doing silly, unreasonable things, she should have been able to make it to the line of position, wherever that might have been in relation to Howland, and eventually turn on it and get to Niku. That's been the presumption. I understand that you're presenting math that says it's not working out, and I think you should probably bring that to the attention of TIGHAR. If you don't have the fuel to get there, that's always been what they call, "an eliminatory trait," and people have tried to use it. People have always tried to attack it from that angle.

I'm not a PR person for TIGHAR. The only thing I can represent in any of this is my *own opinion*.

Jen Taylor

What I'm hearing from *you* is that the best person to ask these questions to would be Ric Gillespie.

Joe Cerniglia

Right. In terms of the Earhart search, he might be the person to ask, but maybe not in an *absolute sense*.

I think he would agree with that, too.

Jen Taylor

Unfortunately, Ric isn't *here*, and he's not *going to be here*. So I am not going to have the opportunity to talk to him.

I have no further questions, Your Honor.

"Short of finding skeletal remains elsewhere or finding the aircraft on the bottom of the ocean, I think the only way to falsify my hypothesis is to deal with what I have put forth and show that it's not accurate in some sense."

Chris Williamson

Your Honor, the project calls *Dr. Richard Jantz* to the stand.

Can we start today by asking you to tell the court exactly where your professional background lies, and what your specialty is?

Dr. Richard Jantz

I'm a biological anthropologist. I studied for my PhD at the University of Kansas in 1970.

So it's been a long time. I have been interested in bones and in statistics from the very beginning. What I do, basically, is quantitative analysis of bone dimensions. I have been at the University of Tennessee since 1971, and I retired in 2010. Nowadays, I have a lot more time to do the things that I like.

Chris Williamson

When were you *first* made aware of the Nikumaroro bones, and how did you come into this investigation?

Dr. Richard Jantz

I came into it in 1998, professionally. TIGHAR was working with an anthropologist named Carl Burns. In 1998, the report of Dr. Hoodless was found in the archives in London, and it had these measurements. Carl recommended that TIGHAR bring me on to analyze these numbers. We did a paper that was presented to the American Anthropological Association in 1998. It was preliminary in nature, but we said that these bones were consistent with Amelia Earhart. The matter lay more or less dormant until 2015, at which time a paper by Pam Cross and Richard Wright came out. I felt that they had misrepresented what Dr. Hoodless could do – that they gave him more credit for being able to accurately develop what we call the "biological profile of a skeleton." That is, age, sex and ancestry. There was no criticism of Dr. Hoodless's competence – I think he was as competent as any physician of the time.

However, the science of forensic anthropology was in its infancy, and we know that forensic anthropologists *today* still make errors. I evaluated the methods he used, and they were to a considerable extent prone to errors. So the paper really has two parts: one part addresses Dr. Hoodless and the possibility that he may not have been correct. The second part goes into much more detail about what we can tell about Amelia Earhart in order to match her to the Nikumaroro bones and make an informed decision about whether they fit her, or whether they do not. Whether she can be included or *excluded*.

Chris Williamson

Dr. Jantz, I'm going to get right to the point. We have a figure looming over this particular theory, and I'm sure you're aware of where I'm going with this. 99% – that's a number that doesn't leave a lot of room for error. Here's a quote directly from the abstract of your paper:

> "This analysis reveals that Earhart is more similar to the Nikumaroro bones than 99% of individuals in a large reference sample. This strongly supports the conclusion that the Nikumaroro bones belonged to Amelia Earhart."

Upon reading the complete report, it's clear that you completed many different analyses of the data using various reference samples. So it appears that in the quote that I just read to you, you're referring to one of those samples. Now with that being said, in addition to the passage of time, do you still stand by your assessment of these bones and that 99% figure?

Dr. Richard Jantz

I think, in general, yes. But as you know, 99% is not 100%, and rare events *do* occur. I would say that if it's *not* Amelia, it's someone very similar to her. As the results of this paper show, that's an unlikely event. So if it's not Amelia Earhart, then it's a random person, and that random person has a high probability of having bone proportions similar to Amelia Earhart.

Chris Williamson

Okay, we'll get back to that. At this point though, so the jury is aware, I'd like to break down a few fundamental anthropological terms. As you state in your report, "All these bones are very weather beaten and have been exposed to the open air for a considerable time. Except in one or two small areas, all traces of muscular attachments and the various ridges and prominences have been obliterated." Even when Hoodless observed these bones, they seem to have been exposed to and affected by taphonomic changes. So, to begin, the first term I'd like you to explain to the court is "taphonomy."

Dr. Richard Jantz

Taphonomy is the study of what happens to a body from the time of death until it is discovered. It includes anything at all that can happen to it. Obviously, a body decomposes.

The way in which it decomposes depends upon the environmental circumstances it's in; it depends upon scavengers, whether they're present or not, and which ones *are* present.

It depends on the weather, and it depends on the insects as well. It's simply whatever happens to the bones or to the body from the time it is dead until someone comes upon it.

When you discover human remains of any kind anywhere, you try to make taphonomic inferences about what kind of circumstances led to those bones as you now see them.

Chris Williamson

Before we go any further, let's talk about the Nikumaroro crabs and the effect these animals can have on a set of bones like this and a hypothesis like this. In your study you state that "damage to the bones was most likely due to scavenging by crabs." This was originally observed by Gerald Gallagher, and it's been investigated by Dr. Tom King. Can you tell the court what *type* of taphonomic changes to the Nikumaroro bones can be attributed to an animal like a crab?

Dr. Richard Jantz

Well, I want to say that I'm not an *expert* in taphonomy. All I know about the crabs is that they are capable of taking down a body fairly fast. What they do to the bones, I don't really have a lot of personal knowledge of. Going off what others have said, it's more likely the activity of the crabs versus "weather-beating," as Hoodless described. The thing about taphonomy is that there are many outcomes. Without knowing the situation better than we do, you can't really say what all has happened to the bones. One of the principal uses of taphonomy, especially now in modern forensic anthropology, is to estimate how long the body has been dead. When you find bones, they are in some stage of decomposition. We know enough about taphonomy and modern people now to be able to, in many cases, make a pretty good estimate of how long the bones have been there. In the case of the Nikumaroro Island bones, we don't really know the circumstances. I know that there were estimates at the time, that maybe these bones had been there a very long time. Maybe the three years between Earhart's disappearance and the discovery of the bones was *not enough time* for the types of changes that were observed to occur. I would just state that I don't think we can say that with much confidence.

Chris Williamson

It's been pretty well established that the island of Nikumaroro can be both beautiful and quite deadly. If we're speaking about taphonomy, it's evident that there were other changes there on that island.

Whether it was environmental, or other changes that could have affected these bones plays an overall part in your research. Is that correct?

Dr. Richard Jantz

Sure, it could have. And I really didn't concern myself much with that, because although Hoodless was not so precise in how he described the bones, it *did* seem that they were in good enough shape that he was able to obtain lengths for them. He did not qualify his length measurements. He also took the cranium and did not qualify it as having been affected by taphonomic changes. As Hoodless said, the muscle attachment areas, the ridges, crests, and things like that had worn down, which could certainly be crabs. That might be other things too.

Chris Williamson

As we know from your report, which has been admitted into evidence for the jury, Dr. D. W. Hoodless measured the skeletal material based on the *Pearson study* from 1899, which has also been admitted into evidence for the court. As per Pearson and more recent methods of skeletal measurement and forensic anthropology, it's often understood that skeletal measurements are taken by measuring from one specific point on a bone to another for the purpose of accuracy across researchers. Can you tell the court about skeletal measurements in forensic anthropology, and how this data specifically is most accurately obtained?

Dr. Richard Jantz

Well, measuring bones is as old as anthropology. That was one of the first things that early anthropologists started doing. In the early days, in the late nineteenth century and early twentieth century, a lot of the measuring of bones and skulls was used in racial typology. That is, you use measurements to say, "This is what Mongoloids look like, and this is what Negroids look like; this is what Caucasoids look like." A lot of what the early anthropologists did with those measurements has been debunked. In some cases, that was categorized as scientific racism. In any case, there often was a kind of a hierarchical view of the human race with Europeans, of course, at the pinnacle and other groups below that. Since the mid to late twentieth century, measuring has become much more extravagant.

We used to do it with calipers, where you had specific points on the skull or the other bones that you would measure. There were definitions given for these, which go back mainly to early German anthropologists. The idea is that if I follow the definitions and measure a bone, and you do the same thing, we will get the same answer or an answer very similar, so that the measurements are comparable across different observers. Now we do a lot of measuring with 3D equipment, and we have a digitizer.

That means we have XYZ coordinates of these points, or you can get information from a CT scan or a laser scan about the size and shape of the bone, the skull, or postcranial bone.

Statistics have evolved to the point where you can do a lot more with those measurements.

The emphasis now is depending on what you're doing. If you're interested in paleoanthropology, you might look at the kinds of changes that have occurred from some millions of years up to the present. If you're interested in human variations of present-day people, you'll want to look at the data you have from people from different regions of the world and ask how they're related, how similar or different they are, and how evolutionary forces might have brought these differences into being. In forensic anthropology, we use measurements to identify what is normally called "ancestry." It used to be called "race." So now, when a forensic case comes into your laboratory, it's unidentified and you know nothing about it. The investigating agency usually brings the bones in, or we will go out and uncover them for an investigating agency. We develop a biological profile as the first step. We use the measurements to estimate the sex, ancestry, height, and age. These estimates are made by using reference samples where we already know these things to be true. We have criteria. We can say that this person is American, African American, or Hispanic-American. In other parts of the world, there are similar kinds of complex population structures, but the questions you would ask in Brazil, for example, are different from what you'd ask in the US.

Chris Williamson

Can you speak to a forensic anthropologist's ability to accurately measure skeletal material that is missing some or all of its prominences? That's got to play a role in the work that you're doing here.

Dr. Richard Jantz

Oh, sure, it can. It depends on what's missing. In modern forensic cases, it is often the case that carnivores such as dogs, coyotes, or other creatures find the body, and normally the first thing they do is chew off the ends. So we have a bone that doesn't have its ends, which makes it impossible to get an accurate length. On the skull, animal activity is usually less destructive, but other questions arise such as, is the body buried? Has pressure from the earth distorted the skull or broken it? When there's taphonomic destruction, it puts some limitations on what information you can get.

Chris Williamson

In Dr. Hoodless's original analysis of the skeletal material, he states that "a mandible with only four teeth in position" was uncovered along with the rest of the material. Do you have any idea as to why Dr. Hoodless would not have analyzed a dentition?

Dr. Richard Jantz

Well, if I have any thoughts, they're purely speculative. It's a very interesting question of whether Hoodless was aware that he might be looking at the remains of Amelia Earhart; he makes no mention of it. But what you would do now if you had the remains that he was looking at is determine whether those teeth had any reconstructions and dental work. Then we would ask whether the suspected missing person, in this case Amelia Earhart, also had dental work. I think I have read – though I'm not certain about this – that she did not have any dental work. I'm not sure if Hoodless mentioned that there were no restorations; one of the early people who saw the skeleton did mention that there weren't any. If we had that mandible now and if Amelia Earhart had ever been to the dentist and there were X-rays, we could carry out a typical match and include or exclude.

Chris Williamson

Dr. Jantz, it has been argued by Les Kinney and others representing the Japanese capture hypothesis that on June 26, 1935, at Cedars of Lebanon Hospital in Los Angeles, California, a Dr. Joseph Goldstein performed a medical procedure on Amelia Earhart known as the "Caldwell Luc procedure."

Dr. Richard Jantz

Oh yeah.

Chris Williamson

Of course, that is something that would have factored into Hoodless's original report on the bones if he was looking at a skull that had two dime-sized incisions in it. If that was something that Dr. Hoodless would have been able to identify, would that have helped include or exclude this skull and these bones as belonging to Amelia Earhart?

Dr. Richard Jantz

I don't really know much about that procedure. I understand there are resulting marks on bone, so one should expect to see evidence of the surgery to remove the sinus issue. I think what we have to remember is that just because Hoodless doesn't mention it, that doesn't mean it wasn't there. His report was very superficial.

He estimated sex, and he was very certain of his estimate. If you look at his report, he says this is "DEFINITELY A MALE," and it's capitalized and underlined. He kind of hedges on some of the other things he says. "Probably European", or perhaps what he called a "half-cast", which is a European and islander mix.

He wasn't going to make a definite pronouncement there. In the height he gave, he was fairly certain based on Pearson's formula. There is an error in one of Hoodless's formulas, and a medical text that has the very same error – it suggests that Hoodless did not consult Pearson's original paper.

Whatever he consulted, we do not know. I think that would be kind of an interesting historical question, because there might have been some English text of the time concerning forensic pathology that included this stature stuff and included the error that was used in this formula. It didn't make much difference in the actual stature estimation, but it *does* suggest that he did not consult Pearson himself. That's also suggested by the fact that he did not mention a paper by Pearson that actually gave good sexing information. For the femur, he did not do any extensive extra work to try to get this matter nailed down as well as he could.

Chris Williamson

Dr. Jantz, isn't it more likely that these Nikumaroro bones are that of one of the victims of the SS *Norwich City* wreckage, which famously ran ashore off Nikumaroro Island?

According to Kenton Spading, there are eight unaccounted-for people from that wreckage.

Isn't it more likely that the Nikumaroro bones can be attributed to one of those men?

Dr. Richard Jantz

Sure, that's always been a possibility. I think what has not been documented is any of the men counted for actually having survived. I don't remember the exact number now, but I think there were thirty-five crew, and eleven of them either perished or were unaccounted for. What it would have to mean is that one of those individuals who was unaccounted for made it to the island but was unable to find the others who were subsequently rescued. I think that is a possibility. I think that needs to be looked at in more detail. We do have some estimates on the documentation of the heights of some of the ones who were accounted for, and those would be the European or the English people. We *do not* have any heights from the era of Arabs or the Yamanis. Now it *is* the case that if one of them happened to be a Yamani, that person would probably qualify as a stocky male because they are shorter, and they tend to be more mesomorphic. From what I have read about the Yamani head form, they tend to have very short broad crania, and the Nikumaroro skull is rather narrow and long.

Without doing any analysis, I would say that the head form of the Nikumaroro skull, using the measurements given by Hoodless, would be *inconsistent* with most Yamanis. I think, and we haven't done this yet, but we *should* be able to include or exclude the people for which we have height. There's more research that needs to be done on that score, but the *other thing* that I think you have to deal with if you want to propose that it's a *Norwich City* survivor is the artifacts that were found in 1940 at the site where the skeleton was found. That would be the sextant box, the Benedictine bottle and then the part of the woman's shoe. I know the sextant box was discussed earlier.

Chris Williamson

TIGHAR is a name and an acronym that has been synonymous with this investigation, and they built this list of what many people believe is circumstantial evidence from the island of Nikumaroro. How much of that data and those findings by TIGHAR has carried influence on your findings in your paper; what role did that play?

Dr. Richard Jantz

Well, TIGHAR was indispensable, Ric has all these connections, and as I began to think about what we might say about Amelia Earhart, I started asking them about photographs that might have a scalable object, and we found this one that's reproduced in the paper of her holding an oil can. Ric put me in touch with Jeff Glickman the forensic photographer and Jeff actually purchased an oil can like the one she's holding on eBay, measured it and then provided a comparable scale. So, he was able to tell me how many pixels per inch were in that photo and that enabled me to estimate where her radius started and ended and where her humorous started and convert those pixels into absolute dimensions.

So that was really the Rosetta stone that kind of broke it open. As far as I'm aware, nothing like that has been accomplished in the past. There's also the issue of the length of her tibia, and there are no photos that we have found that show her tibia or show her calf exposed so you could estimate where her tibia starts and ends with a scalable object. She typically wore trousers and seemed to avoid dresses whenever possible. We got from the Purdue University archives a pair of her trousers, and a historic seamstress took very precise measurements of those trousers. One of the measurements was an inseam length, which gave us the information we could use to get a better estimate of her tibia length. We also got her waist circumference from the trousers, and that was important in estimating her weight. That didn't play directly into comparing the Nikumaroro bones to Amelia Earhart, but it *did* enable us to say that the weight recorded on her pilot's license is probably an underestimate.

The pilot's license says she's five feet eight and weighs 118 pounds, which is pretty close to emaciated. We don't think that she weighed 118 pounds; 130 is the most likely.

Chris Williamson

Dr. Jantz, in your paper, you've discussed the limitations of using Hoodless's original cranial measurements to determine ancestry. In your analysis of his original sex estimation, you stated that "the most prudent position concerning the sex of the Nikumaroro bones is to consider them unknown." You later show how some parts of the skeletal material can be suggestive of male while *other parts* can be suggestive of female. Can you explain to the jury the concept of an indeterminant conclusion in forensic anthropology and why elements of a biological profile such as sex and ancestry estimation are *not* always an exact science in that field?

Dr. Richard Jantz

Well, sure. If you have good measurements, and by *good*, I mean *accurate* and *plentiful*, you still can only get about 90% of them correct. So there's a *known error* of 10% under the best of circumstances from the skull alone. What we had from Dr. Hoodless was four measurements: length and breadth of the skull and then height and width of the orbit. It's a little bit of a mystery to me why he chose the orbit; there are other more obvious things and certainly more things that would contribute to sex, such as the width of the face that's pretty dimorphic. But he did not take those measurements, so with the measurements he *did* provide, the Nikumaroro bones classify as female but not with a high level of confidence. What I think I said, is that the skull points to female but you can't put a lot of confidence in the estimate. The bone lengths themselves are clearly in the male range.

So if you sex the Nikumaroro bones on bone length, they would classify as a man. But that's *also true* with Amelia Earhart.

If we knew we had her bone lengths, they would classify as male just because she was taller than most females and even a little taller than the average male at the time.

Chris Williamson

Dr. Jantz, the other term that I would like for you to explain to the jury that I think is important is the "Mahalanobis distance." Can you explain the significance of this distance and why it is important, *especially* in your comparison of the Nikumaroro material to your Earhart estimations?

Dr. Richard Jantz

Well, okay. P. C. Mahalanobis was a very talented statistician of Indian descent. He wrote a paper in the '30s where he worked out this distance, and it has come to be known as the *Mahalanobis distance.*

Now, historically, that's very interesting because Pearson, the guy who did the formula for estimated height, *also* had a way of doing distances among crania. Usually, the thing about measurements of the human body is that these measurements are always correlated. If you take a measurement of humorous lengths, that's going to be correlated with radius. If you take a measurement of face width, that's going to be correlated with head width. With Pearson's distance, they ignore those correlations, and the significance of the Mahalanobis distance is that he worked out how to *uncorrelate* the measurements so that a measurement only contributes its unique information and not the information that overlaps with other measurements. In the case I was dealing with where I had the humorous, radius and tibia, those bones are all highly correlated. So I was able to use the Mahalanobis distance to compare the Nikumaroro bones to my reference sample and to Amelia Earhart by uncorrelating them and getting the combination of size and shape.

Any time you have more than one measurement, there's a size component and a shape component. Both of those components are captured in the Mahalanobis distance while getting rid of the correlation that exists among the bones, and that's a fairly academic point, I suppose, but the Mahalanobis distance is one of the great statistical inventions; it is still used *very commonly* today.

Chris Williamson

In your paper you give a "Z score of -2.38" in your analysis of the sex of the bones, and I'll quote from this paper again: "One might argue that if the Nikumaroro bones are actually those of Amelia Earhart, that distance should be zero but that expectation is unrealistic for at least two reasons: one, it would assume that my estimates of bone lengths were made without error, which is highly unlikely. And two, it would require that Hoodless also measured the Nikumaroro bones without error, which is also highly unlikely." Can you elaborate on this statement and why studying skeletal samples in these specific conditions can be particularly challenging?

Dr. Richard Jantz

Well, yeah, the challenge of course in this case is we do not know the error. Some criticisms have emerged already, and they're valid points, I suppose. I say that we cannot rely on his sex estimation, so how can we rely on his measurements? It's argued that I'm trying to have it both ways: reject the sex estimation when I don't like it and accept the measurements when I do. What I would say is that measuring is a lot easier than sexing, for one thing. I do not have any idea what kind of equipment Hoodless had available and how well trained he was, although it is not difficult to measure the length of a bone. One interesting thing I *did* note is that when he took the measurements of the eye orbit, he records them to a tenth of a millimeter, and we wouldn't do that today; we would take them to the nearest millimeter. So he did have some kind of an instrument that would measure to a tenth of a millimeter, which kind of suggests that he had decent equipment. Of course, he has to know what he's doing in order for those measurements to the tenth of a millimeter to mean anything. My general impression of the measurements that he provided is that they *are* realistic. You know, I've dealt with enough bones and their lengths and the statistics that they provide to know when something is obviously out of kilter. His measurements seem realistic to me. If *I* measure bones and *you* measure bones, they will differ. Usually, those differences will be one or two millimeters and won't make any major contribution to the result. Those are basically the assumptions that I'm operating from.

Chris Williamson

Since the original bones are for all intents and purposes lost, and you had to go off the original report of Dr. Hoodless, who *did examine* those bones *in person*, would it be safe for me to declare in front of the jury that you're confident in the original measurements done by Dr. Hoodless *as recorded* in his original report?

Dr. Richard Jantz

There's nothing in the measurements he took that would make you think he did it incorrectly. The numbers he got are realistic. Who knows what kind of training he had, but like I say, measuring bone lengths is not that difficult. Measuring orbit height and orbit width? That's more challenging. We do not know exactly *how* he did it. He did not give us a definition. But the measurements *are* what you would get on an ordinary skull in that range.

Chris Williamson

If we turn our attention back to your analysis of Earhart's measurements, it seems that you used a variety of intriguing methods to collect the data that made up your study. You spoke earlier about working with a historic clothing seamstress and using a pair of Amelia's trousers from the Purdue collection, and that Jeff Glickman took estimations using items such as a can of oil lubricant. My question is, do you think using many different types of analytical methods makes your study *even stronger*?

Dr. Richard Jantz

Sure, where we are now is that we have the Nikumaroro bones, and evidence that we could develop from Amelia Earhart does not allow us to *exclude* her. In fact, it argues for *including her*. The way I like to frame this whole thing is that we're testing a hypothesis.

There really *are* just three major hypotheses about what happened to Amelia Earhart. One of them is the crash and sink hypothesis. Another one is that she was captured by the Japanese. And then there is the Nikumaroro Island hypothesis, and that's the hypothesis we're testing. Scientific hypotheses normally *can't be* proven. They can be supported or falsified. The Nikumaroro Island hypothesis, I think, is strongly supported by the evidence developed and put in that paper. Now, it is a scientific hypothesis, so it *can be* falsified. My idea is that the hypothesis and the data are out there. If someone can falsify the hypothesis, fine, we'll have learned something. In the case of the *other two* hypotheses, I do not believe there is much scientific evidence that would support them. I think the Nikumaroro Island hypothesis has more support than any other. Crash and sink, that's a difficult one, because they have to find something at the bottom of the ocean in order to find support for that hypothesis.

Chris Williamson

Regarding bone link estimates taken using historical photographic imagery, can you discuss this method in particular and its ability to be valid overall?

Dr. Richard Jantz

I am certainly *not* an expert photographer or even a mediocre one. I rely on Jeff Glickman. My expertise involved estimating where the bones are from. In the picture, of course, she's got flesh, and you cannot see the bones directly, except you can see the end of the radius pretty well. What *I would say* is that my estimates of where the bones start and end *will have* error, but it cannot be major error. It cannot be very large because there are only certain places where these bones can start and end. Maybe to lend it more credibility, there should be an error analysis, and that might be pretty involved. That would involve photographing people holding a scalable object, like Amelia Earhart is doing, and estimating where their bone links are from the photos, and then measuring them on the person so that we could get an error estimate that way. Like I say, it would take some effort.

Chris Williamson

Dr. Jantz, regarding DNA evidence potentially being in play here, if you still had access to the skeletal material from the Hoodless study, do you think DNA would *still possibly be* viable at this point?

Dr. Richard Jantz

No way to know that. Tropical environments are tough on DNA. We have the whole genome from Neanderthals; their DNA survived because they're in cold climates. Extracting DNA from bones in the tropics have been *much less* successful. Now, of course, with Neanderthals, we're talking fifty, sixty thousand years ago, which is a long time for DNA to survive. In the case of the Nikumaroro bones, we're talking eighty-five years. *It is possible* that DNA could be extracted from the Nikumaroro bones if they were present.

Chris Williamson

And what about the soil samples that TIGHAR collected during their trips out to Niku? Is there a likelihood that DNA could be obtained from those?

Dr. Richard Jantz

Well, it's the same thing as getting it from bones. I know they've gotten DNA from Neanderthal caves from the soil. Again, that's a cold environment. The DNA in the soil at Nikumaroro Island presents the same problem. It's an adverse environment for survival of DNA, which isn't to say that someone couldn't.

If you get DNA, then it's going to be very fragmented, but if you still get something, you might be able to make an identification that way.

Chris Williamson

In your study it was also notably mentioned that you were able to eliminate Fred Noonan as a possibility for the bones due to his documented height being six feet one-quarter inch. I mention Noonan because earlier you spoke about the possibility of these bones belonging to one of the men from the *Norwich City* wreckage. For the jury, one more time, what are the odds that these bones, the ones you studied, are from one of those men?

Dr. Richard Jantz

What I would say is that it *is possible but unlikely*. The reason I say it's "unlikely" is that the data in the paper shows that most people would be rather far removed from the Nikumaroro bones. So a person on the *Norwich City* would have been presumably a random person as far as those bones are concerned.

If it's *improbable but possible* that a *Norwich City* castaway could be the Nikumaroro bones, then it would be someone very similar to Amelia Earhart.

Chris Williamson

Although you seem to leave things open to a certain amount of interpretation in your paper, for you personally, what is the single most convincing piece of evidence for this skeletal material belonging to Amelia Earhart?

Dr. Richard Jantz

Well, it'd be the good old Mahalanobis distance. She has a low distance to the Nikumaroro bones, which you would not expect if they *weren't* her. I agree that it's possible for the bones to appear to be her even though they're not. That seems pretty unlikely.

Chris Williamson

Dr. Jantz, in your *expert professional opinion,* is this *case closed* for Amelia Earhart and Fred Noonan?

Dr. Richard Jantz

Even *if it is* closed in my eyes, it's not closed. If you've been following any of the popular press, there have been some pretty critical articles appearing, so I think it's irrelevant what I *personally think.* What *is* relevant is the science that's brought to bear on it, and I think that we are now at the stage where we're approaching hypotheses *scientifically* and that their support or falsifiability is based on evidence. I *do under-stand* that people who hold other views have pretty strong emotional investments in those views and don't want to let go unless they abso-lutely have to. I personally think we'll probably get into some other avenues of investigation on the Amelia case. For example, I think we'll try to rule in or out Yamanis based on head form and maybe the *Norwich City* unaccounted for castaways. So there are still some things that that can be done. What I would *also say* is that people who do not wish to accept or support the Nikumaroro hypothesis should do more than just say, "I don't believe it." I think there should be some evidence that it's *not* correct. That there are some errors, or the data really does not support it, the statistical analysis is flawed, whatever. I hope it stays in the realm of scientific hypothesis testing.

There is a lot of emphasis on what they call "cold cases" now. We have in our collection here at the University of Tennessee a lot of skele-tons that are unidentified. DNA samples from those skeletons are now being submitted, and occasionally we get a hit, and someone is identi-fied. Well, Amelia Earhart is a *very* cold case. I *do* make clear in my paper that the probabilities that I've developed would not qualify as a positive identification in a modern forensic case, where even DNA identification is not 100%. It might be one in a million, but that's still not 100%. I'm saying 99%. You can argue that's too conservative or not conservative enough, but the fact remains that the Nikumaroro bones are very similar to what I've reconstructed for Amelia Earhart.

In order for the Nikumaroro hypothesis to be falsified, it needs to be done with evidence, and the way I see it now is, if someone comes up with bones in Saipan, and those bones can be linked to Amelia Earhart with a high degree of probability, then that would presumably falsify my hypothesis. There have been bones found in Saipan, and they have been examined. They were thought to be Amelia Earhart, but they were pronounced to be those of a Micronesian. Short of finding skeletal remains elsewhere or finding the aircraft on the bottom of the ocean, I think the *only way* to falsify my hypothesis is to deal with what I have put forth and show that it's not accurate in some sense. That would falsify it.

Chris Williamson

Thank you, Dr. Jantz. No further questions, Your Honor.

"There's a lot of room for additional research here, and I completely agree with him. Anything can benefit from additional research and additional studies being done in order to determine if these results are repeatable across researchers."

Chris Williamson

The project calls *Miss Katie Cohan* to the stand.

Miss Cohan, can you tell the court where your background and professional specialty lies?

Katie Cohan

My background overall is in anthropology. I have a broad experience in anthropology; I have my bachelor's degree in anthropology and my master's degree in anthro, as well. As far as work experience and educational experience goes, I have experience in different fields and subfields of forensic anthropology, which is what my master's degree focused on. Over the past six years, I've been teaching cultural anthropology, and I also have experience in archaeology. So I'm a little bit of a mixed bag.

Chris Williamson

Can you give the court an overview of what anthropological evidence can do for a working hypothesis like the one the project has presented here today?

Katie Cohan

If we're talking about anthropology as a whole, we're looking at the study of humans.

Anthropology as a field itself has different subfields. If you're talking about Nikumaroro, what comes up most frequently is going to be forensic anthropology or biological anthropology, which is going to be the study of human skeletal material, and archaeology as well. You could also argue that cultural anthropology ties into this case as well. A lot of it depends on what you *have*. Do you *actually have* skeletal material that you can hold and analyze in your own hands? Do you have a historical record? That's what we have in this case, with the Nikumaroro bones. There can be many different types of anthropological evidence that can be valuable in a case like this. It can also bring up its own challenges, depending on what's *not* recorded about it.

Chris Williamson

Let's talk about the Nikumaroro bones. Before we get into the study performed by Dr. Jantz, I wonder if you can tell the court your thoughts about the bones *pre-Jantz*. Let's discuss the bones in general, the analysis done by Dr. D. W. Hoodless, and the determinations made by that analysis.

Katie Cohan

Yeah, in my mind, there's a lot to talk about there. The interesting thing that we have from TIGHAR is that they found telegrams that are basically almost a record, kind of a vague chain of custody of the skeletal material that was found on the island originally. Where this starts is the officer in charge of the Phoenix Island settlement scheme learns that this material was found six months prior. In early 1940, islanders found a skull and buried it. Gallagher learns about this about six months later, and he starts a chain of questioning regarding how we proceed here, just in case it *is* Amelia Earhart, or just in general, how should we proceed? So he collects the material, and you start seeing this body of evidence pile up within telegrams that are being passed back and forth all around the western Pacific High Commission about this. Ultimately, you actually *have* the bones.

Gallagher finds the skull and then finds some other bones and materials as well. These bones don't actually *get to* Dr. David Winn Hoodless, who is the principal at the central medical school at the time in Fiji. He doesn't get the bones until spring of the next year.

So you have Gallagher, who finds the bones in the fall of 1940. They also get studied by *another* doctor in between this period, whose name is Dr. Lindsay, Isaac. Then the bones make their way to Hoodless in Fiji, who analyzes them and writes a report. This report is available for anyone to look at because TIGHAR posts up their evidence. If you look at it, you'll find that it's a little bit vague.

Sir Harry Luke, the High Commissioner of the WPHC, in his report, he writes a list of the bones, a list of all the skeletal material, and what his general assessments are. In a lot of ways, his assessments are a little bit vague, in that he does not seem to be *entirely* sure about ancestry. He says that he doesn't feel comfortable saying that it is an islander. He says it could be somebody European, or something like that, but he's not entirely sure. Height, he actually estimates using some of the lengths of the long bones, and he estimates about five feet five to five feet five and a half inches. Age is another thing he's really not sure about, and he actually seems to make a guess. He *does* comment on the degraded nature of the skeletal material, but he makes a guess anyway, that it's about forty-five to fifty-five years old, I believe. The one thing he seems to be fairly sure about is that this is the skeletal material of a male. He uses specific methods to come to that conclusion, but it's a little bit unclear. He doesn't really draw anything or write anything down. In some instances, he'll say that he's using a certain part of the skeleton to make an assessment, but he doesn't really describe what his methods are.

You *do* have a report by Hoodless, but for some of it, it almost seems like he's not entirely sure. In other cases, he seems a little bit *more* sure.

As far as evidence goes, that's what they're starting with in this case.

Chris Williamson

It appears by looking at this original report that D. W. Hoodless is *guessing* in certain areas.

This is certainly *not* his area of expertise. He's a medical doctor, he's *not* a forensic anthropologist. Would I be correct if I said that analyzing and creating a subsequent report on that analyzation would be out of his professional scope?

Katie Cohan

I'm not sure if it would necessarily be out of his wheelhouse. If you go back to the original telegram, when Gallagher is talking to the other members of the Western Pacific High Commission, you have Duncan MacPherson, who's actually a doctor, say, "I think we need to send this material out," because it seems like they know that it's out of their wheelhouse.

Even though they *do* make interesting and what seemed like valid observations, it seems like they know it's out of their wheelhouse. So they actually suggest this material should go to either Fiji or Sydney to be studied further. I don't know that they would have sent it all the way to Hoodless without being sure that he had a better understanding than they did. But at the same time, forensic anthropology itself was in its infancy. One really important thing here is that Hoodless *acknowledges* this at the very end of his report. He basically says, "This is my preliminary report. I could do a little bit more with this." He says right there that, if you want a more detailed analysis of this, what he *really* recommends is that you should send it to the University of Sydney to be analyzed there by their anthropologists. I think even Hoodless is recognizing in his *own* report that he is not the number one expert in the area necessarily. I don't know exactly what he would say as far as what his expertise *is* in this area, but he *does seem* to acknowledge that it could benefit from anthropological studies, specifically.

Chris Williamson

So even Hoodless *himself* is admitting that this particular area is not his specialty, and he's recommending sending this sample out to someone a little more suited to investigate it.

Katie Cohan

Right, and not exactly in those words, but it *is* at the very end of his report. He does suggest that.

Chris Williamson

I want to ask you the same question that I asked Dr. Jantz earlier because it's a big point of contention from the folks who are arguing against the Nikumaroro bones and the hypothesis in general. It's been reported by several researchers that support the Japanese capture hypothesis that Amelia Earhart had a procedure performed known as the Caldwell Luc procedure earlier in her career. My question is, wouldn't someone of Hoodless's stature *notice* and certainly *note* in his report that he observed two dime-sized holes in the bridge of the nose of the skull that he was being asked to analyze?

Katie Cohan

Yes and no. Because of the way that he records things, I'm not entirely sure there's things that he leaves out. For instance, he doesn't input the measurements of the femur or the femoral. He has both femurs, and he doesn't put the measurements in there. I'm not totally sure why. He actually *also* comments on the degraded nature of the bones, that they're highly weathered, and a lot of muscular areas can't be seen anymore, but he does shade in the parts of the skeleton that are there. It doesn't seem to show that there were parts of bones missing or anything like that. So I'm not entirely sure. Theoretically, if you *did* have those pieces of the skull still available to see, then, yes, you would think that would be recorded, absolutely. If they were there, they would look out of place because they're *not* tiny holes. That would then lead into the questions about taphonomic influences and what was there. What were they *actually* looking at? How much of it was intact? It is possible that it was too degraded, and he just didn't record that; I'm not really sure. Obviously, I can't guess on that.

. . .

Chris Williamson

Is it possible that he simply could have missed it?

Katie Cohan

I haven't looked up pictures of the procedure. To me, it would seem like they would likely be too large to be missed, but I *also* don't know how that would look as far as it being healed.

Chris Williamson

Before we get into the Jantz report, I want to ask you to tell the court, in a general sense, what Dr. Richard Jantz's reputation is like in the anthropological field.

Katie Cohan

I think it would be pretty surprising if you were a forensic anthropologist and *hadn't* come across his name at some point, especially because of FORDISC, which is probably what I would say he's *most* well known for. That's where I first heard of him, because he *did* create FORDISC, which is a computer program that he created along with Steven Ousley, who has added material and refined it and created new versions of it over the years. It's a statistical program that you can use to help you identify your skeletal material. It's a dynamic program that they're adding data to all the time, and it is still used today. You wouldn't necessarily want to rely on it solely, but it's a tool. There are a lot of different methods and materials in forensic anthropology to build your biological profile. In *this* case, it's a really important piece of that puzzle and a tool to use for forensic anthropologists.

Chris Williamson

Earlier, Dr. Jantz testified on the details of his report. Now that you've *heard* that testimony, and you've read this report, I'd like you to give your professional opinion on this piece of evidence for the court, please.

Katie Cohan

My first reaction as I'm reading it the *first time* is that I need to go back and read through this again, because it is *very* statistically heavy. We were talking about wheelhouses earlier. Some of it is out of my wheelhouse, in that I'm not an expert in statistics or FORDISC analyses. So *some of it*, I can't speak to in that way. Ultimately, to me, this paper served as a rebuttal to an earlier paper by Cross and Wright that was *actually* a rebuttal of one of *his* earlier papers before that. It seems like this is a back-and-forth research discussion, and this is just the next step in that research process.

What I felt, at least initially, was he was trying to take a look at Hoodless as an expert and *really* say whether or not he was an expert in the field. In a lot of ways, I think that Jantz *does* bring up some good points, as far as going back to that idea that forensic anthropology was in its infancy at the time that Hoodless was performing this analysis. So you have to take that into consideration. He didn't *have* all the same methods and data as we do now, even the same population reference samples to use as we have now; things like that. As it relates to Hoodless, it seems to me like he's trying to say ultimately, he could have been a little bit off on some of this. It's not a critique against Hoodless, but just an observation that he could have been off because he didn't have the same tools we do now.

Chris Williamson

Wouldn't someone the stature of Dr. Richard Jantz be the perfect person to pick up where Dr. Hoodless left off, being that he was limited by his time? And wouldn't his declaration of the 99% number carry a lot of weight simply because of who he *is*, and what his place is in the scientific community?

. . .

Katie Cohan

I think you have to take that number within the context of his *Chasing Earhart* interview.

Ultimately it seems like one of Jantz's main points is that if it's *not* Amelia Earhart, it is somebody who's very similar to her, and to me, that statement isn't *incorrect*. That statement is valid in and of itself. But if someone's similar to her, it would be unlikely for it to be somebody *else*. The question would be, was there anybody *else* it could have been? Was there anybody else at all who died on this island? Or around it? That is where I would start to question that, just in favor of looking at the *whole* picture. Even *if* these bones are very similar to her, is there anyone else who could have been similar to her? Is that a possibility? That's where my mind goes. If there wasn't, that's one thing. As long as there's someone else or other people whom it could have been, I think it becomes a little bit unclear what that means. Even though there weren't a ton of people whom we have recorded data of who passed away on this island, there are *some*, and you just need to look at all the pieces.

Chris Williamson

So is this, then, just a case of ruling everyone *else* out who was documented to be there until only one potential remains, Amelia Earhart?

Katie Cohan

That all depends on whether or not you *believe* that Hoodless's initial measurement can be used, which I know Jantz spoke about today in addition to his *Chasing Earhart* episode.

Even though he might not have agreed with all of Hoodless's assessments, measuring a bone from one point to another is not the most challenging thing in the world. In his paper, Jantz is saying that these measurements are *accurate and can be used*. If you believe that the measurements *are* accurate, then yes, you would think that you could go about it as systematically as possible and say, "Well, who could this be? Who fits into this profile?"

Even if you're *just* looking at bone length, are there people *other* than Amelia Earhart whom this could fit? That brings me to thinking about Kenton Spading's articles from the beginning of 2019, in which it appears to me he worked with Jantz on, in some respects.

There was the *Norwich City* wreck in 1929, in which eleven people went missing, but eight people seemingly lost their lives in and around this area. That's what Kenton's article is all about; it's about looking at this and asking, "Do any of these people fit the bill? Could they be similar enough to this material?" And there's also elements of taphonomy. Were these bones *really* able to be analyzed accurately to begin with? You could definitely do your best to determine who could best fit, or determine if there's *multiple* people who could best fit the skeletal material. However, it does go back to the question, were the original measurements and recordings accurate?

Chris Williamson

Miss Cohan, Dr. Jantz just closed his testimony to the court by saying that he welcomes anyone who wants to try to falsify his hypothesis, as long as they present scientific data to do so. Do you agree that until *that* day, this report by Jantz should be regarded as the explanation and the *most probable* outcome for the vanishing of Amelia Earhart?

Katie Cohan

Well, you know, again, going back to Kenton Spading's article, it seems like at least one of these men from the *Norwich City* could fit this material, and he did work alongside Jantz. That's according to his paper. To me, you have other variables in play, so I would not be able to say *for sure*.

I don't think that based on the evidence at hand, you could fully rule Amelia Earhart *out* of this material, but there are enough *other* possibilities. I don't think you can say that it's *definitely her either*. I'm not sure that Jantz would say that at this point. In your original interview, he's a 99%, but there's still that one percent. For me, I think it's a little bit too unclear. We don't even have all of the height or biological information of the other crew members who lost their lives in the area to compare to. I believe Spading introduced four of them, and there's still four more who are unaccounted for. There could be multiple people who might fit this material.

To go back to the other part of your question about him sort of saying, "Bring it on," I think that's a great way to handle research. To say, "Okay, if you want to prove me wrong, go ahead. But do it scientifically. Do it as methodically as possible." I think there's certain parts of Jantz's paper that people could certainly do that to. You could run a blind study of some of this data, and I think a lot of this data actually would *benefit* from a blind study. Ask a forensic anthropologist who doesn't know. You could say, "This is a blind study; this is the information that you have," which would include the data in his report. Ask if they could come up with a biological profile.

You could also do the same with some of Jantz's methods, because he *does* seem to develop new methods in his paper, too. So there's a lot of room for additional research here. I completely agree with him. Anything can benefit from additional research and additional studies being done in order to determine if these results are repeatable across researchers.

I think that's a great idea.

Chris Williamson
Thank you very much. Pass the witness.

Cross-Examination of Katie Cohan

Jen Taylor

It really seems like we have a lot of incomplete data here. Is that normal when you're conducting a study like this?

Katie Cohan

It absolutely *can* be. That's probably one of the most challenging parts of a field like forensic anthropology, or even biological archeology. Going back in time. Sometimes, you just have small pieces of the puzzle that you're trying to fit together. In this case in particular, you don't even have the skeletal material in front of you to look at, and you don't have pictures. Basically, the best picture you have of what's going on is going to be Hoodless's descriptions and some of the other people who were on the island at the time and looked at the material. You have their description, and then you have almost like a map or drawing of a skeleton, which you would typically *do* in a biological profile like this.

Just a kind of shaded-in skeleton showing what material is there. So, yes, I would say probably and unfortunately, that's very common, but that doesn't mean you shouldn't try looking at it.

Jen Taylor

In this situation, we don't, as you said, have the biological material anymore. And so no one can actually look at it. No one can take samples and test it. No one can take the measurements again. How much of a problem would you say that is? Is it enough that we just have the measurements that were taken by Hoodless?

Katie Cohan

For me, I think, especially if you start looking at two people who have done research on this material, it seems to differ based on who's researching it. Even *I* feel a little bit differently. It seems to depend on who's researching it and how you feel about that. As a researcher, do you feel comfortable knowing that you cannot see this material? For me, as I discussed with Chris, a lot of it *does* come back to the taphonomic factor and the changes that are documented to have occurred to these bones. That parts of them are missing or disintegrated. Some of it for me seems to be just the comfort level of the researcher as to whether they're willing to say anything definite or are willing to say anything at all. I'm sure there are some people who probably wouldn't even want to talk about this material because they have not seen it. That's the other side of it.

Jen Taylor

What kind of condition would you expect these bones to be in if only two to five years had passed between the time they ended up there and the time they were discovered?

Katie Cohan

I *did* try to look for different resources that had been done in island environments because that's one of the biggest challenges. The taphonomy is so environmentally dependent.

Within an island, there can be different environments. There was one study that I believe Cross and Wright referenced that discussed the composition of bodies on Pacific Islands.

They said hair specifically could have been intact at that point, and they didn't find any hair with this material. That's one indicator. I don't know exactly *how* accurate that was or if it would have applied to Nikumaroro, but you also have high heat. You have lots of records of crabs scattering this material all over the place; you have Gallagher describing that. You also have Dr. Karen Burns, who worked with TIGHAR to perform a few different studies regarding crab activity on skeletal material on the island. You would definitely expect that if there *was* anything at that point, it would be scattered. Lastly, you have various weathering influences. So it kind of depends on whether or not the material was being covered by water at all; it probably *was* being rained on because there were storms in the area. It definitely *could be* disintegrated if it was out in the sun. It could be bleached and peeling. There are all different types of things that could have affected it.

Jen Taylor

I know that there's been a lot of discussion about the state of this science. As it's been discussed here today, it was in its infancy when Hoodless examined these bones, and what we've learned is we can do a lot more with this kind of data *now* than he could have at the time. We watch so much TV these days that has us all believing you can take pretty much *any* piece of data or *any* piece of evidence that you find, and you can reconstruct a whole entire profile of somebody based on that. How accurate is the science *today*, and if we *did* have those bones today, what are some of the things that we could expect to learn that Hoodless couldn't have learned back in 1944?

Katie Cohan

I really like that question because if you think about a TV show like *Bones* or something, any of these prime-time TV shows where you have a skeleton, and they can identify it and say, "This is definitely a male; they were between forty-two and forty-five years old," they give very accurate data in that TV show. Of course, typically, that's not how it would work in forensic anthropology. That's one of the challenges of studying the human skeleton. If you *just have* the skeleton, everything is going to be on a range.

There will be that certain amount of standard error. With a stature, you would have something that you're guessing at, but it would have a plus or minus in front of it. That's a part of this case as well. As Jantz reanalyzes it, ultimately there would be a range here.

For something like stature, for instance, it's not going to be exact like in his report. He does an average of some long bone measurements using regression equations, and then gives a stature of five feet five or five feet five and a half inches. That really would be too precise a statement to make. You'd want to give it a little bit of a range there, and that's something that has been refined over time.

Actually, that's one of Jantz's points in his most recent article. Hoodless is using an equation based on a nineteenth-century population. So his estimates would have skewed a little bit low, because people overall get taller as time goes on. Things like that, you'd probably be able to do with a little more accuracy. With the passing of time, you'd have the use of things like digitizers or CT scans, and technology advancements in general.

Jen Taylor

When you're doing a biological profile, what are some of the characteristics that you can try to pin down? I know that Jantz talks about stature, sex and ancestry? Are there others?

Katie Cohan

Yeah. Hoodless actually talked about age in his report. To the best of my knowledge, age is not a part of FORDISC. I believe that's probably why Jantz didn't really comment on it.

Age is the factor that is somewhat missing in this discussion. Hoodless says that he's really not sure about the age of this skeleton, because of the weathering and the taphonomic effects on the bones. But he *does* still make a guess on it. He still says between forty-five and fifty-five years old; however, it's really unclear why he says that.

You can look at certain parts of the bone like the pubic symphysis, the part where the two pubic bones come together, to do aging. There are other methods as well. For instance, If it's a child, you can look at their dentition. So yes, age would be a big one on top of the ones you listed. Things like taphonomic influences would be important to include in a biological profile. Also, any trauma that you noted on the bone. There are different types of trauma; you can have trauma before death, like antemortem trauma, or trauma around the time of death, and then postmortem trauma. That would be important to know in a biological profile as well.

. . .

Jen Taylor

Regarding that trauma, I know you discussed notes made about the bones maybe being damaged in transport. But were there any findings that were made by Hoodless or Jantz as to what kind of trauma that person might have suffered? Cause would probably be way too optimistic to try to be able to tell, but is there anything like that?

Katie Cohan

Well, it *is* good that Hoodless in his original report does note that a lot of the prominences and the muscle attachments have been deteriorated. Even just with general weathering, who knows? That's important to know. As far as *actual* trauma, there was a part of the cheekbone, I believe it was the upper right cheek area, that was broken off. It seemed to me, the way they were writing about it, that it was probably postmortem, that it broke down over time. It didn't seem like it had anything to do with a healed fracture or anything like that. Other than that, there's not too much information.

Jen Taylor

I want to go back to when the bones were *not initially* discovered, but discovered again by Gallagher. I know that you had mentioned earlier during direct that those bones were initially suspected to possibly be Amelia Earhart's. Do you have any idea why that was?

My understanding of the hypothesis is that Amelia and Fred being castaways on that island really didn't become popularized until the 1980s. So in the early 1940s, what was it that had Gallagher suspecting that maybe this is Amelia Earhart?

Katie Cohan

There were some things that were found around the skeletal material. One of them that seemed to me to really spark Gallagher's interest in it being Earhart was a piece of a sole of a shoe that to him looked like a female shoe. That, alongside the skeletal material, might be what triggered this idea that this could be Earhart. On top of that, it wasn't that long after Earhart and Noonan had disappeared. Maybe he had that idea in his mind anyway.

"Hey, just in case, since they've disappeared, and we don't know where they went, we should check this out. How should we proceed with this?" Actually, if you read through the telegrams, they're pretty interesting, because he's talking to the other members of the Western Pacific High Commission at the time, and they seem to want to keep it quiet.

They're not sure what this is, but they think they should get it analyzed, just in case.

Jen Taylor

Say we were excavating today, and we found this material. Is there any way to tell whether the person died *where* the bones were found, or whether they had been moved or relocated? I know, you mentioned that the bones would probably be scattered because of animal activity, but can we be confident that the *general area* where they were found is the *general area* where that person would have died?

Katie Cohan

It's a little tricky, because you *do have* the influence of coconut crabs. Dr. Burns did tests with TIGHAR on this, and they basically watched this material disappear over time. They watched the crabs come in, and eventually, you don't see anything anymore, because all of the pieces of bone are gone. These are studies on lamb and pigs, so it's not *exactly* the same.

If you had a case, typically what you'd want to do is handle it archaeologically, which would be to grid everything out and essentially dig down based on layers and record and map everything. If you have layers that tell you a body is moved from one place to another, or if you found different soil, you might be able to guess or even be able to see sometimes that the soil is different. That could indicate that somebody had been moved. In this case what's interesting is that the soil itself was found by an islander six months *prior* to Gallagher learning about this, and the skull was buried by the islander. So the skull was buried, and then they took Gallagher *back* to the skull, and they kind of do a sweep of the area around that. Unfortunately, either they didn't make a map that I'm aware of, or it's not listed in any of the material that TIGHAR transcribed. So there's no map of how far everything was scattered. If you did that *today*, you would want to map everything and take tons of pictures, of course.

Jen Taylor

There was, of course, another person in the plane with her, Fred Noonan. Wouldn't we expect if this was the site where they were castaways and eventually died, to see *two sets* of skeletal remains? Or do you think there's a reason why one of them might not have been found?

Katie Cohan

I've heard people talk about it differently. Some people think that he might not even have made it to land to begin with. Or that he died in a different manner somehow. Technically, *yes*. Especially if you had an airplane, and if it *did* crash on the reef. It all depends on what they think might have happened at the time.

Jantz *does* talk about that a little bit in his papers. Essentially, based on the length of the long bones that Hoodless records, Noonan's skeletal material would be *excluded* from this because he was a little over six feet. He would be too tall to fit the skeletal materials, but he *does* talk about that.

There's not too much information about where he would be at this time, because a lot of it would be guessing. Ultimately, as far as trying to piece together what could have happened, you'd really just be guessing.

. . .

Jen Taylor

One of the things that Jantz mentions early on in his paper is this concept of cognitive bias. He says, "There's no way to know whether or not that played a role in his evaluation," but the fact that he brings it up at all is almost an implication that it *did* play a role in Hoodless's evaluation. Is there any way to know, based on the data that we have, what he was told in terms of these bones? Was he told that Gallagher thought they may have been familiar? Was he told where they were found, or was it just a case of these bones *being* found and them needing a profile?

Katie Cohan

I've read through this a bunch of times at this point, and to me it's a little bit unclear. I don't believe he says anything *specifically* about this not being Amelia Earhart. For me, it's a little bit unclear. I'm not sure if he could have been made aware through other avenues or through other telegrams that aren't there. I'm sure people were talking about this. I'm not entirely sure if the telegrams are a full, complete record. On the other hand, you could say that he might have the same thought in his head. He might be thinking the same thing Gallagher was thinking. *Maybe* it could be Amelia Earhart. You could *also* say the same thing about Fred Noonan, assuming that you know he went down as well; he was less talked about. But the bias could work either way. It doesn't really indicate to me anywhere that he was overly biased in any way.

I think it all comes back to what I was saying before about objectivity and anthropology.

For me, that's really, ***really*** important. I know everybody has biases that they bring to the table, and that's something I've trained in over the years. You're trying as best you can to acknowledge when you have a bias on something. That's why I *do think* ultimately a lot of these methods and materials could benefit from a blind study where you just take Amelia out of it. There's no fame, no fortune involved in the study. *Now* let's see if these results are repeatable. If you're doing research on a case like this, you can't help but get excited because you want there to be a connection, but you have to keep that in check because ultimately this skeletal material *belongs to somebody*. Regardless of *who it was* and how famous they were, you don't want to do an individual a disservice by getting too clouded and being biased. You want to come into every case that you work on or every research project that you participate in with as much objectivity as possible.

This is somebody's life that was lost. You don't want to misclassify that person.

Jen Taylor
No further questions.

*"I can place a person near the island, lost, who has a height that's near what
Dr. Jantz determined was a possibility."*

Chris Williamson

Your Honor, the project calls *Mr. Kenton Spading* to the stand.

Mr. Spading, can you inform the court of your professional specialty?

Kenton Spading

I hold a bachelor of science degree in civil engineering. My specialty is in water resource projects, things like dams and levees, environmental restoration projects, and flood-risk-reduction projects, those types of things.

Chris Williamson

Before taking a harder look at the evidence in this case, did you carry the preconceived notion that Amelia Earhart and Fred Noonan ended up in the ocean after failing to reach Howland Island?

Kenton Spading

Yes. In 1989, I was living in St. Paul, Minnesota, where I currently live, and I picked up the paper one Sunday, and there was an article in there about a gentleman from Minnesota who was on a team specifically comprised of people from the International Group for Historic Aircraft Recovery. They were looking for Amelia Earhart on an island in the Pacific. Before that, I hadn't given any of the theories any thought at all.

There was a process I had to go through to be vetted by the TIGHAR organization, and I ended up going through an aviation archaeology school that they held. I went through some fieldwork with them, and a few years later, I was picked to be on a team that joined TIGHAR on an expedition to the island in 1997.

Before I went on the trip with them in '97 to the island, I *did* research the other theories, and I discovered that the Nikumaroro hypothesis held a lot of promise. It appeared to me they had enough fuel to get there to the island. The island was on their last known line of position, and TIGHAR had found some artifacts, specifically a piece of aircraft skin and a few other artifacts, that pointed toward the Lockheed possibly having been on or near the island. That intrigued me enough to start pursuing the Nikumaroro hypothesis.

Chris Williamson

When you first started looking at the evidence that TIGHAR was presenting, what did you look at *specifically* that swayed you to believe that they might be onto something with this explanation?

Kenton Spading

That's a good question. I mentioned one artifact already, that's the piece of aircraft skin that's maybe roughly three feet by two feet in dimension. It's of the correct type of aluminum, and the correct thickness, and it has rivets. The rivets are not flush mounted, whereas with World War II aircraft, they *were* flush mounted. That particular artifact was very intriguing to me. If you're trying to figure out why other aircraft aluminum was on the island, World War II is by far your most likely explanation.

You have to try to explain aircraft parts on the island as being military if they're not Earhart's. Things could have been brought there by islanders, but generally speaking, it's military or Earhart. There was also a piece of Plexiglas windshield that's, again, the correct thickness and the correct chemical composition. It has the correct curvature to be a piece of a windshield from a Lockheed Electra. In later years, they found some other artifacts, for example, a woman's makeup kit that dates from the 1920s or '30s. The remaining makeup in the kit is of a chemical composition that's almost identical to a makeup kit that's in the Amelia Earhart Museum that we know she owned. That's *three* arti-facts that I think represent pretty good evidence that she *may have* ended up there.

Chris Williamson

What kind of process goes into vetting some of this evidence that TIGHAR has presented that you just spoke of?

Kenton Spading

Another good question. TIGHAR uses what's known as the "scien-tific method." We try to avoid going down trails that are *all* anecdotal. For example, the captured by the Japanese hypothesis is almost *entirely* based on anecdote. We *do have* anecdotes that we use in our investiga-tion, but we try to stick to hard facts. When we deal with something like the makeup kit, we do a spectral chemical analysis of that kit. The aircraft aluminum has undergone quite a detailed examination by Jeff Glickman. He's taken a video of Earhart's predeparture preparation and extracted images from the video; I think over 150 images are in the video. From there, he'll be able to tell if the rivet pattern we're seeing on the aircraft skin artifact lines up with what we see in the video of her Lockheed Electra.

You might say there's lots of Lockheed Electras around, why don't you look at one of those? Well, a piece of a window on her aircraft was patched over in Miami. So that patch has a nonconforming rivet pattern to it. We believe this artifact is part of that nonconforming patch. The plexiglass, like I said, doesn't match anything that would be on World War II aircraft. It does match up with what would be on an Electra. We also did a spectral analysis of its composition, and it's the correct comp. It matches the composition of other known Electra wind-shields.

Chris Williamson

Mr. Spading, referring to TIGHAR artifact 2-2-V-1, if the recently obtained footage that made news headlines is proven to be useful in making a *more* definite determination on that original artifact being from Amelia's Lockheed Electra, does that help close this case for TIGHAR?

Kenton Spading

Perhaps. We found in the past that finding and identifying a smoking-gun artifact is really, *really* challenging to do. You have to convince yourselves *and* the public that that's where it's from. There is another potential possibility, and that's that the Electra crashed *somewhere else*, and somebody found a piece of aluminum *from* that crash site and brought it to Nikumaroro. You might ask why we'd think aircraft artifacts could have been brought there. Well, because we found B-24 aircraft aluminum on the island. So we know islanders have brought aircraft aluminum from *other* islands to *this* island. It does remain a possibility, but I would say if this artifact 2-2-V-1 can be proven beyond a reasonable doubt to be from Earhart's Electra, then with pretty good certainty, I would say that the Electra was there.

Chris Williamson

I've talked about what *I* consider to be the trinity of evidence for *this* particular theory, the Nikumaroro bones, the collection of artifacts found on the island in question, and the post-loss radio signals. I understand that you have a *different* trinity than I do, and you also have a different hypothesis on the Nikumaroro bones than what we've been discussing in court today. Can you advise the court of what *you* believe regarding both of those aspects?

Kenton Spading

I would subscribe to the trinity that I just mentioned to you, which was artifact 2-2-V-1, the aircraft aluminum, the plexiglass and the makeup kit. That would be *my* trinity. I do not discount the fact that the bones *could be* related to Amelia Earhart. I don't 100% discount that, but I suggest in the paper that I wrote that they could *also be* from some of the lost sailors from the wreck of the *Norwich City*. The *Norwich City* was a British steamship that ran aground on Nikumaroro Island on November 29, 1929, roughly eight years or so before Earhart disappeared. Eleven seamen were lost in that wreck, and eight of them were never recovered. So we have a case of a ship going to ground *on the reef at the island* just a few years before Earhart disappeared and roughly eleven years before the bones were discovered by the British in 1940. As a result of that, we have eight missing men.

In my mind, *one* of those eight guys is *definitely* a candidate for the bones because it's a *known* person missing near the island. Earhart certainly *is* a possibility, but we don't for sure know that Earhart was *there*, so there's that. In addition to that, I did a lot of research on seamen who were lost by digging through the public records office archives at the National Archives in Great Britain, and I discovered that the seamen had what amounted to driver's license cards called central registered cards. It lists the height, the name, eye color, hair color and other demographic things for each of the seamen, *including* a picture of them in many cases.

So I went to those cards, and I pulled out their heights, and I discovered that *one of them specifically*, a seaman named Saleh Ragee, who was an Arabian seaman, has a height of five feet six listed on his card. Well, that measurement falls *within* the height range that Dr. Jantz determined was the most likely height for the skeleton found there. We don't specifically have the bones that were found, but we have a forensic report on the bones, and Dr. Jantz was able to run those bone measurements through FORDISC, which has thousands of known skeleton heights and bone links. From *there* he's able to determine that this last castaway who was found on the island was most likely between five feet five and five feet nine inches tall. Saleh Ragee is five feet six; he's certainly within the wheelhouse of that known probability. There's another lost seaman named Thomas Scott, who comes in at five feet nine, so he's in the upper confidence limit of Dr. Jantz's determination, but *still* a possibility as well. There are a couple of other seamen I found heights for who are more on the lower confidence limit.

With Earhart, we've had a little bit of trouble figuring out her height, but generally it's agreed that she was five feet seven, possibly five feet eight. The evidence points to five feet seven. So she was *very* close to Saleh Ragee's height.

So, to recap, I can place a person *near* the island, *lost*, who has a height that's *near* what Dr. Jantz determined was a possibility.

Chris Williamson

Just to reiterate for the court, the folks you just mentioned *are* unaccounted for as of this moment, correct?

Kenton Spading

Yes. There are eight bodies that are unaccounted for, yes.

Chris Williamson

Could we either prove or disprove that these bones belong to Amelia Earhart *without* ever finding these bodies?

Kenton Spading

That's a really good question. TIGHAR has done a lot of archaeology on the island. In particular, they've done a lot of archaeology at a site on the island that is possibly the castaway site. Gerald Gallagher recovered most of the bones that were found on the island.

Some natives found the original bones and notified him, and he went to this part of the island, which he described only as the "southeast part of the island." He describes how far away it was from the high tides and a few other things like that. On the southeast end of the island, we found a site that has a discarded campsite, a fire, which Gallagher said was there, and it has bird and turtle bones, which Gallagher said were also there. It has some artifacts there that you can tell somebody was using to cook with, like jars they apparently had in a fire. Gallagher said that parts of a shoe, or as he put it, "a heavy walking sandal," were found there as well. That part of it really caught my eye because of the eight missing seamen; five of them were Arabian from Yemen, and people of Yemen then, today and for centuries for that matter wore heavy walking sandals. That's their preferred method of footwear. We've uncovered photographs of Arabian, specifically Yemen, seamen wearing sandals on steamships. Again, I think there's some evidence for the bones that Gerald Gallagher found possibly being a lost Arabian from the *Norwich City*.

Chris Williamson

You mentioned a few other standout pieces earlier. Can you expand on those?

Kenton Spading

There's an artifact that we call the "dado." A dado in an airplane is essentially a piece of baseboard like one that would be in your house. As your carpet or hardwood floor goes over the wall, there's a strip of wood that goes along the base of the wall to transition through the floor and ceiling. Airplanes like Earhart's were often used as passenger planes, and we found a dado on the island that *appears to be* of the correct dimension, and specifically, you can see that the rivet holes in the dado are the correct horizontal distance apart in order to match the horizontal distance between the stringers in the fuselage of the aircraft. So the dado is a decent piece of evidence as well.

Earhart *did have* freckles. We can't put freckle cream in her aircraft, but it's what I would call "suggestive evidence." Those are the main ones that I hang my hat on.

Chris Williamson

Mr. Spading, after everything you've studied within this case, is it your professional opinion that Amelia Earhart and Fred Noonan landed on Nikumaroro and lived out their final days on that island?

Kenton Spading

When I throw the post-loss radio messages into the mix along with my trinity of evidence and *then* add the dado, I believe there's a probability that Earhart and Noonan ended up on Nikumaroro Island.

I believe that probability is higher than it is for the other hypotheses that are out there.

Chris Williamson

Thank you, Mr. Spading, no more questions.

"We went down into that area, and I can tell you that the dogs did alert. All the dogs independently working alerted in pretty much the same areas. So we knew someone had perished there."

Chris Williamson

Your Honor, the project calls *Miss Lynne Engelbert* to the stand.

Can you please advise the court of your professional specialty?

Lynne Engelbert

I have been doing work with search dogs since 1989, so around thirty-two years. I have worked with live find dogs, I have worked with human remains detection dogs, and now I am working with a historical human remains detection dog. I started off with live find dogs doing disaster search. I am one of the twenty-eight FEMA urban search and rescue teams. We are a highly trained team that goes into major disasters. Personally, I worked a live find dog in the World Trade Center after 9/11; we worked the shuttle Columbia recovery mission after the shuttle went down. I worked at NASA for twenty-two years. I've worked a couple of hurricanes; I did work at the Oklahoma City bombing without my dog as well. So I have been to some pretty major disasters with my live find dog, my old dog Lucy. She was cross-trained.

Now we use specialty dogs, but she was cross-trained at that point. When we went to work at the World Trade Center after 9/11, her job at that particular point was to do human remains detection. She was quite successful at that. I have also been doing criminal work with law enforcement agencies all over the state of California and some out of the state as well. During her career, Lucy found two murder victims and a drowning victim. She had quite the career in her fifteen years of life.

Chris Williamson

God bless her, and thank you *both* for the incredible work that you do.

Can you tell us a little more about what you do regarding crime scene investigations? Do you only work with law enforcement for that type of investigation?

Lynne Engelbert

The crime scene work that we do with law enforcement is done through a sister organization called "the Canine Specialized Search Team." We are a resource to the Santa Clara County, California, sheriff's office. Any of the law enforcement work that we do is done under the auspices of the sheriff's department; we only work with law enforcement.

We do not go out and do private cases or anything like that. We are *strictly* law enforcement. We will go in looking for any evidence of foul play: it can be blood spatter, it can be locating a body of someone who has perished, and everything in between.

Chris Williamson

Can you tell us how your specialty was called on for the Amelia Earhart investigation on Nikumaroro?

Lynne Engelbert

We work with cultural resource management groups and with native tribes. We do a lot of work with archaeologists as well. About five years before we actually went to Nikumaroro, on the South Pacific, one of our archaeologists that we had been working with asked us if we would be interested in going down to the middle of the South Pacific and seeing if we can find evidence that Amelia Earhart died on that particular island. And we said, "Well, yeah!" Our dogs have never worked in a tropical atmosphere. They had not yet worked in a hot and humid climate at that point in time. So we had to have a lot of discussions. Over the ensuing several years, there was talk of it, and we weren't really sure, but finally we said, "Yeah, we really would be interested in doing this."

In 2017, all of the talk became a reality. So we had a lot of hoops to jump through before we could do this. We had to make sure that we met all the requirements for flying our dogs into Fiji and then taking a ship to Nikumaroro, which is in the Republic of Kiribati. There were a lot of requirements with that. We had to make arrangements to fly our dogs in business class on an airline that had never flown dogs in-cabin before. We won't put our dogs in cargo. They're *normally* pretty safe there, but accidents happen every now and then, and we just could not afford to have that happen to one of our historical human remains detection dogs.

So it took us about five months to get everything in line. But the next thing you know, in June of 2017, we boarded a plane at LAX and headed for Fiji and for the little, tiny island of Nikumaroro in the middle of the Pacific.

Chris Williamson

How do your dogs go through certification to be able to perform the service that they are called on to perform? Can you take us through that process?

Lynne Engelbert

Some of us start with puppies. Some of us prefer to start with an older dog, a young adult, if you will, ten to twenty months. But we start them both about the same way. We introduce them to old human bones, which we get from osteological supply houses. We've been dealing with the supply houses for long enough to where they know that if we call, we will take the old broken bones. They don't have to be *pretty*, they just have to be *human*.

Once we get those bones, then we will test the dogs to make sure that they are *in fact* human. We've not had a problem with that at all. Then we just start introducing the bones, and as soon as the dogs are curious, *because they're innately curious,* they will go over and check the bone.

Of course, they're given a reward. It doesn't take them very long to figure out, "Hmm, if I go smell this, I get a treat." So we work with that for a little while. And then we introduce whatever alert we want them to perform, which is a way for them to tell us that they have found human bone. It's usually a "down" or a "sit" at the source; they are taught to alert very, *very* close to the source. Once they've got that and it has been imprinted in their brain, we start upping the game. We'll start putting the bones in harder to find places, and we just keep upping the game until certification. If you start with a puppy, it can take a year and a half to two years to get them certified. If you start with an older dog, it's sometimes a little bit faster because they've gotten the puppy stage out of them and they're thinking a little bit more adultlike.

Chris Williamson

You mentioned earlier that there was concern among the team regarding the tropical environment of Niku. Was that concern directed at this particular environment having a *negative effect* on the dogs being able to do what they normally do?

Lynne Engelbert

That was a huge question for us. We didn't know what they were going to do, and it's a really hot and very humid atmosphere. We were very honest and straightforward with both TIGHAR *and* National Geographic, who actually sponsored the dogs. We didn't know, and we really have no way of testing it.

We had worked in Hawaii for a few days, and that worked well. When we got to Nikumaroro, the first thing that they did was offload the dogs onto the launch and take us onto the island. They had some known burials from the colonial era, so they took the dogs in there.

Sure enough, the dogs went, "Yep, right here. There's somebody buried right here." So we knew right away that we were going to be able to use the dogs there. That said, what we had to do was adjust our work time and our rest time. When it's hot and humid, it's taxing on the dogs. Their stamina is not quite what it *would be* in a cool, drizzling atmosphere.

We would work for twenty minutes and take them to rest for a while. When they settled down a little bit, we would work them again. We had reflective vests that we used on the dogs, which have been used in Afghanistan and Iraq when they were working detection dogs over there, and they are *highly* efficient. That helped us immensely.

Chris Williamson

You mentioned two teams of dogs. How did you work both teams without the concern of one team influencing the other? Can you talk about that process?

Lynne Engelbert

We always work our dogs what we call "blind." Try *as we do* as handlers, we can influence our dogs, and we know that. So we try to limit those possibilities. One team will go in and work a site, and while they're doing that, the other teams are completely separated and can't hear or see anything. When the first team comes back, they go away; they don't talk to us at all. The second team goes in, and we do the same thing; then the third team and the fourth team come in. Lastly, we can go back in as four separate handlers, and we can look at what happens. We use pin flags to flag our alerts. What we prefer to do is put the pin flags in, take a picture of it, and pull those pin flags out. Again, we don't want *anything* to influence the other handlers. So that's how we try to work on sites where we want total independent searching and alerts performed by the four teams. One day, two of the teams went to the north end of the island and did something different. We swapped over, and we went in, and we took the *other two* teams in and worked them completely blind from each other.

· · ·

Chris Williamson

Just so it's made completely clear to this jury and this court, can forensic canine evidence be used in a court of law to help prosecute a case?

Lynne Engelbert

Absolutely. We have been known to go in and testify in a court of law as the handler regarding what our dogs found. They can use us in that capacity.

Chris Williamson

My final question is this: Did your dogs alert in the *very same location* that the team from TIGHAR is saying Amelia Earhart died?

Lynne Engelbert

When we were about the area they call the "Seven site," we had no idea this was all based on the British administrator's records as to where he had found the thirteen bones. We went down into that area, and I can tell you that the dogs *did* alert. All the dogs independently working alerted in pretty much the same areas.

So we *knew* someone had perished there.

Chris Williamson

Thank you. Your Honor, pass the witness.

Cross-Examination of Lynne Engelbert

Jen Taylor

It's my understanding that when the dogs alert, that can tell us that there was a body there, that *somebody* passed away there, but it can't tell us *who* that person was. Is my understanding correct?

Lynne Engelbert

Your understanding is absolutely correct.

Jen Taylor

In order to really know *who* it was who passed away on seven site at Nikumaroro Island, we have to wait for the additional testing that National Geographic is going to be conducting, is that correct?

Lynne Engelbert

Absolutely.

Jen Taylor

No further questions.

Chris Williamson

Your honor, at this time the project rests. We'd like to break and reconvene next to present evidence and experts for the *Buka hypothesis*.

Bailiff

ALL RISE!

Post-Trial Discussion

Chris Williamson

This day is *finally* done; we spent weeks and weeks preparing to question this list of people.

You've done this before many times now, but *not* in a historical case and certainly not in a case this old. We packed a lot of data into this, and the readers have been following along, forming their own opinions, *I'm sure*. You heard me talk about the trinity with Kenton Spading earlier. We have some large pieces of evidence here, the post-loss radio signals, the much-discussed Nikumaroro bones. Lots of all-star pieces of evidence to unpack here.

What do you think coming out the other side? What are your first impressions?

Jen Taylor

First impressions? That's a *very* loaded question.

Chris Williamson

I figured we'd start there.

Jen Taylor

My first impression is I *still* have a lot of questions. There are things that are still definitely left unanswered for me, and holes that still need to be filled in my mind. That's a general overview of my first impressions.

. . .

Chris Williamson

What are your takeaways? Positive wise, let's start with that. Give me some of the positives of this particular theory. Did they prove certain things that you had initial questions about? Did they make some good points in certain areas? Talk to me about some of the standout areas on the positive side for castaway.

Jen Taylor

The *strongest* thing for me is the fact that there were signals picked up *after* she supposedly went missing that were coming from her transmission. She was transmitting on 3105 kilohertz, and at that time, there actually were very few aircraft that would have been transmitting on that frequency, even *less so* in the area of the world where we know she was. That for me is very compelling. I'm not 100% convinced that even the vast majority of the signals are credible. I know TIGHAR has their catalog, and anyone can go look at and make their own determination as to whether they're credible or not. I don't think you need to believe the vast majority of those so long as *one of them* came from her.

That's evidence that she survived. That *alone* gives me reasonable doubt toward crash and sink. Now, do I think that that means she went to Nikumaroro? That's a *different* question.

Chris Williamson

And I should note here for everybody who's reading this, we're recapping and giving our own thoughts post-trial, but you *will notice* and perhaps you *did* notice as you read through the entirety of castaway that there are some glaring holes in the text, *particularly* when it comes to cross-examination. You might notice that everyone who testified on behalf of crash and sink was able to be cross-examined by Jen. For castaway, Jen was *not* able to cross-examine some of the biggest players for that theory, Ric Gillespie and Dr. Richard Jantz among others.

It's not for lack of trying.

When creating the original episodes, we actually *did* reach out to

Ric, and we tried to reach out to Dr. Jantz. Ric declined, and we never heard back from Dr. Jantz. I felt it was *particularly* important to have them both appear in the original episode for *Vanished and* this text as well, because they covered some of the most important factors at play for castaway, and you can't have a castaway piece like this *without* including them. It just wouldn't feel right.

Luckily for us, we have their audio from the *Chasing Earhart* archives, and we were able to bring them into the conversation based on those archives. We would have loved to have presented a cross-examination where Jennifer could have gone back and forth with Gillespie and with Jantz on certain things. I know you had burning questions you really wanted to ask them, but we just didn't get that opportunity, which really *is* unfortunate for the sake of the show and this book. We want to make sure that we present the strongest argument possible for all of these different theories, and if we can't do that because of a technicality or because somebody didn't want to participate, well, that's really unfortunate.

Jen Taylor

Yeah, I agree, but it is what it is. Everyone has a right to not speak to media, so I get it. I don't hold it against them, and I don't think anyone *else* should either. But it *did* make our jobs a little bit more difficult.

Chris Williamson

Right. Look, these are the heavy hitters. When we started this, we really wanted to make sure we did everything we could to put forth the strongest case possible for every theory.

Because of the archive, I still think we were able to do that here, but we also weren't able to stay true to what the ultimate goal of all this is, which would be to allow for *a balanced presentation*. Without full cross-examination, that's just not possible. As far as I'm concerned, there's only two reasons why you would decline an invitation like this:

One, you don't believe in the theory as much as you say you do.

Two, you're concerned about standing up to cross-examination, and you're a little worried about being proven wrong on a platform like this. Unless somebody comes forward and says, "Hey, this is actually why I couldn't do it and it's a legitimate reason," then we're going to have to assume that's why you decided not to participate.

This won't be the first time this will happen either; you'll notice those holes again as we move forward. If every time you spot one, you're wondering, "Did they ask?"

The answer is *yes*, we *absolutely did.*

Jen Taylor

Why don't we talk about some of the evidence that we discussed for castaway because I *do have* several unanswered questions and a number of concerns that were *not* addressed.

Chris Williamson

Okay. Take us through it.

Jen Taylor

We started earlier by talking about the post-loss signals, and I said at the beginning of this chapter that I wanted to know (A) did they come from her, and (B) can they *in any way* be triangulated, or can we use this information to locate her? Does it point to Nikumaroro?

I think there's a pretty good chance that *at least* a handful of them came from her, I *really* do.

Chris Williamson

Agreed, it's possible.

Jen Taylor

That was the strongest piece of evidence for me today. That was the one thing that always made me pause. The second part of that was, can they be triangulated to Nikumaroro Island? That, I have a little bit more uncertainty about. I don't think that the guests we had discuss it were as confident as we thought they were going to be. For example, our first expert, Richard Olson, said that we can triangulate where they came from because there's a number of Pan Am stations in the South Pacific that were picking up signals that *some* believe were coming from her in the days following her disappearance. I think that it's fairly likely that they were coming from her. Oahu had a station, Wake Island had a station, and Midway had a station. Those places all had radio direction finders, which means that they would have been able to take a bearing when they received that transmission. They could take a bearing and try to guess what direction that signal was coming from. So the idea is if you have a bunch of them and they're *all* pointing at the same location, then theoretically, that location *should be* where that signal is coming from.

Chris Williamson
Right.

Jen Taylor
So that's the argument. However, the closer I look at it, the more questions I have.

Chris Williamson
Such as?

Jen Taylor
Let's start with Oahu.

Chris Williamson

Okay.

Jen Taylor

If you run a Google Earth search with that, there are a number of mountain ranges around that area, specifically to the west. There are three signals that Oahu received: *one* of them points in an *entirely different* direction, but *two* of them point towards the Phoenix Islands.

Neither of those really point towards Nikumaroro Island.

Chris Williamson

Yeah.

Jen Taylor

Midway is the same. *One* of them points towards the Phoenix Islands, but a *second* one points in an entirely different direction altogether. For Wake Island, I only see one that's, again, pointing towards the Phoenix group, but that bearing does not cross Nikumaroro Island at all.

Chris Williamson

Right.

Jen Taylor

So it's not as precise as I was led to believe when people were talking about it. Another thing is that if you *actually* dig into the accuracy of radio bearings taken in 1937, they're not *100%* accurate. These are really long distances. Olson explained that once you get distances *that* long, the ionosphere comes into play, and you have skip signals and all of that. They were *so* far away that they couldn't hear her talking. For the majority of the signals here, they're getting noise, but they can't make out who it is. The reason why they believe it's her is *not* because they hear her, but because it's coming in on the 3105 kilohertz frequency.

Chris Williamson

Right.

Jen Taylor

So if it's that far away and you're getting that much skip interference, I don't understand how you can still take a bearing. That was just not explained to me. I still have a lot of questions regarding how *much* we can trust this, and even Richard Olson himself said, "She could have been there." When we first spoke with him though, he was very confident that she was in the South Pacific. When he testified, however, he sounded less confident that those signals were *actually* coming from Nikumaroro Island. You also have to remember that the USS *Colorado* was searching for her after she disappeared; the US Navy and the Coast Guard were out looking for her as well. The *Colorado* came very close to Nikumaroro and sent pilots to fly *over* the island and look for her, and they didn't see anything. If she was sending signals from that island, then you would think that *somebody* would have seen *something*. If you have an instrument telling you that you should see something, but your eyes are telling you that it's not there, what are you going to trust?

Chris Williamson

I think there were some mistakes made in the search. I think they should have definitely deployed ground crews to Nikumaroro. I think that if she was injured or if she couldn't get out into view, it would have been a problem. Ric Gillespie mentioned that it could take ten minutes or so to get out onto the beach if you're deep into the brush. If she couldn't get to them for a number of possible reasons, then that could really add to the tragedy. They flew right over her, and she saw them fly over her, and she couldn't do anything about it. The plane wouldn't have been there anymore, it could have very well been washed over the reef and out to sea even at that point, and that would have been her biggest signal for a potential recovery, right? So if you're Earhart on Niku, and your partner Noonan has been dead for however many days, and you've been on that island *alone*, imagine the punch to the gut that would have been. Flyovers are relatively low over the island, but they don't see anything. I just think they missed the boat there, and they should have deployed ground crews as part of the search. If she was there and they failed to properly search that island, then it was a mistake on their part.

Jen Taylor

Another point that I have is that the hypothesis states she was likely there for several days, and she had the state of mind to send out these signals and call for help. If you believe what TIGHAR is telling us, she was *not only* still alive, but she still had the mental capacity to understand that she'd have to start the Electra's engine in order to charge the battery and that she'd have to run it at a low RPM and cut the plane off so that it can cool off and then turn it back on. She's also going to do all of this at nighttime. She had this whole plan in that she was sending all of these signals out to try to get rescued, but once the plane breaks up and goes into the reef, that's the backbreaker. She completely loses all ability to send SOS signals or start a fire and send up smoke signals. It's still a little difficult for me because it's only been a week at that point, you've been trying *desperately* to get your signals out there, and you know they're probably looking for you. I'm sure she wasn't in the best of health, being stranded on an island for a week, but at the same time, I just find it really hard to believe that a flyover would have seen *nothing*.

Chris Williamson

You make a good point.

. . .

Jen Taylor

No fires, no SOS signals, *nothing*. If she's sending out signals from her plane, then why wouldn't she be doing other things as well?

Chris Williamson

This goes all the way back to Atchison, Kansas. When she was a little girl, she was rough and tumble, a tomboy type. We talked about this in the opening chapter of this text, and there's *a reason why* we did that. *Not only* to explain her foundational makeup and the type of little girl she was, but *also* to illustrate the very point that you just made. If this little girl grows up to be the world-famous aviatrix Amelia Earhart, she presumably would not shy away from a situation like this. She would do what she had to do in order to survive. She would not just curl up into a ball and die unless she was physically *so* injured that she couldn't handle it. You make a compelling point there; she would have probably *immediately* started creating ways on the island to try to track down a potential rescue.

She would have exhausted all resources that she had.

Jen Taylor

Set those trees on fire or something!

Chris Williamson

Right. A lot of people who oppose this particular theory would say that there are multiple ways for her to live off this island. There's an abundance of coconuts there, and there's no way she would have died of dehydration. That's one of the areas that would have been pretty well covered because of the abundance of coconuts. There's a lot of things that we'll talk about when we get to the Japanese capture segment that will contradict a lot of the testimony here, or at least oppose a lot of the testimony that we just heard. What will *you* believe? What will make the most sense to you? As we wrap up here, let me ask you about "beyond a reasonable doubt." In the beginning of this segment, I mentioned that I would need to prove beyond a reasonable doubt that this was not only *plausible* but *probable.*

Was I able to do that, or do you think there are *still* just too many holes here?

Jen Taylor

I think there are too many holes and too many unanswered questions. I think when you have multiple witnesses who were *there* a week later who didn't see her or any evidence of her being there, that's really compelling to me. I understand that we have a lot of artifacts. I understand that there were human remains. I understand that they have found airplane parts. I understand *all of that.* But if there are other explanations as to how those things got there, and a week after she disappeared, no one saw evidence of her ever being there, it seems *more and more likely* that these other explanations for how these artifacts got there are probably the correct explanations.

Chris Williamson

I guess the *obvious question* now is, TIGHAR has built this case around a mountain of circumstantial evidence. We just heard all of it. Is this a case of evidence being *too* circumstantial?

Jen Taylor

I don't know if that's how I would characterize it. I don't think it's a matter of it being too circumstantial. I just think that you can have a case built off of nothing but circumstantial evidence, and it *can prove something beyond a reasonable doubt,* but I don't think this is one of those cases. Some of it is just *too much* speculation. There's not enough connecting what we have to her or to the plane. It just depends on *how* in depth you want to get with all of this stuff. For example, artifact 2-2-V-1 and the Plexiglas artifact and those things that they believe came from her plane. Dr. King told you that we know some of the aluminum that has been found came from other planes that were *not* hers. So how are we so confident that 2-2-V-1 came from her plane and not these other planes? Same goes for the plexiglass. Well, the way we know is because somebody has taken *pictures* of her plane, and they have done this cool little trick where we don't have the data from her *specific plane,* so we take pictures, and we try to compare the artifacts to photos, even though the artifacts are degraded, and the photos aren't very good. It just becomes too much of a stretch for me at the end of the day.

Chris Williamson

One of the things readers might have noticed, too, is throwbacks to your first appearance in this case and a really interesting rule of law. You objected *twice* under the federal rules of evidence, 705 and Daubert.

Jen Taylor

Yeah, essentially, I objected stating that I would like to challenge this person as an expert.

The relevant rules of evidence are rule 702 and rule 705. We talked about this at length during "Trial by Jury," which was my first appearance on the show and in this book. I would encourage anyone who wants a more in-depth analysis of those rules to go back and reread that. The *reason why* I made those objections is because if you remember my conversation earlier with Katie Cohan, you will remember that, for example, in Jantz's paper, he relied on Jeff Glickman to take photos of Amelia Earhart and then *use* those photos to extrapolate data about her. Her height, her weight, her bone structure, and things like that.

After that, they compare that data to the measurements that were taken of the Nikumaroro bones. If you remember that conversation that I had with her, she said that method is not something that has really been subject to peer review. That's important because that is a *huge part* of the analysis. You'll notice that I objected twice under those rules. Jantz's paper was the second time I objected to it. The reason is because we have testimony *on the record.* Katie Cohan told us that this method *has not* been used before in this field. It's really easy to test it, you can do a double-blind study on it, and that hasn't happened, so we don't have a rate of error. We don't have *any information* on how reliable this method is regarding getting data we can trust.

Chris Williamson

Right.

Jen Taylor

And that is key for Daubert. In order for something to be admitted under rule 702 and 705, it *has to be* reliable, and that's why I made that objection. I didn't object to the *whole* paper. I objected in part, because any part of the paper that relied on *those* methods, I thought was objectionable under those legal principles. I didn't get to cross-examine Jeff Glickman, so I have less information available on how reliable *his* methods are. If you'll remember, his testimony was related to the Bevington object. Part of the reason why I made those objections is because I *could not actually* cross-examine him on those things.

If you'll remember, the Bevington object is an object that was supposedly inadvertently photographed off the coast of Nikumaroro Island. The image itself is a wallet-sized image.

In that image, there's a tiny, little, grain-sized dark spot on the photo. What Jeff Glickman has done is he's blown the photo up. He believes that if you blow it up *enough*, you can see a landing gear from a plane. There's a *long* history of problems with testimony like that in court. Yeah. If this were a real trial, and I was really defending somebody, it would almost be **malpractice** for me *not* to object under Daubert.

Chris Williamson

That's one aspect that I've personally had a problem with regarding castaway as a whole.

You have this photo, and it's a small image, and as you said, you have this little grain, and you blow it up. What do you know, it's a landing gear! And it's *not only* a landing gear, but it's a Lockheed Electra 10-E landing gear!

Jen Taylor

That's *very specific* information. No one who was there and took the picture that day noticed anything and investigated? It's *really* suspect to me.

Chris Williamson

What are the odds, right? A million to one, *ten million* to one, maybe?

Jen Taylor

How convenient for the project.

And you see that all the time. Suffice it to say, there have been *big* problems with this kind of testimony. There's not enough data out there; there's very little in the way of statistics.

Because of that shortcoming, it's *incredibly* subjective to the person looking at it. On top of that, the person doing the analysis is *not* a neutral third party, he is a board member for TIGHAR.

When you add the cognitive bias to the incredibly subjective nature of this method, it's *highly* objectionable to me to allow that kind of thing into a court of law. If it were *just* the Bevington object, that would be one thing. But he *also* played a huge role in Jantz's analysis of the bones. Kenton Spading mentioned his name as well. And remember, regarding artifact 2-2-V-1 *and* artifact 2-3-V-2, the aluminum panel and the plexiglass, we don't have any data available about her Electra to actually compare what was found to *her* plane because it was modified so many times. Even TIGHAR will tell you that they think the aluminum panel came from a modification that was made later. The only thing they can do is take old photos that were taken of her plane at the time and compare those to the artifacts they found. Well, Jeff Glickman is working on *that* as well, and he's using the *same* methods.

This photo-comparison analysis permeates the *entire* hypothesis.

Almost *every piece* of evidence that has been touched by the experts and by science has been touched by Glickman at some point. So it's really *not just* the Bevington object, it's a lot of it. When you talk about the trinity, two of the three really rely on this. I'm won't say *definitively* that it wouldn't be allowed in, because judges are going to do what judges are going to do. What I *am saying* is that I would stand up and object, and I *would* ask for that hearing. I *would* fight that, and if I lost, I would appeal. That's how strongly I feel about it.

Chris Williamson

From one island to another. Away from Nikumaroro we go. This is *really* going to get good.

Jen Taylor

I'm feeling tired, but we're doing important work. So I'm ready. Let's go.

Chris Williamson

Remember when I told you that we were going to run as deep as anyone ever has on this investigation? Well, we're just getting started. Nikumaroro is now *behind* us. We've asked a lot of questions of this theory, and I only have *one more*.

Are *you* convinced?

From the shores of Nikumaroro, we travel all the way to Buka for the next segment in this investigation.

This is taking a toll on *everyone* involved. But I made the declaration earlier in this story that, "We're all involved now." And we *all* have to see this thing through.

Follow the evidence.

Wherever it leads.

Take a break, reader. You've earned it.

A SIMPLER EXPLANATION?

-5.2313909 | 154.6314813

*"Everybody talks about the 157, but she never flew that far east before turning back west. At 12:00 hours, not at 18:00, she'd already made the turn, and the sunline would have been chasing down her plane as she flew west. Yes, the sunline would have gone through Howland at 18:00, but her plane was never anywhere **near there**."*

Chris Williamson

Crime scenes might be a running theme for this book.

Here's a scenario that I want to explain to people who aren't familiar with this case. It's an easy visual, so follow me. Imagine you're a detective called in to investigate a murder. Let's say in this case, the victim is a woman, and the likely suspect is their husband in a domestic situation gone terribly wrong. When you arrive at the crime scene, let's say it's the home of this couple, one thing is obvious. There's no body.

At the crime scene, there's multiple pieces of evidence to investigate. It looks like there may have been a struggle of some kind; maybe you find a little blood. You might even find a murder weapon – all solid evidence. Yet no body in sight. Then suddenly, you learn that a body of a woman was discovered several miles away in an alley that appears to have several similarities to your apparent victim. Now here's the question:

Do you go investigate that body?

Or do you ignore it and try to prove your case based *solely* on the crime scene?

Next, we're going to talk about a theory that recently has been at the forefront of the investigation into the vanishing of Amelia Earhart and Fred Noonan. This theory happens to have a body, and that body is none other than that of an airplane carrying multiple similarities to the plane they vanished in eighty-five years ago.

Pre-Trial Discussion

Chris Williamson

This is one of those theories that hasn't been around as long as some of the other ones. It's a relatively new theory by the standards of the Earhart investigation. Papa New Guinea has sort of been a breeding ground for a lot of random information as well as a lot of *misinformation*. This particular crash site at Buka that Bill Snavely is investigating is now going to be put through the same process as the ones we've covered thus far, and we're going to talk to all the relevant experts and hear about all the relevant witnesses.

I think it's important though that I mention this right at the top of the text as we did with the original show. What we're about to do now is discuss a highly active investigation. There has been a lot of information that has been uncovered since we did the original show, and if you're reading this right now, that means that you'll likely read some words at the end of this chapter from Bill himself that will give you an update as to where they are with this investigation. It's kind of the same situation as discussion or updates regarding a missing person and/or something high profile. They'll go out and do a press conference, but they can only answer certain questions due to its unfinished nature. This is kind of the same concept. So we're going to do something that's going to feel very similar if you're a true crime fan, but if you're a historical mystery fan, it might not be as common. We get to actually take a bit of a detour and dip into a true crime concept, which I think is super cool and super rare for these cases.

Jen Taylor

Yeah, I think we've been kind of doing that a little bit, but I hear what you're saying. I have also in my head really compared it to a crime scene investigation. The way I look at this is it *is* different from the other theories because it's really hard to put something on trial when the investigation is not concluded. That has been a challenge for us. In many ways, these other theories have their "crime scene," and they have their evidence, and we're arguing over how to interpret that and what it means.

With this next theory, we're still arguing over whether or not we've located a crime scene, right?

Chris Williamson

Right.

Jen Taylor

How can you really complete the investigation until we know what we're looking at?

Chris Williamson

That's a good point.

Jen Taylor

So that also makes it a little difficult. We can talk all day about how she could have gotten there, why she was there; we can speculate on all of that. But at the end of the day, this is an actual site, and there are people who are actually looking at it, and it seems incredibly possible to figure out whether or not this is or is not the plane. We can do that without having to speculate about any of that stuff. Those seem to be two different questions. If it turns out to be her plane, then we can ask all of those questions, and we can try to figure out what happened. I'm sure that will open a whole other area of inquiry and things that we can discuss and debate. But this is a very disprovable thing. Did we find the crash scene, or did we not find the crash scene? That *has to be* the focus.

Chris Williamson

I've used the above body analogy before. A big point of contention during castaway was how far away Nikumaroro Island is from Howland Island and the vicinity where their last communication was picked up by the *Itasca*. If you're arguing that *Niku* would be difficult to get to, Buka is an *even longer stretch*.

The smoking gun, for lack of a better term, is the fact that there is this aircraft there. When you and I have talked about this on the phone, you've made a really great point when you say that somebody died in this plane. This is the end for somebody here, it may not be Amelia Earhart, but somebody had their life come to an end, maybe some *people*. If that's the case, I think we owe it to the people who flew that plane regardless if it was AE or not.

The jury's still out on that.

At the end of the day, there's one thing that I can promise you, and that is that *this plane* remains unidentified. The people who are there don't know who was in the plane, they don't know whom it belonged to, and they don't know who crashed and perished in it. If this plane had been identified before, I can almost guarantee you that Bill Snavely would have figured that out himself or would have found out that somebody had already investigated this wreck site and identified the aircraft. We don't know the origin of this plane at Buka.

Hopefully, by the end of this particular part of the book, everybody reading is going to be caught up and will have a really good understanding of where that investigation lies, at least to the point that we can discuss it.

Jen Taylor

It's not that we might have a crime scene, we do have one. We have a crash site. If it turns out that it's not her plane, then we can definitively rule this out. What I don't want to see is for people to lose interest in this story.

Chris Williamson
Yeah, agreed.

. . .

Jen Taylor

It is heartbreaking to me that somebody has to be famous for us to care about their death.

One hundred percent somebody died there. For me, this is going to be a really heavy section to work on because we can debate all of these other theories, and we can debate whether or not somebody even died in some of these locations. But here, we have found a plane. It just seems sacred because somebody *did* die there.

Opening Statements

Chris Williamson

Ladies and gentlemen, I want to ask you to imagine something for a moment. I want you to imagine a puzzle. Think about everything you've ever learned about how a puzzle gets put together. How do you do it? Do you start with the corners and work your way inward until the bigger picture slowly starts to form? Do you work on a specific section of the puzzle? Maybe you start with the area that serves as the main focal point, and then build everything around that. What if you didn't know what the picture *was* that you were trying to piece together? What if you had a brand-new way of arriving at the realization of what that puzzle was?

For years, Bill Snavely has been working on a puzzle. Perhaps the biggest and most complex one ever.

At the conclusion of that puzzle lies the answer to the greatest mystery of all time. What happened to Amelia Earhart and Fred Noonan? Today, you're going to hear from multiple people, including Bill himself, and they're all going to give you two things:

One, their idea of what happened on the morning of July 2, 1937.

And two, they're going to give you a fresh attitude and a fresh approach to solving this mystery. One that's sorely needed.

At the center of their investigation, they're going to present to you, our jury, a piece of evidence that you've never seen before and will likely never see again.

We're going to present a plane.

You heard me correctly. In the eighty-five years that this investigation has been in place, **no one** has ever presented a plane until now. Today, the project is going to put time, distance and fuel in place that all align for the first time.

Finally, we're going to have a plane at the end of a conclusion. Furthermore, the project will tell you the story of a lone witness, a little boy on a beach of Buka, who witnessed the whole thing. Now, you may ask yourself what makes this witness's story any more powerful than the number of other witnesses in this case? That answer is simple. This witness's testimony has a piece of physical tangible evidence to

505

verify his story. Imagine that for years, you've been working on an idea that no one ever gave you credit for. A theory that had been largely dismissed by other experts in the field.

Now imagine that you finally get the opportunity to prove to everyone that you were right all along. The pieces are starting to fit together. The puzzle is nearly complete. Imagine that you were the one after all this time who gets to tell the ending to the story, but nobody was ever going to believe you.

Until they had no choice *but to*.

Jen Taylor

On July 2, 1937, the Coast Guard cutter *Itasca* received a message from Amelia Earhart.

That transmission, according to the logs, was "KHAQQ to *Itasca*. We are on the line 157/337." According to Leo Bellarts and according to the logs, that signal was received at a signal strength 5, which indicated to Bellarts that she was close. So close that he believed if he walked outside and looked up into the sky, he would see her. I know that we have talked about these logs ad nauseum over the past several days of the trial. I would like to talk about them again. Because those logs are key to understanding what happened to her, what she was doing, and where she was when she disappeared. According to the project, at the very time that this last signal was received, Amelia Earhart and Fred Noonan were actually almost two thousand miles away, caught in a thunderstorm and going down off the coast of Buka. The project talks to you about puzzle pieces, about putting together a cohesive picture of what happened piece by piece, one at a time. What the project doesn't want to mention are the pieces that we *don't have*. So let's talk about those for a second.

"KHAQQ to *Itasca*." Did she say that? The log says she did. Who was she talking to if not the *Itasca*? The project is going to have a theory for you about what that means. But at the end of the day, that is speculation, backed by nothing, and it's a piece of the puzzle that we don't have.

Another piece that we don't have is, why was the *Itasca* receiving this signal at signal strength 5 if she was, in fact, almost two thousand miles away? The project is going to have an explanation for that as well. But again, they have no evidence to back that up. They have conjecture, and they have a hypothesis. They have a theory, but no evidence.

What about the one crucial message that the project is going to tell you Amelia Earhart sent that the *Itasca* didn't hear? She was turning back. She knew she was low on fuel; she knew she wasn't going to make it. So, she let the *Itasca* know, "I'm turning around, I'm not going to make it. We're going to go back the way we came." That would be a huge piece of evidence. If it were true and it appeared in the logs, that would be huge. Well, we don't have that. There is no evidence that Amelia Earhart ever said that. She *might have*. It *could fit*. But that piece is missing.

Let's talk about the last piece that we're missing, and that's a positive identification of this plane. There is no doubt in my mind that there is a plane off the coast of Buka Island. But whose plane is it? Even the project's witnesses will tell you that this is an ongoing investigation. There is still work to be done, there are still tests to be run, and there are still things that we can look at. Because of that, we have not been able to identify this plane.

If they could, then we wouldn't even be here today; it would be case closed, and mystery solved. We can't say that, and not one of the witnesses that you hear from today is going to tell you that we can. So you're going to hear all of the evidence, and you're going to hear all of the work that has been done. You're going to hear theories and speculation and what-ifs. But you're not going to hear proof beyond a reasonable doubt that the plane off the coast of Buka Island is Amelia and Fred's plane

"I don't want to make a statement saying that we have found Amelia's plane. That wouldn't be professionally accurate. We're excited, and what we've found so far is compelling. The only thing I'll say is we found a plane that's consistent with the Electra. The more we piece together, the more likely it seems that we could be on the right track."

Chris Williamson

Your Honor, to begin, we'd like to call *Mr. Bill Snavely* to the stand.

Mr. Snavely, I'd like for you to start at the beginning. For everyone who doesn't know and for the people who aren't familiar with the story and for our jury here today, how did this all begin for you?

Bill Snavely

In 2003, I was curious to know why no one had found the airplane or traces of the remains of either Amelia or Fred Noonan. I looked at the fuel usage, and I realized fairly quickly that there was no way the plane could have gotten close to Howland and then returned farther back toward the west.

Two years later in 2005, my curiosity grew. There were a number of groups scattered at other locations, but the thrusts seemed to be closer to Howland Island. It surprised me a little bit because I'm used to looking at puzzle pieces. When I put them together in a puzzle, I like to have all four corners in place, but I could only see two as I was looking at things.

I could see those that were in the east, but I couldn't see anything that started close to the beginning of her route. I lived overseas for three years as a kid growing up, and I'm very appreciative of oral history for various groups that are around the world.

I just decided to go over and plunk myself down near Rabaul and find out what the natives can tell me and see what they thought had happened to the plane. I wanted to find out if there was any knowledge whatsoever about it before assuming that I knew where the plane went down. So in 2005, I did that. I traveled to Rabaul alone. At that time, *Dominic Chara*, one of the corrections guys from Buka, happened to be at a meeting with two other individuals from different provinces that were connected with the police.

They asked me what I was doing there because it was a little bit unusual for somebody to be over in Rabaul at that time and not be in a tour group. I just told him that I was interested in finding out more about Amelia Earhart and her airplane. And the quietest guy behind the dominant Chara said, "I may know where there's a plane. Can you give me specifics about it and call me in about three weeks?" Initially, a number of the characteristics seemed to be similar. It appeared to be a twin-engine, twin-tail plane, with the entrance to the aircraft located in the cockpit through the top hatch, and it had a door toward the back.

I was surprised that those elements had matched up. That's what got me originally going over there and looking at things. Originally, I'd planned to start with Rabaul and move across to the east, one location per year, and read in the meantime until I'd gone at least as far as the Gilberts because I knew that everything from the Gilberts going east had pretty much been searched.

Chris Williamson

There were five original factors that you asked Dominic Chara to help you confirm?

Bill Snavely

There were five originally, and those I just mentioned were among the five I originally asked for.

Chris Williamson

There is only one witness to the events at Buka on the morning in question, and that witness happened to be a child at the time this occurred. Can you tell the court about the events of that morning from the witness's point of view as you learned them?

Bill Snavely

I had been told that story by the local natives, David Mona in particular. Since then, our divers have been over, and the details of it are a bit different. I want to be as honest and correct as I can. What I originally heard was that the kid was on the beach at the time.

Later we discovered that he was returning to the island quickly, because there was a terrible storm that was occurring. As he got back to the beach, the plane came in.

According to him, the left wing was on fire, and they put the plane down in the water pretty close to where he was standing.

Chris Williamson

And the witness informed the rest of the village of what he saw?

Bill Snavely

As it was reported to me, the kid told the villagers what he'd seen. By then, the plane, which had landed on a K, had been taken up from the tide, drifted, and had sunk, and it was early morning at that time. The storm provided a lot of racket, lightning, thunder, etc. None of the others had seen the plane come in, but there were enough bangs from the thunder that nobody thought of the plane hitting anything at the time, and it was no longer in sight.

So they called the kid a liar.

For years, he lived with that up until about 1995 when, reportedly, a local sponge diver went down with another individual free diving for sponges and actually saw the remains of the plane. When they surfaced, they told everybody in the village that there really was a plane.

Chris Williamson

So when the sponge divers vouched for the plane being there, that original witness was now an old man, and he was vindicated, at least to the point that he was telling the truth that morning, correct?

Bill Snavely

In 1995, he was an old man. The village heads apologized because there really was a plane down there. That must have laid some pretty good scarring on that kid who had to live with that, knowing what he'd seen and being called a liar his entire life.

Chris Williamson

Your Honor, at this time, the project would like to admit exhibit 1 into evidence, which is a Papa New Guinea news article dated one week after the vanishing, highlighting an interview conducted with world flight navigator Fred Noonan. This article states that Mr. Noonan informed local news media that the Electra would be taking off from Lae, New Guinea, with approximately 950 gallons of fuel and not the 1,100 gallons previously reported. Do we agree on this?

Jen Taylor

No objection.

Judge

Project's exhibit 1 is admitted.

Chris Williamson

Mr. Snavely, a lot of this hypothesis, *your hypothesis*, relies on three factors: time, distance and fuel. You started investigating this case, and you put those together, leading to a point at the end of your calculations, which we'll get to in a moment. First, tell us about time, distance and fuel.

Bill Snavely

The thing that was unusual for us is we actually had an airplane, which was different from the other groups. From there, we were forced to look for a theory on how it could possibly arrive at that location.

Other groups that were searching had theories and were looking for an airplane, so it was done in a complete reverse.

As we looked at it, I knew from doing the fuel metering that there was no way it could have gotten close to Howland and back. I think Paul Rafford was a real genius and good thinker when it came to the original efforts. Paul had been on the routes both flying and as a navigator in the South Pacific shortly after Amelia. He was also in telemetry in Houston when the Apollo 13 spaceship came down crippled, and he had to decide where it was going to land and how to get the assets out to it as quickly as possible. Paul wrote a book called *Amelia Earhart's Radio*, and in it, he said she never got close to Howland, which gave me a little bit of an opportunity to think about things. At least one other party was saying that wasn't the case at all. Paul Rafford said in essence that he was not part of the crash and sink theory in regard to the location where everyone else was looking. I used to email him back and forth. That got me thinking a little bit.

From there, I started looking at other possibilities. I spent about twelve days several years ago checking for any common threads of data that could connect all of the events. Amelia said, "We must be on you but cannot see you," as she was flying at the thousand-foot mark over Howland. The question was, were there any other alternatives?

So I started taking a look at reconstructing the route. I assumed people had probably done that many times, but I found out later that it didn't appear they had. As I said, it took me twelve days to be able to look at the time, distance, fuel, and radio callouts. I was curious most of all to see if the radio callouts could fit any other way.

As I went forward, I was shocked, because it appeared from what I was reading that, in all likelihood, they took off with 950 gallons of fuel. The capacity for the plane, of course, was 1,100 gallons and possibly as high as 1,150 gallons. The question would lie in why they would go off on the flight with less than full capacity? Well, Noonan tried to supply the answer the night before. He said they were going with 950 gallons because of weight issues and the length of the runway. He was challenged by a reporter from New Zealand, who said it would be ridiculous to fly out with less than 10% in reserve fuel. Fred's rebuttal to him was that he didn't understand the plane. For the aircraft to get off the ground, it couldn't weigh any more than 15,300 pounds on takeoff for the length of runway they had.

As they started totaling the weight, I began to understand why they were discarding things like parachutes and rafts and other things. They did that because they were very near that total. At best, the plane weighed 9,200 pounds empty with the engines and the fuel tanks inside it. If you add the weight of 6 pounds per gallon of fuel, at 950 gallons, there would have been 5,700 pounds added to it. Add the weight of the two pilots on board, and even without the suitcases that they also carried along with any charts, they were very close to 15,200 pounds at that point. Keep in mind here that the original 15,300 pounds estimated for takeoff was for a paved runway. Ironically, they tried it on an unpaved runway and almost killed themselves.

Chris Williamson

Mr. Snavely, a lot of people argue that there's no way Amelia Earhart and Fred Noonan could have ended up at Buka. Those people use the exact same reasons that *you use* to say that they *could have* ended up there. So I'll ask you now, how do you use time distance and fuel to theorize that this plane ends up at Buka?

Bill Snavely

The day before takeoff, Amelia mentioned that the clouds and the wind were blowing in the wrong direction. After takeoff, the plane was flying into a twenty-six-mile-an-hour headwind that was sustained over twenty knots all the way to Howland. What was not known at the time was that the South Pacific trade winds blew in one direction for six months and then shifted directions. This wasn't known until the British discovered it in 1943. So what happened was, if you look at the flight, the first third of it was up over the Nukumanu Islands. Just before she got to that point, it would have been 7:00 Greenwich Mean Time. She reported in that she was flying at over 150 miles an hour.

Twenty minutes later at 7:20 while they were over the Nukumanu Islands, they looked at the ground speed, and Noonan realized that they were only going 107 nautical miles an hour, an hour late through the first third of the route. That must have been a little concerning to them. They also had Nauru indicated as a second place to look at. They flew over Nauru at night, and the phosphate lights were turned on for them, which were visible for up to thirty-four miles away. The police chief on the island *did* hear them say that they saw the lights ahead. By then, they were almost two hours late to their destination, pushed back by the force of the wind at that point in time.

According to my calculations, I'm looking at roughly 100 gallons of fuel burned during that first hour in order to get to their desired altitude. Her normal burn rate, as stated by Alan Caldwell, Paul Rafford and others, was around 48 gallons per hour in conditions that didn't include fierce headwinds. That's a conservative number. The plane could burn as little as 38 gallons per hour with a tailwind present. According to what I was seeing in looking at the route, she burned up approximately 638 gallons of fuel by the time they were over Nauru at night.

They were just over *halfway*.

At that point, they were down to 322 gallons remaining in the tanks. They needed a minimum of 428 to make it to Howland on fumes.

Amelia and Fred were brilliant people. I will debate and argue that with anybody. They realized they weren't going to make it through. I asked Ann Pellegreno, who did the route thirty years later successfully, what she would have done in that situation. She said, "I'd turn it around." I asked Lisa Cotham of the Ninety-Nines the same question. Same answer. "I'd turn around." Just after midnight in Nauru, I think they turned around and started heading back for Buka. At that point, a return to Rabaul would have been really questionable; it's about 908 miles just on a straight flight. They retrace their steps, and according to what I'm looking at, Buka was the only available airport. They had a 2,300-foot L-shaped airport at Buka at the time.

I think what happened was they ended up heading back toward Buka. There were a couple of keys to things that are relatively unknown, one of which was callouts at 14:15, 15:15, and 16:24. On each one of those callouts, the *Itasca* could hear them, but could only get a few words of what was said. They knew it was her voice. There were words like "cloudy" and "overcast," etc. I think it was during that time that there's a high possibility that she said, "I'm low on fuel. I'm turning back, trying to land at Buka." If that's accurate, and if that's what was said, she would have repeated it a couple of times and assumed that they heard her. Basically, I think that's what they were doing. If they had continued to go toward Howland, the plane would have fallen out of the air at about 19 hours and 10 minutes Greenwich Mean Time.

It didn't.

The only way it could stay in the air at that point in time is if it had turned back and gone from flying at the cost of 48 gallons per hour to 38 gallons per hour in order to conserve enough fuel to make it back to Buka. That would have been possible. In fact, there were three or four callouts after that. I think that's one more reason to believe that they did turn back.

Chris Williamson

And if this is indeed the plane, are you in agreement with the original witness that storms over Bougainville at the time could have caused the Electra to crash there?

Bill Snavely

If it *is* her plane, yes. It's important to note that I have never claimed that the plane we're looking at is Amelia Earhart's airplane. The only thing I've ever said is so far it appears to be consistent with the plane she flew. On the transmission that everyone looks at in great detail, she says, "We must be on you but cannot see you."

This occurs at 19 hours and 12 minutes. I think she was trying to reach Buka. The confusing factor is, if you look at the radio transmissions, Bellarts writes consistently, "KHAQQ calling *Itasca*."

I don't think she ever said those words.

I think she said the words that came *after* that. I think Bellarts was just being extremely careful to note every time he heard her come on the air. If that's the case, I think what she was referring to in that moment at 19:12 was exactly the point that they had got back over Buka. They would have then gone looking for a sunline. If you look at the callouts, at 19 hours and 28 minutes, the *Itasca* has them circling the plane.

Why the heck would they be circling a plane over Buka? I think it's so they can face *east*.

Why would they do it to face east? To get a sunline. One of the main conundrums that Paul Rafford noted in this thing is that it doesn't make sense at 17:00 and 18:00 for her to call and say, "I'm about two hundred miles out; I'm about one hundred miles out." She should have had a sunline and knew exactly where she was at that point in time. And that would be true if she was still going east.

I think she turned back.

If they turned back west, there's no sunline. They would have had to turn east to face the sunline that was coming up.

They were at 1,000 feet, which is not where they would normally be had they kept on going for Howland. Howland was clear. I don't think anybody's challenged that. We know that Buka had a fierce storm over it.

Chris Williamson

If we circle back to the lone witness, and we factor in your hypothesis and the time, distance and fuel aspects of it, we have a very intriguing alternative idea for what might have happened on the day in question. However, you also have something in play that no one else working this case does. You have a plane. When an eyewitness sees something and that something is proven with a linkable, tangible piece of information, it lends more credibility to that story. Having said that, and having set up everything to this point, tell the court what you found at this wreck site. What have you done there? Where do we stand right now?

Bill Snavely

I tend to not want to get too far ahead on my skis. Because of that, I tend to question pretty much everything.

Question everything that we encounter and look at the null hypothesis. Look at the other alternatives to see what's possible. I couldn't rule in any other plane that this could be, and we looked at every option before we got to where we're at today. The New Guinea planes had all been returned back to Australia in 1941, and none had crashed at the time. I was curious to see what other divers would say. We'd had probably ten dives down with individuals reporting things locally. It's been seven years since we had been down to the site to take pictures. So I wanted to find out what was showing up.

Tracy Wildrix, whom you'll hear from shortly, was kind enough to go over and have a look. Tracy is an incredible diver, metallurgist, and just absolutely tremendous at creating on-the-fly tools from scratch that are needed over there. Tracy was kind enough to volunteer his time to go over. Also, Stephani Gordon, a tremendous underwater photographer, was willing to go over as well. And Richard Pruitt, who had worked at the State Department and worked on other Amelia theories, was also kind enough to lend his talents and go over. What I wanted to know was, can we identify the plane? Can we see it? Is it still there seven years later considering the remarkable underwater environment that it lives in and the countless earthquakes and storms that have occurred?

We were able to find that the plane was still there, but it was in considerably worse condition as far as the coral, compared to the images taken seven years prior. We also wanted to establish good relationships with local natives, which I think the Project Blue Angel team did a masterful job of. We were given permission and were the only individuals now outside the region who were allowed to come in and evaluate the plane.

Out of all that comes one of the things that was located. This item appears to be a possible glass lens. The main focus of the trip was to establish relationships over there, see what we could see by documenting the crash site, and actually get a GPS ping on that plane. All of this was made possible by the top-notch team who went over.

Chris Williamson

Mr. Snavely, I want to ask you this very bluntly for our jury who are consuming and considering this testimony.

After everything you've done within this investigation thus far, are you able to tell me with any kind of certainty that the plane you're investigating at Buka *is in fact* that of Amelia Earhart and Fred Noonan?

Bill Snavely

I don't want to make a statement saying that we have found Amelia's plane. That wouldn't be professionally accurate. We're excited, and what we've found so far is compelling. The only thing I'm going to say is that we found a plane that's consistent with the Electra. The more we piece together, the more likely it seems that we could be on the right track. We're certainly not at the conclusive stage yet.

We're still putting puzzle pieces together to see what we have. What I am shocked by, for example, is the landing light lens that I just mentioned. Clearly, it's old, and the diameter is very similar to that of a Lockheed 10. At this point in time, we're trying to take closer looks at what it is we have and see whether or not it indeed matches. That takes an incredibly and sometimes frustratingly long amount of time.

It's the number of things that are coming together that is continuing to surprise me.

Chris Williamson

With that being said, what you're finding thus far in your investigation is giving you cause to believe that you're on the right track?

Bill Snavely

What it tells us is that we have to really look at the glass if we're going to lean on it effectively to any degree. The glass is interesting, as I said, because the diameters are similar. We know that the plane she flew was a Lockheed 10-E. Looking at what we've got underwater, there appears to be a stubby fender and also a configuration for a landing gear that Lockheed typically used on their planes. So, it appears that based on the light, it could be a Lockheed 10-E. If it is, seven other 10s went down between Australia and New Zealand. There's one still missing. What we're looking at could be it.

Chris Williamson

And if you are able to determine in the near future that the plane at Buka is a Lockheed Electra, do the odds of it being *the Electra* become greater?

Bill Snavely

It would be greater, yes. I would not be willing to say even at that point conclusively that it's her plane, but it would give us greater odds.

Chris Williamson

Thank you. Your Honor, pass the witness.

Cross-Examination of Bill Snavely

Jen Taylor

The first thing that I want to start with is how much fuel Amelia and Fred left Lae, New Guinea, with. I understand that you've come to a number. One more time for our jury, can you explain what that number is and how you got there?

Bill Snavely

Yes. The number I'm looking at is 950 gallons of fuel, as said by Fred Noonan the night before they took off. This was then challenged by a chap from New Zealand who said, "It's ridiculous that you would be able to take off and think you'd be able to make it with less than a 10% reserve for any emergency problems." The *Daily Telegraph* in Sydney Australia dated July 6, 1937, indicated that exchange went out to readers in Australia, New Zealand, and New Guinea. Amelia herself was asked the question, and she stated that she was "not planning to fly with more than 1,000 gallons." In looking at the Lockheed specs on it, the maximum envelope or takeoff weight for the plane was 15,300 pounds for a three-thousand-foot paved runway. They actually tried taking off on an unpaved runway. Her words as I have them from Mary Lovell's book *The Sound of Wings* are that she said she was at "weighted capacity." It can be an understandably confusing point. I couple it with the 950 number that we had from Fred the night before.

Jen Taylor

At this point, I would like to offer defense exhibit 1, which is a letter from James A. Collopy to the Civil Aviation board.

Chris Williamson

No objection.

. . .

Judge

Defense's exhibit 1 is admitted.

Jen Taylor

I want to talk a little bit more about this because this was one subject that when I first started looking into this case was most interesting to me. I went to Mary Lovell's book and appendix B, which you referenced earlier, and I wanted to know where she got this information. I couldn't track down all of the old newspaper articles, but I was able to track down *one of them,* and I want to go ahead and read it; it's really short.

This is from the *Daily Telegraph,* the one that you cited earlier. I'm not going to read the whole thing, I'll just read a quote: "When the Lockheed Electra left Lae, it carried 950 gallons of petrol sufficient to give a still air cruising range of 2,750 miles. The distance from Lae to Howland Island is 2,500 miles." It also says according to the navigator, Captain Noonan, "*Lady Lindy* was overloaded to the extent of two tons when she left Lae on the longest trip for the whole flight." Then it continues on, and it goes into rations and everything else that was on the plane. When you read that they're overloaded by two tons, what does that mean?

Bill Snavely

That's an excellent question. I did read that, and I think that part was quoted as having said that, but I don't think they were overweight by two tons. What he might have said was they were over the empty weight by two tons. We'd have to do the math on that. But the total weight number of 15,300 pounds comes from Lockheed for a takeoff on a runway that is three thousand feet long.

Jen Taylor

At this point, I would like to offer defense exhibit 2, which is the specifications for Amelia Earhart's Lockheed Electra 10-E as reported by TIGHAR.

Chris Williamson

No objection.

Judge

Defense's exhibit 2 is admitted.

Jen Taylor

What number are we starting with when we're calculating how much fuel the plane can carry?

Bill Snavely

Well, it's important to note that we're dealing with a particular plane that was built differently from the other 10s that Lockheed had. It had the fuel tanks inside, and it also had 550-horsepower engines. Mary's quote in the book is 9,200 pounds empty weight.

Jen Taylor

The only reason why I ask that is because there are different numbers out there. I want to see what your thoughts are regarding the discrepancy in the information that is available online. So I'll just tell you that TIGHAR's website is where I found this number. They say on their website that the empty weight is actually 7,265 pounds. Why the discrepancy between what they're claiming and what Mary Lovell seems to have found?

Bill Snavely

Great, great point, in fact, I've heard as low as 6,700 pounds. I've also heard it at 7,000 pounds for a Lockheed Electra. That's the typical weight given for the 450-horsepower engines, without the extra build-ins and the tanks.

Jen Taylor

Okay. Do we know how much one empty tank weighs?

Bill Snavely

About 115 pounds give or take. I should say that there are a lot of pieces that I may well not know.

Jen Taylor

Okay, *there's* the discrepancy then, because we have an empty weight of 7,265 pounds that TIGHAR claims was obtained from the license authorization. And you're saying that number doesn't account for the modifications that were made to the plane later. Am I understanding that right?

Bill Snavely

Yeah, that was the typical weight for an Electra, but most of them had the 450s. Hers, of course, had the 550s, which weighed a good deal more. Combine that with the tanks and any further modifications that I'm not aware of.

Jen Taylor

Another point of interest is something Mary Lovell kind of touches on, but she doesn't really go in depth, so I wanted to get your thoughts on it. She points out that in Lae, they used imperial gallons, which is actually different from US gallons. One of the thoughts that Chris and I have both had has been that maybe that accounted for the confusion between some people reporting the 950 number and others reporting

1,100. Callopy's report specifically says *US gallons*. Do you have any thoughts on that and whether that discrepancy could explain any of this?

Bill Snavely

Yeah, I've looked at that, and it's a great question, Jen. Imperial gallons actually weigh more.

Jen Taylor

Okay.

Bill Snavely

For the typical US Gallon, we're looking at about 6 pounds per gallon. The imperial gallons are actually more. I'm not thinking for a minute that she could carry even heavier amounts.

Jen Taylor

And that article doesn't specify, it only says 950 gallons. If it's an article coming out of Sydney, can we make an assumption on which they might have been referring to? 950 imperial gallons or 950 US gallons?

Bill Snavely

Well, if it were imperial, that thing would be even heavier, as I said. The Lockheed specs mentioned in Mary's book state that the maximum weight for takeoff is 15,300 pounds.

That would give you 5,700 pounds of US gallons. I think we'd be going even higher. She actually talks a little bit about Callopy's conclusions, saying something to the effect of, "If it really weighed what he was saying, for the full 1,100, the weight would be 15,800 pounds, and there's no way she could have gotten off the ground in that distance."

In fact, it barely made it off the ground with US gallons, as reported, based on what I'm looking at.

Jen Taylor

When we spoke to experts on the crash and sink side of things, they all told me unequivocally that she was receiving consistent S-5 signaling by the *Itasca*. Therefore, she had to have been within one hundred miles of the *Itasca*. How do you explain that?

Bill Snavely

That is something that has quite honestly been said for years. I think it certainly comes from that 19:12 Greenwich Mean Time mark. She says, "We must be on you but cannot see you." She was flying at one thousand feet at the time. That's what in turn got everybody looking very closely at Howland.

What I did probably doesn't make sense to most people. But several years ago, I tried to reconstruct the flight to see if there were commonalities that would allow it to have gone a certain distance and then return back on its route. I was shocked at what I found when I started looking at the communications, and we'll take the S-5s as an example.

When I was a kid, my dad had a ham radio set. I used to listen to it constantly. It would fade in and out, sometimes it would be real loud, and sometimes it wouldn't. But I'd been getting people from Europe on a set that was probably built in the 1930s. What I'm saying is I think there is a good possibility that we had "skip" at the time. Skip with propagation can go for over three thousand miles and still come in with an S-5 signal strength. So the question we're asking is, can you actually take those radio communications and work them backwards? Would it fit in the other direction? As I was looking at it, she was on a 3105 frequency at that time. That 3105 is a short enough deal that you can get skip off the water and the ionosphere and back several times. It might come in strong at times and weak at times.

The other thing is that it was nighttime, it was summer, and it was near the equator.

It was at maximum years for sunspot activity, which were '36 and '37. I think the possibility is there that her signaling could have very well have come in at an S-5. There's really only one thing that I see differently. I think Bellarts did an excellent job recording what was coming in, and I'm not meaning to be critical at all. He starts out with his part, saying, "KHAQQ calling *Itasca*." I don't have any reference that tells me for sure that she ever said that. I think what happened was, as he's recording, he's writing that into the file.

There were two logs going at that same time the S-5 came in, and they were both from the radio room. The other one does not have that piece written in it. It's a slightly different version. She got angry at one point and said, "Speak in English, not in code." She was furious at that point, and they did get that particular reception. I'm not convinced that even though Bellarts wrote it, it was actually what was said by her. I don't think she wasted words. I think she just broke in with Earhart or whatever and started broadcasting, which is what that second log in the radio room indicates.

Jen Taylor

So your point, then, is that you don't think she was directly speaking to the *Itasca*. You think she was maybe talking to somebody else. Is that the point that you're trying to make?

Bill Snavely

You're saying it much more concisely than I am, and yes, I agree with you completely.

I think up until the time of 19:12, she was communicating with the *Itasca*, but hoping that she could raise the ears on Buka. Everyone would have still been asleep at that time; it would be early morning. Buka would not have been expecting her plane, and neither would Rabaul. I think she was desperately calling out, trying to raise them and let them know that she was trying to come in but was never able to. The 19:12 mark is a delicate and important communication. Forgive me, it took me twelve days to try to reconstruct the route. I'm certainly not a rocket scientist, I'm more like a turtle and not particularly fast. When I looked at it, I realized that 19 hours and 12 minutes was an important time because that's when they would have arrived over Buka, according to my calculations.

Look at the next communication, from 19 hours and 28 minutes. The *Itasca* has them circling the plane.

As I said earlier, I think that was so they could face east to obtain a sunline. The sunline came through right after that 19-hour-and-28-minute mark over Buka. I think they were adjusting for that. It also doesn't make sense if you look at that callout.

Why would she say she's flying at 1,000 feet if Howland was reportedly clear?

I'm only a single-engine pilot, but I'd want to be as high up in the air as I could in order to look down at Howland, which was only a mile-long island, instead of looking at the edge of a quarter. Buka did have that storm going over it at the time, according to what the local kid on the beach said. That would indicate a valid reason for why she couldn't get down below 1,000 feet. She also knew that there was reportedly a runway on Buka that was about 2,300 feet long. She'd flown over it during the day.

Jen Taylor

When you say *19:14 or 19:12*, you're talking about how many hours she'd been in the air?

Bill Snavely

I'm talking Greenwich Mean Time.

Jen Taylor

Okay.

. . .

Bill Snavely

They took off, but nobody told her about the winds she was going to encounter. At 7:00 hours, she was going approximately 150 miles an hour. Twenty minutes later, they flew over the Nukumano Islands although they don't call it the Nukumano Islands, they only give the coordinates. Those coordinates they gave were called back in, and they were at 7 hours and 20 minutes. They talk about being over the Nukumano Islands, which was 785 miles from where she took off in Lae. Well, that means that her ground speed was only 107 miles an hour. She was an hour late for the first third of her trip. The next sighting they would have had over ground would have been the lights at Naru. When the local police chief picked it up on his shortwave radio, it was almost two hours later than she would have been expecting to be over Naru. According to my calculations, fuel wise, she would have gone from the original takeoff amount of 950 gallons all the way down to 322 gallons of fuel left.

Jen Taylor

Is it possible that she was estimating the distance because the sun hadn't risen yet?

Bill Snavely

Now *that's more like it*, Mrs. Taylor.

According to my calculations, they'd actually made it within twelve miles of the airport and would have had plenty of gas. Hypothetically, they would have been able to fly straight on for another one hour and two minutes according to my numbers. They were trying to find the airport and couldn't because of the storm.

Jen Taylor

I have the *Itasca* logs in front of me. One of the things that I never understood was that she continues to request a bearing. She says, "Please take a bearing." If she wasn't trying to get a bearing from the

Itasca, who was she talking to? Who did she think could take a bearing on her?

Bill Snavely

Ironically, most any large outfit could. Rabaul would have been able to take a bearing on her. I don't know whether Buka could have, I don't know the setup at the time, but I do know that Rabaul would have been able to at only 158 miles from Buka.

Jen Taylor

Somewhere around 8 a.m. in that area, *Itasca* time, she indicates that she can hear their signals. I guess the *Itasca* assumes that she's talking to them. She says, "I can hear you, but I can't get a minimum." Does that mean somebody was responding to her who wasn't on board the *Itasca*? Was anyone else picking her up and establishing communication?

Bill Snavely

Forgive me, because I don't have all the callouts memorized, but the only time I think she heard from them was when they switched to the 7500 frequency and did the constant *A*'s, which was at the same time that the S-5 was coming through. If you look at the *Itasca* logs, you'll see that she never responded to that.

Jen Taylor

So she was about two hundred miles out when they start sending the *A*'s. Then there's "KHAQQ calling *Itasca*. We must be on you, but cannot see you. Gas is running low. Unable to reach you by radio. We are flying at 1,000 feet."

Bill Snavely

And I think that she was trying to talk to Buka at that time and trying to raise them. As I said earlier, they would not have been expecting her, and there probably wouldn't have been anyone in the radio station.

Jen Taylor

Alright. "KHAQQ calling *Itasca*. We recorded your signals but unable to get a minimum."

Are you saying that's a mistake and the logs should *not say* "calling *Itasca*"?

Bill Snavely

Yeah, in fact, to support my point, there were two logs kept in the radio room at that time, as I mentioned earlier. The other one was also recorded by radiomen. So two different versions. Bellarts would have said "KHAQQ calling *Itasca*" because he was very thorough.

You want to indicate who was calling, and I think that makes perfect sense. But sometimes people don't know what they don't know. I think what *he didn't know* was that she had already turned and was flying away. I don't think he was intentionally trying to put something into record that wasn't accurate. At some point, she lost interest in trying to get word back from the *Itasca*, and I think her idea then was Buka.

Jen Taylor

The last universally accepted signal: the now infamous line, "We are on the line 157/337."

If that's not referring to the sunline 157/337 that passes through Howland Island, what does that mean? We have been told up to this point that the 157/337 sunline passed directly through Howland Island, and also passed through Nikumaroro Island. Is there any other way to interpret this?

. . .

Bill Snavely

Sure. Let me give you my understanding of the 157/337 sunline. It moves; it's a constantly moving line.

It's a question of where? It was due to hit Howland at about 18:00 hours, okay? But here's the deal. If she turned around, she turned around at about 12:00 hours and started flying back *west*. The sunline and her plane were doing two very different speeds. She was going probably at about 111 or maybe 113 at a rough estimate, just hanging in the air with the wind pushing back, trying to save as much fuel as they could. The sunline, on the other hand, is going at 1,036.5 miles an hour, which is really zippin'.

It was due to be over Howland at about 18:00 hours.

Everybody talks about the 157.

But she never flew that far east before turning back west. At 12:00 hours, not at 18:00, she'd already made the turn, and the sunline would have been chasing down her plane as she flew west. *Yes,* the sunline would have gone through Howland at 18:00.

But her plane was never anywhere **near there**.

Jen Taylor

What is a sunline? What does that even mean?

Bill Snavely

The sunline is, in essence, the point in time at which the sun is going to poke itself above the horizon, the exact timing. For that, Noonan had about two or three different clocks on board, because they had to be very, very accurate. They had to be almost right down to the second.

Jen Taylor

Okay. So let me make sure that I'm hearing you. What you're

saying is that if you calculate a sunline, and you're using that to navigate, and you're off by even a few minutes, that makes a huge difference in terms of your navigation. And that because her transmission of "we are on the line 157/337" came around an hour and a half to two hours late, there's no way that means she's on that line at Howland, she's actually closer to Buka. I just want to make sure that I understand that because I know very little about celestial navigation.

Bill Snavely

That's right. It's a moving line, and ironically, it was used to save some lives. Let me explain. Once, near Australia, there were two planes that took off flying across the Pacific; one of them had engine failure on takeoff and didn't go. The other one is flying, but the pilot lost all of his compass and bearings. Well, there was a 747 with an American pilot who was flying out of Australia who tried to help him, but he had to find out exactly where he was along the line. So he had him turn around and give the exact time that he saw the sunset, and he used that to calculate. They were able to actually bring that plane in and land safely in New Zealand. So the sunlines are very, very important, but there's one added thing:

Noonan also had with him an almanac, which had the exact time that the sunline should be coming up over every one of those key points that he was at. If for some reason the clouds obstructed his vision once he got there and made the turn, he would have been able to say, "Oh yeah, even though I can't see it, this is when it's happening."

Jen Taylor

Okay. And you point that out because, as you've said, there was a thunderstorm; there were clouds. So it seems likely that he might not have been able to see the sun at that time in that place.

Bill Snavely

It's quite possible. That's one of the reasons they carried the almanac with them.

Jen Taylor

One of the things I also wanted to ask you about is, there are a number of people who have said she continued to send signals past this time. There's this huge debate amongst pretty much anyone you ask. No one's going to agree on which signals are credible and which might be hoaxes. In your book, you discuss Betty's notebook. Is that something that you have looked at and deemed a credible account of a post-loss signal?

Bill Snavely

Here's the thing, I don't know. I don't like getting too far out on a limb with stuff that I can't eventually prove. When I read over Betty's stuff, I found it interesting. There were certain things in it that would also tend to support our stuff. In talking with Paul Rafford, I learned that there was no way even with skip and power that he thought those could be credible.

What fascinates me are the things the girl wrote down, things that a fifteen-year-old girl normally wouldn't respond to. So I don't know. I don't want to say yes, and I don't want to say no. I put it in my book because people ask me what could have transpired after that?

It's too far out on the limb for me to fully buy into, but I also don't discount it.

Jen Taylor

Do you have any thoughts on whether Amelia and Fred might have survived the crash for any length of time?

Bill Snavely

There was supposedly a scream heard according to Bellarts's report, and I know you've heard about that.

Jen Taylor

Yes, I've heard that.

Bill Snavely

Reportedly, according to the kid on the beach who witnessed the event, the left wing was on fire, which might indicate in that particular situation that they got struck by a bolt of lightning or had another problem that led to a fire. If I'm in that plane, I'm probably going to scream.

Jen Taylor

In going back to the *Itasca* logs, she's consistently sending out signals every so often. She's sending them out fairly consistently, but after "We're on the line 157/337," the *Itasca* doesn't seem to receive anything else. Even if you believe the post-loss signals are all credible, those don't occur until hours later.

Bill Snavely

Correct. The only one that I feel is pretty accurate is the one from Naru. Naru reported, "Female voice. No hum from the engines."

Jen Taylor

Do you happen to know how long after?

Bill Snavely

Right about 20:14 when she went down.

. . .

Jen Taylor

So it seems, at least based on the radio evidence, she's consistently sending out signals, searching for somebody and looking to try to get a bearing. But then the signals stop for at the very least a few hours, possibly indefinitely. Does that tell you that, at that moment, we can pretty well pin down when she crashed based on when the signal stopped?

Bill Snavely

I'm thinking it was probably pretty close after that last callout at 20:14, yeah. Based on my calculations, they would have been pretty much out of gas by then. The kid reportedly said that the plane had the left wing on fire and may not have been running full throttle.

He thought that it might have been out of gas. According to our math, it could have been, and that could explain why the plane didn't blow up while it was still in the air.

Jen Taylor

Based on my understanding of how she would have needed to transmit signals, if she does not have any gas, it seems to me that she wouldn't have been able to send any of the post-loss signals.

Bill Snavely

I talked to Rafford about that, and you can still get a fair amount of time out of it without the engine running.

She landed on a K, which is like a beach. I can't say for sure whether that right engine was capable of running or not. I doubt that it was, but it could have still run.

Jen Taylor

If the plane crashed, and Amelia and Fred didn't die on impact, why wouldn't they have gone and sought help from those who live on Buka? Buka wasn't an uninhabited island; there were people who were there.

Bill Snavely

Great question. Here's the only thing I can put together for that. The kid was alone on the beach. It was a terrible thunderstorm that packed a lot of noise. The others never heard the plane go down.

Reportedly, they all called the kid a liar. So it sat there for a period of time while the kid said they were working their radios. I don't know how he knew they were radios, maybe he saw headsets, but it's hard to say how he would have known that. We don't know if they were stuck or maybe too injured to climb out.

They landed, and almost immediately, the water came flooding in. Over a short period of time, according to what we're understanding, the plane got carried; it floated briefly and then went down. The lone witness was so traumatized by it that he went to his priest because he thought it was the second coming. That's how much of an impact it had on him.

But nobody else saw it, and nobody else heard it.

Jen Taylor

Something that I'm still having a hard time with is, if they were alive, and they were working their radios, why would they have gone down with the plane? How is it that they wouldn't have been able to get out and seek shelter?

Bill Snavely

We don't know that answer until we can get a more definitive expedition and potential recovery together, we just don't. That's something that we'll likely be clearer on once we get to that point.

I don't know if you've ever seen lightning strike water. But you've got a terrible thunderstorm with that possibility. Are you really going to jump into that water when you have lightning in play?

Jen Taylor

Okay, so the plane would have landed in the water, then.

Bill Snavely

It landed in the water, near the beach, still propped up partly at low tide until the current came and took it. It would have gone down within a short period of time. I can't tell you for sure how long, but in a relatively short period of time, that plane was beyond the islands and under water.

Jen Taylor

You always say "consistent." "It's consistent with the plane she flew." Let's talk about how consistent it is. In your book and in media interviews you've done, you've indicated that there are twelve points of consistency to that of Amelia's plane.

Bill Snavely

Let me amend that because there has been wild speculation on this. I want readers to hear directly from me, and I want to be as crystal clear on this as possible.

Jen Taylor

Okay.

Bill Snavely

The original twelve points of consistency were reported by the original local divers who went down. One reason that I got the Project Blue Angel team to go over and check this out was I wanted to verify with our own eyes what had been said. I had not seen those things personally. I want to be able to check those things out as thoroughly as we can. One of the problems with the pictures from several years ago was that they had showed a number of features that are no longer there because of coral damage. There have since been a number of storms and earthquakes that have hit the area, and the coral has done a tremendous job of destroying parts of the plane. At this point, we're doing what we can to try to determine how many of those original consistencies are valid and/or match up.

Jen Taylor

What points have you been able to see *personally* that you can verify are consistent with Amelia's plane?

Bill Snavely

From the original images taken on-site, I can see the twin tails of the plane. I could see the twin engines. I could see the props that we refer to as *toothpick props*, which simply means that there's one straight prop across. During the war, they used three-bladed props for warbirds. That told me that it doesn't appear to be a warbird. They told me that it went down prior to the war. If it's not Amelia's plane, then I don't have a date. It also reportedly had a loop on top, a door in the back, and the entry into the cockpit through the top of the plane. Those are things that were more readily identified.

During this past trip we wanted to see, first, if we could still find the plane. Second, can we establish that relationship with the locals, and can it be a positive one? That's **very important** to me. And is there anything striking that we might happen to find in the brief amount of time we've got over there.

We came across what appears to be a piece of glass that's roughly six inches around that appears to be similar to the landing light they used on some of the Lockheed 10s. Whether it is or isn't, we don't know. We're still checking it out. At this point we have a lot of opinion, but we do not have a definitive answer.

Jen Taylor

From the pictures that you've been able to look at, are you able to get any kind of measurements? For example, how far apart the twin tails are, or how big the actual plane is? Are you able to extrapolate anything from those pictures?

Bill Snavely

The only thing that we have is one of the early divers asked for the length of her plane and reportedly measured it when the tails were still visible. They're not right now. But when he measured it, he determined it was the same length. They also asked me what the aluminum boxes were inside the plane.

I don't know whether they were referencing the long-range fuel tanks or not, because I wasn't there.

Jen Taylor

Do we have any pictures of the boxes that they saw?

Bill Snavely

We don't. That's why I can't give a 100% endorsement of that. I just want to again make this clear. We don't know whose plane this is. A lot of other people have made premature announcements, and I don't want to do that. I'm not going to be dogmatic and automatically think that we found the plane, but the more individual pieces of information that we put together, the more it makes me think that it could be.

Jen Taylor

I have no further questions for this witness, Your Honor.

"I'm very proud to be the first expedition to ever put our hands on an airplane that might possibly be the one. If it is, and we can bring her mystery to rest, that's the least I can do. If it's not, we're going to figure out who it is."

Chris Williamson

Your Honor, the project calls *Mr. Tracy Wildrix* to the stand.

Mr. Wildrix, can I have you start by explaining to the court where your professional background lies?

Tracy Wildrix

When I was very young, I was always inventing and building things, and I liked gadgets and fiddling with things. I was also fascinated with flying from the time I was about five years old. My first airplane ride was when I was two. So I had the aviation bug.

I started flying airplanes when I was thirteen years old. When I graduated from high school, I decided to go into business, but over the years, I took a lot of training in engineering, and I've worked in many different job capacities that have kept me involved in electro-mechanical engineering. I've studied and was fascinated with the ocean. I became a Coast Guard licensed Merchant Marine officer, a captain, a yachtsman, a sailor, an airplane pilot, and a dive master. I've worked in the scientific equipment design industry, studying metal surfaces. I got out of that industry about fifteen years ago and went into private equity, and I'm now the president of my company, which is an international healthcare-based company.

So I still fly, and I travel a lot. I've always had a mind for Amelia Earhart. Not nearly as in depth and detail as Mr. Snavely, but I've always been interested in her.

. . .

Chris Williamson

As you are well aware, there are multiple hypotheses being worked regarding the vanishing of Amelia Earhart and Fred Noonan. Prior to being introduced to the Buka hypothesis, did you have any preconceived conclusions regarding the fate of Amelia Earhart and Fred Noonan?

Tracy Wildrix

Yeah, you know, I listened to what everybody said. Because I was young when I started paying attention to this, I just took it all in and believed in all of it. Every so often, somebody would tell a new story, and I would believe that. In my mind, I always had this idea that she just flew around in circles that morning, said her prayers and went down into the open ocean somewhere, knowing full well she had no control over the situation.

I would be lying if I didn't have some doubt in my mind. What about an oil slick? There *had to be something*. I'd never seen anything that just completely overwhelmed and impressed me. I think that people bend the will of the listener and push for a certain result. I'm highly resistant to that. I'm interested in things that are real. I'm very much a show-me person.

Show me what you've got if you want to be taken seriously.

Chris Williamson

So what was it about this particular hypothesis, the Buka hypothesis, that convinced you that this is the most probable explanation for the disappearance of Amelia and Fred?

Tracy Wildrix

It wasn't something that I set out to do. I didn't want to go look for somebody who was hunting for Amelia Earhart.

I met a very prominent local businessman who lives in the same community as myself and Mr. Snavely. This man is somebody whom I have a lot of trust in. I was in one of his businesses one day, and he said, "You know, there's a man you ought to meet." I'd never heard of Bill Snavely, and he and I live within a few blocks of each other. I first called Bill, and after that conversation, I decided immediately to meet with him to talk about this Amelia thing. He asked me if I was a pilot, and I said, "Yep, I'm a pilot, with a lot of experience. I've had a lot of experiences occur in airplanes where I'd have to take control and survive." It all comes down to this one question: If you're flying from point A to point B, and you're not quite halfway there, and you don't have enough fuel to make it, what are you going to do?

Well, I don't take unnecessary risks. I would immediately go back exactly where I came from, and that's what I told him when he asked me. If I had to find a beach, I would.

Hopefully an airstrip, something like that, that way I wouldn't be lost flying in triangles or circles or something. The theory basically mirrored what myself and many other highly skilled and experienced pilots would do. In every fiber of my being as a pilot, I know this is reasonable. It's even extremely plausible. It immediately cured me of that original thought that I had for most of my life that she just flew around in circles. I never did like that idea, but that was what I had. She had previously flown right over the Autonomous Region of Bougainville, and specifically, she had flown right over Buka. Even more specifically, she had flown right over the crash site. So that made a very powerful impression on me. We sat there for about three hours talking about this, and at that point, I already knew what I thought. When something feels really right, it's pretty easy to make up your mind about it.

Chris Williamson

Your Honor, at this time the project would like to admit exhibit 2, the landing light lens found at the wreck site at Buka.

．　．　．

Jen Taylor

No objection.

Judge

Project's exhibit 2 is admitted.

Chris Williamson

Mr. Wildrix, let's discuss this landing light, the artifact at the center of your evidential investigation. Can you educate the court on how this particular artifact was discovered and advise us regarding your professional opinion of its origins and representation?

Tracy Wildrix

This is a good one. It's really one of my favorite subjects. The first twenty minutes that I spent with the landing light, I made some observations about it, and those observations seem to be proving themselves.

One of my first observations when I saw the landing light was that it appeared to be transportation related. I ruled out that it would have been for the purpose of being affixed to land like a streetlight or a light on a home or business. It appeared to have a way to be sealed, and I spotted that right off the bat.

It has a smooth face on it, which tells me that it may have been intended for either sea use or aviation use. Aviation lights tend to be smooth on the front, it makes them a little bit more aerodynamic, but it also makes them resistant to icing. It seems to be the right size, character, and style of a light that would be located in the front of a Lockheed 10-E similar to the one that Amelia flew. As a matter of fact, it seems to specifically be the left front light that's in the nose of the plane.

I had an inkling that if this was indeed an airplane from the 1930s, I'd need to find glass evidence. This piece seems to be absolutely unique. I believe, after studying it a great deal, it seems to be from the right era. I believe that I will be able to solve the mystery of exactly what era it's from, and I also believe that I'll be able to figure out what region of the world it was made in. That would go a long way in helping us ultimately decide if this is the real deal.

It's not everything, but it's a lot. This light lens is something that'll fit in your hand. When I looked at it, I figured that it was a non-sealed headlight. In other words, it has a little small bulb that goes behind it that lights it up, and it's just a glass cover. When you look at this lens, it even looks like it was slightly worked on by human hands to make it fit exactly. Like it fit into a special opening.

When we recovered it, it was quite obvious that it was very old because it was overgrown with coral. It would take years to have that stuff growing on it because glass doesn't allow coral to grow very well. That was part of the reason that this airplane was discoverable at all; the coral could not grow on the glass that had since been broken out.

Chris Williamson

I want to change the focus of your testimony from artifacts to radio signals. As the jury is well aware, radio signal is something that has been discussed heavily in this case thus far.

We know what the official explanation for the vanishing is at this point, and it's been well argued that the Electra must have been in the vicinity of Howland Island at the time of the last signal. Buka is approximately 1,700 miles away from Howland Island. Mr. Snavely testified earlier regarding how the time, distance, and fuel factored into getting Amelia and Fred there. Can you expand on what skip is, what it does, and how skip could account for the Electra being at Buka while giving off an S-5 signal strength to the *Itasca* at Howland?

Tracy Wildrix

When you talk on a radio at certain frequencies, you're susceptible to skip, and the frequencies that Earhart and Noonan used weren't immune. Following what Bill said earlier, it's a phenomenon that happens between sundown and sunrise. It happens especially well just before the sun comes up, and immediately after it's gone down. There are reasons for this. There's a place in the sky called the ionosphere. What happens is when you make a radio transmission during the day, that radio transmission goes up and hits the ionosphere and is propagated differently; it's absorbed because there's a lot of ionosphere up there. There's a level in the ionosphere called the "D level," it's the lowest level; it's between thirty-seven miles and, I think, sixty-four miles up roughly. Well, at night, this thing goes way up high, and the D level of the ionosphere disappears.

Picture yourself standing in your kitchen and taking a tennis ball and bouncing it off the floor. If you bounce it off the floor hard, it likely hits the ceiling. When it hits the ceiling, it bounces back down, and it hits the floor again. At night, rather than the signal being absorbed and fading away, it bounces back off a very, very different version of that ceiling. The ionosphere changes during the day; it's different from what it is at night.

During the day, you just transmit with a radio, and it goes a certain distance, and that's that. Well, the Electra had a *nighttime signal* and a *daytime signal.*

If they were in the location that Bill says they were in, it would have been exactly before sunrise, because they would have been looking for the sun to get ready to show itself. Skip radio communications can bounce up to 3,000 miles away. It's completely plausible to have skip radio talk that could reach 1,700 miles back to the *Itasca* just off the shores of Howland where they were expected to show up. It could have come to them with great signal strength, especially considering the time of day, *or night* I should say. They had thunderstorms to their west and their southwest. I believe that also adds a little bit to it.

That's the way radio signals work; they work within the ionosphere, which is a very interesting thing all by itself. If you've ever been to a river or lake and thrown a rock across the water, you'll have a good idea of what skip does. In the absence of having a ceiling over the lake, it's kind of the same idea. The rock will hit once and go up into the air, then come back down, hit again, go up into the air and come back down. If you toss the rock just right, this will happen several times. This is referred to in a technical sense as something called "propagation." Propagation of a signal covers a huge distance of the

Earth, even overcoming the curvature of the Earth. It's not a line-of-sight thing. It's an excellent way for radio stations to be able to transmit out of valleys and over mountains and back down to the city on the other side of those mountains. People don't fully understand how it works; it just *does*.

Chris Williamson

Mr. Wildrix, one more time, is it possible or even probable that the Electra's radio signals could have been affected by the phenomenon of skip to transmit the signals heard by the *Itasca*?

Tracy Wildrix

It's absolutely possible. It happens every day and night at even greater distances. This is not a mysterious Roswell type thing here that we're talking about, this is something that is very normal. If you get in your car tonight, and you tune in to AM radio just before sunset and wait and listen, you'll start hearing other stations from far away interfere and overcome.

On the face of it, to those who don't know, it might sound crazy. Well, I'm not crazy, I'm experienced. Check it out; you'll see. It's all there, and it happens every single day.

Chris Williamson

Mr. Wildrix, is this Amelia Earhart's plane at Buka?

Tracy Wildrix

Well, I'm very proud to be the first expedition to ever put our hands on an airplane that might possibly be the one. If it is, and we can bring her mystery to rest, that's the *least* I can do.

If it's not, we're going to figure out who this is.

We're looking at every angle, and I'm still proud to do that as well. I can't afford to make a mistake. I don't think anybody else on our team can either. I want to draw attention to the people whose backyard this airplane is in. There are some things that I want to do for those people and that Bill wants to do for those people. This is a big deal to them, it's a big deal to us, and it's a big deal to the entire world. We don't take any of that lightly.

Chris Williamson

Thank you, Mr. Wildrix. Pass the witness.

Cross-Examination of Tracy Wildrix

Jen Taylor

I don't know if you were listening, but during crash and sink, we spoke to a number of people who were associated with a company called Nauticos. Nauticos spends a considerable amount of time with their engineers and their radio operators trying to use the data that we have available to try to pinpoint a location or a range of locations where they might be. When we talked to those guys, they seemed incredibly certain that based on that data, and the radio signals especially, that she had to have gone down near Howland Island. When I asked them about this skip phenomenon that you're discussing, they said that they took that into consideration; however, this is still what they came up with. Do you have a response to what they said and the fact that they were so confident in their conclusions?

Tracy Wildrix

I'm not aware of any other people's interviews for your original program or this book. I'm only a few years into this case, and I really didn't even know until a few days before we're recording this that I'd be talking about this subject. I don't know what they've said. I had heard one man speak at the Chasing Earhart panel in 2018, and he had this beautiful map of where all of the listening stations were located and their respective signal strengths. I have no argument with that, but I still say it can happen. Understand that I'm not saying definitely that skip would have caused this to happen, and what we have up to this point has been wrong based on that. I'm simply stating that we really can't say definitively that the signal was coming from one place based only on that signal strength. The fact is that you can get a perfect signal strength from a great distance after a lot of skip and a lot of balance. I can't really comment very far into *their* statements though, I'm sorry.

Having not seen that study in detail, I would assume that all they would have to go on would be the signal strength. What we're presenting is an alternate hypothesis that could very well account for their conclusions.

Jen Taylor

To say that signal strength is the only thing would be oversimplifying it, but I think that was the most important thing.

Tracy Wildrix

Well, the most important thing would be the positioning of all the listening stations. But there's one added complication to it also that may or may not make some difference on that subject, and that's the weather. Sometimes, weather can really create havoc on radios and make them surge in and out, causing the signal strength to either intensify or decrease. It's extremely plausible that skip could interact with all of those listening stations, to give you the result that they're coming to. I don't really have an argument with them, and I don't really have an argument with Mr. Snavely. I think all of it is plausible together as one large theory.

Jen Taylor

Let's move on from that topic and back to the glass piece that was discovered. I understand that there are some things that we can't talk about, and I don't know if this is one of those things, but can we talk about the discovery and the recovery of the landing light?

Tracy Wildrix

It was found and recovered from what *we're calling* a crash scene. It was underwater and had some coral growth on it. It was brought up by Stephani Gordon, our cinematographer/photographer, after I had already come out of the water. She came up with it, and she handed it to me, and I began surmising the character of that light as soon as I saw it. We're very fortunate to have that piece.

Jen Taylor

What makes you believe that this piece of glass came from an aircraft and not, for example, a boat?

Tracy Wildrix

Among the things I mentioned earlier, it looks to me like the manufacturing methods used in the style seem to place it from the '30s. It seemed like it had part of a sealing surface left, where there would be a rubber gasket around the outside edge of it. That would make it fit the character of a landing light very well. One of the nice breaks that I got out of this investigation is that on Matsungan Island where the crash site is located, there's never been any automobiles. It's so uncanny that it came from the crash site, and we haven't found any other lights that amount to anything. This is the only one we found.

Jen Taylor

But can you definitively say that this piece of glass came from Amelia's plane?

Tracy Wildrix

Of course not, we're not there yet. We're glad to have it, but I can't make any claims to that degree about it yet. I can't say whether it's even an aircraft light for sure. It could have come from a scooter or something. But it sure does come from the right location at our crash site, and it has a high amount of character that seems to indicate to us that it's in the running. So we're just going to keep investigating and see whether this is going to hold up for us or not.

Jen Taylor

Is there anything else that might be down there that you would like to investigate further?

Tracy Wildrix

I have always been interested in one artifact that's on the bottom that we're not able to bring up because the degradation of what apparently was an aircraft is so bad that it's just turned into something like a Flintstone village. Coral has been the worst enemy of this airplane, but in a way, it has also been our best friend in preserving the likeness of the airplane. The metal is deteriorated, but the coral has preserved the shapes and the positions of everything. Before I went on the first expedition, I examined Bill's photographs from his book, and I was able to identify one specific part that I believe to have been an engine cowling. It's just this round thing down there. I was looking at it first and thinking all these bad thoughts.

But I kept looking at it, and you know what? That's actually what that is. It's an engine cowling, and it was metal. When the pictures were taken years ago by the first divers, the front of the airplane was metal. You could see the tail fin, and I was able to determine that those were aluminum. One of the things I was fascinated with was what appears to be a landing gear. Lockheed had a shaped landing gear fork that is just really specific. It's just different; it has a little fender like on a bicycle. It's very cleverly made, it's riveted, and it has two layers of aluminum. It's just enough to keep water from splashing up onto the underside of that engine and shock cooling the cylinders. I saw what I believe to be a very delicate remnant of that fender with the style and character of the fork that goes over the wheel. I saw the wheel in those original pictures from Bill's book.

Jen Taylor

I know exactly what picture you're talking about.

Tracy Wildrix

That's what sold me on the whole idea that this is a plane down there. This thing sits in roughly 150 feet of water; it's very badly deteriorated even from what the original photographs show. I can even tell the difference in the deterioration between dives. If you have a rubber tire that was inflated to, say, twenty pounds, or whatever they were inflated to during that time, and you sank it to 110 feet, it would shrink a little bit. Well, this thing looks to me to be exactly the right size for an aircraft tire. Aircraft tires are really soft, even on a big heavy plane like this one. It was smaller in size than what it would have been on land, which just impressed me very much. So it has that character in a lot of ways, like the light does.

Then I remembered something else that was very interesting to me. The airplane had a radar loop on the top of it. At the site, embedded in the wall of the coral, there is the strangest copper-colored circle with an appendage coming out of the top of it. I've never seen that anywhere else in a coral formation.

It's right below the cabin of the airplane. It looks like a radar loop except it's just a little line, and the line is only about a half an inch in diameter. My thinking is that it might possibly be the inner windings of the radar loop. I look at that and posited that it looks like the radar loop was hanging down by a wire, and that wire just stayed there for years and disintegrated in place on the face of that coral reef. The coral reef there grows up all the time because there's continuous avalanches of coral that roll down onto the airplane to entomb and dissolve it. There's all this galvanic activity going on that's dissolving everything, and it just turns into coral. Some of it looks like a plane, and some of it doesn't.

Jen Taylor

Is there anything that you have seen so far that would be inconsistent with the Lockheed Electra 10-E?

Tracy Wildrix

There's nothing that I've found that's been a negative detractor from an airplane, or even from a Lockheed. On the second trip, as soon as we went down to the site, I could just see the character and the shape of the front of the cockpit. When you see the nose, it's like looking at a face. You can actually see the angle of the *eye sockets*, which we'll call the windshield holes. You can see where there used to be windshields.

I had hoped for a little validation, so hopefully in the future, I'll get that. So far, there's nothing that I've seen yet that *disproves it*.

Jen Taylor

Is there any part of the plane that you think we will be able to recover in the future?

Tracy Wildrix

I have a lot of ideas. At this point specifically, I'm looking for more glass evidence. I had predicted that we'd find metal, but we might not be able to retrieve it because if we brought it up to the surface, it would disintegrate within a few hours. We need a larger crew and better equipment to attempt that.

I did some metal detecting on the very bottom underneath the sand, and I got a few hits during the final few minutes of the last dive on the last day before we came back from the second trip. I want the nav lights. I would love to find the other landing light. Onboard, they had a special navigational tool called a sextant. My belief is that thing's probably dissolved. But inside it, it would have some special glass lenses. I want those lenses really bad. We're also after ceramics that were in components of the engine.

Whether I'll be able to find those minor little pieces or not, I don't know. It's going to be tough.

Think of everything that has occurred in this environment over the course of the past eighty five years. Think of what you've got here. Storms, typhoons, earthquakes, marine activity, shifting of potential tectonic plates, and on top of that, the human activity. The one good thing that it has going for it is the depth. I had a lot of ambitions for things that I wanted to recover early on. I had hoped that we would be able to do a lot more than we're able to do right now.

Jen Taylor

I have no further questions, Your Honor.

"There's a lot of disbelief because skeptics generally respond by saying, 'Well, if a young boy saw something like that, why isn't it documented and written down anywhere?' The culture of people on this island is such that they share stories and pass things down verbally. They don't write things down, especially back then."

Chris Williamson

Your Honor, the project calls *Miss Jill Meyers* to the stand.

Miss Meyers, can you advise the court and our jury of your professional background?

Jill Meyers

My aviation expertise started with being a pilot. I got my private pilot's license at the age of seventeen while still in high school. I unfortunately didn't become a professional pilot because there weren't a lot of female role models at that time. So I ended up joining the military. I joined the air force, not as a pilot, but as ground support. While I was in the military, I was able to finish college. My degree is in aerospace engineering, and I have spent the last thirty years as an aerospace engineer, building and supporting development and operations of various avionics systems and aircraft. Avionics, for those who don't know, is most of the equipment in the cockpit of any airplane. It's all sort of lumped into the term "avionics."

So navigation systems, communication systems, radar, control systems, everything that the pilot would interface with in the cockpit is generally considered avionics.

I've helped companies with development and delivery of a lot of avionics systems. Mostly military systems and a few commercial companies thrown in there that I've supported over the years. And then there are some companies where I served as a systems engineer, in charge of integrating the build and operation of an entire aircraft. So not just what's in the cockpit, but the entire aircraft. Systems engineering is technically the function of engineering that I fell into after I got my degree, and I like to describe it as the glue. The systems engineer is the person who really pulls all of the different engineering disciplines together, the mechanical folks, the electrical folks, the software folks, and just makes sure that the entity, the aircraft, or whatever part of the aircraft I was responsible for, works as a single system.

Chris Williamson

Before you got involved in this case in a professional sense, had you ever given any thought to what might have transpired on the morning of July 2, 1937?

Jill Meyers

I really didn't give it much thought. My whole focus of Amelia my entire life was really about her life and not about how she ended. As a young woman getting into aviation, obviously, I knew of Amelia Earhart, and had read a few books about her when I was younger. But I was much more focused on and much more impressed by how she lived her life and the successes that she had with the challenges that were put in front of her. I don't know why I didn't, but I really never focused on what happened that day. I was not even aware of all of the theories about her disappearance, and I didn't have any particular one that I was favoring.

Chris Williamson

Having an engineer mindset and actually sharing that same type of mindset with some of the experts supporting crash and sink, what was it about this particular theory when Bill pitched it to you that made you feel compelled to help try to figure out if he's right and whose plane this actually is?

Jill Meyers

First and foremost, I remain very impressed by the fact that unlike other people involved in this search, he's really not about himself. He tells me all the time that he doesn't want fame or fortune; he just wants to know whose aircraft this is down there. Somebody died down there; let's figure out who that is.

From an engineering and pilot perspective, I really centered on the facts and the data. You have to remove all emotion from it, which all of us engineers tend to do, right or wrong.

When I saw the list of the similarities between this wreck site and Earhart's Lockheed Electra 10-E, it was very surprising to me. I remember right after I met Bill, and he told me the story of how he even came upon this wreck in the first place, I immediately went and purchased a copy of the book that he wrote. I knew then, from talking to him, that it had a lot of the details in it, and it really went through his entire theory end to end.

I've got to tell you, honestly, Chris, after I read the book, I called Bill and I asked, "Why is anyone even questioning that you have not found Amelia Earhart?"

I'm not standing here today saying that I'm 100% confident at all, because this is all secondhand hearsay of what I've heard and seen. But the sheer list of things that were reported by the local divers, meaning the folks in and around Buka who dove on the wreck site during the early years of 2005 through 2012, is remarkable. These very unique things that were attributed to Earhart's plane, for example, not just the twin tails and twin engines, which alone could be a number of aircraft. But they talked about these *aluminum boxes* in the back behind the cockpit that obviously would have been what we call *ferry fuel tanks*. There's a whole set of pilots who have the title of *ferry pilots,* and they do nothing but ferry aircraft from point A to point B. Anyone who ferries an aircraft a very long distance does exactly what Amelia did; they take out everything in the back and replace it with aluminum fuel tanks.

When it was reported again many years ago by local divers that they saw large metal boxes inside the aircraft behind the cockpit, to me, those can really be nothing else but fuel tanks.

Secondly, Earhart did something to her plane that I believe is unusual. It's for sure not done in modern times at all. She had external ports cut into the fuselage of the aircraft in order to fuel them from the outside. Most ferry fuel tanks even today are not fueled in that way. You have to open a door and stick a fuel pump inside the aircraft. You don't go through the fuselage and cut a hole into those tanks. Earhart's Electra had an external port on every single fuel tank cut into one side, and this was reportedly seen.

Additionally, the configuration of the cockpit and the things they saw: most aircraft back then had what we call a "stick" for a control. Earhart's plane had steering wheels that looked just like they did in cars. Any engineer looking at an aircraft and trying to identify it would obviously look first for the things that are unique to that model or unique to that specific serial number. That was what really got me interested. You have a list, and you go down that list. Bill really is trying to be honest and do the best that he can to stick to the facts and the data when it comes to identifying this aircraft and really determining how much of it aligns with the details we know of Earhart's plane.

Chris Williamson

A lot has been said in court today about this landing light lens, the piece of glass found at the site in Buka. You've done some important research regarding this artifact for the Project Blue Angel team. Can you discuss that research for the jury and explain how you've been able to assist in moving the investigation into this particular piece of evidence forward?

Jill Meyers

I happened to have connections at the Smithsonian, within the National Air and Space Museum staff. I contacted them shortly after I joined the team because the engineer in me knew very early on that if you're going to positively identify pieces of the aircraft, you need some documentation to compare it to.

With my contacts at the Smithsonian and in the aerospace industry, including at Lockheed Martin, I did spend quite a bit of time trying to get folks to help us identify people or locations that have documentation on the Electra. For instance, the repair records from what was done at Lockheed Martin in Burbank after her ground loop incident in Hawaii.

Unfortunately, most of those avenues didn't pan out. For some unknown reason, Lockheed is very reluctant to share anything about Amelia Earhart with anybody, but I did go down that path and try to get some documentation. When Bill shared with me that Stephani Gordon found this 6-inch round piece of glass down there, I decided to try to see what I could do.

I was given a list by Doug Westfall of what was believed to be all of the existing Lockheed model 10s in the world. There are multiple versions of the 10; there's the A, the B, the C, all the way through E. Earhart's of course was an E, and there's very few Es. My understanding is that the primary difference between the different models of Lockheed Electra 10s were the engines. Fuselage, surface and electronics were relatively the same.

So I had a list, and I was very lucky to already have business travel for other reasons, nothing to do with this project. But I travelled to two locations where there are 10s.

London, England, has an Electra 10-B at the Science Museum in London. I also had a trip to Pensacola, Florida, where sitting in the museum at Pensacola is a Lockheed 10-A. One of the challenges with looking at all these aircraft is that some of them have been restored, and everything's been replaced with new parts. So what I was trying to do was look at the landing light of the current existing Lockheed 10s. Bill's belief and Stephani's belief is that the piece of glass that they found at the wreckage is very likely to be one of the two landing lights in the nose of the aircraft right under the cockpit windows. The particular glass that Stephani found has two points on the circumference that are slightly dented; I think they refer to them as being "pinched." Well, that also aligns with the shape of the glass that needed to be installed, because the structure that the glass is inserted into does have two areas where it looks like it's not a complete circle and has to go into holders inside the metal structure. So it really looks like this is very likely to be a landing light belonging to an Electra 10.

The challenge you have is you need something to match it to. There is an emblem on the glass that was found at Buka, and we cannot find any other Electra with that emblem. This, of course, could lead to it maybe *not* being what we hope it is. Back in the 1930s, the way that aircraft were repaired and the way that parts were found was not nearly as rigid and stringent and controlled by the FAA as it is today. If her landing light was damaged in any way or there was damage around the light, there's nothing to say that a team of engineers and mechanics could not have just gone and found a piece of glass that was the same size and dropped it in. The best way engineering wise to determine that something is 100% what you think it is, is to match it to paperwork or records or maybe another like item, and that's proven to be difficult when it comes to this landing light.

If this is Earhart's plane, and it's been down there for eighty-five years now, there could have very well been other aircraft that dropped away in the area, even miles away.

Wreckage from those were maybe brought in by the tides. I've been trying to gather as much data about the light itself and the potential installation of the light. It's important to understand that we are looking at every single Electra around the world, and a couple of us have had a hand in that. A lot of this is just trying to do analysis of like items and to see what lines up. We need to find another piece of glass that's similar to try to match it.

We at least need to try to find another piece of glass that can be analyzed by a lab that may be confirmed to have been built in the same era as Earhart's plane.

Chris Williamson

There's going to be lots of talk cross theory regarding eyewitnesses in this case. Your lone eyewitness *does have* the advantage of having a tangible piece of evidence linked to his story. Now the team has been out there on-site, investigating this wreckage and finding artifacts that give cause for a lean toward this being the plane. Does finding an artifact like this one boost your confidence when it comes to making a final determination on whether this plane at Buka could be *the* plane and not just *a* plane?

Jill Meyers

It does add confidence. My understanding from Stephani Gordon, who physically found it, is that it was either right under metal parts of the wreckage or right adjacent to it.

You mentioned the witness, and I feel I can add something on that, that hasn't been covered yet today.

In talking to Bill initially, he told me that when he tells people this story, there's a lot of disbelief because skeptics generally respond by saying, "Well, if a young boy saw something like that, why isn't it documented and written down anywhere?" Bill is someone who, like me, has lived in other countries and is very culturally savvy. The culture of people on this island is that they share stories and pass things down verbally.

They don't write things down, especially back then. I'm Jewish, and there is very much a similar style of sharing stories in the Jewish faith, passing stories down verbally from generation to generation. When I heard that there was a young boy who told the story, and that story's been carried on through the generations verbally, I think I have the opposite response to most people. That factor adds to my confidence level rather than subtracting from it. One of the things that I did for Bill was help manage Project Blue Angel social media. One day we received a message through Facebook from a gentleman who believes he has a video tape somewhere where he or someone in his family filmed the superior telling the story before he passed away. He believed the superior was the young boy who had spent his life telling the story about this airplane. It's not just one person recalling a young boy who's now gone telling this story as a firsthand witness. It may or may not be true, obviously, but this person happens to be related to someone who has been helping us locally in the area when our dive team goes out there.

So there's a whole lot of things that maybe individually wouldn't have someone analytically come to the conclusion that it might be Earhart's plane. But there sure are enough pieces that I think do pull together.

As a pilot, there is a very common process that every pilot goes through on every single flight, which is to determine *the point of no return*. The point of no return is the point just past the halfway point on your route, where you need to decide if you have enough fuel to keep going or not. Every single pilot does it, as you will know, but your readers may not.

I was the primary support person to Shaesta Waiz, who in 2017 became the youngest woman to fly solo around the world in a single-engine aircraft. She flew many flight legs, with roughly thirty stops in five continents around the world, flying through some very challenging areas, like the Pacific Ocean and land masses like Saudi Arabia. Weather does change unexpectedly, especially in the South Pacific. Every pilot has to determine at every checkpoint along the way, and certainly at the point of no return, if they're going to make it or not. If they're not, they do need to turn around. If we take this back to one of your opening questions, regarding what made me really want to help, it's that Bill said to me, "I really think maybe she turned around and realized she wasn't going to have enough fuel."

No one's ever had that concept, at least of the people publicly searching for Earhart that I have heard. It makes total sense as a pilot. If the winds really *did* shift, as they do in that region minute by minute, and if her fuel burn was not what she needed it to be to make it all the way to Howland, I absolutely believe that she was a smart enough pilot and Noonan was a smart enough navigator to turn around. The fact that that is a normal process for every pilot to do and the fact that Buka is on her route from Lae to Howland Island is just another data point that, as an engineer and a pilot, made me want to see if this is what we think it might be.

Chris Williamson

Thank you, Miss Meyers. You've been a lovely witness. Pass the witness, Your Honor.

Cross-Examination of Jill Meyers

Jen Taylor

I just want to clarify, this is an ongoing investigation, right?

Jill Meyers

Yes, ma'am, it is. Bill Snavely, our team leader, has been looking at this particular wreck site off the coast of Buka island for almost fourteen years now. And it is ongoing, definitely.

Jen Taylor

And because it's an ongoing investigation, you can't say today to our jury that you have been able to identify the plane, am I right about that?

Jill Meyers

You are correct.

Jen Taylor

Okay. Have you been able to rule out any particular type of plane?

Jill Meyers

What we know from reports of early dive teams who went down is that they have confirmed *many times* that it is in fact a twin-engine, twin-tail aircraft. So we do know that, and that, of course, rules out a whole category of aircraft. My understanding is that very early on, military personnel also ruled out it being a military plane because of some of the shapes of the surfaces, which are definitely different between military aircraft and civilian aircraft of that era. The long and short of it is that we do strongly believe it is a twin-tail, twin-engine civilian aircraft.

. . .

Jen Taylor

And do you know how many twin-tailed, twin-engine civilian aircraft may have been in that area in the 1930s? Or even the 1940s or 1950s?

Jill Meyers

No, I don't personally know the number. Aviation was relatively new back then as far as the kinds of aircraft that were in service. I think the number of aircraft that would have been anywhere in that region is really small, because it's a very remote place. Any airplane that would be flying over that part of the Pacific Ocean would have to be customized and tailored to handle that long a flight with no refueling.

For example, one of the things that was reportedly seen in this wreckage are metal boxes behind the cockpit, which would have very likely been the long-range fuel tanks that were installed. Other things inside the aircraft would have been taken out to account for that add. You could not cross the ocean without a modified aircraft at that time. Even today's smaller aircraft still can't make that stretch across the Pacific.

The things that were reportedly seen in this wreckage very early on do seem to be very similar to unique modifications that would have been done to an aircraft trying to cross the ocean and not just some regular airplane flying from a normal point A to point B.

Jen Taylor

Are there any pictures of the aluminum or metal boxes that were reportedly seen on the plane?

Jill Meyers

I have not personally seen any photos other than what Bill put in the book that he published several years ago. All you really see in those photos are hunks of coral, to be honest, that are potentially hiding an aircraft underneath them. As it's been discussed here today, if this is an airplane that crashed in the '30s, it would have been overtaken by the coral reef there in the eighty-five years since that day. So I have not personally seen any photograph that makes me 100% sure that anything I'm seeing is relative to an airplane.

Jen Taylor

Along those same lines, then, do you think that the aircraft is recoverable at this point, or do you think that it's been too long with too much disintegration, and it's going to have to stay there?

Jill Meyers

I don't think the airframe is recoverable. My understanding is that anything made of metal will be either replaced by or eaten away by coral, or just be gone. There are other materials that survive in salt water and do not get replaced by coral. For example, glass.

There's definitely no chance of hauling up the entire airplane or even a large piece of it.

The challenge with any recovered piece, and this glass we have is no different, is how do you positively identify it?

There's not a lot of documentation about airplanes built in the '30s. In modern times, we're very spoiled by very solid engineering documentation and FAA documentation. Not so much in the 1930s. We've put a lot of time into our attempts to find documentation that would match anything that may have been seen down there. Over the course of years that the teams have been diving on this wreck site, there's been environmental changes as well that have been very hurtful to our efforts.

Jen Taylor

So other than aluminum and glass, what kind of material might we expect to still be down there?

. . .

Jill Meyers

You know, I'm not sure. I'm not an expert on that particular era of aircraft builds. But I would imagine, and am told by metallurgy experts, that there are some types of metal that survive better than aluminum. The bad news for us is the majority of the aircraft is aluminum. But there are parts of the aircraft that are not the fuselage that are made of metals other than aluminum, and those may not have been as damaged.

The question is, can we *get to them?*

Jen Taylor

Are planes still made of aluminum today?

Jill Meyers

Not many, as that metal is too heavy. As aviation has grown over the decades, metals that airplanes have been built out of have changed. In fact, almost all aircraft built after 2000 are made of much more composite material that looks and feels like plastic or ceramic.

These are made of many different materials that are hand-blended for tensile strength, which basically means they will not break easily in conditions like strong wind. One of the biggest challenges to flying aircraft is what's called "wind shear," which is a very strong wind that comes at you from a different direction than the direction you're flying. There is a long history of aircraft accidents caused by wind shear; the airplane just gets into a situation where the pilot can't recover. The Dreamliner that Boeing builds is actually the first airplane I believe to be completely composite. I don't think there's a piece of metal on a Boeing 787; it's all composites. As the technology has grown through the years, there are fewer and fewer airplanes being made of pure metal, and for sure, hardly anything made of aluminum.

. . .

Jen Taylor

Based on that, is it possible to date the plane that has been found off the coast of Buka, or am I being too optimistic?

Jill Meyers

If it can be proven that it was made of aluminum, that would only narrow it down to a series of decades.

As far as identifying the aircraft positively, the engineer in me says that we need to find a hunk of metal with a serial number stamped on it. That would be the ultimate discovery as far as an ID on this aircraft.

Something that allows us to trace the serial number to a Lockheed Martin drawing today, which would have to be in their archives. We haven't been able to find anyone who will hand us over drawings for that particular aircraft's serial number. The main goal has always been to find things that were *so* unique to her Lockheed Electra 10-E that they couldn't be disputed once we presented them.

As I mentioned earlier, we're looking for things like the inside fuel tanks, or the steering-wheel-style controls. The navigator door is different than on other Electras. The way the fuel tanks were installed with the holes cut into the fuselage that would allow them to refuel from the outside. That, I believe, was unique to her aircraft and was reportedly seen early on before a lot of the damage was done to the wreckage. If the things that were reported to Bill verbally or via emails are *in fact true*, then there is a whole list of things that are very much in line with the uniqueness of her aircraft.

Jen Taylor

I heard you say to Chris earlier that the difference between all of the different Lockheed Electra 10s lies in their engines. So *what about* those engines? Do you think they're recoverable, or are they gone?

Jill Meyers

I have heard that there are significant parts of the engines still down there, at least as of the August dive.

The 10-E, which is what Earhart's plane model was, was actually called a *10-E special*. It had a series of engines called *Wasp engines*. There were two types of Pratt & Whitney engines put into all of the Lockheed 10s. They were either identified as a *Wright* or a *Wasp.*

Within the Wasp series, there were different ones as well. Only the 10-Es had this particular engine that was put into her aircraft. The information that I've been able to gather is that there's really only one other aircraft in the world today still intact. They call it her *sister airplane,* and it currently sits in the Amelia Earhart Hangar Museum in Atchison, Kansas, her hometown. That serial number is one of the few remaining aircraft that was built from the ground up as a model 10. What's interesting is, some people who own 1930s-era Electra 10s have converted them from one model to another. There's one that sits in New Zealand that was built as a 10-A, but they changed out the engines and made it into a 10-E. Part of the challenge when we've gone out and looked at different Electra 10s is that none of them are in service today; they're in museums or in private hands. It's encouraging, because if we do bring up something substantial, we could get some of these owners that have other 10s or even converted 10s to allow us to do some comparisons of parts. That would be really wonderful if anything is salvageable.

Jen Taylor

You also mentioned the landing light. We know that Amelia's aircraft was customized from the very beginning. We also know that she had the accident in Hawaii and had to have the plane rebuilt with new parts. How difficult does that factor make it for you when you're trying to identify whether or not this piece could have come from her plane?

Jill Meyers

It's extremely difficult.

The good news is that the engineering measurements that have been done on this piece of glass are exactly the right size of the landing light that goes into a Lockheed Electra 10.

I've talked to two experts in glass analyzation; one of them runs one of the top labs in the country related to the National Science Foundation.

When I talked to him about his lab doing some analyzation work for us, I was told that they can't give us a 100% confirmation unless we provide a piece of glass that we know was manufactured in the same manufacturing facility. We need that for comparison, and we can't do that because any manufacturing company that was building Lockheed Electras in the '30s isn't in existence anymore. I'm certain that if I went to any of the owners of current Lockheed Aircraft and said, "Hey, can I borrow your landing light? We're gonna take a chip out of it," they'd say no.

The other challenge is that not only does it have to come from the same manufacturing company, but it has to come from the same manufacturing house. Back then, who knows how many companies in the country, or in the world even, were making glass light lenses?

It's very likely that other aircraft do have the same size light lens.

So to positively identify the piece of glass that we found, we would really have to know where it was manufactured. As you just mentioned, there were a number of repairs that were done on her aircraft, and as I said earlier, they didn't keep records like we do now.

Today, you would just go grab an FAA-approved repair drawing, or repair record, and it would contain all the information you could ever want to know about what piece of glass they stuck in that hole. Well, they didn't do that back then.

There's almost this enigma around Earhart's aircraft where if there *are* records, nobody wants to provide them, or they don't want to admit that they *don't* have them, I don't know.

I know what needs to be done, but I don't know that it's possible to do.

Jen Taylor

Given all the things that we've talked about today, do you think that it's possible to solve the mystery of whose plane this is? Do you think that we are ever going to be able to positively identify the plane, what serial number it was, and who was flying it?

Jill Meyers

I actually do.

I've talked to three people personally who have dove on that wreck. What I'm told is that the structure sits at an extremely steep angle, nose down in a lot of sand. A big challenge to our dive team when they go down there is, because of the depth, they cannot dive for very long. They're using heavy equipment down there, and it's very tiring.

What I would hope to be possible are continued dives to bring up something that is positively identifiable. There might be engine parts or things that were inside the cabin or the cockpit that do have serial numbers on them. A lot of things did. If we brought up something with a serial number on it, we could call the Smithsonian or Lockheed and ask, "We have this thing with a serial number on it. Can you check your records to match it?"

I think for that kind of question, they might say yes. You never know what could be brought up or maybe *has already been brought up* that could change everything.

Then of course, the other question is, is there anything that could be brought up that might possibly be related to human remains that could be DNA tested? That would be the other thing that would be, I think, definitive. As an engineer and an aviator, I've been focused primarily on the aircraft itself.

I would just say that you never know what could be brought up *or* maybe has already been brought up that would change everything.

Jen Taylor

I have no further questions for this witness, Your Honor.

"Twenty years ago, there was an airplane sitting there on the sea floor. If we could have got there then, we'd have a lot easier mystery to solve."

Chris Williamson

Your Honor, the project calls Mr. Mike Orange to the stand.

Mr. Orange, can you first inform the court as to your professional background to this point?

Mike Orange

Sure. I started my life as an aircraft engineer. In the US, I guess you'd call it an A&P tech.

I've always had a passion for airplanes. I love pretty much anything to do with aviation. I used that skill to travel the world, basically fixing airplanes worldwide. Then I came back to New Zealand, and I got more into the business side of things and ended up working for startup companies doing high-tech robotics and managing those operations. I ended up with Boxfish Research, which is a startup New Zealand company that manufactures underwater robotic camera platforms.

Chris Williamson

And speaking of the technology you just mentioned, can you inform the court on how technology like the one you use can assist in the identification of historical aircraft, ships and other ruins that lie underwater?

Mike Orange

The key thing that we can capture is high-definition, uncompressed video. That means that we can capture essentially raw footage that can be reviewed again and again, and you can reveal greater detail in reviewing that footage than even divers can, seeing underwater.

• • •

Chris Williamson

Although you're able to see what the ROV is looking at while it's observing, are you ever surprised at the level of detail that this technology can provide once you get a chance to look at the uncompressed imagery that it gives you?

Mike Orange

Every single time. Whenever we review the footage on a large monitor or big-screen 4K TV, it blows me away how much additional detail you didn't see on the day. The screen that we have on the control station is a large screen, but when you blow it up and you see it on a larger scale, the level of detail is incredible.

Chris Williamson

Is there a better than average chance that you might be able to potentially identify an aircraft like this one based on the level of detail the ROV captures?

Mike Orange

Most definitely. There is one example I can give you. We dove on a shipwreck in New Zealand called the *Mikhail Lermontov*, a Russian cruise liner that sank thirty years ago. We went down there, and you could see the wood grain on the teak deck. You could see the fine grain in the wood. We can achieve that even in murky water because the camera has a wide-angle lens to it. In murky water, that wide-angle lens means you can get up close to a subject and still see a meaningful-sized picture.

Chris Williamson

Mr. Orange, can you tell me how you got involved in this investigation into the wreckage at Buka?

• • •

Mike Orange

I would have to name check another podcast.

Chris Williamson

They're my friends. Please *do*.

Mike Orange

I heard Bill being interviewed on *Astonishing Legends*. I have a long commute in the mornings, and I listen to a number of podcasts. When I heard Bill speak, he spoke with a real knowledge. You could tell that he had researched his subject material well. He also has this train of thought where it was obvious that he didn't really mind so much whether he's right or wrong. He just wants to either rule his idea out or in. I thought that was a good approach and clearly displays an open mind. From there, I thought that Boxfish Research has technology that could really help the cause. As a result of that, I reached out to Scott and Forrest of *Astonishing Legends* and asked if they would be so kind as to connect me to Bill. That's how my involvement began.

Chris Williamson

Before you heard Mr. Snavely on *Astonishing Legends*, had you given much thought to the fate of Amelia Earhart, Fred Noonan and their Lockheed Electra?

Mike Orange

Yes and no. It's a fascinating mystery. Whenever something would come up in the media, I would show an interest. Over the years, that interest turned into assuming that whatever came up was just another theory, and my thought process then was that she's more than likely never going to be found. But tying Bill's theory together with her flight path and the decisions that an aviator would have made as well as the discovery of the headwinds factor made sense to me.

. . .

Chris Williamson

Was this experience in Buka your first in that region?

Mike Orange

Absolutely. It was my first time popping up anywhere in New Guinea altogether.

Chris Williamson

And now, you're one of a very small handful of people who have visited this wreck site in person. Can you give our jury an idea of the atmosphere in Buka, especially the nautical environment that this wreckage currently sits in?

Mike Orange

For a start, it's a tropical island. It's a beautiful location; the water is crystal clear and very warm. The island itself has sand coming away from it, and that sand turns into a coral reef that drops away down to about one hundred feet deep and becomes sand again. That reef has got lots of crevices and lots of protrusions, but the general topography is of a gradual slope downhill.

Chris Williamson

Did the topography there present any unique challenges to you regarding what you were there to do?

Mike Orange

On the first couple of days, it was very hard to find landmarks or familiar pieces of land, basically, that I could get a reference from. But that's the same as anywhere; you need to become familiar with the environment that you're in to be able to navigate your way around.

Chris Williamson

There's been a fair amount of controversy when it comes to this particular aircraft, and no shortage of rumor and innuendo over the years. The images in Bill's book were taken many years ago; the aircraft seems to be more identifiable in those images than the high-resolution images that have been provided by the Project Blue Angel group in press releases and online. Because of that, there are people who have argued that this isn't even a plane at all. The coral there makes it so difficult to tell. But you're one of the only people who have been there. So I'll ask you to clarify for the jury now, is there a plane underneath all of that coral there at Buka?

Mike Orange

I have absolutely no doubt that it is an airplane.

There are features there that leave me no doubt. Basically, yes, it's a lump of coral. But there's definitely two clear windows that I take to be the cockpit windows. As you're retreating from the nose of the aircraft, you can see wreckage, both on the sea floor but also attached to the front of the airplane, that looks very much like there was the nose cone structure there. The structural members have disappeared, but the coral that grew around them is still there. When you descend further, there's without a doubt a wheel sitting on the sea floor.

Chris Williamson

Is the environment there at Buka, especially the dominant amount of coral there, destroying this wreckage as we speak?

• • •

Mike Orange

Yeah, and there's two facets to that, really. One is that the coral is definitely corrosive to the aluminum. Basically, it acts like a lime, and it dissolves it. So that's the first facet. The second facet is that the methods in creating the aluminum for Amelia's aircraft were older techniques that introduced lots of impurities. So it was more liable to corrode. You see World War II wrecks that sit on the sea floor, and they basically look like they could be ten or fifteen years old. Pre-World War II aircraft weren't as durable, there were more impurities in the material, and they corroded away. So two factors at play here.

If her aircraft was where we think it originally might have been on the sea floor, there would be a lot more material there to see.

Chris Williamson

How about the water itself there? Is there any danger being imposed on the aircraft by that?

Mike Orange

The water by itself doesn't. What would do the damage is the amount of oxygen in the water. It does provide a little bit of a barrier to stop that oxygen from beginning its chemical process that corrodes the material away. So it can, but it doesn't because it's providing that little bit of barrier there.

Chris Williamson

Earlier you mentioned that after you heard Bill on *Astonishing Legends*, you reached out because you felt that Boxfish had the technology to assist with the identification of this aircraft. Can you tell our jury what it is you did at Buka and how you used that technology to assist Project Blue Angel?

Mike Orange

Boxfish Research is a young company. I wanted to find an opportunity to get our technology out there and show the world how good it is. What better opportunity than to document something that is potentially cementing itself into history?

I went over there with the intention of being able to document the work that the divers were doing underwater and do that in the best quality possible, and I think I did that. What really surprised me was my mission over has actually turned into a little bit of an outreach mission as well. The locals had a very high level of suspicion about outsiders going to what they essentially consider a treasure that they own.

They never knew what the divers were doing underwater. I was able to take some villagers out on the boat with us, and they could see exactly what the divers were doing. They could see that they weren't taking treasure off it and hiding it away for later recovery. That factor removed all doubt from the locals' minds about the condition of the rig and what the divers were doing. I think that was powerful, and it allowed us to be a lot more welcome.

Chris Williamson

Since coral seems to be the primary concern when it comes to this aircraft, is there anything that the technology you're deploying at the site can do to assist in working around that coral to try to identify what lies beneath?

Mike Orange

On the ROV, we can laser scale. When you're laser scaling something, you're using a pair of lasers that you can place onto the structure or whatever you're looking at. Those lasers are a set distance apart, and that helps you scale objects that you're viewing. Where you see the lasers, that's a certain distance. We can also bring in additional equipment like a magnetometer or sonar equipment, lots of different add-ons.

In all honesty, I think that the level of deterioration in the structure really rules out any of those external sensors apart from scaling and looking at what remains.

Chris Williamson

Now that this experience is behind you, give me your professional opinion. What are the odds that we're looking at the holy grail here?

Mike Orange

Well, I'm 100% certain that this is a plane. There is not enough detail at this stage to possibly say it is or it isn't Amelia's aircraft. Now, we should be able to expand on that using actual scientific evidence. At this stage, I believe it could be, but I can't say I'm positive that it is.

Chris Williamson

What needs to happen next, in your opinion, when it comes to trying to identify this aircraft definitively?

Mike Orange

Let me place a precursor in here, Chris. There's this opportunity at the moment regarding the lens that would positively identify whether it's her airplane or not, and we need to see if that comes off. If that does, it'll be 100% confirmed. If that happens, the next step would be to gain a lot more funding because Project Blue Angel has been run on a shoestring budget entirely funded by Bill himself. There's also been the wonderful people who supported the GoFundMe who have contributed some funds that went into the second trip I took part in. All of us on this team were there voluntarily, volunteering our own time and not charging Project Blue Angel at all.

What needs to happen now is we need to get some professional underwater archaeologists to begin a full-scale excavation of the wreck. By that, I mean that the fuselage is completely full of debris, full of sand and full of coral, and it's highly compacted. We were there for ten days with divers working to try to break away some of that internal material and bring it up in bags, having the locals sift through all the debris that was there. In my opinion, that needs to be scaled way up. There needs to be a dredge brought in with the right equipment to begin vacuuming the inside of the rig. Whatever is inside that airplane has survived the degradation process, and it might be the key. That's what's required.

Chris Williamson

You mentioned something that struck me, and that's that when you came away from this experience, you felt a bit dejected. Can you expand on that for the jury?

Mike Orange

I came away from Buka in some respects a bit dejected because after talking to the locals, they described it so clearly as being a twin-engine, twin-tailed airplane sitting on the sea floor when it was first observed.

It was on the sandy area before the coral reef sitting in about twenty meters or so of water. In the intervening years, there have been a couple of large earthquakes, and I know firsthand the destruction that an underwater earthquake causes. The forces are a lot stronger because they're shaking in a much heavier medium. We saw this firsthand on the shipwreck that we dived on in New Zealand. That suffered a severe earthquake, and the top three decks of this ship had sheared off from the forces generated during the earthquake.

I don't think that happened to the aircraft that we found at Buka, but what I think *has* happened is that as the seabed has been shaken by earthquakes, and the aircraft has traveled downhill into the reef. Once it's touched the reef, the reef then has something to grow on. The reef can't grow out across sand, but while the airplane is sitting on the reef, it can engulf it.

It looks to me like the aircraft has fallen into a crevasse, and that's why when you look at the footage that we've got, it appears to be peeking out of the reef. I think it's fallen into that crevice, and the reef has grown over the top of it.

Twenty years ago, there was an airplane sitting there on the sea floor. If we could have gotten there then, we'd have a lot easier mystery to solve.

Chris Williamson

For the people who are arguing that there's no way this could be the plane, and for the people who are quick to say, "It shouldn't take long to identify this plane," can you please explain exactly how difficult this actually is considering the environment you're facing in an attempt to identify this aircraft?

Mike Orange

It's virtually impossible to identify the type of aircraft at the moment. All you can see of the aircraft is the two cockpit windows, a bit of structure, a wheel, and a bit of undercarriage structure on the ground along with a little bit of the nose cone. As the coral grows around it, it changes the scale. You can imagine that as you have a piece of aluminum and coral grows on it, it grows bigger than the original piece of aluminum was.

It distorts the scale of what you're looking at.

The things that are going to identify it as an Electra are the other things that remain inside. The bits that won't degrade are glass and copper, things of that nature. There are parts there that will degrade slower than the aluminum. That's really what needs to be hunted for.

The people who say those things you mentioned don't really appreciate what the environment is like down there. This fuselage is full of compacted coral and sand, and it sits like concrete. Imagine taking this plane and wrapping a block of concrete around it that's four feet thick all around. Now go down there and scratch a serial number off for me while having a very limited amount of equipment and air at your disposal.

Easy peasy, *right?*

The divers are down there with little air-powered jackhammers, trying to chisel off parts of it that are basically jailed inside the fuselage. People that have these thoughts of us going down and just bringing something up miraculously just don't have any idea of what we're dealing with. There is no stuff to just grab and bring up. We can't just go down and get a serial number. If it were *that* easy, anyone could do it and would have by now.

It's so hard to identify it because you're looking at the ghost of the airframe. You're looking at the coral that has grown around the structure, and that structure is gone. I think what needs to really happen is a true excavation of the inside of the airplane in the hope that you'll find some artifacts that have survived. Items maybe made out of material that is not as liable to corrode or disappear. They're in there. I feel it in my bones that there will be artifacts in that airplane.

Chris Williamson

So, to recap, you're on a shoestring budget, with a volunteer team. You're in the middle of a remote part of this planet and down in a very unstable nautical environment. You're looking at a wreckage that's eighty-five years old and engulfed in coral, and you're trying to identify a plane that detractors seem to have a very easy time dismissing as possibly the holy grail of aviation.

Did I miss anything?

Mike Orange

That's absolutely what we're dealing with, and it really *is* impossibly hard.

Chris Williamson

Thank you, Mr. Orange. Pass the witness, Your Honor.

Cross-Examination of Mike Orange

Jen Taylor

I want to clarify your background a little bit. I think that you said that you had worked on planes before, is that right?

Mike Orange

Yeah, sure. I did an apprenticeship in New Zealand for mechanical aircraft engineering, and it's been probably close to ten years of my life working on aircraft.

Jen Taylor

Okay, so you're pretty familiar with being able to identify a plane even in conditions such as these when you don't necessarily see the entirety of the aircraft, but only maybe specific airplane parts?

Mike Orange

Yes, absolutely.

Jen Taylor

In Bill's book, he talked about a number of characteristics between the plane that has been found off the coast of Buka and Amelia Earhart's plane. I want to go through a few of those with you and just find out whether or not you were able to personally verify any of these things. I understand that we have pictures of some things, other things we don't, but you *are able* to actually see the plane. The first thing that he has on his list is the twin-tail structure. Are we still able to see that today?

Mike Orange

No, unfortunately. The aircraft that I was seeing underwater has moved significantly into the reef, and the reef has basically taken over that aircraft. So it's very difficult to spot any identifying features. There are parts that look very similar to the Lockheed Electra, particularly from the cockpit going forward. There's a luggage compartment in the nose structure. You can see the remains of that nose structure hanging down from the front of the airplane.

Jen Taylor

I know one of the things that was reported early on was the additional fuel tanks, the long-range fuel tanks. Were you able to see any indication that those were there?

Mike Orange

No, the inside of the fuselage is completely full of debris, coral and sand. You can't see down deep into the aircraft.

Jen Taylor

So it's accurate to say that so far, despite all of the work that you guys have been doing, you have not been able to definitively identify that this plane is her Lockheed Electra 10-E. Is that correct?

Mike Orange

That's correct.

Jen Taylor

You talked with Chris about needing professional archaeologists to go down there and do an excavation. If that were to happen, how much of that plane would be recoverable still today? Do you think we would get enough information to be able to identify the plane if that was done?

Mike Orange

I think if we go back with a proper dredging operation, we will positively identify the airplane through the artifacts that should be inside.

The fuselage itself is not recoverable.

It essentially doesn't exist. What you've got is a skeleton of the fuselage that's been formed by the coral growing around that element. The element itself has corroded away due to the lime in the coral, which is extraordinarily corrosive to the element.

Jen Taylor

Is there anything that you think is still there that would constitute a smoking gun? I know you guys talked about the likelihood of finding a serial number after all this time, but given what you know about the plane's makeup and its rate of degradation, is there anything that you're hoping to find that would prove beyond a shadow of a doubt that this is her plane?

Mike Orange

Well, it'll sound a bit morbid, but the number one thing would be to recover parts of Amelia or Fred. To be able to bring something that could be DNA tested that would prove conclusively that it's her inside that airplane. The aircraft itself should have artifacts inside that would correspond to the equipment that she had on board.

. . .

Jen Taylor

Based on what you know of the theory and the wreckage that you've seen, when this particular plane crash-landed, regardless of whether this was Amelia or someone else, do you think that they were able to land the plane on land? Or was this something that crash-landed in the water?

Mike Orange

I believe it's something that crash-landed in the water very close to the beach. In seeing the topography of the land, you could discern that she was trying to land on the beach but ended up in the water. One of the other reasons why I believe that is because of the witness who saw a fireball coming out of the sky, aiming for land. Later that morning, there was no wreckage on the beach.

Jen Taylor

I might be wrong about this, and if I'm wrong, then I'm wrong. But I thought earlier we heard a story about somebody seeing the plane as well as a man and a woman inside it, using the radio.

Mike Orange

That's not a story that I heard while witnessing the interviews of people on the island.

Jen Taylor

Okay.

Mike Orange

The feeling I got was that the records really weren't seen until the late '90s, when there was a local who was free diving, and he saw the wreck sitting on the sea floor. He gave quite a strong description of the airframe. He talked about the twin tails and twin engines, and I've got the feeling that the aircraft was still largely intact at that stage.

Jen Taylor

I think what I'm getting at with this line of questioning is that there have been a number of theories in this case. There's a lot of people discussing what they would call the post-loss signals. Even in Bill's book, he discusses Betty Klenck's notebook a little bit. What I want to know is, based on your understanding of the wreckage and of how the crash would have happened, would she have been able to send any signals at all after she had crashed?

Mike Orange

From what we've seen and what we believe is lying in the cockpit, I don't have the feeling that she or whomever was piloting the aircraft would have moved or been able to send any signals. It doesn't give me that impression. Perhaps whilst sitting there, she could have used her radio. But it really is speculation; we have no way of knowing.

Jen Taylor

The fact that all of these identifying features were there in the beginning and are no longer there now, does that make this all the more difficult to solve as time goes on? Is it getting less and less likely that we're going to get an answer on whose plane this is?

Mike Orange

Yes, it is. As the reef takes over, it really does make it harder and harder. I'm so disappointed we weren't able to get to this wreck sooner before it carried on its journey down the hill, essentially. That doesn't mean it's going to be impossible to recover any artifacts off the aircraft. There will still be stuff inside. It just needs large funding spent on a proper expedition that would allow us to go deeper inside the wreckage.

Jen Taylor

Basically, what you're saying is, at this point, we've done as much as we can hope to do, and now we need to have somebody get in there and excavate, right?

Mike Orange

Yeah. Our divers were there going in through the cockpit window. But we're using rudimentary handheld air hammers powered off a dive cylinder, and it's just painfully slow work. The finds that were brought up were being sorted by the locals on a table. I'm not sure they were the best people to be sorting through the spoils that were brought up, but we were there on a shoestring budget.

It just needs to be done on a larger scale.

Jen Taylor

Earlier, I asked Miss Meyers a question about being able to date the plane. What is it about what you're seeing that makes you confident that it could be Amelia's plane?

Mike Orange

When I tie both the stories that I've heard – the original sighting of the aircraft and the rediscovery of it in the late '90s – they seem to fit together. It seems very possible to me that the aircraft is a pre-World War II aircraft, just because of the way that the aluminum has disappeared and corroded. Some aircraft of the World War II era are still sitting on the seabed today, and even when they're in contact with the reef, they are less likely to corrode. That's a big one for me.

· · ·

Jen Taylor

What about the engines? Do we expect that maybe we can recover all or part of those engines?

Mike Orange

Yes. There is a high chance that you can recover part of them. The engines themselves will be made out of various types of steel, as well as aluminum bracketry and stuff like that. As Tracy mentioned earlier, sparkplugs would be big because they have that ceramic portion to them; fairly easy to identify as well if we can get one in good enough condition.

We believe that we saw an engine, but because it was so encrusted in coral, it's very hard to get to the metal.

Jen Taylor

I know that in certain parts of the world, digging through certain environmental formations might cause some legal issues. Have you run into that at all in trying to get through the coral? I know that it's protected to a certain extent.

Mike Orange

No, because the coral inside the aircraft has been compacted and starved of oxygen and is likely very dead coral. We're not digging into active reef. In that area of the world, things of an environmental nature aren't well policed. So it really is up to the environmental consciousness of the people who are working the wreck. We took painstaking measures to ensure that we're being very respectful of the environment there and of the wreckage itself.

Jen Taylor

Who has control over that area? My understanding is that when you go out there, you have to jump through a thousand hoops to get there. Does the government own that area where the plane sits? Or can anyone theoretically go down there and investigate it if they wanted to?

Mike Orange

It seemed to me that the local islanders own whatever is in the vicinity of the island. A personal point of reference for that is, I wanted to go and see a World War II wreck that was nearby, and it was close to *another* island. The villagers informed me that in order to do that, we would need to go and speak to the chief of that island and gain permission to be able to go and have a look. I have a bit of background around the environmental issues as well. Very close to Matsungan Island, there is a commercial freighter ship that has been wrecked and left to rot. Now, I know in New Zealand if that happened, the owners of the ship would be liable to remove the wreck and make the environment pristine again. When the ship ran aground in this particular location, the owners and the crew on board just walked away scot-free. They can almost get away with dumping it because there's not that sort of policing there.

The local villagers really do want the mystery to be solved, and they also want to have artifacts remaining there because they want to be able to turn it into an income stream. They want to be able to bring tourists and divers into the area who are wanting to go diving in this particular spot to be a part of that history. They're fully aware that they have an opportunity to maybe lift social and living standards of the island through this potential opportunity that is on their doorstep.

Jen Taylor

Those who are critical of this theory might say, "Well, if the locals have an interest in this being her plane in the name of tourism and bringing people to the island, they will have an incentive to embellish the things that they have seen." We discussed earlier things like the long-range fuel tanks and other aspects that people had laid eyes on but never took pictures of. By the time that divers actually go down, the plane is disintegrated too much to be able to actually see them. Those who are critical would say, "Well, how can we really trust what was seen early on if there's an incentive to bring in tourism?"

How would you respond to that?

Mike Orange

I would respond by saying any evidence that is relied upon to say this is Amelia's aircraft has to be scientifically backed. It can't just be hearsay and recollections of something that was observed at the time. Those things might give us clues, but any verification has to be scientific in nature.

There's no other way around that.

And it *should be possible.*

Jen Taylor

I have no further questions for this witness, Your Honor.

Chris Williamson

Your Honor, at this time, the project rests for Buka.

We'd like to call an end to this presentation and continue next with witnesses, experts and exhibits for *Japanese capture.*

Bailiff

ALL RISE!

Post-Trial Discussion

Chris Williamson

Alright, you just heard the Buka hypothesis. It's a very hot theory at the moment. You've heard the evidence; you've talked to the people who are involved in it, including some of the primary players. Does it hold water for you?

Jen Taylor

Well, yes and no.

I think that the Project Blue Angel team are doing a really good job of doing their due diligence; they're not taking anything for granted. If somebody says something, they don't just accept it and move on. They want pictures of that thing; they want to go and try to recover that thing. Let's see if we can test these observations. They are searching for hard evidence, and they're not simply hanging their hat on rumors and stories that they've been told, even though those things *are* there. They're not satisfied with that, they're continuing to search, and I think that's really admirable.

That being said, they've found what they've found, and it is still inconclusive, but they're very confident in it. They have enough, I think, to keep moving forward, and I wouldn't expect anything less from Bill Snavely.

I don't think that they have found anything that has told them they should stop the investigation or take it in a different direction. But for me, this is just kind of a *wait and see.*

Chris Williamson

Yeah.

Jen Taylor

How can I be convinced of something beyond a reasonable doubt when they are the ones telling us that they're not done searching and investigating? I mentioned this before their presentation even began. That factor kind of makes it a challenge for us to put on trial. I think we're doing this prematurely, but I'm *waiting*, and I'm *curious*.

Chris Williamson

I love that phrase, *wait and see*. That's exactly what we're doing; it really does sum this up. I want to walk this theory backwards a little bit and talk about some of the evidence, and it starts with the lone witness. If you compare this to something like Japanese capture, which we'll get to next, there's no shortage of witnesses for that particular theory.

We have a single witness when it comes to Buka.

The question is, what makes a good witness? Does it matter that we can link a tangible piece of evidence to his story? Does that make this witness's testimony any more powerful than, say, a couple of dozen witnesses whom you *cannot* do that with?

Jen Taylor

Well, I'm going to give you two answers to that question: For the first one, I promise I'm not trying to be snarky. But a good witness comes to court. Now I know there are obviously some exceptions to that rule, like death, for example. That's the ultimate exception.

We didn't get to talk to the person who saw what they saw, right? Because that person isn't here.

Chris Williamson

Right.

Jen Taylor

I really think it's important to point that out. I think that it does mean something that that person isn't here anymore to tell us first-hand. We're relying on hearsay essentially.

. . .

Chris Williamson

Sure.

Jen Taylor

Which is why I don't think that should have been the focus of the evidence. It was definitely mentioned, but it's not the focus of their evidence, and it shouldn't be. It's only a part of it.

My second answer to that question is, say we didn't have that problem, and we had somebody telling us firsthand what they saw. It is important to be able to corroborate what somebody says with tangible evidence. We have this thing in Texas, and I know other jurisdictions have it as well. Certain testimony must be corroborated in order to be considered by a jury, just based on the nature of what it is. Some good examples would be confessions or jailhouse snitches, things like that, that kind of have this almost inherent unreliability. Even when the person is on the stand testifying, you want it to be corroborated by something in order for the jury to really be allowed to look at it. When I say "corroboration," it doesn't have to be much. Even a tiny piece of evidence being corroborated with the story they're telling is usually enough. The bar is not very high.

I would take those concepts, and I would apply them here. He's telling us what he's saying he saw. If any part of that is corroborated by the physical evidence that we find, even if there are pieces that don't make sense, those are things that can be talked about.

Chris Williamson

If he says that the plane landed in this area, and in 1995, all those years later, it's found, and it turns out there really *is* a plane there, is that not the corroboration that we need?

Jen Taylor

Yeah, I think that's what I'm saying.

Chris Williamson

Okay, gotcha.

Jen Taylor

I know that certain aspects of the story don't 100% match up. It depends on whom you're talking to. If there are human remains in this plane that is now underwater, and she and Fred died there, then none of the post-loss signals could have happened. Anyone who saw her messing with a radio couldn't have been right. So there's things like that, that don't really 100% match up.

Chris Williamson

Right.

Jen Taylor

But is that enough to say that the statement wasn't corroborated? My point is, legally, usually no. But as a jury, if you're trying to determine what you think happened, those are all things that you can take into consideration. Everyone's going to disagree. It's hard enough to get a unanimous verdict when you have twelve people. We have countless people who will read this [hopefully], and you know those opinions are going to be all over the map for many different reasons.

The fact that a plane is seen where he said it would be and it appears to be from that same time period certainly doesn't tell us *what* he saw. But it *does* tell us that he saw *something*.

He's not making it up.

Chris Williamson

That's always been the thing. There's a lot of talk regarding witnesses in this case, cross theory. And we're going to experience next how difficult it can be to put witnesses and evidence together. But this particular witness has a story that matches up with a physical piece of evidence, and that piece of evidence happens to be a plane of all things.

Not a *part* of a plane, not a *piece* of something, but an *actual plane itself.*

What I think is really heartbreaking is the condition of the plane. I want to make it very clear that a couple of the people you just heard from have actually been down there.

Tracy Wildrix dove on the plane, and Mike Orange dove on the plane, and they're both saying this plane is in terrible condition. These men know what they're talking about. Jill Meyers is saying this plane is in terrible condition, and there is no one more honorable than Jill in my opinion. My only regret is that our readers didn't hear from Stephani Gordon, who found the landing light lens and shot all the footage on Buka for both trips.

Her energy and passion are undeniable and remarkably infectious, and that's our loss. But the history has not been good to it, and the environment has not been good to it.

I think people who speculate online in forums from behind keyboards say, "It's super easy; just go and scrape some of the coral off and get a serial number and you have it solved!"

They're armchair quarterbacking. They've never been there. I prefer to hear from the people who have actually been there and have touched the wreckage.

It is not that simple. It's an underwater grave now.

This thing is covered in coral. Mike Orange mentioned that laser scaling can't even determine the actual size of the plane because there's so much coral around it. It's really a heartbreaking scenario.

This plane might be too damaged to ever extract.

Jen Taylor

Yeah, that is incredibly heartbreaking. I always hate to see missing persons cases that never get solved, and bodies recovered that no one can ever identify.

I think that may be what we're dealing with here, and it does break my heart.

I *hate that.*

I understand the desire to say, "No, the *Itasca* logs disprove this whole theory." At this point, I don't know that they do. I have enough questions that I don't know if they do.

If this is a murder case, the *Itasca* logs are the last text messages, the last phone call, the last person who spoke to her. The last person who speaks to *anyone* who disappears is going to be your prime suspect. That's why it matters so much what she said on those logs, and that's why it matters so much if she said anything else. That's why it matters so much if the post-loss signals are credible or not because *what* she said last and *when* she last said it matters.

Chris Williamson

I couldn't agree more.

Jen Taylor

If you're going to tell me that she didn't die at this time, she died at a different time, and she didn't die at this location, she died at a different location, then you have the burden of proof to back that up. You have to be able to explain what the records show and how to interpret them. You have to authenticate them, and you have to prove that this evidence can be trusted. You have to show us what it means. That's why I keep going back to those questions, because anyone who wants to say she was not near Howland Island, like we've been told, *has to explain* those radio logs. And that's going to include this next group of people.

. . .

Chris Williamson

I'm right there with you. As much as my heart is with Bill and what he's trying to do, I agree. I also feel like their explanation for what you're saying is a valid one. I've since spoken to half a dozen ham radio operators, and all of them have told me that what Bill and Tracy are saying here is possible. But I understand your position and agree that it's been one of the things that has been difficult to establish. At this point, everybody is putting them at very far distances from that roughly 200-mile mark. I should remind our readers that Nikumaroro Island is roughly 405 miles away. The Marshall Islands are over 800 miles away, and Buka is over double that distance at 1,700 miles away. During our crash and sink conversations, Tom Dettweiler said something that's really stuck with me.

"We have to trust Amelia and what she was saying."

She said she was low on fuel. You have to explain how she could have been saying that while winding up 400, 800, or even 1,700 miles away. That's something that I think is very difficult to do without hard evidence in play.

Jen Taylor

If that's the theory, then yes, I agree. The thing about the Buka theory, though, is that it actually doesn't rely on that kind of scenario. It has her crashing around the time that she said she was low on fuel. It just has her doing it at a different place because, according to the theory, she never made it to Howland Island.

She turns around, but it still matches up. I certainly think that there are more questions we could ask, but it's just not the right time to ask them. We're not there yet.

This is the only theory that does not have her flying for an additional three to five hours *after* she says she's low on fuel.

I'll give it that.

Chris Williamson

Yeah, it's an interesting dichotomy, and like everything in this case, it just depends on what you believe.

If you believe that she was in fact around Howland Island, then you're stating that she obviously would not have had anywhere near the fuel to make it back to Buka.

Jen Taylor

She would have run out of fuel at Howland Island or, according to the logs, just before.

Chris Williamson

Right. The folks who are working Buka are saying that's not even in play, because she never got anywhere near Howland Island; in fact, she wasn't even talking to the *Itasca*.

That would explain why two-way communication was never established between the two.

So you have to really buy into a whole other outcome. It's like a choose-your-own-adventure book. Of course, this is really difficult to prove. But if this is the plane, well then, we're dealing with something else entirely.

Jen Taylor

If it turns out that it is, then yes. If this turns out to be her, then there is no possible way that she was as close to the *Itasca* as the crash and sink experts say she was. Even TIGHAR acknowledges that she made it over to that area. It is entirely possible to say "yes, this is it" or "no, this isn't."

Chris Williamson

Hence, the hashtag *rewrite history*, which is what they've been pushing on social media for Project Blue Angel. This really would rewrite history if this ended up being the plane because now you have to figure out how the hell this plane got to Buka. Is it exactly as Bill Snavely says *or* is there something else in play? What in the world happened here?

You're going to have to reverse engineer the entire last few moments of her life. I've said that to Bill during private conversations.

If he's right, and it's a *big if*, it's going to change everything we think we know about what's historically reported and what's real.

Jen Taylor

Regardless of who this is, whether it's Amelia Earhart or not, they have an amazing story to tell. I think it's amazing that Bill wants to figure out what that story is.

You don't die in a plane crash off the coast of Buka and *not have* an amazing story.

3 Years Later: A Retrospective

After my interview with Jennifer Taylor for *Vanished*, I went over the rough copy from the *Itasca* on Galten's watch, during which Leo Bellarts sat in. Galten indicates an S-5 at 19:28 GMT. This is the first time that the *Itasca* reports the plane circling [probably to get a sunline facing east]. This is important since Amelia's plane would be facing Howland and the *Itasca*. Radio signals would be louder and clearer without interference and signal reduction from the tail. Signal meters do not yield accurate signal intensity readings and are not calibrated in microvolts. A signal meter is useful only for making relative measures of signal strengths. For just a minute, let's assume that it was an S-5. Due to propagation, the 3105 night signal could skip on one hop and come in as an S-5 from 3,000 miles away according to the AARL antenna book. Amelia's plane would have been only 1,750 miles from Howland. It was ideal conditions for radio transmission for the following reasons: It was summer, nighttime, near the equator and had the highest sunspot activity since 1871. Amelia's plane was in nighttime while the *Itasca* was in daylight. This further explains why they could hear her, but she couldn't hear them.

The sunrise came in over Buka at 19:35 GMT. A half hour later, at 20:14 GMT, Amelia reports she is "on the line 157/337," and Galten writes "S-5?"

Why the question mark at the end? Was this transmission not as strong as the signal had been forty-six minutes earlier when the plane was circling and facing them? You would anticipate that the call at 20:14 would be louder than the call at 19:28 GMT. However, they had flown no closer to Howland in forty-six minutes, and the front of the plane was no longer facing them.

Amelia reported she is planning to switch to 6210, which was her daytime frequency, because it was now early morning at Buka. I called Jennifer regarding my latest finding.

Regarding fuel capacity, Fred Noonan said at a press conference the night before takeoff from Lae that they would be taking off with 950 gallons of fuel due to the weight of the plane, which had to be under the 15,300-pound mark to take off from a paved runway. This is documented in newspapers in New Zealand, Australia, and Papua New Guinea as well.

Callopy indicated that she took off with full tanks, but he likely misunderstood what Amelia said when she said she was "at weighted capacity." Further proof of the delicate nature of the fuel is twofold. First, she had never taken off with as much as 950 gallons of fuel, and she was under the microscope by the British. I reference her letter to Sir Francis dated February 13, 1937. She wrote him over the longest routes on the Pacific: "I will probably carry about 1,000 gallons." She knew Sir Francis would not allow 1,130 gallons, and he gave her permission to fly directly to Aden and land there as long as she didn't fly over Mascat or Oman and kept outside the three-mile limit from the Arabian coast.

Sir Francis's words from that letter are "you have been made aware why the flight over Mascat and Oman is impossible."

The third discovery I've come across in the years since we recorded *Vanished* is six Lockheed Electra 10s went down near New Zealand and Australia. All have been documented, but only *one* is missing.

Amelia's.

Near Buka, we have underwater photos of a short stubby fender used only on Lockheeds.

We also have a round landing light that measures exactly the right diameter for the Electra 10 based on the diameter of a Lockheed 10 light sitting in a museum in Auckland, New Zealand. Lockheed had to gain permission from the FAA to put round landing lights in the hatch cover of the Lockheed 10. Lockheed only used it on the 10, not on any other models, earlier or later.

Thank you to all of you who have supported *Project Blue Angel* and a special thank you to Chris and Vanessa Williamson for helping to get our theory out there.

Bill Snavely
Winter 2022

Chris Williamson

We're hitting our stride in this investigation.

Now, it's about to get deeper than you ever thought possible. We've taken you from the vicinity of Howland Island to the shores of Nikumaroro and now Buka. What we're going to showcase next is a theory that the world may not be ready to accept.

If the running theme for Buka is *a simpler explanation*, then theory four might just be the opposite, spotlighting the most complex explanation and the deepest rabbit hole you can ever imagine.

And it all begins with yet *another* question.

Were Amelia Earhart and Fred Noonan captured by the Japanese?

Fasten your seat belts.

PRISONER

15.1909825 | 145.746743

"The Truth. At Last."

Chris Williamson

What happened to Amelia Earhart and Fred Noonan?

Were they simply lost at sea like the United States government claims? Or did they fly to Nikumaroro, *or maybe* reverse course just over their halfway point to Buka? It's been eighty-five years to the day of release for this book, and *still*, we're no closer to the truth. In the early 1960s, CBS correspondent Fred Goerner began digging. What followed has become an exhaustive pursuit of the truth, as Goerner's search turned over information that the world wasn't ready to believe.

Sometimes you don't have to go out *looking for a story. Sometimes* that story finds *you.*

Listen to Fred Goerner describe how this whole ordeal began for him.

Fred Goerner

It began in 1960 with CBS. I was a correspondent here in San Francisco. And we received information there was a possibility that Amelia Earhart might have reached Saipan in the western Marianas.

Chris Williamson

As tips began pouring in, Goerner surmised that the idea of Amelia Earhart and Fred Noonan being in the hands of the Japanese *might be much more* than an alternative explanation. Goerner explained *one such story* in a 1966 CBS radio broadcast.

Fred Goerner

The story begins with a little girl, a native of Saipan, taking lunch to her brother-in-law working at the Japanese naval base. As she approached the shore, an exciting and unusual scene unfolded: A silver two-engine plane flew low over the water, its engine sputtering and missing. It was not a Japanese plane *she knew*. And then it disappeared hidden behind a cliff. She hurried on, reached the naval base, and there at the beach, a *white American lady pilot and a man*.

The little girl never saw them again.

Chris Williamson

Early on in his search, he came across a woman who *at the time* recalled memories from her childhood. That woman's name is Josephine Blanco, now Blanco Akiyama.

Listen for yourself as Josephine recounts her story during that same radio broadcast to writer Lynn Day of the *San Mateo Times*.

Josephine Blanco Akiyama

In 1937, I took lunch to my brother-in-law Jose Matsumoto. On the way to give him his lunch, I saw a two-engine plane. When I got there to that place, Tanapag Harbor, I saw a crowd of people. So I just wondered what happened. I stood there behind the tree, and I watched the people. I saw an American lady, dressed like a man, with her companion. The Japanese were so excited. They took them to a car, a black sedan. I think they took them into custody. They took them to Garapan City.

I never saw an American lady before. She had a short haircut like a man, and she was *dressed like a man* too; she was wearing a jacket and slacks. When I stood by the tree, I heard Japanese people saying the lady is a pilot, an *American lady,* and the other one is the *navigator* for her. One night we were playing by the house in Garapan City, and one sailor passed by and stopped and talked to us because we knew him. He mentioned that the lady is the pilot, and the man is the navigator, and they'd been shot.

They *executed* them.

Chris Williamson

After his investigation was over, and he'd immersed himself in the story and talked to dozens and dozens of witnesses, Fred Goerner published *The Search for Amelia Earhart,* which became a national best-seller, sitting on the *New York Times* bestselling list for *six months,* a feat not repeated *since.*

For Goerner there *was no mystery,* there was *only the truth.*

Fred Goerner

It is *my belief* that Amelia landed on a small reef area between Howland Island and Canton in the northern Phoenix group. She was picked up *after our search* by the Japanese, taken to *Saipan,* and she died in Japanese custody. The proof of her Japanese custody is contained in records of the Counterintelligence Corps captured from the Japanese at the end of World War II.

Chris Williamson

You just heard from eyewitness Josephine Blanco Akiyama; *that's one.*

Next, we'll hear from over *twenty-five more* of the documented eyewitnesses throughout the Marshall Islands, Saipan and the *United States military* who were stationed there. All of this leads to a single important question.

Is the Japanese capture hypothesis *truly* the *truth at last?*

The time has come. The most requested piece of our trial is upon us. It's time to hear witnesses' evidence and experts for *Japanese capture.*

Pre-Trial Discussion

Jen Taylor

When you *first* approached me with this, the first question you asked me was "What if I had two hundred eyewitnesses who all said they saw the same thing?" That's kind of been on my mind from the very beginning of all this. How do you deal with that? What would that look like, *really?* In preparation for this episode, I've done *a lot* of reading, and a consistent theme is that people get *convicted of murder* with *less evidence.*

Chris Williamson

Is that true?

Jen Taylor

It's a really *loaded* thing to say. It's not enough that you have evidence, you have to have evidence that's admissible in court, and you have to have evidence that's reliable and trustworthy.

I'm not ready to make comments on that right now, in this case. I'm just saying that's *typically* how it works. Something that's always kind of bothered me about that comment is, it's a comment on *how easy it is* to convict someone of a crime.

I'm not sure I'm comfortable with that.

There are many, many people sitting in prison *right now* for crimes they didn't commit, serious crimes. I know *you will know* of notorious cases where people were inches away from the death penalty for crimes that they could not have committed, that they did not commit.

Chris Williamson

How were they put away in the first place?

Jen Taylor

A combination of eyewitness testimony and junk science. Oftentimes, they and their loved ones know that they didn't do anything. They might have an alibi witness or whatever, but they know it's not possible, yet the evidence that they *didn't do it* never makes it in front of a jury. It's a complicated thing to make a statement like that; it's a loaded thing to say. There are rules of evidence for a reason. I think it oversimplifies everything. We really have to break this down and ask ourselves, "Is this something that would even be in front of a jury? If it is, what would they think of it? Should they be allowed to consider something like this?"

Chris Williamson

That's the big question, right? Can we *even get to step one?* Is this something that I would even be able to have admitted into evidence, all of this hearsay? If we have a witness take the stand and talk about all of the eyewitness accounts for people whom *you cannot cross-examine,* then can we even get there? Is our system flawed before it ever gets a chance to get off the ground? That's one of the areas that the people who are arguing for this theory would say, "Of course you should let it go; you should let it be admitted." *Yes,* this is a book based on a show that at the end of the day is for both *educational and entertainment purposes.* We're trying to get all the theories out there. At first, it seems like we should just let it *all go* because it's part of the theory, it's part of the evidence that represents that theory. But at the same time, we're trying to put *a* legal process together that maybe bends the rules for the sake of entertainment purposes but does so very *lightly.* That's where we kind of have a problem.

Jen Taylor

And like we said at the very beginning of this trial, this isn't *the only way* to handle a historical mystery. A trial by jury is not the only way to approach the questions we've been asking.

Experts in this case make statements all the time like, "People are put away for murder for much less" or "I've proven this beyond a reasonable doubt." If you make statements like those, but when it comes time to actually try to put this on trial and follow the rules of evidence, your response is, "Well, it's not a real trial. Why does it matter? This isn't a legal problem. Why do you have to follow these rules?" Well, *now* we have an issue here.

You *can't have it both ways.*

Chris Williamson

Preach!

Jen Taylor

Do you think the evidence is strong enough to hold up in court today or don't you?

Chris Williamson

If you don't, then don't lean on that. Don't tell me your evidence is bulletproof and then walk backwards when we attempt to challenge it. I'm advocating *for you*; I want to put you on the stand and have you shine. If you're not prepared to do that, I would rather you just say *"I'm out"* from the very beginning and *not present your case.* Otherwise, you're wasting *everyone's time*, and what a sad thing that is.

Jen Taylor

There's a reason why we have, for example, the Sixth Amendment, a right to a speedy trial. It's because of *this very thing*, because witnesses pass away or forget, and the evidence is lost. Those are all things that have happened. In *this case*, it's been eighty-five years. I can't think of any example of someone being tried for a murder that happened eighty-five years ago; it just doesn't happen.

We're faced with this situation that isn't typical for the legal system, and we're having to come up with a way to solve this problem and answer a *legal question*. Is something *like this* hearsay or not? That's quite honestly never been addressed by the courts. We're being faced with a question like *that* that has no answer. If you're frustrated by the fact that the evidence for your theory might not be admissible in court because of this issue, well then, imagine what it must feel like to be awaiting trial as someone who's innocent and can prove it, but the government is taking its time and delaying while you're sitting in prison, and you're not being allowed to prove that innocence. Imagine that! And it happens *all the time*.

Chris Williamson

What's going to be argued in court next, and throughout the Japanese capture hypothesis, is that Amelia Earhart and Fred Noonan were casualties of war *well before Pearl Harbor*, they were executed under Japanese custody, and they should receive medals for that.

They should be recognized for that properly. If that was the case, what's sad about it is that Amelia Earhart *never got* her speedy trial; Fred Noonan *never got* his speedy trial. If these two were actually executed by the Japanese, then somebody should have paid the price for that. Somebody should have been tried for that, and this should have happened many, *many* years ago. We come along eighty-five years later, and we're working on the series, and we're trying to apply the rules of law to this very complex story.

Really, it's one of those things where, historically speaking, everybody needs to know the answer.

Everybody needs to know *the truth*. If you believe in what we're about to tell you, then you believe that two people *did die* terribly. Whether she died of dysentery alone in a jail cell in Garapan prison or whether she was executed and kicked into a grave and is buried somewhere on Saipan is almost irrelevant.

That is no way for an American icon's life to end.

It just gets me so *angry*.

It's no way for Fred Noonan's *life to end*, and I think it adds to the tragedy. I've read Fred Goerner's book, I've read Vincent Loomis's book, I've read Thomas E. Devine's book, and I've read Mike Campbell's book. I see the passion in what's being argued there. I see how invested they are in it.

I've talked to Dick Spink, and you'll hear from Les Kinney shortly. These are people who are all highly invested in the pursuit of the truth. The title of Mike Campbell's book is *Amelia Earhart: The Truth at Last*. What we're doing is very important here, and I think it should be taken very seriously because we're arguing, essentially, for two people's lives.

Yes, long gone by now, but that's not the point. When two people get executed, regardless of the time that has passed, I think it should be taken deadly *serious*.

Jen Taylor

Oh, I agree 100%. You mentioned that that's no way for an American icon to die. Well, that's no way for *anyone* to die. She was a *human*. Part of me thinks that if she weren't as famous as she was, and this exact thing happened to her, maybe we *wouldn't care*. Maybe we wouldn't even know or have any interest in talking about it at all, and that's what makes *me sad*.

We're at the beginning of this, and we haven't seen or heard any of the evidence yet. I'm still personally working through a lot of it and trying to decide what *I believe* happened and what could have happened. So I'm not making a comment on what I believe. But *I do* strongly believe that if this is what Mike Campbell and Fred Goerner say it is, then it is a deep failure of our government. It *really is*.

Chris Williamson

Absolutely. We need to do everything we can for this one. You're going to hear from people who say what happened to Earhart and Noonan was swept under the rug and covered up by the United States government and the Japanese government to some extent.

When all is said and done, we are a third party coming in and trying to investigate this as fairly and balanced as we can. Like *everything else* you're read up to this point, it's going to be up to you to listen to everything, hear this out, and make your decision. Will you be convinced? Is what you're about to read going to be *enough* for you? If I'm playing the devil's advocate here, I'm going to tell you there are major plot holes in this theory that you're going to read that won't make a lot of sense. There are some things that you can really question. You're certainly going to bring in somebody who's going to help you point out some of that a little later. I've been excited about some of the evidence that we're going to present and some of the eyewitness testimony that we're going to present.

It's *very powerful* eyewitness testimony, but can it be used?

Should it be used?

Or should it be thrown out? I think that's really the elephant in the room going into this piece.

Jen Taylor

And remember, the judge is the gatekeeper.

The judge is the one who gets to decide *what evidence you hear*. The judge is the one who decides issues of law. The jury decides issues of fact. So if you have a legal question or a legal issue that comes up during trial, you approach the judge. That's why when people make objections, the judge is the one who rules on those, because they are legal questions.

Can somebody say this?

Can this piece of evidence be admitted?

Things like that. The jury listens carefully to all of the evidence, and *then* at the end of the trial, they decide all issues of fact. In a criminal case, that issue is typically one question:

Is the defendant guilty or not guilty, as charged in the indictment? *That* is a question of *fact*.

Did it happen *this way*? Or did it *not*?

The reason why I bring this up is because the issue of hearsay has been debated just as much as the issue of whether or not this even happened the way Fred Goerner said it happened.

That's a legal question. Should a certain person's testimony be admitted into evidence even though they have passed away long ago? They're not here in court. They can't testify.

That is a question for the judge. The judge is the one who gets to interpret those rules, right?

What does the hearsay rule *mean*?

How do we apply it *in this case*?

What are the *exceptions*?

Do *any of them apply*?

In *this case*, we don't have a judge necessarily, so the reader has to be both judge and jury. We've been referring to our readers as the jury because, ultimately, we want them to decide what they believe happened.

Chris Williamson

After everything we've spoken about so far, let's address that elephant in the room. We talked about it a little bit when we introduced you to this series and this book, but now that we're really about to get into it, let's refresh that topic. What's hearsay?

Jen Taylor

For this trial, we're going to be using the Federal Rules of Evidence. The rule against hearsay actually has a pretty strict definition. Let me read from Rule 801:

> *"Hearsay means a statement that (1) the declarant does not make while testifying at the current trial or hearing, and (2) a party offers in evidence to prove the truth of the matter asserted in the statement."*

That's a pretty loaded definition, so I can break it down for everybody. The *first part* of this definition is, "The declarant does not make the statement while testifying at the current trial or hearing." Obviously, the declarant is the person who made the statement.

For example, if we have somebody on the stand, and they said, "Fred Goerner interviewed Josephine, and Fred said that Josephine said this," both Fred Goerner's statements and Josephine's statements are hearsay, because neither of them are in court testifying today.

That's the *first part* of that definition.

Chris Williamson

Let me ask you this, does it automatically disqualify everything, then, at that point?

Jen Taylor

No.

Chris Williamson

So what are some exceptions to that, then? Because that's a pretty straightforward statement.

Jen Taylor

Well, that's only the first part of the hearsay definition. In order to *be hearsay*, you have to meet the first part of the definition and the second part of the definition. The second part of the definition is that "A party offers in evidence to prove the truth of the matter asserted in the statement." Well, that's a big one too. Because if you're not offering that statement to prove what's called "the truth of the matter asserted," then it's *not* hearsay.

Let me just give you a simple example of what that means.

Chris Williamson

Okay.

Jen Taylor

Say, for example, we're probating a will. Someone close to you has died, maybe someone in your family, somebody you've known forever. *That person* has died. When you probate their will, to your surprise, you learn that person has given their entire fortune away to a complete stranger, somebody you don't know. You do a little bit of digging, and you find out that your loved one who died was losing their mind during the last part of their life. This mysterious stranger wiggled their way in, took advantage of that, and is now the benefactor of your loved one's fortune. So we're probating this will, and of course, the issue at trial is the state of mind of your loved one when they passed away. You want to admit a statement during your testimony that your loved one said, and it goes something like this: "I heard my deceased uncle say, two weeks before he died, that he had a vision in which Ronald McDonald from the McDonald's commercials came to him in a dream and told him that the Earth is flat, and that we were visited by UFOs." Some crazy story, whatever it is, right?

Chris Williamson

I think I'm following you so far.

Jen Taylor

Good, *stay with me.*

This is a *very oversimplified explanation,* but you're obviously not offering that statement to prove that the world is flat or that we were visited by UFOs. That's not the purpose of that statement. The purpose of that statement is to show that your uncle had lost his mental faculties at the end of his life. So that wouldn't be hearsay because in order for it to be *hearsay,* you have to offer that statement *in order to prove that the statement is true.* That's built into the definition of hearsay. *Why* you're offering the statement matters.

If those two prongs of the definition are met, *if it is hearsay,* does that mean it automatically gets thrown out? And the answer, of course, is *no,* because there are a number of exceptions to the hearsay rule. *A lot* of them.

Some of them are only exceptions to the hearsay rule if the witness is actually unavailable, and some of them are exceptions to the hearsay rule that can be used regardless of whether the declarant is available or unavailable.

For the record, being unavailable can be satisfied by just refusing to testify. Legally, that's enough. That's not a distinction I'm going to focus too heavily on because *all* of our declarations are unavailable. There are a number of commonly used exceptions to the hearsay rule almost to the point where the exceptions really swallow the rule. But they're all very specific, and they can only be used in very specific situations. Many of them are not going to apply here, and trust me, I've looked at this *a lot*. I've tried to fit a lot of these exceptions into this situation; a lot of them are not going to apply. One really important one in the Federal Rules of Evidence that I wanted to mention, because I think it could save us, is what's called "Rule 807." Rule 807 is just titled "Residual Exception." For Rule 807 to apply, the declarant *must be* unavailable. Like I said, for the most part, that's going to apply here. Most of our declarants are unavailable due to death.

Chris Williamson

Yeah, that's a big one.

Jen Taylor

So in order to use Rule 807, you have to overcome that hurdle, which I think we'll easily do. I'm going to read you the rule, and I want you to tell me what *you think about it.*

Chris Williamson

Okay.

Jen Taylor

Here's what the rule says: "Under the following circumstances, a hearsay statement is not excluded by the rule against hearsay even if the statement is not specifically covered by a hearsay exception in Rule 803 or 804." These are the circumstances. There are four:

1. "The statement has equivalent circumstantial guarantees of trustworthiness."
2. "It is offered as evidence of a material fact."
3. "It is more probative on the point for which it is offered than any other evidence that the proponent can obtain through reasonable efforts."
4. "Admitting it will best serve the purpose of these rules and the interests of justice."

Chris Williamson

I like that last one. And I like the second one.

Jen Taylor

All four of those prongs *have to be met before* you can use the residual exception.

Chris Williamson

Well, I understand that, but I think that "evidence offered in support of material fact" is going to be argued passionately.

Jen Taylor

Number four, "admitting it will serve the purposes of these rules," is arguable, we can argue about that, in the interest of justice. Is justice served by allowing this in? And then of course, number one, "the statement has the equivalent circumstantial guarantees of trustworthiness."

Chris Williamson

That's the entire case right there.

Jen Taylor

That's going to be debated. How can we guarantee it's trustworthy? For number three, "it is more probative on the point for which it is offered than any other evidence that the proponent can obtain through reasonable efforts," you have to show that you reasonably attempted to get this same evidence in another way.

Chris Williamson

Well, that's where the Freedom of Information Act comes in. You've had people like Les Kinney file hundreds of FOIA requests, and they've all been denied. Those would certainly qualify as reasonable attempts to try to obtain evidence.

Jen Taylor

I think that one's going to be easy to show, honestly. You have so many people who have made visit after visit after visit. I think we'll find that the people pushing this hypothesis have made more than reasonable efforts to show what they're trying to show through other means.

And so I don't think number three is going to be heavily litigated. I think that we can *probably agree* that prong number three has been met. But here's the other part of that rule, there *is* a notice requirement, which I think is interesting to mention. It says, "The statement is admissible only if before the trial, the proponent gives the adverse party," which would be *me*, "reasonable notice of the intent to use the statement." I have, obviously had more than adequate notice of your intent to use these statements. *But according to the rule*, you *also* have to give me the declarant's name and address so that I have a fair opportunity to investigate it. So that's a little technical requirement for Rule 807.

Chris Williamson

That's a technicality, and *I* don't worry about those.

Jen Taylor

This is not something that I see used a lot, at least not in state court in Texas, but I came across it. I think it's something that we should really talk about.

Chris Williamson

Well, it sounds like 807 is about to play a huge role in what our jury is about to read.

Jen Taylor

The question is going to be, *can it be used? Does it meet* the four prongs?

Chris Williamson

Like I said at the top of the segment, this is the most passionately argued and defended theory of them *all*. It's the one that's got the largest umbrella of all of them, and since this idea of *trial by jury* has been introduced, it's the one that's been most requested. How are you feeling going into this? Are you concerned; are you relaxed?

Jen Taylor

I'm feeling excited. It's a lot of stuff to dig through. Like I have always said from the very beginning, I think that the best way to get to the truth is to have zealous advocates on *both sides*.

I'm trying to do that. I'm trying to zealously defend against what you're going to put up.

I'm going to be doing the absolute best I can to convince our readers that it's not true. Not because *I've made up my mind that it's not true*, but because the only way to get to the truth is to have somebody really come at them with everything they've got and see how well this thing holds up.

Opening Statements

Chris Williamson

Good morning, ladies and gentlemen. When last we met, we spoke of Buka and the work Bill Snavely and his team are doing to try to identify a piece of aircraft wreckage off the coast there.

If you recall that story contained an eyewitness. An eyewitness who has become a large part of the credibility for that story. But what makes a story stick? What makes an anomaly stand out?

In the early 1960s, CBS reporter Fred Goerner got a tip that sent him to Saipan to investigate rumors that Amelia Earhart and Fred Noonan may have ended up there. When he arrived there, he quickly realized that this was much more than just a story. Dozens and dozens of eyewitness accounts from people all over the Marshall Islands, Saipan and even the military personnel stationed there in the years after would be enough to convince Fred Goerner that this was not a theory. This was the truth. In the time since then, hundreds have come forward with eyewitness accounts that put Amelia Earhart, Fred Noonan and their Lockheed Electra on Saipan.

Now, the defense will have you believe that the witnesses we're about to present are nothing more than ghost stories with no physical evidence to back them up. What *I* am going to prove is that these accounts are *so* compelling that by the time we're done here, like Fred Goerner himself, you will have absolutely no doubt in your mind that Amelia Earhart and Fred Noonan were the first casualties of World War II, and they should in fact be recognized as such.

What you hear today should make you angry. It should make you want to demand the information that is being purposefully and willfully withheld by our United States government.

I want you to think about Amelia Earhart. Think about Fred Noonan. American icons, treated like prisoners of war, being held to the most horrible of conditions, being interrogated as spies, and then being executed and tossed into a shallow grave like garbage.

These witnesses have been telling this truth since they first spoke with Fred Goerner in the 1960s. They continue to tell their story, the same story, many of them until their deathbeds. They told it to Thomas

E. Devine, to Bill Prymak, to Vincent Loomis, and to every other individual brave enough to seek the truth about what happened on July 2, 1937, and thereafter.

If this doesn't anger you today, then I haven't done my job. Do we have all the answers here?

No, we don't.

But should that stop us from using the information that we *do have* to seek the undisputed truth about what occurred in the moments after Amelia Earhart landed her Lockheed Electra in the Marshall Islands? Do we ignore the mountain of evidence that is screaming at us to pay attention and look closer?

We're in the endgame now.

Today, we don't present a theory or an idea.

Today we give you the ending to the story of Amelia Earhart and Fred Noonan.

Jen Taylor

Today, the project will try to prove to you that Amelia Earhart and Fred Noonan went down in the Marshall Islands, were taken captive by the Japanese, were transported to Saipan, and were later killed there.

Or maybe Amelia *wasn't killed.*

Maybe she died of dysentery.

It really depends on who you ask.

But that's the nature of a rumor, isn't it? Everyone is going to have a slightly different version of what happened. I have absolutely no doubt in my mind that the people of the Marshall Islands and Saipan believe this story, but the existence of folklore is not proof of historical fact. For that you need evidence. The key piece of the project's evidence is going to be the hearsay statements from dozens of so-called "witnesses" to Amelia and Fred's presence in the South Pacific. These alleged witnesses are not present here today. Many of them are no longer with us. Very few of these statements have been corroborated by physical evidence, but the project will tell you that they have no reason to lie, and will encourage you to trust them.

But what about Amelia's statements?

What about her last words?

I will leave you with a reminder, as I do before each trial, of the last thing she said: "KHAQQ calling *Itasca*. We must be on you but cannot see you, but gas is running low. Been unable to reach you by radio. We are flying at one thousand feet." An hour later, she says, "KHAQQ to *Itasca*, we are on the line 157/337. Will repeat message. Will repeat this on 6210 kilo cycles. Wait." Those last transmissions were received by the *Itasca* at signal strength 5, indicating that the Electra was very close, just as Amelia said they were. Not over eight hundred miles away at Milli Atoll. As we have seen already, other transmissions were sent out by someone who may or may not have been Amelia Earhart, but no one has ever been able to say for sure. This transmission that I just read to you is the last authenticated message she sent out before she disappeared forever.

So who do you trust, gossip and rumor?

Or Amelia Earhart herself?

At the end of this trial, I don't believe that will be a difficult decision.

"If we ever release the report of the Itasca *on Amelia Earhart, any reputation she's got is gone. I know now that Amelia Earhart disregarded all orders. If we ever release this thing, goodbye Amelia Earhart's reputation."*

Chris Williamson

The project calls *Mr. Rob Ellos* to the stand.

Jen Taylor

I'm going to object to this. The project intends for Mr. Ellos to discuss a number of alleged witnesses to Amelia and Fred's presence in the Marshall Islands and Saipan. None of those witnesses are present here today. This is all second- and thirdhand hearsay.

Chris Williamson

Judge, I believe this falls under Rule 807 as an exception to hearsay. Under Rule 807, hearsay statements may be brought in if they meet a number of requirements:

1. The person originally making the statement must be unavailable, *which is true.*
2. The statement has a circumstantial guarantee of trustworthiness, *which we'll prove.*
3. The evidence is offered as a material fact and the statement is better evidence than anything else we have been able to obtain through reasonable efforts, which *we'll also prove.*
4. And admitting the statement will serve the purpose of these rules and the interest of justice, which is the foundation for this case.

I believe all of these criteria have been met here.

. . .

Jen Taylor

First, the project has put up zero evidence yet, so I see no evidence that these statements are trustworthy, which you'd need before you can rule something admissible. Second, this hearsay evidence is basically the project's entire case. It is corroborated only by other hearsay evidence, and admitting it will entirely defeat the purpose of the rules of evidence.

Would you want to set a precedent that would allow someone to lose their life or liberty based on nothing but gossip and rumor?

Chris Williamson

No one's losing their life or liberty; this is not a criminal trial. This is a historical mystery, and I just want the truth. It's been eighty-five years. As I intend to show, there's a reason to believe physical evidence is being hidden and withheld. Counsel is wrong; we *do have* some corroborating physical evidence. I believe that the jury should be allowed to decide what to believe. They can't do that if they don't hear about the witness statements *first*.

Jen Taylor

If you let this in, you might as well completely throw out the rules of evidence. If you can't prove your case without hearsay, you have no case. How am I supposed to cross-examine witnesses who aren't here? I have a *right* to do that.

Chris Williamson

Again, this isn't a criminal trial.

Judge

I'm going to overrule your objection, Miss Taylor. Since this is a historical mystery trial and not a criminal trial, I think the jury should decide for themselves whether or not Rule 807 applies.

. . .

Chris Williamson

Thank you, Your Honor.

Jen Taylor

I'm going to request a running objection to Mr. Ellos's *entire testimony* as well as any reference to hearsay statements from witnesses who aren't present today.

Judge

Granted.

Chris Williamson

Mr. Ellos, we have a lot to get to today. You've been called to provide testimony before this jury regarding the eyewitness accounts of Amelia Earhart, Fred Noonan and their Lockheed Electra in and around the Marshall Islands and Saipan shortly after July 2, 1937. Now the way this is going to go, Mr. Ellos, is very simple. I have here a list of names that have been provided, and I'm simply going to give you a name and then allow you to tell our jury that person's respective account. Once we've finished with all the names, I'll give you the opportunity to summarize what all this means for the court. I'd like to begin today with Josephine Blanco Akiyama.

Rob Ellos

I talked with Josephine Blanco Akiyama twice in 2017. She's been on many TV shows, and her story is consistent. She said that as a young girl, on Saipan, when she was about eleven years old, she was taking lunch to her brother-in-law, Jose Matsumoto, who was working in a restricted area at Tanapag Harbor. She approached the gate, and she showed her pass to the gate guard, and she saw a Japanese seaplane land in Tanapag harbor. As she got closer to her brother-in-law, Jose Matsumoto, he and others said, "Come see the American woman!" When she got there, there was a tall, thin man, and there was a woman standing next to her who had hair cut short like a man and was wearing a man's shirt and trousers.

When Fred Goerner later on had heard of this story, which initially was told in the book *Daughter of the Sky* by Paul Briand, Goerner showed her several pictures of different women, including one of Amelia Earhart. Josephine picked Amelia out right away. She said, "That's it. That's the woman." Initially, when this story came up, Josephine told this story to her parents immediately after she came home, but they said, "Do not say anything about this." So she really didn't because they knew the Japanese were punitive about anything that might be secretive.

Years later, Dr. Casimir Sheft had her on Saipan as a dental assistant. When Josephine was working as a dental assistant, the subject came up between her and Dr. Casimir Sheft. He wondered if Amelia Earhart had ever come down into the islands, and Josephine told him the story: "I saw a white woman on Saipan before the war." Then of course, they started questioning her, and she told the same story she'd told all those years before. Paul Briand put it in a book. Fred Goerner saw an article from the *San Mateo Times* in California that said, "Local woman says Amelia Earhart held as spy on Saipan." Fred Goerner starts looking into this, and of course, after that, he made many visits to Saipan and a few other islands and started working on his book called *The Search for Amelia Earhart*. Goerner went there to look for more eyewitnesses among other things.

Chris Williamson

Now, Mr. Ellos, going forward, we're going to present the following accounts *chronologically*. What I mean by that is we're going to present them in the order in which they occurred so that we can paint a time-line for our jury today. This begins with Jororo Alibar and Lijon followed by Mrs. Clement and Queen Bosket Diklan.

Mr. Ellos, please continue.

. . .

Rob Ellos

Jororo Alibar and his friend Lijon were fishing near one of the three small Endriken islands just east of Barre Island in Mili Atoll. Mili Atoll has, like, ninety-two islands. It's the most eastern of the Marshall Islands and, again, a likely place for a plane to land if they were low on fuel. Well, Jororo Alibar and Lijon said that they saw a strange-sounding and strange-looking silver twin-engine plane approaching near Barre Island, and it was silent like it was out of fuel. They saw it semi-crash-land on the ocean side about one hundred yards east of Barre Island. It appeared that one of the wings was broken. They saw two individuals come out of the plane, and they got into a yellow boat that "grew." This is an important point: "A yellow boat that grew." Obviously, the natives had never seen an inflatable raft before, but it was on a manifest for Earhart and Noonan to have a rescue raft, and there are pictures you can see of her sitting and practicing with the oars.

Once they came ashore, they buried a silver container under a kanal tree. Shortly after that, some Japanese soldiers started arriving. Jororo and Lijon hid in the bushes so as not to be seen by the Japanese. It's important to note that the Japanese are very punitive of natives regarding anything happening that they saw. So they hid in the bushes and watched as two persons came forward. After a short while, the Japanese officer started arguing with the two persons, and he went and slapped one of them. When he did, the person screamed with the voice of a woman. They looked closer, and sure enough, it was *not* two men. One of them was a woman with hair cut short like a man and wearing a man's trousers. The next person to have seen the plane was a Mrs. Clement. She actually saw the Electra. Queen Bosket Diklan of Mili saw the plane as well.

Chris Williamson

Mr. Ellos, there was something specific about the plane that was interesting, wasn't there?

That brings us to Joro and Bill Prymak.

Rob Ellos

Bill Prymak, who was in the Amelia Earhart Research Association, sent me something called the Enajet document. If you look at Mili Atoll, it's kind of a like a big rectangle with some corners on it, and Barre Island and Endriekein Island are kind of the northwest part of Mili Atoll. Enajet Island is directly to the east.

Bill Prymak talked to a native named Joro who was one of the elders there. He said, one night, a Japanese naval ship came into the harbor. And he said, "Joro, I want you to gather together all of the able-bodied men that you can find, get in your boats and head for the channel near Barre Island." When they got there, what they saw was a Japanese boat with a barge on the back, and the barge had been tilted in the water, and there was an airplane on it. A twin-engine silver airplane with no military insignia. The winch was not powerful enough to actually pull the plane completely up onto the barge; part of it was dragging in the water. Joro said that the natives, almost forty of them, were pushing on the wing, the tail and the fuselage, and they were able to get it up on a barge. The Japanese officer had a meeting with the assembled natives from Enajet, and he told them, "Do not say a word of what has just happened. If you do, we will cut your heads off." This story wasn't repeated for many years until Bill Prymak was in the Marshall Islands and was told this by Joro, who was, by that time, one of the kings there on the islands.

Chris Williamson

Bilimon Amaron is one of the most well-known local accounts in support of this investigation, but it *wasn't* Amelia Earhart he interacted with. Can you tell the court about his account?

Rob Ellos

Bilimon Amaron was working as a medical corpsman in a naval hospital at Jaluit Atoll [in the Marshall Islands] when he was about eighteen years old. One day, midmorning, a Japanese naval ship came into the harbor, and the chief medical officer came along and said, "Bilimon, come with me in a little boat. We're going to go out to the ship. We're going to treat a man who has some injuries." When he got to the boat, he was very surprised. There was a woman with hair cut short like a man, wearing men's trousers, sitting on a deck chair. Sitting on a deck cover was a tall, thin man. The man had a cut on his forehead and a cut on his knee.

The cut on his knee was quite deep, so he applied something called PuraPly, a type of flexible bandage. He was very surprised at the man because he had blue eyes. Bilimon his entire life said that he had never seen a person with blue eyes. Noonan was known to have dark piercing blue eyes. The officers took Bilimon on to the back of a ship, and they showed him a two-engine silver plane with no military insignia. Bilimon knew Japanese military planes, and this was not one of them. They called the American woman pilot "Amira."

That's perfect for Amelia because many of the Japanese replace their *L*'s with *R*'s. If you tell a person who's Japanese to say "Palooza," they'll say "Parooza." So instead of saying "Amelia," he said "Amira."

Bilimon took care of that and then went back with the chief medical doctor. He also noted that the woman and man did not seem to be under any kind of duress or chains or anything like that. They were just freely sitting on a deck chair and deck cover. Bilimon has told this story to Bill Prymak and many other researchers over the years, and he's always told the same story over and over again. When he was near death, he told his son John Prymak to, "Please tell Fred and all the other researchers that the story I've told is true."

Chris Williamson

Up until his dying day, on his *deathbed* even, he never wavered from his original story?

Rob Ellos

No, he didn't.

Chris Williamson

Your Honor, at this time the project would like to enter its first exhibit: the dock photo at Jaluit found by Les Kinney in the US National Archives.

Jen Taylor

No objection.

Judge

Project's exhibit 1 is admitted.

Chris Williamson

Since at this point in the timeline, we've arrived at Jaluit, I think it's relevant to discuss the content of this image for the jury. Can you please do that now, sir?

Rob Ellos

Okay, I have the photo here. It says, "Photograph copyright Les Kinney, US National Archives." It's a photo of a tropical scene. It also says, "Marshall Islands, Jaluit Atoll, Jaluit Island, Office of Naval Intelligence No. 14381." When you look at this photograph, which has been widely distributed around the world, there are two things that really stand out: First, Fred Noonan. He's standing right near an electric telephone pole, and he has a very distinctive widow's peak. That was a part of his hairstyle. When I look at it, boy, it sure looks like Noonan to me. This man sure is a Caucasian. He's holding on to a little pole, and that might have to do with his knee. Remember he had a deeply cut knee, so he was probably favoring the other leg. Next to him, it looks like there are two Marshallese or Japanese. Then there's a person sitting on the dock with hair cut short like a man, wearing a shirt that does show a physique similar to Amelia Earhart's. She was fairly thin, and you can tell that *her face* looks Caucasian. Next is a woman with a long dress and long hair, a Marshallese woman, and another person, partially obscured.

The boat in the background is definitely the *Koshu*. This has been verified by many people, and I presume that shortly, Les Kinney will tell you that it was there at that time. On the back of the boat, you can see a barge with a plane that measurements have shown to be exactly the size of an Electra.

A Japanese blogger has said this was in a travel book that had a copyright date of 1935 on it, so it could *not have been* Earhart.

Well, the trouble with that is that the photo has these lines hanging in the air. You can see telephone lines and electrical lines.

Those were not put there until after 1936.

Additionally, the *dock* was not even there until 1936.

This is based on a statement made to a local elder by the Marshallese government. At the time of the photo, there was no actual Marshallese government. These were just Marshallese people under Japanese rule. The elders *did remember* that the dock did not start until 1936. Robert Siemens, who was given free run of the islands because he encouraged trade, *also said* the dock was not there until 1936. So 1935 is just something that had been put on this scrapbook. This in no way is a copyrighted book. It's a loosely bound scrapbook, and there's a few of them out there. It's tied with string, and there are some pages missing. So there may have been some additions. This is something that could have been put in later. In later editions, they seem to have stuck with the 1935 as kind of a floating copyright date, even though it's not an official book.

I really think it's Amelia Earhart sitting on a dock with Fred Noonan. To me, there are no signs of duress up to that point. They were not under Japanese custody. The Japanese probably did not have any orders to imprison them or shackle them or anything because, at that point, they were probably in a goodwill status. In fact, a newspaper article in Tokyo said that Amelia Earhart and Fred Noonan had been found on a Japanese fishing boat. The article caused widespread alarm in Japan and was quickly removed. Shortly after this dock photo would have been taken, they found out that Amelia was a hot potato, and they were not going to return her to the United States, but rather hold on to her instead. The Japanese military were not happy with the United States. A couple of years earlier, FDR had cut off 88% of their oil imports.

Just *think about that.*

He cut off 88% of their oil imports because they were militarizing the Pacific and getting ready to invade China. So when FDR made that cut, it really hurt Japan.

I think the people at the time said, "Return Earhart? **No way.**"

Chris Williamson

Moving on to further witness accounts, please tell the court about Mera Phillip and John Tobeke.

Rob Ellos

Mera Phillip was somebody who cooked and translated for Amelia when they were at Kwajalein, and John Tobeke also saw Amelia at Kwajalein. These are two people who directly saw her. Amelia and Fred were seen walking around from a causeway on Kwajalein in Roi-Namur. They fit the description of a woman with hair cut short like wearing man's trousers, and a tall thin man going across the causeway at Roi-Namur. There also was a native man who said he had gone out to a Japanese seaplane that had landed in the harbor.

He went out with a little boat and brought back some Japanese officers. He said, "There are two American spies: an American woman and an American man." When he was asked, "Where do they land?" He said, "Well, look at this tree, look at this house over here and look about halfway in between. That is the area there where the seaplane was. I had to go out and pick them up. They were called 'two American spies' by the Japanese, but that's all that I was told."

When the war came along and Kwajalein was taken over, there

were some troops who found a room fitted up for a woman. They found a suitcase with articles about Amelia Earhart, and a locked diary that said, "The 10-Year Diary of Amelia Earhart." This was W. B. Jackson and Victor Maghokian. They're the ones who claim to have found these in Kwajalein. I know Les will expand on them later, so I'll leave it for him.

Chris Williamson

How about Mrs. Joaquina Cabrera?

Rob Ellos

Mrs. Joaquina Cabrera worked at the Kobayashi Ryokan Hotel, in Garapan city. She knew of the American white woman who stayed there on the second floor. This is a place where a lot of times, they sent political prisoners. After a while, sometimes they'd send them on to Garapan prison, but sometimes they'd have them stay at the Kobayashi Ryokan Hotel, which is two stories tall. It was her job to wash Amelia's clothes, and of course, she saw her there several times.

Chris Williamson

The next witness actually *received something* from Amelia Earhart *herself.* Can you tell the jury about Matilde San Nicolas?

Rob Ellos

Yes. Matilde San Nicolas lived practically right next door to the Kobayashi Ryokan Hotel.

She saw Amelia a lot when Amelia was out for her walks to get some exercise. The Japanese guards of course followed her very closely. One time during those walks, Matilde gave Amelia some fruit. Matilde noticed that Amelia would have to go to the outhouse a lot, and that she appeared to have dysentery effects.

Amelia actually gave her her ring.

Years later, Fred Goerner and others came to look for the ring, but the ring was never recovered.

Chris Williamson

Jesús Salas had a very different experience with Amelia Earhart and Fred Noonan. Can you tell us his story?

Rob Ellos

Jesús Salas lived on Saipan. There's a nice picture of him and Father Conover in Goerner's book. Jesús Salas witnessed a processional of a native Chamorro on Saipan, and a Japanese naval officer spit on the processional as the ceremony was going by. Jesús started fighting with them, and as a result, they threw him in Garapan prison. While he was in Garapan prison, he saw and heard about a woman who was brought there and resided in a cell next to him. She was referred to as the "American white woman pilot."

He did not know her name, but they said she was a white American woman pilot and that she was a spy. Others have said that he actually knew of Noonan being way on the other end of the jail because they separated them.

Jesús observed that when the guards were out of range, Amelia and Fred would yell short phrases to each other. When the guards came back, they'd shut up.

That's how they communicated.

Chris Williamson

Antonio and Pedro Cepada along with Carlos Palacios.

Rob Ellos

These are people who live very close to the Kobayashi Ryokan Hotel. They saw her looking out of a second-story window there and saw that she was a white American woman.

Antonio Cepada, Carlos Palacios and Pedro Cepada all have testified to priests that they saw Amelia Earhart at the Kobayashi Ryokan
Hotel in Saipan. A lot of these witnesses, including Father Conover
and others, were very religious people. Catholicism was brought there
in a missionary status to the Chamorro. They're very religious people,
and they're unlikely to lie to a priest. Testimonies of those who were
willing to come forward were considered to be very trusted sources.

Chris Williamson

Mr. Ellos, let's continue the story and shift locations to Garapan
prison. This is a location that has become a cornerstone of this investigation. We come into contact with three additional witnesses here:
Sister Angelica, Sister Remedios Castro, and Dr. Manuel Aldan. Can
you tell the jury about their accounts of what occurred there?

Rob Ellos

My friend Jim Crowder worked in Saipan and Majuro in the
Marshall Islands, and he met Sister Angelica once. She told Jim that
she had been in prison a short time, and she saw an American woman
prisoner there, and she knew the woman's name was Amelia. They
met each other when they were let out in the courtyard to get some
exercise under Japanese guard. A lot of times, Amelia would smile at
her and nod, but generally, she looked like her mind was far away.
Sister Remedios Castro had not seen her, but she heard that her name
was Amelia. Furthermore, Dr. Manuel Aldan was a dentist on Saipan
who understood Japanese very well. He heard them talking about
Amelia a lot.

The last name they used was "Earharto."

One time he heard the Japanese officers joking that the American
men were chicken and not brave enough to come spy, so they had to
send a woman to come over and spy for them.

Chris Williamson

Before we transition to the military side, we have two final witnesses to discuss: Nieves Cabrera Blas and Anna Magofna.

Rob Ellos

Nieves Cabrera Blas was working on a local farm, and she said she saw Amelia Earhart arrive in a Japanese motorcycle in a sidecar. Amelia had her hands tied behind her back and was wearing a blindfold. There were other Japanese officers on motorcycles as well.

They came to a hole that had been dug near the farm that Nieves was working on.

They had Amelia Earhart kneel in front of the hole, and they tore the blindfold from her face.

They shot her, and Amelia fell back into the grave.

Nieves ran away so as not to be seen by the Japanese. Later on, she *did come back,* and the hole was filled up with dirt by this time. That was her testimony.

All this testimony has been given on TV, and it's also recorded in Joe Davidson's book *Amelia Earhart Returns from Saipan.* It's listed in there. What's interesting about a lot of these eyewitnesses is they've been on reel-to-reel film and videotape. There are signed documents by priests, they've had their words put in books, and many artifacts have been seen by people. There's a lot of evidence to support this being the way that Amelia lost her life.

On the other hand, some people say that she died of dysentery. It has been said that at the prison, Amelia and Fred were given a really weak Japanese soup called "miso." It's a lot like chicken noodle soup, but without chicken. It caused a lot of dysentery. So it might have led to her death from dysentery.

Anna Magofna said that she saw some motorcycles approach, and Fred Noonan, the tall thin man, was in one of those motorcycles.

They had him stop by a hole that had been dug, and they had him bend over.

They cut his head off with a samurai sword.

For many years, Anna was haunted by all the blood and how horrible it was to see the tall white man's head cut off.

Chris Williamson

We just laid out over a dozen accounts of the locals in the Marshall Islands and Saipan. It's important to note that what we just went over is *only a portion* of the witnesses found throughout these two areas.

It's easy for detractors to say that these people didn't know what they were seeing, and thus didn't know what they were recalling.

It's easy to say that they can't be trusted.

But there's *another aspect* of eyewitness testimony to this investigation. And that aspect is the United States military who were stationed in Saipan in the years after the disappearance. They have lots to add to this mountain of testimony that we've just gone over.

Mr. Ellos, please tell the court about Thomas E. Devine.

Rob Ellos

Thomas E. Devine arrived at the 244th Army Postal Unit in southern Saipan. There's an airfield that was called "Aslito Field" at that time by the Japanese. Lieutenant Fritz Liebig was his commander, and Thomas Devine was the second in command of the 244th Army Postal Unit. Shortly after they arrived, Lieutenant Liebig asked Tom to drive him up to Aslito field for a meeting.

They drove up in a Jeep, and as they came around the corner of what appeared to be an administration building, at a nearby hangar stood a man who was not military. He had a white shirt with an open collar, and he was not wearing a sidearm, which would be a must in a combat zone. He didn't appear to be military, but seemed to act with authority. He stepped forward with his hand upraised and said, "Halt, this is off-limits!" As they stopped the Jeep, they heard an angry marine officer shout, "What do you mean it's off-limits? We know Earhart's plane is there. What are you guys trying to pull?" Other people were saying that Colonel Wallace Greene had found the plane inside the hangar, and that plane was now locked in there. He considered that it was Amelia Earhart's plane. The angry marine went on: "What are they trying to pull? I suppose some guy sitting in Washington will get credit for finding the plane when our guys laid their lives on the line!"

Shortly after that, Tom went to the back side of the administration building where they had parked the Jeep, and when he got there, an MP told him, "You're going to have to move it; this place is off-limits." Tom asked this MP, "Is it true that Amelia Earhart's plane is inside the locker?" And he said, "Yes, but don't tell anybody I said so. I don't know why the heck they are keeping it safe; why they're keeping this covered up." Devine and Liebig got back in the Jeep, and they discussed the plane on their way back to the unit. When Tom got back to the unit, he thought he would check on the plane even though it was off-limits.

He and Private First-Class Paul Anderson of Chicago walked very carefully up to Aslito field and kind of stayed low so they wouldn't be noticed. When they got there, they saw a civilian two-engine silver plane sitting on a runway, and it had no military insignia on it.

They walked up on the wing of the plane, and he looked inside.

They walked on the back of the plane, and they read **NR16020** on the tail rudders.

They looked inside the back part of the plane and saw a lot of broken glass on the floor.

Suddenly, behind them, a photographer stood up from a crouch, took their picture and ran away. Anderson and Devine were looking at some containers full of gasoline, and they thought maybe the gasoline containers were to add some fuel to the plane. While they're doing this, the photographer again stood up, took their picture, and ran away. There was an airplane nearby in another hangar with its propeller idling, and out of the hangar came two people: one was a pilot with an aviator's helmet on, the other one was the man in the white shirt from earlier. The man in the white shirt had a bandolier full of ammunition over his shoulder. Later on, it was found out that it was James Nichols from the ONI, the Office of Naval Intelligence. They called him "the rabbit." He was very fast at coming up with surveillance on things.

Devine and Anderson went back to the unit because they didn't want to be caught. On the way back, they saw a sudden explosion to the north, and a huge fireball went up into the air. Devine ran really low by himself, and when he got there, the silver plane was being consumed in flames. Just before the explosion, they heard tracing bullets. They figured that those gasoline cans had been poured all over the airplane.

That was the main experience of Tom Devine, having seen the airplane.

Later, when he got back stateside, he wrote a book, *Eyewitness: The Amelia Earhart Incident*, and it didn't sell really well. But he *did* put an article in *Leatherneck Magazine*, which is the official magazine of the US Marines, and he asked if there was anybody back on Saipan in 1944 who had either seen Amelia Earhart's airplane or heard about her airplane.

Twenty-four GIs replied.

There were many who saw the plane there: Earl Ford, Arthur Nash, Jerrell Chatham, Robert Sosbe, Henry Duda, and Howard Ferris to name a few. I'm not going to go on, but there are many who replied to Devine and said, "Yeah, we saw Amelia's plane there, and some of us saw it torched and destroyed."

Someone else very important to all of this is a person named David Finlayson, who walked into a conversation in Washington, DC, between Franklin Delano Roosevelt, Henry Wallace and Harry Truman. He heard Roosevelt say they found Amelia's plane. Then he heard them discussing it a little bit, and shortly after, he heard Roosevelt pointedly say, "Destroy the airplane."

When Tom Devine tried to get ahold of David Finlayson to find out more about these comments made by Roosevelt, David Finlayson was furious. He said a federal officer came and picked him up at his house and took him to a red-brick building in Quantico, Virginia.

Once there, he reminded him that the Security Act of 1941 was still in effect for him, implying that if Finlayson said any more about the comments made by Roosevelt, he could lose a twenty-year government pension. No wonder he was furious with Devine.

. . .

Chris Williamson

Let's move on to Earskin Julious Nabers, please.

Rob Ellos

Julious Nabers was a code clerk on Saipan and overheard messages that they had found Amelia Earhart's plane on there. Of course, this is very interesting to him. He also later overheard that they were going to burn her airplane. So he and a few friends went and stood off at a distance at Aslito field, and it never happened. They went back to their unit, and again the next day, they heard the decoded message that they were going to burn Amelia Earhart's airplane. He and his friends went back, but *this time* they did it, and they saw it torched. As it turns out, in between those two days, he actually guarded the airplane for an almost twenty-four-hour period.

He had been told it was Amelia Earhart's airplane. During the night, some army brass came through in a Jeep, and they said they wanted to take a look at Amelia Earhart's airplane. Nabers said, "Orders are orders. I can't let you in." And they said, "Your orders will shortly be changed." They take off in a Jeep, and they never return.

Chris Williamson

Douglas Bryce.

Rob Ellos

When Douglas Bryce came back to the United States, he'd go to American Legion meetings, and he would tell them, "Hey, I saw Amelia's plane," and they used to laugh at him for that.

Later on, he hooked up with Rich Martini, and Rich Martini got him on videotape saying that he definitely saw the Electra on Saipan. That's *another* direct eyewitness.

Chris Williamson
  Robert Wallack.

Rob Ellos

Robert Wallack was coming ashore in the second wave during the invasion of Saipan near the town of Chalan Kanoa. Luckily, he made it ashore. They went to Mount Tapochau, which is the tallest mountain in Saipan, and they were trying to attack the Japanese who were there. Robert was a machine gunner and used his right hand. Unfortunately, on the way up Mount Tapochau, he got shot in his right hand. A few years ago, just before he died, he said, "When I look down, I can still see the scar here from where I got shot." He was not injured bad enough to have to go offshore to a medical naval ship, but he was not able to be a machine gunner because of it. So they sent him Garapan city, where some of the other injured were.

One day in Garapan city, he and eleven of his friends were looking around at old buildings for souvenirs. They were kicking things left and right. A lot of buildings had collapsed. Naval forces had been bombarding Garapan city for months and months, and the place was really a mess. They're looking for souvenirs, and they went by what looked like an administration building of some kind where the roof had caved in on the building.

They almost walked by it, but they looked back in a corner, and one part of the roof was being held up by something sturdy, so they decided to go investigate. They pulled away the shingles, tar paper, and boards, and there was some concrete and twisted steel as well.

Under all of that, they found a safe.

Robert told me the safe was about five feet tall and a little bit over three feet wide. It had two doors on it, and it had a handle with a lock. Of course, they tried to open it, but it would not unlock. Interestingly enough, they *did have* a demolition expert with them, and he applied some gel to the lock. They backed up and stood at a safe distance, and all was quiet.

Suddenly, there was a big explosion! Boards, steel, concrete, dust and dirt filled the air, and it took a while to settle down. When it finally did, Robert said he was the first one in.

He opened the doors of the safe, and he reached up on a top shelf, and he pulled out a briefcase. He turned to the guys and said, "Look at this! We're going to be rich in Japan! We're going to be zillionaires because this is going to be full of Japanese yen!" They started to open it, but when they did, to their surprise, there was no money inside. Instead, he found many of Amelia Earhart's passports to get in and out of various countries around the world. They found Amelia Earhart's maps and flight itineraries for where she was supposed to fly and her many stops around the world. Furthermore, he found health certificates for her and Noonan, their official papers letting them come and go from countries in order to prove that they didn't have tropical diseases, etc. Robert was really surprised by this because he asked, "What is this doing up here in a locked safe in Garapan city? I thought Amelia Earhart and Fred Noonan went down in the ocean thousands of miles away. These papers are bone dry; they've never been in water."

He wanted to keep it as a souvenir, but his buddies kept telling him, "Robert, they won't let you keep this. This is too important. They won't let you keep this; you've got to turn it in."

After a couple of days, he sided with his buddies, and he walked down onto the shore to give it to an officer. Officers on Saipan did not wear any military rank because snipers would take them out *first*, being in a chain of command. He approached a man on the shore who had what Robert called "scrambled eggs" on his cap. That's a reference to this gold emblem that was a symbol of authority. He gave the briefcase to the officer, and this officer actually wrote on a receipt: "Received from Robert E. Wallack: Amelia Earhart's briefcase with passports, permits, etc."

That was the last time that Robert Wallack saw the briefcase, but it was not the last that *any soldier* saw it. Julious Nabers said that he saw the briefcase being picked up by the man in a white shirt, James Nichols, near a command post. He saw him pick up the briefcase and head out with it. I'm sure Robert really prized this receipt showing he had Amelia Earhart's effects, but when he went to Okinawa, he was shot in the leg, and it was a very serious injury. They were pulling off his clothes to try to save his life with this grievous injury, and he kept saying, "Save the money belt!"

In all the confusion of them trying to save his life, the money belt was lost.

Chris Williamson

Having laid out all of these witnesses for you here today, we've established far more than a running story. We've established a timeline of consistency with dozens and dozens of people all saying the same thing. And I know what you're thinking: people make up stories.

This is just a bunch of locals and a handful of military personnel hearing a rumor and spinning it into the greatest multilayered story ever. It couldn't possibly go beyond that, right?

Admiral Chester W. Nimitz, Mr. Ellos.

Rob Ellos

Chester W. Nimitz was the commander of the fleet in the Pacific in the war against Japan. In talking to Fred Goerner, Fleet Admiral Chester W. Nimitz said, "Now that you're going to Washington, Fred, I want to tell you, Earhart and her navigator did go down to the Marshall Islands and were picked up by the Japanese." Furthermore, General Alexander A. Vandergrift was told by General Tommy Watson that it had been substantiated that Miss Earhart met her death on Saipan. I've *seen* his handwritten letter.

In addition, Admiral James Russell was told that Amelia Earhart was captured by the Japanese and died on Saipan. General Graves Erskine told two KCBS newsmen, "I'm telling you; Earhart was on Saipan. But that's all I'll tell you. You'll have to dig out the rest on your own."

Chris Williamson

Mr. Ellos, we've only covered a portion of the enormous eyewitness accounts for this investigation here today. What does all this say to you, an expert who has dedicated their life to the study of this case and all the investigations contained within it?

Rob Ellos

There are forty-one documented eyewitnesses who saw and accurately described Amelia Earhart, Fred Noonan, their plane, or their artifacts. We have this photograph of them standing by Japanese soldiers near the aircraft. We have written testimonies that were taken by priests. So these things are all documented. You can see these online; you can see films; you can see the writings and many books. There's a very high consistency of these eyewitnesses' accounts. Keep in mind that Amelia Earhart would have been a very unusual-looking woman in Saipan and the Marshall Islands.

There was a Russian woman writer who was blonde haired who was on Saipan for a while, and we also know of a white family who came there from Guam for a very brief time. But here, we're talking about a very strange-looking woman. The women in the Marshall Islands and Saipan, according to Les Kenney and Jim Crowder, were generally short to medium height, whereas Amelia Earhart, she was very tall. I'm not knocking anybody's body type here, I'm just being descriptive, but both of these experts said that the Chamorro women in the Marshalls and Saipan generally had a heavy-bodied to plump body type, whereas Amelia was rail thin. Their skin color in both the Marshalls and Saipan was brown, whereas Amelia's skin was very white. So you've got a woman who looks very unusual for the area, and you have the fact that woman pilots were unheard of in Japan. It would have been a very strange thing to call her "American woman pilot."

I think the high consistency of these eyewitness accounts to both Amelia and Fred, along with what the airplane looked like, "silver two-engine airplane with no military insignia," is very telling. And that's before we add the fifty-one documented eyewitnesses accounts. I know the number *two hundred* has been bandied about, and that's probably very close to the overall number. But a lot of those are prob-

647

ably undocumented as to who exactly they are. Fifty-one of those *are documented eyewitnesses*, and I think that's very strong.

I've studied all the different scenarios for what might have happened to Earhart and Noonan, and this is the one that I would stake my life on if I had to. From Goerner to Mike Campbell to Les Kinney, the government has suppressed all efforts to get information. The government knows what happened to Earhart. They knew long ago in 1937, they knew more in 1944, and they know *now* and are refusing to inform us.

Chris Williamson

Thank you, Mr. Ellos. Pass the witness, Your Honor.

Cross-Examination of Rob Ellos

Jen Taylor

You guys started with Josephine Blanco Akiyama. I understand that she gave a pretty consistent statement from the first time she was talked to, all the way up to her death. My understanding is that she saw a plane go down in a harbor at Saipan. Am I right about that?

Rob Ellos

She said she saw a plane land in the water in the harbor, yes.

Jen Taylor

You told Chris that she said she saw a *seaplane*. Did she say she saw a seaplane?

Rob Ellos

There can be different versions of her account.

Jen Taylor

This is one thing I want to make sure that I clarify. Some of the accounts I have read have said that she saw an airplane crash in the water, which of course is very different from a seaplane landing in the water. If a landplane crashed in the water, those are two very different things. Do you know whether she said "crashed" or whether she said "landed," either then or now or at any time in between? Do you know whether she clarified her statements by stating definitively, "I definitely saw a seaplane," or, "I saw a landplane that crash-landed in the water?" Or is this just an interpretation from others who have interviewed her and read her statements? It must have been a seaplane because it was in the harbor as opposed to being in the airfield.

. . .

Rob Ellos

I don't know her exact statement on that. Her main details regarding Earhart are definitely consistent. The main thing is that when she got by her brother-in-law, he said, "Come and see the American woman!" She saw a woman with hair cut short like a man, wearing trousers like a man, standing by a tall, thin man. That's the most important part of her story. Whether the plane crashed into the harbor or whether it made a seaplane landing, the most important part is how she described the woman and that she was able to pick her out from the pictures provided by Goerner. Goerner brought her several pictures of women, and she easily picked Amelia out.

Jen Taylor

How did her brother-in-law know that it was an American woman as opposed to some other nationality?

Rob Ellos

It's just something he said.

Jen Taylor

I want to ask you about the photo identification. When was that done, and who was the one who showed her the photos?

Rob Ellos

Fred Goerner was the one who went over to Saipan and questioned her. He showed her these photographs. I don't know the exact date; some research would have to go into that.

Originally, he heard of this from the *San Mateo Times,* and she lived in San Mateo, California. He became interested in this, and he interviewed her. He showed her these pictures, and she picked Amelia out really easily.

· · ·

Jen Taylor

How did the *San Mateo Times* find out about her and this story?

Rob Ellos

I'm not sure. There was a reporter there named Linwood Day. She probably approached the newspaper with this information, that would be my guess. And it *is* a guess.

Jen Taylor

Was she actually living on the mainland at that point, or was she still on the island?

Rob Ellos

She was on the mainland, and her picture was on the front page of the newspaper. It was the headline of the newspaper.

Jen Taylor

When Fred Goerner initially spoke to her, she had already spoken to the *San Mateo Times*, and that paper had already linked her story with Amelia Earhart. So Fred Goerner *was not* the first person to mention Amelia Earhart's name to her?

Rob Ellos

No, he heard about this article from the *San Mateo Times* at KCD3, which was the news organization and radio station that he worked for that wanted him to look into it, and he did so. That led to many trips to Saipan and talking with Catholic priests and others who helped him interview people who were on Saipan.

Jen Taylor

I'm sure I know the answer to this, but do we still have the photos that he used to do the photo identification? Do we know how many of them there were, or what the other photos looked like? I'd love to be able to show them to our jury so they can see these images for themselves.

Rob Ellos

I have never seen the pictures presented anywhere. I've only seen them described in his book. I've never heard any experts mention that the pictures were published or shown in any books.

Jen Taylor

But *it is* possible that since she was living in California and had already spoken with the *San Mateo Times*, Earhart's name had already been thrown around in connection with her story. *It is* possible that she had seen a picture of Amelia Earhart *before* Fred Goerner approached her and knew *exactly* who she was. That would have certainly influenced which picture she picked out, correct?

Rob Ellos

Yeah, that's possible.

Jen Taylor

You guys talked about Jororo and Lijon earlier. To refresh the court's memory, these were the two men fishing near Barre Island on Mili Atoll. They actually may have witnessed the plane go down. How far away would you say they were from the beach?

Rob Ellos

I would say they were about three to four hundred feet away, somewhere in that range. They described the plane as being quiet, like it was out of fuel, and that it came down with a huge splash in the water. If they said a "huge splash," it could not have been miles away; it would have been close to them. Also, they did say that when the pilots came ashore, the first thing they did is bury a silver container near a kanal tree. So they must have been pretty close initially, or they might have moved closer.

Jen Taylor

Did anyone ever go back and find that same spot and attempt to look for whatever it is that was buried under the tree?

Rob Ellos

Yes, there was a person who went back and dug it up, and they found a rusty, small object maybe about the size of a lighter. I don't think any positive identification was made on that.

Jen Taylor

And you don't remember who found it?

Rob Ellos

I believe it was someone named Oliver Knaggs.

Jen Taylor

Do you know where that rusty object is now?

Rob Ellos

I do not.

. . .

Jen Taylor

In your description of their account, you say that they saw two individuals, and one of them screamed when they were hit. That made them think that one of them was a woman and one of them was a man. Did they ever give any physical description of them? How tall, how large or small, their hair or anything like that?

Rob Ellos

Initially, they just thought they were two pilots. They were surprised that one was a woman. When they looked closer, they saw that her hair looked short like a man.

Jen Taylor

But they couldn't visually verify that that was a woman. So as far as we know, it could be either a woman or a man who screams like that.

The two next witnesses that I want to ask you about are Mrs. Clement with no first name and Queen Bosket Diklan. You mentioned before that both of them saw the Electra. What were the circumstances of that? Because that was glossed over.

Rob Ellos

There is very little information on that. It was brought forward that Mrs. Clement had seen it, her husband was mentioned, and there was never a first name given to her. Queen Bosket Diklan was interviewed by people, and she said during those interviews that she also saw that silver airplane. There's very little information from those two, to my knowledge.

Jen Taylor

Do we know if they gave a description of a plane that they saw? Or if they saw a photo or anything like that?

. . .

Rob Ellos

No, I don't know. Again, there's very little information; it's just mentioned in research books and some things.

Jen Taylor

Okay. Do you know roughly when either or both of these women were interviewed?

Rob Ellos

I don't know when they were interviewed.

Jen Taylor

Do you know when Jororo and Lijon were interviewed?

Rob Ellos

I don't know that either.

Jen Taylor

Next, you mentioned that Bill Prymak talked to Joro, and this is actually a different person than the person who was fishing on Barre Island, correct?

Rob Ellos

Right. Joro lived at Enajet Atoll, which is much farther away; it's on the other side of Mili Atoll.

Jen Taylor

When did Bill Prymak interview him?

Rob Ellos

I don't know the exact dates of when Bill Prymak interviewed Joro, but he did send me a document called the Enajet document that he had made up that described what Joro had said happened.

Jen Taylor

He described what appears to be a plane that's very similar in description to the one that crashed into the ocean seen by the two men: a twin-engine silver airplane with no military insignia. I don't know a whole lot about planes, so can you tell us how common it would be to see a twin-engine silver airplane in the Pacific? Is that a common descriptor of planes that would fly around in that area?

Rob Ellos

I don't know. I would not be an expert in that area.

Jen Taylor

The fact that it had no military insignia, does that indicate that it was a civilian plane? Or could it have been a military plane that was flying incognito?

Rob Ellos

It could have been that, yes.

Jen Taylor

The next witness you guys talked about was Bilimon Amaron. What did he do for a living?

. . .

Rob Ellos

At the time, he was a junior medical corpsman in the hospital on Jaluit. He is one of the key witnesses. He's been interviewed probably by more researchers than anybody, and his story never wavered.

Jen Taylor

I have a question about Fred Goerner. He was the first one out there, and he wrote this bestselling book about it. My understanding is that after all of the research he had done, he came to the conclusion that the Marshall Islands were not involved, which means that he had to have decided that he didn't believe this story after all. Can you tell us why that might have been? Why didn't Fred Goerner buy this story if he's such a strong witness?

Rob Ellos

I can't recall Goerner being in touch with any Marshall Island eyewitnesses, and I can't recall Goerner ever going to the Marshall Islands.

Jen Taylor

So he actually never interviewed any of the Marshallese himself?

Rob Ellos

I can't remember Goerner going into the Marshalls at all. That was just an opinion of his, I think, based on a tip he received: "Maybe it's better if you're searching the Marshall Islands." There was good reason to say that. They didn't want reporters snooping around Saipan because in the northern part of Saipan, there was an illegal guerrilla warfare training base called the NTTU, where the United States CIA and such were training either Chinese or Korean insurgents to go and

657

fight against the Japanese. That was illegal and something that the United States, being a part of the League of Nations and such, was not something that was permitted. So I think the tip he got saying, "Maybe you're better off searching the Marshall Islands; I heard that they may have come down there," was an idea and perhaps a diversion too.

Jen Taylor

I guess I'm just trying to understand why he would come to that conclusion after all the research he had done. Even though he may not have personally interviewed Amaron or some of the other Marshallese, he indicated before he died that he didn't believe the Marshall Islands were part of this story.

Correct me if I'm wrong, but he's done more work on this than anyone. So I've been really trying to understand why he changed his mind about the Marshall Islands, especially when you're telling me that we have *such strong witnesses* there.

Rob Ellos

I don't really know why he changed his mind.

Jen Taylor

Was Fred Goerner able to use any witnesses from the Gilbert Islands who could corroborate this theory of his?

Rob Ellos

I don't think in his book, he said anything about the Gilbert Islands. This is something he said when he was very old. It may have been mentioned that Eugene Vidal and William Miller had told Amelia that if she missed Howland, she should try to turn back west and head for the Gilbert Islands and try to land on the beach there somewhere. During the time his book was written and published, he was not of that view. That is something he changed later in his life. Again, this was surprising to Mike Campbell and myself. I don't know where he came up with this idea that they had landed in the Gilbert Islands. It may have been a hunch, or it may have been some of his later research that led him to think that way.

Jen Taylor

Going back to Amaron's description of the two Americans he saw, first of all, did he ever indicate that he knew for sure that they were Americans? Did someone tell him that?

What was his description *exactly* of their nationality or ethnicity?

Rob Ellos

He said that the people on board the naval ship were surprised that there was an American woman pilot, because women pilots were unheard of in Japan.

Jen Taylor

Okay. So he heard from *someone else* that this was an American woman pilot?

Rob Ellos

Somebody on the ship told him that it was American woman pilot, yes.

Jen Taylor

Other than her short hair and her wearing men's trousers, did he provide any more detail regarding her physical description?

Rob Ellos

No, he didn't.

. . .

Jen Taylor

Regarding the man he was treating, we know that he noticed his blue eyes; you mentioned that during direct. Did he give any other physical description regarding height, weight, or hair?

Rob Ellos

No, there were no other descriptions that I can recall other than that these were some of the first white people he had ever seen. But he was really surprised at the blue eyes. That really struck him.

Jen Taylor

This is something that we hear very often; Fred and Amelia would have been the first white people in this area or amongst the first white people in this area.

Rob Ellos

The only white people in the mandated islands in the Marshall Islands were priests and nun missionaries. According to my friend Jim Crowder, who was a tenant of Bilimon Amaron actually, Bilimon was his landlord on Majuro in the Marshalls for one year. A man named Robert Reimer, who was a white person, was there. The Japanese would not allow inter-island travel, but they *did let* Robert go because he was clever with industry and such, and he encouraged trade among the islands. He manufactured some things, and he helped encourage trade, so they let him move about freely because they trusted him. Another gentleman, Carl Heine, was an educator, and *he was* a white person. But there were no other white people on the islands that I know of. On Saipan, there was a white family there briefly who came from Guam. For a while, there was a Russian nationalized writer there as well. But there were very few white people in the Marshalls.

Jen Taylor

Do we have photos of the Russian writer?

Rob Ellos

I've never seen a photo of the Russian writer.

Jen Taylor

The next thing you guys talked about was the Jaluit dock photo. I know you already discussed the obvious question that I would ask, which is, of course, the claim that came after it was released that it was found in a book that was published in 1935. When Chris asked you about it, you mentioned electrical lines and a dock that were not there until 1936.

My question is, is there anything else in the photo that can narrow down that date? I understand that you and others believe that Amelia and Fred are in that photo, but just taking that out for a moment and dating the photo *generally*, is there any other way that we can do that?

Rob Ellos

Les Kinney has said that he has records from the *Koshu Maru* being there in July of 1937, and it's clearly seen in the background of that image. And of course, that would be the period in which Earhart disappeared. July 2 would have been the day they semi-crash-landed at Mili Atoll. So this would have been many days later that they were brought there by boat.

Jen Taylor

Were there any other times that the *Koshu* was there that would explain it being in this image?

Rob Ellos

I don't know. Movement of Japanese naval and survey vessels is not my big area of expertise.

Jen Taylor

If this is a picture of Amelia and Fred as some claim, why is it that we don't see many or *any* Japanese military in the picture? Why do we mostly see civilians?

Rob Ellos

They would not have been in trouble at that point. The Japanese at that point had a newspaper article come out very quickly in Tokyo that Fred Noonan and Amelia Earhart were found by a Japanese fishing boat, and then the article was retracted immediately.

In fact, the Japanese were probably thinking that a goodwill mission was going to occur.

They were going to take Earhart and Noonan and maybe bring them to Tokyo and then bring them back to the United States as a kind of goodwill-type gesture. However, after this photo was taken, the Japanese military probably thought, "Earhart and Noonan are spies," because they had a real spy fetish. Anybody who landed in the mandated islands would have been prohibited. They would not let us search the islands when Earhart went down there in any way. They considered all foreign people spies. The Japanese military probably changed their mind and said, "No, they're spies. We're not going to release them."

That would have been the start of Amelia's troubles. At this point on the dock though, the only distress showing is that Noonan seems to be holding onto a pole due to his knee injury.

Bilimon Amaron said that he had a big gash in his knee. He said that the woman did not appear to be in any distress. He certainly did not mention anything about shackles around their ankles or their hands being tied or cuffed or anything of that nature. At this point, Earhart and Noonan probably thought, "Hey, we're going to be returned to the United States," and the Japanese were probably thinking about this too until the military stepped in.

Jen Taylor

So we have Amaron, who claims that Amelia and Fred were not in distress, everything is fine so far. Is that then inconsistent with Jororo and Lijon's sighting where they come on to the beach, they're immediately accosted by Japanese soldiers, and one of them even hits her?

Rob Ellos

It could be inconsistent, yes, but that could also have been a junior soldier who was trying to interview her and slapped her for intimidation purposes. People in charge might have said, "We're not going to strike these people. They're not going to be treated as hostages yet. We're going to see what Tokyo says, and what the Japanese military says." The act of slapping her was done by an individual person, and I don't think that act necessarily represented the position of the Japanese government or military.

Jen Taylor

Kwajalein, where is that?

Rob Ellos

Kwajalein is a little bit farther up in the Marshall Islands. The Marshall Islands have a western side of islands that go down in a line and an eastern side of islands that go down in a line. Kwajalein is on the western side. It's quite a bit of ways above Jaluit. That's where they were seen next, according to research by Mike Campbell, based on research in a magazine or article, rather a newspaper article, called *The Kwajalein Hourglass*. This is where Mike first heard about it.

· · ·

663

Jen Taylor

Next, we have, based on your conversation with Chris, three more witnesses. We have Phillip, Tobeke, and Jackson.

Rob Ellos

Yeah, Phillip is a witness who translated and cooked for Amelia. Mr. Tobeke also saw her there, and then the old native man said that a Japanese seaplane landed, and he went out with a boat and brought back what *he said* were two American spies. The person interviewing at the time pointed to an area between some trees and between the beach and a house just approximately where he had to go out and get them.

Jen Taylor

Do we know the date to any degree of specificity? I know that the story goes that they first landed near Barre Island, then they went to Jaluit, then they went to Kwajalein, and finally, Saipan.

Rob Ellos

No dates that I'm aware of.

Jen Taylor

Okay. I'm just curious why Jaluit before Kwajalein and not Kwajalein before Jaluit. Is it just the geography that makes it make more sense?

Rob Ellos

It's a lot closer, especially if they were towing the Electra behind them. They likely wouldn't have dragged the plane up to Kwajalein. In fact, they probably hoisted it onto the ship after a little while and let the barge do the work because it was a barge that was local or belonged to people in the area at either Mili Atoll or most likely Jaluit.

. . .

Jen Taylor

You discussed a physical description of the woman given as a woman with short hair, alongside a tall, thin man. Is that the extent of the descriptions we have from Kwajalein witnesses?

Rob Ellos

I can't even recall anybody giving the descriptions. Only Mera Phillip saying that she translated for Amelia and cooked for her, and Mr. Tobeke says he saw her. There was an eyewitness, not mentioned, who saw them walking the causeway between Roi and Namur.

That's an area that we fought in during the war. At the time, someone said they saw a tall, thin man and woman walk across the causeway from Roi to Namur. It's like a low-lying bridge near the water. No names were given, and no time, date or anything else was given.

Jen Taylor

To follow up on that, we do have a lot of witnesses later on Saipan who include talk of a bandage around Noonan's head, but no one really ever mentions a bandage around his knee or that he's walking with a limp or a stick maybe. Is that an issue for you when you're assessing these witness statements?

Rob Ellos

It is, yes. I don't know about the bandage on his head. If they saw a bandage separately, there probably was a need for it. Noonan may have reinjured himself or fell and hit his head or something. It could also be an inconsistency.

Jen Taylor

What about the fact that no one mentioned anything regarding his knee or mentioned him walking with a limp? To you, would that mean that it couldn't be Fred Noonan, or do you think there's an explanation as to why no one noticed an injury to his leg that was apparently very serious?

Rob Ellos

I don't know why they didn't notice that. I think maybe on Saipan, their focus was not on Noonan as much as it was on Amelia because she was so unusual looking with all her different physical features and what she would have been wearing. They could have missed a limp on Noonan and not paid as much attention. I cannot say that the limp was or wasn't there while they're on Saipan, but the big focus seemed to be on Amelia Earhart.

Jen Taylor

Who found the supposed bedroom that was fitted for a woman with Amelia's suitcase and diary?

Rob Ellos

W. B. Jackson and Victor Maghokian.

Jen Taylor

Do we know that she had a suitcase that matched the description?

Rob Ellos

We know she had a briefcase that had her official papers in it. I read a quote from her in that she carried a small amount of clothing from Lae. It could have been in a suitcase, but I don't know what they had at that time as far as luggage. I would think a suitcase would be a very common object. I just don't really know. It's a little surprising that she would carry articles around about herself. She knew who she was. As far as the diary, I don't know. That's a hard one to discuss.

Jen Taylor

We know that she *did* keep a diary. I might be wrong about this, but my understanding is that it was sent back with some of her other things and published later.

Rob Ellos

Yes, they wrote a book. A ghostwriter named Janet Mabie wrote the book and put the notes together, and Amelia's husband, George Palmer Putnam, took credit for it. He said that *he* was the author. They put together all her notes from along the journey and such, and they made a book called *Last Flight* that was published after the disappearance.

Jen Taylor

Does it make sense, then, that she would have kept a second diary on her trip? Like you said earlier, they were trying to reduce weight load. It doesn't make sense that she would have (a) kept two diaries and then (b) kept one and sent the other one back.

Rob Ellos

I don't think she would have taken a diary with her, but again, that's just my opinion. It could have been a quirk and something she decided to do. After all, she was the most famous woman in the world at the time. After her disappearance, she was even more famous.

Jen Taylor

Assuming that this *did happen*, and that this was her room and her stuff, the briefcase was found in Saipan. What scenario would explain her leaving behind her clothing and her personal items but taking her documents and papers? Why not leave those behind as well?

Rob Ellos

She left her notes at Khartoum and all kinds of different places around the world. She landed on five continents, she had twenty-two landings and takeoffs, and she left notes at each of those places.

Jen Taylor

But this is an entire suitcase, and it seems like a very nice one.

Rob Ellos

If they say it was a suitcase, I'd depict it as being a nice and decent-sized suitcase.

Jen Taylor

You said it was leather matte and embossed in gold.

Rob Ellos

Oh no, I'm talking about the leather map case that was found at the airport hangar at Kwajalein.

Jen Taylor

Okay, so that was *not* found in her room?

Rob Ellos

No, they found a leather map case, a case for carrying aviation maps and such, with "AE" embossed in gold really big on it. She always described herself as "AE."

Jen Taylor

So a suitcase *and* a map case were left behind?

Rob Ellos

There was a map case found at Kwajalein, and the person who discovered it said, "She was here, all right." They had been scrounging around for stuff, and they found that leather map case there.

Jen Taylor

And when was the stuff found?

Rob Ellos

This was found during or after the war by US soldiers. Remember in the mandated islands, we weren't allowed there at all. Nobody was allowed there. These were all things that after were discovered both after and during the war when soldiers were able to go to each place and look. These are things that were found, and these were the stories that were told.

Jen Taylor

We're talking mid to late 1940s?

Rob Ellos

I would say so.

Jen Taylor

For this stuff to have been hers, it would have had to sit in this bedroom and in this hangar essentially *undisturbed and untouched* for ten years, even though there was a war raging on?

Rob Ellos

Well, 1937 until 1942 or something. I'm not sure. But yeah, it would have sat there and been deemed important by somebody.

Jen Taylor

I'm sure you know where I'm going with this, of course. The artifacts that we've been discussing, the suitcase, the map case, and the personal diary: do we know where those things are today?

Rob Ellos

No. We have no idea. I would guess that they're in the National Archives. As far as the map case goes, that could have sat there for all those years because they said they found it in some rubble in the corner of a hangar. The suitcase would have been larger, and whether Mera Phillip thought that was significant to keep that could have played into it.

It's a long time for that big an item to be hanging around.

Jen Taylor

The next witness on your list was Mrs. Joaquina Cabrera. She worked at a hotel in Garapan city. What was the name of that hotel?

Rob Ellos

The Kobayashi Ryokan Hotel.

· · ·

Jen Taylor

Her job was to wash clothes. Several times, she says she saw a white woman who stayed there on the second floor.

Rob Ellos

Yes. She saw Amelia many times, she said.

Jen Taylor

Other than saying this was "a white woman," did she ever give a description?

Rob Ellos

A white woman, that's all she said.

Jen Taylor

Did she say she was an *American* white woman?

Rob Ellos

That I can't recall. That's something I would have to research.

Jen Taylor

So we're not sure if she did, but those who *did say* "I saw an American white woman" as opposed to just *a white woman,* how was it that *they knew* that she was from America?

Rob Ellos

It might have been gossip by local people who lived there. It might have been a slip by Japanese officials or military police. It's hard to know. There's also another woman who washed her clothes, a second woman, and she also said she saw her there many times in a second-story window. She saw Fred Noonan there initially as well.

Jen Taylor

She didn't give a name? Her identification wasn't, "I saw Fred Noonan"? She just said she saw a male companion?

Rob Ellos

A male companion, yes.

Jen Taylor

She washed her clothes. Did she ever at any time give a description of the types of clothes she was washing?

Rob Ellos

One of the articles of clothing that she had was a leather flying jacket. She called it that. She mentioned it was stiff, so she couldn't wash it in the normal way. She rubbed it with some kind of wooden board and soap or something like that. She rubbed it and washed it with water and soap, but it was "made out of leather," she said.

Jen Taylor

Okay, and did she ever speak to the woman, or did she just see her?

Rob Ellos

I can't recall.

Jen Taylor

The next witness that you guys talked about was Matilde San Nicolas. You say she lived next door to the hotel, and that she would see a woman come outside under guard watch to get exercise in the courtyard. The first thing I want to know is, did she ever give a description of this woman? Because according to my notes and conversation earlier, you're saying, "She saw Amelia." Who did she *actually* see?

Rob Ellos

I think she knew that she was an American white woman or at least a Caucasian, and that she knew the woman had geographical information because she shared it with her daughter, and she gave her daughter a ring. I just can't recall her version of the description.

Jen Taylor

My image of what's going on here is that there's probably a private residence next to this hotel, and there's, in my head at least, a fence separating the two. Maybe they would go talk at the fence, and she might get a piece of fruit at the fence. Do you think that's an accurate idea?

Rob Ellos

I would say that regardless of there being a fence there or not, they certainly communicated to the degree that she offered Amelia some fruit, and Amelia accepted it.

Amelia was even allowed to interact with this woman's daughter and show her different places on a map regarding where Saipan would be in relation to some other geographic points. We don't even know if they were talking, or if they could understand each other, but she *did mention* that she pointed out to her daughter where Saipan was and also where these other geographic places were in the world. So there was some kind of communication going on, at least in one single instance. The Japanese guards must have allowed her to talk with her daughter.

· · ·

Jen Taylor

Everything that *I've heard* about the Japanese soldiers and the situation shows that if you saw anything, you were to keep quiet. They were very strict. What do you make of this story? It's strange that they're allowing her to speak to a local who lives next door, and they're not concerned about the security risk of that.

Rob Ellos

The Kobayashi Ryokan Hotel is where they kept political prisoners before they brought them to Garapan prison. If I ran a hotel that from time to time would house political prisoners, I would certainly be familiar with the people next door and in the immediate neighborhood. People like Antonio Cepada lived in the neighborhood, and he said he saw the *American white woman* looking out of that upstairs window. People knew she was there. Even though the Japanese were very punitive, I think they had some trust, at least in the local neighbors. If, again, Amelia was under guard, and somebody gave her some fruit, I don't think they would really talk to each other. It might very well have been a wordless gesture. Amelia likely didn't understand Chamorro. I think these might have been incidental contacts, and the guards didn't make a big deal of it.

Jen Taylor

This ring Amelia gave, do we know where *that* is?

Rob Ellos

No, and not for lack of trying. They searched and searched, but they never found it.

Jen Taylor

Jesús Salas, what did *he* witness?

. . .

674

Rob Ellos

Jesús Salas said that he was in Garapan prison, and a *white American lady pilot* was held briefly in the cell next to him. He either heard or was told that. Given that he was Chamorro, he may well have overheard that from guards talking about it. Maybe he understood Japanese as well. He also mentioned to somebody else that Fred Noonan had been in the fourth cell of that block near him. This was from an interview conducted by Father Conover. Father Conover always said it would be very unlikely that these people would lie to a priest because they were very religious people. In fact, that is how Salas got into prison to start with, and I told that story earlier.

Jen Taylor

But we just heard a second ago that she was held prisoner in a hotel. Now we're hearing that she was held prisoner at Garapan prison. Was it *both*?

Rob Ellos

Yes, both. Initially, she would have been at the Kobayashi Ryokan Hotel and then later at Garapan prison.

Jen Taylor

If we have a number of people spotting her at the hotel and a number of people spotting her at the prison, do we then have enough detail to establish a timeline regarding when she was moved or which place she was at first?

Rob Ellos

I don't think we have a timeline.

Jen Taylor

How far away geographically are these two places from one another?

Rob Ellos

About eight hundred yards apart.

Jen Taylor

Pretty close. Why would they have put her at the hotel first and then moved her to the prison?

Rob Ellos

It's hard to say. It could have been a staging area, or it could just have been an administrative type of decision at the moment. They might not have been quite sure how to handle her. If you were holding an American national in a prison, and our government ever got wind of that, and that person turned out to be *Amelia Earhart*, you'd have a very hot potato on your hands. I don't know what the US response would have been. I don't think Roosevelt would have wanted to go to war in the Pacific over Amelia Earhart, but there would have been big trouble.

Jen Taylor

Did Salas have a good view of her or the male companion she was with? I don't know how the cells are laid out.

Rob Ellos

I don't think he mentioned the male companion. He said the male companion would talk to her from the other end, and they would yell back and forth. Some of his testimony is a little inconsistent; I'm just going to say that right now. But Father Conover has said that their initial conversations were regarding how he got into prison and him being surprised by the *American white woman pilot* who was in the cell next to him for a while. That was always Salas's main claim.

Jen Taylor

Earlier, we talked about how Josephine Blanco Akiyama actually picked her out in a photo lineup. I know that some of these other witnesses did as well, but I don't know if we've mentioned which ones. Was Salas one of them?

Rob Ellos

Salas, to my knowledge, did not give a description. When Father Conover came along with Fred Goerner, they asked the locals to, "Tell us about the war. Before the war, have you had any interesting experiences?" This is where some of these we're discussing today came from.

Jen Taylor

Do we have the question-and-answer transcript from those interviews or notes even?

Rob Ellos

No, there's no transcript of it. It's said that these priests are the only people who these Chamorro natives of Saipan trusted because the Japanese were still so punitive. There was no proof that they would not come back in the future, even after they lost the war. So, even later on, it was hard to pry things out of these people.

Jen Taylor

Let's move on to Antonio Cepada, Pedro Cepada, and Carlos Palacios. Did *they* give a description other than *white woman*?

. . .

677

Rob Ellos

I can't recall off the top of my head, I would have to double-check. They told Goerner and the priests that they knew of her, and they'd seen her. There's a gentleman who says he saw Amelia Earhart in the back of a truck with a bunch of men going down a road.

Jen Taylor

Yeah, *about that*, I've heard so many different versions of that story. I've heard that she was in the back of a truck; I've heard she was in a motorcycle sidecar; I've heard that they were walking. What do you make of those inconsistencies?

Rob Ellos

The sidecar on a motorcycle *does* make a lot of sense. It was an efficient way of travel. As far as the back of the truck, I don't know what was going on there. There has also been testimony from someone seeing her get into a large sedan with a Japanese officer.

Jen Taylor

She's traveling a lot, it seems.

Rob Ellos

Yeah, she's moving around a little bit.

Jen Taylor

Based on everything we've talked about so far, it seems like what is physically being witnessed is a white woman with short hair. Occasionally, we get a little bit more detail.

We know that her companion had blue eyes, and we have some detail on his injuries. But for the most part, it seems to me like this information that this is an American pilot woman is coming from rumor and gossip. It sounds like rumor and gossip is being, either intentionally *or not*, spread by the Japanese government. From what you and I are talking about, that seems to be what's likely happening here. Almost everyone we've discussed so far says, "Well, they said it was an American pilot." I ask, "How do you know?" The answer always traces back to rumor, gossip, or that the Japanese military told them.

Rob Ellos

Well, I think that, yeah, it turned into gossip. But the fact that she was called an American white woman pilot *initially* was the startling information.

Jen Taylor

But the source of that information, that it was an American pilot, seems to have originated *first* with the Japanese military. All of the civilians whom we are talking about heard it from someone *else* who heard it from someone *else*. If you trace it back based on what we've been talking about, it seems like the original source of that information was the Japanese military.

Rob Ellos

Yes. Bilimon Amaron said that the naval officers on board told him that they were surprised that the white pilot was a woman.

Jen Taylor

Can you think of any reason why a rumor like this started by the Japanese military might be wrong or untrustworthy?

Rob Ellos

No.

. . .

Jen Taylor

We know that the Japanese told the Americans searching for her that they would help in that search. Logs later revealed that they were lying about that. We also know that the Japanese and the American governments were not exactly friends, as you mentioned before.

Rob Ellos

The Japanese were preparing the mandated islands, they were preparing for the war in the Pacific to come, and the United States was very wary about that. They sent over a spy, a real American spy, a soldier named Pete Ellis, and he pretended to be a trader and was going from island to island. The Japanese poisoned him. Anybody who landed on any of those mandated islands knew they'd be considered a spy. I've seen a picture of Jaluit, and they had, like, four big radio towers; there probably were more.

They were no doubt monitoring Amelia's flight around the world to make sure she didn't come near the mandated islands.

Jen Taylor

Well then, based on *that*, why is it reasonable to think that in the beginning, this was not necessarily a happy thing for them? Maybe in the beginning, they had good intentions.

You said yourself that they were going to send her back on her way, that they weren't under guard, that it was not a big deal. But you're also telling me that they were suspicious from the very beginning. They were monitoring her flight because we were enemies with them. It *does* seem to make more sense that if it really *was her* and she landed there, they would have immediately treated her as a spy.

Rob Ellos

You have to realize that there would be administrative people or government people, like the emperor or high military officials, who would make decisions regarding how she would be handled. Although they hated our country, a goodwill gesture could maybe mend fences long enough for them to build more things in the islands and have more fortifications and pillboxes and things of that nature. For a very short period of time, they probably weren't quite sure what they were going to do with her. She was, in a sense, a commodity. They could have held her as a prisoner, but not let anybody know. Then later, if the war to come did not go in Japan's favor, they could have maybe traded Amelia for a high-ranking Japanese officer who might have been captured or someone of that status. "Hey, we have Amelia Earhart; we want a trade." There is an awful lot of foresight that would be behind all of this. Somewhere, there were meetings by either the military or Japanese officials.

Again, she was a hot potato. She's an international celebrity, and she would have had some real value and clout. How they handled Amelia Earhart could affect everything. I think Amelia could have been a bargaining chip in their minds *at the moment*.

Jen Taylor

Before court today, you mentioned you wanted to discuss something else. What is that?

Rob Ellos

Yes, I wanted to mention Deanna Mick, who along with her husband flew out of Saipan International Airport in 1978, on a trip to the neighboring islands. When they were going to later return to the United States, a former employee and one of their best friends Ramon San Nicolas gave Mrs. Mick an artifact.

It was a small steel door about seven inches by eight inches and about a quarter inch thick with broken hinges on one side and a hasp lock on the other. On one side of the door was this inscription:

It said, "July 29, 1937, A. Earhart."

Ramon said that the door came from a Japanese prison in Saipan and that it was used to pass food and other articles to and from the cells. Ramon said he felt that he should give this to Mrs. Mick as a ceremonial artifact because she was the only woman pilot to fly in the Marianas since Amelia Earhart. Ramon said he got the door from a cousin on Saipan, who was positive it was in the Garapan jail during the time indicated on the door, and that Amelia probably had scratched the words onto the door.

Tom Devine tried to get a hold of the door in order to conduct tests on it to try to find out when the inscription was made. She really did not want to sell the door or part with the door, but what she *did do* is enclose a sheet of paper with a pencil tracing from the door.

She also mentioned that the hinges had broken off, and if the other parts of the broken hinges are still on the cell at Saipan, which very well could be, it could certify authenticity.

Devine tried to give her some money for temporary custody of it, but she really didn't want to do it.

That sheet I just mentioned was taken to the cell where they said Amelia was supposedly held, and it fit *exactly*.

So that's an artifact I think is interesting. It cannot be proven that somebody after the fact wrote "July 29, 1937," and her name, but it looks very interesting to me. It looks like whoever scratched it on there was using an object that was not real precise, but it's very readable. If indeed it was matched to the door, it could be authenticated. I wish we could get our hands on that artifact.

Jen Taylor

We don't know where it's at?

Rob Ellos

We don't know where it's at.

Jen Taylor

Just to reiterate for our jury, as far as artifacts go, so far we've mentioned a rusty object that was found near Barre Island or on Barre Island, a suitcase, a map case, a personal diary, a ring, and now a steel door with broken hinges that she may have inscribed her name on.

But *all of these things* that could have corroborated all of these eyewitness statements are gone. None of those are here. We don't have any of that stuff. Correct?

Rob Ellos

Correct, we don't.

We mustn't forget the photographs because the photographs make a lot of sense. Joseph Garofalo found a dead Japanese soldier, and in his wallet, he had a picture of a very weary-looking Amelia Earhart.

Some other soldiers in California that had been in the war at Saipan had pictures of Amelia Earhart standing by a Japanese aircraft on Aslito field.

They said they had them, but they searched and searched and couldn't find them. Remember that photographer who snapped those pictures of Tom Devine and Paul Anderson while they were observing the Electra? Those should be out there. There are also probably official US photographs that were taken by official photographers of the armed services before the plane was burned at the hangar at Aslito Field. They no doubt took pictures from many angles. Those are probably in the National Archives or something like that, waiting to be discovered.

Jen Taylor

But we don't have any of the photographs you're talking about?

Rob Ellos

Right. We have nothing physical we can touch. We just have people who have said these things. This all seems to fit rather consistently.

. . .

Jen Taylor

Of the military witnesses. The first guy you discussed during direct is Tom Devine. He indicated that he saw a hangar, but he was not allowed to go inside. There was a mysterious civilian telling them not to go in, and this civilian was not wearing a sidearm.

Rob Ellos

This is when they first pulled up in the Jeep. He hadn't seen the plane at that point. He wanted to snoop around and see if this was Amelia's plane. They *did see it* and walk on the wing, and they saw the broken glass in the background.

Jen Taylor

He even made the claim that he saw her serial number.

Rob Ellos

Oh yeah, **NR16020.** He said he wrote that down and put it in his wallet. Private First Class Paul Anderson was with him while they were, like, looking at the twin tail fins, and they read the serial number from the twin tail fins.

Jen Taylor

Here's my issue with Devine. We've known him to lie. He *has* lied before to attempt to support his claims. He's not *above lying.*

Rob Ellos

I think Tom was a person who liked to favor pet theories. When this stuff came up about the Marshall Islands, he kind of just waved that off like, "No, they landed at Saipan," which would have been a 90-degree error on Noonan's part. Noonan was one of the premier navigators in the world at that time; he was getting ready to start his own navigation school when he returned from the flight. Devine feels that the Electra semi-crash-landed in Tanapag harbor in Saipan, and he was stuck on that idea. He would not leave it. When Vincent Loomis, Oliver Knaggs, Mike Campbell and others came up with what appears to be proof that they had been in the Marshalls, he refused to accept that proof. So, yeah, he was a person who was capable of lying. Having said that, I think he was an honorable person and a nice person. But if it didn't fit the paradigm of what he thought happened in the initial book, he wasn't interested. Devine ignored the Marshalls thing even though Mike Campbell was trying to bug him about it and said, "Hey, look, there's people who have gone and interviewed these people. It appears that they had landed there." Devine was not interested in that. That was kind of like a lie to continue on that path.

Jen Taylor

No, that's *ignoring evidence*. That's ignoring something because it doesn't fit with your theory. What I'm talking about is fabricating evidence.

Rob Ellos

I don't know that much about him. He could have made up some lies. In some areas, people have been known to lie to keep their pet theory alive.

Jen Taylor

When someone does that, do you think that it hurts their credibility?

Rob Ellos

These initial statements by Devine I think are very solid and very strong. Maybe later on, he may have lied about some things, I don't know. I wish you could ask Mike Campbell because Mike Campbell knew him well, and they corresponded a lot. He visited with Robert Wallack and Tom Devine. I'm not aware of any lies, but he certainly would be capable. All human beings can tell lies.

Jen Taylor

You just mentioned that I should ask Mike Campbell; I haven't really been able to talk to him. But this next story here came *from his book*. I know that you say you haven't heard of it before, but I'll go ahead and tell you what Campbell claims: This has to do with who the civilian we spoke of earlier was, and for the record, I don't particularly think that who the civilian was necessarily matters. That being said, Tom Devine was *convinced* that the civilian he saw was James Vincent Forrestal. He was *so convinced of that*, that no one could tell him otherwise. I believe it was Nabers who had done a bunch of research on it, had looked into it, had obtained his appointment book, and had come to the conclusion that it couldn't have been him. Devine could never accept it, but he didn't stop at just *not* accepting it. Here's a quote in the form of a question taken directly from Devine as found in Campbell's book: "Why did Forrestal summon Amelia Earhart's husband to his office on July 19, 1944?" The implication being that he had seen his appointment book and had evidence that James Forrestal and George Putnam spoke in his office on July 19, 1944.

When Mike Campbell went to go check that out, that was not supported at all. There was nothing in the appointment book that would support that. It never happened, yet Devine competently claimed that it had, and I've *yet* to see evidence that it had.

Rob Ellos

There have been people who have talked very convincingly about actual experiences that they had and then later, for various reasons, have told lies. A lie could be something that could maintain the economic viability of your book so that your readers can have an authentic experience like Devine did. I think a person can tell a lie at one point in their life but be completely authentic earlier on. I think that's something that humans can do. I don't think that has to diminish the initial things that he said. The initial report to me is so convincing and so odd and so unusual. It's not something that a young trooper would make up. When Julious Nabers came along and said, yes, he overheard that Earhart and Noonan's plane had been found, and he was ordered to guard it for twenty-four hours, he knew it was Amelia's plane. And he heard they were going to destroy it, so he went there. I mean, there are twenty-four GIs who corroborated it.

Jen Taylor

But the only reason why we know about that at all is because they told Devine, and Devine wrote about it.

We've just established that we can't trust him.

Rob Ellos

He sent that article to *Leatherneck* magazine, asking for people who served as GIs on Saipan, and he got that really large response. He has pictures of these people. They all have shared pictures with him. They're at least putting their family reputations on the line.

Jen Taylor

Again, I'm not asking about the credibility of anyone *but* Thomas Devine.

Rob Ellos

Yeah, I think his initial statements were true. Maybe he lied later on, given that he wanted to sell books, or maybe he just wanted to save face. He didn't want to accept any information that threw some of his ideas into disfavor, and maybe he *did* make up some lies for that. Devine, Wallack and Nabers have never ever wavered in their stories, and it's all available online to watch. These things have been documented by priests. They're on videotapes and old-fashioned audiotapes. I mean, these things can be *seen*; they can be *heard* on audiotapes. I wish we had the photographs. I wish we had Wallack's briefcase, but since we don't, we've got to lean on these eyewitnesses. Are we calling these twenty-four GI patriots liars?

Jen Taylor

I am not calling *anyone* a liar *other* than Tom Devine. Like I said, *he's the one* who spoke to them. Once *his* credibility has been called into question, you don't think that tarnishes everything he touched?

Rob Ellos

I think his initial account is so powerful and so convincing that it would not. I don't think he would lie about comments made to him that he included in a nationally released book where they've published the pictures of these people while they were in the military. They were young, and they had their names under their pictures. I don't think he would publish those pictures and make these comments if they were not true. Otherwise, these people could say, "Hey, I didn't say that; defamation of character!" There could be legal problems there.

I'm not saying Tom Devine *didn't lie*; he may well have lied. But I think his initial observations regarding what happened were shocking and convincing.

Jen Taylor

They were *also* very detailed, and I think that's my problem with it. I don't question that he believed the things he was saying on a big-picture level. For me, that's probably his motivation for lying in the first place.

It's not that I think that everything he says cannot be trusted. I believe that he believes the overarching message, but his account was so detailed.

After so much time had passed, he was able to remember the serial number on the plane.

To me, that's a *massive* detail. If *he did see* that serial number, that's *so big* that it's almost a smoking gun.

How can we trust that he didn't make that up to support other things that he saw the same way he made up notations in James Forrestal's book that he supposedly saw? That is the problem for me. I don't know now what to trust and what not to trust. I believe that he's being genuine about what he thinks happened, but he's capable of lying, and he's shown that. When confronted with it, he apparently doesn't back out.

Rob Ellos

Sometimes people take their account, and they sculpt it a little bit to make it look nicer.

Whether it's to sell a book or to feel more believable, I think the gist of the message from Devine's initial account is true, because Julious Nabers also confirmed it. Doug Bryce said he saw the Electra on Saipan, and he says that in a Rich Martini video that you can see right now online. There are a lot of troops who saw this plane and described where it was and how it was burned and that type of thing. He may have altered some details, I don't know.

If you've ever painted yourself into a corner, *any of you*, about *anything* in life, if you're on the record widely about that, it's pretty hard to just step out of that corner and say, "I was wrong. I'm sorry, but I was wrong."

Jen Taylor

Moving on from Divine, the next witness is Julious Nabers, the code clerk on Saipan who overheard messages saying they had found Amelia Earhart's plane there. I want to know, and this court wants to know, do we have a transcription of what the message *actually said*?

Rob Ellos

It would have been in military code. I would think things that are in code would not be intelligible by people. But it may be in some records. If I'm the US government, I probably would have gotten rid of those records by now.

Also, he *did see* the briefcase that Wallack found.

Jen Taylor

Is there a description of the briefcase?

Rob Ellos

By Wallack. I have a drawing by his son Bill Wallack. It shows a leather briefcase type deal that's got a hasp that goes over the top kind of like the jail cell hasp for earlier. It's got a little swivel that turns and holds that down, and it has a handle on the top. Robert Wallack also sent me two photos from Purdue University from when they were loading the Electra, and sure enough, right by her right foot, there's the briefcase as Robert described.

Jen Taylor

Since you're bringing up Robert Wallack, we know he gave the briefcase containing all of these crucial, personal documents to someone *he believed to be* an officer. Do we know whom he gave it to?

Rob Ellos

No, we don't know. The officers didn't advertise their rank because snipers would take them immediately. So they had what he called little scrambled eggs on their hat, which was like a symbol of authority, and that is the person he gave it to, and he actually gave Robert a receipt.

Jen Taylor

And the receipt had her name on it? It said "Amelia Earhart's."

· · ·

Rob Ellos

It said "Amelia Earhart's maps, charts, health certificates, passports." He gave this to Robert, and he put it in his money belt, which he always kept on him throughout the war.

Unfortunately though, it was lost in all the confusion while he was being tended to after suffering a leg injury later in battle.

Jen Taylor

Just to recap on all the artifacts, we have the rusty object found on an island, the suitcase, the map case, her diary, a ring, a small steel door that she may have signed; now we add to that photographs of her as well as Robert Wallack's receipt. All of these things could have corroborated *all* of this witness testimony, and we don't have *any of it*.

Rob Ellos

None of it here, but I would suspect that the Wallack briefcase is in the National Archives.

Jen Taylor

Burks, Henson and Griswold. We'll hear about them at length shortly, I'm sure. But in short, their story is that they went out and dug up a grave, correct?

Rob Ellos

Henson and Burks were led on a digging detail led by Marine Captain Tracy Griswold.

They went around the northern part of Liyang cemetery, and he had a map. He had some coordinates to look at on the map regarding where to dig. When they got down to about three feet deep, they found these bones. Griswold recovered them, and he put them in canisters, and when it was all over, Henson asked, "Who did we dig up?" Griswold said, "Well, have you ever heard of Amelia Earhart?" Henson said, "Why sure." Griswold said, "Well, that's enough said, and keep quiet about this."

Jen Taylor

Okay, before we get any further, what bones were actually found, do we know?

Rob Ellos

I have not seen or read descriptions as to how many bones. There's a very wide reported variation. Fred Goerner and other people went to talk to Griswold in Washington, and he would not talk to them unless he was in the presence of his lawyer. When Goerner or the other interviewers asked, he always maintained he didn't know anything about any bones, and he didn't know anything about Amelia Earhart.

Jen Taylor

Did Fred Goerner believe Griswold's story? Because Griswold told him that he didn't participate in any digging. He basically denied that the whole incident happened. He denied knowing anything about Amelia Earhart. Did Fred Goerner *buy that*?

Rob Ellos

Fred Goerner seemed to be a person who was sometimes naive of authority. If somebody like Griswold said it didn't happen, it didn't happen, and that was it. That was the impression I got.

Jen Taylor

At one point, Devine actually believed that he knew where she was buried. He had spoken to someone, and from my understanding, he and Goerner had a disagreement about *that* as well.

· · ·

Rob Ellos

You had one person with a *big* ego, and another who had these things happen to them. Devine was trying to get that across and trying to contribute, but that contribution was maybe not being given the weight that it should have been.

Jen Taylor

I have no further questions for this witness, Your Honor.

"I believe there are all kinds of smoking guns out there, if the right person can identify where they are, and use the right key to unlock them. From what I understand, the only person who has the power to do that is the President of the United States."

Chris Williamson

The project calls *Jon Hagadorn* to the stand.

Mr. Hagadorn, can you advise the court as to your professional background and expertise?

Jon Hagadorn

My professional background lies in research and history. I have a podcast heard worldwide called *1001 Heroes, Legends, Histories and Mysteries*. With a name like that, you get an opportunity to dig into a lot of different types of stories.

Chris Williamson

Tell us how you got involved in this case and why it's so interesting to you?

Jon Hagadorn

It's just the mystery of it. One of the most interesting stories that I've ever dug into, both before I had this podcast and now having the podcast, is the disappearance of Amelia Earhart. It's a tremendous story when you start to look at it. There's a lot of people lined up on different sides of the field with different opinions of what actually happened to her. Did she crash and sink in the Pacific not far from Howland Island? Did she reverse the planes direction and ditch in Buka? Did they end up on Nikumaroro? *Or* did they ditch the plane in the Marshall Islands?

. . .

Chris Williamson

You've mentioned on your show previously that there's a single piece of evidence that *you have seen* that has caused you to believe in this theory more than any other one in this case. First, please tell the court where you found this piece of evidence and give us a little background on the situation in that time. Then enlighten our jury regarding the document known as "the message in a bottle."

Jon Hagadorn

I came across it in the Office of Naval Intelligence reports. Before that, it was found in the United States National Archives, which are housed, by the way, in a number of places. If you try to search the archives, it's a lifetime job getting in there and finding information. This is one of the most compelling reports I've ever found. Let me set the scene for you:

July 2, 1937, when Fred and Amelia's plane went down to the best of our knowledge, the situation in the Pacific was that the Japanese were building fortifications on various Pacific islands. That information was given to the Office of Naval Intelligence, which was responsible for gathering intelligence on the Pacific for our *own* national security purposes. It was illegal for them to do so; they signed a mandate for it back in 1920. They agreed to a policy where they could inhabit the islands of the Pacific, but they could not build military fortifications on them.

The US believed very strongly that they were doing this in secret, so there was a great deal of concern. At the same time, they knew that Japan was building up their military fortifications and building up their military. Their first objective was neighboring China, to the west of them.

On the day that Earhart and Noonan went down, July 2, 1937, Japan was just five days away from attacking mainland China. In the process of that attack of mainland China, their purpose was to kill as many as they could and steal the wealth of China to help them gain resources, materials, and everything else they needed in order to build their military and take over most of the Pacific.

Conquering China would help them do that, and that's exactly what they did on July 7. Here's the document we call *the message in a bottle*. This document was an Office of Naval Intelligence document, which was kept classified. Once you've heard the contents of this document, the first thing you need to do is ask yourself why in the world they would keep this classified? Someone had to put in that classified order. Who was it? It's signed "Declassified." It says "908 intelligence." It's dated "Seventh of January 1959." This document came to our State Department from our embassy in France. It's titled ~~"Confidential,"~~ which is crossed out. And initialed. "Report of Amelia Earhart as prisoner in Marshall Islands." No one was talking about or had written anything about the possibility that Amelia Earhart and Fred Noonan may have been taken captive. At this point, to the entire world, they were lost at sea. It would have been a very prescient idea to come up with something like this as a hoax.

Chris Williamson

Your Honor, at this time the project would like to admit exhibit 1 into evidence, the document known as the "message in a bottle" found on the southwestern shores of France.

Jen Taylor

No objection.

Judge

Project's exhibit 1 is admitted.

Chris Williamson

Okay, Mr. Hagadorn, you've got our attention. Would you please read that document for the court now, sir?

. . .

Jon Hagadorn

"Mr. Happenot, the chief of the French Foreign office, allowed the writer to read some papers found in a bottle washed ashore near Bordeaux. This communication will be delivered to the American embassy here."

Here's how it reads:

"On the 30th of October, Mrs. Barrett, aged 37, while walking on the beach, near Soulac-sur-mer on the Atlantic coast, found a bottle of about a half pint size, peppered with a cork over which wax had been poured. Found in the bottle, were a lock of chestnut colored hair, a paper with the words in French, 'God guide this bottle, I confirm my life and that of my companions to it.'"

The third paper mentioned above contained on one side written in French the following:

"I have been a prisoner at Jaluit in the Marshals by the Japanese. In the prison there, I have seen Amelia Earhart aviatrix, and in another cell her mechanic, a man, as well as several other European prisoners held on charge of alleged spying on large fortifications erected on the Atoll. Earhart and companion were picked up by Japanese hydroplane and will serve as hostages. I was in prison because I disembarked on Mili Atoll. My yacht VEVEO sunk, crew, three Maoris killed. My yacht, 26 tons sailing ship was equipped with radio."
On the other side of this paper, the story continues: *"After having been kept longtime at Jaluit, I was forcibly enrolled as stokehold hand [coal shoveler] on board, Nippon nori bound for Europe. Will try to escape when ship gets near to coast. Carry this message to Gendarmerie immediately so that we can be freed. This message is to be thrown overboard probably near Santander, [Spain] and should arrive in Brittany towards September or at latest, October 1938. This is message number 6. To have a good chance of freeing Miss Earhart and her companion and also other prisoners, police should arrive incognito at Jaluit I shall be with [next word is indecipherable.] And if I succeed in escaping...because if the Japanese are asked to free the prisoners, they will say that they have none are detained at Jaluit.*

> *"One must be tricky. The hair is Miss Earhart's and will prove the veracity of this story, and that I've seen Amelia Earhart."* [Supposedly dead.] *"This bottle will serve as a float for a second bottle containing some objects of Miss Earhart. I am writing on my knees because I have only a little paper, some left-over when police took fingerprints."*

The second bottle referred to has never been found. This bottle that *was found* has on the bottom the following stamp inscription: *V.B.2*

Chris Williamson

Can you tell us anything else regarding the chain of command for this document?

Jon Hagadorn

If you look deeply into this missive, this will tell you that the actual document and the bottle came to the far eastern section of the French Foreign Office. All they say is that they retyped it and gave it to the American Embassy. They might still have the original tucked in a base-ment or a box somewhere. I don't think anybody's ever followed up.

Chris Williamson

So the French Foreign Office *did* officially acknowledge that this document is a legitimate document that came to them.

Jon Hagadorn

Yes.

Chris Williamson

Moving on, Mr. Hagadorn, and I'd like to discuss the Office of Naval Intelligence report for the Amelia Earhart-Fred Noonan disappearance case. Right off the bat, there's something odd about this report, isn't there?

Jon Hagadorn

Indeed. The only ONI report is the one done in 1960, probably as a response because the first books had been published. I think Paul Briand's book had elicited a real uproar that prompted the ONI to do a classified report in 1960. But they declassified it and said it was made available in 1967 as a declassified document.

But it's not out there anywhere; you can't find it.

Chris Williamson

Don't you think it's odd that you can't find the report that you just referenced?

Jon Hagadorn

It was really a whitewash. Of all the witnesses who had been talked to, a lot of them didn't come up until after that report. They discounted a lot of the major witnesses and took the minor witnesses and didn't make them look good. It looked very much like the ONI report was meant to pull people off course.

Chris Williamson

That sounds a lot like the foundation for a cover-up to me.

Jon Hagadorn

Yeah, I believe so. And of course, all you've got is hearsay. You've got Goerner, who said he was allowed to see that report, but not photograph or copy any part of it. The one he saw actually was much more open-minded than the one that was finally released. Here it is, the seventh, eighth, ninth, tenth, eleventh, and twelfth day of July 1937, and we're sending missives back and forth to the Japanese.

They're saying they would get ships out to search for her. They're doing everything they can, so there's no need for us to come up to the Marshall Islands. In fact, we *did have* researchers that went back to check on that. To see if those same ships were out searching like the Japanese said they'd be, and it was confirmed they *were not*. That's a real killer. You can read the copy of their report that states the *Kamoi* was in on the search. Well, the *Kamoi* was still docked in Saipan.

They also said the *Koshu* was out looking, but actually, the *Koshu* was in dock and then sent to Jaluit on the seventh. That's probably the same day that they were picked up.

Chris Williamson

Would it be fair for me to say that Amelia Earhart and Fred Noonan should have government recognition as casualties of World War II?

Jon Hagadorn

I believe that Amelia Earhart and Fred Noonan are **heroes.**

I actually believe that they made a decision somewhere east of the Gilbert Islands to turn that plane north and to take a daytime look at the Marshall Islands so they could photograph any fortifications, airstrips or large ships that they saw there. I believe they were hoping they could make that pass and come back. I believe they were keeping radio silence for the most part so they could get away with it. I also believe that their transmissions were kept short so that the Japanese couldn't get a fix on them. Whether they were *asked to do that* or whether they knew it was very important to our intelligence and to FDR personally doesn't really matter.

I believe they put their lives at risk, and they got caught as a result of that risk. I believe that they should be given medals of honor for their ultimate sacrifice. To do that, the United States government would have to come out and say, "Yes, this has been kept quiet way too long. We owe it to Earhart and Noonan's memory."

They were the first Americans to die as a result of Japanese aggression in the Pacific, in 1937, pre-Pearl Harbor.

Chris Williamson
Thank you. Your Honor, pass the witness.

Cross-Examination of Jon Hagadorn

Jen Taylor

I want to ask you some follow-up questions regarding the message-in-a-bottle story that you and Chris talked about. I'm going to keep coming back around to this because it's important. What you're reciting is from a three-page report. It's *not the actual message itself.* We don't have the message *or* the bottle. We have a report describing the message in a bottle. Do you know when that report was first discovered?

Jon Hagadorn

The report was first sent from the embassy in France to the US in January of 1939.

Jen Taylor

Okay.

Jon Hagadorn

That's found in the document. The document was originally marked confidential. It's dated the seventh of January, 1939, which I find to be quite interesting. It was declassified March 1, 1977.

Jen Taylor

Between 1977 and now, somebody had to have discovered it. As far back as I can find, it was first mentioned and researched somewhere in the 1980s by Oliver Knaggs. He told the story in his book, and that's the earliest mention anywhere that I can find. Is there anything before then?

Jon Hagadorn

Not that I'm aware of.

Jen Taylor

Okay. So, before that, it was, I guess, technically declassified. But no one knew that it existed?

Jon Hagadorn

That sounds correct. It was declassified in March of '77.

Jen Taylor

As far as we know, he's the one who found the document and wrote about it in his book. He wasn't relying on somebody else's research. He's actually the one who went and found it?

Jon Hagadorn

On that, I'm not sure. I can't say yes to that statement because I'm not actually sure if he was who discovered it.

Jen Taylor

Who wrote this message in a bottle? Do we know anything about the author?

Jon Hagadorn

We do not know about the author. What we know is that it was discovered along the French coast in 1938, by a lady who turned it in to the local police. They thought it was very interesting information, so they sent it along to the French Embassy. The French Embassy contacted the United States, and they rewrote the letter. They retyped the letter word for word. For all we know, the French Embassy still has the original letter and the bottle. We *do know* that it was sent to our intelligence people exactly as it was originally written.

Jen Taylor

Is there anything in the transcription of the letter that can help us identify anything about the author? Do we know if they're a male or a female?

Jon Hagadorn

Excellent question. It does not indicate if the author was male or female.

Jen Taylor

What about the person who wrote the actual letter found in the bottle?

Jon Hagadorn

The person who wrote the letter found in the bottle never named himself. He names his yacht, which was called the "VEVEO," in capital letters. He says that he had a crew of three, but the Japanese killed that crew. They took him and imprisoned him on a tanker ship. It was from that tanker ship that he was trying to drop message bottles, which were his only way of trying to communicate to the outside. His name wasn't given there. I have no record of the yacht. I couldn't find it in any searches anywhere. What really makes this whole story unusual is that *if this was a hoax*, this report was written in 1939. The bottle was found in 1938. Earhart disappeared in 1937. Nobody in '37, '38, '39, or '40 was saying that Amelia had landed or had been seen anywhere near Jaluit.

Nobody.

That's what makes this story and this letter so unusual and so precious. It wasn't until many years later that the pieces started to come together, and people like Goerner started to investigate. When he wrote his book, people contacted him. One of the people who contacted him had connections in the Marshall Islands. They told him then that there's a lot going on the Marshall Islands with respect to the legend of Amelia Earhart. All that *began thirty* years *after the fact.*

Jen Taylor

You've been talking about hoaxes. This could not have been a hoax because of the dates. Because people weren't writing about this in 1938 and 1939. This was not something that had been talked about yet.

We see the date that's written on the document. But it wasn't, as you say, "declassified" until the '70s. It wasn't *found* until the '80s. I would imagine that there would be some kind of effort made to verify that the document is *actually* from the 1930s and doesn't just have the date *1939* written on it. If a hoaxer had done this, I can completely understand why putting that date on there would be something they might do to give it an air of credibility. Has anyone made any attempt to verify the date of the actual document?

Jon Hagadorn

Not that I know of or have heard of. I can vouch for the skill of naval intelligence in that they're not going to classify a document unless they believe that there's information there that would be valid information worth classifying. I would say they probably didn't classify every hoax that came along. They had a certain means by which they would determine if it had a high degree of accuracy or not. We know this document was released by the ONI. That is a fact.

Jen Taylor

When you run a Google search for this and you try to look for information online, there really isn't a whole lot of information out there. Around the time that the History Channel ran their documentary *Amelia Earhart: The Lost Evidence,* they also ran a number of blog posts and news stories leading up to the documentary, and one of the articles was on this subject. According to the History Channel, the actual document didn't show up in the National Archives until just a *few days before* the History Channel's documentary aired.

I understand that people had seen it since long before then, because people were talking about it in books and things like that, so I'm not claiming that it *wasn't there*. I'm claiming that according to *this* article, people *had* tried to find it. Almost coincidentally, it shows up on the National Archives website right before the History Channel show hits.

I guess my question is why? Why was it so hard to find? How did it disappear? It seemed to have appeared, disappeared and reappeared again. I don't understand why or how that could be?

Jon Hagadorn

Well, I think those are excellent questions. I can't answer them. With regard to this particular letter, I can only say, let's look at the Office of Naval Intelligence. We know that this report came from *them*. They did a report on Earhart in Saipan in 1960. It was classified, and then they declassified it in '67.

But *try to find it*.

Certain things want to remain buried. I'm not sure of all the ways and means that our intelligence community uses to make things hard to find, but they certainly have an excellent knack of doing that when they want to.

Jen Taylor

I'm not so interested in the report as much as I am the original message in the bottle, and I want to talk about those contents. We know it was written by a man. We know it was written in French. Can we then deduce that it was written by a Frenchman, or is that going too far?

Jon Hagadorn

We really don't know.

Jen Taylor

This message was probably thrown off near Santander. Santander is in Spain, correct?

Jon Hagadorn

Yes.

Jen Taylor

Okay, so he's *in* Spain, or *near* Spain, and he says the message "should arrive in Brittany towards September or, at the latest, October 1938." And the bottle *was found,* according to the report, in October of 1938. He's been taken prisoner. He's writing a note in French.

We don't know if it's *because* he's French, but we *do know* that he speaks fluent French.

He's writing this note, and he's going to throw it into the water. And he was able to accurately guess *exactly* when that bottle was going to be found. Coincidentally, he's writing it in French, and it was found in France.

That seems like *a lot* of coincidences going on. That would point more towards this being a hoax than it being real.

Jon Hagadorn

I can answer you with regard to that. Nowhere in this letter does it say it was written in French. I think that's an assumption that we really can't afford to make.

Jen Taylor

So we *don't know* that it was actually written in French?

Jon Hagadorn

That's correct. All we know is that it was found on the coast of France, and it was handed to the chief of the far eastern section of the French Foreign Office. But we don't know what language it was written in.

Jen Taylor

Interesting…The report doesn't indicate?

Jon Hagadorn

Correct.

Jen Taylor

What about the fact that the person who wrote the note accurately predicted that it would end up in France in October 1938? Is that something that he should have been able to know if he's just throwing a bottle off the side of a boat?

Jon Hagadorn

Well, he had his own yacht. I believe it says somewhere in there that his yacht was a French-registered yacht, though I'm not sure on that. If he was a yachtsman, he probably knew ocean currents pretty well. So we're going to jump to the assumption that he knew ocean currents and had at least a vague idea of where he was when he dropped the bottles off. He probably would have had a vague idea of where they would end up, because he was close to that coast.

Jen Taylor

Okay. You mentioned that you and maybe others have tried to verify a yacht sinking in that area at that time and have been unable to do so. There are other things that I'm curious about as well, for example, would it have been common practice for the Japanese to take prisoners and use them as slave labor on a ship?

Jon Hagadorn

I don't know, but I can tell you this: It was on July 2, 1937, that Amelia Earhart and Fred Noonan's plane went down. We *do know* that the Japanese were on a war footing. The taking of prisoners was not new to them. On July 7, 1937, only five days after Amelia disappeared, the Japanese launched a full-scale invasion of China. Most of us know from our research exactly what happened there. It was an all-out attack. They attacked the coast of China, at Shanghai, and then went inward toward Nanking. By all reports, they killed tens of thousands of people, including innocents. That war in China kept going for a number of years. They were building fortifications against mandates that they had agreed to years earlier. They were doing it, and they were keeping it secret; they were protecting information from getting out. Anyone who had seen those fortifications and could possibly radio out about them or take pictures of them would have been considered a spy. That's a fact.

Jen Taylor

Which would explain why prisoners were taken. I understand that Japanese prisoners were not treated gently. I'm trying to understand the decision to take a prisoner and use him as slave labor as opposed to, say, his crew, which they killed. If the stories are to be believed, they viciously killed and definitely did not treat most of the prisoners that they took well. Yet this particular prisoner was being used for labor. He doesn't indicate that he's being *mistreated*. He was able to sneak away and write a letter and toss it overboard. He at least had the mental faculties available to him to do that. While I can't really argue from reading the letter that he was treated *well*, he did seem to have escaped the same fate as most prisoners.

· · ·

Jon Hagadorn

I'm sure they used him until his slave services were no longer needed, and then they just threw him overboard to the sharks. The Japanese were famous for working prisoners throughout those island fortifications in the Pacific. A lot of the work in China was done by prisoners, Korean and Chinese prisoners. Your chances of surviving a Japanese prison camp were very low. The way they treated prisoners was horrendous. Many Japanese were indicted and tried for war crimes and subsequently died for their war crimes. That's all documented. It doesn't surprise me at all that they committed this guy to the confines of a tanker. A stokehold hand was a job that probably killed a lot of people. They were shoveling coal into the furnaces that powered those ships. They probably used them as long as they could and just threw him overboard once he served his purpose.

Jen Taylor

It looks like he tried to name the ship that he was on board. In quotations he puts "Nippon Noa."

It looks like he's almost trying to phonetically spell out what he thinks the ship is named. Is that how you read that?

Jon Hagadorn

Yeah, I think it might have been the "Nippon Nori." Nippon could be a reference to "The Land of the Rising Sun," which is, of course, Japan. And then we have "Nori."

Jen Taylor

Have any attempts been made to verify whether a ship like that, with that name, was controlled by the Japanese at that time?

Jon Hagadorn

None that I've seen, but that would be a good investigation to run.

Jen Taylor

We *do have* logs from the *Koshu*, from my understanding. It seems like this should be something that somebody with more skill than me should be able to find.

Jon Hagadorn

It would be a good one to check on, absolutely. I would also try to find that wreck. I know it's been a lot of years, but where would the Japanese have sunk that? If they were going to wreck it, they probably would have towed it out a ways and set it on fire. I'm sure they didn't want to wreck their own channels, of which they had been in the process of digging deeper.

I would say that the wreck of the VEVEO is not too far off the coast of Jaluit.

Jen Taylor

I'm trying to do the best that I can to read this and figure out what we can learn about the person who wrote it. Would having a yacht indicate socioeconomic status at that time? Is that something that *only* wealthy people would have? The name, "VEVEO," is there anything we can get out of that? What language or maybe what nationality? I don't recognize that word as being an English word.

Jon Hagadorn

I looked it up one time, and I believe it might have been Portuguese.

Jen Taylor

I think the overarching point that I'm trying to make is that there are *a lot* of questions here.

There are a lot of things that could be verified. It seems that either no attempt has yet been made to verify it, *or* attempts that *were made* have been unsuccessful.

Jon Hagadorn

I've searched like you have. I haven't found any record of that ship. I've drawn a blank on it. I think you could search the American Embassy in France, to see where those documents from 1937 through 1940 are now. I think that could be a very interesting search. That would be a tremendous item to try to research and locate.

Amelia must have made herself known to him. So he knew that she was a pilot. He likely assumed Noonan was the mechanic. I thought that part was fascinating.

Jen Taylor

And he somehow was able to get a lock of her hair.

Jon Hagadorn

That doesn't surprise me as much. Maybe he got more even. Remember this was "message number 6." I think he indicated that he had tried more than once.

Jen Taylor

Does this indicate to you that Amelia wanted to be rescued? If she's working with someone, giving her hair and saying, "Please do everything you can to get me rescued," does that tell us anything?

Jon Hagadorn

Absolutely. By the time they got them to Jaluit, they had been questioned by Japanese intelligence. They likely began to realize that they were not going to be treated as guests, and there wasn't going to be an easy way out of this. I think they became real desperate real fast. They may have seen this guy as their only lifeline. It's kind of what it sounds like.

Jen Taylor

"I am writing on my knees because I have only a little paper, some left over when police took fingerprints." What does that sentence mean?

Jon Hagadorn

I wish I could clarify that. I don't have an answer for that.

Jen Taylor

Do you think maybe it's a *mistranslation*? Because again, we don't know the original language.

Jon Hagadorn

It could be.

Jen Taylor

Would the average person in the 1930s understand the geography of the South Pacific? Who controlled what and the names of the islands, things like that? Is that something that you could find in a geography book in the 1930s?

Jon Hagadorn

I wasn't alive in the '30s. I can't recall looking at any geography books that featured those times.

I would tend to believe that they were still mapping islands during that time. It was probably a constant game of catch-up in terms of mapping what was out there and what wasn't. I think the Japanese had the Pacific pretty well mapped out. Whether or not it was in our US history books, I have no idea.

Jen Taylor

I'm just trying to decide whether or not somebody who's trying to hoax it would have known that Jaluit was an island there controlled by the Japanese.

Jon Hagadorn

I'm at a loss regarding who could have hoaxed this, I really am. Anything is *possible*. You might say it's all confirmation bias, that we're finding every reason to make this as true as it can be. Because of the date, I find the story fascinating. I find the fact that the Office of Naval Intelligence classified it, which tells me they *had a reason* for classifying it. They probably had a reason for classifying thousands of other documents that would likely be a much bigger smoking gun than this one. We looked at all the different theories and hypotheses that are out there about what possibly could have happened, and nobody has turned up a solid piece of evidence yet.

What's been found so far has been found by accident. Everything's been found in places where they might have been missed.

There was a classified order put out by FDR that made everything regarding the actual truth of what happened to Earhart top secret, and they just locked down on it.

I believe there are all kinds of smoking guns out there, if the right person can identify where they are, and use the right key to unlock them. From what I understand, the only person who has the power to do that is the president of the United States.

Jen Taylor

For our jury, let me summarize my concerns with the message. The first one is that we don't have what I would call a "chain of custody." We can't map the point that it was found to the time of the declassification report; there's too many gaps. We don't know where the original message is; we don't know where the original bottle is. It was declassified, someone found it, and then it disappeared. Then someone found it *again*. Because of that, even though the paper says 1939, there's always the possibility that it was produced at a later date and dated as 1939. Until we can really trace the chain of custody, or someone can do some kind of study on the paper or the ink or something that can actually verify when this was written, there's always a possibility that it was written decades later and made to look like it was written in the noted time.

Jon Hagadorn

Sure. How would you feel if this were researched, and everything was found to be just as I'm saying here today?

Jen Taylor

If I was convinced that it *was* written when it *says* it was written, I would feel a little bit differently. The issue for me is that this was declassified in the 1970s and written about for the first time in the 1980s. There's still a possibility in my mind that somebody knew about this theory and produced this document and backdated it.

Jon Hagadorn

Fair enough.

I think that would exist in anyone's mind who might come across this. It would be nice to be able to lock that down and find out exactly what the truth behind this is.

Jen Taylor

The issue here is that we just don't have enough information. I don't know if that's because not enough people have done the work on it. It's very hard to find any information about this at all.

I think there's a lot of stuff that could be done. There are so many little clues in here. It's not that I don't believe it. It's obvious that there's not enough information out there to say this is authentic.

Jon Hagadorn

I have that in the back of my mind, too. Nothing's proven until it's *proven*. I think it's a fascinating story. I think people tend to overlook it. A message in a bottle just sounds kind of flighty. So people overlook that and say, "Well, you know, it's probably some hoax or some creative person."

There's more on these three pages that we *didn't* talk about, which is fascinating as well. We have information regarding the Japanese fortifications there in the Marshalls, as seen by another witness to that. We have that in addition to the message-in-a-bottle letter. It's all part of this long intelligence report, of which the message in a bottle is only a *part*. That tends to tell me that this document you and I are looking at is actually an intelligence report based on what they knew about Jaluit and the Marshalls at that time, which wasn't a whole lot. I encourage people to go to the National Archives and search Amelia Earhart and pull this report up and read it. There is a missing paragraph at the bottom of page 2; it looks like a piece of the original typewritten paper maybe had coffee spilled on it or whatever, but it's not there. And wouldn't you know it, that's *one* piece that you'd really like to see every word in.

I think it needs to be worked on by someone who's really serious with it. I think they could really dig up some interesting information. If they prove that this was actually done when they say it was done, I think it becomes a very convincing piece.

I've always said follow the witness trail.

Nobody has a smoking gun. In fact, nobody has a shred of evidence yet other than the mountain of circumstantial evidence that is attached to Japanese capture. I can't think of another theory that has as much support behind it as this one.

We'll just have to see where this goes and see how the jury takes it.

Jen Taylor

I have no further questions for this witness, Your Honor.

"I don't quite understand the navy's official position on this. It appears that the navy's position, or at least what the press was telling us, was that Earhart crashed and sank. Now you're saying you went to Saipan to investigate her disappearance and possible death. Who ordered the investigation?"

Chris Williamson

The project would like to continue by calling *Les Kinney* to the stand.

Can you please state your full name and your background for our jury, sir?

Les Kinney

Yes, my name is Les Kinney or Leslie Kinney, and I'm a retired federal agent. I was a senior federal agent assigned to a variety of locations within the United States as well as our headquarters in Washington, DC, where at one time, I was the branch chief and the head of the organized crime task force. I was also liaison for some period of time to the Central Intelligence Agency and the National Security Agency as well as the United States State Department. I was a field agent for many years, and I worked undercover.

Earlier in my life, I did a variety of investigations that related to smuggling and early terrorism, so to speak. We also did fraud cases, and I was with the US Treasury department under the office of investigations, which later turned into ICE. After retirement, I still continue to do security investigations under a contract basis for both the FBI and the US State Department. I still currently hold two top-secret security clearances, which I use quite frequently with my work with the FBI.

Chris Williamson

Can you tell the court how your work with the Earhart investigation began?

. . .

718

Les Kinney

Early in my career, actually right out of college, I was fortunate enough to be hired by the office of naval intelligence as a civilian agent. And this was a time when they were transitioning over to what we now know as NCIS, or the Naval Criminal Investigators Service. I was working in Chicago as a young agent, and I don't remember the *exact date*; I really wish I knew. But I had a moment where I was walking in front of one of the assistant special agents in charge's office; his name was Joe Patton. Joe was talking to a bunch of agents in the office, and they're kind of brownnosing, and they all had coffee cups and etc.

Somehow, I stopped by, and the name Amelia Earhart came up. Well, I had just read Goerner's book *The Search for Amelia Earhart,* and I was intrigued by it. I was brand new to it. All of a sudden, I realized that this guy was *involved* with the investigation on Earhart. At the time, he was in Guam, and he had just traveled up to Saipan. This is several years earlier, he was in his mid-forties at the time, so it was a while back.

When he was talking, I interrupted him and said, "I don't quite understand the navy's official position on this. It appears that the navy's position, or at least what the press was telling us, was that Earhart crashed and sank. Now you're saying you went to Saipan to investigate her disappearance and possible death. Who ordered the investigation?" And he didn't really want to discuss this, and he kind of glared at me, I remember that, and I kind of dropped it, and that was the end of it. At that moment in time, I was a little bit intrigued by what was going on. I thought, "There's something wrong here; there's something not right." Joe Patton might not have known all the information and details and the complexity of what was happening when he got his inquiry. I *know that* because that's how these inquiries work. But *still*, I knew that there was *something* wrong, and it's stuck with me from that time. I then started dabbling with it, even a little bit when I was working. But mainly after I retired, I decided to go full blast and see if I could resolve the Earhart issue itself, *whatever* happened to her.

· · ·

Chris Williamson

At the time that your investigation began, were you of the mind that Amelia Earhart and Fred Noonan simply crashed in the ocean near Howland?

Les Kinney

I was really quite young at that time, and no, I did not have any preconceived ideas. Goerner's book, to me, appeared somewhat credible. Because of my background as a criminal investigator, I know that where there's smoke, there's *usually* fire. That old adage holds true here; he had interviewed so many people who said they had seen this white woman and white man in the Japanese mandated territories and/or saw an airplane that possibly belonged to her. There were so many, I had to believe that there *must be* some credibility. And I started gravitating towards the Saipan/Marshall Island capture theory.

Chris Williamson

Earlier in this trial, it was argued by me, the project, that Fred Goerner was really the spark that lit the fire that *became* the investigation we all know today. Can you talk about Mr. Goerner's overall impact and influence in this case?

Les Kinney

Oh, sure. He wasn't *the first* individual who actually started looking into Earhart, by the way; Paul Briand preceded him by a couple of years. Fred Goerner had the clout, being a CBS correspondent who was on the radio every evening in San Francisco and sometimes *nationally*. He certainly *was* an impressive figure. When he started his inquiries, which later turned into the book, people started to listen, and he really *actually* did a fantastic job, there's no question. I went through his files, which are down in Texas at the War in the Pacific Museum; the Nimitz library, so to speak.

I'm always questioning another investigator and/or researcher's information: how they discovered and how they source information. Frankly, most of the early researchers took things as a fact when *in fact* they could not substantiate it or back it up by source material. Goerner did that as well but only to a *limited degree*. As a trained correspondent in the news industry, he realized that source information was important. I was impressed by what he did, and considering it was pre-internet days, he did an outstanding job; there's no question about that. He was on the right track leading all the way through to the book. He went off on a tangent a little bit regarding what happened to her airplane, and it was understandable, and I hope that we will talk about her airplane a little later on, on the basis of it being in Saipan. But he did an *extremely* credible job, and even *after* that book was published, he wrote hundreds and hundreds of letters to former command officers and former military officials, hoping to get some information. Where he failed badly was his ego and the inability that he could possibly gain some information from some *other* early researchers by conducting inquiries.

At the time, they never shared information; fellas like Joe Gervais, who later lost a little bit of his credibility. His early work on trying to resolve the mystery was *really* good.

Vincent Loomis is another great one; he knew these guys. Don Kothera, the guy out of Cleveland in 1968; unfortunately, even with Kothera, Goerner was realizing maybe deep in his mind that he was getting close to solving this, and he tried to discredit Don Kothera and the Cleveland group, and that's really quite sad. But overall, Fred Goerner did a magnificent job, there's no question about it.

Chris Williamson

Why do you think he tried to discredit Kothera?

Les Kinney

Possibly because of competition. He thought he was going to write another book. Don Kothera got involved in 1967 to try to resolve the Earhart mystery, and Goerner's book was published in November of

1966. He always had plans on running a sequel to that book *In Search of Amelia Earhart.*

Consequently, anything that anybody *else* did certainly caused him to reconsider writing a book, and maybe he needn't go any further. I don't know, but he tried to discredit Don Kothera in numerous ways, and it really is quite sad because Kothera and the four other guys in this Cleveland group did probably the *most significant* source information inquiries relating to Amelia Earhart, even *more so* than Fred Goerner, although Goerner had a mass of information.

Chris Williamson

You just mentioned *sourcing*. For our jury and for everyone reading, can you talk about the process of taking a piece of information and walking it back to the source to determine *how viable* or *not viable* that might be?

Les Kinney

Yeah, it *is very important*, and it's important to the newspaper industry, the television industry and everybody else. If you receive information, whether it's secondhand or firsthand from the source witness themselves, you just can't take his or her word that what they're saying is true and accurate. A great example of what's happening in our society today, especially with social media, is people will post things, and now we're starting to realize that probably 80 or 90% of what is written is not real; it's not factual.

Unfortunately, today, it concerns a deliberate attempt at malfeasance in relationship to putting out false and libelous information. As far as the Earhart research was concerned, you had so many people stating things about what happened to her, and some of it was second- and thirdhand, which is okay to a degree because you can track it back. But you got to find out if that source was in a position to offer whatever they stated, to make it a *credible* statement? If it's a document, could the document *itself* potentially be a document that was falsified? So you have to try to go back as far as you can to determine the credibility of that particular witness; otherwise all of your research, all the investigation that you or anybody *else* would be attempting to do, loses this credibility almost immediately. Most of the research that I've done, I would say 90% of it, is really *nothing more* than trying to figure out whether the person who's supplying that information is credible.

Chris Williamson

When Mr. Ellos was on the stand, he walked us through twenty-seven of the multitude of eyewitnesses throughout the Marshall Islands, Saipan and the US military who were stationed there. Of *all* the eyewitness testimony, are there any that stand out to you especially?

Les Kinney

I guess it depends on what segment of the Earhart mystery that you wanted to talk about at that moment in time.

I believe Amelia Earhart and Fred Noonan were captured by the Japanese in the Marshall Islands, and they spent some time there *before* they went to Saipan. But I'm just going to haphazardly throw this out, because I think it's probably *the most* credible. The two young marines, Everett Henson and Billy Burks, who dug up that grave in the summer of 1944, outside Liyang cemetery, on the island of Saipan. They're credible; there's just absolutely no question about it. They have offered witness statements; they offered to testify. And everything that they did, I have documented by timelines to show that *they were there*. In fact, there was no reason for them to lie. The fact that they hadn't seen each other for twenty-five years; they had no idea where the other person was. They didn't bring this up to the press. They were found *originally* by Fred Goerner and then later by Don Kothera. And what they said was corroborated completely.

They were brought to the Liyang cemetery, an abandoned cemetery south of Garapan, and they were told to dig up a grave. They were told this by a gentleman who, at first, they couldn't remember his name, but they thought he was associated with some sort of manufacturing company back east. They thought he came from at least a semi-wealthy family. As time went on, we discovered that, in fact, that man *was identified* as Captain Tracy Griswold. And in fact, his family *indeed* owned the Griswold manufacturing company, which had a huge plant in Erie, Pennsylvania. They manufactured all sorts of steel and iron pots and pans, and Griswold stoves, etc., etc. Once they were asked if it could be this guy by the name of Griswold, they said, "Yes, that's it, that's the guy!" and etc.

And you can carry that on and trace back Tracy Griswold, who he *was*, what *unit* he was in, and what his MOS (military official position) was. And he *was* a part-time intelligence officer in that 18th engineering battalion. He was in a position to do all these things. So it just adds up; everything adds up. They did *indeed* pick up bones; the timeline corresponds *exactly* to what happened after the battle. In fact, I even know *the date* when this grave was dug up, because it corresponded to one of the two marines' birthday. It can be sourced *all the way* back. Unfortunately, what happened to the bones *after that*, that's a different story.

Chris Williamson

Has any progress been made as far as the location of those bones? That would be a big smoking gun, would it not?

Les Kinney

Yes, it would. They gave the bones to Captain Tracy Griswold after they dug out this waist-high grave outside the Liyang cemetery, and they never heard any more about it. They had seen Griswold afterwards, and of course, Griswold denied all of this. He was a reserve marine officer after he left the Battle of World War II at Saipan, and he actually served to 1963. It was incumbent upon him to carry on the rules and regulations of the Marine Corps. Then Fred Goerner started snooping around and following him in the 1960s.

When Fred first talked to him, one of his notes said, "This guy dances around like a shortstop trying to field a hot grounder." That's a great line. And it's a very *truthful* line, because that's exactly what Captain Tracy Griswold did. And then he receives a letter from the marines in the mid-1960s that says, "In the unlikely event that you had something to do with digging up a grave on Saipan, which we seriously doubt, please let us know your thoughts on this matter before you speak to anybody regarding it." Well, what would *you* do? If you were still in the marine reserves, and you're an officer, and you receive this from the commandant of the Marine Corps, you're going to follow *exactly* what you perceive that message meant. And that's exactly what happened.

Chris Williamson

Mr. Kinney, at the conclusion of the History channel documentary *Amelia Earhart: The Lost Evidence*, you and your team excavated a potential grave site where remains were thought to be. Just now, you spoke about the bones from the Henson and Burke location.

What is your opinion on the status of potential remains, now?

Les Kinney

Here's the point that I'd like to make. I was unsure, first of all, whether *anybody* could find the grave site that was dug up by Henson and Burke. They described it pretty well; they said it was outside the cemetery, and Captain Tracy Griswold had some sort of map with him. The cemetery was intact. You have to keep in mind that at that point in time, there was *no* jungle around that particular cemetery. That was seeded later on to cause it to be almost inaccessible. The cemetery had been used, literally, up until the time of the war. Griswold told them, "You guys, come with me," and I believe it was Billy Burks who *actually went* with him. "We're going to walk around this cemetery on one side," and he told him to, "Walk on the other end." He said, "Look for something that looks like a fresh grave; it might be outside the cemetery. And when you get to that location, just let me know."

All of a sudden, Henson says, "Hey, Captain, how about over here?" According to the statement of *both* of those men, Griswold looked at his map and said, "I think this is it. Okay, guys, start digging." The location was outside the cemetery, maybe no more than fifteen to twenty feet. It was near a kind of oddly shaped tree. They noticed that, at the time, there was a fence around that cemetery, an iron rod fence. It was a pretty decent cemetery, but it wasn't large; it was probably no more than seventy-five to a hundred yards by sixty yards, and there were a lot of graves there. So they started digging, and they got down beyond the knee level.

And they were asked by Goerner and Kothera later, "How far did you go?" and they said, "It was more than just jumping out, we kind of had to hop out. It was probably close to waist-high. All of a sudden, we started finding some stuff, bone fragments. And we started finding what looked like the remains of possibly two skeletons."

Unfortunately, they could not remember whether they had *clearly* found skulls. But they said, "We weren't really interested in that. We're just trying to figure out what this guy wanted. And we dug this stuff up. And it was kind of gruesome work, and we got what we needed. And he seemed satisfied."

And while they're down there digging, one of them asked the captain, "Hey, Captain, what are we doing? What the heck is going on here?" And he said, "Have you ever heard of Amelia Earhart?" And they said, "Of course!" And he said, "Enough said. Keep digging." Now there are groups like TIGHAR, for instance, that are said to poo-pah this and say, "Oh, yeah, everybody knew the story about Earhart and Noonan, a movie had just come out, and everybody laughed about it, and he was just joking." That is unadulterated nonsense. And the reason I say that is this: in the middle of a war zone, you're not going to have two marines *go out there* and dig up the remains of somebody without it being *somebody important*. There were a lot of marines and army personnel killed in the Battle of Saipan. There was a *reason* they were there, and I *don't think* the guy was joking.

Another reason was Captain Griswold told them as they got back to their unit to keep this quiet. This was considered a secret matter. In so many words, they were paraphrasing that because they couldn't remember *exactly* what he said. Griswold took possession of a "canister" full of bones, they didn't know whether it was a canister, but they kept on utilizing the word "canister." I'm not sure if that's accurate, or it was kind of adopted, we don't know. Nobody knows what happened to it after that point. As far as Henson and Burke and Tracy Griswold, that was the end of it.

This story dovetails through another gentleman by the name of James H. Nichols, whom we'll get into a little later, but *he* came to Saipan on orders of somebody in Washington, DC, to *find the evidence* of Earhart being there, and if it *was there*, to bring it back to Washington and/or ***destroy it*** if needed. Obviously, there are more details to that, whatever that order was, but I don't know what they were.

In 1968, Don Kothera had knowledge of *where* Fred Goerner had dug up the grave based on where *Goerner thought* Henson and Burke had dug in 1944. He *also had* some further information. Don and the Cleveland group were told by this woman, who was a young girl who couldn't have been older than eight or nine in 1944, that *she* witnessed a white man with "a long nose, good looking," she said, being executed. But she said there was two people, but she couldn't remember whether the second person was standing up, sitting down or lying down. But she *absolutely remembered* the beheading by Japanese outside that cemetery. And she told Don Kothera that she knew where that was at. She said that she had walked by there from school on so many occasions, and it was embedded in her memory. And even though it had been overgrown, she knew where the site was. She said the same thing as Henson and Burke; she said it was near a breadfruit tree with a crazy fork, and it was about ten paces away from that tree *outside* the cemetery, and she pointed to exactly where she thought it was.

When Don and the Cleveland group started digging in 1968, they dug up about 185-190 bone fragments, the largest being no bigger than an inch and a half to two inches. They brought those back to Cleveland, Ohio, and they had them tested. This is pre-DNA days. The anthropologist, who had an extremely good portfolio and had been doing this kind of work for years and years for Ohio State University, said that in his opinion, it was that of a *white woman*, and *one* of the bone fragments was from a *white man*. I don't know whether I would entirely believe his analysis; I don't think it would stand up in a court of law. But it certainly *would be admissible* in a court of law, because of the chain of custody and everything else associated with it. When Don Kothera and the Cleveland group, with the advent of DNA about ten years later, *went back* to *retrieve those bones* from the Ohio State Archives, they were missing. And unfortunately, the doctor who did the *original* analysis died.

I did an *extensive amount* of work to try to find out how this could possibly be. The curator told me that they would never throw away artifacts of any kind, never ever. But we have no idea where they're at. And yes, we *do know they were here*. I tried to track those bones down for a long, *long* time, and I could not do it. I have a suspicion, and it's *only that*. It's one of those eyebrow-raising suspicions where people would say, "Oh, God, Kinney, you don't know what you're talking about." That there's a *chance* that government agents came and *retrieved those bones* while they were in the custody of the doctor at the museum, maybe a year or two or even less than that after he had completed his original analysis. But I don't have any proof of that, and I certainly don't have any source material.

There was a young navy yeoman who came off a ship during this time in the summer of 1944, and he was accompanied by a couple of officers. And they're looking for a place to put a navy distillation plant. By the way, *I have* sourced this; *I have* found out that the navy *indeed* was looking for a place for a navy distillation plant. And he said they wandered around by this cemetery, and while they were there, there were several men digging up a grave, which they had just completed. They asked, "What's going on?" And they said, "We're digging up the grave of a naval aviator who had been buried here." "Oh, you're kidding!" One of the men pointed *literally* near where the navy aviator's grave was, meaning just a few feet away, and he said this: "And right here is where Amelia Earhart is buried." Now *that guy*, he's a **direct witness**. He made those comments. He's dead now, of course, but he said he was outside the Liyang cemetery. Okay, that's pretty good, but *where* outside the Liyang cemetery? We don't have that to work on.

Well, I *know* where the Kothera group dug, and I *know* where Goerner dug. And I *also know* where Billy Burks and Everett Henson dug. But they never *named a location* outside. He just said "a few feet."

I *then* found in the National Archives the report of that naval aviator whose remains were uncovered outside Liyang cemetery, and that report was very, *very* specific. And it said it was "a few feet outside the northeast corner of the Liyang cemetery." Well, that is the *exact spot* where Anna said she had witnessed this white man being beheaded and dumped into a grave along with another body or person at the same location. I'm confident that would hold up in trial in a court of law, simply because *now* we have documented proof from the JAG report of 1944 of where that naval aviator was buried. Now, granted, we *have the testimony,* but we *really don't* because he's dead. However, we have this navy yeoman who *has been identified* write a letter that stated, "I witnessed this navy aviator's remains being uncovered, and they said to me 'and right here literally next to it Amelia Earhart is buried'" I have the date, I know *exactly the date,* and it corresponds to *exactly* when Everett Henson and Billy Burks dug that grave *four days later.*

Chris Williamson

Who tipped off Griswold to the location of that original set of bones, do we know?

Les Kinney

Yeah, I *think we know,* and no, I *don't have* that source because I'm trying to put this together in a manner that would provide a solid timeline. But it *would* hold up in court simply because what we have here in a sense is a conspiracy, don't we? We have a bunch of co-conspirators, and when we have that, hearsay is admissible. This is what I would utilize if anybody tried to argue this point. To answer your question *specifically* would be so extensive and complex.

But who tipped them off?

I believe it was an intelligence officer from the V Amphibious Corps, meaning he came from the oversight group on the flagship that oversaw the *entire* Saipan operation. I think he tipped him off, and that man's name I *don't know*, but I have to give you the background, and the background is this: A few years ago, I spoke to a gentleman who received his doctorate and was a professor of history at San Jose University. He spoke fluent Japanese, and he *also* understood Kanji. The reason he did was he was born and raised in Japan pre-war by his parents, who were missionaries. As a young man when the war broke out, he joined the navy, and immediately they put him into service as a linguist and a translator.

At the Battle of Saipan, he was assigned as the civil affairs officer, and *one of his jobs* was the oversight of this huge camp where they're putting all the prisoners. It was called "Camp Susupe." In that camp as the battle unfolded, people were picked up, including natives, who were put in one part of the camp, Koreans were put in another part of the camp, Japanese civilians in another part, and of course, Japanese soldiers put in another part.

He said he was there and was approached one day by an intelligence officer who wanted to speak to a *specific individual.* I asked him, "Well, who was the individual?" and he said, "I don't remember." Of course, that's understandable, we're talking *forty years earlier.* But he said it was regarding Amelia Earhart. He said, "I knew who he wanted. I knew that, so I found that person." I asked if that person was a man or a woman; were they a Japanese soldier? And he again said, "I don't remember." All this is good because you *know* that he's not trying to embellish anything that he was telling me. He said, "I found this person," and I asked him what happened then? "We went and sat down, and I remember sitting on the ground maybe inside a tent, I'm not sure. And this intelligence officer was there, and he was asking questions of this person, relative to Amelia Earhart." I asked, "Did you overhear the conversation?" And again, he said, "I don't remember." He said, "I just know it was about Amelia Earhart." He said, "I'm sorry, I should have paid more attention. But I do know that whoever this person was that this intelligence officer was talking to, I wasn't needed that much because his English was fairly good."

I have a fairly good idea who that person might have been. I think it was an individual who was one of the earliest Saipan Chamorro leaders, one of the native leaders who would have been in a position to know these things. My thoughts are that this intelligence officer was trying to determine where Earhart had been buried. To put a little icing on the cake, after I had this long, extensive conversation with this retired history professor, he called me back, and he said, "You know, there is one thing. I know that that guy was from the V Amphibious Corps." I said, "You mean he came off the flagship?" And he answered, "Yes." I asked him how he knew that, and he said, "I don't know. But I'm telling you right now, my thoughts going back, I know positively that he came from the fifth amphibious core, meaning he came from the overall intelligence command, not from one of the units on the ground in Saipan." And so my thoughts are that the fifth amphibious core then *knew* where Earhart had been buried from this conversation I just described to you. And the orders came down for somebody to go and dig up that grave. And of course, *that would have been* Captain Griswold. So that's how I think the events unfolded regarding Earhart's and Noonan's remains being *removed* from the cemetery.

Chris Williamson

Mr. Kinney, much has been made about the location and the retrieval of the Lockheed Electra 10-E. Where do you stand on this location, as you testify here today?

Les Kinney

According to the witnesses who *saw* this aircraft, all military soldiers and officers on Saipan, sometime in July of 1940 the plane was burnt, and it was then shredded and run over by a bulldozer back and forth and shoved to the side of the airport runway. At that point in time, if you saw or have ever seen any of the pictures from 1944, there's dozens of abandoned, crashed, and wrecked Japanese and American aircraft along the edges of the other runway at Aslito field, which name was later changed. That plane is crunched, cracked, and broken up; it was burned. And that's where it remains; that's where it is today.

Chris Williamson

You think the odds are good that at *some point* the remains of the plane will ever be recovered?

Les Kinney

Never.

I would have to show you some photographs of 1944 and late 1945. We're talking hundreds of aircraft. That runway was used shortly *after* this happened by B29s taking off to bomb Tokyo. These B29s were wrecked and taken apart. There are dozens and dozens of them, all mashed together and thrown off to the side of the runways for maybe a mile. The idea of trying to separate all of this carnage to determine a serial number from one of the Electra's engines would be *nearly* impossible. It would be a project that would cost maybe $50-100 million; it would be an impossible task. And I'm not quite sure that that we *could anyway* because there was tremendous scrap activity on Saipan after the war.

I'm not sure how much of this material wasn't picked up and *actually brought back* to Japan and repurposed for new metal contents. In essence, I guess, *maybe*, Earhart's plane, partially, could be a 1969 Nissan.

Chris Williamson

Mr. Kinney, I'd like to switch gears a bit, if I may, and discuss the idea that Amelia Earhart, due to her incredible sinus issues, had a procedure known as the "Caldwell Luc" performed on her. We spoke about this in court during castaway. As you know, much was made about the Nikumaroro bones study by Dr. Richard Jantz in 2018, and I'd like our jury to *remember* that piece of evidence as we move further today.

First, can you tell us what the Caldwell Luc procedure entails? And can you tell the court what your research has told you regarding this event in her life?

Les Kinney

Yes, what you're describing is, of course, regarding some skeletal remains found on Gardner Island (now Nikumaroro) that TIGHAR insists has a strong possibility, based upon analysis, that it could be Amelia Earhart. As I said before, that is just pure *poppycock*. It's impossible. Even the British doctors at the time said that they believed *strongly* that the bones had been there for maybe forty to fifty years.

The evidence to show that it was *not* Amelia Earhart is this: She had a procedure done on two occasions to alleviate sinus headaches and sinus bacterial infections, an *awful procedure* called Caldwell Luc, where they will drill a hole inside her mouth up *into* her nasal passages, and it's the size of a dime. This was done to *alleviate that tension* and pressure *as well* as allow for the drainage of mucus. She had that done for *the first time* in 1926. Do I have any source material to back that up? No. But I *do know* that her sister, Muriel, *clearly stated* that Amelia had *had that procedure* done in Boston in 1926 to alleviate the pain that she was experiencing for years and years. That's pretty good, and of course she would be utilized as a witness to back that statement up.

The *second procedure* that Amelia had done was in Los Angeles at a hospital in 1934 or '35, and *that one* has been documented. The son of the doctor who *actually* completed the operation stated that he recalled *vividly* the notes in his office that that took place at that time. Lastly, Amelia Earhart *herself* in one of her letters *clearly indicates* that she had that procedure, and she names the doctor, she names the time, and it *exactly* corresponds to what the doctor had mentioned in the letter to Fred Goerner back in the 1960s. So we *know* she had that procedure done *once* in 1926 and a *second time* in the '30s on both sides of her face. That would have been *clearly visible* by any person; you would have *known* that the skull had that.

TIGHAR and the two British doctors make *no mention* whatsoever of that procedure, and they examined that skull clearly and carefully. The whole Hoodless bones theory is a bunch of poppycock.

Lastly, the bones were discovered in an area a long way from where TIGHAR believes her plane had crash-landed. It makes no sense that Earhart and Noonan would have walked three miles away and, for some reason, died at that location. They would have never done that.

Chris Williamson

One of the elephants in the room throughout this case has been a photo that you were responsible for discovering in the National Archives; it's become known as the "Jaluit dock photo." It was at the center of *Amelia Earhart: The Lost Evidence* in 2017. For our jury here today, can you give us an overview of that photo, that discovery, *and* the story? And can you tell us where we stand on that piece of evidence right now?

Les Kinney

When I *first* found that photo in the National Archives, it was in 2012. I got into the habit of *not* copying documents. It was simply too time consuming and too expensive. All of a sudden, you have hundreds and hundreds of documents that you've copied, and it's just labor intensive, and it just doesn't work. So what I started doing was I just started shooting pictures of every document that I felt was important, including photographs. And *that was one of them*, so I did that in 2012. When I glanced at it, of course I didn't give it much thought at all because I was moving fast, and I just had other things to do. A couple of years later, while I'm going through thousands and thousands of documents and photographs that I had picked up during the course of my research, I looked at it carefully, and I said, "Oh my God, what is this?"

I called my wife, who is an artist, and she's very good at observing details. I said, "Jane, what do you think of this, look at this?" and she said without any further hesitation, "That's Amelia Earhart, no question." And she's referring to the woman in the image with her back to the camera. I said, "What about this guy?" And she said, "Oh my God, it looks like Fred Noonan." And she said, "I'm more convinced that even though her face isn't showing, that is Amelia Earhart."

And of course, I looked a bit further, and I see all these *other* points of interest. It's at Jaluit, where I *knew she was.* According to the witnesses, she had been there. I identified the ship *absolutely positively* through navy records and Japanese records as being the *Koshu.* The *Koshu* is towing a barge, and *sitting on the barge,* of course, is this object that appeared to be an airplane. One wing you can't see very well. I put all this together and thought this has to be mid-July or earlier of 1937 at Jaluit because the ONI picture is clearly labeled. And I just felt that the points of interest are *just so pronounced* as being associated with everything that other various witnesses had said.

There's a record of a little boy saying he was brought down to the dock by a Japanese schoolmaster, who showed him children waving little Japanese flags as the ship comes in towing the barge with the silver airplane on it. There is another older gentleman who was Japanese who was at the seaplane base at Mili, I believe. He said, "While I was working there before the war, there was a ship that came in towing a barge, and on that barge was a silver airplane with two engines. They unloaded that plane, and they brought it somewhere." He said he didn't remember what happened to it because that just wasn't his interest; he had work to do. Then of course, there's the Marshallese witnesses at Mili Atoll who said, "We as youngsters were tasked by the Japanese to go help them remove a plane off a reef at Mili Atoll and load it onto a barge, which sailed away on the back of a ship."

All this added up, and I thought this *has to be* Earhart and Noonan.

Of course, the forensic evidence is irrefutable in that regard. With the intelligence available *now,* the facial-recognition software, new software, even *after* the production came out, the author says that with 99.99% certainty he believes that's right. I know I'm sounding like TIGHAR when I talk that way. So that's it.

I felt very confident of that.

I was devastated and embarrassed, really, but for different reasons. The reason I was embarrassed is that I *should have* looked a little bit further to see whether this photograph was somewhere else. I never thought that it would have shown up in a Japanese picture book, but it makes sense that it did. What *it is* is a coffee table book loosely bound, the kind that had strings holding it together. There's no question the copyright date on that picture book is 1935, and therefore since Earhart and Noonan had landed at Milli Atoll in 1937, there's *no way* that the photograph could be credible. To be honest with you, if I tried to introduce this into a court of law right now, I doubt if a judge would allow it simply because of that copyright date. With that said, I *did* go back to Japan, and I tried to find out more information relative to this 1935 picture book, and I *did* find it. It's not in the library, by the way; they just have the digital images there.

I found it in the university library, and I looked at it carefully; it is what it is, and the copyright date *is in* the fall of 1935. I actually found *another one*; there is *another* picture book almost *identical* to the one that is described in the 1935 picture book. There's a couple of pictures that are different, the index is slightly different, and there's a few other things that are different, like page numbering. In the 1935 picture book, a couple of the page numbers are wrong; they're not sequential. So it was kind of a haphazard job how that was put together. It was meant for a *local audience* and probably sold as a curio piece for any Japanese visitors in Palau during the 1930s. More significantly, the second picture book that I found that same picture in had the almost identical order of pictures. That picture book copyright date is *1933*. So therefore that means that picture could not have been taken *after* 1933, and it makes sense, right?

Except there was *no electricity* on that dock in 1933. I have evidence and source material that the electricity in Jaluit did not occur until the fall of 1935, and it wasn't everywhere. So therefore, I know that since this picture has an electrical line running down to the dock, it is *impossible* it was taken in 1933.

That means that picture book is not credible on its face, because we know there was not electricity there. That means the 1935 picture book *should also* come into question as far as the credibility. And why is this? According to the Japanese librarians I talked to, it would not have been uncommon for the little local man who decided to put that book together and pay some publisher in Japan to put it in a little picture book format, to use whatever copyright date he had *originally*. And I believe that's exactly what happened.

It would be tough to have this photograph be convincing *enough* to be admitted into evidence, but maybe it *would be* admitted in a court of law. At the same time, whoever was trying to *refute that photograph* would have ample reason to do so. The evidence that I just went over regarding the electrical lines and the 1933 book are *valid*. But more importantly, I don't think anybody would argue that the two individuals, the man on the far left and the woman with her back to you, are *both* Caucasians. And everybody says, "Yeah, okay, they're Caucasian." And the woman, of course, there's no question, she has a female body with the shoulders coming down into the narrow waist, and she has short hair. She's a Caucasian.

Amelia Earhart was a swimmer. If you look at that picture again and look at her swimming pictures, you could see that it's a body of a swimmer. Amelia actually was a strong swimmer, and she swam quite frequently.

My question to the jury in this particular case is, well then, *who are they?* And people have said, "Well, you know, there are probably other white people there." No. *There were no other white people there.* And I have the source documents from the navy *and* from the missionary logs that there was nobody there. The last missionaries had left Jaluit in the Marshall Islands in 1934. The navy *tried really hard* to find somebody who was there in 1939, 1940 or 1941, and *all the reports* said that the last people they knew of who were white who were there was in 1934. So my question to your jury is, who are these people? Who is this white man with the pronounced widow's peak and the white woman with short hair; who are they? They could be *anybody?* Well, that's silly, because we both know there are no other individuals who *could have been there* at that time other than Amelia Earhart and Fred Noonan.

And the other points of interests *are* valid. The *Koshu was* there. We have the plane on the back of the barge *at* Jaluit. And we have not touched on this, but I *do have Koshu's* logs; it was *indeed* at Jaluit, *docked*, during this time period that air Earhart was missing. When you put *all those things together*, I think I can make a convincing case and I still

737

believe it. I couldn't convict somebody for a capital crime based upon that picture, but there's *overwhelming evidence* to prove that picture is *probably valid*. Notice how I used the word "probably."

Chris Williamson

Is there anything else you'd care to share with me and our jury that you feel helps your case here?

Les Kinney

There *is* another tangible piece of evidence, and its documentary evidence that will *prove my case*, and I think it's irrefutable *except* that the name Earhart *is not* mentioned. Let me explain:

In the Marshall Islands, Earhart and Noonan, according to the source witnesses, left Jaluit, and then they were next seen on the on the atoll of Kwajalein. They were seen at Roi-Namur, which is a series of two islands, Roi and Namur, connected by a little passageway, which later the Japanese built into a naval land-based airfield. And of course, later they were seen on Saipan by a multitude of witnesses, but they were seen on Kwajalein at random by at least *two* witnesses. During the battle of Roi-Namur by the Americans, there was this young man, a twenty-eight-year-old marine; he was a sergeant. He and a group of younger marines came across a bombed-out building, and they pulled *out of that building* a suitcase.

When they opened the suitcase, they found what appeared to be women's clothes and some other incidental items that they could not remember. But *more specifically* they found a diary, and it was embossed with the words "The 10-year Diary of Amelia Earhart." His name was W. B. Jackson.

Fred Goerner found a man through a radio station in Texas, and this man was a good friend of that radio station. Goerner had done a series of prepublication broadcasts of his book, and this man heard of them. He told Fred Goerner that he has "this friend here in Texas who was a marine, and he has a story that you should hear." Of course, Goerner found out about him and interviewed him, and he wrote

Goerner a letter. And he said, that "the unit he was in was in the fourth marines. He was at Roi-Namur," and he named the date, which, by the way, is off by *one day*, but I think that's totally understandable. And he said *exactly* what I just described to you, and we have it. It's a witness statement, and that's all we have. But does he have anything to corroborate this? No. Nothing further other than what he saw, and they turned it over to regimental intelligence.

Now, here is *my evidence*. It's not much, but it *absolutely is* a smoking gun. I go to the National Archives, and I find a series of documents describing the battle of Roi-Namur, and the whole Marshalls for that matter, and I find a note. This note is regarding a phone call from the commanding general of the 4th Marine Division, and that part is *very* significant because that *same commanding general* was *also* assigned to Saipan. His name was Harry Schmidt. There was a phone call from Harry Schmidt to the commanding general of the V Amphibious Corps, who was "Mad Dog Smith" on board the ship, and here's what that note regarding that call said: "We found a suitcase belonging to a confidential US citizen. Turned over to intelligence." I saw this, and it was buried among thousands of other little entries, and I don't know how I saw it, but I could not believe it. Because I knew that *that must be* associated with what W. B. Jackson told Fred Goerner.

So I started looking. Not *only* was it a suitcase found at Roi-Namur, but it *happened to be found* by the same 4th Marine Division at the time that W. B. Jackson said he found the suitcase. Now we have *documented evidence* to tie those two together. Sadly, it doesn't say the name. It says, "found a suitcase belonging to a confidential US citizen." There's *no question in my mind*. The date is off by *one day*, going back to W. B. Jackson's memory. It *clearly is* a smoking gun. I think it's *even more* significant than the photograph, Amelia Earhart and Fred Noonan at Roi Namur and it is corroborated by the letter, it's corroborated by the official document that I found, and it's corroborated by one or more witnesses who said they were there.

Chris Williamson
Mr. Kinney, I have one more area that I'd like to touch on with you

before we go to the defense. I'd like you to tell our jury about the Freedom of Information Act and the requests that you've placed over the years to *get information* on the Earhart/Noonan case released so that we might discover *more information* on what happened to them in Saipan. Can you do that for the court now, please?

Les Kinney

Sure. The Freedom of Information Act was enacted in the mid-1960s, and it was meant to have an open government. At that point in time, they're *very* sincere about it. Prior to that, you'd write a letter, and if you didn't get a response back from that particular agency, then you'd probably enlist the services of a congressman to help you. Everybody thought that FOIA would open the doors, but all of a sudden, the agencies did not like it at all, and they put a lot of stipulations into that bill before it was passed. So you have eight or nine exemptions; one is *national security*, one is an *active criminal investigation*, one is *sensitive personnel records*, etc., etc. It's been around now for a long time, and I started using it.

If the material has been *declassified*, and it is at the National Archives or some *other* government repository, you don't use FOIA, you just request the documents.

We are talking about documents that *still have not been released* by the United States government. That's the whole purpose of FOIA. I have filed maybe a couple of hundred relating to the Earhart/Noonan disappearance, and **I have only gotten two** of those things back with *any* positive information that I could use. It's not that the agencies are so restrictive that they *don't* help you. They say that it is "beyond their means" or that "you were not being specific enough with the information that you're requesting"; there's a myriad of reasons why they come back negative. Probably for the most part, they couldn't find it, and they're being honest with you. I have filed appeals on *several of them*, and I've gotten information on *two or three of them*, which did not really relate to Amelia Earhart, by the way.

The process is labor intensive; when you file it, they have twenty-one days to respond. Normally, they'll take two to four months because they don't care about what the law says. They don't care about following the guidelines of the statute, and you'll get an answer back in two or three months. More than likely, you'll have to write them *again* and say, "Look, I want the information I requested per law." And maybe a month or two later they will respond back and say, "We're working on it." Then you might get a *final response* back in six months to a year; in *some cases*, it's taken me *four to five years* to get that agency to respond to my FOIA. So it's a terribly wasteful effort of my time to have to wait for this information, and you're frustrated by it.

A great example of this is James Nichols, whom we talked about earlier. He goes to Saipan on orders of the highest level of government to either *bring back* information relative to Amelia Earhart being captured by the Japanese or destroy that evidence if need be. He accompanied the American fleet to the Battle of Saipan, and he did his business; *he is the one* who ordered the destruction of the Lockheed Electra, Earhart's plane, at Aslito field. He *also is the one* who took possession of the briefcase that you briefly touched on earlier, which was found by another marine. He brought that material, everything that he had found that was relative, back to the United States on its own private PBY plane. Pretty impressive.

Of course, it's only from the retell, so to speak, the account of a family member who heard about this from this guy back in 1960, a long time ago. I filed a FOIA with the Central Intelligence Agency because I had strong belief that the guy *must have been* an OSS agent. And everything corroborated; everything that I found out about him, including his personnel records when he was in the navy prior to World War II, was *spot on* with the information that I received from the family member. Despite this, the CIA *denied* my requests based upon this nebulous phrase they use the "Glomar response," which we've all heard before: "We neither confirm nor deny the existence or the nonexistence of the materials you're seeking."

Of course, I filed an appeal because I felt strongly about it, and I thought that they should *at least* tell me whether this man *actually existed* as an officer or an agent of the OSS. There may be a few readers who would know that, in fact, all of the OSS employees' names were released, and *yes, they were*. But those employees who transitioned over to the CIA after the demise of the OSS *were never* released. According to this family member, he had transitioned to the Central Intelligence Agency, or at least it was *believed that he did.*

So I filed my appeal, and I got no answer. I waited a month or two, still with no answer. I *finally* got an inside number, and I got ahold of *my* case appeals manager for my FOIA. And this woman knew my background; she was very helpful. She said, "Mr. Kinney, we should have an answer back for you in two to three weeks. It shouldn't take that much longer; we have to get answers from another agency before we can act upon your request." And I thought, that means they had to get *some other agency's permission* before the releases. I got my appeal results back about a month later, and they *denied* my appeal. At that point in time, I filed a civil suit in the US district court in Seattle, Washington, asking *again* for the material. The CIA said that, "We believe that if there is any material that Mr. Kinney is requesting, it is national security sensitive, and we're not going to release it if in fact that material exists."

I appeal it *again* to the ninth circuit in San Francisco, and I lost on the same grounds. "Mr. Kinney has no further rights to this material. We must acquiesce to the affidavit from the CIA indicating that 'if there was material, it can't be released because it might endanger national security.'" And that's it.

It leaves me hanging, and I'm *very* frustrated. And I have to go on with this. You mentioned earlier the two hundred witnesses; there's probably *at least* one hundred *direct source witnesses* who said they saw a white man and woman. A hundred. You have *at least* ten or fifteen military personnel who saw something that would be considered Earhart's plane, her grave site, picking up bones. These are good, solid witnesses, and they're *direct* witnesses. I have a hard time not believing them. And then the *most important* thing is this: You have *three* high-ranking military officers: the commander of the War in the Pacific, Admiral Chester Nimitz; you have Erskine Graves; and you have *another* marine general who won the Medal of Honor *at* Saipan.

All three of those men said that Earhart and Noonan had met their end at Saipan. Nimitz told Goerner (through a friend, because he wouldn't say it openly); he said, "Fred, keep on going because what you will find will **stagger your imagination**." There's *no question* that's Earhart. Nimitz said that "Earhart and Noonan met their end in Saipan."

I have a hard time understanding why *anybody, including the press,* would believe *any* other theory.

This is not a theory anymore; this is fact.

These men were honorable. They served in the war and were the *highest-ranking officers in the Pacific.* They *all* said that Earhart and Noonan died on Saipan. And for some reason, the vast majority of the general public says, "Oh, I don't believe it." It's **crazy**. We don't just have a preponderance of evidence to bring this to a logical conclusion that she died in Saipan. We don't have evidence that is *beyond a reasonable doubt.* We have **overwhelming evidence** that she died in Saipan, *in captivity* and in the custody of the Japanese.

Chris Williamson

Are you confident that this case is going to see an ending?

Les Kinney

Oh, eventually absolutely.

It might be beyond *our lifetime.*

This government is stubbornly resisting. What *it is* is that all of these files and all of this material that we're talking about is dispersed in a variety of places that *might contain* Earhart information. That might happen to be uncovered after we're dead, simply by somebody sifting through some old warehouse at the National Archives.

The information is *also available* in Japan, but it's such a nightmare. It's really, really difficult for a researcher to go over there and uncover any writings or documents in Kanji that the Japanese *still* might have, including in private families. Old Kanji is very difficult to read. Anybody under the age of sixty-five or seventy, they labor over a document, and there would have to be thousands and thousands of documents to be looked at, especially from the Sai Pan prison and the hospital. So the answer lies in Saipan. Maybe in fifty to a hundred years, somebody will have the answer. But am I *confident* it will be solved shortly? I would say right now that if we can get information on James Nichols and from the captain of the *Koshu*'s upper flat, there's a chance.

Maybe *not a good chance.*

But there's a *chance.*

Chris Williamson

Thank you. No further questions, Your Honor.

"When people try to remember things from a long time ago, there is a much greater chance that the memory they report could be a distorted memory. The account they give is therefore distorted."

Jen Taylor

The defense calls *Christopher French* to the stand.

Can you introduce yourself to our jury, please?

Christopher French

I'm Professor Chris French. I am a professor of psychology in the department of psychology at Goldsmiths University of London.

Jen Taylor

And what area of research do you specialize in there?

Christopher French

I am the head of the anomalistic psychology research unit, and anomalistic psychology really focuses on the psychology of weird stuff. I'm interested in things like why people might *claim to have been* abducted by aliens or seen ghosts, etc., etc. *One aspect* of that is, of course, the *reliability or unreliability* of eyewitness testimony.

Jen Taylor

Is it possible for somebody to have a very real, *real to them*, memory of something having happened to them or something having happened that they saw, for that to be *entirely not real*?

Christopher French

That is *totally possible*. There's a mountain of very, *very strong* empirical evidence to show that *we can,* under very controlled experimental conditions, *implant* those so-called rich false memories in a sizable minority of the population.

Jen Taylor

Most of us have *our own* memories, we have *our own* experiences, and most of us have never had reason to doubt that what *we believe happened* is not *exactly what happened.* Based on your research, how is that?

Christopher French

Many people *do believe wrongly* in that memory works in a way similar to a video recorder: It's accurately recording every detail of everything you experience. Even though you may not be able to *recall* all those details when asked, *they are there,* if only you could find some way of getting at them.

And that's just a total misconception. Memory is a reconstructive process. Whenever you remember *anything,* whether it's something from yesterday or from years ago, you are *reconstructing* that memory, *partly on the basis* of more or less accurate memory traces that *do* correspond to what you may have experienced, partly filling in gaps, and maybe elaborating on things. And of course, it's because memory is a reconstructive process that is prone to errors. Sometimes, when we are producing those memories, we might fill in the gaps in a way that was *wrong.*

And as I say, we've got various very well-tried and trusted techniques to *actually deliberately* implant false memories. One of these is to get people to just imagine the things that *never actually happened.* And then later on, on an apparently unrelated occasion, we ask them whether these things *ever did actually happen?* We give them a whole range of different possible scenarios. And you find that if people have *imagined* something, *particularly people with very good imaginations,* quite likely *some of them* will say, "Yes, I did actually experience that." And of course, what they're doing is they're confusing their memory for what *they imagined* with being a memory for something that *really did* happen.

Jen Taylor

You're talking about situations where an experimenter has deliberately implanted a false memory into somebody else's head, giving them a story that they *knew* didn't happen. What about somebody who's just asking questions? What about somebody who maybe is a detective or investigator, somebody who's trying to interview witnesses to an event that *they believe* happened? Is that a situation where a false memory can be inadvertently implanted into somebody's mind?

Christopher French

It absolutely is. There's a whole body of research looking at the effects of leading questions. Just to give you a couple of examples. This is from the work of Elizabeth Loftus, who's probably *the major researcher* in this area. Research that she carried out back in the '70s, for example, showed people videos of two cars crashing into each other. Now, if you *then show* people that video and ask them, "How fast were the cars traveling when they smashed into each other?" versus, "How fast were they traveling when they contacted each other, or hit each other?" In other words, you just *change the word* that you use. And it looks like on the surface that you're asking the *same* question, but of course you're not. "Smashed into" implies *much higher* speeds than "contacted." That's reflected in the answers that people give, even though they all saw the same video.

Similarly, if you ask the question, "Did you see a broken headlight?" versus, "Did you see the broken headlight?" The latter question implies that *there was* a broken headlight? Did you see it? People are *much more* likely to say that they saw *a* broken headlight in this case, even though *there wasn't one*, as opposed to you asking the question in the form of, "Did you see a broken headlight?" The way that the questions are asked can have a very, *very* big impact on what people report.

. . .

Jen Taylor

How about we talk about a specific example. Say someone witnessed a plane coming down in a harbor.

If, for example, we asked about a plane that *crashed into a harbor* versus a plane that *landed in a harbor*; with those different variations in how the question is asked, would you expect a possibility that that could have an effect on the person's answer, or what the person remembers?

Christopher French

It's interesting that you should choose that example because, in terms of experimental studies that imply that *maybe sometimes* people can remember things that they didn't actually witness at all, another of the kinds of techniques that's used is something that's referred to as the "crushing memories paradigm," and this was a technique that was *first used* in the Netherlands, I think it was. There *had been* a genuinely terrible plane crash where a plane had crashed into a block of flats, and many lives were lost. Of course, it was a big national news story for a long time. People were asked in this study if they could remember seeing the news footage of the plane crashing into the building, and many of them reported that they *could remember the footage*, and they could describe things like the angle of the plane as it approached and so on and so forth.

*The truth is it was **never** caught on camera.*

What was *happening here* was the event had happened, but presumably when people would hear about the event, they would imagine it in their heads, and for some of them, when they're subsequently asked if they *had seen* this nonexistent footage, they're remembering the time that they *imagined the footage*, and they're basing their answers on that. I think it's a really nice illustration of the way that this can happen.

Jen Taylor

Are you familiar with the hypothesis that Amelia Earhart and Fred Noonan crash-landed in the South Pacific and were captured by the Japanese?

Christopher French

I'm familiar with that in broad terms, yeah.

Jen Taylor

Before we get too much into that theory, I want to ask about the passage of time and whether or not that would play a role in a person's memory. The first witness to come forward about this incident did so twenty-five to thirty years *after the fact*, and then after that, the flood-gates opened, and many *more witnesses* followed.

So before we get into all of that, just focusing on the passage of, say, twenty-five to thirty years before the first witness came forward, does that raise any red flags for you?

Christopher French

When people try to remember things from a long time ago, there is a *much greater chance* that the memory that they report *could be* a distorted memory, and the account they give is therefore distorted.

There's a nice study by my friends Richard Wiseman and Peter Lamont, it's very different contents than what we're talking about here, but they were interested in reports of the so-called "Indian rope trick." This is a kind of classic conjuring trick, which many people who lived in India around about the turn of the last century reported that they had witnessed the trick with their own eyes. Whereas Western conjurers were saying this could not be done in the open air, there's no way you could do that trick, and there were large monetary rewards for anyone who *could*. What Richard and Peter did was, they looked at the various accounts in terms of *how full they were*, some of them were just kind of describing what they saw, a trick that involved *part of the*

749

classic whole trick, and others gave the *full account*. They got independent judges to rate how impressive the account was, and then they plotted the degree of impressiveness with the distance in time between *when it was supposed to have happened* and *when it was reported*. They got a really nice straight-line graph. In other words, the *longer the time period had passed* between this event supposedly happening and it being reported, the *more elaborate and impressive* the memory had become. This strongly suggests that we were seeing memories being distorted in the direction of making them *more impressive*. I think this is a general thing, that we would expect that the longer time passes, the *more likely* it is that that your memory will *not be* accurate regarding what *you think* you've witnessed.

Jen Taylor

The *first* witness who came forward was already living in the States at this time. She had spoken to a newspaper in California, and then later a *second* journalist came to interview her further about what happened, and he brought with him a photo array of different women. He asked her to pick out which woman she saw, and she picked out Amelia Earhart.

Now my question to *you is* we haven't yet made it to the part of the story where all of the researchers are visiting Saipan and the Marshall Islands; we're still in California. she's living in America; she's already been interviewed by *another newspaper*, which then published a story with a headline about Amelia Earhart. Under *those circumstances* do you think that there's reason to doubt her account and memory of what happened? What kinds of things would you be looking for in those interviews to help you determine whether or not that might be the case?

Christopher French

I would be very keen to know whether she'd had any opportunity to look at pictures of Amelia Earhart, which would seem to be very likely given what had made her interested in the first place, this idea that *maybe* she was a witness. Even if by that point, for some bizarre reason, she'd never taken any great interest in Amelia Earhart's life, I'm sure *at that point* she would have. There would be photographs in library books and newspapers; the fact that she could then *subsequently correctly identify* Amelia from a lineup, so to speak, it wouldn't have very much evidential value in my eyes.

Jen Taylor

And what about the effect of positive feedback? She's saying, "This is what I saw," and, "This is who I saw," and the people that she's talking to are getting excited about it, and they're following up with additional questions. We see this in criminal cases all the time, where sometimes the person being interviewed *knows that they're lying, knows that they're making a false confession,* and is trying to say what they need to say to get out of that room. Other times though, we might see a case of a person with maybe a diminished mental capacity or sometimes even just a person who's very stressed, and they will say what they *think happened* based on suggestions and positive feedback that they're getting from the interviewer.

Is that something that's possible here? This, obviously, isn't a *criminal case,* and she's probably not under any kind of duress. I've seen no evidence that this particular first witness has any kind of diminished mental capacity. Can a normal person with normal intelligence and capabilities have *real memories* about something that didn't happen based on the reaction they're getting in the media and from the journalists whom she's talking to?

Christopher French

That's *absolutely* the case. I suppose what comes to mind then is the "satanic panic." Back in the 1980s and '90s and still today, we get instances where this happens. Admittedly, we're typically dealing with children who are being interviewed on bizarre allegations of things that are said to have taken place at daycare centers and so on. What you can *clearly see* when you're looking at those transcripts is the children will deny and deny and deny that anything had happened until *eventually,* they imply that *maybe* it did. And they'll get lots of positive feedback and rewards, and *some of those kids* no doubt come out of there *genuinely believing* that they were victims of these bizarre crimes.

Putting that in the context of someone who is obviously not a child and presumably of normal intelligence and not under any great duress, there is *still* a tendency that people have to want to give answers that are in line with what they're sensing is being asked. I don't know the details of this lady *in particular,* but the idea that she may well have actually quite enjoyed being in the limelight and quite quickly picked up on what it was that was going to get the most attention, that *may well have* swayed her, however unintentionally, in the direction of giving those answers and then maybe even *ultimately herself* believing that those things *really did* happen the way she described them.

Jen Taylor

That journalist who interviewed her then took a trip *himself* to Saipan in order to interview natives there.

He was followed by a number of *other* researchers, so many people have gone and interviewed a number of people both in Saipan and also the Marshall Islands because part of this hypothesis involves that group of islands. And they did this in the '60s, '70s and '80s. Subsequently, *more and more people* began to come forward and say, "Actually, yes, I did see a plane. I did see an American woman with a male companion."

Some of them even named names, but they never said the exact name. They would say things like "Earharto" or "Amira," things that are very close but never exact. What are your initial thoughts on this phenomenon; one witness followed by a *few more* and a *few more* and then the floodgates opening, and now we have two hundred plus witnesses?

Christopher French

What springs to my mind is a study that was looking at memory for a sniper attack on a school that *did* take place in America. One of the interesting things was that a lot of the kids who actually *hadn't witnessed* the sniper attack at all came up with very, *very* detailed accounts of having seen it. So one child who was actually away from school that day came up with a very detailed account of what he'd witnessed.

I think there is kind of a natural tendency to want to be part of the action. You don't want to miss out on this big story, and I think in *some cases*, of course, what *we can't tell* without a lot of further digging into the details, and even then perhaps not, is whether the person coming up with the account *actually knows* that they are just making the whole thing up, versus them actually believing that they *really did* witness it. I think the overall weight of evidence was, yes, at least *some of those people* genuinely *do come to believe* that they did see something.

Again, I go back to classic studies by Sir Frederick Bartlett back in the 1930s. We know that stories become *better* the more they are retold. The most human experience tells you that bits of the stories are inconsistent; they don't quite seem to fit. It makes sense that details either change or drop out of the story altogether; other embellishments get added in to make it more consistent with what we know to be the facts of the case that are available etc., etc. So I would kind of expect that to happen. It doesn't necessarily mean to imply that any of those people are *deliberately lying*, although some of them *may be*; it's just the way that memory works and the way that stories develop and are retold and passed on.

Jen Taylor

Bottom line: if we have *that many witnesses* and we have *no other physical evidence*, no corroborating evidence other than witnesses corroborating *each other*, is it possible that this *could be* a phenomenon of mass amounts of people remembering things that either didn't happen, or having their memory distorted to fit what others *believed* happened?

· · ·

753

Christopher French

I certainly think it's *possible*. How *likely* is it? I wouldn't like to say one way or the other without digging a lot deeper into the details of the case. There are all kinds of questions in my mind, listening to you describe how this story has developed. You'd like to go and interview all these individual witnesses and people around them to find out if they have always spoken about this event, or is this something that they only started speaking about in the 1960s onwards? That would be *crucially important* information. To what extent all of these accounts *actually* mutually support each other. There are some other very, *very* big contradictions in there that indicate that *at least one* of those two contradictory accounts *must be wrong*.

Those are the kind of questions I would be asking. The thing that came to my mind very clearly as you were describing the way this story unfolded is some of the classic UFO cases. In particular, stories from Roswell in America or Rendlesham Forest in the UK, instances that were kind of minor events way back in the past suddenly becoming reignited decades later, and all of a sudden, you have several witnesses coming forward saying they witnessed this. You have investigators coming in with a particular hypothesis, searching for evidence for that hypothesis. One of the strongest cognitive biases that we all suffer from is something called "confirmation bias." We notice, take note of and accept the evidence that supports our beliefs and the hypothesis that we're putting forward. We tend to find reasons to reject or ignore or *not accept* any evidence that seems to contradict it. So these investigators are coming in, and they've got a particular story that they're trying to find evidence for, and that influences *the way* they interview witnesses, unintentionally perhaps. But it might push them in one particular direction and lead them in various ways. Certainly, you find that with these classic cases within the world of the paranormal.

At the end of the day, in the absence of any strong physical forensic evidence to support the various claims, memory on its own typically *is not enough*.

. . .

Jen Taylor

The proponents of this theory will tell you that the *reason why* the folklore exists and the *reason why* this belief exists is because it actually happened. Those who would *discredit this theory* say the opposite, that the reason *why* this folklore exists is because people were *there* asking questions, and the folklore was caused by the *investigation* not the other way around. Is there any way to tell which is the truth in this case? Which came first?

Christopher French

I don't think there is. What would be of interest, going back to the point I made earlier, is to what extent was this an important part of the folklore *prior* to it becoming a big story in the west? If up until the 1960s, this was not something that was part of the general folklore of that particular area, then I think we'd have very strong reasons to believe that it's the interest from the west that has caused the folklore to take root.

Again, unfortunately if you were to ask people if this was something that was talked about prior to the 1960s, *could you even trust their answers* anyway, because of the natural tendency that we have to distort memory in the various ways I've described.

Jen Taylor

There has been the claim made that Amelia and Fred were the only, *or* among the only, white people visiting that area, and therefore if a native witness identified them in, say, a photo lineup, we should trust that evidence more because this was something that was unusual for them. They have reason to trust that their identification is more accurate for that reason. Can you address whether or not that is an accurate assumption?

Christopher French

In general terms, I'd say no. What people will know from their own experience; *most people* have what's somehow referred to as an "own race bias" or "cross race bias." There is a tendency that people have to find faces from their own people or their own race easier to differentiate from people of different races.

Without wishing to be racist in any sense whatsoever to lots of white westerners or Chinese people who are saying all black American people or all African people look the same and so on. But the bias works *the other way around as well*, that white people are all harder to differentiate. If you happen to be Chinese or you happen to be African, it depends on lots of factors. It depends upon whether you grew up in a situation where you very rarely saw people or those of other races. If you did, then you will not have the bias so strongly. But it's a very robust effect that we typically are *not as good* at recognizing faces from people of other races as we are from people of our own race.

Jen Taylor

We were to believe 100% that this witness *did see* a white woman and a white man with her. We also believe that was the first or only white people they had ever seen. Then, thirty years later, they were given a photo lineup and were asked to identify who it was they saw. How much trust would you place in that photo identification?

Christopher French

If it's a photo lineup situation, then that is a different form of asking the question than just showing you a picture of Amelia and asking, "Is this the woman that you saw?" In a photo lineup, if they can't really tell the difference between white women, then the question is why would they *then choose* Amelia and get it correct? You might argue that there were ten pictures in the array: there's a one-in-ten chance of them choosing the right one. If in fact they *don't know,* what I'd be more concerned about *there* would be the possibility of contamination in the sense of having had the opportunity to already look at pictures of Amelia and therefore knowing what she looked like. Again, without knowing the details of exactly how these tests were carried out, it strikes me as kind of very likely that someone who knows they're going to be interviewed about this white woman that they claim to have seen many decades earlier, who *may or may not have been* Amelia, it strikes me as quite likely that person would have probably seen a picture of her at some point *before* the lineup was done. I want to see very clear evidence that that *didn't happen* **before** I placed much faith in the results of that particular lineup.

Jen Taylor

I have no further questions, Your Honor.

Chris Williamson

Your Honor, at this time, the project rests and would like to turn this case over to our jury for deliberation.

Bailiff

ALL RISE!

Post-Trial Discussion

Chris Williamson

Alright, we've finished Japanese capture. This is a really robust piece. You just heard me walk through twenty-seven of the eyewitnesses with Rob Ellos. We also talked about one of my favorite stories, "the message in a bottle," as well as the ONI report with Jon Hagadorn, and we heard from Les Kinney; it doesn't get any bigger than him. You also brought Chris French aboard, which was a nice balancing act for what we're doing.

Lots to unpack here; what are your thoughts on all of that?

Jen Taylor

I think we got a really nice, succinct overview of the timeline of witnesses; I think that Rob did a really good job laying that out. Obviously, I think there are problems, and I thought that I conveyed that in my questions. I think that there are issues with the fact that there's just no physical evidence as of yet. So far in trial, we haven't seen any physical evidence. Can I say that's a little convenient?

Chris Williamson

You can.

Jen Taylor

Every time there's a story that involves a potential piece of corroborating physical evidence, conveniently there's some story about it being mysteriously lost. I don't want to be disrespectful, but it does start to carry a little bit of a mythological fairy-tale kind of feel. When you have this story and you have these artifacts that are involved, but they're mysteriously lost or they've vanished and we don't know where they are, it does seem like we're starting to chase ghosts. That's not to say that I'm not convinced. I'm still trying to keep an open mind, and we haven't finished the trial yet. There's still a lot of evidence and witness testimony that readers are going to consume. But I was also expecting two hundred witnesses.

Chris Williamson

If I presented all two hundred witnesses, we'd need a dedicated book.

Jen Taylor

This was your moment! We still got over twenty witnesses, which is still a substantial number.

Chris Williamson

It is. It's a good snapshot.

Jen Taylor

But we got to actually dig through it and look at the details of what they actually had to say, and it was fun. I really enjoyed going through all of that.

Chris Williamson

There's really an abundance of witnesses whom we could pull from. But I remember asking Rob Ellos beforehand to pick the most crucial eyewitnesses that he felt he could come up with, and that's the list that we got. And I think he did a great job of separating the list by people who have been documented in the news or on film or on camera, audio, affidavits or whatever. So that's how we built the structure when it came to presenting these witnesses. Twenty-seven eyewitnesses really served as a representation of the over two hundred that are floated around, and that is a **big** number.

Going back to your point regarding the physical, tangible evidence just not working out for this particular hypothesis, I sort of look at it from another perspective. You'll hear me ask Les Kinney later about frustration because if you're a modern-day investigator and you're working on this case, and the physical evidence just seems to keep on eluding you, that has to be incredibly frustrating that you have to just work with eyewitness testimony. Not to discount that at all, but it sure would be great if you could have a physical, tangible piece of evidence.

If you go back to our segment on Buka, you'll recall that we have one eyewitness, this little boy, and he tells a story much like a lot of these people in the Marshall Islands and Saipan are telling. The key difference there though is that his original story can point to something that actually exists, that's there right now. They can go look at it, they can put their hands on it, they can actually study this piece, and they can try to determine if that little boy's story matches up with this piece and vice versa. We can't do that here because it seems like everything just seems to slip through people's fingers. It seems to be just out of reach, and it's one of those things that can add a lot of frustration to someone investigating this case.

Jen Taylor

When you have a situation like this with very little physical evidence and 95% of the case is on the credibility of eyewitnesses, I still have to go back to my position of "we don't have those witnesses here."

I can't cross-examine somebody who claims to have seen something, and we can't have that kind of conversation because those people aren't here anymore. I know that goes back to the hearsay argument that I made before, but in my mind that's why we have that. Being on the defense, I should have the right to confront witnesses against my client. I know this is a little bit more theoretical than an actual criminal case, but that's the whole point of the confrontation clause, and it's the whole point of the hearsay rule.

Chris Williamson

Sure.

. . .

Jen Taylor

I know that you talked with Rob beforehand regarding who the strongest witnesses would be, and I loved hearing that. But what we don't get is people on the other side, maybe the strongest witnesses against this theory. Fred Goerner and others who went out there to investigate a particular theory likely spoke to many, many people. Of the people whom they talked to, how do I know and how does our jury know that those who made it into his book or our podcast were the only ones who had anything to say? What if there's fifty other people who say, "No, I was there around that time, and I saw somebody who looks completely different?" Or, "I saw something completely contradictory?" Unless we can talk to the people who were actually there with an unbiased mindset, we can't really get the whole story. What we get is a cherry-picked number of witnesses who support the Japanese capture theory.

Chris Williamson

My counter to that would be that the twenty years I've been researching this case, I have never once come across anybody who was in or around Saipan or the Marshall Islands who did not support this theory. I would think that in the time I've been researching it, I would have come across something, anything, **one thing**, that would not support this case, and I have never been able to do that.

What I found really interesting and what kind of made me sweat a little bit was your back and forth with Ellos during his testimony. You really hammered on Thomas Devine's credibility, and I want to know what your reasoning was behind that.

Jen Taylor

In my experience, sometimes you meet somebody who truly and honestly believes something so much that they're willing to do whatever it takes to prove to others that they're right.

761

. . .

Chris Williamson
Right.

Jen Taylor
I was not trying to imply that everything he ever said about this case is a lie; that is not it at all. I think he has an honest belief that he saw what he saw. He interpreted what he saw a certain way, and that is what he believed. He's put genuine effort into trying to work on this story and to prove his truth. However, I noticed that he had no problem bending the truth or lying about evidence in order to promote his truth and his story. In particular for him it was because he believes James Forrestal was in Saipan when that could not have possibly been true, and it was a hill he was going to die on. He did whatever it took to prove that to others. If he's willing to do that about one thing, what else is he willing to do that about? The reason why this is so important is out of all of these witnesses, he was the only person who was able to identify a serial number. That's **huge**.

Chris Williamson
Yeah.

Jen Taylor
That's a big piece of evidence. The serial number on the plane is what everyone wants; it's what everyone talks about. It's one of the biggest smoking guns other than DNA, and he claimed to have seen it. We know that he is capable of bending the evidence and lying about it just a little bit. How do we trust that? It's, of course, up to the people reading this to decide how much, if any, credibility to give each witness.

The fact that he was willing to lie does have some bearing on his credibility.

How much?

That's up to each individual person to decide.

Chris Williamson

After this, readers should have a good representation of what Japanese capture stands for. It was the most requested theory for us to put on trial, and now that trial is over. So much information here, it's almost overwhelming trying to keep up. I can imagine how our readers must be feeling right now.

Jen Taylor

I think that there *is* something there. I think that it's a really, *really* interesting theory.

It's probably one of my favorite ones to research. There's just so many little rabbit holes you can go down, so many aspects to this story, and it was a lot of fun working on it. That being said, I still have tons of reasonable doubt, I really do, and we can go over that if you want, but I don't think that we're there yet. I don't think that we're at a "beyond a reasonable doubt" place in my mind. I have a lot of things that I still have doubts about, things that I still have questions about.

Chris Williamson

Sure.

Jen Taylor

For example, what plane did Josephine see? At the very beginning of all the Japanese capture evidence, you played a clip from her, and it was pretty unequivocal that she *didn't see* a Japanese plane, that it was not a Japanese plane, right?

Chris Williamson
Right.

Jen Taylor
However, the theory as I understand it is that she landed in the Marshall Islands, was taken by the Japanese, her plane was put aboard the *Koshu*, and that's how they made it to Saipan.

Chris Williamson
Yeah.

Jen Taylor
If that's true and Josephine saw Amelia Earhart and Fred Noonan landing on Saipan, she couldn't have seen the Electra; she had to have seen a Japanese plane. So that doesn't really add up. When I asked Rob Ellos about that, he seemed to brush it off like it didn't matter. But I think it *does matter*. If she's seeing someone land in that harbor, and *it's not* a Japanese plane, that definitely opens up the possibility that what she's seeing *isn't the same event* that is being described in Fred Goerner's book. His book states that somebody landed in the Marshall Islands, their plane was taken, and then they were moved to Saipan that way. That's *not* the same event that she's seeing. It's also really unclear whether or not she was seeing a seaplane or a landplane, because again, if it was an Electra, that's a landplane.

There's no reason for it to try to land at the sea harbor. There's an airstrip. If they're being transported on a Japanese seaplane, well, then it makes sense for them to go into the harbor. If not, then they should have gone to the airstrip that's on Saipan. There are just still so many questions there, and I have reasonable doubt as to whether what Josephine saw is the same event being described by the other witnesses.

· · ·

Chris Williamson

Did your conversation with Professor French help sway you or help fill in the blanks on some of that reasonable doubt?

Jen Taylor

I think it did. In talking to him, I kind of just assumed that if somebody saw something and they relate to you that they're confident in what they saw, and they tell the same story over and over again, well then, 100%, we should take that as gospel. That's what they saw, and why would they lie? *After talking to him,* I realized that just because they are confident in what they saw and repeat the same story over and over again and they're probably not lying, that *doesn't mean* that that's *actually* what they saw. It doesn't even mean that's *even close* to what they saw. There's a lot of other things that have to be considered. Just because a lot of people saw something similar over a period of time that *also isn't* necessarily indicative of its accuracy. Speaking with him kind of made me realize that there's a lot of things that could be going on here. And I guess I just kind of reiterate my position from the very beginning. That I understand Fred Goerner and all of these other researchers were able to talk to those people, but they're not here to speak to us *directly*. They're not here to speak to the jury and to the readers directly. We don't have transcripts of their questions and answers, what they talked about, what they were asked; we *just have* what we have.

Books that researchers wrote and summaries of what they said, and I just don't think that's enough in this case. Now, like I said, it's an interesting story, and it's certainly a reason to investigate further. But that in and of itself *isn't enough* evidence. Let's put it that way

Chris Williamson

Since you came on board and started working with me, a lot of people have said, "Wait until you get to Japanese capture; it's going to be so incredible and so overwhelming!" And they're not wrong about that; it is *very* robust. But now that you've now gone through that, do you feel like the evidence, the data, the witnesses, and everything as a whole lived up to that pre-trial hype for you?

Jen Taylor

Yes and no, there was a lot there. There's a lot of stories there that I didn't really expect.

There are lot of things that *did* give me pause overall, from when it was pitched to me at the very beginning. People saying things like, "This is the truth, and once you look at it, you're not going to have any doubt in your mind that this is the truth." I mean, *that* certainly hasn't happened.

Chris Williamson

You know, it's funny, you're mentioning the way it was pitched to us: "This is not a theory; this is the truth at last." When somebody comes at you with something like that, does that hinder their case? Does it help it?

Jen Taylor

In a way, I almost want to say it hinders it because what you're doing is you're raising the burden of proof for yourself. If you're in a criminal court, and you're the prosecution, you have to prove your case *beyond a reasonable doubt.* And prosecutors will tell you every day that that *does not mean **beyond a shadow of a doubt.*** There *is* room for a little bit of unknown, maybe a few questions. If you knew everything that happened, that necessarily means that you were there, and you saw it. And that's never going to be the case here; no one's going to know 100% what happened. That's why the standard is *beyond a reasonable doubt.* And they'll try to soften that a little bit, because that helps them. What *I* want to do on the defense is say, "No, no, no, no, beyond a reasonable doubt, that's the highest burden in the land. No legal standard is above beyond a reasonable doubt." I want to make it seem like an insurmountable obstacle for them. So when someone comes to me and says, "I know beyond a shadow of a doubt that this is the truth. And when you hear all of this evidence, you will know that too," that almost raises the bar for them. It makes their work a little bit more difficult. Yeah, I think that does hinder it a little bit.

Chris Williamson

When you hear someone like Les Kinney make a statement as he did on the stand with me, "This is not proof beyond a reasonable doubt. This is a preponderance of evidence. It's overwhelming," what do you think of something like that?

Jen Taylor

Yeah, that goes back to kind of what I said before; he's trying to lower that burden of proof. And I don't think he's doing it in a sneaky kind of way. Like I said from the very beginning, this trial-by-jury, beyond-a-reasonable-doubt format is one of many ways to look at it. I think he kind of sees that there are some...not necessarily *problems* with some of the evidence, but I think that he also understands that if you tried to put certain things into evidence in a court of law, it might not get very far. There might still be questions, and he wants to continue researching. And I think the reason why he wants to is because he understands that maybe he might have *reached* the preponderance of the evidence standard. I think he even maybe said "**clear and convincing**." He understands the burdens of proof *enough* to understand that maybe we haven't made it to "beyond a reasonable doubt" yet.

Chris Williamson

Yeah, that's a good point. You mentioned you had a couple of issues with some of the things, you mentioned Josephine seeing the plane that she saw, was it indeed *the plane* or just *a plane*? Were there any other areas of the testimony that stuck out to you?

• • •

Jen Taylor

One thing that I continue to have a reasonable doubt about is the frequency of Caucasian visitors to the South Pacific and the late 1930s. It was said many times, "Well, if it's not Amelia and Fred, who else could it be? White people just did not go there." And that's interesting. If that's true, I didn't really see a whole lot of *evidence* on whether it is or isn't. I didn't get a whole lot of data or statistics on how many travelers there were, how many missionaries there were. I understand in speaking about the photo, Les Kinney *did say* that in Jaluit, there were no missionary trips there past I think he said 1934.

Chris Williamson

Right.

Jen Taylor

He didn't necessarily *bring us* anything to back that up. But that's *at least* a specific statement that we can take into consideration. That was really all we got, though, from any front for the entire thing. We didn't really have anyone bringing forward evidence of who was traveling there. How difficult was it to travel there? All of those things are still questions I have in my mind. So *before* I can say to myself, "It had to have been them, because who else could it have been?" I just needed to hear more.

Chris Williamson

Yeah, that makes sense.

Jen Taylor

Another thing that I still have reasonable doubt about is the missing physical evidence. We heard all throughout Rob Ellos's testimony stories that involved tangible pieces of physical evidence that, *if found*, would go a long way to corroborate some of these stories, right?

. . .

Chris Williamson

Right.

Jen Taylor

Every single instance, the physical evidence is missing. *Every single one.* While I'm not faulting anyone for that, it still raises doubts in my mind. At the end of the day, if all we have are stories repeated and rumors, you *do want to see something physical* to corroborate that.

Chris Williamson

Yeah.

Jen Taylor

For the story of the plane being burned through Rob's testimony, we had a couple of witnesses who said that they *saw the plane* being burned. They said *unequivocally* that it was Amelia Earhart's plane being burned. One of the reasons why we're to believe that is because Thomas Devine saw the serial number on the plane. And I know that we already talked about this, so I'm not going to go over all of it again. But I *do have* reasonable doubt as to whether or not Thomas Divine is a credible witness and how much of his testimony we can and cannot trust. I don't believe he was lying about *everything*. I don't even think he was lying about *most things*. But I have lost *enough confidence* in his ability to tell the truth that I take almost everything he says with a grain of salt at this point. And so that's another point of reasonable doubt for me.

Another piece of reasonable doubt I have is the whole story about them digging up her grave and finding the bones. When the three men go out there to dig and one of them says to the other, "Who are were digging up?" and the response was, "Have you ever heard of Amelia Earhart?" Well, they dig up these bones, and of course, the bones have been lost. That story has a lot of holes in it for me. It appears that the *main thing* connecting Amelia Earhart to that story is that single verbal exchange. Other than that, is there really anything else that connects her to that story and to those bones? I don't know what that comment means; it's a hearsay comment. And I'll just take this time to clarify what the co-conspirator exception to the hearsay rule means.

As we discussed earlier, hearsay is *any out-of-court statement* offered for its truth. So it doesn't matter if the person who made that statement is the person on the witness stand. Now, if they said it a week ago, and they're not saying it on the stand today, it's hearsay. It is *incredibly* broad.

But there *are* a number of exceptions to the hearsay rule, which is why many times, you *do hear* evidence like this coming in, but it has to meet a specific exception. And if it doesn't, and you can't find one, it's not going to be able to come in. Les Kinney indicated that the comment, "Have you ever heard of Amelia Earhart?" is conversation between co-conspirators; therefore that is an exception to the hearsay rule. And there *is* an exception that is defined that way; statements made by co-conspirators. But it's not just *any* co-conspirator, it has to be a co-conspirator to the *defendant*. The reason why we have this rule is because we have what's called "party admissions." When somebody gets arrested, you hear part of their Miranda warnings are "Anything you say can and will be used against you in a court of law."

Chris Williamson

Oh, yeah.

Jen Taylor

That's because anything you say is a party admission. You're a defendant. Literally *anything you say* to anyone *other than* your lawyer can be used against you in court. It's an exception to the hearsay rule.

Well, in a situation where, say, you have a robbery and three people were involved, or you have a drug ring and multiple people are, they're all co-conspirators. It doesn't matter if they're tried together or not. Anything that they're saying to *each other* in furtherance of the crime is all going to be considered party admission. So because it's a co-conspirator saying it and not you, you don't get the benefit of getting to keep that out. That's where that rule comes from. That's how it's used.

Chris Williamson

I like it. Okay. I feel like after all this testimony that we've done for Japanese capture, this *really is* another one of those "wait and see" situations. You've got all of this behind-the-scenes work that's being done on the Japanese capture hypothesis. And it's a very slow-moving theory; there's a lot that has to go on here. A lot of documentation has to be combed through; a lot of research has to be done. It's not the most exciting theory in the world; you're not getting out into the ocean and excavating potential aircraft, things like that. You're just basically walking backwards on what *might have happened* and tracing down someone's particular statement or someone's particular story and seeing if you can find corroborating evidence in an archive somewhere to fit that piece together before you move on to the next piece.

This whole thing sort of left me feeling a little indifferent, to be honest with you, because I just feel like we don't know what we don't know. On the other side of this door, potentially, there's so much more information that can just flood through and could break this case *wide* open. If anybody can do it, it's Les Kinney. It's Dick Spink. It's the people who are working this case *right now*. I think that we'll have something in the near future, hopefully from them, that will give us excitement and the idea that maybe this *really did* happen.

But for now, you have a lot of stories, like you mentioned, and story is not necessarily a bad thing. Everything begins with a story. But until we find some of that corroborating hard physical, tangible evidence, whatever you want to call it, until you find that smoking gun, it's going to be frustrating.

Proving this beyond a reasonable doubt to the general public is going to be difficult without anything physical to back up the testimony and the eyewitness stuff. You need more than that, and I think they're working on it. I think it's going to come our way, and it'll be exciting to see what happens when it actually *does* come our way. This has the most far-reaching effect of any theory that's out there, because if this is what happened to them, it's going to affect the lives and legacies of not only Amelia Earhart, but FDR, and potentially Eleanor Roosevelt, just about anybody who was involved. Jackie Cochran as well, potentially, which we'll get to shortly.

It's one of those situations that could send shock waves through historical accuracy and the way we look at what history tells us, if Amelia Earhart and Fred Noonan were *indeed* executed by the Japanese pre-World War II before Pearl Harbor. If that's the case, then they were, *in fact*, the very *first* prisoners of war. They were also the very *first* casualties of war. I agree 100% with Jon Hagadorn that *if* that's proven to be true, beyond a reasonable doubt, that means Earhart and Noonan need to be honored in a way that we would never imagine they needed to be. They need to be looked at in a whole different way.

And with that, we come to an end on our investigation into the Earhart/Noonan vanishings. There is so much more to this case if you can believe it. But we have to end this *sometime*. We've covered in depth now, crash and sink, Buka, castaway, and now Japanese capture. We've painted this picture with the broadest strokes possible in order to give you, our jury, the chance to really consume everything you've just read and make your *own* decision. Have you been convinced? Did one of these presented theories hit home for you? Or is there *more?* Is there something out there that *you* believe is the reason for the vanishing of Amelia Earhart and Fred Noonan?

What evidence has convinced *you?*

3 Years Later: A Retrospective

First, I must credit Chris Williamson for "chasing" his dream and bringing his far-reaching *Chasing Earhart* podcast to fruition. Although this book focuses on the first season of *Vanished*, I would strongly encourage everyone who picks up this book to listen to the entire *Chasing Earhart* collection, as it includes not only additional material on the disappearance of Amelia Earhart and Fred Noonan, but also on Earhart's life and continuing legacy. It was the *Chasing Earhart* podcast that prompted my correspondence and friendship with Chris and eventually resulted in him asking me to write this retrospective.

Credit also to Jennifer Taylor for making *Vanished* possible with her critical and objective analyses of the four theories presented in this book. Until *Vanished*, the discussion had centered almost entirely on why a particular theory was correct as opposed to why a particular theory might be incorrect. Good theories welcome critique and, as a result, emerge stronger than they began.

Finally, thanks to Rob Ellos, Jon Hagadorn and Les Kinney for sharing with us all of their considerable knowledge and research, and to Professor Christopher French for presenting an opposing view.

Like many people who grew up in the 1970s, I first became interested in the fates of Earhart and Noonan after watching the *In Search Of* episode in 1977. At that time, I had a slight bias toward "ditched and sank," which seemed logical, although there is only so much to be gleaned from a half hour of television. My interest then fell dormant and remained so until TIGHAR's 1997 expedition to Nikumaroro, which garnered significant media coverage. So seemingly persuasive was TIGHAR's ostensible evidence at the time to a layperson such as myself, and so far-fetched a tale Japanese capture seemed, that I took it for granted that Earhart and Noonan had wound up on Nikumaroro. It was only upon watching the 1998 Earhart and Noonan episode of *In Search of History* that I started to grasp that there just might be something to the theory of a Japanese capture. But it wasn't until 2003, when I started regularly traveling to Saipan for business, that I started becoming a believer.

Among the Saipanese, it is common knowledge that Earhart and

Noonan met their fates on the island that, at the time of the duo's disappearance, served as the headquarters of the Japanese military in the Pacific. A deeper dive into the existing research on this topic only cemented my belief. The Japanese capture theory is as compelling for the sheer volume of supporting evidence as it is for its concurrent timelines emerging from divergent geographic sources and the way that evidence clicks into place almost seamlessly.

Early evidence originated from three very distinct groups: the Saipanese, the Marshallese and the US military. Saipan [part of the Northern Mariana Islands] and the Marshall Islands, although both part of Micronesia, are politically, culturally, linguistically and geographically distinct. Both were under Japanese control at the time of Earhart and Noonan's disappearance, which explains how the pair could have landed in the Marshalls and wound up on Saipan.

Mili Atoll, in the Marshall Islands where they are thought to have landed, is 1,869 miles from Saipan. Today, thanks to the internet, we take for granted that even the most trivial events that occur in remote outposts are made known to the rest of the world mere moments later. This was not the case back in 1937, when news traveled slowly [if at all] in two separate societies that were strongly discouraged from discussing such matters even internally. The idea that false rumors at that time could have started in one place and quickly migrated to the other, 1,869 miles away, or for that matter that they could have developed independently, seems absurd. Equally as fanciful is the idea that so many witnesses [not only on Saipan and in the Marshalls but also in the US military] would, in isolation from each other, concoct stories that happened to coincide with each other and, when pieced together, form a compelling and cohesive account of Earhart's and Noonan's respective fates [a series of "impossible coincidences," to co-opt Bill Prymak's term].

Taylor makes a good case for how many [but not even close to all] eyewitness accounts *could* have alternative explanations: potentially unreliable witnesses, witnesses being led, the power of suggestion, testimony being taken years after the fact, etc. Alternatively, Occam's razor, mentioned countless times in the podcast, seeks the simplest solution. Applied here, why not consider that these witnesses are simply telling the truth?

Furthermore, the alternatives that Taylor proffers do not explain the contentions from the many, varied members of the US military. Taylor skillfully calls Sergeant Thomas Devine's credibility into question, but even if Devine's account were to be dismissed entirely, which even she does not suggest, what about Private Robert Wallack's credibility? Either Wallack [who, like other servicemen, and contrary to what Taylor says, we heard from directly, not only through Devine] had Earhart's briefcase, or else he lied; there is no room for any other conclusion. What about Corporal Earskin Julious Nabers, who contrary to podcast testimony, did not "overhear" a discussion of a message about the Lockheed Electra 10-E aircraft, but was in fact the very person to decode the message? Nabers either decoded the message, or he lied. Privates Billy Burks and Everett Henson either heard Captain Tracy Griswold mention Earhart when digging up the gravesite at Liyang cemetery, or else they lied. Either Joseph Garafolo, a US Marine, saw a photo of Earhart with a Japanese officer, or else he lied. Either Admiral Chester Nimitz [yes, *that* Nimitz], General Alexander Vande-grift and General Graves Erskine – all of whom would be in a position to know – told Fred Goerner and his associates the truth: that Goerner was on the right track with his Saipan investigation. Or else they lied.

There is still more evidence that is difficult to ignore, some of which was not covered in the podcast. What are three rusted dolly wheels doing on an uninhabited Endriken Island on Mili Atoll, exactly where Earhart and Noonan were seen landing, if not to move the aircraft? Why were airplane parts consistent with the 10-E found on that same island, where no aircraft are known to have crashed during World War II? What about the message in the bottle that was discovered in 1938? What about the July 13, 1937, Bethlehem [Pennsylvania] *Globe-Times* article reporting that the Japanese had "rescued" Earhart and Noonan? What about the multiple post-loss radio signals received by Pan Am stations throughout the Pacific with bearings that could have inter-sected near Mili? Notwithstanding the controversy as to the Jaluit dock photo's date, what are obviously Caucasian Noonan and Earhart lookalikes doing on Jaluit [in the Marshalls] in the 1930s with what indisputably is the *Koshu Maru* [known to be at Jaluit in July 1937] carrying what looks like a 10-E in a scene that bears eerie resemblance to the Marshall Islands stamp issued three decades before that photo surfaced?

The lack of physical evidence does not particularly frustrate me, given the totality of the rest of the case. What does frustrate me, but does not surprise me, is the relative lack of evidence from Japan [although there is some of that, too], where firsthand witnesses have undoubtedly since passed. Nevertheless, this remains a largely untapped treasure trove, and I wish Les Kinney luck in pursuing it.

Does the preponderance of the evidence prove the Japanese capture case beyond a reasonable doubt? The case is strong. Keep in mind that it was Taylor's job to attack all four theories, *one* of which must be true. Having listened to Taylor make quick work of the other four, Japanese capture emerges all the stronger for having withstood her attempts to bring it down.

Sean Keatts
Winter 2022

Bonus Retrospective The Orona Hypothesis

The Orona (Hull Island) lagoon image is the basis for my hypothesis. The image is an undeniable clue and fits with what we know about the two experienced flyers. Both Amelia and Fred could make good survival decisions. When the search for Howland Island failed, both knew they must find a quiet surface upon which to set the Electra down. From his work at Pan Am, Fred knew of just such a place; the totally enclosed lagoon(s) of the Phoenix Islands. While on a different and wrong 157-337 line of flight, the Orona hypothesis initially parallels the Nikumaroro hypothesis, but diverges into a totally different path after the pilots successfully put the plane down in the Orona lagoon.

This is not a castaway theory, but rather a Japanese capture theory.

Tojo had installed a listening post on Nikumaroro in order to monitor the radio activity of the USS *Avocet* and HMS *Wellington* as they supported the solar eclipse expedition of June 1937 at Canton. The Japanese were interested in intercepting encrypted messages of the US and UK for study. On the reports from the listening post on Nikumaroro and learning the flyers were only ninety miles away on Orona, Tojo ordered the capture of the fliers. After the kidnap of the fliers, the Nikumaroro post was abandoned, leaving "evidence of recent habitation" as reported later by US Navy search pilots.

Amelia was not a spy but became an accused spy after capture by the Japanese as a part of the Imperial Army's pressure campaign to move the IJN to offense. The idea has a motive: a spy hoax with Amelia as the American spy and proof the US was planning war.

The spy charge was kept secret among the upper echelon of the Japanese military and was part of a greater effort to force the IJN into an aggressive first-strike strategy and capability [see the Mahan principle]. The IJN under Yamamoto had implemented the Mahan principle in a defensive strategy. The Imperial Army under Tojo and other pro-Axis elements sought an offensive Naval first-strike capability. Other Japanese capture ideas have no motive, and readers might ask, "Why would Japan do that?" The Orona/Saipan theory answers two of the many big questions that surround the Amelia Earhart mystery: where is the airplane, and what was the reason the Japanese took Amelia captive?

The image of an airplane in the Orona lagoon clearly shows the outline of a L10-E aircraft.

Google Earth measurements and compensation for the refractive index of water shows the same dimensions as the L10-E airframe. 2006 Google Earth image measurements, in addition to symmetry studies, prove this to be the best clue so far in the long study of the mystery. The presence of an oval object measuring the same [four by eight feet] as the two-person raft carried on the world flight leads to the conclusion that the fliers survived the splash, landing in the lagoon. Because the raft lies close to the airframe, the raft sank to the bottom at the same time as the aircraft.

Extreme speculation would be required to connect this with Japanese capture were it not for a claimed 1937 photo discovered by Les Kinney in the National Archives: a picture of the Marshall Islands Jaluit dock that shows two Caucasian persons. One looks like Fred Noonan and the other could be Amelia. Different Japanese sources, including the National library of Japan, refute the claim and expound counterclaims that the photo was published in 1935, making it impossible to show the missing fliers.

Analysis of the Jaluit dock photo details a discrepancy in the horizon line behind the persons standing on the dock. This disparity can only be explained by coconut palm trees.

The Marshallese government claims the dock photo must be *post 1936*, as the dock was not constructed until 1936. An article in *Pacific Islands* magazine dated September 1935 details the July 1935 visit to Jaluit by the Japanese Navy and the fact the dock used in 1935 was the old dock from the German period. Study of the direction from which the old German dock looks across the lagoon reveals that the distance [sixteen miles] is too great across the lagoon to see coconut trees.

Earth curvature disallows any view of trees when observing straight away from the 1935 dock. Earth curvature allows trees [nine miles away] to be seen in the straight-away view from the 1936 dock. The end of the Jaluit coconut tree plantation at the island's end results in the photo horizon disparity as the horizon falls from treetops to absolute sea level.

While the Japanese continue to double down on the 1935 claim, simple science, recorded history, and the horizon disparity in the photo indicate the photo is post 1936 and most likely was taken in the summer of 1937.

These two images as clues make Orona/Japanese capture the best of the theories explaining the Amelia Earhart mystery.

Thomas Maxwell
Winter 2022

Chris Williamson

We've been working on this together for a *long* time. It feels like forever.

Jen Taylor

Like nine months now.

Chris Williamson

Yeah. And that's nothing when you think about all the people who have been working on this for twenty, thirty or even forty years at this point. We've been working on this pretty consistently, and you've been neck deep in this Earhart/Noonan case for nine months coming into the night we're recording this. When we first connected before our "Trial by Jury" segment, you didn't really know a whole lot about the story or the case or the theories that are contained within it. What are your final thoughts now on this experience as we come to an end, as you maybe walk away from this forever?

Jen Taylor

Well, it's been really fun, and it's been incredibly educational. I've learned a lot about a woman I didn't really know very much about before. In studying her disappearance, I learned a lot about who she is and a lot about her life, which I think is good, I really appreciated that. I think that was probably the best part about doing this whole thing. Theory wise, I tend to have a hard time picking one because I think that there are certain theories that *absolutely* need to be investigated further.

Chris Williamson

Agreed.

· · ·

Jen Taylor

And I don't say that just to be nice. I believe that for all of them except for the castaway theory because I think that one has been investigated to the ground. I think there is still a lot of work to do on the other ones. If we run through them in the order that we covered them, I think crash and sink was the most compelling just in terms of who we had and what they were talking about, how confident they were. Just their overall credibility, I thought that that was a very well put together case for the project, which is why I wanted to start there for every other theory. I wanted to start with those *Itasca* logs. Any theory, *including* this last one, needs to explain that. That point is where she was last heard, and any investigation into what happened to her *has* to start there even if it takes you somewhere else. Now, am I convinced beyond a reasonable doubt that that's what happened? I'm actually not because I *do have* reasonable doubt. I have reasonable doubt in the form of witnesses who saw her in Saipan. I have reasonable doubt in the form of weird documents that can't be explained. I have reasonable doubt in the form of a plane that's at Buka *right now.* So, because of those things, I can't say that I know what happened to them. That's why we need to keep going.

Chris Williamson

We set out to do what I felt was possibly *impossible.* Do you think we were able to pull it off? Was it a success in that sense?

Jen Taylor

It was. With the original podcast and now this book, you tried to do something that no one's ever done before. You tried to apply real-life courtroom rules and rules of evidence and procedural rules, and you tried to apply them to something that they weren't really meant to apply to. In essence, you forced a round peg into a square hole. But we did it, and I think that we did it pretty well too. At the end of the day, what we were able to do is get all of the evidence out there for people to really scrutinize and criticize. To get both sides out there is something we should be proud of, *you* should be proud of. To allow people who are zealously advocating for either side to present their cases and present the pros and cons of each theory, that's what trial is really for. That's really how the truth comes out. I think that we did that as best anyone could have done it.

Chris Williamson

I feel like I can't properly put into words what a genuine pleasure this has been to be with you for the back half of this and for you to come on board and really breathe life into a crazy idea that I had. I really didn't know this was even possible until I reached out to you and we started fleshing it out. It was really *all* you. You took an idea that I had a really long time ago and made it real and made it possible. I am forever in debt to you for that. At this point, with this book release now, I feel like we have taken this investigation as far as we can take it. Now it's up to the reader. You've got other cases that need your attention, and I have to be able to walk away from this with a degree of finality. It's been a wild ride.

Jen Taylor

I really appreciate that you asked me to come on board, it was a complete surprise when you reached out to me. I had no idea what this would turn into, but I'm very grateful that I got the opportunity to learn all of this stuff and to learn about a really amazing person who has become quite a bit of an inspiration to me and my family as well. So *thank you* for that.

EPILOGUE

Chris Williamson

When we began our journey, I stood on the corner of North Terrace in Santa Fe Street in Atchison, Kansas, across from the home that Amelia Earhart was born in.

I find it only fitting that I return here as we end. It's winter in Atchison, and it's cold. But it's eerily quiet on the bluffs overlooking the Missouri River.

Jennifer has departed us, on to cases that need her attention. So I end like I began. On my own.

We've covered a lot of information during our journey together, and I hope you've enjoyed the ride. We've traveled all over the world with Amelia, from her humble beginnings here in Atchison just a few feet from where I'm standing *right now*, to her incredible world flight that she unfortunately never came home from.

Or did she?

It was never my job to convince you of *anything* except this.

Amelia Earhart is a legend. In every way that someone can be.

And now our job is done. The trial of the century is over. All cases have been made, all voices have been heard, and now it's up to *you*.

You decide.

You write the ending.

Because as I've said so many times before on our podcast and here in this text, Amelia Earhart and Fred Noonan belong to **all of us** *now*.

AFTERWORD

More than eight decades have passed since Amelia Earhart, her navigator Fred Noonan, and their Lockheed Electra 10-E Special disappeared over the Central South Pacific on 2 July 1937. The ensuing search involved dozens of ships, scores of aircraft, and thousands of sailors. It cost a staggering $250,000 a day, and when the search ended on 19 July 1937, the total cost was $4 million. It was the biggest and most expensive search in United States history. Amelia's fame and the mysterious circumstances of her disappearance have ensured it remains one of the twentieth century's most enduring mysteries.

In the years that followed, three main theories developed that form the Holy Trinity of Earhart lore: crashed and sank, Japanese capture and castaway.

Crashed and Sank:

From the outset, the simplest explanation was that our intrepid flyers, having failed to locate Howland Island, ran out of fuel and crashed into the vast Pacific Ocean where, despite the best efforts of the US Coastguard and US Navy, they were never found. This was the conclusion reached by the US Navy's official report published on 31 July 1937.

In 1999 the US Navy's report was endorsed by Elgen Long, a record-breaking American aviator, who proposed his "Crashed and Sank" theory in *Amelia Earhart: The Mystery Solved*.

Yet in the days following their disappearance, post-loss radio signals were overheard from the missing flyers, which could not have been sent had they ditched at sea. These reports originated from a variety of independent sources.

Official sources included Pan Am radio stations in the Pacific, the British ocean liner MV *New Zealand Star*, and the British cruiser HMS *Achilles*.

Unofficial sources included ham radio operators and members of the public back in the United States, such as Betty Klenck and Nina Paxton, who, listening at home on makeshift radios, reported hearing Amelia's desperate pleas for help and her possible location.

Most of these reports were dismissed as hoaxes, but before long, additional evidence emerged to contradict the official report. This suggested Amelia and Fred may have survived.

Japanese Capture:

The mystery took a dramatic turn in 1960 with the publication of *Daughter of the Sky* by air force Captain Paul L. Briand Jr., which contained the eyewitness account of Josephine Blanco Akiyama. In 1937, aged eleven, she claimed to have seen Amelia and Fred at Tanapag harbor, a key Japanese naval base on Saipan. What was unclear is how they arrived on Saipan, some 2,750 miles northwest of their intended destination.

Other researchers were quick to pick up the story, notably KCBS newsman Fred Goerner. In 1966 he published *The Search for Amelia Earhart*, a New York Times best-seller and widely regarded as the seminal work of Earhart research. Drawing on eyewitness accounts, Goerner concluded that Amelia and Fred had gone down in the Marshall Islands and were picked up by the Japanese. From here they were taken to Saipan, where they died as prisoners. Some eyewitnesses claimed they had been executed, whereas others said Amelia died from dysentery.

Goerner's research firmly established the "Japanese capture" theory in the American psyche, not least because it was endorsed by the former commander in chief of the US Pacific Fleet, Admiral Chester Nimitz. It also prompted further research by Earhart luminaries like Vincent Loomis, Oliver Knaggs, Don Kothera, Rollin Reineck and Donald Wilson to name but a few. These researchers identified additional eyewitnesses, and some of their accounts were videoed and preserved for the historical record by filmmaker Richard Martini.

Another key piece of research was Thomas E. Devine's 1987 book *Eyewitness: The Amelia Earhart Incident.* Sergeant Devine, who arrived on Saipan in June 1944, described learning of the presence of Earhart's Electra at Aslito Field (now Saipan International Airport). Later he claimed to have witnessed its destruction by US military personnel and to have been shown the location of Amelia and Fred's graves.

Crucially, Devine invited fellow Saipan veterans to contact him if they knew anything about Amelia Earhart's presence on Saipan. Twenty-six responded, with stories more incendiary than his own. Chief among these were US Marines Robert E. Wallack and Erskine Julious Nabers.

In addition, several sub-theories developed. It was even suggested Amelia was "Tokyo Rose," one of the many female English-speaking voices of Japanese propaganda broadcasts during World War II. These claims were investigated and subsequently dismissed by Amelia's husband, George P. Putnam, who listened to many of the broadcasts.

Castaways:

In June 1982 Frederick J. Hooven, an engineer and inventor, suggested the post-loss radio signals strongly supported the theory that Earhart landed in the Phoenix Islands, probably on McKean or Gardner Island (now known as Nikumaroro). He subsequently dismissed this theory due to lack of evidence and agreed with Fred Goerner's Japanese capture scenario.

Nevertheless, his theory was adopted by the International Group for Historic Aircraft Recovery (TIGHAR), founded by Ric Gillespie in 1985. TIGHAR believe Earhart and Noonan, flying along the line of position 157/337, missed Howland Island and landed instead at Nikumaroro some four hundred miles to the southeast, where they died as castaways.

The Newcomers:

Although the big three theories are well established, this has not prevented the emergence of new theories.

In 2004, David Billings, a retired aircraft engineer, suggested the Electra crashed in the jungle of New Britain, Papua New Guinea. He found evidence that in 1945, an Australian army patrol discovered the wreckage of an unpainted, all-metal, twin-engine aircraft in the jungles of New Britain. One of the soldiers retrieved a metal tag from an engine mount. Although this has since been lost, he believes the reference number was transcribed onto a wartime map rediscovered in the 1990s, and that it identifies an engine belonging to Earhart's Electra. To date all attempts to rediscover the wreckage have proved unsuccessful.

Finally, there is Bill Snavely's Buka theory, the newest of all the theories. In 2005 Bill learned of an aircraft wreck site off the coast of Buka Island in Papua New Guinea. This supported the eyewitness account of a boy who claimed to have witnessed the crash in or close to 1937 during a fierce tropical storm. Divers investigating the wreck confirmed it is consistent with Earhart's Electra, as is a six-inch piece of glass they recovered, which may be one of the aircraft's landing lights.

Snavely theorizes the Electra was not fully fueled when it took off from Lae and, after encountering strong headwinds, used more fuel than anticipated. Realizing they had insufficient fuel to reach Howland Island, they were forced to turn back. He believes they intended to land at Buka, which lay along their outward flight path, but crashed during the storm, as witnessed by the boy.

The current state of Earhart research:

Yet as we approach the eighty-fifth anniversary of Amelia and Fred's disappearance, it could be argued that we are no closer to the truth. During this time, the three main theories have all tried to advance their cause, with varying degrees of success.

Several attempts to verify the Crashed and Sank theory have been undertaken by Nauticos LLC, a specialist deep-sea exploration company owned and operated by David Jourdan, in collaboration with Elgen Long. In 2002 and 2006 they undertook a 1,200-square-mile underwater search to the north and west of Howland Island at a cost of $4.5 million but found nothing. In 2017 a third search, entitled the "Eustace Earhart Discovery Expedition," surveyed a further 725 square miles, but again no trace of the Electra was found.

TIGHAR have undertaken over a dozen trips to Nikumaroro, collecting numerous archaeological finds, including a piece of aircraft aluminum thought to originate from Earhart's Electra (artefact 2-2-V-1) and a 1940/41 report by the British documenting the discovery of human remains. However, despite decades of research, TIGHAR has yet to find verifiable evidence that Amelia and Fred landed on Nikumaroro.

In 2019 their theory was undermined when Bob Ballard's two-week, multimillion-dollar search of the waters surrounding Nikumaroro failed to find any trace of the Electra. Ballard himself said he felt he was adding: "nail after nail after nail" to the coffin of the Nikumaroro theory. Undeterred, he plans to map the undersea areas around Howland and Baker Islands soon.

Tantalizing evidence to support Japanese capture surfaced in 2017 when Les Kinney, a former US Treasury agent, discovered a recently declassified photo in the US National Archives. The photograph, from the Office of US Naval Intelligence, shows a group of people standing on a dock in Jaluit Harbor, Jaluit Atoll, in the Marshall Islands in the 1930s. The seated figure with their back to the camera could be Amelia Earhart, while a man standing to the far left could be Fred Noonan. On the far right a ship is towing a barge, upon which is an object resembling Earhart's Electra.

Within days, however, a Tokyo-based blogger claimed to have discovered the same photo in a South Seas travelogue published in 1935, two years before Earhart's disappearance. This prompted a swift response from the Republic of the Marshall Islands Ministry of Foreign Affairs. In a letter dated 15 July 2017, they confirmed the photograph showed the dock at Jabor on Jaluit Atoll and that it could not have been taken in 1935, since it was built in 1936.

In contrast, Bill Snavely, and Project Blue Angel are in a unique position because they have what many consider the holy grail of the Earhart mystery: physical wreckage of an aircraft that could be the Electra. This wreckage has the potential to prove or disprove their theory and perhaps solve the mystery.

Some mysteries, however, are destined to endure, and there are elements to this case that I think may ensure this. Nevertheless, I am optimistic that in the future evidence to help solve the mystery might be declassified, found in a national archive, or discovered through advancements in science and technology.

On the other hand, I enjoy the mystery. I have vanished down the rabbit hole, and I often wonder what it would be like to emerge again if the mystery is solved. How would I feel? The honest answer is, I do not know.

But until *that day*, the rabbit hole is a fun place to be.

Chris Hare
Winter 2021

ACKNOWLEDGMENTS

This book is *all of me*. It is the *best* in me, and it is the *worst* in me. It's the obsession that took me away from my wife and son most nights over the course of the last couple of years.

It's also a reminder of the absolute love and devotion that I've put toward this case. A love that's *not uncommon* among the hundreds of Earhart researchers who over the years have painstakingly done the same. It's countless late nights of being stuck at my desk after working my "day job" or sitting in bed with my wife curled up beside me. Most of all, it's a reminder of all the times I would hear my son ask, "Are you done working so we can play?"

Only to have to remind him that Dad has a deadline. For a *podcast,* or for a *panel* or a *documentary shoot.*

Or a book.

Amelia has been the other woman in my life for as long as I can remember. And now, she lives in the following pages; her triumphs, her tragedies, her disappointments, and her victories, they all live here.

I want to thank everyone who has been willing to work with me, even carrying a difference of opinion along the way. Some of the following acknowledgments might surprise you.

Wherever our relationships might be at *this moment,* I wouldn't have been able to do this without them.

First, to my editors, Chris Hare, Lisa Payne, Sean Keatts, Tessa Di'Amico and Nicky Broughton, thanks for all the hard work. This case needs you *all.*

To Amber, Andrew and the rest of my *Straight Up Strange* family, thank you for sharing my love for the mysterious and unexplained. Here's to solving mysteries!

To Henrique Peirano, thank you for the amazing cover. You've been a joy to work with. Here's to many more.

Ric Gillespie – you picked up the phone and gave me your time when you didn't *have to*. I forever remain grateful.

Dr. Tom King – you were my first *Chasing Earhart* guest when it was impossible to even get a guest. Thank you for being open to this dumb kid's questions. You made the show credible.

Mike Campbell – Forever the dream guest for my show. If you ever change your mind, I'll be here. Thank you for all you've done in pursuit of the truth.

Marianne Miller – you offered us your home and a chance to change our lives forever. We love you.

Les Kinney – The walking encyclopedia. Nobody is more dedicated to this case than you. When we find an answer, you'll be part of it, I just know it.

Dick Spink – Vanessa and I both adore you. You're always incredibly honest, and you've been more than generous with your time. Thank you for everything.

Chris Hare – You're a once-in-a-lifetime researcher. You have what I like to call *"it"*. You're the captain of this ship now. I'm honored to know you.

Tom Dettweiler – A giant among giants. It's been an honor to speak with you and feature a guest of your stature in some of our work.

Dr. Alex Mandel - Thank you for always being willing to engage me in conversation. I truly appreciate your years of knowledge on this case.

Michelle Cervone - I never had the honor of meeting you in person, but I feel like I've gotten to know you through Marianne and Alex. Thank you for everything you did to further the AES and this case.

Sean Keatts – Always willing to keep an open mind. Thanks for always being there to challenge me and talk things out when I need someone to put me in check.

Nicholas Augusta – Thank you for your incredible knowledge of Amelia's relationship with Hawaii and your willingness to spotlight

Fred Noonan, a pioneer in aviation history. Thank you for introducing me to Burl.

Doug Westfall – You've become like a second father to me. I will always cherish our talks on AE *and on* other things. I know this won't be the last time we work together.

Gary LaPook - Thank you for always being so willing to converse with me and entertain my questions. It's been a pleasure learning from you.

Sammie Morris – I'm *still* starstruck.

Jill Meyers – What can I say? You're a true friend. I love you.

Lisa Cotham – You're so much fun to be around, you make everyone feel like they can share their thoughts on the case without judgment, and I'm forever grateful that you've been willing to work with me.

Lou Foudary – I love you. We *all do.*

Ann Pellegreno – Thank you for everything. The long conversations, the suggestions and the honest feedback. You are a national treasure, and I am lucky to know you. Vanessa and I love you very much.

Bob Wheeler – You have been a true friend. Even if it's been months, I know I can always pick up the phone and call and you'll be there to engage and stimulate my thoughts. It always feels like we're picking up right where we left off. Thank you, sir, it's a real honor.

Grace McGuire – You *are* Amelia's legacy. Thank you for always being there.

Scott & Forrest – You've both become *true* brothers. I could never imagine we'd become as close as we have. Love you both.

TJ – You're the kind of friend that people brag about having. Thanks for always being there.

Adam and Matt – Thank you for having Jen and I on your show on our final night for this case. You have become friends and podcast brothers. Love to you both.

Bill Snavely – Thank you for trusting me to work with you and help you tell your story. It's been a *true* honor. You're one of the good ones.

My Parents - that you for always being encouraging in everything I do. I'm proud to be your son.

Vic – This is as much yours as it is mine. The only reason I was able to do this is because I've had your example to look up to my whole life. Love you.

Gus "Big Sexy" Brooks – I love you, brother. You are the truest of friends. Thanks for always being there.

Jennifer Taylor – My co-host and my friend. I'm so *very proud* of you. You are a *star*. I knew it the first time we sat down to record. You've swept over this case like an enigma, and you breathed life into this crazy idea I had so long ago. I can't wait to see what you do next. I'm your biggest fan.

To the town of Atchison, thank you for embracing us and allowing us to be part of Amelia's legacy. To Karen, Jacque, and everyone else, you keep the spirit of Amelia *alive*.

Benjamin - you have been the driving force behind everything I've done with Earhart. Always there to engage in conversation that inspires me and keeps me calm. You can talk me through anything. I love you for that. Thank you.

My wife, Vanessa Marie. You are the life of this *entire project* from start to finish. You championed and believed in me without hesitation from the beginning. You're the best friend I ever had. Without you, none of this happens. *I love you more than anything.*

And to my son.

You may not know this now, but you sacrificed *a lot* for me to follow my dream. I dedicate this book to you. Dream big and follow those dreams wherever they may take you. Dad has your back forever and ever.

I dedicate this moment to all who believe that the biggest dreams can still come true.

ABOUT THE AUTHOR

Chris Williamson has always been fascinated with the story of Amelia Earhart and the mystery surrounding her disappearance. He wrote his very first report in 3rd grade on Amelia and ever since then, he has been searching for the absolute truth behind her disappearance. *Rabbit Hole* was conceived with the hopes of bringing even more attention to the worldwide fascination with Amelia. Chris hopes that this book will serve as an ongoing case study that will inspire more and more people to research and form their *own* fascinations and opinions with one of the most iconic figures of our time.

facebook.com/vanishedpod

twitter.com/vanishedpod

instagram.com/vanishedpod

"Wait."

CPSIA information can be obtained
at www.ICGtesting.com
Printed in the USA
BVHW091801240622
640596BV00012B/337